LIFE

OF

ABRAHAM LINCOLN

A. Lincoln

LIFE

OF

ABRAHAM LINCOLN

JOSEPH H. BARRETT

1865 EDITION

STACKPOLE
BOOKS

Stackpole Classic Reprint 2006 by Stackpole Books

Published by:
Stackpole Books
5067 Ritter Road
Mechanicsburg, PA 17055
www.stackpolebooks.com

Printed in the United States of America

10   9   8   7   6   5   4   3   2   1

Originally published by Moore, Wilstach & Baldwin of Cincinnati and
New York: 1865

Cover design by Wendy A. Reynolds

Library of Congress Cataloging-in-Publication Data

Barrett, Joseph H. (Joseph Hartwell), 1824–1910.
    Life of Abraham Lincoln / by Joseph H. Barrett.
        p. cm.
    Originally published: Cincinnati ; New York : Moore, Wilstach &
Baldwin, 1865.
    ISBN 0-8117-0159-X
    1. Lincoln, Abraham, 1809–1865. 2. Presidents—United States—
Biography. 3. United States—Politics and government—1861–1865.
I. Title.

E457.B273 2006
352.23'8097309034—dc22
                                                          2005056317

ISBN 978-0-8117-0159-4

LIFE

OF

ABRAHAM LINCOLN,

PRESENTING

HIS EARLY HISTORY, POLITICAL CAREER, AND SPEECHES IN
AND OUT OF CONGRESS; ALSO, A GENERAL
VIEW OF HIS POLICY AS

President of the United States;

WITH HIS

MESSAGES, PROCLAMATIONS, LETTERS, ETC.,

AND A

HISTORY OF HIS EVENTFUL ADMINISTRATION, AND OF THE
SCENES ATTENDANT UPON HIS TRAGIC
AND LAMENTED DEMISE.

BY

JOSEPH H. BARRETT,

COMMISSIONER OF PENSIONS, WASHINGTON, D.C.

―――――――――

PUBLISHERS:

MOORE, WILSTACH & BALDWIN,

25 WEST FOURTH STREET, CINCINNATI.
NEW YORK, 60 WALKER STREET.

1865.

PREFACE.

THE first part of the sketch of Mr. Lincoln's life herewith presented to the public, was mainly prepared for the press in June, 1860—only slight modifications having been made, and brief additions, so as to embrace the period terminating with his inauguration. This portion of the work embodies a condensed view of Mr. Lincoln's speeches, which can not fail to interest the attentive student, who seeks for information concerning his early political life. The second part, after a summary of National events immediately preceding March 4, 1861, gives a condensed history of Mr. Lincoln's Administration, including a narrative of military operations, down to the present time. The most important public papers, addresses and occasional letters of the President, will also be found in the following pages.

It has been the fortune of Mr. Lincoln to be called to the Chief Magistracy, at an epoch when a long-maturing conspiracy for the dismemberment of the Union has culminated in a war of unprecedented magnitude. The President, tried as none of his predecessors ever were, has so wisely exercised his power as to command the hearty support of all loyal men at home, and the admiration of enlightened thinkers, unperverted by anti-democratic prejudice in Europe. It was a late member of the British Parliament who pointed out single passages from an address of Mr. Lincoln, as worth "all that Burke ever wrote." His able statesmanship has justified the confidence of the people, while his sterling qualities of heart, his humane sympathies, his purity of life, and his power of winning the love and trust of his countrymen, have contributed to deepen the earnestness of the popular wish for his continuance, during another term, in the high office he providentially fills.

It is hardly to be hoped that the present attempt to treat so wide a subject, within so small a compass, will satisfy all readers. Many minor details, of special interest to individuals, have necessarily been omitted. Some accounts of military and naval undertakings, which might, of themselves, have filled an entire volume, have been given with perhaps a disappointing brevity. It must suffice to say, here, that no pains have been spared—as no requisite facilities for obtaining correct data have been lacking—to make the work not only trustworthy and complete in regard to matters of salient interest, but also as acceptable as possible to all classes of loyal readers.

WASHINGTON, D. C., May 14, 1864.   J. H. B.

The Third Part of this work comprises the events of the last year of Mr. Lincoln's life, with his public papers and addresses of the same period, as well as many letters and speeches of an earlier date, not given in the previous parts. The summary of the closing campaigns of the war has been prepared with care, as well as the political history of the time. No year of the nation's existence has been more memorable than that commencing on the 1st of May, 1864. Before its close, a gigantic rebellion was finally crushed, and our great and good President, after witnessing the triumph of his labors, fell a martyr to the cause he had so firmly upheld through the darkest hours. Would that the work were more worthy the theme. No name will be more sacred in our country's annals, or more perpetual in the memory of the world, than that of ABRAHAM LINCOLN.

WASHINGTON, D. C., July 20, 1865.   J. H. B.

CONTENTS.

PART I.

CHAPTER I.

CHAPTER XI.

CHAPTER XII.

CHAPTER XIII.

PART II.

CHAPTER I.

CHAPTER II.

CHAPTER III.

CHAPTER IV.

CHAPTER V.

CHAPTER VI.

PART III.

CHAPTER I.

CHAPTER IV.

CHAPTER V.

CHAPTER VI.

CHAPTER VII.

CHAPTER VIII.

CHAPTER IX.

CHAPTER X

CHAPTER XI.

PART I.

CHAPTER I.

MR. LINCOLN'S EARLY BOYHOOD IN KENTUCKY.

Ancestry of Abraham Lincoln.—Their residence in Pennsylvania and Virginia.—His Grandfather Crosses the Alleghanies to join Boone and his Associates.—"The Dark and Bloody Ground."—His Violent Death.—His Widow Settles in Washington County.—Thomas Lincoln, his Son, Marries and Locates near Hodgenville.—Birth of Abraham Lincoln.—La Rue County.—His Early Life and Training in Kentucky.

THE ancestors of ABRAHAM LINCOLN were of English descent. We find the earliest definite traces of them in Berks county, Pennsylvania, though this was almost certainly not the first place of their residence in this country. Their location, and their adherence to the Quaker faith, make it probable that the original emigration occurred under the auspices of William Penn. It was doubtless a branch of the same family that, leaving England under different religious impulses, but with the same adventurous and independent spirit, settled, at an earlier date, in Old Plymouth Colony. The separation may possibly have taken place this side of the Atlantic, and not beyond. Some of the same traits appear conspicuously in both these family groups. One tradition indeed affirms that the Pennsylvania branch was transplanted from Hingham, Massachusetts, and was derived from a common stock with General Benjamin Lincoln, of Revolutionary fame. There is a noticeable coincidence in the general prevalence, in each American branch, of Scriptural names in christening—the Benjamin, Levi, and Ezra, of Massachusetts, having their counterpart in the Abraham, Thomas, and Josiah, of Virginia and Kentucky. The peculiarity is one to have been equally expected among sober Friends, and among zealous Puritans.

Berks county was not very long the home of Mr. Lincoln's immediate progenitors. There can hardly have been more than a slender pioneer settlement there, when one or more of the number made another remove, not far from the year 1750, to what is now Rockingham county, Virginia. Old Berks was first settled about 1734—then, too, as a German colony—and was not organized as a county until 1752; before which date, according to family traditions, this removal to Virginia took place.

This, it will be observed, was pre-eminently a pioneer stock, evidently much in love with backwoods adventure, and constantly courting the dangers and hardships of forest life.

Rockingham county, Virginia, though situated in the beautiful valley of the Shenandoah, and inviting, by its natural resources, the advances of civilization, must nevertheless have been, at the time just mentioned, in the very heart of the wilderness. Now, it is one of the most productive counties of Virginia, having exceeded every other county in the State, according to the census of 1850, in its crops of wheat and hay. A branch of the family, it is understood, still remains there, to enjoy the benefits of so judicious a selection, and of the labors and imperfectly requited endurances of these first settlers.

From this locality, about the year 1782, Abraham Lincoln, grandfather of him who was to make the name illustrious, started Westward across the Alleghanies, attracted by the accounts which had reached him of the wonderfully fertile and lovely country explored by Daniel Boone, on and near the Kentucky river. During all his lifetime, hitherto, he could have known little of any other kind of existence than that to which he had been educated as an adventurous frontiersman. The severe labor of preparing the heavily-timbered lands of Shenandoah for cultivation, the wild delights of hunting the then abundant game of the woods, and the exciting hazards of an uncertain warfare with savage enemies, had been almost the sole occupation of his rough and healthful life. Perhaps the settlements around him had already begun to be too far advanced for the highest enjoyment of his characteristic mode of living; or possibly, with others, he aspired to the possession of more fertile fields, and to an easier subsistence. Whatever the reason, he set out at the time just stated, with his wife and several young children, on his long journey across the mountains, and over the broad valleys intervening between the Shenandoah and the Kentucky.

At this date, and for ten or twelve years later, the present State of Kentucky formed part of the old Commonwealth of Virginia. "The dark and bloody ground," as afterward named for better reasons than the fiction which assigns this meaning to its Indian appellation, had then been but recently entered upon by the white man. Its first explorer, Daniel Boone, whose very name suggests a whole world of romance and adventure, had removed, when a mere boy, among the earlier emigrants from Eastern Pennsylvania, to Berks county. Here he must have been a contemporary resident, and was perhaps an acquaintance, of some of the younger members of the Lincoln family. At all events, as substantially one of their own neighbors, they must have watched his later course with eager interest and sympathy, and caught inspiration from his exploits. At eighteen, Boone had again emigrated with his father, as before, to the banks of the Yadkin, a mountain river in the north-west of North Carolina, at just about the same date as the removal of the Lincolns to Virginia. Some years later, Boone, in his hunting excursions, had passed over and admired large tracts of the wilderness north of his home, and especially along a branch of the Cumberland river, within the limits of what is now Kentucky. It was not until 1769, however, that, with five associates, he made the thorough exploration of the Kentucky valley, which resulted in the subsequent settlements there. The glowing descriptions, which ultimately got abroad, of the incredible richness and beauty of these new and remote forest-climes of Trans-Alleghanian Virginia, and of their alluring hunting-grounds, must have early reached the ears of the boyhood-companions of Daniel Boone, and spread through the neighboring country. The stirring adventures of the pioneer hero, during the next five or six years, and the beginnings of substantial settlements in that far-west country, must have suggested new attractions thitherward, to the more active and daring spirits, whose ideal of manhood Boone so nearly approached.

From the borders, in various directions, hundreds of miles away, emigration had now begun. These recruits were from that class of hardy frontiersmen most inured to the kind of toils they were to encounter anew in the Kentucky forests. They went forward, fearless of the dangers to be encountered from the numerous bands of Indians already re-commencing hostilities, after a temporary pacification. Here was a common territory and place of meeting for the tribes, both of the North and the South, and here, before and after this date, there were many exciting adventures and deadly conflicts with these savages, whose favorite haunts had been thus unceremoniously invaded.

It was not far from the date of the disastrous battle of the Lower Blue Licks, in 1782, that the grandfather of Mr. Lincoln, with his young family, reached the region which had, perhaps, long been the promised land of his dreams. The exact place at which he settled is not known. According to the family tradition, it was somewhere on Floyd's creek, supposed to be near its mouth, in what is now Bullitt county. On the other hand, in the field-book of Daniel Boone, who was a deputy-surveyor under Col. Thomas Marshall, father of Chief Justice Marshall, is the following memorandum: "Abraham Lincoln enters 500 acres of land, on a Treasury Warrant—No. 5,994—beginning opposite Charles Yancey's upper line, on the south side of the river, running south 200 poles, then up the river for quantity, 11th December, 1782."* Yancey's land, as appears from the same book, was on the north side of the "main" Licking Creek, as then designated.

The emigrant had made but a mere beginning in his new pioneer labors, when, while at work one day, at a distance from his cabin, unsuspecting of danger, he was killed by an Indian, who had stolen upon him unaware. His widow, thus suddenly bereaved

---

* Boone's field-book is now in the hands of L. C. Draper, Esq., of Madison, Wisconsin, to whom I am indebted for the copy given in the text. The "treasury warrant" was issued by the State of Virginia.

in a new and strange land, had now their three sons and two daughters left to her sole protection and care, with probably little means for their support. She soon after removed to what became Washington county, in the same State, and there reared her children, all of whom reached mature age. One of the daughters was married to a Mr. Crume, and the other to a man named Bromfield. The three sons, named Thomas, Mordecai and Josiah, all remained in Kentucky until after their majority.

Thomas Lincoln, one of these sons, was born in 1778. He was a mere child when his father removed to Kentucky, and was but six years old at the time of the latter's death. The date of this event was consequently about 1784. Of the early life of the orphan boy, we have no knowledge, except what can be learned of the general lot of his class, and of the habits and modes of living then prevalent among the hardy pioneers of Kentucky. These backwoodsmen had an unceasing round of hard toils, with no immediate reward but a bare subsistence from year to year, and the cheering promise of better days in the future. But even their lands, as in the case of Boone, they were not always so fortunate as to retain in fee.

More comfortable days, and a much improved state of things had come, before Thomas arrived at maturity; but in his boyhood and youth, he must have known whatever was worst in the trials and penury of the first generation of Kentucky frontiersmen, with few other enjoyments than an occasional practice with his rifle. His training was suited to develop a strong, muscular frame, and a rugged constitution, with a characteristic quickness of perception and promptness of action. The Kentuckian of that, and the succeeding generation had generally a tall, stalwart frame, a frank and courteous heart, and a humorous and slightly quaint turn of speech; a fondness for adventure and for the sports of hunting; a manly self-respect, and a fearless independence of spirit.

> "Pride in their port, defiance in their eye,
>   *   *   *   *
> Intent on high designs, a thoughtful band,
> By forms unfashioned, fresh from nature's hand,
> Fierce in their native hardiness of soul,
> True to imagined right, above control."

This generation began its life with the independent existence of the nation, and partook largely of the spirit of exultant self-confidence then abroad through the land.

These were the circumstances and associations under which, in those primeval days in Kentucky, Thomas Lincoln passed through the period of boyhood and youth. At the date of the political separation from Virginia, in 1792, and the formation of a new State, this orphan boy, struggling to aid his mother in the support of the ill-fortuned family, had reached the age of fourteen. The currents of emigration had become enlarged and accelerated, meantime, until the population was swelled, as early as 1790, to more than 73,000; and during the next ten years it was more than trebled, reaching 220,000. The wilderness that once was around Boonesborough, Harrodsburg, and Lexington, was now blossoming as the rose. Still, however, there was ample space unoccupied, within the limits of the new State, for those who craved the excitements and the loneliness of a home in the wilderness.

In 1806, Thomas Lincoln, being then twenty-eight years of age, was married to Nancy Hanks, a native of Virginia, and settled in what was then Hardin county, Kentucky. It does not appear that the parents of Miss Hanks ever removed to Kentucky, though others of the family did so. Of the history of her ancestry, we have no definite particulars. Her position in life appears to have been not dissimilar to that of her husband. That she possessed some rare qualities of mind and heart, there is reason to believe; although, dying at an early age, and having, from the time of her marriage, passed her days on obscure frontiers, few recollections of her remain.

ABRAHAM LINCOLN was born of these parents on the 12th day of February, 1809. The place where they at this time resided, is in what is now LaRue county, about a mile and a half from Hodgenville, the county-seat, and seven miles from Elizabethtown, laid off several years previously, and the county-seat of Hardin county. He had one sister, two years his senior, who grew up to womanhood, married, and died while young. He had a brother, two years younger than himself, who died in early childhood. Mr. Lincoln remembers to

SITE OF ABRAHAM LINCOLN'S BIRTHPLACE.

The House stood in front of the Pear Trees, which were planted by his Father.

2

have visited the now unmarked grave of this little one, along with his mother, before leaving Kentucky. These were the only children of Thomas Lincoln, either by the present or by a subsequent marriage, hereafter to be noticed. ABRAHAM has thus, for a long time, been the sole immediate representative of this hardy and energetic race.

LaRue county, named from an early settler, John LaRue, was set off and separately organized in 1843, the portion containing Mr. Lincoln's birthplace having been, up to that date, included in Hardin county. It is a rich grazing country in its more rolling and hilly parts, and the level surface produces good crops of corn and tobaccco. In the northern borders of the county, on the Rolling Fork of Salt river, is Muldrough's Hill, a noted eminence. Hodgenville, near which Mr. Lincoln was born, is a pleasantly situated town on Nolin creek, and a place of considerable business. About a mile above this town, on the creek, is a mound, or knoll, thirty feet above the banks of the stream, containing two acres of level ground, at the top of which there is now a house. Some of the early pioneers encamped on this knoll; and but a short distance from it a fort was erected by Philip Phillips, an emigrant from Pennsylvania, about 1780 or 1781, near the time Mr. Lincoln's ancestor arrived from Virginia. John LaRue came from the latter State, with a company of emigrants, and settled, not far from the same date, at Phillips' Fort. Robert Hodgen, LaRue's brother-in-law, purchased and occupied the land on which Hodgenville is built. Both these pioneers were men of sterling integrity, and high moral worth. They were consistent and zealous members of the Baptist church, and one of their associates, Benjamin Lynn, was a minister of the same denomination. Such were the influences under which, more than twenty years before Thomas Lincoln settled there, this little colony had been founded, and which went far to give the community its permanent character.

It is needless to rehearse the kind of life in which Abraham Lincoln was here trained. The picture is similar in all such settlements. In his case, there was indeed the advantage of a generation or two of progress, since his grandfather had

2   2

hazarded and lost his life in the then slightly broken wilderness. The State now numbered some 400,000 inhabitants, and had all the benefits of an efficient local administration, the want of which had greatly increased the dangers and difficulties of the first settlers. Henry Clay had already, though little more than thirty years of age, begun his brilliant political career, having then served for a year or two in the United States Senate.

Yet, with all these changes, the humble laborers, settled near " Hodgen's Mills," on Nolin Creek, had no other lot but incessant toil, and a constant struggle with nature in the still imperfectly reclaimed wilds, for a plain subsistence. Here the boy spent the first years of his childhood. With apparently the same frowning fortune which darkened the early days of Robert Burns, it was not destined that young Lincoln's father should succeed in these first endeavors to secure a competency. Even before the date of his earliest distinct recollections, he removed with his father to a place six miles distant from Hodgenville, which was also ere long to be surrendered, as we shall presently see, for a home in the far-off wilderness, and for frontier life, in its fullest and most significant meaning.

The period of ABRAHAM LINCOLN'S Kentucky life extends through a little more than seven years, terminating with the autumn of 1816. If it be true as a rule (as Horace Mann was wont to maintain), that the experiences and instructions of the first seven years of every person's existence, do more to mold and determine his general character, than all subsequent training, then must we regard Mr. Lincoln as a Kentuckian (of the generation next following that of Clay), by his early impressions and discipline, no less than by birth.

In those days there were no common schools in that country. The principal reliance for acquiring the rudiments of learning was the same as that to which the peasant-poet of Ayrshire was indebted. Education was by no means disregarded, nor did young Lincoln, poor as were his opportunities, grow up an illiterate boy, as some have supposed. Competent teachers were accustomed to offer themselves then, as in later years, who opened private schools for a neighborhood, being supported by tuition fees or subscription. During his boyhood days in Kentucky, Abraham Lincoln attended, at different times, at least two schools of this description, of which he has clear recollections. One of these was kept by Zachariah Riney, a Roman Catholic, whose peculiarities have not been wholly effaced from the memory of his since so distinguished pupil. But although this teacher was himself an ardent Catholic, he made no proselyting efforts in his school, and when any little religious ceremonies, or perhaps mere catechising and the like, were to be gone through with, all Protestant children, of whom, it is needless to say that young Abraham was one, were accustomed to retire, by permission or command. Riney was probably in some way connected with the movement of the "Trappists," who came to Kentucky in the autumn of 1805, and founded an establishment (abandoned some years later) under Urban Guillet, as superior, on Pottinger's Creek. They were active in promoting education especially among the poorer classes, and had a school for boys under their immediate supervision. This, however, had been abandoned before the date of Lincoln's first school-days, and it is not improbable that the private schools under Roman Catholic teachers were an offshoot of the original system adopted by these Trappists, who subsequently removed to Illinois.

Another teacher, on whose instructions the boy afterward attended, while living in Kentucky, was named Caleb Hazel. His was also a neighborhood school, sustained by private patronage.

With the aid of these two schools, and with such further assistance as he received at home, there is no doubt that he had become able to read well, though without having made any great literary progress, at the age of seven. That he was not a dull or inapt scholar, is manifest from his subsequent attainments. With the allurements of the rifle and the wild game which then abounded in the country, however, and with the meager advatages he had, in regard to books, it is certain that his perceptive faculties, and his muscular powers, were much more fully developed by exercise than his scholastic talents.

While he lived in Kentucky, he never saw even the exterior of what was properly a church edifice. The religious services he attended were held either at a private dwelling, or in some log school-house, or in the open grove :

> " Fit shrine for humble worshiper to hold
> Communion with his Master. These dim vaults,
> These winding aisles, of human pomp or pride
> Report not. No fantastic carvings show
> The boast of our vain race, to change the form
> Of Thy fair works. But Thou art here, Thou fill'st
> The solitude."*

Unsatisfactory results of these many years' toil on the lands of Nolin Creek, or a restless spirit of adventure and fondness for more genuine pioneer excitements than this region continued to afford, led Thomas Lincoln, now verging upon the age of forty, and his son beginning to be of essential service in manual labor, to seek a new place of abode, far to the west, beyond the Ohio river.

---

*Bryant.

CHAPTER II.

MR. LINCOLN'S EARLY LIFE IN INDIANA.

The Removal from Kentucky.—An Emigrant Journey.—The Forests of Southern Indiana.—New Home of the Lincoln Family.—Indiana in 1816.—Slavery and Free Labor.—Young Lincoln at His Work.—His Schools and Schoolmasters.—Self-Education.—A Characteristic Incident.—Acquaintance with River Life.—His First Trip to New Orleans as a Flatboatman.—Death of His Mother.—His Father's Second Marriage.—Recollections of an Early Settler.—Close of an Eventful Period in Young Lincoln's History.

EARLY in the autumn of 1816, an immediate departure for the new wilds of Indiana, was determined on by Thomas Lincoln. It was no very imposing sight, certainly, as the little family, bidding the old Kentucky home adieu, moved forward upon their long and winding pioneer march. Many sad thoughts there undoubtedly were in that small group, and perhaps some forebodings, also, as their former place, gradually receding, at length disappeared from their reverted eyes. But these emotions must soon have been lost in the excitements of their journey.

It was no novel picture which they presented, for that period, as they advanced on their lonely way, for the days required to bring them to the place whence they were to cross the "Beautiful River." The plain wagon, with its simple covering as a shelter for its lading of household utensils, articles of food, and "varieties," was drawn by a not too-spirited or over-fed horse, in a harness probably compounded of leather and hempen cords of an uncertain age. In the forward part of this conveyance, sat the emigrant wife and her daughter, nine years old, while the father and his son, now past seven, walking in the rear, took care that the indispensable cow kept pace to the music of the jolting wheels.   Underneath the wagon, or scouting at pleasure through the surrounding woods, was of course a large dog, constant to the fortunes of his master's family, and ready for any fate to which their migrations might lead him. Arrived at the appointed landing on the banks of the Ohio, it only remained to embark the little caravan upon a flatboat, and to cross the stream, now swelled to fair proportions by the autumn rains.   Finally, after reaching the Indiana side, the adventurers landed at or near the mouth of Anderson's Creek, now the boundary between the counties of Perry and Spencer, about one hundred and forty miles below Louisville, by the river, and sixty above Evansville.   In a direct line across the country from their former residence, the distance is, perhaps, hardly one hundred miles.

The place at which Mr. Lincoln settled, at the end of this journey, is some distance back from the Ohio river, near the present town of Gentryville.   Under the earliest organization, this was in Perry county, of which Troy was the county-seat. Two years later, Spencer county was formed, embracing all that part of Perry west of Anderson's Creek, and including the place at which Mr. Lincoln had located himself.

Here his emigrant wagon paused, and aided by the busy hands of his son, a log cabin was speedily built, which was to be their home through many coming years.   The particular site of his dwelling was doubtless determined, as usual, by the discovery of a living spring of water, after fixing on his selection for a farm.   This completed, and a shelter provided for their stock, the next business was to clear up a space in the forest which should produce a crop of grain for their sustenance the next season.   Hard work had begun in good earnest for the young Kentuckian.   He was to learn the realities of genuine pioneer life, such as he had before but imperfectly understood, unless by tradition and the evening tales of his father.

Indiana, at this date, was still a Territory, having been originally united under the same government with Illinois, after the admission of Ohio as a State, "the first-born of the great North-west," in 1802.   A separate territorial organization was made for each in 1809.   A few months before the arrival of Thomas Lincoln, namely, in June, 1816, pursuant to a Congressional "enabling act," a Convention had been held which adopted a State Constitution, preparatory to admission into the Union. Under this Constitution, a little later, in December, 1816, Indiana became, by act of Congress, one of the United States.

The population of Indiana was now about 65,000, distributed chiefly south of a straight line drawn from Vincennes, on the Wabash, to Lawrenceburg, on the Ohio. Vincennes was long the territorial capital, and with the surrounding country, had been occupied by French emigrants, many years before the Revolution. In 1800, the whole number of residents in these colonies was less than 5,000. These, like other French settlements, made little progress of themselves. From 1800 to 1810, there had been a large increase, mostly by emigrations to Southern Indiana from Kentucky, swelling the population to 24,520, at the latter date. In 1811 had occurred serious difficulties with the Indians, terminating in the decisive victory over them at Tippecanoe. So general had become the settlements, eastward from Vincennes and up the Ohio river, that the capital was removed far eastward to Corydon, in 1813, as a central location. This place, the capital of Harrison county, is about twenty-five miles west from Louisville, and more than a hundred south of the present metropolis of the State. But one county intervened between Harrison and Perry, and Gentryville is hardly forty miles, in a direct line, from Corydon. This place continued to be the seat of government for the State until 1824, as it had been for the Territory during the three years next preceding 1816. It was but natural, therefore, that emigration should be prominently directed to this part of the State, at the period under consideration. In 1820, the population had increased to over 147,000, or more than six-fold during ten years, and nearly thirty-fold since 1800.

There is little doubt that, in emigrating, Thomas Lincoln had fallen in with a prevalent contagion in his own State, and that he took up his residence in the part of Indiana then deemed most desirable of all that was unoccupied. It is common to attribute these extensive migrations from the border slaveholding States into the non-slaveholding North-west, to a preference for institutions based upon free labor to the exclusion of slavery. This was, beyond question, a powerful inducement with many, yet, by no means the only one; and, with some, it did not exist at all. In the earlier days of Kentucky, the proportion of slaves to the free white population was small, and in many places slavery can hardly have been an appreciable element. But in 1816, the number of slaves must have exceeded 100,000, and their ratio of increase was becoming very high. Upon a man in the circumstances of Mr. Lincoln, with a young family to rear, this consideration undoubtedly had its weight, among the others we have suggested as the cause of his removal to Indiana. We have at least the fact, that, though painfully, and with an exile's sadness, he yet turned his back forever on a State that tolerated slavery, to seek a new home where free labor had been sacredly assured exclusive rights and honors.

The next thirteen years Abraham Lincoln spent here, in Southern Indiana, near the Ohio, nearly midway between Louisville and Evansville. He was now old enough to begin to take an active part in the farm labors of his father, and he manfully performed his share of hard work. He learned to use the ax and to hold the plough. He became inured to all the duties of seed-time and harvest. On many a day, during every one of those thirteen years, this Kentucky boy might have been seen with a long "gad" in his hand, driving his father's team in the field, or from the woods with a heavy draught, or on the rough path to the mill, the store, or the river landing. He was specially an adept at felling trees, and acquired a muscular strength in which he was equaled by few or none of those about him. In the sports of hunting and fishing, he was less skilled.

A vigorous constitution, and a cheerful, unrepining disposition, made all his labors comparatively light. To such a one, this sort of life has in it much of pleasant excitement to compensate for its hardships. He learned to derive enjoyment from the severest lot. The "dignity of labor," which is with demagogues mere hollow cant, became to him a true and appreciable reality.

Here, as in Kentucky, he attended private schools, and in other ways increased his little stock of learning, aided by what he had already acquired. The same want of systematic public instruction, and the same mode of remedying this lack, prevailed in Indiana, as in his former home. One of his teachers was named Andrew Crawford, to whom he used to be occasionally indebted for the loan of books, to read at such leisure hours as he could command. His last teacher was Azel W. Dorsey, who had the satisfaction, in later years, of taking his former scholar by the hand, rejoicing to recognize the once obscure boy as one of the foremost leaders of the people. Dorsey was lately residing in Schuyler County, Illinois, where he also had sons living.

That we may estimate Mr. Lincoln in his true character, as chiefly a self-educated man, it should be stated that, summing up all the days of his actual attendance upon school instruction, the amount would hardly exceed one year. The rest he has accomplished for himself in his own way. As a youth he read with avidity such instructive works as he could obtain, and in winter evenings, by the mere light of the blazing fireplace, when no better resource was at hand.

An incident having its appropriate connection here, and illustrating several traits of the man, as already developed in early boyhood, is vouched for by a citizen of Evansville, who knew him in the days referred to. In his eagerness to acquire knowledge, young Lincoln had borrowed of Mr. Crawford a copy of Weems' Life of Washington—the only one known to be in existence in the neighborhood. Before he had finished reading the book, it had been left, by a not unnatural oversight, in a window. Meantime, a rain storm came on, and the book was so thoroughly wet as to make it nearly worthless. This mishap caused him much pain; but he went, in all honesty, to Crawford with the ruined book, explained the calamity that had happened through his neglect, and offered, not having sufficient money, to "work out" the value of the book.

"Well, Abe," said Crawford, "as it's you I wont be hard on

3

you. Come over and pull fodder for me for two days, and we will call our accounts even."

The offer was accepted and the engagement literally fulfilled. As a boy, no less than since, Abraham Lincoln had an honorable conscientiousness, integrity, industry, and an ardent love of knowledge.

The town on the Ohio river, nearest his home, was Troy, the capital of Perry county down to the date of its division. This place, at the mouth of Anderson's Creek, had been settled as early as 1811, and was a place of some consequence, both for its river trade and as the county-seat. After this latter advantage was lost, by the formation of a new county in 1818, Troy dwindled away, and is now a place of only about five hundred inhabitants. Rockport, nearly twenty miles south-west of Gentryville, became the capital of Spencer county, and thenceforward a point of interest to the new settlers. It is situated on a high bluff of the Ohio river, and receives its name from "Lady Washington's Rock," a picturesque hanging-rock at that place. At these two points young Lincoln gained some knowledge of the new world of river life and business, in addition to his farm experience, and to his forest sports with rod and rifle. For several months he is said to have been ferryman at Anderson's Creek Ferry.

It was during one of the later of these thirteen years, that Abraham, at nineteen, was permitted to gratify his eager longing to see more of the world, and to try the charms of an excursion on the Beautiful River. He had inherited much of the adventurous and stirring disposition of his Virginian grandfather, and was delighted with the prospect of a visit to New Orleans, then the splendid city of Western dreams. He performed this journey on a common flatboat, doing service as one of the hands on that long yet most exhilarating trip. We have no particulars of this his sole excursion as a flatboatman during his Indiana days, yet to his own mind it probably long afforded many not unpleasing recollections. He was undoubtedly the life of the little company, delighting them with his humorous sallies no less than with his muscular superiority, and with his hilarious activity and intuitive tact in all that immediately concerned their voyage.

If there had been any forebodings at the time of departure from their first home on Nolin Creek, these were to be ere long realized by the Indiana emigrants. Scarcely two years had passed, in this changed climate, and in these rougher forest experiences, before the mother of young Abraham—perhaps too gentle to encounter the new trials added to those she had before partially surmounted, and to endure the malarious influences in which this wild country abounded—was called to a last separation from those she had so tenderly loved. She died in 1818, leaving as her sole surviving children, a daughter less than twelve years old, and a son two years younger, of whose future distinction, even with a mother's fondness, she probably had but an indefinite hope. A grave was made for her—

> "Where the wind of the West breathes its softest sigh;
> Where the silvery stream is flowing nigh—
> Where the sun's warm smile may never dispel
> Night's tears o'er the form that was loved so well—
> Where no column proud in the sun may glow,
> To mock the heart that is resting below." *

A year or two later, Thomas Lincoln contracted a second marriage with Mrs. Johnston, a widow with three children, that were brought up with those of Mr. Lincoln. Besides these step-children, there were no additions to the family as before enumerated.

In concluding this brief account of the thirteen important years which were spent by Abraham Lincoln as an Indianian, the personal recollections of a distinguished lawyer and statesman of an older generation, who emigrated to Indiana at nearly the same date, will aid in conveying a correct impression of those times, and of the circumstances with which the youth was surrounded.

Indiana, says the late Hon. O. H. Smith,† "was born in the year 1816, with some sixty-five thousand inhabitants—only about forty years ago. A few counties only were then organ-

---

* J. B. Dillon.

† Early Indiana Trials and Sketches. Reminiscences by Hon. O. H. Smith, page 285.

ized. The whole middle, north, and north-west portions of the State were an unbroken wilderness, in the possession of the Indians. Well do I remember when there were but two families settled west of the Whitewater Valley—one at Flat Rock, above where Rushville now stands, and the other on Brandywine, near where Greenfield was afterward located. When I first visited the ground on which Indianapolis now stands, the whole country, east to Whitewater and west to the Wabash, was a dense, unbroken forest. There were no public roads, no bridges over any of the streams. The traveler had literally to swim his way. No cultivated farms, no houses to shelter or feed the weary traveler, or his jaded horse. The courts, years afterward, were held in log huts, and the juries sat under the shade of the forest trees. I was Circuit Prosecuting Attorney at the time of the trials at the falls of Fall Creek, where Pendleton now stands. Four of the prisoners were convicted of murder, and three of them hung, for killing Indians. The court was held in a double log cabin, the grand jury sat upon a log in the woods, and the foreman signed the bill of indictment which I had prepared, upon his knee; there was not a petit juror that had shoes on—all wore moccasins, and were belted around the waist, and carried side-knives used by the hunter. The products of the country consisted of peltries, the wild game killed in the forest by the Indian hunters, the fish caught in the interior lakes, rivers and creeks, the pawpaw, wild plum, haws, small berries gathered by the squaws in the woods. The travel was confined to the single horse and his rider, the commerce to the pack-saddle, and the navigation to the Indian canoe. Many a time and oft have I crossed our swollen streams, by day and by night, sometimes swimming my horse, and at others paddling the rude bark canoe of the Indian. Such is a mere sketch of our State when I traversed its wilds, and I am not one of its first settlers."

Thus it was that young Lincoln grew up to the verge of manhood; he led no idle or enervating existence. Brought up to the habits of sobriety, and accustomed to steady labor, no one of all the working-men with whom he came in contact was a better sample of his class than he. He had now become a Saul among his associates, having reached the hight of nearly six feet and four inches, and with a comparatively slender yet uncommonly strong, muscular frame. He was even then, in his mental and moral characteristics, no less than in his physical proportions, one not to be forgotten or unappreciated by those who knew him. Many reminiscences of those days of his hardy endeavor and rough experience linger in the minds of the plain, earnest people among whom his lot for a long period was thus cast, and will some time be repeated, with such exaggerations or fabulous glosses as are wont gradually to gather, like the sacred halo of the painters, around the memorials of a recognized hero. And a hero, ever hereafter, in the traditions of Southern Indiana, will be the youthful Abraham Lincoln, gigantic and stalwart in his outward form, no less than in the glowing and noble spirit already beginning to foresee and prepare for a high destiny. Wherever he has dwelt becomes classic and consecrated ground, and to have known him, even in his obscurest days, will be deemed a circumstance to be recounted with pride. To gather up such recollections and to perpetuate them with the pen, will be the work of future times and other hands.

This period of young Lincoln's life was terminated by another removal of his father, as will appear in the next chapter

CHAPTER III.

FIRST YEARS IN ILLINOIS.—1830-32

The French Settlements.—The North-west.—The Advance of Emigration.—Four Great States Founded in the Lifetime of Mr. Lincoln's Father.—North and South Meeting in Ohio, Indiana and Illinois.—Sentiments of Southern Emigrants.—The First Emigrations.—A Coincidence of Dates.—Mordecai and Josiah Lincoln.—Removal to Illinois.—Settlement on the Sangamon, in Macon County.—The Locality Described.—Abraham Lincoln Engaged in Splitting Rails.—Another Removal of his Father.—He Settles in Coles County.—Abraham Lincoln makes Another Trip as a Flatboatman.—Becomes Clerk in a Store on his Return.—Postmaster at New Salem.

THE early French settlements of Illinois, at Kaskaskia and Cahokia, had proved as little successful or permanent as those of Indiana around Vincennes. The territory had come into the possession of the British Government just before the Revolution, and emigration from Virginia had commenced almost simultaneously to that quarter and to Kentucky. In 1787, as is well known, the settlements here, in common with those scattered throughout the great expanse of United States territory, north-west of the Ohio river, were brought under a territorial government, as wide in its local scope as it was apparently insignificant in the extent of its population and power. Time speedily demonstrated the error of such an estimate of the remarkable region between the Ohio, the Mississippi, and the Lakes, yet, even to this day, the people of the East accept the idea of this greatness and coming power rather as an abstract proposition than as a living reality, deeply affecting their own relative interests and the common resources and grandeur of the country.

The rapid growth of Kentucky on the one side, and of Ohio and Indiana on the other, we have incidentally seen in these pages. The birth of Mr. Lincoln's father, Thomas Lincoln, was anterior to, or nearly coeval with, the very first settlements in all those States, excepting only the lifeless French colonies of Indiana. The State of Illinois may be added to those of which it may be said, in like manner, his own life was the measure of their age, dating from the first substantial and growing existence of their colonial settlements. In Illinois, as in Indiana, the earliest waves of a healthful emigration had come from Kentucky and Virginia, and in both cases alike, the Southern portion was the earliest to be occupied. Between these early outflowings of free labor from the land of slavery, and those later ones from the free States of the East, on more northern parallels, there is a marked difference, still traceable—creating, in a certain sense, in all the States of the North-west which touch the imaginary line of Mason and Dixon, a division of North and South. Experience and increased commingling between these localities are fast abating the distinctness of this somewhat indefinite separating line, but for years to come it can not be wholly obliterated. These two elements, combined and consolidated, growing into unity instead of being arrayed against each other in widening separation, will go to constitute the strongest of States. The Southern emigration gave character to the earlier legislation of Indiana and Illinois especially. With evidences of a lurking attachment to the peculiar institution of the States on the other side of the Ohio river, the general tenor of public sentiment and action was as positive and distinct, as were the opinions of the more Northern multitudes who came in to fill up these new commonwealths. And yet, the views of slavery prevalent in southern Indiana and Illinois, were at that time not much diverse from those which were entertained in the communities from which these settlers had come. They regarded slavery as an evil to be rid of; and to make sure of this, those who were not already too much entangled with it, left in large numbers for a region which, by request of Virginia herself, was "forever" protected from the inroads of this moral and social mischief.

As we have seen, Indiana had more than 100,000 people concentrated in the south, before any real advance had been made in the central and northern parts. Nearly the same thing was true of Illinois. The territory had been separately organized in the same year with the birth of Abraham Lincoln—1809. The next year's census showed its entire white population to be only 11,501. These were almost exclusively located south of the National Road, which crosses the Kaskaskia river at Vandalia, extending nearly due west to Alton. Notwithstanding the severe labors of opening the forests on the rich western soil, and the long period that must necessarily elapse between the first clearing therein and the perfect subjugation of the selected lands into cultivated farms, there seems to have been a general avoidance, even down to comparatively a late period, of the open prairie, which is now thought to offer such pre-eminent facilities for cultivation, with almost immediate re-payment for the toil bestowed. The settlers who had gone into Illinois, evidently placed a low estimate upon the prairie lands, and always settled on the banks of some stream, on which there was plenty of timber, seeking the forest by preference for their homes. The open character of the country undoubtedly repelled emigration, and caused it to be concentrated on the chief streams, for a long time, when at last it commenced in earnest.

In 1820, two years after admission into the Union, the entire population, still almost entirely confined to the same region, and to similar localities as ten years before, amounted to only 55,211. From that time to 1830, there was some extension of the settlements northward, toward the center of the State, and up the Mississippi to Galena, where the mines were already worked. The rivers along which the principal settlements had been made, aside from the great boundary rivers—the Mississippi, the Ohio, and the Wabash—were the Kaskaskia, the Embarras, the Sangamon, and their branches. There were a few settlements, also, in the Rock-river country, and on the range of Peoria. The population, thus chiefly distributed, had now (1830) reached 157,445.

The brothers of Thomas Lincoln had previously removed

THE EMIGRATION FROM KENTUCKY.

to a more northern location in Indiana, than that which he had occupied. Both settled in the Blue river country—Mordecai in Hancock county, where he not long after died, and Josiah in Harrison county. Their example, perhaps, had its influence upon Thomas, who, however, took a course of his own. Whatever the immediate or remote occasion, he left Indiana in the spring of 1830, to seek another place of abode, in the State of Illinois. He had seen the growth of Kentucky from almost the very start, to a population of nearly 700,000 and he had lived in Indiana from the time its inhabitants numbered only 65,000, until they had reached nearly 350,000. As he first set his foot within the limits of Illinois, its vast territory had, comparatively, but just begun to be occupied, scarcely at all, as we have seen, except in the extreme southern portion, and here almost exclusively along the principal streams. In a country so poorly supplied with wood and water, as Illinois, such sites would naturally be the first to be taken up, and, with a prairie addition, they suited the tastes even of those to whom the level, open country was forbidding in appearance.

Mr. Lincoln's father pushed forward to the central part of the State, where such locations were abundant. A more beautiful country than that of the Sangamon valley, could not easily have been anywhere discovered by an explorer. It was not strange that the report of such lands, if he heard it in his Southern Indiana home, should have attracted even so far one who was bred to pioneer life, and inherited a migratory disposition. He first settled on the Sangamon "bottom," in Macon county.

Passing over the Illinois Central Railroad, as you approach Decatur, the county-seat of Macon, from the south, a slightly broken country is reached two or three miles from that place, and presently the North Fork of the Sangamon, over which you pass, a mile from the town. This stream flows westwardly, uniting with the South Fork, near Jamestown, ten miles from Springfield. Following down this North Fork for a distance of about ten miles from Decatur, you come to the immediate vicinity of the first residence of Abraham Lincoln (with his father's family), in Illinois.

3

Here, for the first season of his abode in the new State he continued to assist the father in his farm-work. One of the first duties was to fence in a field on the rich bottom-lands, which had been selected for cultivation. For this purpose, with the help of one laborer, Abraham Lincoln, it is said split three thousand rails*—the crowning work of a long laborious period of his life. The hand who aided him in this exploit, named John Hanks, a distant relative of his mother, bears earnest testimony to the strength and skill with with which the maul and the wedge were employed on this occasion.

For some unexplained reason, the family did not remain on this place but a single year. Abraham was now of age, and when, in the spring of 1831, his father set out for Coles county, sixty or seventy miles to the eastward, on the upper waters of the Kaskaskia and Embarras, a separation took place, the son for the first time, assuming his independence, and commencing life on his own account. The scene of these labors he never again visited. His father was soon after comfortably settled in the place to which he had turned his course, and spent the remainder of his adventurous days there, arriving at a good old age. He died in Coles county, on the 17th day of January, 1851, being in his seventy-third year. The farm on the Sangamon subsequently came into the possession of a Mr. Whitley, who erected a mill in the vicinity.

While there was snow on the ground, at the close of the year 1830, or early in 1831, a man came to that part of Macon county where young Lincoln was living, in pursuit of hands to aid him in a flatboat voyage down the Mississippi. The fact was known that the youth had once made such a trip, and his services were sought for the occasion. As one who had his own subsistence to earn, with no capital but his hands, and with no immediate opportunities for commencing professional study, if his thoughts had as yet been turned in that direction, he accepted the proposition made him. Perhaps there was something of his inherited and acquired fondness for exciting adventure, impelling him to this decision. With him, were

*The number is uncertain, but the main fact rests on the best authority.

also employed, his former fellow-laborer, John Hanks, and a son of his step-mother, named John Johnston. In the spring of 1831 Lincoln set out to fulfill his engagement. The floods had so swollen the streams that the Sangamon country was a vast sea before him. His first entrance into that county was over these wide-spread waters, in a canoe. The time had come to join his employer on his journey to New Orleans, but the latter had been disappointed by another person on whom he relied to furnish him a boat, on the Illinois river. Accordingly, all hands set to work, and themselves built a boat, on that river, for their purposes. This done, they set out on their long trip, making a successful voyage to New Orleans and back. It is reported by his friends, that Mr. Lincoln refers with much pleasant humor to this early experience, so relating some of its incidents as to afford abundant amusement to his auditors. In truth, he was a youth who could adapt himself to this or any other honest work which his circumstances required of him, and with a cheerfulness and alacrity—a certain practical humor—rarely equaled. He could turn off the hardest labor as a mere pastime; and his manly presence, to other laborers, was as a constant inspiration and a charm to lighten their burdens.

It was midsummer when the flatboatman returned from this his second and last trip, in that capacity. The man who had commanded this little expedition now undertook to establish himself in business at New Salem, twenty miles below Springfield, in Menard county—a place of more relative consequence then than now—two miles from Petersburg, the county-seat. He had found young Lincoln a person of such sort that he was anxious to secure his services in the new enterprise he was about to embark in. He opened a store at New Salem, and also had a mill for flouring grain. For want of other immediate employment, and in the same spirit which had heretofore actuated him, Abraham Lincoln now entered upon the duties of a clerk, having an eye to both branches of the business carried on by his employer. This connection continued for nearly a year, all the duties of his position being faithfully performed.

It was to this year's humble but honorable service—one that would have been ennobled by his alacrity in discharging it, as a necessity of his lot, were the employment far less dignified than it really was—that Mr. Douglas tauntingly alluded, in one of his speeches during the canvass of 1858, as "keeping a grocery." In his reply, Mr. Lincoln declared his adversary to be "woefully at fault" as to the fact, in alleging him to have been a grocery-keeper, though it might be no great sin had the statement been well founded. He added that, in truth, he had "never kept a grocery anywhere in the world."

The business of this country merchant at New Salem did not prove remarkably successful. In any event, the employment was not such as could have permanently suited an active, muscular person, like young Lincoln, with a lurking passion for adventure, and for more exciting scenes. His clerkship days, however, were brought to an abrupt close, probably much sooner than they otherwise would have been, by the breaking out of the Black-Hawk war, in which he was eager to bear an honorable part.

It was during this year that he was appointed Postmaster at New Salem—not from political affinity with the administration of Jackson, to which he was, in fact, opposed, but because he was thought better fitted for the place than any of his neighbors. He discharged his duties well; and instead of even temporarily using any of the public money to supply his then pressing wants, he carefully laid up whatever belonged to the Government, from day to day, and at the final settlement he had a bag of coin, containing the proper amount, ready to be paid over.

CHAPTER IV.

SERVICE IN THE BLACK-HAWK WAR—1832.

Breaking out of the Black-Hawk War.—The Invasion of 1831.—The Rock-river Country Threatened.—Prompt Action of Gov. Reynolds.—Retreat of Black-Hawk. — Treaty of 1804 Re-affirmed. — Bad Faith of the Indians.—Invasion of 1832.—Volunteers Called For.—Abraham Lincoln one of a Company from Menard County.—He is chosen Captain.—Rendezvous at Beardstown.—Hard Marches across the Country to Oquawka, Prophetstown and Dixon.—Expected Battle Avoided by the Enemy.—Discontent among Volunteers.—They are Disbanded.—Captain Lincoln Remains, Volunteering for Another Term of Service.—Skirmishing Fights.—Arrival of New Levies.—Encounter at Kellogg's Grove.—Black-Hawk at the Four Lakes.—He Retreats.—Battle on the Wisconsin.—Hastens Forward to the Mississippi.—Battle of the Bad-ax.—End of Lincoln's First Campaign.—Autobiographic Note.

WHILE Abraham Lincoln was quietly performing his duties in the pioneer "store," in Menard county, reports were received of an alarming Indian invasion, on the western border of the State. In the spring of 1831, the noted Black-Hawk, an old chief of the Sac tribe of Indians, repudiating the treaty by the terms of which they had been removed beyond the Father of Waters, re-crossed the river with his women and children, and three hundred warriors of the Sacs, together with allies from the Kickapoo and Pottawatomie nations. His object was again to take possession of his old hunting-grounds, and to establish himself where the principal village of his nation before had been, in the Rock-river country. The Indians began committing depredations upon the property of the white settlers, destroying their crops, pulling down their fences, driving off and slaughtering their cattle, and ordering the settlers themselves to leave under penalty of being massacred.

In response to the representations of Gov. Reynolds, to whom the settlers applied for protection, Gen. Gaines, commander of the United States forces in that quarter, took prompt and decisive measures to expel these invaders from the State. With a few companies of regular soldiers, Gen. Gaines at once took up his position at Rock Island, and at his call, several hundred volunteers, assembled from the northern and central parts of the State, upon the proclamation of Gov. Reynolds, joined him a month later. His little army distributed into two regiments, an additional battalion, and a spy battalion, was the most formidable military force yet seen in the new State. The expected battle did not take place, the Indians having suddenly and stealthily retired again, in their canoes, across the river. The troops had been advanced to Vandruff's Island, opposite the Indian town, where the engagement was anticipated, and there was much dissatisfaction among the volunteers, and some complaints against the generals, Gaines and Duncan, for permitting the enemy to escape.

Whether or not either of these commanders was chargeable with blame, this retreat of Black-Hawk only prolonged the difficulties impending, and prepared the way for a more formidable and eventful campaign the next season. Gen. Gaines, however had taken measures to preclude any such possibility, so far as the deliberate engagements of the uneasy chief could avail for that purpose. Intimidated by the threats of Gaines to cross the river, and to prosecute the war on that ground, Black-Hawk sued for peace. A treaty was entered into, by which he agreed that he and his tribe should ever after remain on the west side of the river, unless by permission of the State Governor, or of the President. Thus was the treaty of 1804 re-affirmed, by which the lands they were claiming had been distinctly conveyed to the United States Government, which, in turn, had sold them to the present settlers.

In express violation, however, of this second deliberate engagement, Black-Hawk and his followers began, early in the spring of 1832, as we have seen, to make preparations for another invasion. Many and grievous wrongs have undoubtedly been inflicted upon the savage tribes by the superior race, that has gradually, but steadily driven the former from their ancient homes. But the bad faith shown in this case, and the repeated violation of deliberate and voluntary agreements, was wholly without justification or excuse. No provocation or plausible pretext had arisen after the treaty of the previous June; yet Black-Hawk, under the misguided influence and false representations of the "Prophet," who persuaded him to believe that even the British (to whom Black-Hawk had always been a fast friend), as well as the Ottawas, Chippewas, Winnebagoes and Pottawatomies, would aid them in regaining their village and the adjoining lands. Under this delusion, to which the wiser Keokuk refused to become a dupe, though earnestly invited to join them, Black-Hawk proceeded to gather as strong a force as possible. He first established his headquarters at the old site of Fort Madison, west of the Mississippi. After his preparations, of which the people of Illinois were advised, had been completed, he proceeded up the river with his women and children, his property and camp equipage, in canoes, while his warriors, armed and mounted, advanced by land. In spite of the warning he had received, that there was a strong force of white soldiers at Fort Armstrong, on Rock Island, he continued on to the mouth of Rock river, where, in utter recklessnes and bad faith—paying not the slightest regard to his solemn agreement of the last year—the whole party crossed to the east side of the Mississippi, with a declared purpose of ascending Rock river to the territory of the Winnebagoes. This was in the early part of April, 1832. Black-Hawk, after he had gone some distance up this latter river, was overtaken by a messenger from Gen. Atkinson, who had command of the troops on Rock Island, and ordered to return beyond the Mississippi. This was defiantly refused.

Gov. Reynolds again issued a call for volunteers to protect the settlers from this invasion. A company was promptly raised in Menard county, in the formation of which Abraham Lincoln was one of the most active. From New Salem, Clary's Grove, and elsewhere in the vicinity, an efficient force was gathered, and in making their organization, Lincoln was elected Captain. This was the first official honor he had ever received by the suffrages of his fellows, and one that afforded particular satisfaction to his not unaspiring, though modest spirit, as he, long afterward, frankly admitted.

Their first march was to the rendezvous appointed by Gov. Reynolds, at Beardstown, one of the earlier settlements on the Illinois river, forty miles west of New Salem. Here eighteen hundred men were speedily assembled, under the direction of the Governor. The forces were organized into four regiments, with an additional spy battalion. Gen. Samuel Whiteside, of the State militia, who had commanded the spy battalion in the campaign of the previous year, was now intrusted with the command of the whole brigade. Gen. James D. Henry was placed at the head of the spy battalion.

This little army, a more imposing force than that of the preceding year, set out from Beardstown on the 27th of April, for the scene of action. Three or four days' hard marching across the country brought the volunteers to Oquawka, on the Mississippi, from whence they proceeded, without delay, northward to the mouth of Rock river. Here it was arranged with Gen. Atkinson, commander of the regulars, that the volunteer force should march up the latter stream a distance of about fifty miles, to Prophetstown, where they were to encamp, awaiting the arrival of the regulars, with provisions, by the river. Gen. Whiteside, however, instead of following out this plan, set fire to the Prophet's village, on arriving, and pushed forward toward Dixon's Ferry, forty miles further up the river.

These incessant marches must have severely taxed the endurance of many of the inexperienced soldiers, but to Capt. Lincoln, reared as he had been, they rather hightened the exhilaration which attended these adventures from the start. The prospect of speedily overtaking and encountering the enemy in battle, and the hope of winning, in the fight, some special honors for the little contingent under his command, relieved the sense of fatigue. A short distance below Dixon's Ferry, it was ordered that the baggage-wagons should be left behind, and that a forced march should be made upon that place. Arrived there, Gen. Whiteside halted, and sent out scouting parties to ascertain the position and condition of the enemy. Here two battalions of mounted volunteers, numbering two hundred and seventy-five men, joined them from McLean, Peoria, and other counties, eager to distingish themselves by participating in the war. Some of these fiery spirits, advancing without orders, and having no other duty assigned them than that of scouts, had a little skirmish on the 12th of May, a mile distant from their encampment, in Ogle county, with a number of mounted Indians, in which three of the latter were killed. Black-Hawk and his principal forces were not far off, and rallying seven hundred men, he promptly repelled the assaults of these scouts, pursuing them in a disorderly condition, to their camp. These rash adventurers now showed greater eagerness in flight, than they had before to gain distinction in battle, and ran helter-skelter over the prairie, producing such confusion and dismay as to render it difficult to prevent the most serious effects from their insubordinate conduct. As it was, eleven of the men were killed, the confidence of the Indians was greatly raised, and the survivors, who came straggling into the camp of General Whiteside, were full of panic, anticipating an immediate and general attack from their pursuers. Such was "Stillman's defeat."

The consequence of this affair was a council of war at the tent of the commander-in-chief, and a decision to march, early next morning, to the scene of that evening's misadventure. The great battle which Capt. Lincoln and his fellow-volunteers had come so far to participate in, seemed now on the point of becoming a reality. Notwithstanding the premature advance of Whiteside from Prophetstown had left them without the necessary supplies, and subjected them to the privations so well known to experienced soldiers, yet seldom encountered so early in a campaign, they made up for the absence of their regular provisions as best they might, and were ready, with the dawn, for the day's undertaking. But their enemy did not await their coming. Arrived at the scene of yesterday's skirmish and flight, they found not a straggler of all the savage forces. They had partly gone further up the river, and partly dispersed, to commit depredations in the

4

surrounding country. One party of them came suddenly upon a settlement near Ottawa, and massacred fifteen persons, carrying two young women into captivity. This circumstance alone is sufficient to show how utterly unfounded was the pretense of some that Black-Hawk had no hostile purpose, in this repudiation of his treaty engagements, and to remove any ground for the mistaken sympathy which many have expended upon him.

After this energetic but vain attempt to fall in with the enemy and give him battle, Gen. Whiteside, having buried the dead of the day before, returned to camp, where he was joined, next day, by Gen. Atkinson, with his troops and supplies. The numbers of the army were thus increased to twenty-four hundred, and a few weeks more would have enabled this force to bring the war to a successful close. But many of the volunteers, whose time had nearly expired, were eager to be discharged. They had seen quite enough of the hardships of a campaign, which, without bringing as yet any glory, had turned out in reality quite different from what their imaginations had foretold. With the prevailing discontents, but one course was possible. The volunteers were marched to Ottawa, where they were discharged by Gov. Reynolds, on the 27th and 28th of May.

This sudden disbanding, without a battle, and with no results accomplished, was a disappointment to the young captain from Menard county. Gov. Reynolds had previously issued a call for two thousand new volunteers, to assemble at Beardstown and Hennepin. In accordance with the wishes of Lincoln, and others, who were still ready to bear their share of the campaign, to its close, the Governor also asked for the formation of a volunteer regiment from those just discharged. Lincoln promptly enrolled himself as a private, as did also General Whiteside.

Before the arrival of the other levies, a skirmishing fight with the Indians was had at Burr Oak Grove, on the 18th of June, in which the enemy was defeated, with considerable loss, and on the side of the volunteers, two killed and one wounded.

The Winnebagoes and Pottawatomies now showed a decidedly hostile disposition toward the whites, and an inclination to join the movement of Black-Hawk. Accordingly, with the appearance of the new levies, which had been divided into three regiments, and their junction with the regular and volunteer forces already in the field—the whole number of volunteers alone being thirty-two hundred—the army was placed in a formidable and effective attitude for offensive warfare. Meantime the Indian atrocities continued, their acts of signal treachery and cruelty rendering an efficient prosecution of the war, to its termination, indispensable. Galena, then a village of about four hundred inhabitants, was surrounded by the desperate enemy, and in imminent danger of attack. Apple River Fort, twelve miles from Galena, had already been made the object of a fierce and persevering attack, by Black-Hawk himself and a hundred and fifty of his warriors, and obstinately defended by twenty-five men, during fifteen hours of constant fighting, ending with the retreat of the Indians, with no slight loss. Within the fort, one man was killed and another wounded. Straggling parties of Indians, at various points, made attacks upon the whites, producing constant alarm and excitement through that part of the country.

The new forces, under command of Gen. Atkinson, of the regular army, were at length put in motion, detachments being sent out in different directions. A severe fight was had at Kellogg's Grove, in the midst of the Indian country, on the 25th of June, resulting in the retreat of the Indians, with much loss. Five whites were killed, and three wounded. A detachment under Gen. Alexander was stationed in a position to intercept the Indians, should they attempt to re-cross the Mississippi.

Meanwhile, it was understood that Black-Hawk had concentrated his forces, in a fortified position, at the Four Lakes, awaiting the issue of a general battle. Gen. Atkinson moved in that direction, with all possible celerity, and encamped a mile above Turtle Village, on the open prairie, not far from Rock river, on the 30th of June. The appearance of hostile Indians, prowling around his encampment, showed that their progress was watched, but they were not attacked. Next day, with numerous re-enforcements, Gen. Atkinson's troops reached Burnt Village, a Winnebago town on the Whitewater river. They were now in a strange country, in which, for want of correct information, they were obliged to advance slowly and cautiously. There were traces of hostile Indians in the vicinity, and next day two soldiers, at a little distance from the camp, were fired upon by them, and one seriously wounded. But from this point it was difficult to discover the trail of the enemy.

Nearly two months had now passed since the opening of the campaign, and its purpose seemed as remote from accomplishment as ever. The new volunteers had many of them become discontented, like the former ones. Their number had in fact become reduced one-half. The wearisome marches, the delays, the privations and exposures, had proved to them that this service was no pastime, and that its romance was not what it seemed in the distance. They sickened of such service, and were glad to escape from its restraints. Not so, however, with Lincoln, who had found in reality the kind of exciting adventure which his spirit craved. While others murmured, and took their departure, he remained true and persistent, no less eager for the fray, or ambitious to play a genuine soldier's part, than at the beginning. Hardship was not new to him, and he had a physical energy and endurance that would not be wearied into untimely discouragement.

It was not destined, however, that he should be actively engaged in any battle more serious than those encounters already mentioned. The forces were divided and dispersed in different directions, on the 10th of July, with a view to obtaining supplies. Two days later, news was received that Black-Hawk was thirty-five miles above Gen. Atkinson, on Rock river. A plan of Generals Alexander, Henry, and others, to take him by surprise, without awaiting orders, was frustrated by their troops refusing to follow them. Gen. Henry finally set out in pursuit of the Indians, on the 15th of July, but was misled by treachery. He continued on for several days, acquiring better information, passing the beautiful country around the Four Lakes, the present site of Madison, Wisconsin, and after another day's hard march came close upon the retreating Indians, and finally overtook them on the 21st. They were immediately charged upon, and driven along the high bluffs of the Wisconsin, and down upon the river bottom. The Indians lost sixty-eight killed, and of the large number wounded, twenty-five were afterward found dead on their trail leading to the Mississippi. The regulars, in this engagement on the Wisconsin, were commanded by Gen. (then Colonel) ZACHARY TAYLOR, afterward President of the United States. Gen. Henry, of Illinois, and Col. Dodge (afterward United States Senator), were chief commanders of the volunteers.

Waiting two days at the Blue Mounds, the forces still in the field were all united, and a hard pursuit resumed through the forest, down the Wisconsin. On the fourth day, they reached the Mississippi, which some of the Indians had already crossed, while the others were preparing to do so. The battle of the Bad-Axe here brought the war to a close, with the capture of Black-Hawk and his surviving warriors.

Mr. Lincoln, as yet a youth of but twenty-three, faithfully discharged his duty to his country, as a soldier, persevering amid peculiar hardships, and against the influences of older men around him, during the three months' service of this his first and last military campaign.

Sarcastically commenting on the efforts of Gen. Cass' biographers to render him conspicuous as a military hero, Mr. Lincoln, in a Congressional speech, delivered during the canvass of 1848, made a humorous and characteristic reference to his own experience as a soldier. We give his language on this occasion, as a suitable pendent to our sketch of this period of Mr. Lincoln's youth :

" By the way, Mr. Speaker, did you know I am a military hero ? Yes, sir, in the days of the Black-Hawk war, I fought, bled, and came away. Speaking of Gen. Cass' career, reminds me of my own. I was not at Stillman's defeat, but I was about as near it as Cass to Hull's surrender ; and like him, I saw the place very soon afterward. It is quite certain I did

not break my word, for I had none to break ; but I bent a
musket pretty badly on one occasion.   If Cass broke his sword,
the idea is, he broke it in desperation ; I bent the musket by
accident.   If Gen. Cass went in advance of me in picking
whortleberries, I guess I surpassed him in charges upon the
wild onions.   If he saw any live, fighting Indians, it was more
than I did, but I had a good many bloody struggles with the
mosquitoes ; and although I never fainted from loss of blood,
I can truly say I was often very hungry.

"Mr. Speaker, if I should ever conclude to doff whatever
our Democratic friends may suppose there is of black-cockade
Federalism about me, and, thereupon, they should take me up
as their candidate for the Presidency, I protest they shall not
make fun of me as they have of Gen. Cass, by attempting to
write me into a military hero."

CHAPTER V.

EIGHT YEARS IN THE LEGISLATURE OF ILLINOIS—1834–41.

A New Period in Mr. Lincoln's Life.—His Political Opinions.—Clay
and Jackson.—Mr. Lincoln a Candidate for Representative.—His
Election in 1834.—Illinois Strongly Democratic.—Mr. Lincoln as a
Surveyor.—Land Speculation Mania.—Mr. Lincoln's First Appear-
ance in the Legislature.—Banks and Internal Improvements.—Whig
Measures Democratically Botched.—First Meeting of Lincoln with
Douglas.—The Latter Seeks an Office of the Legislature and Gets it.—
Mr. Lincoln Re-elected in 1836.—Mr. Douglas also a Member of
the House.—Distinguished Associates.—Internal Improvements
Again.—Mr Lincoln's Views on Slavery.—The Capital Removed to
Springfield.—The New Metropolis.—The Revulsion of 1837.—Mr.
Lincoln Chosen for a Third Term.—John Calhoun of Lecompton
Memory.—Lincoln the Whig Leader, and Candidate for Speaker.—
Close Vote.—First Session at Springfield.—Lincoln Re-elected in
1840.—Partisan Remodeling of the Supreme Court.—Lincoln Declines
Further Service in the Legislature.—His Position as a Statesman at
the Close of this Period.—A Tribune of the People.

WE now approach the period of Mr. Lincoln's transition to
the more natural position in which, as a professional man and
a statesman, he was to attain that success and eminence for
which his rare endowments fitted him.   Hitherto, he had been
unconsciously undergoing a varied training, the whole tendency
of which, if rightly subjected afterward to a high purpose in
life, could not fail to be advantageous.   He had learned much
of the world, and of men, and gained some true knowledge of
himself.   The discipline of those hard years of toil and penury,
so manfully and cheerfully gone through with, was of more
value to him, as time was to prove, than any heritage of wealth
or of ancestral eminence could have been.   Still the conflict
with an adverse fortune was to continue; but from this time

onward, a more genial future began to shape itself in the hopes and aspirations of the self-reliant youth. His later experiences had shown him more clearly that he was not to be a mere private in the great battle of life, but that he had certain qualities which could place him at the head of a brigade or of a column, if he were so minded. Nor was he indifferent to the good opinion of his fellow-men. The confessed satisfaction which the captaincy of a company of volunteers had given him, as the expressed preference of a hundred or two of associates for him above all others, as a leader, showed that, however distrustful as yet of his own powers, he was not without ambition, or unable to appreciate popular honors.

This campaign likewise, besides the excitements of varied adventure which it afforded, so much to his natural inclination, had brought him in contact with inspiring influences and associations, and had demonstrated, and doubtless improved, his powers of fixing the esteem and admiration of those around him. He had been, as is told of him, a wild sort of a boy, and in his peculiar way he had attached his associates to him to a remarkable degree. This will be seen from a circumstance to be presently related. His horizon had been enlarged and his dreams ennobled. Meantime, it is to be remembered, that he had come home from the Black-Hawk war with no definite bnsiness to resort to, and still under a necessity of devoting his chief and immediate energies to self-support.

He has, then, reached a new epoch of his youth, at this date, and entered on another distinct period of his history. Proof of this we shall find in the fact that he became, on returning home, a candidate for representative in the State Legislature, the election of which was close at hand. A youth of twenty-three, and not at all generally known through the county, or able, in the brief time allowed, to make himself so, it may have an appearance of presumption for him to have allowed the use of his name as a candidate. He was not elected, certainly, and could hardly have thought such an event possible; yet the noticeable fact remains that he received so wonderful a vote in his own precinct, where he was best if not almost exclusively known, as may almost be said to

HOUSE NEAR GENTRYVILLE, INDIANA.

The Home of Lincoln for thirteen years, and where his Mother died.

4

have made his fortune. His precinct (he had now settled in Sangamon county) was strongly for Jackson, while Lincoln had, from the start, warmly espoused the cause of Henry Clay. The State election occurred in August, and the Presidential election two or three months later, the same season. Political feeling ran high, at this the second election (as it proved) of Jackson. Notwithstanding this, such was the popularity which young Lincoln had brought home with him from the war, that out of the two hundred and eighty-four votes cast in his precinct, two hundred and seventy-seven—the entire vote wanting seven—were cast for him. Yet, a little later in the same canvass, Gen. Jackson received a majority of one hundred and fifty-five for the Presidency, from the very same men, over Mr. Clay, whose cause Lincoln was known to favor. So marked an indication as this of his personal power to draw votes, made him a political celebrity at once. In future elections it became a point with aspirants to seek to combine his strength in their favor, by placing Lincoln's name on their ticket, to secure his battalion of voters. When he was elected to the Legislature for the first time, two years later, his majority ranged about two hundred votes higher than the rest of the ticket on which he ran.

Such was the beginning of Mr. Lincoln's political life, almost in his boyhood. This is the proper place to pause and review, in a brief way, the state of political affairs in Illinois, at the time of his first appearance upon this public arena. We shall find the revolution which has been wrought—Mr. Lincoln, though for long years in an apparently hopeless minority in the State, having been always a foremost leader on the side opposed to the Democracy—to be scarcely less remarkable than his youthful successes at the polls.

At the date of Mr. Lincoln's arrival—when just of age—in the State of Illinois, Gen. Jackson was in the midst of his first Presidential term. Since 1826 every general election in that State had resulted decisively in favor of his friends. In August, 1830, the first election after Lincoln became a resident of the State, and before he was a qualified voter, the only rival candidates for Governor, were both of the same

5

4

strongly predominant party.. The Legislature then elected
had a large majority on that side. In 1832, Gen. Jackson
received the electoral vote of Illinois, for the second time,
by a decisive majority. The Legislature of 1834 was so
strongly Democratic, that the Whig members did not have
any candidates of their own, in organizing the House, but
chose rather to exercise the little power they had in favor of
such Democratic candidate as they preferred. Against such
odds, as we shall see, the opponents of that party struggled
long and in vain. Even the great political tornado which
swept over so large a portion of the Union in 1840, made no
decisive impression upon Illinois. In spite of all these difficulties and discouragements, Mr. Lincoln adhered steadily to
his faith, never once dreaming of seeking profit in compliance,
or in a compromise of his honest principles. Henry Clay was
his model as a statesman, and always continued such, while
any issues were left to contend for, of the celebrated American
system of the great Kentuckian.

During the time Mr. Lincoln was pursuing his law studies,
and making his first practical appearance with political life,
he turned his attention to the business of a surveyor as a
means of support. The mania for speculation in Western
lands and lots was beginning to spread over the country at this
time ; and while our young student of law had neither means
nor inclination to embark in any such enterprise for himself, it
was the means of bringing him some profitable employment
with the chain and compass. From the earliest grand center
of these operations in lands and town lots, Chicago, which had
also itself furnished, even then, most remarkable examples of
fortunes easily made, the contagion spread everywhere through
the State. Towns and cities without number were laid out in
all directions, and innumerable fortunes were made, in anti-
cipation, by the purchase of lots in all sorts of imaginary cities,
during the four or five years preceding the memorable crisis
and crash of 1837. It was during the year previous to that
consummation, that this business had reached its hight in
Illinois. With the revulsion, came also a brief period of
adversity to the successful surveyor, whose occupation was now

gone. It is said that even his surveying instruments were sold under the hammer. But this change only served to establish him more exclusively and permanently in his profession of the law.

Mr. Lincoln's first election to the Illinois Legislature, as has been stated, was in 1834. His associates on the ticket were Major John T. Stuart (two or three years later elected to Congress), John Dawson and William Carpenter. All were decided Clay men, or, as the party in that State was first styled, Democratic Republicans. About this time, the name of Whigs had begun to be their current designation. Lincoln was the youngest member of this Legislature, with the single exception of Hon. Jesse K. Dubois, of Lawrence county, afterward State Auditor of Illinois, who served with him during his entire legislative career. He had not yet acquired position as a lawyer, or even been admitted to the bar, and had his reputation to make, no less, as a politician and orator. At this time he was very plain in his costume, as well as rather uncourtly in his address and general appearance. His clothing was of homely Kentucky jean, and the first impression made by his tall, lank figure, upon those who saw him, was not specially prepossessing. He had not outgrown his hard backwoods experience, and showed no inclination to disguise or to cast behind him the honest and manly, though unpolished characteristics of his earlier days. Never was a man further removed from all snobbish affectation. As little was there, also, of the demagogue art of assuming an uncouthness or rusticity of manner and outward habit, with the mistaken notion of thus securing particular favor as " one of the masses." He chose to appear then, as in all his later life, precisely what he was. His deportment was unassuming, though without any awkwardness of reserve.

During this, his first session in the Legislature, he was taking lessons, as became his youth and inexperience, and preparing himself for the future, by close observation and attention to business, rather than by a prominent participation in debate. He seldom or never. took the floor to speak, although before the close of this and the succeeding special session of the same Legislature, he had shown, as previously in every other capacity in which he was engaged, qualities that clearly pointed to him as fitted to act a leading part. One of his associates from Sangamon county, Major Stuart, was now the most prominent member on the Whig side of the House.

The organization of this Legislature, was, of course, in the hands of the Democrats. The Speaker was Hon. James Semple, afterward United States Senator. In the selection of his committees, he assigned Lincoln the second place on the Committee on Public Accounts and Expenditures, as if with an intuition, in advance of acquaintance, of the propriety of setting " Honest Abe " to look after the public treasury.

Hon. Joseph Duncan, then a member of Congress, had been elected Governor at the same time this Legislature was chosen, over Mr. Kinney, also a Democrat, and of what was then termed the " whole hog " Jackson school. Notwithstanding the strong preponderance of the Democrats in both branches of the Legislature, and in the State, it is noticeable that in the distinguishing measures of Whig policy, in this as in subsequent years, the minority found their principles repeatedly in the ascendant, though unable to control the details of their practical application. This was true more particularly in regard to banks and internal improvements. Though inferior in numbers, the Whigs had superiority in ability, and in the real popularity and genuine democracy of their doctrines.

General attention had now come to be strongly fixed upon the remarkable natural advantages and resources of the new State of Illinois. Land speculation, as we have seen, had already begun to bring in Eastern money, and the population was rapidly increasing. According to the Whig policy, it now became desirable that every proper and reasonable legislative aid should be afforded to further the development of the latent power of this young commonwealth, and its progress toward the high rank among the States of the Mississippi valley, which had been indicated and provided for by nature. Despite the strong Democratic predominancy in this Legislature, therefore, a new State bank, with a capital of one million and five hundred thousand dollars, was incorporated, and the Illinois bank at Shawneetown, which had suspended for twelve years, was re-chartered, with a capital of three hundred thousand dollars. It is to be noticed, however, that this bank legislation, just like that of many other States, similarly circumstanced, while it fully indorsed the Whig policy, in its fundamental principle, was by no means so skillfully done or so safely guarded as it should have been, and habitually was done in those States where the Whigs were in the ascendant. Whatever troubles have accrued in Illinois, under this head, have been chiefly due to the fact that Whig measures were not rightly shaped and executed by Democratic hands. Whig measures, framed and carried out by Democrats, have too often ended in a mere botch. At the same time, it is observable that these imperfect, yet plausible concessions to the public welfare, have often saved the Democratic party, at the expense of the real interest involved. The State bank charter passed the House of Representatives by one majority.

This Legislature also gave some attention to what are technically called internal improvements within the State. In behalf of the Illinois and Michigan Canal, the company for constructing which had been incorporated in 1825, a loan was agitated at the first session. Congress had granted for this work, in 1826, about 300,000 acres of land on the proposed route of the canal. But for a special message of Gov. Duncan, maintaining that the desired loan could be effected on a pledge of these canal lands alone, it is probable that the loan bill, reported by a Senator from Sangamon county, named George Forquer, would have passed. At the next session, in 1835, this measure was carried, a bill pledging the credit of the State in behalf of the Canal Company, to the amount originally proposed, having become a law. The loan was negotiated by Gov. Duncan the next year, and the work on this important canal was commenced in June, 1836. At the same special session, a large number of railroads, without State aid, were chartered, including the Illinois Central and the Galena and Chicago routes.

It is hardly necessary to state more distinctly that these measures, securing, with all the defects of their origin, immense benefits to the people of Illinois, and in their spirit accordant with the great principles of the "American system," were sup-

ported by Mr. Lincoln and his Whig associates. Not all they
desired, these measures were yet the nearest approach to their
wishes that could be obtained of the majority.

It was during the regular session of this Legislature, that
Stephen A. Douglas, not himself a member, became first known
to Mr. Lincoln. Late in the year 1833, Mr. Douglas, then in
his twenty-first year, had migrated to Illinois (Vermont being
his native State), and commenced teaching a district school in
Winchester, Scott county. During the succeeding year, he
gave a portion of his time to the study of law, taking part also
in the political affairs of his locality. The Legislature, at this
session, had taken from the Governor the power of appointing
State's attorneys for the several judicial districts, and provided
that these officers should be elected by the Legislature, in joint
convention. Though he had been but a little more than a year
in the State, and was scarcely to be regarded as an expert in
the profession of the law, Mr. Douglas presented himself before
the Legislature as a candidate for State's attorney for the first
judicial district, against Mr. Hardin, a distinguished lawyer,
then in office. The movement was so adroit, that the youthful
advocate distanced his unsuspecting competitor, receiving thir-
ty-eight votes to thirty-six cast against him. Mr. Lincoln had
not only preceded Mr. Douglas as a resident of Illinois,
but, also, as thus seen, in gaining a political standing in the
State.

In 1836, Mr. Lincoln was elected for a second term, as one of
the seven representatives from Sangamon county. Among his
associates were Mr. Dawson, re-elected, and Ninian W. Edwards.
Mr. Douglas was one of the representatives from Morgan
county (to which he had recently removed), and along with
him Mr. Hardin, whom he had managed to supersede as State's
attorney in 1835. The latter (who was subsequently in Congress, and who fell at Buena Vista) was the only Whig elected
from that county, the other five representatives being Democrats. This canvass in Morgan county is memorable for
introducing in Illinois, through the aid of Douglas, the
convention system, the benefit of which he was subsequently

to reap in the local contests of that State. He had been put on the representative ticket to fill a vacancy occasioned by the declinature of one of the candidates, having failed himself in this instance to secure a nomination from the convention. He was never again elected to the Legislature, having in fact vacated his seat after the first session, and accepted the federal appointment of Register in the land office at Springfield.

In this House, as in that which immediately preceded, the Democrats had a decided majority. Gen. Semple was re-elected Speaker. Mr. Lincoln was assigned a place on the Committee on Finance. In addition to those we have already named, the House included many men of ability, who have been distinguished in the politics of the State or of the nation, among whom were James Shields, Augustus C. French, Robert Smith, John Dougherty, W. A. Richardson, and John A. Mc-Clernand. At the two sessions of this Legislature, in 1836 and '37, Mr. Lincoln came forward more prominently in debate gradually, becoming recognized as the leading man on the Whig side.

The subject of internal improvements became one of the most prominent ones before this Legislature, as had happened with the last. Of this policy, in a judiciously guarded form, Mr. Lincoln had been from the first a stanch and efficient advocate. He held it to be the duty of Government to extend its fostering aid, in every Constitutional way, and to a reasonable extent, to whatever enterprise of public utility required such assistance, in order to the fullest development of the natural resources, and to the most rapid healthful growth of the State. The Democratic party, while professing the let-alone (*laissez faire*) principle in general, was compelled to follow pretty closely in the wake of its adversary, in some of its most distinctive features of public policy. The question of internal improvements was one of these. And while the Democrats had a decided majority of the members of each House, it was understood that, by the aid of pledges made contrary to Democratic teaching in general, a majority for liberal legislation in regard to internal improvements had likewise been secured. The business, in fact, under the grand excitement of the flush times of 1836, was somewhat overdone, and through subsequent mismanagement and the revulsion of the next year, matters were eventually made still worse. The voice of the people was overwhelmingly in favor of the legislation which was granted. Even Whigs like Mr. Lincoln, were outstripped by some ardent Democrats—Mr. Douglas among them—in zeal for these improvements'; they having unfortunately, as noticed in the case of bank-legislation, in appropriating the principle, failed to understand its most skillful and safe application in practice.

At the first session of 1836–7, about 1,300 miles of railroad were provided for, in various quarters, the completion of the Illinois and Michigan Canal, from Chicago to Peru, and the improvement of the navigation of the Kaskaskia, Illinois, Rock, and Great and Little Wabash rivers; requiring in all a loan of $8,000,000. This included the novel appropriation of $2,000,000 to be distributed among those counties through which none of the proposed improvements were to be made. The system voted by the Legislature was on a most magnificent scale, such as New York, Pennsylvania, Ohio or Indiana had not surpassed. This system of internal improvement, with Democratic variations, having scarcely been inaugurated when the crash of 1837 came, did not entirely correspond in practice with what it had promised in theory.

There was also a considerable addition made to the banking capital of the State at this session.

During the winter, resolutions of an extreme Southern character on the slavery question, were introduced, and, after discussion, adopted by the Democratic majority. The attempt was, of course, made to affix a character of abolitionism to all those who refused assent to these extreme views. At that time, the public sentiment of the North was not aroused on the subject, as it became a few years later, in consequence of pro-slavery aggressions. Yet Mr. Lincoln refused to vote for these resolutions, and exercised his Constitutional privilege, along with one of his colleagues from Sangamon county, of entering upon the Journal of the House his reasons for thus acting. As showing his sentiments twenty-three years ago, on this now so prominent national question, the protest referred to, as it appears on the journal, is here appended in full:

MARCH 3, 1837.

The following protest was presented to the House, which was read and ordered to be spread on the journals, to wit:

"Resolutions upon the subject of domestic slavery having passed both branches of the General Assembly, at its present session, the undersigned hereby protest against the passage of the same.

"They believe that the institution of slavery is founded on both injustice and bad policy; but that the promulgation of abolition doctrines tend rather to increase than abate its evils.

"They believe that the Congress of the United States has no power, under the Constitution, to interfere with the institution of slavery in the different States.

"They believe that the Congress of the United States has the power, under the Constitution, to abolish slavery in the District of Columbia; but that the power ought not to be exercised, unless at the request of the people of said District.

"The difference between these opinions and those contained in the said resolutions, is their reason for entering this protest.

"(Signed)   "DAN STONE,

"A. LINCOLN,

"*Representatives from the County of Sangamon.*"

On the formation of the separate territory of Illinois, in 1809, Kaskaskia, perhaps the oldest town in all the Western country, had been designated as the capital. Such it continued to be until Illinois was admitted into the Union as a State, in 1818, when Vandalia, far up the Kaskaskia river, was laid out as the new capital. For some time it continued to be relatively a central location. But during several years immediately preceding 1837, the middle and northern portions of the State had filled so rapidly that the removal of the capital to a point nearer the geographical center had become manifestly expedient. At this session, accordingly, an act was passed changing the seat of government to Springfield, the principal town in the interior of the State, from and after the 4th day of July, 1839. To the people of Sangamon county, whom Mr. Lincoln represented, this was of course a most satisfactory measure, and by the State at large it was received with general approbation. Vandalia, which had reached a population of about two thousand, dwindled away for a time, until it had but about one-fourth that number of inhabitants, though of late years it has revived. Springfield has steadily advanced, since this period, and is one of the most beautiful interior towns of the West. The prairie country for scores of miles around is as charming in appearance and as fertile in its productions as any tract of like extent on the face of the earth. It is greatly to the credit of Mr. Lincoln's good taste and sagacity that, when he came to his majority, he fixed upon such a locality for his home, foreseeing for this spot a successful future, to which (altogether beyond his anticipations) his influence, in 1836, added a material advantage, and his presence, in 1860, gave a national luster of renown.

The financial disasters of the spring of 1837 were the occasion of an extra session of the Legislature of Illinois, in July of that year. The Governor asked for the legalization of the suspension of specie payments by the banks of the State, which a majority of both Houses granted. He also asked a repeal or modification of the internal improvement system, which was refused. The condition of affairs was deemed critical, and particularly so to the prospects of the Democratic party, which had just been congratulating itself on the election and inauguration of the successor of Gen. Jackson, Martin Van Buren, as President. In Illinois, that party had held unbroken and decisive sway, from the days of the younger Adams down. Whatever looseness of legislation had contributed to these evils at home, they were responsible for. And in the nation, the political dangers were felt to be imminent—so much so that the President had called an extra session of Congress. There was a want of Democratic harmony, however, at Washington and at Vandalia. The doctors of the party sat in council at the latter place, during the special session, but in the Legislature they only accomplished what has been stated. It now required the most desperate exertions to save the Democracy from defeat, and the

Whigs actively followed up their advantages. So overwhelming had been the strength of their opponents, however, from the time that Mr. Lincoln first appeared on the political stage, and long before, that while a great change was visible in the results of the next election, the revolution was not yet to be completed.

In 1838, Mr. Lincoln was for the third time elected a representative in the Legislature, for the two years ensuing. Among the other six representatives of Sangamon county was John Calhoun, since notorious for his connection with the Lecompton Constitution. Availing himself of some local issue or other, and being a man of conceded ability, of highly respectable Whig antecedents and connections, he had slipped in by a small majority, crowding out the lowest candidate on the Whig ticket. The remaining five were Whigs, including E. D. Baker, Ninian W. Edwards, and A. McCormick. The strength of the two parties in the House was nearly evenly balanced, the Democrats having only three or four majority, rendering this unexpected gain particularly acceptable.

So well recognized was now the position of Mr. Lincoln in his party that, by general consent, he received the Whig vote for the Speakership. There was a close contest, his Democratic competitors being Col. William Lee D. Ewing, who had served with Lincoln in the Black-Hawk war. On the fourth ballot, Ewing had a majority of one over all others, two Whigs (including Mr. Lincoln) and two Democrats having scattered their votes.

At the State election, in August, 1838, the Whig candidate for Governor made an excellent run, but was defeated by Thomas Carlin, Democrat. State affairs were hardly brought in issue in the general canvass. A majority of the Legislature, at the first session, was opposed to the repeal or modification of the public works system, but voted additional expenditures thereon, to the amount of $800,000. At a special session, however, this body repealed the system, and made provisions for its gradual winding up. Mr. Lincoln, as the Whig leader, had his position on the Committee on Finance, and exerted his influence in favor of wise counsels, and such a determination of affairs as would best remedy the evils resulting from this loose Democratic tampering with measures of Whig policy.

Aside from these financial questions, there were few matters of any general interest before this Legislature. This session of 1838–9 was the last held at Vandalia. A special session in 1839, inaugurated the new state-house at Springfield. The great contest of 1840 was already casting its shadow before, and began chiefly to engross the attention of persons in political life. Whig candidates for electors were nominated in November of this year, and discussions commenced in earnest. Mr. Lincoln, who was deemed one of the strongest champions of the cause before the people, was repeatedly called on to encounter the foremost advocates of the Democratic party— what no man in Illinois, it was now manifest, could do more successfully.

For the fourth time in succession, Mr. Lincoln was elected to the Legislature in 1840—the last election to that position which he would consent to accept from his strongly attached constituents of Sangamon county. In this Legislature, like all previous ones in which he had served, the Democrats had a majority in both branches, and the responsibility of all legislation was with them. It was at this session that, to over- rule a decision unacceptable to Democrats, and for political and personal reasons of common notoriety in Illinois, the judicial system of the State was changed, as desired by Mr. Douglas, against the judgment of many leading Democrats, and five new judges, of whom Mr. Douglas was one, were added to the Supreme Court of the State. This is now gen- erally felt to be a measure conferring little credit upon those concerned in concocting the scheme, and was never heartily approved by the people.

There was but one session during the two years for which this Legislature was chosen. Mr. Lincoln, as in the last, was the acknowledged Whig leader, and the candidate of his party for Speaker. First elected at twenty-five, he had continued in office without interruption so long as his inclination allowed, and until, by his uniform courtesy and kindness of manners, his marked ability, and his straight-forward integrity, he had won an enviable repute throughout the State, and was virtually, when but a little past thirty, placed at the head of his party in Illinois.

Begun in comparative obscurity, and without any adventitious aids in its progress, this period of his life, at its termination, had brought him to a position where he was secure in the confidence of the people, and prepared, in due time, to enter upon a more enlarged and brilliant career, as a national statesman. His fame as a close and convincing debater was established. His native talent as an orator had at once been demonstrated and disciplined. His zeal and earnestness in behalf of a party whose principles he believed to be right, had rallied strong troops of political friends about him, while his unfeigned modesty and his unpretending and simple bearing, in marked contrast with that of so many imperious leaders, had won him general and lasting esteem. He preferred no claim as a partisan, and showed no overweening anxiety to advance himself, but was always a disinterested and generous co-worker with his associates, only ready to accept the post of honor and of responsibility, when it was clearly their will, and satisfactory to the people whose interests were involved. At the close of this period, with scarcely any consciousness of the fact himself, and with no noisy demonstrations or flashy ostentation in his behalf from his friends, he was really one of the foremost political men in the State. A keen observer might even then have predicted a great future for the " Sangamon Chief," as he was sometimes called in Illinois; and only such an observer, perhaps, would then have adequately estimated his real power as a natural orator, a sagacious statesman, and a gallant TRIBUNE OF THE PEOPLE.

CHAPTER VI.

HIS SETTLEMENT AT SPRINGFIELD AND HIS MARRIAGE.— 1837-42.

Mr. Lincoln's Law Studies.—His Perseverance under Adverse Circumstances.—Licensed to Practice in 1836.—His Progress in his Profession.—His Qualities as an Advocate.—A Romantic and Exciting Incident in his Practice.—A Reminiscence of his Early Life.—He Renders a Material Service to the Family of an Old Friend.—An Affecting Scene.—Mr. Lincoln Removes to Springfield in 1837.—Devotes Himself to his Profession, Giving up Political Life.—His Marriage.—The Family of Mrs. Lincoln.—Fortunate Domestic Relations.—His Children and their Education.—Denominational Tendencies.—Four Years' Retirement.

DURING the time of his service in the Legislature, Mr. Lincoln was busily engaged in mastering the profession of law. This he was, indeed, compelled to do somewhat at intervals, and with many disadvantages, from the necessity he was under to support himself meanwhile by his own labor, to say nothing of the attention he was compelled to give to politics, by the position he had accepted. Nothing, however, could prevent his consummating his purpose. He completed his preliminary studies, and was licensed to practice in 1836. His reputation was now such that he found a good amount of business, and began to rise to the front rank in his profession. He was a most effective jury advocate, and manifested a ready perception and a sound judgment of the turning legal points of a case. His clear, practical sense, and his skill in homely or humorous illustration, were noticeable traits in his arguments. The graces and the cold artificialities of a polished rhetoric, he certainly had not, nor did he aim to acquire them. His style of expression and the cast of his thought were his own, having all the native force of a genuine originality.

The following incident, of which the narration is believed to be substantially accurate, is from the pen of one who professes to write from personal knowledge. It is given in this connection, as at once illustrating the earlier struggles of Mr. Lincoln in acquiring his profession, the character of his forensic efforts, and the generous gratitude and disinterestedness of his nature:

Having chosen the law as his future calling, he devoted himself assiduously to its mastery, contending at every step with adverse fortune. During this period of study, he for some time found a home under the hospitable roof of one Armstrong, a farmer, who lived in a log house some eight miles from the village of Petersburg, in Menard county. Here, young Lincoln would master his lessons by the firelight of the cabin, and then walk to town for the purpose of recitation. This man Armstrong was himself poor, but he saw the genius struggling in the young student, and opened to him his rude home, and bid him welcome to his course fare. How Lincoln graduated with promise—how he has more than fulfilled that promise—how honorably he acquitted himself, alike on the battle-field, in defending our border settlements against the ravages of savage foes, and in the halls of our national legislature, are matters of history, and need no repetition here. But one little incident, of a more private nature, standing as it does as a sort of sequel to some things already alluded to, I deem worthy of record. Some few years since, the oldest son of Mr. Lincoln's old friend Armstrong, the chief support of his widowed mother—the good old man having some time previously passed from earth—was arrested on the charge of murder. A young man had been killed during a riotous melee, in the night-time, at a camp-meeting, and one of his associates stated that the death-wound was inflicted by young Armstrong. A preliminary examination was gone into, at which the accuser testified so positively, that there seemed no doubt of the guilt of the prisoner, and therefore he was held for trial. As is too often the case, the bloody act caused an undue degree of excitement in the public mind. Every improper incident in the life of the prisoner—each act which bore the least semblance of rowdyism—each school-boy quarrel— was suddenly remembered and magnified, until they pictured him as a fiend of the most horrid hue. As these rumors spread abroad, they were received as gospel truth, and a feverish desire for vengeance seized upon the infatuated populace, while only prison-bars prevented a horrible death at the hands of a mob. The events were heralded in the news-papers, painted in highest colors, accompanied by rejoicing over the certainty of punishment being meted out to the guilty party. The prisoner, overwhelmed by the circumstances in which he found himself placed, fell into a melancholy condition, bordering upon despair; and the widowed mother, looking through her tears, saw no cause for hope from earthly aid.

At this juncture, the widow received a letter from Mr. Lincoln, volunteering his services in an effort to save the youth from the impending stroke. Gladly was his aid accepted, although it seemed impossible for even his sagacity to prevail in such a desperate case; but the heart of the attorney was in his work, and he set about it with a will that knew no such word as fail. Feeling that the poisoned condition of the public mind was such as to preclude the possibility of impanneling an impartial jury in the court having jurisdiction, he procured a change of venue, and a postponement of the trial. He then went studiously to work unraveling the history of the case, and satisfied himself that his client was the victim of malice, and that the statements of the accuser were a tissue of falsehoods. When the trial was called on, the prisoner, pale and emaciated, with hopelessness written on every feature, and accompanied by his half-hoping, half-despairing mother—whose only hope was in a mother's belief of her son's innocence, in the justice of the God she worshipped, and in the noble counsel, who, without hope of fee or reward upon earth, had undertaken the cause—took his seat in the prisoner's box, and with a "stony firmness" listened to the reading of the indictment.

Lincoln sat quietly by, while the large auditory looked on him as though wondering what he could say in defense of one whose guilt they regarded as certain. The examination of the witnesses for the State was begun, and a well-arranged mass of evidence, circumstantial and positive, was introduced, which seemed to impale the prisoner beyond the possibility of extrication. The counsel for the defense propounded but few questions, and those of a character which excited no uneasiness on the part of the prosecutor—merely, in most cases, requiring the main witness to be definite as to time and place. When the evidence of the prosecution was ended, Lincoln introduced a few witnesses to remove some erroneous impressions in regard to the previous character of his client, who, though somewhat rowdyish, had never been known to commit a vicious act; and to show that a greater degree of ill-feeling existed between the accuser and the accused, than the

THE CRAWFORD PLACE.   [See Pages 25 & 26.]

accused and the deceased. The prosecutor felt that the case was a clear one, and his opening speech was brief and formal. Lincoln arose, while a deathly silence pervaded the vast audience, and in a clear but moderate tone began his argument. Slowly and carefully he reviewed the testimony, pointing out the hitherto unobserved discrepancies in the statements of the principal witness. That which had seemed plain and plausible, he made to appear crooked as a serpent's path. The witness had stated that the affair took place at a certain hour in the evening, and that, by the aid of the brightly-shining moon, he saw the prisoner inflict the death-blow with a slung-shot. Mr. Lincoln showed, that at the hour referred to, the moon had not yet appeared above the horizon, and consequently the whole tale was a fabrication. An almost instantaneous change seemed to have been wrought in the minds of his auditors, and the verdict of "not guilty" was at the end of every tongue. But the advocate was not content with this intellectual achievement. His whole being had for months been bound up in this work of gratitude and mercy, and as the lava of the overcharged crater bursts from its imprisonment, so great thoughts and burning words leaped forth from the soul of the eloquent Lincoln. He drew a picture of the perjurer, so horrid and ghastly that the accuser could sit under it no longer, but reeled and staggered from the court-room, while the audience fancied they could see the brand upon his brow. Then in words of thrilling pathos, Lincoln appealed to the jurors, as fathers of sons who might become fatherless, and as husbands of wives who might be widowed, to yield to no previous impressions, no ill-founded prejudice, but to do his client justice; and as he alluded to the debt of gratitude which he owed the boy's sire, tears were seen to fall from many eyes unused to weep. It was near night when he concluded by saying, that if justice was done—as he believed it would be—before the sun should set it would shine upon his client, a freeman. The jury retired, and the court adjourned for the day. Half an hour had not elapsed, when, as the officers of the court and the volunteer attorney sat at the tea-table of their hotel, a messenger announced that the jury had returned to their seats. All repaired immediately to the court-house, and while the prisoner was being brought from the jail, the court-room was filled to overflowing with citizens of the town. When the prisoner and his mother entered, silence reigned as completely as though the house were empty. The foreman of the jury, in answer to the usual inquiry from the court, delivered the verdict of "Not Guilty!" The widow dropped into the arms of her son, who lifted her up, and told her to look upon him as before, free and innocent. Then, with the words, "Where is Mr. Lincoln?" he rushed across the room and grasped the hand of his deliverer, while his heart was too full for utterance. Lincoln turned his eyes toward the West, where the sun still lingered in view, and then, turning to the youth, said, "It is not yet sundown, and you are free." I confess that my cheeks were not wholly unwet by tears, and I turned from the affecting scene. As I cast a glance behind, I saw Abraham Lincoln obeying the divine injunction, by comforting the widowed and the fatherless.

On becoming well established in his profession, Mr. Lincoln took up his permanent residence at Springfield, the county-seat of Sangamon county. This occurred in the spring immediately following the passage of the act removing the State capital to that place, but more than two years before it was to go into effect. The date at which he became settled in Springfield, which has ever since been the place of his residence, was April 15, 1837.

For several years after his removal, Mr. Lincoln remained a bachelor, and was an inmate of the family of the Hon. William Butler, in later years the Treasurer of the State. For three or four years he continued to represent his county in the Legislature, but after 1840, he refused further public service, with a view to the exclusive pursuit of his profession, the highest success in which he could not hope to obtain while giving so much of his time, as had been hitherto required of him, to political affairs.

On the 4th of November, 1842, Mr. Lincoln was married to Miss MARY TODD, daughter of the Hon. Robert S. Todd, of Lexington, Kentucky. This lady is one of four sisters, the eldest of whom had previously married the Hon. Ninian W. Edwards, and settled at Springfield. Her two other sisters, subsequently married, became residents of the same town. Mr. Lincoln's domestic relations were happy, and his devoted attachment to his home and family was always one of the marked traits of his personal character. Of the four sons born to him, Robert T., the oldest, was at school at Exeter Academy, in New Hampshire, when Mr. Lincoln was first nominated for the Presidency, and soon after entered Harvard

University, where he completed his course in 1864, when in his twenty-first year. The second son died when four years old. The third, Willie, died at the White House in 1863, at the age of twelve years. Thomas, familiarly called "Tad," was two years younger.

It is proper to mention that Mrs. Lincoln is a Presbyterian by education and profession (two of her sisters are Episcopalians), and that her husband, though not a member, was a liberal supporter of the church to which she belongs. It should further be stated that the Sunday-School, and other benevolent enterprises associated with these church relations, found in him a constant friend.

In this quiet domestic happiness, and in the active practice of his profession, with its round of ordinary duties, and with its exceptional cases of a more general public interest, Mr. Lincoln disappears for the time from political life. Its peculiar excitements, indeed, were not foreign to the stirring and adventurous nature which, as we have seen, was his by inheritance. Nor could the people, and the party of which he was so commanding a leader, long consent to his retirement. Yet such was his prudent purpose—now especially, with a family to care for—and to this he adhered, with only occasional exceptions, until, four years after his marriage, he was elected to Congress.

CHAPTER VII.

CANVASSES OF 1844 AND 1846.

Mr. Lincoln's Devotion to Henry Clay.—The Presidential Nominations of 1844.—The Campaign in Illinois.—Mr. Lincoln Makes an
Active Canvass for Clay.—John Calhoun the Leading Polk Elector.—
The Tariff Issue Thoroughly Discussed.—Method of Conducting the
Canvass.—The Whigs of Illinois in a Hopeless Minority.—Mr. Lin-
coln's Reputation as a Whig Champion.—Renders Efficient Service
in Indiana.—Mr. Clay's Defeat and the Consequences.—Mr. Lincoln
a Candidate for Congressman in 1846.—President Polk's Adminis-
tration.—Condition of the Country.—Texas Annexation, the Mexican
War and the Tariff.—Political Character of the Springfield District.—
Mr. Lincoln Elected by an Unprecedented Majority.—His Personal
Popularity Demonstrated.

MR. LINCOLN had, from his first entrance into political life,
recognized Henry Clay as his great leader and instructor in
statesmanship. His reverence and attachment for the great
Kentuckian had been unlimited and enthusiastic. When, therefore, Mr. Clay had been nominated by acclamation for the Presidency by the National Whig Convention, held at Baltimore on
the 1st of May, 1844, and when a Democrat of the most offensive school was put in nomination against him, Mr. Lincoln
yielded to the demands of the Whigs of Illinois, and, for the
first time breaking over the restrictions he had placed upon
himself in regard to the exclusive pursuit of his profession, he
consented to take a leading position in canvassing the State
as an elector. In a State that had stood unshaken in its Democratic position, while so many others had been revolutionized
during the great political tempest of 1840, there was, of course,
no hope of immediate success. It was deemed an opportunity not to be lost, however, for maintaining and strengthening
the Whig organization, and a spirited canvass was consequently
made.

On the Democratic side, John Calhoun, then one of the strongest and most popular speakers of that party, and in many respects quite another man than he subsequently became, held the laboring oar for Mr. Polk. Mr. Lincoln traversed various parts of the State, attracting large audiences and keeping their fixed attention for hours, as he held up to admiration the character and doctrines of Henry Clay, and contrasted them with those of his Presidential opponent. On the tariff question, which was the chief issue in Illinois that year, he was particularly elaborate, strongly enforcing the great principles on which the protective system, as maintained by Clay, was based. He had always a fund of anecdote and illustration, with which to relieve his close logical disquisitions, and to elucidate and enforce his views in a manner perfectly intelligible, as well as pleasing to all classes of hearers. This campaign, so barren in immediate results, as it was expected to be in Illinois, was not without its excellent fruits, ultimately, to the party. It had also the effect of establishing Mr. Lincoln's reputation as a political orator, on a still broader and more permanent foundation. From this time forward he was widely known as one of the soundest and most effective of Whig champions in the West.

After doing in Illinois all that could have been required of one man, had this arena been of the most promising description, Mr. Lincoln crossed the Wabash, at the desire of the people of his former State, and contributed largely toward turning the tide of battle for Clay in that really hopeful field. Here he worked most efficiently, losing no opportunity up to the very eve of the election. In Indiana, those efforts were not forgotten, but were freshly called to mind, at a later juncture, by great numbers of Old Whigs in Southern Indiana.

If any event, more heartily than another, could have discouraged Mr. Lincoln from again participating in political affairs, it was the disastrous result, in the nation at large, of this canvass of 1844. He felt it more keenly than he could have done if it were a mere personal reverse. Mr. Clay was defeated, contrary to the ardent hopes, and even expectations of his friends, down to the last moment. Of the causes and the consequences which followed that event, the impartial historian, at some future day, can more candidly and philosophically speak than any of those who shared in this disappointment. That the election of Mr. Polk over Mr. Clay, made the subsequent political history of our country far different from what it would have been with the opposite result, all will concede.

Two years later, in 1846, Mr. Lincoln was induced to accept the Whig nomination for Congress in the Sangamon District. The annexation of Texas had, in the meantime, been consummated. The Mexican war had been begun, and was still in progress. The Whig tariff of 1842 had just been repealed. This latter event had been acccomplished in the Senate by the casting vote of Mr. DALLAS, the Vice-President, and with the official approval of Mr. POLK, the President, both of whom had been elected by the aid of Pennsylvania, and had carried the vote of that State solely by being represented to the people as favoring the maintainance of the tariff which they thus destroyed.

The Springfield district had given Mr. Clay a majority of 914 in 1844, on the most thorough canvass. It gave Mr. Lincoln a majority af 1,511, which was entirely unprecedented, and has been unequaled by that given there for any opposition candidate, for any office since. The nearest approach was in 1848, when Gen. Taylor, on a much fuller vote than that of 1846, and receiving the votes of numerous returned Mexican volunteers, of Democratic faith, and who had served under him in Mexico, obtained a majority of 1,501. In the same year (1848) Mr. Logan, the popular Whig candidate, was beaten by Col. Thomas L. Harris, Democrat, by 106 majority. There was no good reason to doubt, in advance, that Mr. Lincoln would have been elected by a handsome majority, had he consented to run for another term, nor has it been questionable, since the result became known, that the strong personal popularity of Mr. Lincoln would have saved the district. It was redeemed by Richard Yates in 1850, who carried his election by less than half the majority (754) which Mr. Lincoln had received in 1845. The district, after its reconstruction, following the census of 1850, was for ten years Democratic. Under all the circumstances, therefore, the vote for Mr. Lincoln was a remarkable one, showing that he possessed a rare degree of strength with the people. His earnest sincerity of manner always strongly impressed those whom he addressed. They knew him to be a man of strong moral convictions. An opponent seemed to intend a sneer at this trait, when he called Mr. Lincoln " conscientious," but it was a quality to which the people were never indifferent.

There was a universal confidence in his honest integrity, such as has been rarely extended to men so prominent in political life. The longer he was tried as a public servant, the more his constituents became attached to him. A popularity thus thoroughly grounded is not to be destroyed by the breezes of momentary passion or prejudice, or materially affected by any idle fickleness of the populace.

CHAPTER VIII.

MR. LINCOLN IN CONGRESS.—1847–49.

The Thirtieth Congress—Its Political Character—The Democracy in a Minority in the House.—Robert C. Winthrop Elected Speaker.— Distinguished Members in both Houses.—Mr. Lincoln takes his Seat as a Member of the House, and Mr. Douglas, for the first time, as a Member of the Senate, at the same Session.—Mr. Lincoln's Congressional Record, that of a Clay and Webster Whig.—The Mexican War.—Mr. Lincoln's Views on the Subject.—Misrepresentations.— Not an Available Issue for Mr. Lincoln's Opponents.—His Resolutions of Inquiry in Regard to the Origin of the War.—Mr. Richardson's Resolutions Indorsing the Administration.—Mr. Hudson's Resolutions for an Immediate Discontinuance of the War.—Voted Against by Mr. Lincoln.—Resolutions of Thanks to Gen. Taylor.— Mr. Henley's Amendment, and Mr. Ashman's Addition thereto.— Resolutions Adopted without Amendment.—Mr. Lincoln's First Speech in Congress, on the Mexican War.—Mr. Lincoln on Internal Improvements.—A Characteristic Campaign Speech.—Mr. Lincoln on the Nomination of Gen. Taylor; the Veto Power; National Issues; President and People; the Wilmot Proviso; Platforms; Democratic Sympathy for Clay; Military Heroes and Exploits; Cass a Progressive; Extra Pay; the Whigs and the Mexican War; Democratic Divisions.—Close of the Session.—Mr. Lincoln on the Stump.—Gen. Taylor's Election.—Second Session of the Thirtieth Congress.— Slavery in the District of Columbia.—The Public Lands.—Mr. Lincoln as a Congressman.—He Retires to Private Life.

MR. LINCOLN took his seat in the National House of Representatives on the 6th day of December, 1847, the date of the opening of the Thirtieth Congress. In many respects this Congress was a memorable one. That which preceded, elected at the same time Mr. Polk was chosen to the Presidency, had been strongly Democratic in both branches. The policy of the Administration, however, had been such, during the first two years of its existence, that a great popular re-action had followed

The present House contained but one hundred and ten Democrats, while the remaining one hundred and eighteen, with the exception of a single Native American from Philadelphia, were nearly all Whigs, the balance being "Free-Soil men," who mostly co-operated with them. Of these, only Messrs. Giddings, Tuck and Palfrey refused to vote for the Hon. Robert C. Winthrop for Speaker, who was elected on the third ballot.

Among the members of the House, on the Whig side, were John Quincy Adams (who died during the first session, and was succeeded by Horace Mann), and George Ashman, of Massachusetts; Washington Hunt, of New York; Jacob Collamer and George P. Marsh, of Vermont; Truman Smith, of Connecticut; Joseph R. Ingersoll and James Pollock, of Pennsylvania; John M. Botts and William L. Goggin, of Virginia; Alexander H. Stephens, Robert Toombs and Thomas Butler King, of Georgia; Henry W. Hilliard, of Alabama; Samuel F. Vinton and Robert C. Schenck, of Ohio; John B. Thompson and Charles S. Morehead, of Kentucky; Caleb B. Smith and Richard W. Thompson, of Indiana, and Meredith P. Gentry, of Tennessee. On the Democratic side, there were David Wilmot, of Pennsylvania; Robert M. McLane, of Maryland; James McDowell and Richard K. Meade, of Virginia; R. Barnwell Rhett, of South Carolina; Howell Cobb, of Georgia; Albert G. Brown and Jacob Thompson, of Mississippi; Linn Boyd, of Kentucky; Andrew Johnson, George W. Jones and Frederick P. Stanton, of Tennessee; James S. Greene and John S. Phelps, of Missouri; and Kinsley S. Bingham, of Michigan. Illinois had seven representatives, of whom Mr. Lincoln was the only Whig. His Democratic colleagues were John A. McClernand, Orlando B. Ficklin, William A. Richardson, Robert Smith, Thomas J. Turner and John Wentworth.

At this session, Stephen A. Douglas took his seat in the Senate, for the first time, having been elected the previous winter. In that body there were but twenty-two Opposition Senators, against thirty-six Democrats. Among the former were Daniel Webster, Wm. L. Dayton, S. S. Phelps, John M. Clayton, Reverdy Johnson, Thomas Corwin, John M. Berrien, and John Bell. On the Democratic side were John C. Cal-

houn, Thomas H. Benton, Daniel S. Dickinson, Simon Cameron, Hannibal Hamlin, Sam Houston, R. M. T. Hunter, and
William R. King.

Mr. Lincoln was comparatively quite a young man when he
entered the House, yet he was early recognized as one of the
foremost of the Western men on the floor. His Congressional
record, throughout, is that of a Whig of those days, his votes
on all leading national subjects, being invariably what those of
Clay, Webster or Corwin would have been, had they occupied
his place. One of the most prominent subjects of consideration before the Thirtieth Congress, very naturally, was the
then existing war with Mexico. Mr. Lincoln was one of those
who believed the Administration had not properly managed its
affairs with Mexico at the outset, and who, while voting supplies and for suitably rewarding our gallant soldiers in that war,
were unwilling to be forced, by any trick of the supporters of
the Administration, into an unqualified indorsement of its
course in this affair, from beginning to end. In this attitude,
Mr. Lincoln did not stand alone. Such was the position of
Whig members in both Houses, without exception. Yet his
course was unscrupulously misrepresented, during the campaign of 1858, as it has been more or less, on other occasions
since. That many men who supported Mr. Lincoln, approved
President Polk's course in regard to the Mexican War, as well
in its inception as in its management from first to last, is not
improbable. But all those who, at that time, were induced by
their party relations, to sustain the Administration, at heart
approved the method in which hostilities were precipitated, or
felt satisfied that the most commendable motives actuated the
Government in its course toward Mexico, is certainly not true.
This is not an issue that any existing party need be anxious to
resuscitate. Still less would the friends of Mr. Lincoln be
reluctant to have his record on this question scrutinized to the
fullest extent.

Early in the session, after listening to a long homily on the
subject from the President, in his annual message, in which
the gauntlet was defiantly thrown down before the Opposition
members, and after his colleague, Mr. Richardson, had pro-

posed an unqualified indorsement of the President's views, Mr. Lincoln (December 22, 1847) introduced a series of resolutions of inquiry in regard to the origin of the war. They affirmed nothing, but called for definite official information, such as, if conclusively furnished in detail, and found to accord with the general asserrations of Mr. Polk's messages, would have set him and his administration entirely right before the country. Either such information was accessible, or the repeated statements of the President on this subject were groundless, and his allegations mere pretenses. If the Democratic party was in the right, it had not the least occasion to complain of this procedure, if pressed to a vote. Mr. Lincoln's preamble and resolutions (copied from the *Congressional Globe*, first session, thirtieth Congress, page 64) were in the following words :

WHEREAS, The President of the United States, in his message of May 11, 1846, has declared that " the Mexican Government not only refused to receive him (the envoy of the United States), or listen to his propositions, but, after a long-continued series of menaces, has at last invaded *our territory*, and shed the blood of our fellow-citizens on *our own soil :*"

And again, in his message of December 8, 1846, that " We had ample cause of war against Mexico long before the breaking out of hostilities ; but even then we forbore to take redress into our own hands until Mexico herself became the aggressor, by invading *our soil* in hostile array, and shedding the blood of our citizens :"

And yet again, in his message of December 7, 1847, that " The Mexican Government refused even to hear the terms of adjustment which he (our minister of peace) was authorized to propose, and finally, under wholly unjustifiable pretexts, involved the two countries in war, by invading the territory of the State of Texas, striking the first blow, and shedding the blood of our citizens on *our own soil :*" and,

WHEREAS, This House is desirous to obtain a full knowledge of all the facts which go to establish whether the particular spot on which the blood of our citizens was so shed was or was not at that time " *our own soil :*" therefore,

Resolved, by the House of Representatives, That the President of the United States be respectfully requested to inform this House—

1st. Whether the spot on which the blood of our citizens

was shed, as in his message declared, was or was not within the territory of Spain, at least after the treaty of 1819, until the Mexican revolution.

2d. Whether that spot is or is not within the territory which was wrested from Spain by the revolutionary Government of Mexico.

3d. Whether that spot is or is not within a settlement of people, which settlement has existed ever since long before the Texas revolution, and until its inhabitants fled before the approach of the United States army.

4th. Whether that settlement is or is not isolated from any and all other settlements by the Gulf and the Rio Grande on the south and west, and by wide uninhabited regions on the north and east.

5th. Whether the people of that settlement, or a majority of them, or any of them, have ever submitted themselves to the government or laws of Texas or of the United States, by consent or by compulsion, either by accepting office, or voting at elections, or paying tax, or serving on juries, or having process served upon them, or in any other way.

6th. Whether the people of that settlement did or did not flee from the approach of the United States army, leaving unprotected their homes and their growing crops, *before* the blood was shed, as in the messages stated ; and whether the first blood, so shed, was or was not shed within the inclosure of one of the people who had thus fled from it.

7th. Whether our *citizens*, whose blood was shed, as in his messages declared, were or were not, at that time, armed officers and soldiers, sent into that settlement by the military order of the President, through the Secretary of War.

8th. Whether the military force of the United States was or was not so sent into that settlement after General Taylor had more than once intimated to the War Department that, in his opinion, no such movement was necessary to the defense or protection of Texas.

These resolutions were laid over, under the rule. Many other propositions, embracing the substance of this question were also brought before the House, besides Mr. Richardson's, which ultimately failed. Mr. Lincoln did not call up his resolutions, nor were they acted upon ; but he commented on them in a speech subsequently made.

On the third day of January, 1849, Mr. Hudson, of Massachusetts, offered a resolution, directing the Committee on Military Affairs " to inquire into the expediency of requesting the President of the United States to withdraw to the east bank of the Rio Grande our armies now in Mexico, and to propose to the Mexican Government forthwith a treaty of peace on the following basis, namely : That we relinquish all claim to indemnity for the expenses of the war, and that the boundary between the United States and Mexico shall be established at or near the desert between the Nueces and the Rio Grande; that Mexico shall be held to pay all just claims due to our citizens at the commencement of the war, and that a convention shall be entered into by the two nations to provide for the liquidation of those claims and the mode of payment."

This was a test question on abandoning the war, without any material result accomplished. Mr. Lincoln voted with the minority, in favor of laying this resolution on the table. On the question of adopting the resolution, which was defeated, yet voted for by John Quincy Adams, Ashmun, Vinton, and many others on the Whig side, Mr. Lincoln voted in the negative. (See *Congressional Globe, first session,* 30*th Congress, page* 94.)

On the same day, almost immediately following the above action, joint resolutions of thanks to General Zachary Taylor and our troops in Mexico, having been offered, an amendment was proposed by Mr. Henley, a Democratic member from Indiana, as an adroit political maneuver, by which it was designed to secure an indorsement of the war from the Whigs, or a refusal of the vote of thanks. He moved the addition of this clause to the resolutions : " engaged, as they were, in defending the rights and honor of the nation." As an amendment to the amendment, in order to defeat its underhand purpose, Mr. Ashmun promptly moved to add the words : " In a war unnecessarily and unconstitutionally begun by the President of the United States," Mr. Lincoln voted for Ashmun's amendment to Henley's amendment. So also did Messrs. Clingman and Barringer, of North Carolina ; A. H. Stephens, Robert Toombs and Thomas Butler King, of Georgia ; Goggin, of Virginia ; Gentry, of Tennessee ; and a majority of all those voting. [See page 95, as above.] The object intended, of defeating the brilliant movement of Mr. Henley, was accomplished. The amendment, as amended, was not carried. The resolutions in their original shape, were subsequently re-introduced by Mr. Stephens, and adopted without opposition. (*Congressional Globe, page* 304.)

On the 12th day of January, 1848, Mr. Lincoln expressed his views, frankly and fully, in regard to the war with Mexico. It was the first speech made by Mr. Lincoln in Congress, and is subjoined entire, as reported in the Appendix to the *Congressional Globe* [1st session, 30th Congress, page 93]:

MR. LINCOLN'S SPEECH ON THE MEXICAN WAR.

(*In Committee of the Whole House, January* 12, 1848.)

Mr. Lincoln addressed the Committee as follows:

MR. CHAIRMAN: Some, if not all, of the gentlemen on the other side of the House, who have addressed the Committee within the last two days, have spoken rather complainingly, if I have rightly understood them, of the vote given a week or ten days ago, declaring that the war with Mexico was unnecessarily and unconstitutionally commenced by the President. I admit that such a vote should not be given in mere party wantonness, and that the one given is justly censurable, if it have no other or better foundation. I am one of those who joined in that vote; and did so under my best impression of the *truth* of the case. How I got this impression, and how it may possibly be removed I will now try to show. When the war begun, it was my opinion that all those who, because of knowing too *little*, or because of knowing too *much*, could not conscientiously approve the conduct of the President (in the beginning of it), should, nevertheless, as good citizens and patriots, remain silent on that point, at least till the war should be ended. Some leading Democrats, including ex-President Van Buren, have taken this same view, as I understand them; and I adhered to it, and acted upon it, until since I took my seat here; and I think I should still adhere to it, were it not that the President and his friends will not allow it to be so. Besides, the continual effort of the President to argue every silent vote given for supplies into an indorsement of the justice and wisdom of his conduct; besides that singularly candid paragraph in his late message, in which he tells us that Congress with great unanimity (only two in the Senate and fourteen in the House dissenting) had declared that " by the act of the Republic of Mexico a state of war exists between that Government and the United States ;" when the same journals that informed him of this, also informed him that, when that declaration stood disconnected from the question of supplies, sixty-seven in the House, and not fourteen merely, voted against it; besides this open attempt to prove by telling the *truth*, what he could not prove by telling the *whole truth*, demanding of all who will not submit to be misrepresented, in justice to themselves, to speak out; besides all this, one of my colleagues (Mr. Richardson), at a very early day in the session, brought in a set of resolutions, expressly indorsing the original justice of the war on the part of the President. Upon these resolutions, when they shall be put on their passage, I shall be *compelled* to vote ; so that I can not be silent if I would. Seeing this, I went about preparing myself to give the vote understandingly, when it should come. I carefully examined the President's messages, to ascertain what he himself had said and proved upon the point. The result of this examination was to make the impression, that, taking for true all the President states as facts, he falls far short of proving his justification ; and that the President would have gone further with his proof, if it had not been for the small matter that the *truth* would not permit him. Under the impression thus made I gave the vote before mentioned. I propose now to give, concisely, the process of the examination I made, and how I reached the conclusion I did.

The President, in his first message of May, 1846, declares that the soil was *ours* on which hostilities were commenced by Mexico ; and he repeats that declaration, almost in the same language, in each successive annual message—thus showing that he esteems that point a highly essential one. In the importance of that point I entirely agree with the President. To my judgment, it is the *very point* upon which he should be justified or condemned. In his message of December, 1846, it seems to have occurred to him, as is certainly true, that title, ownership to soil, or anything else, is not a simple fact, but is a conclusion following one or more simple facts ; and that it was incumbent upon him to present the facts from which he concluded the soil was ours on which the first blood of the war was shed.

Accordingly, a little below the middle of page twelve in the message last referred to, he enters upon that task ; forming an issue and introducing testimony, extending the whole to a little below the middle of page fourteen. Now, I propose to try to show that the whole of this—issue and evidence—is, from beginning to end, the sheerest deception. The issue, as he presents it, is in these words: "but there are those who, conceding all this to be true, assume the ground that the true western boundary of Texas is the Nueces, instead of the Rio Grande; and that, therefore, in marching our army to the east bank of the latter river, we passed the Texan line, and invaded the territory of Mexico." Now, this issue is made up of two affirmatives and no negatives. The main deception of it is, that it assumes as true that *one* river or the *other* is necessarily the boundary, and cheats the superficial thinker entirely out of the idea that *possibly* the boundary is somewhere *between* the two, and not actually at either. A further deception is, that it will let in *evidence* which a true issue would exclude. A true issue made by the President would be about as follows: " I say the soil *was ours* on which the first blood was shed ; there are those who say it was not."

I now proceed to examine the President's evidence, as applicable to such an issue. When that evidence is analyzed, it is all included in the following propositions :

1. That the Rio Grande was the western boundary of Louisiana, as we purchased it of France in 1803.

2. That the Republic of Texas always *claimed* the Rio Grande as her western boundary.

3. That, by various acts, she had claimed it *on paper*.

4. That Santa Anna, in his treaty with Texas, recognized the Rio Grande as her boundary.

5. That Texas *before*, and the United States *after* annexation, had *exercised* jurisdiction *beyond* the Nueces, *between* the two rivers.

6. That our Congress *understood* the boundary of Texas to extend beyond the Nueces.

Now for each of these in its turn :

His first item is, that the Rio Grande was the western boundary of Louisiana, as we purchased it of France in 1803; and, seeming to expect this to be disputed, he argues over the amount of nearly a page to prove it true ; at the end of which, he lets us know that, by the treaty of 1819, we sold to Spain the whole country, from the Rio Grande eastward to the Sabine. Now, admitting for the present, that the Rio Grande was the boundary of Louisiana, what, under heaven, had that to do with the *present* boundary between us and Mexico? How, Mr. Chairman, the line that once divided your land from mine can *still* be the boundary between us *after* I have sold my land to you, is, to me, beyond all comprehension. And how any man, with an honest purpose only of proving the truth, could ever have *thought* of introducing such a fact to prove such an issue, is equally incomprehensible. The outrage upon common *right*, of seizing as our own what we have once sold, merely because it *was* ours *before* we sold it, is only · equaled by the outrage on common *sense* of any attempt to justify it.

The President's next piece of evidence is, that " The Republic of Texas always *claimed* this river (Rio Grande) as her western boundary." That is not true, in fact. Texas *has* claimed it, but she has not *always* claimed it. There is, at least, one distinguished exception. Her State Constitution— the public's most solemn and well-considered act; that which may, without impropriety, be called her last will and testament, revoking all others—make no such claim. But suppose she had always claimed it. Has not Mexico always claimed the contrary? So that there is but *claim* against *claim*, leaving nothing proved until we get back of the claims, and find which has the better *foundation*.

Though not in the order in which the President presents his evidence, I now consider that class of his statements, which are, in substance, nothing more than that Texas has, by various acts of her Convention and Congress, claimed the Rio Grande as her boundary—*on paper*. I mean here what he says about the fixing of the Rio Grande as her boundary, in her old Constitution (not her State Constitution), about forming congressional districts, counties, etc. Now, all this is but naked *claim;* and what I have already said about claims is strictly applicable to this. If I should claim your land by word of mouth, that certainly would not make it mine, and if I were to claim it by a deed which I had made myself, and with which you had nothing to do, the claim would be quite the same in substance, or rather in utter nothingness.

I next consider the President's statement that Santa Anna, in his *treaty* with Texas, recognized the Rio Grande as the western boundary of Texas. Besides the position so often taken, that Santa Anna, while a prisoner of war—a captive— *could* not bind Mexico by a treaty, which I deem conclusive; besides this, I wish to say something in relation to this treaty, so called by the President, with Santa Anna. If any man would like to be amused by a sight at that *little* thing, which the President calls by that *big* name, he can have it by turning to Niles' Register, volume 50, page 336. And if any one should suppose that Niles' Register is a curious repository of so mighty a document as a solemn treaty between nations, I can only say that I learned, to a tolerable degree of certainty, by inquiry at the State Department, that the President himself never saw it anywhere else. By the way, I believe I should not err if I were to declare, that during the first ten

6

years of the existence of that document, it was never by any-body *called* a treaty; that it was never so called till the President, in his extremity, attempted, by so calling it, to wring something from it in justification of himself in connection with the Mexican war. It has none of the distinguishing features of a treaty. It does not call itself a treaty. Santa Anna does not therein assume to bind Mexico; he assumes only to act as President, Commander-in-Chief of the Mexican army and navy; stipulates that the then present hostilities should cease, and that he would not *himself* take up arms, nor *influence* the Mexican people to take up arms, against Texas, during the existence of the war of Independence. He did not recognize the independence of Texas; he did not assume to put an end to the war, but clearly indicated his expectation of its continuance; he did not say one word about boundary, and most probably never thought of it. It *is* stipulated therein that the Mexican forces should evacuate the territory of Texas, *passing to the other side of the Rio Grande;* and in another article it is stipulated, that to prevent collisions between the armies, the Texan army should not approach nearer than within five leagues—of *what* is not said—but clearly, from the object stated, it is of the Rio Grande. Now, if this is a treaty recognizing the Rio Grande as the boundary of Texas, it contains the singular feature of stipulating that Texas shall not go within five leagues of *her own* boundary.

Next comes the evidence of Texas before annexation, and the United States afterward, exercising jurisdiction beyond the Nueces, and *between* the two rivers. This actual *exercise* of jurisdiction is the very class or quality of evidence we want. It is excellent so far as it goes; but does it go far enough? He tells us it went *beyond* the Nueces, but he does not tell us it went *to* the Rio Grande. He tells us jurisdiction was exercised *between* the two rivers, but he does not tell us it was exercised over *all* the territory between them. Some simple-minded people think it possible to cross one river and go beyond it, without going all the way to the next; that jurisdiction may be exercised *between* two rivers without covering *all* the country between them. I know a man, not very unlike myself, who exercises jurisdiction over a piece of land between the Wabash and the Mississippi; and yet so far is this from being *all* there is between those rivers, that it is just one hundred and fifty-two feet long by fifty wide, and no part of it much within a hundred miles of either. He has a neighbor between him and the Mississippi—that is, just across the street, in that direction—whom, I am sure, he could neither *persuade* nor *force* to give up his habitation; but which, nevertheless, he could certainly annex, if it were to be done, by merely standing on his own side of the street and claiming it, or even sitting down and writing a deed for it.

But next, the President tells us the Congress of the United States *understood* the State of Texas they admitted into the Union to extend *beyond* the Nueces. Well, I suppose they did—I certainly so understand it—but how *far* beyond? That Congress did *not* understand it to extend clear to the Rio Grande, is quite certain by the fact of their joint resolutions for admission, expressly leaving all questions of boundary to future adjustment. And, it may be added, that Texas herself is proved to have had the same understanding of it that our Congress had, by the fact of the exact conformity of her new Constitution to those resolutions.

I am now through the whole of the President's evidence; and it is a singular fact, that if any one should declare the President sent the army into the midst of a settlement of Mexican people, who had never submitted, by consent or by force to the authority of Texas or of the United States, and that *there*, and *thereby*, the first blood of the war was shed, there is not one word in all the President has said which would either admit or deny the declaration. In this strange omission chiefly consists the deception of the President's evidence—an omission which, it does seem to me, could scarcely have occurred but by design. My way of living leads me to be about the courts of justice; and there I have some times seen a good lawyer struggling for his client's neck, in a desperate case, employing every artifice to work round, befog, and cover up with many words some position pressed upon him by the prosecution, which he *dared* not admit, and yet *could* not deny. Party bias may help to make it appear so; but with all the allowance I can make for such bias, it still does appear to me that just such, and from just such necessity, are the President's struggles in this case.

Some time after my colleague (Mr. Richardson) introduced the resolutions I have mentioned, I introduced a preamble, resolution, and interrogatories, intended to draw the President out, if possible, on this hitherto untrodden ground. To show their relevancy, I proposed to state my understanding of the true rule for ascertaining the boundary between Texas and Mexico. It is, that *wherever* Texas was *exercising* jurisdiction was hers; and wherever Mexico was exercising jurisdiction was hers; and that whatever separated the actual exercise of jurisdiction of the one from that of the other, was the true boundary between them. If, as is probably true, Texas was exercising jurisdiction along the western bank of the Nueces, and Mexico was exercising it along the eastern bank of the Rio Grande, then *neither* river was the boundary, but the uninhabited country between the two was. The extent of our territory in that region depended not on any *treaty-fixed* boundary (for no treaty had attempted it), but on revolution. Any people anywhere, being inclined and having the power, have the *right* to rise up and shake off the existing government, and form a new one that suits them better. This is a most valuable, a most sacred right—a right which, we hope and believe, is to liberate the world. Nor is this right confined to cases in which the whole people of an existing government may choose to exercise it. Any portion of such people that *can* may revolutionize, and make their *own* of so much of the territory as they inhabit. More than this, a *majority* of any portion of such people may revolutionize, putting down a *minority*, intermingled with, or near about them, who may oppose their movements. Such minority was precisely the case of the Tories of our own Revolution. It is a quality of revolutions not to go by old lines, or old laws; but to break up both, and make new ones. As to the country now in question, we bought it of France in 1803, and sold it to Spain in 1819, according to the President's statement. After this, all Mexico, including Texas, revolutionized against Spain; and still later, Texas revolutionized against Mexico. In my view, just so far as she carried her revolution, by obtaining the *actual*, willing or unwilling submission of the people, *so far* the country was hers, and no further.

Now, sir, for the purpose of obtaining the very best evidence as to whether Texas had actually carried her revolution to the place where the hostilities of the present war commenced, let the President answer the interrogatories I proposed, as before mentioned, or some other similar ones. Let him answer fully, fairly and candidly. Let him answer with *facts*, and not with arguments. Let him remember he sits where Washington sat; and so remembering, let him answer as Washington would answer. As a nation *should* not, and the Almighty *will* not, be evaded, so let him attempt no evasion, no equivocation. And if, so answering, he can show that the soil was ours where the first blood of the war was shed—that it was not within an inhabited country, or, if within such, that the inhabitants had submitted themselves to the civil authority of Texas, or of the United States, and that the same is true of the site of Fort Brown—then I am with him for his justification. In that case, I shall be most happy to reverse the vote I gave the other day. I have a selfish motive for desiring that the President may do this; I expect to give some votes, in connection with the war, which, without his so doing, will be of doubtful propriety, in my own judgment, but which will be free from the doubt, if he does so. But if he *can not* or *will not* do this—if, on any pretence, or no pretence, he shall refuse or omit it—then I shall be fully convinced, of what I more than suspect already, that he is deeply conscious of being in the wrong; that he feels the blood of this war, like the blood of Abel, is crying to heaven against him; that he ordered General Taylor into the midst of a peaceful Mexican settlement, purposely to bring on a war; that originally having some strong motive— what I will not stop now to give my opinion concerning—to involve the two countries in a war, and trusting to escape scrutiny by fixing the public gaze upon the exceeding brightness of military glory—that attractive rainbow that rises in showers of blood—that serpent's eye that charms to destroy— he plunged into it, and has swept *on* and *on*, till, disappointed in his calculation of the ease with which Mexico might be subdued, he now finds himself he knows not where. How like the half insane mumbling of a fever dream is the whole war part of the late message! At one time telling us that Mexico has nothing whatever that we can get but territory; at another, showing us how we can support the war by levying contributions on Mexico. At one time urging the national honor, the security of the future, the prevention of foreign interference, and even the good of Mexico herself, as among the objects of the war; at another, telling us that, "to reject indemnity by refusing to accept a cession of territory, would be to abandon all our just demands, and to wage the war, bearing all its expenses, *without a purpose or definite object* " So, then, the national honor, security of the future, and everything but territorial indemnity, may be considered the *no purposes* and *indefinite* objects of the war! But having it now settled that territorial indemnity is the only object, we are urged to seize by legislation here, all that he was content to take a few months ago, and the whole province of Lower California to boot, and to still carry on the war—to take *all* we are fighting for, and *still* fight on. Again, the President is resolved, under all circumstances, to have full territorial indemnity for the expenses of the war; but he forgets to tell us how we are to get the *excess* after those expenses shall have surpassed the value of the *whole* of the Mexican territory. So, again, he insists that the separate national existence of Mexico shall be maintained; but he does not tell us *how* this can be done after we shall have taken *all* her territory. Lest the question I here suggest be considered speculative merely, let me be indulged a moment in trying to show they are not.

The war has gone on some twenty months; for the expenses of which, together with an inconsiderable old score, the President now claims about one-half of the Mexican territory, and that by far the better half, so far as concerns our ability to make anything out of it. It is comparatively uninhabited; so that we could establish land offices in it, and raise some money in that way. But the other half is already inhabited, as I understand it, tolerably densely for the nature of the country; and all its lands, or all that are valuable, already appropriated as private property. How, then, are we to make any thing out of these lands with this incumbrance on them, or how remove the incumbrance? I suppose no one will say we should kill the people, or drive them out, or make slaves of them, or even confiscate their property! How, then, can we make much out of this part of the territory? If the prosecution of the war has, in expenses, already equaled the *better* half of the country, how long its future prosecution will be in equaling the less valuable half is not a *speculative* but a *practical* question, pressing closely upon us; and yet it is a question which the President seems never to have thought of.

As to the mode of terminating the war and securing peace, the President is equally wandering and indefinite. First, it is to be done by a more vigorous prosecution of the war in the vital parts of the enemy's country; and, after apparently talking himself tired on this point, the President drops down into a half despairing tone, and tells us that, " with a people distracted and divided by contending factions, and a government subject to constant changes, by successive revolutions, *the continued success of our arms may fail to obtain a satisfactory peace.*" Then he suggests the propriety of wheedling the Mexican people to desert the counsels of their own leaders, and, trusting in our protection, to set up a government from which we can secure a satisfactory peace, telling us that " *this may become the only mode of obtaining such a peace.*" But soon he falls into doubt of this, too, and then drops back on to the already half-abandoned ground of "more vigorous prosecution." All this shows that the President is in no wise satisfied with his own positions. First, he takes up one, and, in attempting to argue us into it, he argues himself *out* of it; then seizes another, and goes through the same process; and then, confused at being able to think of nothing new, he snatches up the old one again, which he has some time before cast off. His mind, tasked beyond its power, is running hither and thither, like some tortured creature on a burning surface, finding no position on which it can settle down and be at ease.

Again, it is a singular omission in this message that it nowhere intimates *when* the President expects the war to terminate. At its beginning, General Scott was, by this same President, driven into disfavor, if not disgrace, for intimating that peace could not be conquered in less than three or four months. But now at the end of about twenty months, during which time our arms have given us the most splendid successes—every department, and every part, land and water, officers and privates, regulars and volunteers, doing all that men could do, and hundreds of things which it had ever before been thought that men could *not* do; after all this, this same President gives us a long message without showing us that, *as to the end*, he has himself even an imaginary conception. As I have before said, he knows not where he is. He is a bewildered, confounded, and miserably-perplexed man. God grant he may be able to show that there is not something about his conscience more painful than all his mental perplexity.

Mr. Lincoln was an industrious member of the Committee on Post-offices, and Post-roads, and thoroughly acquainted himself with the details of that prominent branch of the public service. On the 5th of January, 1848, he made a clear and pertinent speech in regard to a question of temporary interest which then excited considerable attention, the " Great Southern Mail " contract. Some of the Virginia Whig members had taken issue with the Postmaster-General, in regard to his action on this question, and there were indications of an attempt to give a partisan turn to the affair. Mr. Lincoln sustained the action of that Democratic official, insisting that his construction of the law in this instance, which was the more economical, was also the more correct one. It is unnecessary to enter into the details of the case here. We subjoin two or three paragraphs from the speech, which was purely a practical one, for the purpose of showing the general spirit and tenor of Mr. Lincoln's mode of dealing with business matters :

I think that abundant reasons have been given to show that the construction put upon the law by the Postmaster-General is the right construction, and that subsequent acts of Congress have confirmed it. I have already said that the grievance complained of ought to be remedied. But it is said that the sum of money about which all this difficulty has arisen is exceedingly small—not more than $2,700. I admit it is very small; and if nothing else were involved, it would not be worth the dispute. But there is a principle involved; and if we once yield to a wrong principle, that concession will be the prolific source of endless mischief. It is for this reason, and not for the sake of saving $2,700, that I am unwilling to yield what is demanded. If I had no apprehensions that the ghost of this yielding would rise and appear in various distant places, I would say, pay the money, and let us have no more fuss about it. But I have such apprehensions. I do believe, that if we yield this, our act will be the source of other claims equally unjust, and therefore I can not vote to make the allowance.

Mr. L. insisted that the true and great point to which the attention of this House or the committee should be directed was, what is a just compensation? Inasmuch as this railroad and steamboat company could afford greater facilities than any other line, the service ought to be done upon this route; but it ought to be done on just and fair principles. If it could not be done at what had been offered, let it be shown that a greater amount was just. But, until it was shown, he was opposed to increasing it. He had seen many things in the report of the Postmaster-General and elsewhere that stood out against the river route. Now, the daily steamboat transportation between Troy and New York was performed for less than one hundred dollars per mile. This company was dissatisfied with two hundred and twelve or two hundred and thirteen dollars per mile. It had not been shown, and he thought it could not be shown to them why this company was entitled to more, or so much more, than the other received. It was true, they had to encounter the ice, but was there not more ice further north? There might possibly be shown some reason why the Virginia line should have more; but was there any reason why they should have so much more? Again, the price paid between Cincinnati and Louisville for daily transportation was not two hundred and thirteen dollars per mile, or one hundred dollars, or fifty; it was less than twenty-eight dollars per mile. Now, he did not insist that there might not be some peculiar reasons connected with this route between this city and Richmond that entitled it to more than was paid on the routes between Cincinnati and Louisville, and Troy and New York. But, if there were reasons, they ought to be shown. And was it supposed that there could be any, or so peculiar reasons as to justify so great a difference in compensation as was claimed by this company? It did seem that there could be none.

These reasons actuated him in taking the position he had taken, painfully refusing to oblige his friend from Virginia, which he assured the gentleman he had the greatest inclination to do.

In relation to the report of the committee, let him state one thing: It proposed that the Postmaster-General should again offer this company what he had already offered and they had refused. It was for the reason that the Postmaster-General, as he understood, had informed them that he was not himself going to renew the proposition. The committee supposed, at any rate he (Mr. L.) supposed—that as soon as the company should know that they could get what he he had offered them, and no more—as soon as all hope of greater compensation was cut off—that instant they would not take ten thousand dollars a year for the privilege of doing it. Whether this was actually the case he did not profess positively to know; it was a matter of opinion, but he firmly believed it. In proposing to offer them the contract again, as he had already said, the committee yielded something, viz.: the damage that the Government would have to pay for the breaking up of the present arrangement. He was willing to incur that damage; some other gentlemen were not; they were further away from the position which his friend from Virginia took. He was willing to yield something, but could not consent to go the whole length with the gentleman.

The subject of internal improvements, as before indicated, had long been one in which Mr. Lincoln had taken a special interest. In the Illinois Legislature, he had favored the policy of developing the resources of the State by the fostering aid of the local government, in so far as he might, under the constant restraints of a Democratic majority. The great River and Harbor Improvement Convention, held at Chicago, not long before the commencement of his Congressional life—and to which he refers in his subjoined speech on this policy—he had participated in, as one of its most active and earnest members. A brief, fifteen-minute speech of his on that occasion, of which there appears to be no report extant, is still remembered by many of those who heard it, as one of the most eloquent and impressive efforts of that memorable convention, which was presided over by the Hon. Edward Bates.

8

of St. Louis. Aside from the celebrated speech of the latter, a theme of constant praise from that day to the present, no more electrifying address was made before the convention than that of Mr. Lincoln.

On the 20th day of June, 1848, after the Presidential nomination of Mr. Cass, whom "circumstances," it will be remembered, prevented from being present at that convention, Mr. Lincoln took occasion to address the House on this subject. Below is his speech entire, as reported in the Appendix to the *Congressional Globe* for that sesson (p. 709):

MR. LINCOLN'S SPEECH ON INTERNAL IMPROVEMENTS.

(In Committee of the Whole House, June 20, 1848.)

Mr. Lincoln said:

MR. CHAIRMAN—I wish at all times in no way to practice any fraud upon the House or the Committee, and I also desire to do nothing which may be very disagreeable to any of the members. I therefore state, in advance, that my object in taking the floor is to make a speech on the general subject of internal improvements; and if I am out of order in doing so, I give the Chair an opportunity of so deciding, and I will take my seat.

The Chair.—I will not undertake to anticipate what 'the gentleman may say on the subject of internal improvements. He will, therefore, proceed in his remarks, and if any question of order shall be made, the Chair will then decide it.

Mr. Lincoln.—At an early day of this session the President sent to us what may properly be termed an internal improvement veto message. The late Democratic Convention which sat at Baltimore, and which nominated General Cass for the Presidency, adopted a set of resolutions, now called the Democratic platform, among which is one in these words:

"That the Constitution does not confer upon the General Government the power to commence and carry on a general system of internal improvements."

General Cass, in his letter accepting the nomination, holds this language:

"I have carefully read the resolutions of the Democratic National Convention, laying down the platform of our political faith, and I adhere to them as firmly as I approve them cordially."

These things, taken together, show that the question of

internal improvements is now more distinctly made—has become more intense, than at any former period. It can no longer be avoided. The veto message and the Baltimore resolution I understand to be, in substance, the same thing; the latter being the more general statement, of which the former is the amplification—the bill of particulars. While I know there are many Democrats, on the floor and elsewhere, who disapprove that message, I understand that all who shall vote for General Cass will thereafter be considered as having approved it, as having indorsed all its docrines. I suppose all, or nearly all, the Democrats will vote for him. Many of them will do so, not because they like his position on this question, but because they prefer him, being wrong in this, to another, whom they consider further wrong on other questions. In this way the internal improvement Democrats are to be, by a sort of forced consent, carried over, and arrayed against themselves on this measure of policy. General Cass, once elected, will not trouble himself to make a constitutional argument, or, perhaps, any argument at all, when he shall veto a river or harbor bill. He will consider it a sufficient answer to all Democratic murmurs, to point to Mr. Polk's message, and to the "Democratic platform." This being the case, the question of improvements is verging to a final crisis; and the friends of the policy must now battle, and battle manfully, or surrender all. In this view, humble as I am, I wish to review, and contrast as well as I may, the general positions of this veto message. When I say *general* positions, I mean to exclude from consideration so much as relates to the present embarrassed state of the Treasury, in consequence of the Mexican war.

Those general positions are: That internal improvements ought not to be made by the General Government:

1. Because they would overwhelm the treasury;

2. Because, while their *burdens* would be general, their *benefits* would be *local* and *partial*, involving an obnoxious inequality;

3. Because they would be unconstitutional;

4. Because the States may do enough by the levy and collection of tunnage duties; or, if not,

5. That the Constitution may be amended.

"Do nothing at all, lest you do something wrong," is the sum of these positions—is the sum of this message; and this, with the exception of what is said about Constitutionality, applying as forcibly to making improvements by State authority as by the national authority. So that we must abandon the improvements of the country altogether, by any and every authority, or we may resist and repudiate the doctrines of this message. Let us attempt the latter.

The first position is, that a system of internal improvement would overwhelm the treasury.

That, in such a system, there is a *tendency* to undue expansion, is not to be denied. Such tendency is founded in the nature of the subject. A member of Congress will prefer voting for a bill which contains an appropriation for his district, to voting for one which does not; and when a bill shall be expanded till every district shall be provided for, that it will be too greatly expanded is obvious. But is this any more true in Congress than in a State Legislature? If a member of Congress must have an appropriation for his district, so a member of a Legislature must have for his county ; and if one will overwhelm the national treasury, so the other will overwhelm the State treasury. Go where we will, the difficulty is the same. Allow it to drive us from the halls of Congress, and it will just as easily drive us from the State Legislatures. Let us, then, grapple with it, and test its strength. Let us, judging of the future by the past, ascertain whether there may not be, in the discretion of Congress, a sufficient power to limit and restrain this expansive tendency within reasonable and proper bounds. The President himself values the evidence of the past. He tells us that at a certain point of our history, more than two hundred millions of dollars has been *applied for*, to make improvements, and this he does to prove that the treasury would be overwhelmed by such a system. Why did he not tell us how much was *granted?* Would not that have been better evidence? Let us turn to it, and see what it proves. In the message, the President tells us that " during the four succeeding years, embraced by the administration of President Adams, the power not only to appropriate money, but to apply it, under the direction and authority of the General Government, as well to the construction of roads as to the improvement of harbors and rivers, was fully asserted and exercised."

This, then, was the period of greatest enormity. These, if any, must have been the days of the 200,000,000. And how much do you suppose was really expended for improvements during those four years? Two hundred millions? One hundred? Fifty? Ten? Five? No, sir, less than two millions. As shown by authentic documents, the expenditures on improvements during 1825, 1826, 1827 and 1828, amounted to $1,879,627 01. These four years were the period of Mr. Adams' administration, nearly, and substantially. This fact shows that when the power to make improvements was " fully asserted and exercised," the Congresses *did* keep within reasonable limits ; and what has been done it seems to me, *can* be done again.

Now for the second position of the message, namely, that the burdens of improvements would be *general*, while their *benefits* would be *local* and *partial*, involving an obnoxious inequality. That there is some degree of truth in this position I shall not deny. No commercial object of Government patronage can be so exclusively *general*, as not to be of some peculiar *local* advantage ; but, on the other hand, nothing is so *local* as not to be of some general advantage. The navy, as I understand it, was established, and is maintained, at a great annual expense, partly to be ready for war, when war shall come, but partly also, and perhaps chiefly, for the protection of our commerce on the high seas. This latter object is, for all I can see, in principle, the same as internal improvements. The driving a pirate from the track of commerce on the broad ocean, and the removing a snag from its more narrow path in the Mississippi river, can not, I think, be distinguished in principle. Each is done to save life and property, and for nothing else. The navy, then, is the most general in its benefits of all this class of objects ; and yet even the navy is of some peculiar advantage to Charleston, Baltimore, Philadelphia, New York, and Boston, beyond what it is to the interior towns of Illinois. The next most general object I can think of, would be improvements on the Mississippi river and its tributaries. They touch thirteen of our States—Pennsylvania, Virginia, Kentucky, Tennessee, Mississippi, Louisiana, Arkansas, Missouri, Illinois, Indiana, Ohio, Wisconsin, and Iowa. Now, I suppose it will not be denied, that these thirteen States are a little more interested in improvements on that great river than are the remaining seventeen. These instances of the navy, and the Mississippi river, show clearly that there is something of local advantage in the most general objects. But the converse is also true. Nothing is so *local* as not to be of some *general* benefit. Take, for instance, the Illinois and Michigan canal. Considered apart from its effects, it is perfectly local. Every inch of it is within the State of Illinois. That canal was first opened for business last April. In a very few days we were all gratified to learn, among other things, that sugar had been carried from New Orleans, through the canal, to Buffalo, in New York. This sugar took this route, doubtless, because it was cheaper than the old route. Supposing the benefit in the reduction of the cost of carriage to be shared between seller and buyer, the result is, that the New Orleans merchant sold his sugar a little *dearer*, and the people of Buffalo sweetened their coffee a little *cheaper* than before ; a benefit resulting *from* the canal, not to Illinois, where the canal *is*, but to Louisiana and New York, where it is *not*. In other transactions Illinois will, of course, have her share, and perhaps the larger share too, in the benefits of the canal ; but the instance of the sugar clearly shows that the *benefits* of an improvement are by no means confined to the particular locality of the improvement itself.

The just conclusion from all this is, that if the nation refuse to make improvements of the more general kind, because their benefits may be somewhat local, a State may, for the same reason, refuse to make an improvement of a local kind, because its benefits may be somewhat general. A State may well say to the nation: "If you will do nothing for me, I will do nothing for you." Thus it is seen, that if this argument of "inequality" is sufficient anywhere, it is sufficient everywhere, and puts an end to improvements altogether. I hope and believe, that if both the nation and the States would, in good faith, in their respective spheres, do what they could in the way of improvements, what of inequality might be produced in one place might be compensated in another, and that the sum of the whole might not be very unequal. But suppose, after all, there should be some degree of inequality : inequality is certainly never to be embraced for its own sake ; but is every good thing to be discarded which may be inseparably connected with some degree of it ? If so, we must discard all government. This Capitol is built at the public expense, for the public benefit ; but does any one doubt that it is of some peculiar local advantage to the property holders and business people of Washington ? Shall we remove it for this reason ? And if so, where shall we set it down, and be free from the difficulty ? To make sure of our object, shall we locate it nowhere, and leave Congress hereafter to hold its sessions as the loafer lodged, "in spots about ?" I make no special allusion to the present President when I say, there are few stronger cases in this world of "burden to the many, and benefit to the few"—of "inequality"—than the Presidency itself is by some thought to be. An honest laborer digs coal at about seventy cents a day, while the President digs abstractions at about seventy dollars a day. The *coal* is clearly worth more than the *abstractions*, and yet what a monstrous inequality in the prices ? Does the President, for this reason, propose to abolish the Presidency ? He *does* not, and he *ought* not. The true rule, in determining to embrace or reject anything, is not whether it have *any* evil in it, but whether it have more of evil than of good. There are few things *wholly* evil or *wholly* good.

Almost every thing, especially of government policy, is an inseparable compound of the two ; so that our best judgment of the preponderance between them is continually demanded. On this principle, the President, his friends, and the world generally, act on most subjects. Why not apply it, then, upon this question ? Why, as to improvements, magnify the *evil*, and stoutly refuse to see any good in them?

Mr. Chairman, on the third position of the message (the Constitutional question) I have not much to say. Being the man I am, and speaking when I do, I feel that in any attempt at an original, Constitutional argument, I should not be, and ought not to be, listened to patiently. The ablest and the best of men have gone over the whole ground long ago. I shall attempt but little more than a brief notice of what some of them have said. In relation to Mr. Jefferson's views, I read from Mr. Polk's veto message :

" President Jefferson, in his message to Congress in 1806, recommended an amendment of the Constitution, with a view to apply an anticipated surplus in the treasury ' to the great purposes of the public education, roads, rivers, canals, and such other objects of public improvements as it may be thought proper to add to the Constitutional enumeration of the Federal powers.' And he adds : ' I suppose an amendment to the Constitution, by consent of the States, necessary, because the objects now recommended are not among those enumerated in the Constitution, and to which it permits the public moneys to be applied." In 1825, he repeated, in his published letters, the opinion that no such power has been conferred upon Congress."

I introduce this, not to controvert, just now, the Constitutional opinion, but to show, that on the question of *expediency*, Mr. Jefferson's opinion was against the present President— that this opinion of Mr. Jefferson, in one branch at least, is, in the hands of Mr. Polk, like McFingal's gun :

" Bears wide and kicks the owner over."

But, to the Constitutional question. In 1826, Chancellor Kent first published his Commentaries on American Law He devoted a portion of one of the lectures to the question of the authority of Congress to appropriate public moneys for internal improvements. He mentions that the question had never been brought under judicial consideration, and proceeds to give a brief summary of the discussions it had undergone between the legislative and executive branches of the Government. He shows that the legislative branch had usually been *for*, and the executive *against*, the power, till the period

of Mr. J. Q. Adams' administration ; at which point he considers the executive influence as withdrawn from opposition,
and added to the support of the power. In 1844, the Chan-
celor published a new edition of his Commentaries, in which
he adds some notes of what had transpired on the question
since 1826. I have not time to read the original text, or the
notes, but the whole may be found on page 267, and the two
or three following pages of the first volume of the edition of
1844. As what Chancellor Kent seems to consider the sum
of the whole, I read from one of the notes :

" Mr. Justice Story, in his Commentaries on the Constitution of the United States, vol. 2, page 429–440, and again,
page 519–538, has stated at large the arguments for and
against the proposition that Congress have a Constitutional
authority to lay taxes, and to apply the power to regulate commerce, as a means directly to encourage and protect domestic
manufactures ; and, without giving any opinion of his own on
the contested doctrine, he has left the reader to draw his own
conclusion. I should think, however, from the arguments as
stated, that every mind which has taken no part in the discussions, and felt no prejudice or territorial bias on either side of
the question, would deem the arguments in favor of the Congressional power vastly superior."

It will be seen, that in this extract, the power to make
improvements is not directly mentioned ; but by examining
the context both of Kent and of Story, it will appear that the
power mentioned in the extract and the power to make
improvements, are regarded as identical. It is not to be
denied that many great and good men have been *against* the
power ; but it is insisted that quite as many, as great, and as
good, have been *for* it ; and it is shown that, on a full survey
of the whole, Chancellor Kent was of opinion that the arguments of the latter were *vastly* superior. This is but the
opinion of a man; but who was that man? He was one of
the ablest and most learned lawyers of his age, or of any
other age. It is no disparagement to Mr. Polk, nor, indeed,
to any one who devotes much time to politics, to be placed far
behind Chancellor Kent as a lawyer. His attitude was most
favorable to correct conclusions. He wrote coolly and in
retirement. He was struggling to rear a durable monument
of fame ; and he well knew that *truth* and thoroughly sound
reasoning were the only sure foundations. Can the party
opinion of a party President, on a law question, as this purely
is, be at all compared or set in opposition to that of such a
man, in such an attitude, as Chancellor Kent?

This Constitutional question will probably never be better

LITTLE PIGEON BAPTIST CHURCH,

Where the Lincoln's worshipped, in Spencer County.

7

settled than it is, until it shall pass under judicial consideration; but I do think that no man who is clear on this question of expediency need feel his conscience much pricked
upon this.

Mr. Chairman, the President seems to think that enough
'may be done in the way of improvements, by means of tunnage duties, under State authority, with the consent of the
General Government.   Now, I suppose this matter of tunnage
duties is well enough in its own sphere.   I suppose it may be
efficient, and perhaps *sufficient*, to make slight improvements
and repairs in harbors already in use, and not much out of
repair.   But if I have any correct general idea of it, it must
be wholly inefficient for any general beneficient purposes of
improvement.   I know very little, or rather nothing at all, of
the practical matter of levying and collecting tunnage duties;
but I suppose one of its principles must be, to lay a duty, for
the improvement of any particular harbor, *upon the tunnage
coming into that harbor.*   To do otherwise—to collect money
in *one* harbor to be expended on improvements in *another*—
would be an extremely aggravated form of that inequality
which the President so much deprecates.   If I be right in this,
how could we make any entirely new improvements by means of
tunnage duties?   How make a road, a canal, or clear a greatly
obstructed river?   The idea that we could, involves the
same absurdity of the Irish bull about the new boots: "I shall
niver git 'em on," says Patrick, " till I wear 'em a day or two,
and stretch 'em a little."   We shall never make a canal by
tunnage duties, until it shall already have been made awhile,
so the tunnage can get into it.

After all, the President concludes that possibly there may
be some great objects of improvements which can not be
effected by tunnage duties, and which, therefore, may be expedient for the General Government to take in hand.   Accordingly, he suggests, in case any such be discovered, the propriety of amending the Constitution.   Amend it for what?
If, like Mr. Jefferson, the President thought improvements
expedient, but not constitutional, it would be natural enough
for him to recommend such an amendment; but hear what he
says in this very message:

"In view of these portentous consequences, I can not but
think that this course of legislation should be arrested, even
were there nothing to forbid it in the fundamental laws of our
Union."

For what, then, would *he* have the Constitution amended?
With *him* it is a proposition to remove *one* impediment,
merely to be met by *others*, which, in his opinion, can not be

7 9

removed—to enable Congress to do what, in his opinion, they ought not to do if they could.

[Here Mr. Meade, of Virginia, inquired if Mr. L. understood the President to be opposed, on grounds of expediency, to any and every improvement?]

To which Mr. Lincoln answered : In the very part of his message of which I am now speaking, I understand him as giving some vague expressions in favor of some possible objects of improvements; but, in doing so, I understand him to be directly in the teeth of his own arguments in other parts of it. Neither the President, nor any one, can possibly specify an improvement, which shall not be clearly liable to one or another of the objections he has urged on the score of expediency. I have shown, and might show again, that no work— no object—can be so general, as to dispense its benefits with precise equality; and this inequality is chief among the " portentous consequences " for which he declares that improvements should be arrested. No, sir ; when the President intimates that something in the way of improvements may properly be done by the General Government, he is shrinking from the conclusions to which his own arguments would force him. He feels that the improvements of this broad and goodly land are a mighty interest ; and he is unwilling to confess to the people, or perhaps to himself, that he has built an argument which, when pressed to its conclusion, entirely annihilates this interest.

I have already said that no one who is satisfied of the expediency of making improvements need be much uneasy in his conscience about its constitutionality. I wish now to submit a few remarks on the general proposition of amending the Constitution. As a general rule, I think we would do much better to let it alone. No slight occasion should tempt us to touch it. Better not take the first step, which may lead to a habit of altering it. Better rather habituate ourselves to think of it as unalterable. It can scarcely be made better than it is. New provisions would introduce new difficulties, and thus create and increase appetite for further change. No, sir ; let it stand as it is. New hands have never touched it. The men who made it have done their work, and have passed away. Who shall improve on what *they* did?

Mr. Chairman, for the purpose of reviewing this message in the least possible time, as well as for the sake of distinctness, I have analyzed its arguments as well as I could, and reduced them to the propositions I have stated. I have now examined •them in detail. I wish to detain the committee only a little while longer, with some general remarks on the subject of improvements. That the subject is a difficult one, can not be denied. Still, it is no more difficult in Congress than in the State Legislatures, in the counties, or in the smallest municipal districts which everywhere exist. All can recur to instances of this difficulty in the case of county roads, bridges, and the like. One man is offended because a road passes over his land; and another is offended because it does *not* pass over his; one is dissatisfied because the bridge, for which he is taxed, crosses the river on a different road from that which leads from his house to town; another can not bear that the county should get in debt for these same roads and bridges; while not a few struggle hard to have roads located over their lands, and then stoutly refuse to let them be opened, until they are first paid the damages. Even between the different wards and streets of towns and cities, we find this same wrangling and difficulty. Now, these are no other than the very difficulties against which, and out of which, the President constructs his objections of "inequality," "speculation," and "crushing the Treasury." There is but a single alternative about them— they are *sufficient*, or they are *not*. If sufficient, they are sufficient *out* of Congress as well as *in* it, and there is the end. We must reject them as insufficient, or lie down and do nothing by any authority. Then, difficulty though there be, let us meet and overcome it.

> "Attempt the end, and never stand to doubt;
> Nothing so hard, but search will find it out."

Determine that the thing can and shall be done, and then we shall find the way. The tendency to undue expansion is unquestionably the chief difficulty. How to do *something*, and still not to do *too much*, is the desideratum. Let each contribute his mite in the way of suggestion. The late Silas Wright, in a letter to the Chicago Convention, contributed his, which was worth something; and I now contribute mine, which may be worth nothing. At all events, it will mislead nobody, and therefore will do no harm. I would not borrow money. I am against an overwhelming, crushing system. Suppose that at each session, Congress shall first determine *how much* money can, for that year, be spared for improvements; then apportion that sum to the most *important* objects. So far, all is easy; but how shall we determine which *are* the most important? On this question comes the collision of interests. *I* shall be slow to acknowledge that *your* harbor or *your* river is more important than *mine*, and *vice versa*. To clear this difficulty, let us have that same statistical information which the gentleman from Ohio [Mr. Vinton] suggested

at the beginning of this session.   In that information we shall
have a stern, unbending basis of *facts*—a basis in nowise subject to whim, caprice, or local interest.   The pre-limited
amount of means will save us from doing *too much*, and the
statistics will save us from doing what we do, in *wrong places*.
Adopt and adhere to this course, and, it seems to me, the difficulty is cleared.

One of the gentlemen from South Carolina (Mr. Rhett)
very much deprecates these statistics.   He particularly objects,
as I understand him, to counting all the pigs and chickens
in the land.   I do not perceive much force in the objection.
It is true, that if everything be enumerated, a portion of such
statistics may not be very useful to this object.   Such products
of the country as are to be *consumed* where they are *produced*,
need no roads and rivers, no means of transportation, and have
no very proper connection with this subject.   The *surplus*, that
which is produced in *one* place to be consumed in *another;* the
capacity of each locality for producing a *greater* surplus; the
natural means of transportation, and their susceptibility of
improvement; the hindrances, delays, and losses of life and
property during transportation, and the causes of each would
be among the most valuable statistics in this connection.   From
these it would readily appear where a given amount of expenditure would do the most good.   These statistics might be
equally accessible, as they would be equally useful, to both the
nation and the States.   In this way, and by these means, let
the nation take hold of the larger works, and the States the
smaller ones; and thus, working in a meeting direction, discreetly, but steadily and firmly, what is made unequal in one
place, may be equalized in another, extravagance avoided, and
the whole country put on that career of prosperity which shall
correspond with its extent of territory, its natural resources,
and the intelligence and enterprise of its people.

The first session of the Thirtieth Congress was prolonged
far beyond the date of the Presidential nominations of 1848,
and the canvass was actively carried on by members on the
floor of the House.   Mr. Lincoln warmly sustained the nomination of Gen. Taylor, and before the adjournment of Congress, he made, in accordance with precedent and general
practice, one of his characteristic campaign speeches.   He
showed himself a man of decided partisan feelings, and entered
into this contest with zeal, not only repelling the violent attacks
upon the Whig candidate, but showing that there were blows

to be given as well as taken. He said some things in a vein of sarcastic humor, which could only have been mistaken for actual bitterness, by those who did not know the really genial character of the man. Argument, ridicule and illustrative anecdotes were brought into requisition, with great ability and unsparing boldness, in setting the real issues of the canvass, political and personal, in what he deemed a proper light before the people.

Although containing so many things of mere temporary interest, this speech will be read with avidity at the present time, and particularly on account of several passages which have especial significance from the position Mr. Lincoln himself afterward occupied—what had then probably never seriously entered his thoughts as among the events of the future. This effort will perhaps give occasional offense to the purist in style, but its manly earnestness and force, and its adaptedness to popular effect as a campaign document, will not be called in question. It is obvious that there was some change in Mr. Lincoln's manner of speaking subsequently to those days, yet his first appearance in the national arena of politics exhibited that rugged strength and that earnest directness of expression which have given him permanent power with popular auditories.

MR. LINCOLN'S SPEECH ON THE PRESIDENCY AND GENERAL POLITICS.

(*Delivered in the House, July* 27, 1848)

GENERAL TAYLOR AND THE VETO POWER.

Mr. Lincoln said—

Mr. SPEAKER :—Our Democratic friends seem to be in great distress because they think our candidate for the Presidency don't suit *us*. Most of them can not find out that Gen. Taylor has any principles at all ; some, however, have discovered that he has *one*, but that that one is entirely wrong. This one principle is his position on the veto power. The gentleman from Tennessee (Mr. Stanton) who has just taken his seat, indeed, has said there is very little if any difference on this question between Gen. Taylor and all the Presidents ; and he seems to think it sufficient detraction from Gen. Taylor's position on it, that it has nothing new in it. But all others, whom I have heard speak, assail it furiously. A new member from Ken-

tucky (Mr. Clarke*) of very considerable ability, was in particular concern about it.   He thought it altogether novel and
unprecedented for a President, or a Presidential candidate, to
think of approving bills whose Constitutionality may not be
entirely clear to his own mind.   He thinks the ark of our
safety is gone, unless Presidents shall always veto such bills
as, in their judgment, may be of *doubtful* Constitutionality.
However clear Congress may be of their authority to pass any
particular act, the gentleman from Kentucky thinks the President must veto if *he* has *doubts* about it.   Now I have neither
time nor inclination to argue with the gentlemen on the veto
power as an original question; but I wish to show that Gen.
Taylor and not he, agrees with the earliest statesmen on this
question.   When the bill chartering the first Bank of the
United States passed Congress, its constitutionality was questioned, Mr. Madison, then in the House of Representatives,
as well as others, had opposed it on that ground.   Gen. Washington, as President, was called on to approve or reject it.   He
sought and obtained, on the constitutional question, the separate written opinions of Jefferson, Hamilton and Edmund Randolph, they then being respectively Secretary of State, Secretary of the Treasury, and Attorney General.   Hamilton's
opinion was for the power; while Randolph's and Jefferson's
were both against it.   Mr. Jefferson, after giving his opinion
decidedly against the constitutionality of that bill, closed his
letter with the paragraph which I now read :

" It must be admitted, however, that unless the President's
mind, on a view of everything which is urged for and against
this bill, is tolerably clear that it is unauthorized by the Constitution ; if the pro and the con hang so even as to balance
his judgment, a just respect for the wisdom of the Legislature
would naturally decide the balance in favor of their opinion ;
it is chiefly for cases where they are clearly misled by error,
ambition or interest, that the Constitution has placed a check
in the negative of the President.   THOMAS JEFFERSON.

" *February* 15, 1791."

Gen. Taylor's opinion, as expressed in his Allison letter, is
as I now read :

" The power given by the veto is a high conservative power;
but, in my opinion, should never be exercised, except in cases
of clear violation of the Constitution, or manifest haste and
want of consideration by Congress."

It is here seen that, in Mr. Jefferson's opinion, if on the
constitutionality of any given bill, the President *doubts*, he is

---

*The late Hon. Beverly L. Clarke.

not to veto it, as the gentleman from Kentucky would have him to do, but is to defer to Congress and approve it. And if we compare the opinions of Jefferson and Taylor, as expressed in these paragraphs, we shall find them more exactly alike than we can often find any two expressions having any literal difference. None but interested fault-finders, can discover any substantial variation.

THE NATIONAL ISSUES.

But gentlemen on the other side are unanimously agreed that Gen. Taylor has no other principle. They are in utter darkness as to his opinions on any of the questions of policy which occupy the public attention. But is there any doubt as to what he will *do* on the prominent questions, if elected? Not the least. It is not possible to know what he will or would do in every imaginable case; because many questions have passed away, and others doubtless will arise which none of us have yet thought of; but on the prominent questions of currency, tariff, internal improvements, and Wilmot proviso, General Taylor's course is at least as well defined as is General Cass'. Why, in their eagerness to get at General Taylor, several Democratic members here have desired to know whether, in case of his election, a bankrupt law is to be established. Can they tell us General Cass' opinion on this question? (Some member answered, "He is against it.") Aye, how do you know he is? There is nothing about it in the platform, nor elsewhere, that I have seen. If the gentleman knows anything which I do not, he can show it. But to return: General Taylor, in his Allison letter, says:

"Upon the subject of the tariff, the currency, the improvement of our great highways, rivers, lakes, and harbors, the will of the people, as expressed through their Representatives in Congress, ought to be respected and carried out by the Executive."

A PRESIDENCY FOR THE PEOPLE.

Now, this is the whole matter—in substance, it is this: The people say to General Taylor, "If you are elected, shall we have a national bank?" He answers, "*Your* will, gentlemen, not *mine?*" "What about the tariff?" "Say yourselves." "Shall our rivers and harbors be improved?" "Just as you please." "If you desire a bank, an alteration of the tariff, internal improvements, any or all, I will not hinder you; if you do not desire them, I will not attempt to force them on you." "Send up your members of Congress from the various districts, with opinions according to your own, and if they are for these measures, or any of them, I shall have nothing to oppose; if they are not for them, I shall not, by any appliances whatever, attempt to dragoon them into their adoption." Now, can there be any difficulty in understanding this? To you, Democrats, it may not seem like principle; but surely you can not fail to perceive the position plainly enough. The distinction between it and the position of your candidate is broad and obvious, and I admit you have a clear right to show it is wrong, if you can; but you have no right to pretend you can not see it at all. We see it, and to us it appears like principle, and the best sort of principle at that—the principle of allowing the people to do as they please with their own business. My friend from Indiana (Mr. C. B. Smith) has aptly asked, " Are you willing to trust the people?" Some of you answered, substantially, "We are willing to trust the people; but the President is as much the representative of the people as Congress." In a certain sense, and to a certain extent, he is the representative of the people. He is elected by them, as well as Congress is. But can he, in the nature of things, know the wants of the people as well as three hundred other men coming from all the various localities of the nation? If so, where is the propriety of having a Congress? That the Constitution gives the President a negative on legislation, all know; but that this negative should be so combined with platforms and other appliances as to enable him, and, in fact, almost compel him, to take the whole of legislation into his own hands, is what we object to—is what General Taylor objects to—and is what constitutes the broad distinction between you and us. To thus transfer legislation is clearly to take it from those who understand with minuteness the interest of the people, and give it to one who does not and can not so well understand it. I understand your idea, that if a Presidential candidate avow his opinion upon a given question, or rather upon all questions, and the people, with full knowledge of this, elect him, they thereby distinctly approve all those opinions. This, though plausible, is a most pernicious deception. By means of it measures are adopted or rejected, contrary to the wishes of the whole of one party, and often nearly half of the other. The process is this: Three, four, or half a dozen questions are prominent at a given time; the party selects its candidate, and he takes his position on each of these questions. On all but one his positions have already been indorsed at former elections, and his party fully committed to them: but that one is new, and a large portion of them are against it. But what are they to do? The whole are strung together, and they must take all or reject all. They can not take what they like and leave the the rest. What they are already committed to, being the majority, they shut their eyes and gulp the whole. Next election, still another is introduced in the same way. If we run our eyes along the line of the past, we shall see that almost, if not quite, all the articles of the present Democratic creed, have been at first forced upon the party in this very way. And just now, and just so, opposition to internal improvements is to be established, if Gen. Cass shall be elected. Almost half the Democrats here are for improvements, but they will vote for Cass; and if he succeeds, their votes will have aided in closing the doors against improvements. Now, this is a process which we think is wrong. We prefer a candidate who, like Gen. Taylor, will allow the people to have their own way, regardless of his private opinion; and I should think the internal-improvement Democrats, at least, ought to prefer such a candidate. He would force nothing on them which they don't want, and he would allow them to have improvements, which their own candidate, if elected, will not.

GEN. TAYLOR AND THE WILMOT PROVISO.

Mr. Speaker, I have said Gen. Taylor's position is as well defined as is that of Gen. Cass. In saying this, I admit I do not certainly know what he would do on the Wilmot Proviso. I am a Northern man, or, rather, a Western free-state man, with a constituency I believe to be, and with personal feelings I know to be, against the extension of slavery. As such, and with what information I have, I hope, and *believe*, Gen. Taylor, if elected, would not veto the proviso; but I do not *know* it. Yet, if I knew he would, I still would vote for him. I should do so, because, in my judgment, his election alone can defeat Gen. Cass; and because, *should* slavery thereby go into the territory we now have, just so much will certainly happen by the election of Cass; and, in addition, a course of policy leading to new wars, new acquisitions of territory, and still further extensions of slavery. One of the two is to be President; which is preferable?

CASS ON INTERNAL IMPROVEMENTS.

But there is as much doubt of Cass on improvements, as there is of Taylor on the proviso. I have no doubt myself of Gen. Cass on this question, but I know the Democrats differ among themselves as to his position. My internal-improvement colleague (Mr. Wentworth) stated on this floor the other day, that he was satisfied Cass was for improvements, because he had voted for all the bills that he (Mr. W.) had. So far so good. But Mr. Polk vetoed some of these very bills; the Baltimore Convention passed a set of resolutions, among other things, approving these vetoes, and Cass declares, in his letter accepting the nomination, that he has carefully read these resolutions, and that he adheres to them as firmly as he approves them cordially. In other words, Gen. Cass voted for the bills, and thinks the President did right to veto them; and his friends here are amiable enough to consider him as being on one side or the other, just as one or the other may correspond with their own respective inclinations. My colleague admits that the platform declares against the constitutionality of a general system of improvements, and that Gen. Cass indorses the platform; but he still thinks Gen. Cass is in favor of some sort of improvements. Well, what are they? As he is against *general* objects, those he is *for*, must be *particular* and *local*. Now, this is taking the subject precisely by the wrong end. *Particularity*—expending the money of the *whole* people for an object which will benefit only a *portion* of them, is the greatest real objection to improvements, and has been so held by Gen. Jackson, Mr. Polk, and all others, I believe, till now. But now, behold, the objects most general, nearest free from this objection, are to be rejected, while those most liable to it are to be embraced. To return: I can not help believing that Gen. Cass, when he wrote his letter of acceptance, well understood he was to be claimed by the advocates of both sides of this question, and that he then closed the door against all further expressions of opinion, purposely to retain the benefits of that double position. His subsequent equivocation at Cleveland, to my mind, proves such to have been the case.

PLATFORMS.

One word more, and I shall have done with this branch of the subject. You Democrats, and your candidate, in the main are in favor of laying down, in advance, a platform—a set of party positions, as a unit; and then of enforcing the people, by every sort of appliance, to ratify them, however unpalatable some of them may be. We, and our candidate, are in favor of making Presidential elections and the legislation of the country distinct matters; so that the people can elect whom they please, and afterward legislate just *as* they please, without any hindrance, save only so much as may guard against infractions of the Constitution, undue haste, and want of consideration. The difference between us is clear as noonday. That we are right, we can not doubt. We hold the true Republican position. In leaving the people's business in their hands, we can not be wrong. We are willing, and even anxious, to go to the people on this issue.

MR. CLAY'S DEFEAT AND DEMOCRATIC SYMPATHIES.

But I suppose I can not reasonably hope to convince you that we have any principles. The most I can expect is, to assure you that we think we have, and are quite contented with them. The other day one of the gentlemen from Georgia (Mr. Iverson), an eloquent man, and a man of learning, so far as I can judge, not being learned myself, came down upon us astonishingly. He spoke in what the Baltimore *American* calls the "scathing and withering style." At the end of his second severe flash I was struck blind, and found myself feeling with my fingers for an assurance of my continued physical existence. A little of the bone was left, and I gradually revived. He eulogized Mr. Clay in high and beautiful terms, and then declared that we had deserted all our principles, and had turned Henry Clay out, like an old horse, to root. This is terribly severe. It can not be answered by argument; at least, I can not so answer it. I merely wish to ask the gentlemen if the Whigs are the only party he can think of, who sometimes turn old horses out to root? Is not a certain Martin Van Buren an old horse, which your own party have turned out to root? and is he not rooting a little to your discomfort about now? But in not nominating Mr. Clay, we deserted our principles, you say. Ah! in what? Tell us, ye men of principles, what principle we violated? We say you did violate principle in discarding Van Buren, and we can tell you how. You violated the primary, the cardinal, the one great living principle of all Democratic representative government—the principle that the representative is bound to carry out the known will of his constituents. A large majority of the Baltimore Convention of 1844 were, by their constituents, instructed to procure Van Buren's nomination if they could. In violation, in utter, glaring contempt of this, you rejected him—rejected him, as the gentleman from New York (Mr. Birdsall), the other day expressly admitted, for *availability*—that same "general availability" which you charge upon us, and daily chew over here, as something exceedingly odious and unprincipled. But the gentleman from Georgia (Mr. Iverson), gave us a second speech yesterday, all well considered and put down in writing, in which Van Buren was scathed and withered a "few" for his present position and movements. I can not remember the gentleman's precise language, but I do

remember he put Van Buren down, down, till he got him
where he was finally to "stink" and "rot."

Mr. Speaker, it is no business or inclination of mine to
defend Martin Van Buren.   In the war of extermination now
waging between him and his old admirers, I say, devil take
the hindmost—and the foremost.   But there is no mistaking
the origin of the breach ; and if the curse of "stinking" and
"rotting" is to fall on the first and greatest violators of principle in the matter, I disinterestedly suggest, that the gentleman
from Georgia and his present co-workers are bound to take it
upon themselves.

[Mr. Lincoln then proceeded to speak of the objections
against Gen. Taylor as a mere military hero ; retorting with
effect, by citing the attempt to make out a military record for
Gen. Cass ; and referring, in a bantering way, to his own services in the Black-Hawk war, as already quoted.   He then
said :]

CASS ON THE WILMOT PROVISO.

While I have Gen. Cass in hand, I wish to say a word about
his political principles.   As a specimen, I take the record of
his progress on the Wilmot Proviso.   In the Washington
Union, of March 2, 1847, there is a report of the speech of
Gen. Cass, made the day before in the Senate, on the Wilmot
Proviso, during the delivery of which Mr. Miller, of New
Jersey, is reported to have interrupted him as follows, to wit :
" Mr. Miller expressed his great surprise at the change in
the sentiments of the Senator from Michigan, who had been
regarded as the great champion of freedom in the North-west,
of which he was a distinguished ornament.   Last year the
Senator from Michigan was understood to be decidedly in favor
of the Wilmot Proviso ; and, as no reason had been stated for
the change, he (Mr. Miller) could not refrain from the expression of his extreme surprise. '

To this Gen. Cass is reported to have replied as follows,
to wit :
" Mr. Cass said, that the course of the Senator from New
Jersey was most extraordinary.   Last year he (Mr. Cass)
should have voted for the proposition had it come up.   But
circumstances had altogether changed.   The honorable Senator
then read several passages from the remarks as given above,
which he had committed to writing, in order to refute such a
charge as that of the Senator from New Jersey."

In the "remarks above committed to writing," is one numbered 4, as follows, to-wit:

"4th. Legislation would now be wholly imperative, because no territory hereafter to be acquired can be governed without an act of Congress providing for its government. And such an act, on its passage, would open the whole subject, and leave the Congress, called on to pass it, free to exercise its own discretion, entirely uncontrolled by any declaration found in the statute book."

In Niles' Register, vol. 73, page 293, there is a letter of Gen. Cass to A. O. P. Nicholson, of Nashville, Tennessee, dated December 24, 1847, from which the following are correct extracts:

"The Wilmot Proviso has been before the country some time. It has been repeatedly discussed in Congress, and by the public press. I am strongly impressed with the opinion that a great change has been going on in the public mind upon this subject—in my own as well as others; and that doubts are resolving themselves into convictions, that the principle it involves should be kept out of the National Legislature, and left to the people of the Confederacy in their respective local Governments. *   *   *   *   *   *

"Briefly, then, I am opposed to the exercise of any jurisdiction by Congress over this matter; and I am in favor of leaving the people of any territory which may be hereafter acquired, the right to regulate it themselves, under the general principles of the Constitution. Because,

"1. I do not see in the Constitution any grant of the requisite power to Congress; and I am not disposed to extend a doubtful precedent beyond its necessity—the establishment of territorial governments when needed—leaving to the inhabitants all the rights compatible with the relations they bear to the Confederation."

AN OBEDIENT DEMOCRAT.

These extracts show that, in 1846, Gen. Cass was for the Proviso *at once;* that, in March, 1847, he was still for it, *but not just then;* and that in December, 1847, he was *against* it altogether. This is a true index to the whole man. When the question was raised in 1846, he was in a blustering hurry to take ground for it. He sought to be in advance, and to avoid the uninteresting position of a mere follower; but soon he began to see glimpses of the great Democratic ox-gad waving in his face, and to hear indistinctly, a voice saying, "back," "back, sir," "back a little." He shakes his head and bats his eyes, and blunders back to his position of March, 1847; but still the gad waves, and the voice grows more distinct, and sharper still—"back, sir!" "back, I say!" "further back!" and back he goes to the position of December, 1847; at which the gad is still, and the voice soothingly says—"So!" "Stand still at that."

Have no fears, gentlemen, of your candidate; he exactly suits you, and we congratulate you upon it. However much you may be distressed about *our* candidate, you have all cause to be contented and happy with your own. If elected, he may not maintain all, or even any of his positions previously taken; but he will be sure to do whatever the party exigency, for the time being, may require; and that is precisely what you want. He and Van Buren are the same "manner of men;" and like Van Buren, he will never desert *you* till you first desert *him*.

[After referring at some length to extra "charges" of Gen Cass upon the Treasury, Mr. Lincoln continued :]

WONDERFUL PHYSICAL CAPACITIES.

But I have introduced Gen. Cass' accounts here, chiefly to show the wonderful physical capacities of the man. They show that he not only did the labor of several men at the same *time*, but that he often did it, at several *places* many hundred miles apart, *at the same time.* And at eating, too, his capacities are shown to be quite as wonderful. From October, 1821, to May, 1822, he ate ten rations a day in Michigan, ten rations a day here, in Washington, and near five dollar's worth a day besides, partly on the road between the two places. And then there is an important discovery in his example—the art of being paid for what one eats, instead of having to pay for it. Hereafter, if any nice young man shall owe a bill which he can not pay in any other way, he can just board it out. Mr. Speaker, we have all heard of the animal standing in doubt between two stacks of hay, and starving to death; the like of that would never happen to Gen. Cass. Place the stacks a thousand miles apart, he would stand stock-still, midway between them, and eat them both at once; and the green grass along the line would be apt to suffer some too, at the same time. By all means, make him President, gentlemen. He will feed you bounteously—if—if—there is any left after he shall have helped himself.

THE WHIGS AND THE MEXICAN WAR.

But as Gen. Taylor is, par excellence, the hero of the Mexican war; and, as you Democrats say we Whigs have always opposed the war, you think it must be very awkward and embarrassing for us to go for Gen. Taylor. The declaration that we have always opposed the war, is true or false accordingly as one may understand the term "opposing the war." If to say "the war was unnecessarily and unconstitutionally commenced by the President," be opposing the war, then the Whigs have very generally opposed it. Whenever they have spoken at all, they have said this; and they have said it on what has appeared good reason to them: The marching an army into the midst of a peaceful Mexican settlement, frightening the inhabitants away, leaving their growing crops and other property to destruction, to *you* may appear a perfectly amiable, peaceful, unprovoking procedure; but it does not appear so to *us.* So to call such an act, to us appears no other than a naked, impudent absurdity, and we speak of it accordingly. But if, when the war had begun, and had become the cause of the country, the giving of our money and our blood, in common with yours, was support of the war, then it is not true that we have always opposed the war. With few individual exceptions, you have constantly had our votes here for all the necessary supplies. And, more than this, you have had the services, the blood, and the lives of our political brethren in every trial, and on every field. The beardless boy and the mature man—the humble and the distinguished—you have had them. Through suffering and death, by disease and in battle, they have endured, and fought, and fallen with you. Clay and Webster each gave a son, never to be returned. From the State of my own residence, besides other worthy but less known Whig names, we sent Marshall, Morrison, Baker, and Hardin; they all fought, and one fell, and in the fall of that one, we lost our best Whig man. Nor were the Whigs few in number, or laggard in the day of danger. In that fearful, bloody, breathless struggle at Buena Vista, where each man's hard task was to beat back five foes, or die himself, of the five high officers who perished, four were Whigs.

In speaking of this, I mean no odious comparison between the lion-hearted Whigs and Democrats who fought there. On other occasions, and among the lower officers and privates on *that* occasion, I doubt not the proportion was different. I wish to do justice to all. I think of all those brave men as Americans, in whose proud fame, as an American, I, too, have a share. Many of them, Whigs and Democrats, are my constituents and personal friends; and I thank them—more than thank them— one and all, for the high, imperishable honor they have conferred on our common State.

AN IMPORTANT DISTINCTION.

But the distinction between the cause of the *President* in beginning the war, and the cause of the *country* after it was begun, is a distinction which you can not perceive. To *you*, the President and the country seem to be all one. You are interested to see no distinction between them; and I venture to suggest that *possibly* your interest blinds you a little. We see the distinction, as we think, clearly enough; and our friends, who have fought in the war, have no difficulty in seeing it also. What those who have fallen would say, were they alive and here, of course we can never know; but with those who have returned there is no difficulty. Col. Haskell and Maj. Gaines, members here, both fought in the war; and one of them underwent extraordinary perils and hardships; still they, like all other Whigs here, vote on the record that the war was unnecessarily and unconstitutionally commenced by the President. And even Gen. Taylor himself, the noblest Roman of them all, has declared that, as a citizen, and particularly as a soldier, it is sufficient for him to know that his country is at war with a foreign nation, to do all in his power to bring it to a speedy and honorable termination, by the most vigorous and energetic operations, without inquiring about its justice, or anything else connected with it.

Mr. Speaker, let our Democratic friends be comforted with the assurance that we are content with our position, content with our company, and content with our candidate; and that although they, in their generous sympathy, think we ought to be miserable, we really are not, and that they may dismiss the great anxiety they have on *our* account.

Mr. Lincoln concluded with some allusions to the then divided condition of the New York Democracy.

This session of Congress came to a close on the 14th day of August. The chief points of Mr. Lincoln's Congressional record, thus far, have been noticed, and his principal speeches given at length. He stood firmly by the side of John Quincy Adams, in favor of the unrestricted right of petition, as will be seen by his vote, among others, against laying on the table a petition presented by Caleb B. Smith (December 27, 1847), praying for the abolition of slavery and the slave-trade in the District of Columbia. He favored a liberal policy toward the people in disposing of the public lands, as indicated by

ANDERSON CREEK FERRY,

Where Mr. Lincoln was Ferryman for Nine Months.

his imperfectly reported remarks (May 11, 1848), at the time of the passing of the bill admitting Wisconsin into the Union as a State. He was careful to scrutinize particular claims, to satisfy which he was asked to vote for an appropriation, as in the case of the proposition to pay the Texas volunteers for lost horses (May 4, 1848). All his acts show a purpose to do his duty to the country, no less than to his immediate constituents, without fear or favor.

After the session closed, Mr. Lincoln made a visit to New England, where he delivered some effective campaign speeches, which were enthusiastically received by his large audiences, as appears from the reports in the journals of those days, and as will be remembered by many. His time, however, was chiefly given, during the Congressional recess, to the canvass in the West, where, through the personal strength of Mr. Cass as a North-western man, the contest was more severe and exciting than in any other part of the country. The final triumph of Gen. Taylor, over all the odds against him, did much to counterbalance, in Mr. Lincoln's mind, the disheartening defeat of four years previous. As before stated, he had declined to be a candidate for re-election to Congress, yet he had the satisfaction of aiding to secure, in his own district, a majority of 1,500 for the Whig Presidential candidates.

Mr. Lincoln again took his seat in the House in December, on the re-assembling of the thirtieth Congress for its second session. Coming between the Presidential election, which had effected a political revolution, and the inauguration of the new Government, this session was generally a quiet one, passing away without any very important measure of general legislation being acted upon. A calm had followed the recent storms. There were, indeed, certain movements in regard to slavery and the slave-trade in the District of Columbia, which produced some temporary excitement, but resulted in no serious commotion. On the 21st of December, Mr. Gott, a representative from New York, introduced a resolution, accompanied by a strong preamble, instructing the Committee on the District of Columbia to report a bill prohibiting the slave-trade in the District. The language used was as follows:

8

WHEREAS, The traffic now prosecuted in this metropolis of the Republic in human beings, as chattels, is contrary to natural justice and the fundamental principles of our political system, and is notoriously a reproach to our country throughout Christendom, and a serious hinderance to the progress of republican liberty among the nations of the earth; therefore,

Resolved, That the Committee for the District of Columbia be instructed to report a bill, as soon as practicable, prohibiting the slave-trade in said District.

Mr. Haralson, of Georgia, moved to lay the same on the table, and the yeas and nays were taken on his motion. Mr. Lincoln, Joseph R. Ingersoll, Richard W. Thompson, and George G. Dunn, were nearly or quite the only Northern Whigs who voted in the affirmative. The motion was lost, and the resolution, under pressure of the previous question, was adopted, ninety-eight to eighty-eight, Mr. Lincoln voting in the negative. A motion to re-consider this vote came up for action on the 27th of the same month. A motion to lay on the table the motion to re-consider having been lost (yeas 58, nays 107, Mr. Lincoln voting in the negative), the subject was postponed until the 10th of January. At that date, Mr. Lincoln read a substitute which he proposed to offer for the resolution, in case of a re-consideration. This substitute contained the form of a bill enacting that no person not already within the District should be held in slavery therein, and providing for the gradual emancipation of the slaves already within the District, with compensation to the owners, if a majority of the legal voters of the District should assent to the act, at an election to be holden for the purpose. It made an exception of the right of citizens of the slaveholding States, coming to the District on public business, " be attended into and out of said District, and while there, by the necessary servants of themselves and their families." These were the chief provisions of the measure contemplated by Mr. Lincoln, which compared favorably with the act prohibiting the slave-trade in the District, included among the Compromise measures of 1850. After rehearsing the details of the bill, according to the report in the *Congressional Globe*—

Mr. Lincoln then said, that he was authorized to say, that

of about fifteen of the leading citizens of the District of Columbia to whom this proposition had been submitted, there was no one but who approved of the adoption of such a proposition. He did not wish to be misunderstood. He did not know whether or not they would vote for this bill on the first Monday of April; but he repeated, that out of fifteen persons to whom it had been submitted, he had authority to say that every one of them desired that some proposition like this should pass.

A motion to lay on the table the proposition to re-consider was again lost, and by a much larger majority than before, and the resolution was re-considered, 119 to 81. Mr. Smith, of Indiana, then moved the following substitute :

Resolved, That the Committee on the District of Columbia be instructed to report, as soon as practicable, a bill so amending the present law in this District, as effectually to prevent the bringing of slaves into the District, either for sale here, or to be sold and carried to any place beyond the District.

Mr. Meade, of Virginia, offered the following as an amendment to Mr. Smith's amendment :

And that the said committee is hereby instructed to report a bill more effectually to enable owners to recover their slaves escaping from one State into another.

Here, it is observable, are two of the propositions which were ultimately embraced in the great Compromise "settlement" of 1850, and these several amendments, proposed by Mr. Lincoln and others, may be termed the springs in Congress from which flowed a portion of that celebrated series of measures.

The Speaker (Mr. Winthrop) ruled Mr. Meade's amendment out of order, and without any decisive action thereon, the House adjourned, leaving the resolution and amendments to disappear among the files of unfinished business on the Speaker's table.

An unsuccessful attempt had previously been made by Mr. Palfrey, of Massachusetts, a Free-Soil member who refused to vote for Mr. Winthrop for Speaker, to introduce a bill " to repeal all acts, or parts of acts, of Congress establishing or maintaining slavery or the slave-trade in the District of Colum bia." Mr. Holmes, of South Carolina, having objected, the yeas and nays were taken on granting the leave asked, and the negative prevailed by thirteen majority. The Northern Whigs in general, excepting Messrs. Vinton and Dunn, and many Northern Democrats, including John Wentworth, David Wilmot, and J. J. Faran, of Ohio, voted in the affirmative. Mr. Lincoln's name is recorded among the nays. So sweeping and unqualified a measure he had ever been opposed to, as he avowed himself to be in 1858, and he never hesitated, from a fear of popular misapprehension, to vote in strict accordance with his own convictions.

On the 31st of January, Mr. Edwards, from the Committee on the District of Columbia, reported a bill, suitably guarded in its terms, prohibiting the slave-trade in the District. On a motion to lay this on the table, Mr. Lincoln voted in the negative, with the friends of that measure, who were a majority. This bill, however, passed over among the unfinished business of the session.

In regard to the grant of public lands to the new States, to aid in the construction of railroads and canals, Mr. Lincoln favored the interests of his own constituents, under such reasonable restrictions as the proper carrying out of the purpose of these grants required. This policy had been strongly opposed by Mr. Vinton, while one of the bills of this sort was pending. In the brief remarks which Mr. Lincoln offered in reply, there are some points (*Congressional Globe*, page 533) worth quoting here:

In relation to the fact assumed, that, after awhile, the new States, having got hold of the public lands to a certain extent, would turn round and compel Congress to relinquish all claim to them, he had a word to say, by way of recurring to the history of the past. When was the time to come (he asked) when the States in which the public lands were situated would compose a majority of the representation in Congress, or any thing like it. A majority of Representatives would very soon reside West of the mountains, he admitted; but would they all come from States in which the public lands were situated? They certainly would not; for, as these Western States grew strong in Congress, the public lands passed away from them, and they got on the other side of the question, and the gentleman from Ohio (Mr. Vinton) was an example attesting that fact.

Mr. Vinton interrupted here to say, that he had stood upon this question just where he was now, for five-and-twenty years.

Mr. Lincoln was not making an argument for the purpose of convicting the gentleman of any impropriety at all. He was speaking of a fact in history, of which his State was an example. He was referring to a plain principle in the nature of things. The State of Ohio had now grown to be a giant. She had a large delegation on that floor; but was she now in favor of granting lands to the new States, as she used to be? The New England States, New York, and the Old Thirteen, were all rather quiet upon the subject; and it was seen just now that a member from one of the new States was the first man to rise up in opposition. And so it would be with the history of this question for the future. There never would come a time when the people residing in the States embracing the public lands would have the entire control of this subject; and so it was a matter of certainty that Congress would never do more in this respect than what would be dictated by a just liberality. The apprehension, therefore, that the public lands were in danger of being wrested from the General Government by the strength of the delegation in Congress from the new States, was utterly futile. There never could be such a thing. If we take these lands (said he) it will not be without your consent. We can never outnumber you. The result is, that all fear of the new States turning against the right of Congress to the public domain must be effectually quelled, as those who are opposed to that interest must always hold a vast majority here, and they will never surrender the whole or any part of the public lands, unless they themselves choose so to do. This was all he desired to say.

With the termination of the Thirtieth Congress, by Constitutional limitation, on the 4th of March, 1849, Mr. Lincoln's career as a Congressman came to a close. He had refused to be a candidate for re-election in a district that had given him over 1,500 majority in 1846, and nearly the same to General Taylor, as the Whig candidate for the Presidency in 1848. His name was prominently presented for the position of Commissioner of the General Land Office, under President Taylor, but, though he zealously labored to bring in the new Administration, he made no complaint, and certainly did not afterward seriously regret that his valued services were not thus recognized. He retired once more to private life, renewing the professional practice which had been temporarily interrupted by his public employment. The duties of his responsible position had been discharged with assiduity and with fearless adherence to his convictions of right, under whatever circumstances. Scarcely a list of yeas and nays can be found, for either session, which does not contain his name. He was never conveniently absent on any critical vote. He never shrank from any responsibility which his sense of justice impelled him to take. His record, comparatively brief as it is, is no doubtful one, and will bear the closest scrutiny. And though one of the youngest and most inexperienced members of an uncommonly able and brilliant Congress, he might well have been ranked, without the more recent events which have naturally followed upon his previous career, among the distinguished statesmen of the Thirtieth Congress.

CHAPTER IX.

PROFESSIONAL LIFE.—THE ANTI-NEBRASKA CANVASS.—
1849—1854.

Mr. Lincoln in Retirement for Five Years.—Gen. Taylor's Administration.—The Slavery Agitation of 1850.—The Compromise of Clay
and Fillmore.—The "Final Settlement" of 1852.—How, and by
Whom it was Disturbed.—Violation of the most Positive Pledges.—
The Kansas-Nebraska Bill.—Douglas, the Agitator.—Popular Indignation and Excitement.—Mr. Lincoln takes part in the Canvass of
1854.—Great Political Changes.—The Anti-Nebraska Organization.—
Springfield Resolutions of 1854.—Results of the Election.—A Majority of Congressmen and of the Legislature Anti-Nebraska.—Election
of United States Senator to Succeed Gen. Shields.—Mr. Lincoln and
Mr. Trumbull.—A Magnanimous Sacrifice.—Mr. Trumbull Elected.

DURING the five years immediately following the close of his
Congressional life, Mr. Lincoln attentively pursued his profession of the law. He took no active part in politics through
the period of Gen. Taylor's Administration, or in any of the
exciting scenes of 1850. His great political leader, Henry
Clay, had resumed his place in the Senate, and was earnestly
striving—one of the last great labors of his life—to avert the
dangers to the country, which he believed to be threatened by
the fierce contests over the question of Slavery. It was, with
the slave States, a desperate struggle to retain the balance of
power in the Senate, by rejecting the application of another
free State for admission, the granting of which would destroy
the exact equilibrium then existing. The policy of admitting
a slave State along with every new free one, had substantially
prevailed for years; but, at this time, despite the extensive
additions of Mexican territory, there was no counterbalancing
slave State ready for admission. The exclusion of slavery

from California had, in fact, been rather a surprise, and this application was evidently still more an irritating circumstance for that reason. And yet this movement was in strict accordance with the policy of a Southern President. As a final result, the admission of California was only carried by means of great counterbalancing concessions on the part of the free States. For months after, there was much discontent in both sections, in regard to the compromise measures of 1850, which were defeated in Congress, when first acted upon as a whole, but were ultimately carried in detail. It was not until 1852, when both the great parties of the country agreed to accept those measures as a "final settlement" of the slavery controversy, that public sentiment, North and South, appeared to have become fully reconciled to this adjustment. The Administration, brought into power by the election of that year, was most thoroughly and sacredly committed to the maintenance of this settlement, and against the revival of the slavery agitation in any form. To introduce that subject under any pretence, into the halls of Congress, was an act of wanton incendiarism, in utter disregard of most solemn pledges, by the aid of which the Democratic party had secured whatever real hold it had upon popular confidence. Such was the state of affairs in 1852, and at the time of Mr. Pierce's inauguration in 1853.

Mr. Lincoln, as a private citizen, engrossed with his professional duties, had borne no part in the original controversy, and had taken no share in its settlement. Whether preferring the non-intervention policy of President Taylor, or the compromise course of Clay and Fillmore, he had undoubtedly regarded the peace established, by means of the latter, as one that ought by all means to be preserved, and the pledges of both sections of the country, through the action of both the national parties, as religiously binding upon every public man who had openly or tacitly assented thereto. That he approved all the details of this compromise is not probable. But that, if faithfully adhered to, the practical results would have been satisfactory, he was undoubtedly convinced.

The introduction of the Kansas-Nebraska bill, in 1854, in the midst of this profound peace on the slavery question, was "the alarm of the fire-bell at night" which startled Mr. Lincoln in the repose of his private life, and showed that the incendiary had but too successfully been at his work. The solemn pledge of peace had ·been violated by the very men who were most forward in making it, and most noisy in their professions of a desire that the slavery conflict should cease. This new agitating movement, not only unsettling all the more recent stipulations made for the sake of peace, but even going back to destroy the only condition yet assailable, of the Compromise of 1820, and that the very portion which was agreed on as a consideration to the free States, was led by the ambitious politician of Illinois, Stephen A. Douglas. Not only had Senator Douglas committed himself as fully as any man could do to the maintenance of peace on this question, after the compromise of 1850, but he had, a year previous, called down vengeance upon the hand that would dare disturb the time-honored Missouri compact—that settlement which secured freedom "forever" to the soil embraced within the limits of Kansas and Nebraska. Yet the first hand raised for the commission of this incalculable wrong was his own! Douglas himself reported the act which violated that compact, and which opened the new territories to slavery (professedly, not really, at the option of the people), contrary to the spirit of all the early legislation, and to the hitherto uniform course of the Government. Even he himself had recently voted for the Wilmot Proviso as applied to the territory acquired from Mexico, and Mr. Polk had approved the Oregon bill, containing the same restriction. Never was there more universal indignation among the people of the North, and many of the more sagacious statesmen of the South clearly foresaw the mischiefs that were to follow from this sacrilege. Yet strange to say, this measure sundered and broke up the Whig party forever, through the action of a large portion of the Southern Whig Congressmen, in joining the Democracy in this act of bad faith, for the sake of supposed sectional advantage. The most intense excitement prevailed throughout the country, and the destruction óf the old party lines was effectually accomplished.

11

These events called forth Mr. Lincoln once more to do battle for the right. He entered into the canvass of 1854, as one of the most active leaders of the " Anti-Nebraska" movement. He addressed the people repeatedly from the stump, with all his characteristic earnestness and energy. He met and cowed the author of the " Nebraska iniquity," in the presence of the masses, and powerfully aided in effecting the remarkable political changes of that year in Illinois.

The incendiary act had come to the final vote, in the Senate, on the 26th day of May. About the first of August, Congress adjourned. Douglas lingered by the way on his return to his constituents, and reached Chicago near the close of that month. Here he met a storm of indignation from the people whom, for manifesting their disapprobation of his conduct, he complacently termed a " mob." He had proposed to speak in self vindication, on the evening of the first day of September. He was received with the most decisive demonstrations of popular indignation, which he attempted to face down with an uncompromising insolence of manner, that only tended to increase the excitement against him. After long perseverance in an attempt to *compel* a hearing, he was forced to succumb. All over the State he early discovered the same state of feeling existing among a large portion of his constituents, although there was no refusal to hear him, except in this first unlucky effort to defy and silence a crowd by bullying deportment. The popular rage gradually subsided, but the deliberate sentiment of the people of Illinois on this subject was rather confirmed and strengthened in succeeding years. From commanding a large majority of the popular vote, as he had done previously, his strength dwindled away, until from that time on, he and the party that sustained him, were in a positive minority in the State. The reader can judge how much this, to him, painful truth, had to do with the change of policy adopted by him, in opposing the Lecompton Constitution, the legitimate fruit of the Kansas-Nebraska bill, and substantially approved by him in advance, in a speech made in Springfield, in 1857.

Mr. Douglas visited several parts of the State, vainly attempting, by ingenious but sophistical addresses to the people to avert the impending revolution. Mr. Lincoln met him in debate at Springfield, during the time of the State Fair, early in October, 1854, and the encounter was a memorable one in the great campaign then in progress. They met a few days later at Peoria, where Mr. Douglas had no better fortune. Subsequently to that encounter, he showed a decided preference for speaking at other times and places than Mr. Lincoln did.

The Anti-Nebraska organization, formed at Springfield in October of that year, and embracing men of all parties opposed to the ill-judged measures which had introduced the most violent agitation in regard to slavery ever known in the country, was the beginning from which the Republican party in Illinois was to be matured. Among the resolutions at that time adopted, after setting forth in a preamble that a majority of Congress had deliberately and wantonly re-opened the controversy respecting the extension of slavery under our national jurisdiction, which a majority of the people had understood to be closed forever by the successive compromises of 1820 and 1850, were the following:

Resolved, That the doctrine affirmed by the Nebraska Bill, and gilded over by its advocates, with the specious phrases of non-intervention and popular sovereignty, is really and clearly a complete surrender of all the ground hitherto asserted and maintained by the Federal Government, with respect to the limitation of slavery, is a plain confession of the right of the slaveholder to transfer his human chattels to any part of the public domain, and there hold them as slaves as long as inclination or interest may dictate; and that this is an attempt totally to reverse the doctrine hitherto uniformly held by statesmen and jurists, that slavery is the creature of local and State law, and to make it a national institution.

Resolved, That as freedom is national, and slavery sectional and local, the absence of all law upon the subject of slavery presumes the existence of a state of freedom alone, while slavery exists only by virtue of positive law.

Resolved, That we heartily approve the course of the freemen of Connecticut, Vermont, Iowa, Ohio, Indiana, Wisconsin, New York, Michigan and Maine, postponing or disregarding their minor differences of opinion or preferences, and acting together cordially and trustingly in the same cause of freedom, of free labor, and free soil, and we commend their spirit to the freemen of this and other States, exhorting each to renounce his party whenever and wherever that party proves unfaithful to human freedom.

In behalf of these principles, Mr. Lincoln had already taken the stump, and for them he did valiant service in various parts of the State.

This new party was organized late in the season, and the canvass for Treasurer, the only State officer to be elected, was but imperfectly made. In some parts of the State, there was even no distribution of tickets containing the name of this candidate. The result, even under these unfavorable circumstances, and in spite of the overwhelming Democratic preponderance during the previous twenty-five years, was extremely close, and for a long time doubtful. The Democratic candidate barely escaped defeat. This was the last election in which the party sustaining Douglas has had even the appearance of a majority in Illinois. *The revolution was now substantially accomplished.* From that day to the present, the Republican party has been steadily gaining in strength, and that opposed to it sinking more and more into a hopeless minority. Even the temporary reaction, under the Anti-Lecompton flag, was more apparent than real.

Of the nine Congressional Districts, the Opposition now, for the first time, carried a majority, electing five members, and the Democrats four. The Legislature would have been completely revolutionized, in both branches, with little doubt, but for the large number of Democrats "holding over," as members of the new Senate. In the House, the Anti-Nebraska representatives numbered forty, and the Democratic thirty-five. In the Senate, there were seventeen elected as Democrats, and eight as Opposition men. Of the former, however, there were three, elected two years previously, who repudiated Douglas and his policy, and inclined to the Opposition. These were Norman B. Judd, J. M. Palmer, and B. C. Cook. Reckoning these with the Anti-Nebraska side, the Senate stood, Opposition eleven, Democrats fourteen—leaving a majority against the Douglas Democracy of two on joint ballot.

A United States Senator, to succeed Gen. Shields on the 4th of March, 1855, was to be chosen by this Legislature. For the first time in the history of Illinois, the election of an Anti-Democratic Senator was within the reach of possibility. Mr. Lincoln was the first choice of the great mass of the Opposition for this position. From his prominence, for a long time, in the old Whig party, it was but natural that a portion of the members having Democratic antecedents who had come into the new organization, should hesitate to give Mr. Lincoln their votes. This was especially true of the three Senators above named as holding over, they having been elected as regular Democrats. Under this state of things, it was manifest, after a few ballots, that, with the close vote in joint convention the election of a Democrat, not to be certainly relied on as an opponent of the Douglas policy, and at best uncommitted in regard to the new party organization, might be the result of adhering to Mr. Lincoln. He, accordingly, with the self-sacrificing disposition which had always characterized him, promptly appealed to his Whig friends to go over in a solid body to Mr. Trumbull, a man of Democratic antecedents, who could command the full vote of the Anti-Nebraska Democrats. By these earnest and disinterested efforts, the difficult task was accomplished, great as was the sacrifice of personal feeling which it cost the devoted friends of Mr. Lincoln. On the part of himself and them, it involved the exercise of a degree of self-denial and magnanimity, as rare as it was noble. It demonstrated their honest attachment to the great cause for which old party lines had been abandoned, and their sincere purpose of thoroughly ignoring all differences founded on mere partisan prejudice. It cemented the union of these Anti-Nebraka elements, and consolidated the new organization into a permanent party.

The joint convention for electing a United States Senator met on the 8th day of February, 1855. On the first ballot, James Shields, then Senator, who had been induced by Douglas, against his own better judgment, to vote for the

Kansas-Nebraska bill, received 41 votes, and three other Democrats had one vote each. Abraham Lincoln had 45 votes, Lyman Trumbull 5, Mr. Koerner 2, and there were three other scattering votes. On the seventh ballot, the Democratic vote was concentrated upon Gov. Matteson, with two exceptions, and he received also the votes of two Anti-Nebraska Democrats, making 44 in all. On the tenth ballot, Mr. Trumbull was elected, in the way just explained, receiving 51 votes, and Mr. Matteson 47. Every Whig vote but one was given to Mr. Trumbull.

Among the speeches delivered by Mr. Lincoln in this memorable campaign, which gave the Republicans an able Senator from Illinois, and which effectually accomplished the overthrow of the Democracy in that State, perhaps the ablest and most characteristic was the one delivered at Peoria, important portions of which were quoted by him in the canvass with Douglas, four years later. The following detached passages of this speech are specially memorable :

This declared indifference, but as I must think real zeal for the spread of slavery, I can not but hate. I hate it because of the monstrous injustice of slavery itself; I hate it because it deprives our republican example of its just influence in the world; enables the enemies of free institutions with plausibility to taunt us as hypocrites; causes the real friends of freedom to doubt our sincerity; and especially because it forces so many really good men among ourselves into an open war with the very fundamental principles of civil liberty, criticising the Declaration of Independence, and insisting that there is no right principle of action but self-interest.

When the Southern people tell us they are no more responsible for the origin of slavery, than we are, I acknowledge the fact. When it is said that the institution exists, and that it is very difficult to get rid of it in any satisfactory way, I can understand and appreciate the saying. I surely will not blame them for not doing what I should not know how to do myself. If all earthly power were given me, I should not know what to do, as to the existing institution.

When the white man governs himself, that is, self-government; but when he governs himself, and also governs another man, that is more than self-government—that is despotism. If the negro is a man, why, then my ancient faith teaches me that "all men are created equal;" and that there can be no moral right in connection with one man's making a slave of another.

Slave States are places for poor white people to remove *from*, not to remove *to ;* new free States are the places for poor people to go to and better their condition. For this use, the nation needs these territories.

Slavery is founded in the selfishness of man's nature—opposition to it, in his love of justice.

In our greedy chase to make profit of the negro; let us beware lest we "cancel and tear to pieces" even the white man's charter of freedom.

Some men, mostly Whigs, who condemn the repeal of the Missouri Compromise, nevertheless hesitate to go for its restoration, lest they be thrown in company with the Abolitionist. Will they allow me, as an old Whig, to tell them, good-humoredly, that I think this is very silly? Stand with anybody that stands *right.* Stand with him while he is right, and *part* with him when he goes wrong.

Little by little, but steadily as man's march to the grave, we have been giving up the *old* for the *new* faith. Near eighty years ago we began by declaring that all men are created equal; but now from that beginning we have run down to the other declaration, that for *some* men to enslave *others* is a " sacred right of self-government." These principles can not stand together. They are as opposite as God and Mammon; and whoever holds to one must despise the other.

In the course of my main argument, Judge Douglas interrupted me to say that the principle of the Nebraska bill was very old; that it originated when God made man, and placed good and evil before him, allowing him to choose for himself, being responsible for the choice he should make. At the time, I thought this was merely playful; and I answered it accordingly. But in his reply to me, he renewed it as a serious argument. In seriousness, then, the facts of this proposition are not true, as stated. God did not place good and evil before man, telling him to make his choice. On the contrary, He did tell him there was one tree, of the fruit of which he should not eat, upon pain of certain death. I should scarcely wish so strong a prohibition against slavery in Nebraska.

CHAPTER X.

POLITICAL MOVEMENTS IN 1856 AND '57.

The Republican Party Organized.—Their Platform adopted at Bloom
ington.—The Canvass of 1856.—Mr. Lincoln Sustains Fremont and
Dayton.—His Active Labors on the Stump.—Col. Bissell Elected
Governor of Illinois.—Mr. Buchanan Inaugurated.—His Kansas Pol-
icy.—Mr. Douglas Committed to it in June, 1857.—John Calhoun his
Special Friend.—The Springfield Speech of Douglas.—Mr. Lincoln's
Reply.

MR. LINCOLN took an active part in the formation of the
Republican party as such. The State Convention of that organization, which met at Bloomington, on the 29th of May, 1856,
sent delegates to the Philadelphia Convention of that year, held
for the nomination of Presidential candidates. Among the resolutions of the Bloomington Convention were the following:

Resolved, That foregoing all former differences of opinion
upon other questions, we pledge ourselves to unite in opposition
to the present Administration, and to the party which upholds
and supports it, and to use all honorable and constitutional
means to wrest the Government from the unworthy hands which
now control it, and to bring it back in its administration to the
principles and practices of Washington, Jefferson, and their
great and good compatriots of the Revolution.

Resolved, That we hold, in accordance with the opinions and
practices of all the great statesmen of all parties, for the first
sixty years of the administration of the Government, that, under
the Constitution, Congress possesses full power to prohibit slavery in the Territories; and that while we will maintain all constitutional rights of the South, we also hold that justice, humanity, the principles of freedom as expressed in our Declaration
of Independence, and our National Constitution, and the purity
and perpetuity of our Government require that that power
should be exerted, to prevent the extension of slavery into Territories heretofore free.

Resolved, That the repeal of the Missouri Compromise was
unwise, unjust and injurious; in open and aggravated violation
of the plighted faith of the States, and that the attempt of the
present Administration to force slavery into Kansas against the

known wishes of the legal voters of that Territory, is an arbitrary and tyrannous violation of the rights of the people to govern themselves, and that we will strive, by all constitutional means, to secure to Kansas and Nebraska the legal guarantee against slavery, of which they were deprived, at the cost of the violation of the plighted faith of the nation.

With this creed, and the Philadelphia platform, subsequently adopted, the Republicans of Illinois went into the canvass of 1856. Mr. Lincoln labored earnestly during the campaign, sustaining the nominations of Fremont and Dayton. In the State canvass, Col. Wm. H. Bissell received the united support of the Opposition for Governor, and was elected by a decisive majority. On the Presidential candidates, there being, unfortunately, two tickets in the field, the divided Opposition were unsuccessful, although Fremont, in spite of the heavy Fillmore vote, ran so closely upon Buchanan that the result was for a time in doubt, and only the nearly solid vote of " Egypt " decided the result in favor of the latter. The untiring exertions of Mr. Lincoln on the stump, in enlightening the people as to the real issues involved, did much toward securing this remarkable vote.

Mr. Buchanan came into power in March, 1857, and the hopes which had been entertained of a material change, under his administration, of the unjust and execrable policy hitherto pursued toward Kansas, were speedily dissipated. After some little show of resistance at first, he was soon found acting in accordance with the dictates of the extreme pro-slavery interest. A deep scheme was concocted, into the secrets of which even the Governor and Secretary of that territory were not admitted, for forcing Kansas into the Union as a slave State. This plot began to be suspected, and its existence more and more confirmed by the course of events, not long after Mr. Buchanan's inauguration. The thin veil of "bogus Popular Sovereignty," with which Douglas had tried to hide the naked deformity of the act under which Kansas and Nebraska were organized, was to be rent asunder. People were beginning to look with curiosity for the next evasion or artful afterthought by which he would attempt to escape the force of a public sentiment which was already rapidly bearing him down, before

9

this more complete exposure became inevitable. This interest in his course was the more lively, for the reason that his Senatorial tern. had nearly expired, and that, without some remarkable change of affairs, or some ingenious device, the curse he had himself pronounced in advance upon the disturber of the Missouri compact, was to be most signally realized.

Meantime, the machinery had been put in motion for a Convention at Lecompton, which was to ratify a Constitution prepared at Washington, under Administration auspices, and to secure the great purpose intended by the Southern supporters of the Kansas-Nebraska scheme. How grossly unjust and unequal were the provisions of the act calling this Convention, and how deliberate was its design of excluding the free State men from any effectual voice in determining " the domestic institutions " of a State in which the party of free labor comprised about four-fifths of the people, as had already been distinctly indicated, need not be here rehearsed. To Douglas, at least, the real facts were not unknown. That these iniquities must all ultimately come out, and receive the condemnation of the people, he can not have seriously questioned. Yet, in spite of these facts, it is undeniably true, and is clearly of record, that he committed himself in advance—not at all uncertain, most assuredly, as to what it was substantially to be—in favor of the Lecompton Constitution. John Calhoun the chosen instrument of the Administration for carrying out its plot to defeat "Popular Sovereignty" in Kansas, was one of the special friends of Douglas, and understood to share his intimate confidence. And when, in his speech at Springfield, in June, 1857, Mr. Douglas substantially indorsed the Lecompton Convention and its doings, beforehand, no one had any reason to doubt that he intended fully to sustain the Administration in attempting to force a slave Constitution on the people of Kansas—a process for which his " organic act " had prepared the way. In the course of his remarks on that occasion, he said :

Kansas is about *to speak for herself*, through her delegates assembled in convention, to form a Constitution, preparatory to her admission into the Union on an equal footing with the original States. Peace and prosperity now prevail throughout her borders. The law under which her delegates are about to be elected is believed to be *just and fair in all its objects and provisions.* There is every reason to hope and believe that the law will be fairly interpreted and impartially executed, so as to insure every *bona fide* inhabitant the free and quiet exercise of the elective franchise. If any portion of the inhabitants, acting under the advice of political leaders in distant States, shall choose to absent themselves from the polls, and withhold their votes, with a view of leaving the Free State Democrats in a minority, and thus securing a pro-slavery Constitution in opposition to the wishes of a majority of the people living under it, let the responsibility rest on those who, for partisan purposes, will sacrifice the principles they profess to cherish and promote. Upon them, *upon the political party for whose benefit and under the direction of whose leaders they act,* let the blame be visited of fastening upon the people of a new State institutions repugnant to their feelings and in violation of their wishes.

Words could not have more positively indicated his purpose of sustaining all the acts of the Lecompton Convention, or that he anticipated the formation of a pro-slavery Constitution, for which he meant to charge the blame upon the Free State men and upon the Republican party in general, anticipating then that the non-voting policy would be adopted. In a subsequent part of this same speech, he still more fully and unreservedly indorsed the act providing for the Lecompton Constitutional Convention, committing himself to all its legitimate consequences. He said:

The present election law in Kansas is acknowledged to be fair and just—the rights of the voters are clearly defined—and the exercise of those rights will be efficiently and scrupulously protected. Hence, if the majority of the people of Kansas desire to have it a free State (and we are told by the Republican party that nine-tenths of the people of that Territory are free State men), *there is no obstacle in the way* of bringing Kansas into the Union as a free State, *by the votes and voice of her own people,* and in conformity with the great principles of the Kansas-Nebraska act; provided all the Free State men will go to the polls, and vote their principles in accordance with their professions. If such is not the result, let the consequences be visited upon the heads of those whose policy it is to produce strife, anarchy and bloodshed in Kansas, that their party may profit by slavery agitation in the Northern States of this Union. That the Democrats in Kansas will perform their duty fearlessly and nobly, according to the principles they cherish, I have no doubt, and that the result of the struggle will be such as will gladden the heart and strengthen the hopes of every friend of the Union, I have entire confidence.

The Lecompton Convention was to settle the whole Kansas controversy, "peacefully and satisfactorily," according to the professed faith of Mr. Douglas. He fully indorsed it in its origin, and committed himself to abide by its results, which were accomplished through the instrumentality of one of his warmest personal friends. And what these results would be, in his opinion, he clearly foreshadowed in the extracts above given from his speech. He expected a pro-slavery Constitution, and he repeatedly approved, without any reservation, the convention-act which, by its regular carrying-out, accomplished that expectation. He declared, substantially, that the will of the people could be fully and fairly expressed in forming a Constitution at Lecompton, under that act; and that if they did not obtain such a Constitution as they desired, it would be *their own fault*—plainly implying that they must submit to such action as should be taken. He left himself scarcely a loophole of retreat, whatever might come of the Lecompton Convention.

In the same speech, Mr. Douglas spoke at length in indorsement of the dogmas embraced in what is popularly called the Dred Scott decision, and particularly of the one which denies the power of Congress to exclude slavery from the Territories. He tried, also, to convey the impression that the Republican party was in favor of negro equality, because dissenting in general to a judicial opinion, of which one of the details is a denial to the negro race of any legal redress for wrongs in the higher courts.

A third subject of this speech was the Utah rebellion, which Mr. Douglas proposed to end by annulling the act establishing the Territory of Utah.

To this speech Mr. Lincoln replied at Springfield, two weeks later. It is noticeable that the first two of the topics of Mr. Douglas's speech formed leading subjects of the great canvass of the next year. It is not impossible that this prompt joining of issues may have had its influence in inducing Mr. Douglas so completely to change front, before another twelve-month had passed. In any event, these two speeches have a rare interest, from their immediate relations to the coming contest, of which they are properly the prelude. We give Mr. Lincoln's remarks at length:

SPEECH OF MR. LINCOLN, IN REPLY TO MR. DOUGLAS, ON KANSAS, THE DRED SCOTT DECISION, AND THE UTAH QUESTION.
(*Delivered at Springfield, Illinois, June 26, 1857.*

FELLOW-CITIZENS: I am here to-night, partly by invitation of some of you, and partly by my own inclination. Two weeks ago Judge Douglas spoke here, on the several subjects of Kansas, the Dred Scott decision, and Utah. I listened to the speech at the time, and have read the report of it since. It was intended to controvert opinions which I think just, and to assail (politically, not personally) those men who, in common with me, entertain those opinions. For this reason I wished then, and still wish to make some answer to it, which I now take the opportunity of doing.

I begin with Utah. If it prove to be true, as is probable, that the people of Utah are in open rebellion against the United States, then Judge Douglas is in favor of repealing their territorial organization, and attaching them to the adjoining States for judicial purposes. I say, too, if they are in rebellion, they ought to be somehow coerced to obedience; and I am not now prepared to admit or deny, that the Judge's mode of coercing them is not as good as any. The Republicans can fall in with it, without taking back anything they have ever said. To be sure, it would be a considerable backing down by Judge Douglas, from his much vaunted doctrine of self-government for the territories; but this is only additional proof of what was very plain from the beginning, that that doctrine was a mere deceitful pretence for the benefit of slavery. Those who could not see that much in the Nebraska act itself, which forced Governors, and Secretaries, and Judges on the people of the Territories, without their choice or consent, could not be made to see, though one should rise from the dead.

But in all this, it is very plain the Judge evades the only question the Republicans have ever pressed upon the Democracy in regard to Utah. That question the Judge well knew to be this: "If the people of Utah shall peacefully form a State Constitution tolerating polygamy, will the Democracy admit them into the Union?" There is nothing in the United States Constitution or law against polygamy; and why is it not a part of the Judge's "sacred right of self-government" for the people to have it, or rather to keep it, if they choose? These questions, so far as I know, the Judge never answers. It might involve the Democracy to answer them either way, and they go unanswered.

As to Kansas. The substance of the Judge's speech on ansas is an effort to put the Free State men in the wrong for not voting at the election of delegates to the Constitutional Convention. He says: "There is every reason to hope and believe that the law will be fairly interpreted and impartially executed, so as to insure to every *bona fide* inhabitant the free and quiet exercise of the elective franchise."

It appears extraordinary that Judge Douglas should make such a statement. He knows that, by the law, no one can vote who has not been registered; and he knows that the Free State men place their refusal to vote on the ground that but few of them have been registered. It is possible this is not true, but Judge Douglas knows it is asserted to be true in letters, newspapers and public speeches, and borne by every mail, and blown by every breeze to the eyes and ears of the world. He knows it is boldly declared, that the people of many whole counties, and many whole neighborhoods in others, are left unregistered; yet, he does not venture to contradict the declaration, or to point out how they can vote without being registered; but he just slips along, not seeming to know there is any such question of fact, and complacently declares, "There is every reason to hope and believe that the law will be fairly and impartially executed, so as to insure to every *bona fide* inhabitant the free and quiet exercise of the elective franchise."

I readily agree that if all had a chance to vote, they ought to have voted. If, on the contrary, as they allege, and Judge Douglas ventures not particularly to contradict, few only of the Free State men had a chance to vote, they were perfectly right in staying from the polls in a body.

By the way, since the Judge spoke, the Kansas election has come off. The Judge expressed his confidence that all the Democrats in Kansas would do their duty—including "Free State Democrats" of course. The returns received here, as yet, are very incomplete; but, so far as they go, they indicate that only about one-sixth of the registered voters have really voted; and this, too, when not more, perhaps, than one-half of the rightful voters have been registered, thus showing the thing to have been altogether the most exquisite farce ever enacted. I am watching with considerable interest, to ascertain what figure the "Free State Democrats" cut in the concern. Of course they voted—all Democrats do their duty—

and of course they did not vote for Slave State candidates. We soon shall know how many delegates they elected, how many candidates they had pledged to a free State, and how many votes were cast for them.

Allow me to barely whisper my suspicion, that there were no such things in Kansas as "Free State Democrats"—that they were altogether mythical, good only to figure in newspapers and speeches in the Free States. If there should prove to be one real, living Free State Democrat in Kansas, I suggest that it might be well to catch him, and stuff and preserve his skin, as an interesting specimen of that soon to be extinct variety of the genus Democrat.

And now, as to the Dred Scott decision. That decision declares two propositions—first, that a negro can not sue in the United States Courts; and secondly, that Congress can not prohibit slavery in the Territories. It was made by a divided court—dividing differently on the different points. Judge Douglas does not discuss the merits of the decision, and in that respect, I shall follow his example, believing I could no more improve upon McLean and Curtis, than he could on Taney.

He denounces all who question the correctness of that decision, as offering violent resistance to it. But who resists it? Who has, in spite of the decision, declared Dred Scott free, and resisted the authority of his master over him?

Judicial decisions have two uses—first, to absolutely determine the case decided; and secondly, to indicate to the public how other similar cases will be decided when they arise. For the latter use, they are called "precedents" and "authorities."

We believe as much as Judge Douglas (perhaps more) in obedience to and respect for the judicial department of Government. We think its decisions on Constitutional questions, when fully settled, should control, not only the particular cases decided, but the general policy of the country, subject to be disturbed only by amendments of the Constitution, as provided in that instrument itself. More than this would be revolution. But we think the Dred Scott decision is erroneous. We know the court that made it has often overruled its own decisions, and we shall do what we can to have it overrule this. We offer no resistance to it.

Judicial decisions are of greater or less authority as precedents, according to circumstances. That this should be so, accords both with common sense, and the customary understanding of the legal profession.

If this important decision had been made by the unanimous concurrence of the judges, and without any apparent partisan bias, and in accordance with legal public expectation, and with the steady practice of the departments, throughout our history, and had been in no part based on assumed historical facts which are not really true ; or, if wanting in some of these, it had been before the court more than once, and had there been affirmed and re-affirmed through a course of years, it then might be, perhaps would be, factious, nay, even revolutionary, not to acquiesce in it as a precedent.

But when, as is true, we find it wanting in all these claims to the public confidence, it is not resistance, it is not factious, it is not even disrespectful, to treat it as not having yet quite established a settled doctrine for the country. But Judge Douglas considers this view awful. Hear him :

" The courts are the tribunals prescribed by the Constitution and created by the authority of the people to determine, expound and enforce the law. Hence, whoever resists the final decision of the highest judicial tribunal, aims a deadly blow to our whole Republican system of government—a blow which, if successful, would place all our rights and liberties at the mercy of passion, anarcy and violence. I repeat, therefore, that if resistance to the decisions of the Supreme Court of the United States, in a matter like the points decided in the Dred Scott case, clearly within their jurisdiction as defined by the Constitution, shall be forced upon the country as political issue, it will become a distinct and naked issue between the friends and enemies of the Constitution—the friends and the enemies of the supremacy of the laws."

Why, this same Supreme Court once decided a national bank to be Constitutional; but General Jackson, as President of the United States, disregarded the decision, and vetoed a bill for a re-charter, partly on Constitutional ground, declaring that each public functionary must support the Constitution, "as he understands it." But hear the General's own words. Here they are, taken from his veto message :

" It is maintained by the advocates of the bank, that its constitutionality, in all its features, ought to be considered as settled by precedent, and by the decision of the Supreme Court. To this conclusion I can not assent. Mere precedent is a dangerous source of authority, and should not be regarded as deciding questions of Constitutional power, except where the acquiescence of the people and the States can be considered as well settled. So far from this being the case on this subject, an argument against the bank might be based on precedent. One Congress, in 1791, decided in favor of a bank ; another in 1811, decided against it. One Congress, in 1815, decided against a bank ; another in 1816, decided in its favor. Prior to the present Congress, therefore, the precedents drawn from that source were equal. If we resort to the States the expressions of legislative, judicial and executive opinions against the bank have been probably to those in its favor as four to one. There is nothing in precedent, therefore, which, if its authority were admitted, ought to weigh in favor of the act before me."

I drop the quotations merely to remark, that all there ever was, in the way of precedent, up to the Dred Scott decision, on the points therein decided, had been against that decision. But hear General Jackson further :

"If the opinion of the Supreme Court covered the whole ground of this act, it ought not to control the co-ordinate authorities of this Government. The Congress, the Executive and the Court, must each for itself be guided by its own opinion of the Constitution. Each public officer, who takes an oath to support the Constitution, swears that he will support it as he understands it, and not as it is understood by others."

Again and again have I heard Judge Douglas denounce that bank decision, and applaud General Jackson for disregarding it. It would be interesting for him to look over his recent speech, and see how exactly his fierce philippics against us for resisting Supreme Court decisions, fall upon his own head. It will call to mind a long and fierce political war in this country, upon an issue which, in his own language, and, of course, in his own changeless estimation, was "a distinct issue between the friends and the enemies of the Constitution," and in which war he fought in the ranks of the enemies of the Constitution.

I have said, in substance, that the Dred Scott decision was, in part, based on assumed historical facts which were not really true, and I ought not to leave the subject without giving some reasons for saying this: I, therefore, give an instance or two, which I think fully sustains me. Chief Justice Taney, in delivering the opinion of the majority of the Court, insists at great length, that negroes were no part of the people who made, or for whom was made, the Declaration of Independence, or the Constitution of the United States.

On the contrary, Judge Curtis, in his dissenting opinion, shows that in five of the then thirteen States, to-wit: New Hampshire, Massachusetts, New York, New Jersey and North Carolina, free negroes were voters, and, in proportion to their numbers, had the same part in making the Constitution that the white people had. He shows this with so much particularity as to leave no doubt of its truth , and as a sort of conclusion on that point, holds the following language :

"The Constitution was ordained and established by the

12

people of the United States, through the action, in each State, of those persons who were qualified by its laws to act thereon in behalf of themselves and all other citizens of the State. In some of the States, as we have seen, colored persons were among those qualified by law to act on the subject. These colored persons were not only included in the body of ' the people of the United States,' by whom the Constitution was ordained and established; but in at least five of the States they had the power to act, and, doubtless, did act, by their suffrages, upon the question of its adoption."

Again, Chief Justice Taney says: "It is difficult, at this day, to realize the state of public opinion in relation to that unfortunate race, which prevailed in the civilized and enlightened portions of the world at the time of the Declaration of Independence, and when the Constitution of the United States was framed and adopted." And again, after quoting from the Declaration, he says: " The general words above quoted would seem to include the whole human family, and if they were used in a similar instrument at this day, would be so understood."

In these the Chief Justice does not directly assert, but plainly assumes, as a fact, that the public estimate of the black man is more favorable now than it was in the days of the Revolution. This assumption is a mistake. In some trifling particulars, the condition of that race has been ameliorated; but, as a whole, in this country, the change between then and now is decidedly the other way; and their ultimate destiny has never appeared so hopeless as in the last three or four years. In two of the five States—New Jersey and North Carolina—that then gave the free negro the right of voting, the right has since been taken away; and in the third —New York—it has been greatly abridged; while it has not been extended, so far as I know, to a single additional State, though the number of the States has more than doubled. In those days, as I understand, masters could, at their own pleasure, emancipate their slaves; but since then such legal restraints have been made upon emancipation as to amount almost to prohibition. In those days Legislatures held the unquestioned power to abolish slavery in their respective States; but now it is becoming quite fashionable for State Constitutions to withhold that power from the Legislatures. In those days, by common consent, the spread of the black man's bondage to the new countries was prohibited; but now, Congress decides that it will not continue the prohibition— and the Supreme Court decides that it could not if it would. In those days our Declaration of Independence was held sacred by all, and thought to include all; but now, to aid in making the bondage of the negro universal and eternal, it is assailed, sneered at, construed, hawked at, and torn, till, if its framers could rise from their graves, they could not at all recognize it. All the powers of earth seem rapidly combining against him. Mammon is after him; ambition follows, philosophy follows, and the theology of the day is fast joining the cry. They have him in his prison-house; they have searched his person, and left no prying instrument with him. One after another they have closed the heavy iron doors upon him; and now they have him, as it were, bolted in with a lock of a hundred keys, which can never be unlocked without the concurrence of every key; the keys in the hands of a hundred different men, and they scattered to a hundred different and distant places; and they stand musing as to what invention, in all the dominions of mind and matter, can be produced to make the impossibility of his escape more complete than it is.

It is grossly incorrect to say or assume, that the public estimate of the negro is more favorable now than it was at the origin of the Government.

Three years and a half ago Judge Douglas brought forward his famous Nebraska bill. The country was at once in a blaze. He scorned all opposition, and carried it through Congress. Since then he has seen himself superseded in a Presidential nomination, by one indorsing the general doctrine of his measure, but at the same time standing clear of the odium of its untimely agitation, and its gross breach of national faith; and he has seen that successful rival constitutionally elected, not by the strength of friends, but by the division of his adversaries, being in a popular minority of nearly four hundred thousand votes. He has seen his chief aids in his own State, Shields and Richardson, politically speaking, successively tried, convicted, and executed, for an offense not their own, but his. And now he sees his own case, standing next on the docket for trial.

There is a natural disgust, in the minds of nearly all white people, to the idea of an indiscriminate amalgamation of the white and black races; and Judge Douglas evidently is basing his chief hope upon the chances of his being able to appropriate the benefit of this disgust to himself. If he can, by much drumming and repeating, fasten the odium of that idea upon his adversaries, he thinks he can struggle through the storm. He, therefore, clings to this hope, as a drowning man to the last plank. He makes an occasion for lugging it in from the opposition to the Dred Scott decision. He finds the

Republicans insisting that the Declaration of Independence includes ALL men, black as well as white, and forthwith he boldly denies that it includes negroes at all, and proceeds to argue gravely that all who contend it does, do so only because they want to vote, eat and sleep, and marry with negroes! He will have it that they can not be consistent else. Now, I protest against the counterfeit logic which concludes that, because I do not want a black woman for a slave, I must necessarily want her for a wife. I need not have her for either. I can just leave her alone. In some respects she certainly is not my equal; but in her natural right to eat the bread she earns with her own hands, without asking leave of any one else, she is my equal, and the equal of all others.

Chief Justice Taney, in his opinion in the Dred Scott case, admits that the language of the Declaration is broad enough to include the whole human family; but he and Judge Douglas argue that the authors of that instrument did not intend to include negroes, by the fact that they did not at once actually place them on an equality with the whites. Now, this grave argument comes to just nothing at all, by the other fact, that they did not at once, or ever afterward, actually place all white people on an equality with one another. And this is the staple argument of both the Chief Justice and the Senator for doing this obvious violence to the plain, unmistakable language of the Declaration.

I think the authors of that notable instrument intended to include *all* men, but they did not intend to declare all men equal *in all respects*. They did not mean to say all were equal in color, size, intellect, moral developments, or social capacity. They defined with tolerable distinctness in what respects they did consider all men created equal—equal with " certain inalienable rights, among which are life, liberty, and the pursuit of happiness." This they said, and this meant. They did not mean to assert the obvious untruth, that all were then actually enjoying that equality, nor yet, that they were about to confer it immediately upon them. In fact, they had no power to confer such a boon. They meant simply to declare the *right*, so that the *enforcement* of it might follow as fast as circumstances should permit.

Mr. Lincoln, in conclusion, pointed out in a clear and forcible manner the real distinction between his own views and those of Mr. Douglas on this question, as he has done in other speeches.

CHAPTER XI.

THE LINCOLN-DOUGLAS CAMPAIGN OF 1858.

The Lecompton Struggle.—The Policy of Douglas Changed.—He Breaks with the Administration and Loses Caste at the South.— Republican Sympathies.—Douglas Falters, but Opposes the English Bill.—Passage of that Measure.—Democratic State Convention of Illinois.—Douglas Indorsed, and Efforts for his Re-Election Commenced.—The Democratic Bolt.—Meeting of the Republican State Convention in June.—Mr. Lincoln named as the First and Only Choice of the Republicans for Senator.—His Great Speech Before the Convention at Springfield.—Douglas and Lincoln at Chicago.— Speeches at Bloomington and Springfield.—Unfairness of the Apportionment Pointed out by Mr. Lincoln.—He Analyzes the Douglas Programme.—Seven Joint Debates.—Douglas Produces a Bogus Platform, and Propounds Interrogatories.—"Unfriendly Legislation."—Lincoln Fully Defines his Position on the Slavery Question.— Result of the Canvass.—The People for Lincoln, the Apportionment for Douglas.—Public Opinion.

THE Lecompton Convention did its work according to the programme laid down at Washington. It adopted the Constitution desired, and probably devised, at the national capital, with the design of forcing slavery upon an unwilling people. One of the chief instruments in the execution of this work, so far as it could be consummated at Lecompton, was John Calhoun, an Illinois politician. The act under which that Convention was assembled, had received an unreserved and complete indorsement from Douglas, as "fair and just." He was emphatically committed in advance by his Springfield speech to the action of that Convention, which exercised no powers not distinctly conferred upon it by the act thus indorsed, or not in strict accordance with what was contemplated from the first by its framers. Yet late in the autumn of 1857, a rumor began to be circulated that Douglas was hesitating about sustaining the Lecompton Constitution. Knowing his previous attitude, people were generally incredulous in regard to this report. After a time, however, some of the leading Democratic papers of Illinois began to break ground against the Lecompton scheme, and when Congress assembled, in December, there were serious doubts as to whether Douglas did not intend to break with the Admisistration on this subject. Suspense on this point was soon relieved. Immediately after the annual message of Mr. Buchanan was read in the Senate, Douglas took occasion to announce his disagreement with the President on the Kansas question, and this notice was followed up by an elaborate speech the next day, in which he boldly talked against "forcing this Constitution down the throats of the people of Kansas, in opposition to their wishes and in violation of our pledges." He ignored all his recent attempts to charge the responsibility upon the non-voters if the Constitution did not suit them. He seemed to forget his declaration that the act calling the Lecompton Convention was "just and fair in all its objects and provisions." He now denied the right of the minority represented at Lecompton, in accordance with the well-understood "objects and provisions" of that act, "to defraud the majority of that people out of their elective franchise."

In brief, whatever his motives—and these may be left to himself—he had completely changed his attitude during the last few months, and now co-operated with the Republicans in opposing the Lecompton policy to which the President and the Democratic party had become definitely committed before the world. These two facts, however, are undeniable. The re-election of Douglas as Senator was to depend on the coming election in Illinois, and without some definite change of course, from that he had indicated at Springfield in June previous, he would be compelled to yield his place to Abraham Lincoln, as the associate of Lyman Trumbull.

It is not necessary here to follow the history of the desperate struggle which this change cost him during the long session of Congress. He carried with him but two Democratic Senators out of nearly forty, and only a little larger fraction of the Democratic members of the House. He was generally denounced at the South as a traitor, and this fact, added to the energy with which he carried on his warfare with the Administration against so many odds, gained him not a little sympathy in many Republican quarters. This, however, for the most part, his subsequent course alienated. It is believed that but for the firm stand taken by the lamented Broderick, in opposition to the course intended, Douglas would have made his peace with the Administration by voting for the shabby compromise known as the English Bill. That measure, in spite of his final influence against it, passed both Houses on the 4th of May.

Previous to that date, the Democratic State Convention, of Illinois, had met at Springfield (April 21st), nominated a State ticket and indorsed Douglas and his Anti-Lecompton associates from that State. The issue was thus fairly joined early in the season ; and all the influence of the Administration was brought to bear in getting up a counter Democratic organization sustaining the Lecompton policy. However promising for a time, this undertaking was not brilliantly successful. The friends of Douglas had taken time by the forelock, and made the most of their advantage in having the regular organization, with a State ticket early in the field. They spared no labor from this time forward in preparing for the re-election of Douglas. Without expecting the election of their candidates on the State ticket, they hoped, through an unequal apportionment strongly favoring their side, and from the large number of Democratic Senators holding over, to be able, at least, to get the control of the Senate, and to prevent the choice of a Republican successor to Douglas, if they could not accomplish their full purpose.

On the 16th of June—the day on which the session of Congress closed—the Republicans held their State Convention at Springfield. Richard Yates was the temporary, and Gustavus Koerner the permanent President. Nearly every one of the hundred counties of Illinois was duly represented, the delegates numbering over five hundred. Candidates were nominated for State Treasurer and for Superintendent of Public Instruction, and a Platform was adopted essentially the same as that put forth two years previously at Bloomington, as already quoted. A resolution approving the course of Lyman Trumbull as Senator was carried without opposition. The following resolution was then introduced, which, according to the official report, "was greeted with shouts of applause, and unanimously adopted :"

Resolved, That Abraham Lincoln is the first and only choice of the Republicans of Illinois for the United States Senate, as the successor of Stephen A. Douglas.

Mr. Lincoln had not been present during the Convention, and when called on to speak, at the adjourned evening session, he had no knowledge that such a resolution had been offered. So far was it from being true that his speech on that occasion, as subsequently stated by Douglas, was made on accepting a nomination for the Senatorship, that, of course, he did not allude to that subject. The speech, too, though carefully prepared, as Mr. Lincoln afterward admitted, was never known to any one else than himself until its delivery, notwithstanding the insinuation of Douglas that it was a subject of special consultation among the Republican leaders. It was the result of a broad and profound survey of the slavery question, from the point of view then reached in the progress of parties. It laid down certain propositions as philosophical truths, derived from a close observation of events. Its opening paragraph has already become one of the most celebrated passages in the political literature of the country. However it may be perverted, there is no portion of this speech which can be successfully assailed, when taken in its true meaning. There is a moral sublimity in the rugged honesty and directness with which the grand issues in this whole slavery agitation are presented. The two forces of slavery and free labor in our civil and social system, inevitably antagonistic, *so long as they come into collision in our national politics,* have each their peculiar tendency, the one to make slavery, and the other to make free labor universal. Until slavery is again reduced to its true local and sectional character, from which Douglas, Buchanan, and other agitators had conspired to raise it into national predominance, the antagonism will not cease. What Douglas

10 GRAVE OF MR. LINCOLN'S MOTHER.

always superficially slurred over—assuming an *indifference*, such as no earnest or sound statesman can really feel, whether "slavery is voted up or voted down"—Lincoln treats with true philosophic insight, and in the light of earnest convictions. This famous speech is in entire harmony with the views of the earlier statesmen, even of the South. If any man at first reads this great effort doubtingly, or with an inclination toward dissent—as most assuredly few really earnest, thinking men can—let him carefully look onward and see how it endures the test of a severe campaign, and how its chief positions are maintained against all the assaults of a wily foe, who is himself really on trial, solemnly indicted by that speech, yet vainly imagines that he is placing Mr. Lincoln on the defensive.

"The hall, and lobbies, and galleries were even more densely crowded and packed than at any time during the day," says the official report, as the Convention re-assembled in the evening to hear Mr. Lincoln. "As he approached the speaker's stand, he was greeted with shouts, and hurrahs, and prolonged cheering."

MR. LINCOLN'S FIRST SPEECH IN THE SENATORIAL CANVASS.

(*At the Republican State Convention, June* 16, 1858.)

Mr. Lincoln said—

GENTLEMEN OF THE CONVENTION:—If we could first know where we are, and whither we are tending, we could then better judge what to do, and how to do it. We are now far on into the fifth year, since a policy was initiated, with the avowed object, and confident promise, of putting an end to slavery agitation. Under the operation of that policy, that agitation has not only not ceased, but has constantly augmented. In my opinion, it will not cease, until a crisis shall have been reached, and passed. "A house divided against itself can not stand." I believe this Government can not endure permanently, half slave and half free. I do not expect the Union to be dissolved—I do not expect the house to fall—but I do expect it will cease to be divided. It will become all one thing, or all the other. Either the opponents of slavery will arrest the further spread of it, and place it where the public mind shall rest in the belief that it is in course of ultimate extinction, or its advocates will push it forward, till it shall

10   13

become alike lawful in all the States—old as well as new—North as well as South.

Have we no tendency to the latter condition? Let any one who doubts, carefully contemplate that now almost complete legal combination—piece of machinery, so to speak—compounded of the Nebraska doctrine and the Dred Scott decision. Let him consider not only what work the machinery is adapted to do, and how well adapted, but also let him study the history of its construction, and trace, if he can, or rather fail, if he can, to trace the evidences of design, and concert of action, among its chief master-workers from the beginning.

But, so far, Congress only had acted; and an indorsement by the people, real or apparent, was indispensable, to save the point already gained, and give chance for more. The new year of 1854 found slavery excluded from more than half the States by State Constitutions, and from most of the national territory by Congressional prohibition. Four days later commenced the struggle, which ended in repealing that Congressional prohibition. This opened all the national territory to slavery, and was the first point gained.

This necessity had not been overlooked, but had been provided for, as well as might be, in the notable argument of " squatter sovereignty," otherwise called " sacred right of self-government," which latter phrase, though expressive of the only rightful basis of any government, was so perverted in this attempted use of it as to amount to just this: that if any one man choose to enslave another, no third man shall be allowed to object. That argument was incorporated into the Nebraska bill itself, in the language which follows: " It being the true intent and meaning of this act not to legislate slavery into any Territory or State, nor exclude it therefrom; but to leave the people thereof perfectly free to form and regulate their domestic institutions in their own way, subject only to the Constitution of the United States."

Then opened the roar of loose declamation in favor of " squatter sovereignty," and " sacred right of self-government."

" But," said opposition members, " let us be more specific—let us amend the bill so as to expressly declare that the people of the territory may exclude slavery." " Not we," said the friends of the measure; and down they voted the amendment.

While the Nebraska Bill was passing through Congress, a law case, involving the question of a negro's freedom, by reason of his owner having voluntarily taken him first into a free State and then a territory covered by the Congressional prohibition, and held him as a slave—for a long time in each—

was passing through the U. S. Circuit Court for the District of Missouri; and both the Nebraska Bill and law suit were brought to a decision in the same month of May, 1854. The negro's name was "Dred Scott," which name now designates the decision finally made in the case.

Before the then next Presidential election case, the law came to, and was argued in the Supreme Court of the United States; but the decision of it was deferred until *after* the election. Still, *before* the election, Senator Trumbull, on the floor of the Senate, requests the leading advocate of the Nebraska Bill to state *his opinion* whether a people of a territory can constitutionally exclude slavery from their limits; and the latter answers, "That is a question for the Supreme Court."

The election came. Mr. Buchanan was elected, and the *indorsement*, such as it was, secured. That was the *second* point gained. The indorsement, however, fell short of a clear popular majority by nearly four hundred thousand votes, and so, perhaps, was not overwhelmingly reliable and satisfactory. The outgoing President in his last annual message, as impressively as possible echoed back upon the people the weight and authority of the indorsement.

The Supreme Court met again; did not announce their decision, but ordered a re-argument. The Presidential inauguration came, and still no decision of the court; but the incoming President, in his Inaugural Address, fervently exhorted the people to abide by the forthcoming decision, *whatever it might be.* Then, in a few days, came the decision. This was the third point gained.

The reputed author of the Nebraska Bill finds an early occasion to make a speech at this capitol indorsing the Dred Scott decision, and vehemently denouncing all opposition to it. The new President, too, seizes the early occasion of the Silliman letter to indorse and strongly construe that decision, and to express his astonishment that any different view had ever been entertained. At length a squabble springs up between the President and the author of the Nebraska Bill on the mere question of fact, whether the Lecompton Constitution was, or was not, in any just sense, made by the people of Kansas; and, in that squabble, the latter declares that all he wants is a fair vote for the people, and that he cares not whether slavery be voted down or voted up. I do not understand his declaration that he cares not whether slavery be voted down or voted up, to be intended by him other than as an apt definition of the policy he would impress upon the public mind—the principle for which he declares he has suffered much, and is ready to suffer to the end.

And well may he cling to that principle. If he has any parental feeling, well may he cling to it. That principle is the only shred left of his original Nebraska doctrine. Under the Dred Scott decision, " squatter sovereignty " squatted out of existence, tumbled down like temporary scaffolding—like the mould at the foundry, served through one blast, and fell back into loose sand—helped to carry an election, and then was kicked to the winds. His late joint struggle with the Republicans, against the Lecompton Constitution, involves nothing of the original Nebraska doctrine. That struggle was made on a point—the right of a people to make their own Constitution—upon which he and the Republicans have never differed.

The several points of the Dred Scott decision, in connection with Senator Douglas' " care-not " policy, constitute the piece of machinery in its present state of advancement. The working points of that machinery are :

First, That no negro slave, imported as such from Africa, and no descendant of such, can ever be a citizen of any State in the sense of that term as used in the Constitution of the United States.

This point is made in order to deprive the negro, in every possible event, of the benefit of this provision of the United States Constitution, which declares that—" The citizens of each State shall be entitled to all the privileges and immunities of citizens in the several States."

Secondly, That " subject to the Constitution of the United States," neither Congress nor a Territorial Legislature can exclude slavery from any United States Territory.

This point is made in order that individual men may fill up the Territories with slaves, without danger of losing them as property, and thus to enhance the chances of permanency to the institution through all the future.

Thirdly, That whether the holding a negro in actual slavery in a free State makes him free, as against the holder, the United States courts will not decide, but will leave to be decided by the courts of any slave State the negro may be forced into by the master.

This point is made, not to be pressed immediately ; but, if acquiesced in for a while and apparently indorsed by the people at an election, then, to sustain the logical conclusion that what Dred Scott's master might lawfully do with Dred Scott, in the free State of Illinois, every other master may lawfully do with any other one, or one thousand slaves, in Illinois, or in any other free State.

Auxiliary to all this, and working hand in hand with it,

the Nebraska doctrine, or what is left of it, is to educate and mold public opinion, at least Northern public opinion, not to care whether slavery is voted down or voted up.

This shows exactly where we now are, and partially, also whither we are tending.

It will throw additional light on the latter, to go back, and run the mind over the string of historical facts already stated. Several things will now appear less dark and mysterious than they did when they were transpiring. The people were to be left "perfectly free," "subject only to the Constitution." What the Constitution had to do with it, outsiders could not then see. Plainly enough now, it was an exactly fitted niche for the Dred Scott decision afterward to come in, and declare that perfect freedom of the people, to be just no freedom at all.

Why was the amendment, expressly declaring the right of the people to exclude slavery, voted down? Plainly enough now, the adoption of it would have spoiled the niche for the Dred Scott decision.

Why was the court decision held up? Why even a Senator's individual opinion withheld till after the Presidential election? Plainly enough now; the speaking out then would have damaged the "*perfectly free*" argument upon which the election was to be carried.

Why the outgoing President's felicitation on the indorsement? Why the delay of a re-argument? Why the incoming President's advance exhortation in favor of the decision? These things look like the cautious patting and petting of a spirited horse, preparatory to mounting him, when it is dreaded that he may give the rider a fall. And why the hasty after-indorsements of the decision, by the President and others?

We can not absolutely know that all these exact adaptations are the result of pre-concert. But when we see a lot of framed timbers, different portions of which we know have been gotten out, at different times and places, and by different workmen—Stephen, Franklin, Roger and James, for instance—and when we see these timbers joined together, and see they exactly make the frame of a house or a mill, all the tenons and mortises exactly fitting, and all the lengths and proportions of the different pieces exactly adapted to their respective places, and not a piece too many or too few—not omitting even scaffolding—or, if a single piece be lacking, we can see the place in the frame exactly fitted and prepared to yet bring such piece in—in such a case, we find it impossible not to believe that Stephen and Franklin and Roger and James all understood one another from the beginning, and all worked upon a common plan or draft drawn up before the first blow was struck.

It should not be overlooked that, by the Nebraska Bill, the people of a State, as well as Territory, were to be left "*perfectly free,*" "*subject only to the Constitution.*" Why mention a State? They were legislating for Territories, and not for or about States. Certainly the people of a State are and ought to be subject to the Constitution of the United States; but why is mention of this lugged into this merely territorial law? Why are the people of a territory and the people of a State therein lumped together, and their relation to the Constitution therein treated as being precisely the same?

While the opinion of the Court, by Chief Justice Taney, in the Dred Scott case, and the separate opinions of all the concurring judges, expressly declare that the Constitution of the United States neither permits Congress nor a Territorial Legislature to exclude slavery from any United States Territory, they all omit to declare whether or not the same Constitution permits a State, or the people of a State to exclude it. *Possibly,* this was a mere *omission;* but who can be quite sure, if McLean or Curtis had sought to get into the opinion a declaration of unlimited power in the people of a State to exclude slavery from their limits, just as Chase and Mace sought to get such declaration in behalf of the people of a Territory into the Nebraska Bill—I ask, who can be quite sure that it would not have been voted down, in the one case, as it had been in the other.

The nearest approach to the point of declaring the power of a State over slavery, is made by Judge Nelson. He approaches it more than once, using the precise idea, and almost the language, too, of the Nebraska Act. On one occasion his exact language is, "except in cases where the power is restrained by the Constitution of the United States, the law of the State is supreme over the subject of slavery within its jurisdiction."

In what cases the power of the State is so restrained by the United States Constitution, is left an open question, precisely as the same question, as to the restraint on the power of the Territories, was left open in the Nebraska Act. Put that and that together, and we have another nice little niche, which we may, ere long, see filled with another Supreme Court decision, declaring that the Constitution of the United States does not permit a State to exclude slavery from its limits. And this may especially be expected if the doctrine of "care not whether slavery be voted down or voted up," shall gain upon the public mind sufficiently to give promise that such a decision can be maintained when made.

Such a decision is all that slavery now lacks of being alike lawful in all the States. Welcome or unwelcome, such decision is probably coming, and will soon be upon us, unless the power of the present political dynasty shall be met and overthrown. We shall lie down pleasantly dreaming that the people of Missouri are on the verge of making their State free; and we shall awake to the reality, instead, that the Supreme Court has made Illinois a slave State.

To meet and overthrow the power of that dynasty, is the work now before all those who would prevent that consummation. That is what we have to do. But how can we best do it?

There are those who denounce us openly to their own friends, and yet whisper softly, that Senator Douglas is the *aptest* instrument there is, with which to effect that object. They do not tell us, nor has he told us, that he wishes any such object to be effected. They wish us to infer all, from the facts that he now has a little quarrel with the present head of the dynasty; and that he has regularly voted with us, on a single point, upon which he and we have never differed.

They remind us that *he* is a very *great man*, and that the largest of us are very small ones. Let this be granted. But " a *living dog* is better than a *dead lion.*" Judge Douglas, if not a *dead* lion for this work, is at least a *caged* and *toothless* one. How can he oppose the advances of slavery? He don't care anything about it. His avowed mission is impressing the " public heart" to care nothing about it.

A leading Douglas Democratic newspaper thinks Douglas' superior talent will be needed to resist the revival of the African slave-trade. Does Douglas believe an effort to revive that trade is approaching? He has not said so. Does he *really* think so? But if it is, how can he resist it? For years he has labored to prove it a *sacred right* of white men to take negro slaves into the new Territories. Can he possibly show that it is less a sacred right to buy them where they can be bought cheapest? And, unquestionably, they can be bought cheaper in Africa than in Virginia.

He has done all in his power to reduce the whole question of slavery to one of a mere right of property; and as such, how can he oppose the foreign slave-trade—how can he refuse that trade in that " property," shall be " perfectly free"—unless he does it as a *protection* to the home production? And as the home *producers* will probably not ask the protection, he will be wholly without a ground of opposition.

Senator Douglas holds, we know, that a man may rightfully be wiser to-day than he was yesterday—that he may rightfully change when he finds himself wrong. But, can we for that reason run ahead and infer that he will make any particular change, of which he himself has given no intimation? Can we safely base our action upon any such vague inferences?

Now, as ever, I wish not to misrepresent Judge Douglas' position, question his motives, or do aught that can be personally offensive to him. Whenever, *if ever*, he and we can come together on *principle*, so that our great cause may have assistance from his great ability, I hope to have interposed no adventitious obstacle.

But clearly, he is not now with us—he does not pretend to be—he does not promise ever to be. Our cause, then, must be intrusted to, and conducted by its own undoubted friends—those whose hands are free, whose hearts are in the work—who do care for the result.

Two years ago the Republicans of the nation mustered over thirteen hundred thousand strong. We did this under the single impulse of resistance to a common danger, with every external circumstance against us. Of strange, discordant, and even hostile elements, we gathered from the four winds, and formed and fought the battle through, under the constant hot fire of a disciplined, proud and pampered enemy. Did we brave all then to falter now?—*now*—when that same enemy is wavering, dissevered and belligerent?

The result is not doubtful. We shall not fail—if we stand firm, we shall not fail. *Wise counsels* may *accelerate* or *mistakes delay* it, but, sooner or later, the victory is *sure* to come.

Mr. Douglas, having lingered for more than three weeks on his way homeward, preparing for the struggle before him, arrived in Chicago on the 9th of July, amid the most showy demonstrations of his friends. He made a long speech on the occasion, which Mr. Lincoln was present to hear. Douglas claimed great credit as having defeated the President's Lecompton policy, and imperiously returned thanks to the Republicans for "coming up manfully and sustaining" him and his little band in opposition to the Administration—a course, certainly, for which the Republican party deserved no special thanks, as it required of them no sacrifice of either consistency or partisan fellowship. Subsequently he charged an alliance between the Republicans and the Administration party for his defeat. He took care again to avow an utter indifference as to whether Kansas should be slave soil or free soil, only asking that the popular majority should prevail. At length he came to the great opening speech of Mr. Lincoln, which had been carefully pondered during the last three weeks.

"I have observed," he said with condescending assurance, "I have observed from the public prints, that but a few days ago the Republican party of the State of Illinois assembled in convention at Springfield, and not only laid down their platform, but nominated a candidate for the United States Senate as my successor. I take great pleasure in saying that I have known, personally and intimately, for about a quarter of a century, the worthy gentleman who has been nominated *for my place;* and I will say that I regard him as a kind, amiable and intelligent gentleman, a good citizen, and an honorable opponent; and whatever issue I may have with him will be of principle, and not involving personalities." He then proceeded to specify his two chief points of attack on Mr. Lincoln, after citing a portion of the first paragraph of his Springfield speech. Mr. Douglas endeavored thus to put his opponent on the defensive, by selecting sentences out of their connection, and imputing to them a meaning not intended. His first point he thus states:

In other words, Mr. Lincoln asserts as a fundamental principle of this Government, that there must be uniformity in the local laws and domestic institutions of each and all the States of the Union, and he therefore invites all the non-slaveholding States to band together, organize as one body, and make war upon slavery in Kentucky, upon slavery in Virginia, upon slavery in the Carolinas, upon slavery in all of the slaveholding States in this Union, and to persevere in that war until it shall be exterminated. He then notifies the slaveholding States to stand together as a unit and make an aggressive war upon the free States of this Union, with a view of establishing slavery in them all; of forcing it upon Illinois, of forcing it upon New York, upon New England, and upon every other free State, and that they shall keep up the warfare until it has been formally established in them all. In other words, Mr. Lincoln advocates boldly and clearly a war of sections, a war of the North against the South, of the free States against the slave States—a war of extermination—to be continued relentlessly until the one or the other should be subdued, and all the States shall either become free or become slave.

His other point was made in these words:

The other proposition discussed by Mr. Lincoln in his

speech consists in a crusade against the Supreme Court of the United States on account of the Dred Scott decision. On this question, also, I desire to say to you, unequivocally, that I take direct and distinct issue with him. I have no warfare to make on the Supreme Court of the United States, either on account of that or any other decision which they have pronounced from that bench. The Constitution of the United States has provided that the powers of Government (and the Constitution of each State has the same provision) shall be divided into three departments—executive, legislative and judicial. The right and the province of expounding the Constitution, and constructing the law, is vested in the judiciary established by the Constitution. As a lawyer, I feel at liberty to appear before the court and controvert any principle of law while the question is pending before the tribunal; but when the decision is made, my private opinion, your opinion, all other opinions must yield to the majesty of that authoritative adjudication.

Later in the same speech, Mr. Douglas said on this head:

On the other point, Mr. Lincoln goes for a warfare upon the Supreme Court of the United States, because of their decision in the Dred Scott case. I yield obedience to the decisions of that Court—to the final determination of the highest judicial tribunal known to our Constitution. He objects to the Dred Scott decision because it does not put the negro in the possession of the rights of citizenship on an equality with the white man. I am opposed to negro equality. I repeat that this nation is a white people—a people composed of European descendants — a people that have established this Government for themselves and their posterity, and I am in favor of preserving, not only the purity of the blood, but the purity of the Government, from any mixture or amalgamation with inferior races. I have seen the effects of this mixture of superior and inferior races — this amalgamation of white men and Indians and negroes; we have seen it in Mexico, in Central America, in South America, and in all the Spanish-American States, and its result has been degeneration, demoralization, and degradation below the capacity for self-government.

How completely the positions of Mr. Lincoln were misconstrued in these extracts, will partly appear from reading his speech, made at Springfield on the 26th of June, 1857. These misconceptions were completely disposed of in Mr. Lincoln's reply, at Chicago, on the following evening, July

10th. An instense eagerness to hear his answer drew together a great crowd, and the reception of Mr. Lincoln, on his appearance, was most enthusiastic, the applause continuing for several minutes

MR. LINCOLN'S REPLY TO MR. DOUGLAS.

(At Chicago, on the evening of July 10th, 1858.)

Mr. Lincoln said :

MY FELLOW-CITIZENS : On yesterday evening, upon the occasion of the reception given to Senator Douglas, I was furnished with a seat very convenient for hearing him, and was otherwise very courteously treated by him and his friends, for which I thank him and them. During the course of his remarks my name was mentioned in such a way as, I suppose, renders it at least not improper that I should make some sort of reply to him. I shall not attempt to follow him in the precise order in which he addressed the assembled multitude upon that occasion, though I shall perhaps do so in the main.

THE ALLEGED ALLIANCE.

There was one question to which he asked the attention of the crowd, which I deem of somewhat less importance—at least of propriety for me to dwell upon—than the others, which he brought in near the close of his speech, and which I think it would not be entirely proper for me to omit attending to, and yet if I were not to give some attention to it now, I should probably forget it altogether. While I am upon this subject, allow me to say that I do not intend to indulge in that inconvenient mode sometimes adopted in public speaking, of reading from documents; but I shall depart from that rule so far as to read a little scrap from his speech, which notices this first topic of which I shall speak—that is, provided I can find it in the paper. [Examines the morning's paper.]

" I have made up my mind to appeal to the people against the combination that has been made against me ! the Republican leaders having formed an alliance, an unholy and unnatural alliance, with a portion of unscrupulous federal office-holders. I intend to fight that allied army wherever I meet them. I know they deny the alliance, but yet these men, who are trying to divide the Democratic party for the purpose of electing a Republican Senator in my place, are just as much the agents and tools of the supporters of Mr. Lincoln. Hence I shall deal with this allied army just as the Russians dealt with the allies at Sebastopol—that is, the Russians did not stop to inquire, when they fired a broadside, whether it hit an Englishman, a Frenchman, or a Turk. Nor will I stop to inquire, nor shall I hesitate whether my blows shall hit these Republican leaders or their allies, who are holding the federal offices, and yet acting in concert with them."

Well, now, gentlemen, is not that very alarming? Just to think of it! right at the outset of his canvass, I, a poor, kind, amiable, intelligent gentleman, I am to be slain in this way. Why, my friends, the Judge is not only, as it turns out, not a dead lion, nor even a living one—he is the rugged Russian Bear! [Laughter and applause.]

But if they will have it—for he says that we deny it—that there is any such alliance, as he says there is—and I don't propose hanging very much upon this question of veracity—but if he will have it that there is such an alliance—that the Administration men and we are allied, and we stand in the attitude of English, French and Turk, he occupying the position of the Russian, in that case, I beg that he will indulge us while we barely suggest to him that these allies took Sebastopol. [Great applause.]

Gentlemen, only a few more words as to this alliance. For my part, I have to say, that whether there be such an alliance, depends so far as I know, upon what may be a right defini-nition of the term *alliance*. If for the Republican party to see the other great party to which they are opposed divided among themselves, and not try to stop the division and rather be glad of it—if that is an alliance, I confess I am in ; but if it is meant to be said that the Republicans had formed an alliance going beyond that, by which there is contribution of money or sacrifice of principle on the one side or the other, so far as the Republican party is concerned, if there be any such thing, I protest that I neither know any thing of it, nor do I believe it. I will, however, say—as I think this branch of the argument is lugged in—I would before I leave it, state, for the benefit of those concerned, that one of those same Buchanan men did once tell me of an argument that he made for his opposition to Judge Douglas. He said that a friend of our Senator Douglas had been talking to him, and had among other things said to him: "Why, you don't want to beat Douglas?" "Yes," said he, "I do want to beat him, and I will tell you why. I believe his original Nebraska Bill was right in the abstract, but it was wrong in the time that it was brought forward. It was wrong in the application to a Territory in regard to which the question had been settled ; it was brought forward at a time when nobody asked him ; it was tendered to the South when the South had not asked for it, but when they could not well refuse it; and for this same reason he forced that question upon our party; it has sunk the best men all over the nation, everywhere; and now when our President, struggling with the difficulties of this man's getting up, has reached the very hardest point to turn in the case, he deserts him, and I *am* for putting him where he will trouble us no more.''

Now, gentlemen, that is not my argument—that is not my argument at all. I have only been stating to you the argument of a Buchanan man. You will judge if there is any force in it.

WHAT IS POPULAR SOVEREIGNTY?

Popular Sovereignty! everlasting Popular Sovereignty! Let us for a moment inquire into this vast matter of Popular Sovereignty. What is Popular Sovereignty? We recollect that in an early period in the history of this struggle, there was another name for the same thing—*Squatter Sovereignty*. It was not exactly Popular Sovereignty, but Squatter Sovereignty. What do those terms mean? What do those terms mean when used now? And vast credit is taken by our friend, the Judge, in regard to his support of it, when he declares the last years of his life have been, and all the future years of his life shall be, devoted to this matter of Popular Sovereignty. What is it? Why, it is the sovereignty of the people! What was Squatter Sovereignty? I suppose if it had any significance at all, it was the right of the people to govern themselves, to be sovereign in their own affairs while they were squatted down in a country not their own, while they had squatted on a Territory that did not belong to them, in the sense that a State belongs to the people who inhabit it—when it belonged to the nation—such right to govern themselves was called "Squatter Sovereignty."

Now I wish you to mark. What has become of that Squatter Sovereignty? What has become of it? Can you get any body to tell you now that the people of a territory have any authority to govern themselves, in regard to this mooted question of slavery, before they form a State Constitution? No such thing at all, although there is a general running fire, and although there has been a hurrah made in every speech on that side, assuming that policy had given the people of a Territory the right to govern themselves upon this question; yet the point is dodged. To-day it has been decided—no more than a year ago it was decided by the Supreme Court of the United States, and is insisted upon to-day, that the people of a Territory have no right to exclude slavery from a Territory, that if any one man chooses to take slaves into a Territory, all the rest of the people have no right to keep them out. This being so, and this decision being made one of the points that the Judge approved, and one in the approval of which he says he means to keep me down—*put me down* I should not say, for I have never been up. He says he is in favor of it, and sticks to it, and expects to win his battle on that decision, which says that there is no such thing as Squatter Sovereignty; but that any one man may take slaves into a Territory, and all the other men in the Territory may be opposed to it, and yet by reason of the Constitution they can not prohibit it. When that is so, how much is left of this vast matter of Squatter Sovereignty I should like to know? [A voice—"It is all gone."]

When we get back, we get to the point of the right of the people to make a Constitution. Kansas was settled, for example, in 1854. It was a Territory yet, without having formed a Constitution, in a very regular way, for three years. All this time negro slavery could be taken in by any few individuals, and by that decision of the Supreme Court, which the Judge approves, all the rest of the people can not keep it out; but when they come to make a Constitution they may say they will not have slavery. But it is there; they are obliged to tolerate it some way, and all experience shows it will be so—for they will not take negro slaves and absolutely deprive the owners of them. All experience shows this to be so. All that space of time that runs from the beginning of the settlement of the Territory until there is sufficiency of people to make a State Constitution—all that portion of time popular sovereignty is given up. The seal is absolutely put down upon it by the Court decision, and Judge Douglas puts his on the top of that, yet he is appealing to the people to give him vast credit for his devotion to popular sovereignty. [Applause.]

Again, when we get to the question of the right of the people to form a State Constitution as they please, to form it with slavery or without slavery—if that is anything new, I confess I don't know it. Has there ever been a time when any body said that any other than the people of a Territory itself should form a Constitution? What is now in it that Judge Douglas should have fought several years of his life, and pledge himself to fight all the remaining years of his life for? Can Judge Douglas find any body on earth that said that any body else should form a Constitution for a people? [A voice, " Yes."] Well, I should like you to name him; I should like to know who he was. [Same voice, " John Calhoun."]

Mr. Lincoln—No, Sir, I never heard of even John Calhoun saying such a thing. He insisted on the same principle as Judge Douglas ; but his mode of applying it in fact, was wrong. It is enough for my purpose to ask this crowd, when ever a Republican said anything against it? They never said anything against it, but they have constantly spoken for it; and whosoever will undertake to examine the platform, and the speeches of responsible men of the party, and of irresponsible men, too, if you please, will be unable to find one word from anybody in the Republican ranks, opposed to that Popular Sovereignty which Judge Douglas thinks that he has invented. [Applause.] I suppose that Judge Douglas will claim in a little while, that he is the inventor of the idea that the people should govern themselves; that nobody ever thought of such a thing until he brought it forward. We do remember, that in that old Declaration of Independence, it is said that " We hold these truths to be self-evident, that all men are created equal ; that they are endowed by their Creator with certain inalienable rights ; that among these are life, liberty, and the pursuit of happiness; that to secure these rights, governments are instituted among men, deriving their just powers from the consent of the governed." There is the origin of Popular Sovereignty. [Loud applause.] Who, then, shall come in at this day and claim that he invented it?

[After referring, in appropriate terms, to the credit claimed by Douglas for defeating the Lecompton policy, Mr. Lincoln proceeds :]

I defy you to show a printed resolution passed in a Democratic meeting—I take it upon myself to defy any man to show a printed resolution of a Democratic meeting, large or small, in favor of Judge Trumbull, or any of the five to one Republicans who beat that bill. Every thing must be for the Democrats! They did every thing, and the five to the one that really did the thing, they snub over, and they do not seem to remember that they have an existence upon the face of the earth.

LINCOLN AND DOUGLAS—THE PERVERTED ISSUES.

Gentlemen, I fear that I shall become tedious. I leave this branch of the subject to take hold of another. I take up that part of Judge Douglas' speech in which he respectfully attended to me.

Judge Douglas made two points upon my recent speech at Springfield. He says they are to be the issues of this campaign. The first one of these points he bases upon the language in a speech which I delivered at Springfield, which I believe I can quote correctly from memory. I said there that " we are now far on in the fifth year since a policy was instituted for the avowed object, and with the confident promise, of putting an end to slavery agitation ; under the operation of that policy, that agitation had not only not ceased, but had constantly augmented. I believe it will not cease until a crisis shall have been reached and passed. A house divided against itself can not stand. I believe this Government can not endure permanently half slave and half free. I do not expect the Union to be dissolved"—I am quoting from my speech—" I do not expect the house to fall, but I do expect it will cease to be divided. It will come all one thing or the other. Either the opponents of slavery will arrest the spread of it, and place it where the public mind shall rest in the belief that it is in the course of ultimate extinction, or its advocates will push it forward until it shall have become. alike lawful in all the States, North as well as South."

In this paragraph which I have quoted in your hearing, and to which I ask the attention of all, Judge Douglas thinks he discovers great political heresy. I want your attention particularly to what he has inferred from it. He says I am in favor of making all the States of this Union uniform in all their internal regulations ; that in all their domestic concerns I am in favor of making them entirely uniform. He draws this inference from the language I have quoted to you. He says that I am favor of making war by the North upon the South for the extinction of slavery ; that I am also in favor of inviting, as he expresses it, the South to a war upon the North, for the purpose of nationalizing slavery. Now, it is singular enough, if you will carefully read that passage over, that I did not say that I was in favor of any thing in it. I only said what I expected would take place. I made a prediction only— it may have been a foolish one perhaps. I did not even say that I desired that slavery should be put in course of ultimate extinction. I do say so now, however, so there need be no longer any difficulty about that. It may be written down in the next speech.

Gentlemen, Judge Douglas informed you that this speech of mine was probably carefully prepared. I admit that it was. I am not master of language ; I have not a fine education ; I am not capable of entering into a disquisition upon dialectics, as I believe you call it ; but I do not believe the language I

THE LINCOLN HOME IN ILLINOIS,
Where the 3,000 Rails were Split.

employed bears any such construction as Judge Douglas puts upon it. But I don't care about a quibble in regard to words. I know what I meant, and I will not leave this crowd in doubt, if I can explain it to them, what I really meant in the use of that paragraph.

I am not, in the first place, unaware that this Government has endured eighty-two years, half slave and half free. I know that. I am tolerably well acquainted with the history of the country, and I know that it has endured eighty-two years, half slave and half free. I *believe*—and that is what I meant to allude to there—I *believe* it has endured, because during all that time, until the introduction of the Nebraska Bill, the public mind did rest all the time in the belief that slavery was in course of ultimate extinction. That was what gave us the rest that we had through that period of eighty-two years; at least, so I believe. I have always hated slavery, I think, as much as any Abolitionist. I have been an Old Line Whig. I have always hated it, but I have always been quiet about it until this new era of the introduction of the Nebraska Bill began. I always believed that everybody was against it, and that it was in course of ultimate extinction. [Pointing to Mr. Browning, who stood near by:] Browning thought so; the great mass of the nation have rested in the belief that slavery was in course of ultimate extinction. They had reason so to believe.

The adoption of the Constitution, and its attendant history, led the people to believe so; and that such was the belief of the framers of the Constitution itself. Why did those old men, about the time of the adoption of the Constitution, decree that slavery should not go into the new territory, where it had not already gone? Why declare that within twenty years the African slave-trade, by which slaves are supplied, might be cut off by Congress? Why were all these acts? I might enumerate more of such acts—but enough. What were they but a clear indication that the framers of the Constitution intended and expected the ultimate extinction of that institution? [Cheers.] And now, when I say, as I said in this speech that Judge Douglas has quoted from, when I say that I think the opponents of slavery will resist the further spread of it, and place it where the public mind shall rest with the belief that it is in course of ultimate extinction, I only mean to say, that they will place it where the founders of this Government originally placed it.

I have said a hundred times, and I have no inclination to take it back, that I believe there is no right, and ought to be no inclination in the people of the free States to enter into

11   14

the slave States, and to interfere with the question of slavery at all. I have said that always. Judge Douglas has heard me say it—if not quite a hundred times, at least as good as a hundred times; and when it is said that I am in favor of interfering with slavery where it exists, I know that it is unwarranted by anything I have ever intended, and, as I believe, by anything I have ever said. If, by any means, I have ever used language which could fairly be so construed (as, however, I believe I never have), I now correct it.

So much, then, for the inference that Judge Douglas draws, that I am in favor of setting the sections at war with one another. I know that I never meant any such thing, and I believe that no fair mind can infer any such thing from anything I have ever said.

Now in relation to his inference that I am in favor of a general consolidation of all the local institutions of the various States. I will attend to that for a little while, and try to inquire, if I can, how on earth it could be that any man could draw such an inference from anything I said. I have said, very many times, in Judge Douglas' hearing, that no man believed more than I in the principle of self-government; that it lies at the bottom of all my ideas of just government, from beginning to end. I have denied that his use of that term applies properly. But for the thing itself, I deny that any man has ever gone ahead of me in his devotion to the principle, whatever he may have done in efficiency in advocating it. I think that I have said it in your hearing—that I believe each individual is naturally entitled to do as he pleases with himself and with the fruit of his labor, so far as it in no wise interferes with any other man's rights—[applause] that each community, as a State, has a right to do exactly as it pleases with all the concerns within that State that interfere with the right of no other State, and that the General Government, upon principle, has no right to interfere with anything other than that general class of things that does concern the whole. I have said that at all times. I have said, as illustrations, that I do not believe in the right of Illinois to interfere with the cranberry laws of Indiana, the oyster laws of Virginia, or the liquor laws of Maine. I have said these things over and over again, and I repeat them here as my sentiments. * * * * * * * * *

So much, then, as to my disposition—my wish—to have all the State Legislatures blotted out, and to have one consolidated government, and a uniformity of domestic regulations in all the States; by which I suppose it is meant, if we raise corn here, we must make sugar-cane grow here too, and we must make those which grow North grow in the South. All this I suppose he understands I am in favor of doing. Now, so much for all this nonsense—for I must call it so. The Judge can have no issue with me on a question of established uniformity in the domestic regulations of the States.

DRED SCOTT DECISION.

A little now on the other point—the Dred Scott decision. Another of the issues he says that is to be made with me, is upon his devotion to the Dred Scott decision, and my opposition to it.

I have expressed heretofore, and I now repeat my opposition to the Dred Scott decision, but I should be allowed to state the nature of that opposition, and I ask your indulgence while I do so. What is fairly implied by the term Judge Douglas has used, "resistance to the decision?" I do not resist it. If I wanted to take Dred Scott from his master, I would be interfering with property, and that terrible difficulty that Judge Douglas speaks of, of interfering with property, would arise. But I am doing no such thing as that, but all that I am doing is refusing to obey it as a political rule. If I were in Congress, and a vote should come up on a question whether slavery should be prohibited in a new Territory, in spite of the Dred Scott decision, I would vote that it should.

That is what I would do. Judge Douglas said last night, that before the decision he might advance his opinion, and it might be contrary to the decision when it was made; but *after* it was made he would abide by it until it was reversed. Just so! We let this property abide by the decision, but we will try to reverse that decision. [Loud applause.] We will try to put it where Judge Douglas will not object, for he says he will obey it until it is reversed. Somebody has to reverse that decision, since it was made, and we mean to reverse it, and we mean to do it peaceably.

What are the uses of decisions of courts? They have two uses. As rules of property they have two uses. First—they decide upon the question before the court. They decide in this case that Dred Scott is a slave. Nobody resists that. Not only that, but they say to every body else, that persons standing just as Dred Scott stands, is as he is. That is, they say that when a question comes up upon another person, it will be so decided again unless the Court decides in another way, unless the Court overrules its decision. [Renewed applause.] Well, we mean to do what we can to have the Court decide the other way. That is one thing we mean to try to do.

The sacredness that Judge Douglas throws around this decision, is a degree of sacredness that has never been before thrown around any other decision. I have never heard of such a thing. Why, decisions apparently contrary to that decision, have been made by that very Court before. It is the first of its kind; it is an *astonisher* in legal history. It is a new wonder of the world. It is based upon falsehoods in the main as to the facts—allegations of facts upon which it stands are not facts at all in many instances, and no decision made on any question—the first instance of a decision made under so many unfavorable circumstances—thus placed, has ever been held by the profession as law, and it has always needed confirmation before the lawyers regarded it as settled law. But Judge Douglas will have it that all hands must take this extraordinary decision, made under these extraordinary circumstances, and give their vote in Congress in accordance with it, yield to it and obey it in every possible sense. Circumstances alter cases. Do not gentlemen here remember the case of that same Supreme Court, twenty-five or thirty years ago, deciding that a National Bank was constitutional? I ask if somebody does not remember that a National Bank was declared to be constitutional? Such is the truth, whether it be remembered or not. The Bank charter ran out, and a re-charter was granted by Congress. That re-charter was laid before General Jackson. It was urged upon him, when he denied the constitutionality of the Bank, that the Supreme Court had decided that it was constitutional; and that General Jackson then said that the Supreme Court had no right to lay down a rule to govern a co-ordinate branch of the Government, the members of which had sworn to support the Constitution—that each member had sworn to support that Constitution as he understood it. I will venture here to say, that I have heard Judge Douglas say that he approved of General Jackson for that act. What has now become of all his tirade about "resistance to the Supreme Court?"   *   *   *

THE DECLARATION OF INDEPENDENCE.

We were often—more than once, at least—in the course of Judge Douglas' speech last night, reminded that this Government was made for white men—that he believed it was made for white men. Well, that is putting it into a shape in which no one wants to deny it; but the Judge then goes into his passion for drawing inferences that are not warranted. I protest, now and forever, against that counterfeit logic which presumes that because I did not want a negro woman for a slave, I do necessarily want her for a wife. My understanding is that I need not have her for either; but, as God made us separate, we can leave one another alone, and do one another much good thereby. There are white men enough to marry all the white women, and enough black men to marry all the black women, and in God's name let them be so married. The Judge regales us with the terrible enormities that take place by the mixture of races; that the inferior race bears the superior down. Why, Judge, if you do not let them get together in the Territories they won't mix there.

A voice—"Three cheers for Lincoln." (The cheers were given with a hearty good will.)

Mr. L.—I should say at least that this is a self-evident truth.

Now, it happens that we meet together once every year, some time about the Fourth of July, for some reason or other. These Fourth of July gatherings I suppose have their uses. If you will indulge me, I will state what I suppose to be some of them.

We are now a mighty nation; we are thirty, or about thirty, millions of people, and we own and inhabit about one-fifteenth part of the dry land of the whole earth. We run our memory back over the pages of history for about eighty-two years, and we discover that we were then a very small people in point of numbers, vastly inferior to what we are now, with a vastly less extent of country, with vastly less of everything we deem desirable among men—we look upon the change as exceedingly advantageous to us and to our posterity, and we fix upon something that happened away back, as in some way or other being connected with this rise of prosperity. We find a race of men living in that day whom we claim as our fathers and grandfathers; they were iron men; they fought for the principle that they were contending for; and we understood that by what they then did it has followed that the degree of prosperity which we now enjoy has come to us. We hold this annual celebration to remind ourselves of all the good done in this process of time, of how it was done and who did it, and how we are historically connected with it; and we go from these meetings in better humor with ourselves—we feel more attached the one to the other, and more firmly bound to the country we inhabit. In every way we are better men in the age, and race, and country in which we live, for these celebrations. But after we have done all this, we have not yet reached the whole. There is something else connected with it. We have, besides these—men descended by blood from our ancestors—those among us, perhaps half our people, who are not descendants at all of these men; they are men who

have come from Europe—German, Irish, French and Scandi-
navian—men that have come from Europe themselves, or
whose ancestors have come hither and settled here, finding
themselves our equals in all things.   If they look back
through this history to trace their connection with those days
by blood, they find they have none; they can not carry themselves back into that glorious epoch and make themselves feel
that they are part of us; but when they look through that old
Declaration of Independence, they find that those old men say
that " We hold these truths to be self-evident, that all men are
created equal," and then they feel that that moral sentiment,
taught on that day, evidences their relation to those men, that
it is the father of all moral principle in them, and that they
have a right to claim it as though they were blood of the
blood and flesh of the flesh of the men who wrote that Declaration [loud and long-continued applause], and so they are.
That is the electric cord in that Declaration that links the
hearts of patriotic and liberty-loving men together, that will
link those patriotic hearts as long as the love of freedom
exists in the minds of men throughout the world. [Applause.]

   Now, sirs, for the purpose of squaring things with this idea
of " don't care if slavery is voted up or voted down," for sustaining the Dred Scott decision, for holding that the Declaration of Independence did not mean anything at all, we have
Judge Douglas giving his exposition of what the Declaration
of Independence means, and we have him saying that the
people of America are equal to the people of England.
According to his construction, you Germans are not connected
with it.   Now I ask you in all soberness, if all these things,
if indulged in, if ratified, if confirmed and indorsed, if taught
to our children and repeated to them, do not tend to rub out
the sentiment of liberty in the country, and to transform this
Government into a government of some other form.   These
arguments that are made, that the inferior race are to be
treated with as much allowance as they are capable of enjoying; that as much is to be done for them as their condition
will allow—what are these arguments?   They are the arguments that Kings have made for enslaving the people in all
ages of the world.   You will find that all the arguments in
favor of King-craft were of this class; they always bestrode
the necks of the people, not that they wanted to do it, but
because the people were better off for being ridden.   That is
their argument, and this argument of the Judge is the same
old serpent that says: You work and I eat, you toil and I will
enjoy the fruits of it.   Turn it whatever way you will—
whether it come from the mouth of a King, an excuse for

enslaving the people of the country, or from the mouth of men of one race as a reason for enslaving the men of another race, it is all the same old serpent, and I hold if that course of argumentation that is made for the purpose of convincing the public mind that we should not care about this, should be granted, it does not stop with the negro. I should like to know if, taking this old Declaration of Independence, which declares that all men are equal upon principle, you begin making exceptions to it, where you will stop? If one man says it does not mean a negro, why not another say it does not mean some other man? If that declaration is not the truth, let us get the statute book, in which we find it, and tear it out! Who is so bold as to do it? If it is not true, let us tear it out! [cries of " no, no "]; let us stick to it then ; let us stand firmly by it then. [Applause.]

It may be argued that there are certain conditions that make necessities and impose them upon us, and to the extent that a necessity is imposed upon a man, he must submit to it. I think that was the condition in which we found ourselves when we established this Government. We had slaves among us ; we could not get our Constitution unless we permitted them to remain in slavery ; we could not secure the good we did secure if we grasped for more ; and having, by necessity, submitted to that much, it does not destroy the principle that is the charter of our liberties. Let that charter stand as our standard.

My friend has said to me that I am a poor hand to quote Scripture. I will try it again, however. It is said in one of the admonitions of our Lord: "As your Father in Heaven is perfect, be ye also perfect." The Saviour, I suppose, did not expect that any human creature could be perfect as the Father in Heaven ; but He said : "As your Father in Heaven is perfect, be ye also perfect." He set that up as a standard, and he who did most toward reaching that standard, attained the highest degree of moral perfection. So I say in relation to the principle that all men are created equal, let it be as nearly reached as we can. If we can not give freedom to every creature, let us do nothing that will impose slavery upon any other creature. [Applause.] Let us then turn this Government back into the channel in which the framers of the Constitution originally placed it. Let us stand firmly by each other. If we do not do so we are turning in the contrary direction, that our friend Judge Douglas proposes—not intentionally—as working in the traces tends to make this one universal slave nation. He is one that runs in that direction, and as such I resist him.

My friends, I have detained you about as long as I desired to do, and I have only to say, let us discard all this quibbling about this man and the other man—this race and that race and the other race being inferior, and therefore they must be placed in an inferior position—discarding our standard that we have left us. Let us discard all these things, and unite as one people throughout this land, until we shall once more stand up declaring that all men are created equal.

My friends, I could not, without launching off upon some new topic, which would detain you too long, continue to-night. I thank you for this most extensive audience that you have furnished me to-night. I leave you, hoping that the lamp of liberty will burn in your bosoms until there shall no longer be a doubt that all men are created free and equal.

Mr. Lincoln retired amid long-continued applause.

A week later than his Chicago speech, Mr. Douglas spoke at Bloomington, in continuation of his canvass. Here again, he laid great stress upon his " popular sovereignty " device, and upon his Anti-Lecompton rebellion. He also repeated substantially his two issues against Mr. Lincoln, based upon the Springfield speech of June 16th. Mr. Lincoln was present and heard him. The next day Mr. Douglas made a speech of similar character at Springfield, at which Mr. Lincoln was not present. The latter, however, spoke on the same evening at that place. The following are some of the chief points of Mr. Lincoln's speech on this occasion (July 17, 1858) :

INEQUALITIES OF THE CONTEST—THE APPORTIONMENT, ETC.

FELLOW-CITIZENS : Another election, which is deemed an important one, is approaching, and, as I suppose, the Republican party will, without much difficulty, elect their State ticket. But, in regard to the Legislature, we, the Republicans, labor under some disadvantages. In the first place, we have a Legislature to elect upon an apportionment of the representation made several years ago, when the proportion of the population was far greater in the South (as compared with the North) than it now is ; and inasmuch as our opponents hold almost entire sway in the South, and we a correspondingly large majority in the North, the fact that we are now to be represented as we were years ago, when the population was different, is, to us, a very great disadvantage. We had in the year 1855, according to law, a census, or enumeration of the inhabitants, taken for the purpose of a new apportionment of representation. We know what a fair apportionment of representation upon that census would give us. We know that it could not, if fairly made, fail to give the Republican party from six to ten more members of the Legislature than they can probably get as the law now stands. It so happened at the last session of the Legislature, that our opponents, holding the control of both branches of the Legislature, steadily refused to give us such an apportionment as we were rightly entitled to have upon the census already taken. The Legislature would pass no bill upon that subject, except such as was at least as unfair to us as the old one, and in which, in some instances, two men from the Democratic regions were allowed to go as far toward sending a member to the Legislature as three were in the Republican regions. Comparison was made at the time as to representative and senatorial districts, which completely demonstrated that such was the fact. Such a bill was passed, and tendered to the Republican Governor for his signature; but, principally for the reasons I have stated, he withheld his approval, and the bill fell without becoming a law.

Another disadvantage under which we labor is, that there are one or two Democratic Senators who will be members of the next Legislature, and will vote for the election of Senator, who are holding over in districts in which we could, on all reasonable calculation, elect men of our own, if we only had the chance of an election. When we consider that there are but twenty-five Senators in the Senate, taking two from the side where they rightfully belong, and adding them to the other, is to us a disadvantage not to be lightly regarded. Still, so it is; we have this to contend with. Perhaps there is no ground of complaint on our part. In attending to the many things involved in the last general election for President, Governor, Auditor, Treasurer, Superintendent of Public Instruction, members of Congress and of the Legislature, County Officers, and so on, we allowed these things to happen for want of sufficient attention, and we have no cause to complain of our adversaries, so far as this matter is concerned. But we have some cause to complain of the refusal to give us a fair apportionment.

There is still another disadvantage under which we labor, and to which I will ask your attention. It arises out of the relative position of the two persons who stand before the State as candidates for the Senate. Senator Douglas is of world-wide renown. All the anxious politicians of his party, or who have been of his party for years past, have been looking upon him as certainly, at no distant day, to be the President of the

15

United States.   They have seen in his round, jolly, fruitfu.
face, post-offices, land offices, marshalships, and cabinet
appointments, chargeships and foreign missions, bursting and
sprouting out in wonderful luxuriance, ready to be laid hold
of by their greedy hands. [Great laughter.]   And as they
have been gazing upon this attractive picture so long, they
can not, in the little distraction that has taken place in the
party, bring themselves to give up the charming hope; but
with greedier anxiety they rush about him, sustain him, and
give him marches, triumphal entries, and receptions, beyond
what even in the days of his highest prosperity they could
have brought about in his favor.   On the contrary, nobody
has ever expected me to be President.   In my poor, lean, lank
face, nobody has ever seen that any cabbages were sprouting
out. [Cheering and laughter.]   These are disadvantages all,
that the Republicans labor under.   We have to fight this battle upon principle, and upon principle alone.   I am, in a certain sense, made the standard-bearer in behalf of the Republicans.   I was made so merely because there had to be some
one so placed—I being in no wise preferable to any other one
of the twenty-five—perhaps a hundred—we have in the Republican ranks.   Then I say I wish it to be distinctly understood
and borne in mind, that we have to fight this battle without
many—perhaps without any—of the external aids which are
brought to bear against us.   So I hope those with whom I am
surrounded have principle enough to nerve themselves for the
task, and leave nothing undone, that can be fairly done, to
bring about the right result.

THE DOUGLAS PROGRAMME.

After Senator Douglas left Washington, as his movements
were made known by the public prints, he tarried a considerable time in the city of New York; and it was heralded that,
like another Napoleon, he was lying by and framing the plan
of his campaign.   It was telegraphed to Washington city, and
published in the *Union*, that he was framing his plan for the
purpose of going to Illinois to pounce upon and annihilate the
treasonable and disunion speech which Lincoln had made here
on the 16th of June.   Now, I do suppose the Judge really
spent some time in New York maturing the plan of the campaign, as his friends heralded for him.   1 have been able, by
noting his movements since his arrival in Illinois, to discover
evidences confirmatory of that allegation.   I think I have
been able to see what are the material points of that plan.   I
will, for a little while, ask your attention to some of them.

What I shall point out, though not showing the whole plan, are, nevertheless, the main points, as I suppose.

They are not very numerous. The first is Popular Sovereignty. The second and third are attacks upon my speech made on the 16th of June. Out of these three points—drawing within the range of Popular Sovereignty the question of the Lecompton Constitution—he makes his principal assault. Upon these his successive speeches are substantially one and the same. On this matter of Popular Sovereignty, I wish to be a little careful. Auxiliary to these main points, to be sure, are their thunderings of cannon, their marching and music, their fizzle-gigs and fire-works; but I will not waste time with them. They are but the little trappings of the campaign.

POPULAR SOVEREIGNTY.

Coming to the substance—the first point—"Popular Sovereignty." It is to be labeled upon the cars in which he travels; put upon the hacks he rides in; to be flaunted upon the arches he passes under, and the banners which wave over him. It is to be dished up in as many varieties as a French cook can produce soups from potatoes. Now, as this is so great a staple of the plan of the campaign, it is worth while to examine it carefully; and if we examine only a very little, and do not allow ourselves to be misled, we shall be able to see that the whole thing is the most arrant Quixotism that was ever enacted before a community. What is this matter of Popular Sovereignty? The first thing, in order to understand it, is to get a good definition of what it is, and after that to see how it is applied.

I suppose almost every one knows, that in this controversy, whatever has been said has had reference to the question of negro slavery. We have not been in a controversy about the right of the people to govern themselves in the *ordinary* matters of domestic concern in the States and Territories. Mr. Buchanan, in one of his late messages (I think when he sent up the Lecompton Constitution), urged that the main point to which the public attention had been directed, was not in regard to the great variety of small domestic matters, but it was directed to the question of negro slavery; and he asserts that if the people had had a fair chance to vote on that question, there was no reasonable ground of objection in regard to minor questions. Now, while I think that the people had *not* had given, or offered them, a fair chance upon that slavery question; still, if there had been a fair submission to a vote upon that main question, the President's proposition would have been true to the uttermost. Hence, when hereafter I speak of Popular Sovereignty. I wish to be understood as applying what I say to the question of slavery only, not to other minor domestic matters of a Territory or a State.

Does Judge Douglas, when he says that several of the past years of his life have been devoted to the question of "Popular Sovereignty," and that all the remainder of his life shall be devoted to it, does he mean to say that he has been devoting his life to securing to the people of the Territories the right to exclude slavery from the Territories? If he means so to say, he means to deceive; because he—and every one knows that the decision of the Supreme Court, which he approves and makes an especial ground of attack upon me for disapproving—forbids the people of a Territory to exclude slavery. This covers the whole ground, from the settlement of a Territory till it reaches the degree of maturity entitling it to form a State Constitution. So far as all that ground is concerned, the Judge is not sustaining Popular Sovereignty, but absolutely opposing it. He sustains the decision which declares that the popular will of the Territories has no constitutional power to exclude slavery during their Territorial existence. [Cheers.] This being so, the period of time, from the first settlement of a Territory till it reaches the point of forming a State Constitution, is not the thing that the Judge has fought for, or is fighting for, but, on the contrary, he has fought for, and is fighting for, the thing that annihilates and crushes out that same Popular Sovereignty.

Well, so much being disposed of, what is left? Why, he is contending for the right of the people, when they come to make a State Constitution, to make it for themselves, and precisely as best suits themselves. I say again, that is Quixotic. I defy contradiction, when I declare that the Judge can find no one to oppose him on that proposition. I repeat, there is nobody opposing that proposition on *principle*. Let me not be misunderstood. I know that, with reference to the Lecompton Constitution, I may be misunderstood; but when you understand me correctly, my proposition will be true and accurate. Nobody is opposing, or has opposed, the right of the people, when they form a Constitution, to form it for themselves. Mr. Buchanan and his friends have not done it; they, too, as well as the Republicans and the Anti-Lecompton Democrats, have not done it; but, on the contrary, they together have insisted on the right of the people to form a Constitution for themselves. The difference between the Buchanan men, on the one hand, and the Douglas men and the Republicans on the other, has not been on a question of principle, but on a question of *fact*.

The dispute was upon the question of fact, whether the Lecompton Constitution had been fairly formed by the people, or not. Mr. Buchanan and his friends have not contended for the contrary principle, any more than the Douglas men or the Republicans. They have insisted, that whatever of small irregularities existed in getting up the Lecompton Constitution, were such as happen in the settlement of all new Territories. The question was, was it a fair emanation of the people? It was a question of fact, and not of principle. As to the principle, all were agreed. Judge Douglas voted with the Republicans upon that matter of fact.

He and they, by their voices and votes, denied that it was a fair emanation of the people. The Administration affirmed that it was. With respect to the evidence bearing upon that question of fact, I readily agree that Judge Douglas and the Republicans had the right on their side, and that the Administration was wrong. But I state again that, as a matter of principle, there is no dispute upon the right of a people in a Territory, merging into a State, to form a Constitution for themselves, without outside interference from any quarter. This being so, what is Judge Douglas going to spend his life for? Is he going to spend his life in maintaining a principle that nobody on earth opposes? [Cheers.] Does he expect to stand up in majestic dignity, and go through his *apotheosis*, and become a god, in the maintaining of a principle which neither man nor mouse, in all God's creation, is opposing? [Great applause.]

THE LECOMPTON ISSUE.

How will he prove that we have ever occupied a different position in regard to the Lecompton Constitution, or any principle in it? He says he did not make his opposition on the ground as to whether it was a free or a slave Constitution, and he would have you understand that the Republicans made their opposition because it ultimately became a slave Constitution. To make proof in favor of himself on this point, he reminds us that he opposed Lecompton before the vote was taken declaring whether the State was to be free or slave. But he forgets to say, that our Republican Senator, Trumbull, made a speech against Lecompton even before he did.

Why did he oppose it? Partly, as he declares, because the members of the Convention who framed it were not fairly elected by the people; that the people were not allowed to vote unless they had been registered; and that the people of whole counties, in some instances, were not registered. For these reasons he declares the Constitution was not an emanation, in any true sense, from the people. He also has an additional objection as to the mode of submitting the Constitution back to the people. But bearing on the question of whether the delegates were fairly elected, a speech of his made something more than twelve months ago, from this stand, becomes important. It was made a little while before the election of the delegates who made Lecompton. In that speech he declared there was every reason to hope and believe the election would be fair; and if any one failed to vote it would be his own fault.

I, a few days after, made a sort of answer to that speech. In that answer, I made, substantially, the very argument with which he combated his Lecompton adversaries in the Senate last winter. I pointed to the fact that the people could not vote without being registered, and that the time for registering had gone by. I commented on it as wonderful that Judge Douglas could be ignorant of these facts, which every one else in the nation so well knew.

[Mr. Lincoln then proceeded to notice the attacks made by Douglas on the 6th of June speech of the former. In substance, it is like his reply at Chicago. Some of its more striking passages are here subjoined.]

He charges, in substance, that I invite a war of sections; that I propose that all the local institutions of the different States shall become consolidated and uniform. What is there in the language of that speech which expresses such purpose, or bears such construction? I have again and again said that I would not enter into any of the States to disturb the institution of slavery. Judge Douglas said, at Bloomington, that I used language most able and ingenious for concealing what I really meant; and that, while I had protested against entering into the slave States, I nevertheless did mean to go on the banks of the Ohio and throw missiles into Kentucky, to disturb the people there in their domestic institutions.

I said in that speech, and I meant no more, that the institution of slavery ought to be placed in the very attitude where the framers of this Government placed it, and left it. I do not understand that the framers of our Constitution left the people of the free States in the attitude of firing bombs or shells into the slave States. I was not using that passage for the purpose for which he infers I did use it. * * * Now you all see, from that quotation, I did not express my *wish* on anything. In that passage I indicated no wish or purpose of my own; I simply expressed my *expectation*.

[Further on, Mr. Lincoln said :]

Mr. Brooks, of South Carolina, in one of his speeches, when they were presenting him canes, silver plate, gold pitchers and the like, for assaulting Senator Sumner, distinctly affirmed his opinion that when this Constitution was formed, it was the belief of no man that slavery would last to the present day.

He said, what I think, that the framers of our Constitution placed the institution of slavery where the public mind rested in the hope that it was in the course of ultimate extinction. But he went on to say that the men of the present age, by their experience, have become wiser than the framers of the Constitution ; and the invention of the cotton-gin had made the perpetuity of slavery a necessity in this country.

[Recurring to the Dred Scott case, after citing Jefferson's views on judicial decisions, and alluding to the course of the Democracy, Douglas included, in regard to the National Bank decision, Mr. Lincoln said :]

Now, I wish to know what the Judge can charge upon me with respect to decisions of the Supreme Court, which does not lie in all its length, breadth and proportions at his own door. The plain truth is simply this : Judge Douglas is *for* Supreme Court decisions when he likes, and against them when he does not like them. He is for the Dred Scott decision because it tends to nationalize slavery—because it is part of the original combination for that object. It so happened, singularly enough, that I never stood opposed to a decision of the Supreme Court till this. On the contrary, I have no recollection that he was ever particularly in favor of one till this. He never was in favor of any, nor I opposed to any, till the present one, which helps to nationalize slavery.

Free men of Sangamon—free men of Illinois—free men everywhere—judge ye between him and me, upon this issue.

Near the close of July, various speeches having been made by each at different points, an arrangement for one joint discussion in each of the seven Congressional districts, in which they had not already both spoken, was agreed upon. At this stage of the canvass, the people of the whole country were beginning to take a lively interest in this contest, and the reports of the first debate at Ottawa were eagerly sought for and read, at the East and at the West. The friends of Mr. Lincoln, and the Republicans in general, were well pleased with the manner in which he acquitted himself in this **joint** discussion. At each succeeding encounter of this sort, the impression was strengthened, throughout the country, that Mr Lincoln was obtaining decided advantages over his opponent. At Freeport, he forced Douglas into an attempted reconciliation of the hitherto unexplained inconsistencies between his squatter sovereignty theory, and his support of the Dred Scott decision, which utterly excludes squatter sovereignty in practice. His "unfriendly legislation" device, on that occasion, cost Douglas the loss of the last possibility of any reconciliation with the Southern Democracy. While this answer, most unwillingly given, perhaps, yet announced with apparent alacrity, contributed something toward effecting his immediate temporary purpose, it undoubtedly destroyed all his remoter chances as the Presidential candidate of a united Democracy.

In the Ottawa debate, Mr. Douglas produced a series of "ultra" resolutions adopted at a small local convention held long before the Republican party was organized in that State, representing them as the platform adopted by "the first mass State Convention ever held in Illinois by the Republican party." On these resolutions, to which he assumed to believe that Mr. Lincoln was committed, Douglas based a series of interrogatories, which the former, after duly exposing the misrepresentation, frankly and very explicitly answered at Freeport, the scene of the second debate, as follows:

OPENING PASSAGES OF MR. LINCOLN'S FREEPORT SPEECH.

LADIES AND GENTLEMEN:—On Saturday last, Judge Douglas and myself first met in public discussion. He spoke one hour, I an hour and a half, and he replied for half an hour. The order is now reversed. I am to speak an hour, he an hour and a half, and then I am to reply for half an hour. I propose to devote myself during the first hour to the scope of what was brought within the range of his half-hour speech at Ottawa. Of course there was brought within the scope of that half-hour's speech something of his own opening speech. In the course of that opening argument, Judge Douglas proposed to me seven distinct interrogatories. In my speech of an hour and a half, I attended to some other parts of his speech, and incidentally, as I thought, answered one of the interrogatories then. I then distinctly intimated to him that I would answer the rest of his interrogatories on condition only that he should agree to answer as many for me. He made no intimation at the time of the proposition, nor did he in his reply allude at all to that suggestion of mine. I do him no injustice in saying that he occupied at least half of his reply in dealing with me as though I had *refused* to answer his interrogatories. I now propose that I will answer any of the interrogatories, upon condition that he will answer questions from me not exceeding the same number. I give him an opportunity to respond. The Judge remains silent. I now say that I will answer his interrogatories, whether he answers mine or not [applause] ; and that after I have done so, I shall propound mine to him. [Applause.]

I have supposed myself, since the organization of the Republican party at Bloomington, in May, 1856, bound as a party man by the platforms of the party, then and since. If in any interrogatories which I shall answer I go beyond the scope of what is within these platforms, it will be perceived that no one is responsible but myself.

Having said thus much, I will take up the Judge's interrogatories as I find them printed in the Chicago *Times*, and answer them *seriatim*. In order that there may be no mistake about it, I have copied the interrogatories in writing, and also my answers to them. The first one of these interrogatories is in these words:

Question 1. "I desire to know whether Lincoln to-day stands, as he did in 1854, in favor of the unconditional repeal of the Fugitive Slave law?"

Answer. I do not now, nor ever did, stand in favor of the unconditional repeal of the Fugitive Slave law.

Q. 2. "I desire him to answer whether he stands pledged to-day, as he did in 1854, against the admission of any more slave States into the Union, even if the people want them ?"

A. I do not now, nor ever did, stand pledged against the admission of any more slave States into the Union.

Q. 3. "I want to know whether he stands pledged against the admission of a new State in the Union, with such a Constitution as the people of that State may see fit to make."

A. I do not stand pledged against the admission of a new State into the Union, with such a Constitution as the people of that State may see fit to make.

Q. 4. "I want to know whether he stands to-day pledged to the abolition of slavery in the District of Columbia?"

12

A. I do not stand to-day pledged to the abolition of slavery in the District of Columbia.

Q. 5. "I desire him to answer whether he stands pledged to the prohibition of the slave-trade between the different States?"

A. I do not stand pledged to the prohibition of the slave-trade between the different States.

Q. 6. "I desire to know whether he stands pledged to prohibit slavery in all the Territories of the United States, North as well as South of the Missouri Compromise line?"

A. I am impliedly, if not expressly, pledged to a belief in the *right* and *duty* of Congress to prohibit slavery in all the United States Territories. (Great applause.)

Q. 7. "I desire him to answer whether he is opposed to the acquisition of any new territory unless slavery is first prohibited therein?"

A. I am not generally opposed to honest acquisition of territory; and, in any given case, I would or would not oppose such acquisition, accordingly as I might think such acquisition would or would not agitate the slavery question among ourselves.

Now, my friends, it will be perceived, upon an examination of these questions and answers, that so far I have only answered that I was not *pledged* to this, that or the other. The Judge has not framed his interrogatories to ask me any thing more than this, and I have answered in strict accordance with the interrogatories, and have answered truly that I am not *pledged* at all upon any of the points to which I have answered. But I am not disposed to hang upon the exact form of his interrogatory. I am rather disposed to take up at least some of these questions, and state what I really think upon them.

As to the first one, in regard to the Fugitive Slave law, I have never hesitated to say, and I do not now hesitate to say, that I think, under the Constitution of the United States, the people of the Southern States are entitled to a Congressional Slave law. Having said that, I have had nothing to say in regard to the existing Fugitive Slave law, further than that I think it should have been framed so as to be free from some of the objections that pertain to it, without lessening its efficiency. And inasmuch as we are not now in an agitation in regard to an alteration or modification of that law, I would not be the man to introduce it as a new subject of agitation upon the general question of slavery.

In regard to the other question, of whether I am pledged to the admission of any more slave States into the Union, I state to you very frankly that I would be exceedingly sorry ever to be put in a position of having to pass upon that question. I should be exceedingly glad to know that there would never be another slave State admitted into the Union; but I must add, that if slavery shall be kept out of the Territories during the Territorial existence of any one given Territory, and then the people shall, having a fair chance and a clear field, when they come to adopt the Constitution, do such an extraordinary thing as to adopt a slave Constitution, uninfluenced by the actual presence of the institution among them, I see no alternative if we own the country, but to admit them into the Union. [Applause.]

The third interrogatory is answered by the answer to the second, it being, as I conceive, the same as the second.

The fourth one is in regard to the abolition of slavery in the District of Columbia. In relation to that, I have my mind very distinctly made up. I should be exceedingly glad to see slavery abolished in the District of Columbia. I believe that Congress possesses the constitutional power to abolish it. Yet as a member of Congress, I should not, with my present views, be in favor of *endeavoring* to abolish slavery in the District of Columbia, unless it would be upon these conditions : *First*, that the abolition should be gradual ; *second*, that it should be on a vote of the majority of qualified voters in the District; and *third*, that compensation should be made to unwilling owners. With these three conditions, I confess I would be exceedingly glad to see Congress abolish slavery in the District of Columbia, and, in the language of Henry Clay, " sweep from our Capital that foul blot upon our nation."

In regard to the fifth interrogatory, I must say here, that as to the question of the abolition of the slave-trade between the different States, I can truly answer, as I have, that I am *pledged* to nothing about it. It is a subject to which I have not given that mature consideration that would make me feel authorized to state a position so as to hold myself entirely bound by it. In other words, that question has never been prominently enough before me to induce me to investigate whether we really have the constitutional power to do it. I could investigate it if I had sufficient time to bring myself to a conclusion upon that subject; but I have not done so, and I say so frankly to you here, and to Judge Douglas. I must say, however, that if I should be of opinion that Congress does possess the constitutional power to abolish slave-trading among the different States, I should still not be in favor of the exercise of that power, unless upon some conservative principle as I conceive it, akin to what I have said in relation to the abolition of slavery in the District of Columbia.

My answer as to whether I desire that slavery should be prohibited in all Territories of the United States, is full and explicit within itself, and can not be made clearer by any comments of mine. So I suppose in regard to the question whether I am opposed to the acquisition of any more territory unless slavery is first prohibited therein, my answer is such that I could add nothing by way of illustration, or making myself better understood, than the answer which I have placed in writing.

Now in all this, the Judge has me, and he has me on the record. I suppose he had flattered himself that I was really entertaining one set of opinions for one place, and another set for another place—that I was afraid to say at one place what I uttered at another. What I am saying here, I suppose I say to a vast audience as strongly tending to Abolitionism as any audience in the State of Illinois, and I believe I am saying that which, if it would be offensive to any persons and render them enemies to myself, would be offensive to persons in this audience.

At Jonesboro, in the lower part of "Egypt," where their third debate was held, Douglas reiterated his often-refuted charges of ultraism against Lincoln, which the latter just as coolly and convincingly disposed of, as if there had been no unreasonable pertinacity in making unjust accusations against him. After bringing home the sin of re-opening agitation, to the door of Douglas, he proceeded to show as extravagant radicalism in the recorded professions of the Democracy as of any persons acting with the Republican party. He then completely riddled the "unfriendly legislation" theory of Douglas, exhibiting its utter inconsistency with fidelity to his constitutional oaths, so long as he indorsed the validity of the political dogmas of Judge Taney, in his Dred Scott opinion.

In the fourth debate, at Charleston, the attempts of Douglas to make capital out of the Mexican War question were appropriately disposed of. Here, also, Douglas was convicted, on conclusive testimony, of having *stricken out* of the Toombs' Kansas Bill a clause requiring the Constitution that should be formed under its provisions, to be submitted to the people.

This had an important bearing on one objection upon which Douglas based his Anti-Lecompton rebellion.

The fifth joint discussion was held at Galesburg, the sixth at Quincy, and the last at Alton. The main topics and methods of these debates, as of the rest, did not substantially differ from those of the speeches at Chicago and Springfield.

The Alton debate occurred on the 15th of October. As the day of the election (November 2d) approached, it became more and more evident that strong efforts were making, aided by the advice of Senator Crittenden on the one hand, and of Vice-President Breckinridge on the other, to secure a diversion of " Conservative " votes—American, Democratic, and Whig—in the central and southern parts of the State, in favor of Douglas. These endeavors succeeded to such an extent that, with the immense advantages the Douglas party had in their unequal and utterly unfair apportionment of Legislative Districts, and in the lucky proportion of Democratic Senators holding over, they secured a small majority in each branch of the new Legislature. The Senate had 14 Democrats and 11 Republicans— the House 40 Democrats and 35 Republicans. The popular voice was for Lincoln, by *more than four thousand majority,* over Douglas.

Admiration of the manly bearing and gallant conduct of Mr. Lincoln, throughout this campaign, which had early assumed a national importance, led to the spontaneous suggestion of his name, in various parts of the country, as a candidate for the Presidency. From the beginning to the end of the contest, he had proved himself an able statesman, an effective orator, a true gentleman, and an honest man. While, therefore, Douglas was returned to the Senate, there was a general presentiment that a juster verdict was yet to be had, and that Mr. Lincoln and his cause would be ultimately vindicated before the people. That time was to come, even sooner, perhaps, than his friends, in their momentary despondency, expected. From that hour to the present, the fame of Abraham Lincoln has been enlarging and ripening, and the love of his noble character has become more and more deeply fixed in the popular heart.

CHAPTER XII.

SPEECHES OF 1859-'60.

Mr. Lincoln in Ohio.—His Speech at Columbus.—Denial of the Negro
Suffrage Charge.—Troubles of Douglas with His "Great Princi-
ple."—Territories Not States.—Doctrines of the Fathers.—His Cin-
cinnati Speech.—"Shooting Over the Line."—What the Republicans
Mean to Do.—Plain Questions to the Democracy.—The People Above
Courts and Congress.—Uniting the Opposition.—Eastern Tour.—
The Cooper Institute Speech.—Mr. Bryant's Introduction.—What
the Fathers Held.—What will Satisfy the Southern Democracy ?—
Counsels to the Republicans.—Mr. Lincoln Among the Children.

DURING the year following his great contest with Douglas,
which had resulted in a barren triumph through the injustice
of the previous Democratic Legislature in refusing a fair and
equal apportionment, Mr. Lincoln again gave himself almost
exclusively to professional labors. During the autumn campaign of 1859, however, when Douglas visited Ohio, and
endeavored to turn the tide of battle in favor of the Democracy in that State, so as to secure the re-election of Mr. Pugh,
and to gain other partisan benefits, an earnest invitation was
sent to Lincoln to assist the Republicans in their canvass. He
complied, and delivered two most effective speeches in Ohio, one
at Columbus, and the other at Cincinnati.

In his speech at the former place (September 16, 1859), he
began by noticing a statement which he read from the central
Democratic organ, averring that in the canvass of the previous
year with Douglas, " Mr. Lincoln declared in favor of negro
suffrage." This charge he quickly disposed of, showing by
quotations from his printed speeches of that canvass, that he

distinctly and repeatedly declared himself *opposed* to the policy thus attributed to him.

Mr. Lincoln then noticed the recent Columbus speech of Mr. Douglas, in which he "dealt exclusively" in the "negro topics" of discussion. Mr. L. spoke at some length on these issues, and thoroughly exposed the distinctions between genuine popular sovereignty, and the spurious sort which Douglas and his friends passed off for the reality. He then went on to notice the great amount of trouble which Mr. Douglas had had with his spurious popular sovereignty, and to illustrate how "his explanations explanatory of explanations explained are interminable." The *Harper's Magazine* essay of Douglas on this subject was dissected, and left without any logical vitality or cohesion. Two or three brief points in the remainder of this speech are subjoined :

STATES AND TERRITORIES.

There is another little difficulty about this matter of treating the Territories and States alike in all things, to which I ask your attention, and I shall leave this branch of the case. If there is no difference between them, why not make the Territories States at once? What is the reason that Kansas was not fit to come into the Union when it was organized into a Territory, in Judge Douglas' view? Can any of you tell any reason why it should not have come into the Union at once? They are fit, as he thinks, to decide upon the slavery question—the largest and most important with which they could possibly deal—what could they do by coming into the Union that they are not fit to do, according to his view, by staying out of it? Oh, they are not fit to sit in Congress and decide upon the rates of postage, or questions of *ad valorem* or specific duties on foreign goods, or live oak timber contracts. [Laughter.] They are not fit to decide these vastly important matters, which are national in their import, but they are fit, "from the jump," to decide this little negro question. But, gentlemen, the case is too plain; I occupy too much time on this head, and I pass on.

STAND BY THE DOCTRINES OF THE FATHERS.

I see in the Judge's speech here a short sentence in these word: "Our fathers, when they formed this Government under which we live, understood this question just as well, and even better than we do now." That is true. I stick to that. [Great cheers and laughter.]   I will stand by Judge Douglas in that to the bitter end. [Renewed laughter.]   And now, Judge Douglas, come and stand by me, and faithfully show how they acted, understanding it better than we do. All I ask of you, Judge Douglas, is to stick to the proposition that the men of the Revolution understood this subject better than we do now, *and with that better understanding they acted better than you are trying to act now.* [Applause.]

At Cincinnati, on the 17th of September, Mr. Lincoln addressed an immense audience on the same general political topics, and in his ablest manner. He did not repeat or merely play variations upon his Columbus speech, but adopted new modes of illustrating and enforcing his views. He was listened to with an interest rarely excited by any orator who ever spoke in this city, even in the most exciting campaign. No extracts can give a true idea of its ability and power as a whole. Alluding to Douglas' perversions of his views, and to the charge of wishing to disturb slavery in the States by " shooting over" the line, Mr. Lincoln said :

SHOOTING OVER THE LINE.

It has occurred to me here to-night, that if I ever do shoot over at the people on the other side of the line in a slave State, and purpose to do so, keeping my skin safe, that I have now about the best chance I shall ever have. [Laughter and applause.]   I should not wonder if there are some Kentuckians about this audience ; we are close to Kentucky , and whether that be so or not, we are on elevated ground, and by speaking distinctly, I should not wonder if some of the Ken tuckians should hear me on the other side of the river. [Laughter.]   For that reason I propose to address a portion of what I have to say to the Kentuckians.

I say, then, in the first place, to the Kentuckians, that I am what they call, as I understand it, a " Black Republican." [Applause and Laughter.]   I think that slavery is wrong, morally, socially and politically.   I desire that it should be no further spread in these United States, and I should not object if it should gradually terminate in the whole Union. [Applause.]   While I say this for myself, I say to you, Kentuckians, that I understand that you differ radically with me upon this proposition ; that you believe slavery is a good thing · that slavery is right ; that it ought to be extended and perpetuated in this Union. Now, there being this broad difference between us, I do not pretend in addressing myself to you, Kentuckians, to attempt proselyting you at all; that would be a vain effort. I do not enter upon it. I only propose to try to show you that you ought to nominate for the next Presidency, at Charleston, my distinguished friend, Judge Douglas. [Applause.] In whatever there is a difference between you and him, I understand he is as sincerely for you, and more wisely for you, than you are for yourselves. [Applause.] I will try to demonstrate that proposition. Understand, now, I say that I believe he is as sincerely for you, and more wisely for you, than you are for yourselves.

Mr. Lincoln then went on to show that Douglas was constantly endeavoring to "mold the public opinion of the North to the ends" desired by the South; that he only differed from the South in so far as was necessary to retain any hold upon his own section; that not daring to maintain that slavery is right, he professed an indifference whether it was "voted up or voted down"—thus indirectly advancing the opinion that it is not wrong; and that he had taken a step in advance, by doing what would not have been thought of by any man five years ago, to-wit:—denying that the Declaration of Independence asserts any principle intended to be applicable to black men, or that properly includes them. The tendency of this doctrine "is to bring the public mind to the conclusion that when men are spoken of, the negro is not meant; that when negroes are spoken of, brutes alone are contemplated.

Of the certainty of a speedy Republican triumph in the nation, and of its results, Mr. Lincoln said:

WHAT THE OPPOSITION MEAN TO DO.

I will tell you, so far as I am authorized to speak for the Opposition, what we mean to do with you. We mean to treat you, as nearly as we possibly can, as Washington, Jefferson, and Madison treated you. [Cheers.] We mean to leave you alone, and in no way to interfere with your institution; to abide by all and every compromise of the Constitution, and, in a word, coming back to the original proposition, to treat you, so far as degenerated men (if we have degenerated) may, imitating the examples of those noble fathers—Wash-

16

ington, Jefferson and Madison. [Applause.] We mean to remember that you are as good as we; that there is no difference between us, other than the difference of circumstances. We mean to recognize and bear in mind always that you have as good hearts in your bosoms as other people, or as we claim to have, and treat you accordingly. We mean to marry your girls when we have a chance—the white ones I mean—[laughter] and I have the honor to inform you that I once did get a chance in that way. [A voice, " Good for you," and applause.]

PLAIN QUESTIONS TO THE DISUNION DEMOCRACY.

I have told you what we mean to do. I want to know, now, when that thing takes place, what you mean to do. I often hear it intimated that you mean to divide the Union whenever a Republican, or anything like it, is elected President of the United States. [A voice, " That is so."] " That is so," one of them says. I wonder if he is a Kentuckian. [A voice, " He is a Douglas man."] Well, then, I want to know what you are going to do with your half of it? [Applause and laughter.] Are you going to split the Ohio down through, and push your half off a piece? Or are you going to keep it right alongside of us outrageous fellows? Or are you going to build up a wall someway between your country and ours, by which that movable property of yours can't come over here any more, and you lose it? Do you think you can better yourselves on that subject, by leaving us here under no obligation whatever to return those specimens of your movable property that come hither? You have divided the Union because we would not do right with you, as you think, upon that subject; when we cease to be under obligations to do anything for you, how much better off do you think you will be? Will you make war upon us and kill us all? Why, gentlemen, I think you are as gallant and as brave men as live; that you can fight as bravely in a good cause, man for man, as any other people living : that you have shown yourselves capable of this upon various occasions ; but, man for man, you are not better than we are, and there are not so many of you as there are of us. [Loud cheering.] You will never make much of a hand at whipping us. If we were fewer in numbers than you, I think that you could whip us ; if we were equal, it would likely be a drawn battle ; but being inferior in numbers, you will make nothing by attempting to master us.

WHAT REPUBLICANS MUST DO.

I say that we must not interfere with the institution of slavery in the States where it exists, because the Constitution forbids it, and the general welfare does not require us to do so. We must not withhold an efficient fugitive slave law, because the Constitution requires us, as I understand it, not to withhold such a law, but we must prevent the outspreading of the institution, because neither the Constitution nor the general welfare requires us to extend it. We must prevent the revival of the African slave-trade and the enacting by Congress of a Territorial slave-code. We must prevent each of these things being done by either Congresses or Courts. THE PEOPLE OF THESE UNITED STATES ARE THE RIGHTFUL MASTERS OF BOTH CONGRESSES AND COURTS [applause], not to overthrow the Constitution, but to overthrow the men who pervert that Constitution. [Applause.]

After expressing an earnest desire "that all the elements of the Opposition should unite in the next Presidential election and in all future time," on a right and just basis; and after saying, "There are plenty of men in the slave States that are altogether good enough for me to be either President or Vice-President, provided they will profess sympathy with our purpose in the election, and will place themselves upon such ground that our men, upon principle, can vote for them," Mr. Lincoln brought his remarks to a close.

In the spring of 1860, Mr. Lincoln yielded to the calls which came to him from the East for his presence and aid in the exciting political canvasses there going on. He spoke at various places in Connecticut, New Hampshire, and Rhode Island, and also in New York city, to very large audiences, and was everywhere warmly welcomed. Perhaps one of the greatest speeches of his life, was that delivered by him at the Cooper Institute, in New York, on the 27th of February, 1860. A crowded audience was present, which received Mr. Lincoln with enthusiastic demonstrations. William Cullen Bryant presided, and introduced the speaker in terms of high compliment to the West, and to the "eminent citizen" of that section, whose political labors in 1856 and '58 were appropriately eulogized.

THE COOPER INSTITUTE SPEECH.

Mr. Lincoln then proceeded to address his auditors in an extended and closely-reasoned argument, proving in the most convincing manner that the Republican party stands where

" the Fathers" stood on the slavery question, and eloquently enforcing the sentiment expressed by Mr. Douglas in his Columbus speech of the previous autumn, namely: "Our fathers, when they framed the Government under which we live, understood this question just as well, and even better, than we do now." The argument and its illustrations were masterly; the logic unanswerable. A few pararaphs of his concluding remarks are all that can be given here:

WHAT WILL SATISFY THE SOUTHERN DEMOCRACY?

A few words now to Republicans. It is exceedingly desirable that all parts of this great Confederacy shall be at peace, and in harmony one with another. Let us Republicans do our part to have it so. Even though much provoked, let us do nothing through passion and ill temper. Even though the Southern people will not so much as listen to us, let us calmly consider their demands, and yield to them, if, in our deliberate view of our duty, we possibly can. Judging by all they say and do, and by the subject and nature of their controversy with us, let us determine, if we can, what will satisfy them.

Will they be satisfied if the Territories be unconditionally surrendered to them? We know they will not. In all their present complaints against us, the Territories are scarcely mentioned. Invasions and insurrections are the rage now. Will it satisfy them if, in the future, we have nothing to do with invasions and insurrections? We know it will not. We so know, because we know we never had anything to do with invasions and insurrections; and yet this total abstaining does not exempt us from the charge and the denunciation.

The question recurs, What will satisfy them? Simply this: We must not only let them alone, but we must, somehow, convince them that we do let them alone. This, we know by experience, is no easy task. We have been so trying to convince them, from the very beginning of our organization, but with no success. In all our platforms and speeches, we have constantly protested our purpose to let them alone; but this has had no tendency to convince them. Alike unavailing to convince them is the fact, that they have never detected a man of us in any attempt to disturb them.

These natural and apparently adequate means all failing, what will convince them? This, and this only: cease to call slavery *wrong*, and join them in calling it *right*. All this must be done thoroughly—done in *acts* as well as in *words*.   *   *

If our sense of duty forbids this, then let us stand by our duty, fearlessly and effectively. Let us be diverted by none of those sophistical contrivances wherewith we are so industriously plied and belabored—contrivances such as groping for some middle ground between the right and the wrong, vain as the search for a man who should be neither a living man nor a dead man—such as a policy of "don't care" on a question about which all true men do care—such as Union appeals, beseeching true Union men to yield to Disunionists, reversing the Divine rule, and calling, not the sinners, but the righteous to repentance—such as invocations of Washington, imploring men to unsay what Washington said, and undo what Washington did. Neither let us be slandered from our duty by false accusations against us, nor frightened from it by menaces of destruction to the Government, nor of dungeons to ourselves. Let us have faith that right makes might; and in that faith, let us, to the end, dare to do our duty, as we understand it.

This is the last of the great speeches of Mr. Lincoln, prior to the election of 1860, of which there is any complete report. It forms a brilliant close to this period of his life, and a fitting prelude to that on which he was about to enter.

It was during this visit to New York that the following incident occurred, as related by a teacher in the Five Points House of Industry, in that city:

Our Sunday-school in the Five Points was assembled, one Sabbath morning, a few months since, when I noticed a tall and remarkable-looking man enter the room and take a seat among us. He listened with fixed attention to our exercises, and his countenance manifested such genuine interest, that I approached him and suggested that he might be willing to say something to the children. He accepted the invitation with evident pleasure, and coming forward began a simple address, which at once facinated every little hearer, and hushed the room into silence. His language was strikingly beautiful, and his tones musical with intensest feeling. The little faces around would droop into sad conviction as he uttered sentences of warning, and would brighten into sunshine as he spoke cheerful words of promise. Once or twice he attempted to close his remarks, but the imperative shout of "Go on!" "Oh, do go on!" would compel him to resume. As I looked upon the gaunt and sinewy frame of the stranger, and marked his powerful head and determined features, now touched into softness by the impressions of the moment, I felt an irrepressible curiosity to learn something more about him, and when he was quietly leaving the room, I begged to know his name. He courteously replied, "It is Abra'm Lincoln, from Illinois!"

CHAPTER XIII.

MR. LINCOLN'S NOMINATION FOR THE PRESIDENCY.

The Republican National Convention at Chicago.—The Charleston Explosion.—" Constitutional Union" Nominations.—Distinguished Candidates among the Republicans.—The Platform.—The Ballotings.—Mr. Lincoln Nominated.—Unparalleled Enthusiasm.—The Ticket Completed with the name of Senator Hamlin.—Its Reception by the Country.—Mr. Lincoln's Letter of Acceptance.

THE Republican National Convention met at Chicago on the 16th of May, 1860, to nominate candidates for President and Vice-President of the United States. At the date of its assembling, the great quadrennial convention of the Democratic party had been held at Charleston, and, after nearly two weeks' session, had adjourned without any agreement upon either platform or candidates. Douglas, with his Freeport record, which had become necessary in order to accomplish his temporary purpose, had proved an irreconcilably disturbing element in that convention. The nomination of Douglas by a united Democracy had been demonstrated to be impossible, and the only alternative of his withdrawal or an incurable disruption was presented. Subsequently, a " Constitutional Union" Convention had assembled at Baltimore, and nominated a Presidential ticket, with no other definitely avowed object than that professed in common by all citizens, everywhere, of supporting the Constitution and the Union. All eyes were now turned toward Chicago, as the point at which the problem of the next Presidency was to be definitely solved.

Before the Republican National Convention met, the names

of many distinguished statesmen had been proposed for the first place on the Presidential ticket, and their merits and availability had been extensively discussed. In this preliminary canvassing there had been no bitterness or unseemly personalities. There was a general indication of harmony in ultimate action, and of unbroken union upon whatever ticket should be selected.

The first day of the convention was spent in organizing, and on the second day the committee, selected for that purpose, reported a platform of principles which was unanimously adopted, and has been strongly approved by the people.

On the morning of the 18th, amid the most intense though subdued excitement of the twelve thousand people inside of the "Wigwam" in which the convention was held, and amid the anxious solicitude and suspense of the still greater numbers outside who could not gain admission, it was voted to proceed at once to ballot for a candidate for President of the United States. Seven names were formally presented in the following order:

WILLIAM H. SEWARD, of New York; ABRAHAM LINCOLN, of Illinois; WILLIAM L. DAYTON, of New Jersey; SIMON CAMERON, of Pennsylvania; SALMON P. CHASE, of Ohio; EDWARD BATES, of Missouri; and JOHN McLEAN, of Ohio.

Loud and long-continued applause greeted the first two of these names, in particular, between which it was soon apparent that the chief contest was to be.

On the first ballot Mr. Seward received 173 votes, Mr. Lincoln 102, Mr. Cameron 50, Mr. Chase 49, Mr. Bates 48, Mr. Dayton 14, Mr. McLean 12, and there were 16 votes scattered among candidates not put in nomination. For a choice, 233 votes were required.

on the second ballot (Mr. Cameron's name having been withdrawn) the vote for the several candidates was as follows: Mr. Seward 184, Mr. Lincoln 181, Mr. Chase 42, Mr. Bates 35, Mr. Dayton 10, Mr. McLean 8, scattering 4.

The third ballot was immediately taken, and, when the call of the roll was ended, the footings were as follows: For Mr.

Lincoln 231, Mr. Seward 180, Mr. Chase 24, Mr. Bates 22, all others 7. Immediately, before the result was announced, four Ohio delegates changed their votes to Mr. Lincoln, giving him a majority.

The scene which followed—the wild manifestations of approval and delight, within and without the hall, prolonged uninterruptedly for twenty minutes, and renewed again and again for a half hour longer—no words can describe. Never before was there a popular assembly of any sort, probably, so stirred with a contagious and all-pervading enthusiasm. The nomination was made unanimous, on motion of Mr. Everts, of New York, who had presented the name of Mr. Seward, and speedily, on the wings of lightning, the news of the great event was spread to all parts of the land. Subsequently, with like heartiness and unanimity, the ticket was completed by the nomination, on the second ballot, of Senator HANNIBAL HAMLIN, of Maine, for Vice-President.

These demonstrations at Chicago were but a representation of the common sentiments of the masses of the Republican party, and of thousands among the people, not before included in its ranks in the country at large. From that day to the present, the wisdom of the nomination of Abraham Lincoln for the highest place in the American Government has been more and more confirmed. As a man of the people, in cordial sympathy with the masses, he had the undoubting confidence of the sincere friends of free labor, regardless of party distinctions. As a man of sterling integrity and incorruptible honesty, he was to become the fitting agent for upholding the Federal Government in the days of its greatest trial. As a man of eminent ability, and of sound principles, after the earliest and best standard in our political history, his election was to give to the country an administration creditable to our republican polity, and to result in the complete removal of the great disquieting element which at length convulsed the nation with a gigantic civil war.

The brief letter of Mr. Lincoln, in acceptance of the Presidential nomination, is subjoined.

SPRINGFIELD, ILL., May 23, 1860.

HON. GEO. ASHMUN,

President of the Republican National Convention:

SIR :—I accept the nomination tendered me by the convention over which you presided, and of which I am formally apprised in the letter of yourself and others, acting as a committee of the convention for that purpose.

The declaration of principles and sentiments, which accompanies your letter, meets my approval; and it shall be my care not to violate nor disregard it, in any part.

Imploring the assistance of Divine Providence, and with due regard to the views and feelings of all who were represented in the convention; to the rights of all the States, and Territories, and the people of the nation; to the inviolability of the Constitution, and to the perpetual union, harmony and prosperity of all, I am most happy to co-operate for the practical success of the principles declared by the convention

Your obliged friend and fellow-citizen,

ABRAHAM LINCOLN.

The popular favor with which the nomination of Mr. Lincoln was first received was strengthened by the spirited canvass which followed. The electoral votes of the States of Maine, New Hampshire, Vermont, Massachusetts, Rhode Island, Connecticut, New York, Pennsylvania, Ohio, Indiana, Illinois, Michigan, Iowa, Wisconsin, Minnesota, California, and Oregon, seventeen States, were cast for Lincoln and Hamlin. The votes of Maryland, Delaware, North Carolina, South Carolina, Georgia, Florida, Alabama, Louisiana, Mississippi, Arkansas and Texas, eleven States, were cast for Breckinridge and Lane. The votes of Virginia, Kentucky and Tennessee were cast for Bell and Everett. The electoral vote of Missouri was given for Douglas and Johnson. The vote of New Jersey was divided, four being given for Lincoln and three for Douglas.

The aggregate electoral vote for each Presidential candidate, as found by the official canvass in joint session of the two Houses of Congress, on the 13th day of February, 1861, was as follows: For Abraham Lincoln, 180; for John C. Breckinridge, 72, for John Bell, 39; and for Stephen A. Douglas,

17

13

12. The Vice-President, Mr. Breckinridge, then officially declared Mr. Lincoln elected President of the United States for four years, commencing on the 4th of March, 1861.

The aggregate popular vote for each of the Presidential candidates, at this election, was as follows: For Mr. Lincoln, 1,866,452; for Mr. Douglas, 1,375,157; for Mr. Breckinridge, 847,953; and for Mr. Bell, 590,631. The last speech of Mr. Douglas, in the ensuing spring, urged upon his friends an earnest support of the Administration in putting down the rebellion, as in his speech at Norfolk, Va., during the preceding canvass, he had declared in favor of coercion, as the remedy for secession. Mr. Bell went over to the secession cause, co-operating with Mr. Breckinridge, afterward a General in the Rebel army. The total vote for the two loyal candidates was 3,241,609.

On the morning of February 11th, Mr. Lincoln, with his family, left Springfield for Washington. A large concourse of citizens had assembled at the depot, on the occasion of his departure, whom, with deep emotion, he addressed as follows:

MY FRIENDS: No one, not in my position, can appreciate the sadness I feel at this parting. To this people I owe all that I am. Here I have lived more than a quarter of a century; here my children were born, and here one of them lies buried. I know not how soon I shall see you again. A duty devolves upon me which is, perhaps, greater than that which has devolved upon any other man since the days of Washington. He never could have succeeded except for the aid of Divine Providence, upon which he at all times relied. I feel that I can not succeed without the same Divine aid which sustained him; and in the same Almighty being I place my reliance for support, and I hope you, my friends will all pray that I may receive that Divine assistance, without which I can not succeed, but with which success is certain. Again, I bid you all an affectionate farewell.

The first speech of Mr. Lincoln on his journey was that delivered at Indianapolis, on the evening of the same day, addressed to a multitude of people assembled to welcome him. As containing the earliest direct intimation of his views on the all-engrossing topic of the time, it is appropriately given here:

FELLOW-CITIZENS OF THE STATE OF INDIANA: I am here to thank you for this magnificent welcome, and still more for the very generous support given by your State to that political cause, which, I think, is the true and just cause of the whole country, and the whole world. Solomon says, "there is a time to keep silence;" and when men wrangle by the mouth, with no certainty that they mean the same thing while using the same words, it perhaps were as well if they would keep silence.

The words "coercion" and "invasion" are much used in these days, and often with some temper and hot blood. Let us make sure, if we can, that we do not misunderstand the meaning of those who use them. Let us get the exact definitions of these words—not from dictionaries, but from the men themselves, who certainly deprecate the things they would repre sent by the use of the words.

What, then, is coercion? What is invasion? Would the marching of an army into South Carolina, without the consent of her people, and with hostile intent toward them, be invasion? I certainly think it would, and it would be coercion also, if the South Carolinians were forced to submit. But if the United States should merely hold and retake its own forts and other property, and collect the duties on foreign importations, or even withhold the mails from places where they were habitually violated, would any or all of these things be invasion or coercion? Do our professed lovers of the Union, who spitefully resolve that they will resist coercion and invasion, understand that such things as these, on the part of the United States, would be coercion or invasion of a State? If so, their idea of means to preserve the object of their great affection would seem to be exceedingly thin and airy. If sick, the little pills of the homeopathist would be much too large for it to swallow. In their view, the Union, as a family relation, would seem to be no regular marriage, but rather a sort of "free-love" arrangement, to be maintained on passional attraction.

By the way, in what consists the special sacredness of a State? I speak not of the position assigned to a State in the Union by the Constitution, for that is a bond we all recognize. That position, however, a State can not carry out of the Union with it. I speak of that assumed primary right of a State to rule all which is less than itself, and to ruin all which is larger than itself. If a State and a County, in a given case, should be equal in number of inhabitants, in what, as a matter of principle, is the State better than the County? Would an exchange of name be an exchange of rights? Upon what principle, upon what rightful principle, may a State, being no more than

one-fiftieth part of the nation in soil and population, break up
the nation, and then coerce a proportionably large subdivision
of itself in the most arbitrary way?   What mysterious right
to play tyrant is conferred on a district of country with its
people, by merely calling it a State?   Fellow-citizens, I am not
asserting anything.   I am merely asking questions for you to
consider.   And now allow me to bid you farewell.

Enthusiastic greetings awaited the President elect all along
his route, the people hailing the approach of the day which
was to witness, under his auspices, the beginning of a *new regime*
for the nation.

At Philadelphia, on the 22d of February, he visited Independence Hall, where throngs of people gathered to see him,
and where he raised a national flag to its place on the staff
above, as requested, amid the cheers of the thousands present.
In a brief speech, he referred with much emotion to the men
who had assembled in this Hall in 1776, and to the principles
there proclaimed on the 4th of July—principles which he
declared it to be his purpose never to yield, even if he must
seal his devotion to them by a violent death.   On the next
day he reached Harrisburg.

Positive information had now been received at Washington,
of a plot to assassinate Mr. Lincoln at Baltimore.   When this
was communicated to him, he was averse to any change of the
time fixed upon for his transit through that city.   On the
earnest representations of Mr. Seward, however, who sent a
special messenger to the President elect at Harrisburg, to urge
this course, he left the latter place on the night train, a few
hours in advance of that which he was expected to take, and
passing through Baltimore without recognition, arrived, on
the following morning in Washington.

PART II.

CHAPTER I.

Commencement of President Lincoln's Administration.—Retrospect and Summary of Public Events.—Fort Sumter.

ON the 4th day of March, 1861, Mr. Lincoln took the oath of office, as President of the United States. The administration of James Buchanan, and eight years of intensely southern sway in all branches of the National Government, were now at an end. During the four months that had intervened since the people decreed this change not a moment had been lost by the leaders in the now clearly developed scheme of revolt, in making energetic preparation for its consummation. So well had they succeeded, by the aid of bold treason or of inert complicity at the national capital, that they imagined they had assured the full attainment of their object, almost without the hazard of a single campaign. While professing, however, to believe in a fancied right of peaceable secession, and proclaiming their desire to be left unmolested in the execution of their revolutionary purposes, the chief conspirators well knew that this immunity could only be gained by such use of the remaining days of the outgoing administration that the crisis should already be over, or resistance to their treason be rendered ineffectual, when the new administration should begin. They industriously collected the materials of war, yet spared no efforts to bring about a state of things which should insure either peaceful submission to their will or a sure vantage ground for an appeal to arms.

While yet the question of passing a secession ordinance was pending in South Carolina, President Buchanan, in his annual message, after having urged the unconstitutionality of the pro-

197

posed action, distinctly notified the complotters that he was equally without constitutional power to oppose their carrying out that purpose. When appealed to by the veteran head of the army, at a still earlier day, to take firm military possession of the United States forts on the southern coast, the same public functionary could find no means of adopting this prudent precaution. Consequently, the rebellious South Carolina leaders carried through their ordinance of secession on the 20th of December, 1860. Fort Moultrie, by an overt act of treason, was seized on the 28th, and the Palmetto flag was raised over Government property in Charleston. On the 3d of January, 1861, without even the pretext of a secession ordinance, or any form of authority from his own State, Gov. Brown, of Georgia, seized Forts Pulaski and Jackson, at Savannah; and this example was followed next day, in Alabama, by the occupation of Fort Morgan, at Mobile.

The patient submission with which all these acts were witnessed by the Executive, nay, the meekness with which he had himself invited them, and the ready assistance rendered to these efforts of treason by some of the highest officers immediately about him, were followed by the natural results. On the 9th of January, the steamer Star of the West, tardily dispatched with a small re-enforcement for Fort Sumter, now held by a totally inadequate garrison, was fired into from rebel batteries erected on Morris' Island, and from Fort Moultrie. On the same day, the conspirators in Mississippi, now, as in the times of repudiation, under the lead of Jefferson Davis, followed their co-laborers in South Carolina, in the pretense of secession. Alabama, Florida and Georgia were speedily subjected to a similar process of rebel manipulation. Louisiana, on the 28th of January, and Texas on the 1st of February, were proclaimed as having dissolved their connection with the Union. Meanwhile, the delegates of these States successively withdrew from Congress.

On the 10th of December, Howell Cobb, Secretary of the Treasury, had resigned the position he had so zealously perverted to the aid of the great conspiracy, and departed to the more immediate scene of action, that he might hasten the consummation, for a time delayed, and so earnestly resisted in Georgia as seemingly to involve the result in doubt. The venerable Secretary of State, Lewis Cass, surrendered his place four days later, in disgust at the hopelessness of his efforts to rouse President Buchanan to some effective resistance to the destructive blows aimed at the national life. John B. Floyd soon after (Dec. 29) retired from the office of Secretary of War, which he had used to disarm the loyal portion of the country, and to fill the rebellious States with cannon and muskets, which they were not slow to appropriate to the uses of rebellion. Jacob Thompson, without resigning, absented himself on a tour in the South, throwing all the weight of his influence as a cabinet officer in favor of rebellion in his native State of North Carolina. Bold peculation was meanwhile left to do its work in his department, in aid of the treasonable labors of high officials in crippling the Government, and in rendering the new administration as powerless as possible to meet the approaching crisis. The Secretary of the Navy had notoriously dispersed our war vessels to distant seas, so that months must pass before the incoming administration could bring an effective naval force to bear on the rebellion.

Delegates from the seven States in which this spreading insurrection had become predominant assembled at Montgomery, in Alabama, on the 6th of February, organized their "Confederacy" under a temporary constitution, and, on the 9th, selected Jefferson Davis to be their President, with Alexander H. Stephens as Vice President. The latter had been chosen as a representative of the more conservative sentiment, having strenuously resisted secession, as an utterly needless rebellion against "the best government upon earth," and his acceptance was a token of the general acquiescence of all political leaders of the States concerned in the rebellion now organized. Around this nucleus of seven States, thus completely in revolt, it was expected by the conspirators that every State in which slavery existed would soon be gathered, by a common interest, in the bonds of a common crime. The leaven of rebellion was industriously diffused through every other slaveholding State, and in several, movements were already in progress, which afterward culminated in secession ordinances.

While this confederacy of seven States was forming, a convention, composed of delegates from most of the free States, and from all the border slave States, was in session at Washington, aiming to bring about, by compromise, a peaceable solution of the pending struggle. On the part of leading loyal men this conference was conducted in good faith, in a conciliatory spirit, and with an earnest desire to avert any more serious collision than had already occurred. On the other hand, it was manifest that at least the delegates from Virginia, with John Tyler at their head, were aiming only to use this means to widen the gulf already existing, and to overcome the decided Union majority still existing in all the border slave States. While a series of propositions, therefore, looking to peace on the basis of a preserved Union, were agreed to by a majority of the Convention (which adjourned on the 1st of March), no practical result appeared in the rebellious districts, unless of an adverse character. This action did serve, however, to proclaim to all the world the anxiety of the people of the free States to avert, by any possible concessions, the full initiation of civil war. On the 11th of February, likewise, the Federal House of Representatives unanimously passed a resolution, introduced by Mr. Corwin, of Ohio (soon after concurred in by the Senate), providing for an amendment to the Constitution of the United States, forever prohibiting any legislation by Congress interfering with slavery in any State of the Union— a measure that fully set aside one of the chief pretended occasions for revolt. Going still further, in the way of concession, and in fact surrendering the long controversy about slavery in the Territories, were the resolutions known as the Crittenden Compromise, and which certain Southern Senators deliberately defeated, in their own house, by withholding their votes.

The temper and purpose of the secession leaders were thus distinctly manifested. They would have no compromise. On their own terms, of final separation alone, would they listen to terms of peace. Many of them manifestly desired war, and exulted in the hope of such revenge upon their Northern opponents as war only could bring; while all insisted on yielding nothing, except on the condition of substantially gaining everything they aimed at, by a full recognition of a separate and independent Confederacy comprising all the slaveholding States. For to this end, though less than half the number of those States had already been carried by the revolutionists, they were zealously laboring, and of the final issue no doubt was entertained, when once the Montgomery organization was countenanced as a legitimate government.

It is unpleasant to mention, yet impartial history can not omit the fact, that hopes of peaceable submission to secession were seemingly encouraged in Southern minds by newspapers and orators in the North, at this period, and that a number of political leaders, with scarcely any apparent popular support, it is true, earnestly advocated what they termed the policy of peaceable separation. To this day, perhaps, it may be doubtful to many minds whether, had not a spirit of unbounded insolence and a haughty defiance, that spurned even the slightest concession, been manifested by the secession leaders, this complacent policy—more fatal than any former compromise— might not have gained the ascendency in the popular mind.

So much had been brought to final accomplishment by the conspirators during the closing months of Mr. Buchanan's administration. Such was the spirit manifested by them to repel conciliation in every form, to maintain peace solely on condition of the complete submission of the loyal States to every essential demand of secessionism. And such, on the other hand, was the amicable disposition of loyal men everywhere, and their earnest wish to avoid a collision of arms, if any other solution were possible short of absolute degradation and ruin to the nation. Jefferson Davis, in assuming power as head of the "Confederacy," at Montgomery, February 18, stated the sole conditions of peace in the following unmistakeable language:

If a just perception of mutual interest shall permit us peaceably to pursue *our separate political career,* my most earnest desire will have been fulfilled. But *if this be denied us,* and the integrity of our territory and jurisdiction be assailed, it will but remain for us with firm resolve *to appeal to arms*, and invoke the blessing of Providence on a just cause.

This was immediately followed by the recommendation that a Confederate army be organized and put in training for the emergency; " a well instructed, disciplined army, more numerous than would usually be required, on a peace establishment," being distinctly indicated as essential to his plans.

While it is thus clear that he and all his coadjutors were determined on war from the outset, and at all hazards, unless disunion were recognized as an accomplished fact, and the jurisdiction of the Government over the rebellious districts were abandoned without a struggle, it is equally manifest that not a single grievance complained of could have failed of redress, under our popular institutions, by peaceable methods. While deluding their adherents with smooth words, they deliberately chose an appeal to arms, and scorned a peaceable solution, which was equally at their disposal, under the Constitution and the laws.

Some acts of vigor and patriotic fidelity, during the closing days of Mr. Buchanan's administration, deserve to be remembered, to the honor of those cabinet ministers, to whom alone the country was indebted for these redeeming deeds. Dix, Stanton and Holt had preserved a remainder of popular respect for a Government that all the loyalty of the nation rejoiced to see transferred to the hands of a new executive, untried though he was, and terrible as was the task devolving upon him.

Despite all the threats, constantly repeated for months past, that Mr. Lincoln should never be permitted to occupy the Presidential chair, and desperate as had been the plottings for his assassination, he appeared at the east front of the capitol and received, at the appointed time, the oath from Chief Justice Taney. During the period that had elapsed since the election, Mr. Lincoln had carefully studied the situation, closely watching the course of events. His inaugural address shows the results of his observation, and of the application of his sterling good sense and comprehensive practical judgment to the mastery of the problem to be solved by him as head of the nation. He clearly understood how everything depended, so far as his administration was concerned, on a true insight into the very heart of the question, and on the initiation, at the very outset, of an appropriate policy in dealing with the rebellion.. The great insurrection is the uppermost thought—almost the exclusive theme—of his inaugural address. That this was th wisest utterance of the time, manifesting a rare foresight, a well as a remarkable skill in briefly presenting the true ques tions at issue, in their proper bearings, with a calm, candid appeal to the nation, in all its parts, in behalf of law, order and peace, will more and more clearly appear in the light of after events. Whoever would acquaint himself with the inmost traits of Mr. Lincoln's character, as a public man, and at the same time discover, in honest and plain words, a statement in advance of the fundamental principles by which his administration has been guided, let him carefully study this paper, every sentence of which is full of meaning:

MR. LINCOLN'S INAUGURAL ADDRESS.

FELLOW-CITIZENS OF THE UNITED STATES: In compliance with a custom as old as the Government itself, I appear before you to address you briefly, and to take, in your presence, the oath prescribed by the Constitution of the United States, to be taken by the President before he enters on the execution of his office.

I do not consider it necessary, at present, for me to discuss those matters of administration about which there is no special anxiety or excitement. Apprehension seems to exist among the people of the Southern States, that, by the accession of a Republican Administration, their property and their peace and personal security are to be endangered. There has never been any reasonable cause for such apprehension. Indeed, the most ample evidence to the contrary has all the while existed, and been open to their inspection. It is found in nearly all the published speeches of him who now addresses you. I do but quote from one of those speeches, when I declare that "I have no purpose, directly or indirectly, to interfere with the institution of slavery in the States where it exists." I believe I have no lawful right to do so; and I have no inclination to do so. Those who nominated and elected me, did so with the full knowledge that I had made this, and made many similar declarations, and had never recanted them. And, more than this, they placed in the platform, for my acceptance, and as a law to themselves and to me, the clear and emphatic resolution which I now read:

"*Resolved*, That the maintenance inviolate of the rights of the States, and especially the right of each State to order and control its own domestic institutions according to its own judgment exclusively, is essential to that balance of power on which the perfection and endurance of our political fabric depend; and we denounce the lawless invasion, by armed force, of the soil of any State or Territory, no matter under what pretext, as among the gravest of crimes."

I now reiterate these sentiments; and in doing so I only press upon the public attention the most conclusive evidence of which the case is susceptible, that the property, peace, and security of no section are to be in anywise endangered by the now incoming administration.

I add, too, that all the protection which, consistently with the Constitution and the laws, can be given, will be cheerfully given to all the States when lawfully demanded, for whatever cause, as cheerfully to one section as to another.

There is much controversy about the delivering up of fugitives from service or labor. The clause I now read is as plainly written in the Constitution as any other of its provisions:

"No person held to service or labor in one State under the laws thereof, escaping into another, shall, in consequence of any law or regulation therein, be discharged from such service or labor, but shall be delivered up on claim of the party to whom such service or labor may be due."

It is scarcely questioned that this provision was intended by those who made it for the reclaiming of what we call fugitive slaves; and the intention of the lawgiver is the law.

All members of Congress swear their support to the whole Constitution—to this provision as well as any other. To the proposition, then, that slaves whose cases come within the terms of this clause "shall be delivered up," their oaths are unanimous. Now, if they would make the effort in good temper, could they not, with nearly equal unanimity, frame and pass a law by means of which to keep good that unanimous oath?

There is some difference of opinion whether this clause should be enforced by National or by State authority; but surely that difference is not a very material one. If the slave is to be surrendered, it can be of but little consequence to him or to others by which authority it is done; and should any one, in any case, be content that this oath shall go unkept on a merely unsubstantial controversy as to how it shall be kept?

Again, in any law upon this subject, ought not all the safeguards of liberty known in the civilized and humane jurisprudence to be introduced, so that a free man be not, in any case, surrendered as a slave? And might it not be well at the same time to provide by law for the enforcement of that clause in the Constitution which guarantees that "the citizens of each State shall be entitled to all the privileges and immunities of citizens in the several States?"

I take the official oath to-day with no mental reservations, and with no purpose to construe the Constitution or laws by any hypercritical rules; and while I do not choose now to specify particular acts of Congress as proper to be enforced, I do suggest that it will be much safer for all, both in official and private stations, to conform to and abide by all those acts which stand unrepealed, than to violate any of them, trusting to find impunity in having them held to be unconstitutional.

It is seventy-two years since the first inauguration of a President under our National Constitution. During that period, fifteen different and very distinguished citizens have in succession administered the executive branch of the Government. They have conducted it through many perils, and generally with great success. Yet, with all this scope for precedent, I now enter upon the same task, for the brief constitutional term of four years, under great and peculiar difficulties.

A disruption of the Federal Union, heretofore only menaced, is now formidably attempted. I hold that in the contemplation of universal law and of the Constitution, the Union of these States is perpetual. Perpetuity is implied, if not expressed, in the fundamental law of all national governments. It is safe to assert that no government proper ever had a provision in its organic law for its own termination. Continue to execute all the express provisions of our National Constitution, and the Union will endure forever, it being impossible to destroy it, except by some action not provided for in the instrument itself.

Again, if the United States be not a government proper, but an association of States in the nature of a contract merely, can it, as a contract, be peaceably unmade by less than all the parties who made it? One party to a contract may violate it—break it, so to speak; but does it not require all to lawfully rescind it? Descending from these general principles, we find the proposition that in legal contemplation the Union is perpetual, confirmed by the history of the Union itself.

The Union is much older than the Constitution. It was formed, in fact, by the Articles of Association in 1774. It was matured and continued in the Declaration of Independence in 1776. It was further matured, and the faith of all the then thirteen States expressly plighted and engaged that it should be perpetual, by the Articles of the Confederation, in 1778; and, finally, in 1787, one of the declared objects for ordaining and establishing the Constitution was to form a more perfect Union. But if the destruction of the Union by one or by a part only of the States be lawfully possible, the Union is less than before, the Constitution having lost the vital element of perpetuity.

It follows from these views that no State, upon its own mere motion, can lawfully get out of the Union; that resolves and ordinances to that effect, are legally void; and that acts of violence within any State or States against the authority of the United States, are insurrectionary or revolutionary, according to circumstances.

I therefore consider that, in view of the Constitution and the laws, the Union is unbroken, and, to the extent of my ability, I shall take care, as the Constitution itself expressly enjoins upon me, that the laws of the Union shall be faithfully executed in all the States. Doing this, which I deem to be only a simple duty on my part, I shall perfectly perform it, so far as is practicable, unless my rightful masters, the American people, shall withhold the requisition, or in some authoritative manner direct the contrary.

I trust this will not be regarded as a menace, but only as the declared purpose of the Union that it will constitutionally defend and maintain itself.

In doing this there need be no bloodshed or violence, and there shall be none unless it is forced upon the National authority.

The power confided to me *will be used to hold, occupy, and possess the property and places belonging to the Government,* and collect the duties and imposts; but beyond what may be necessary for these objects there will be no invasion, no using of force against or among the people anywhere.

Where hostility to the United States shall be so great and so universal as to prevent competent resident citizens from holding the Federal offices, there will be no attempt to force obnoxious strangers among the people that object. While the strict legal right may exist of the Government to enforce the exercise of these offices, the attempt to do so would be so irritating, and so nearly impracticable withal, that I deem it better to forego, for the time, the uses of such offices.

The mails, unless repelled, will continue to be furnished in all parts of the Union.

So far as possible, the people everywhere shall have that

sense of perfect security which is most favorable to calm thought and reflection.

The course here indicated will be followed, unless current events and experience shall show a modification or change to be proper; and in every case and exigency my best discretion will be exercised according to the circumstances actually existing, and with a view and hope of a peaceful solution of the National troubles, and the restoration of fraternal sympathies and affections.

That there are persons, in one section or another, who seek to destroy the Union at all events, and are glad of any pretext to do it, I will neither affirm nor deny. But if there be such, I need address no word to them.

To those, however, who really love the Union, may I not speak, before entering upon so grave a matter as the destruction of our National fabric, with all its benefits, its memories, and its hopes? Would it not be well to ascertain why we do it? Will you hazard so desperate a step, while any portion of the ills you fly from have no real existence? Will you, while the certain ills you fly to are greater than all the real ones you fly from? Will you risk the commission of so fearful a mistake? All profess to be content in the Union if all constitutional rights can be maintained. Is it true, then, that any right, plainly written in the Constitution, has been denied? I think not. Happily the human mind is so constituted, that no party can reach to the audacity of doing this.

Think, if you can, of a single instance in which a plainly-written provision of the Constitution has ever been denied. If, by the mere force of numbers, a majority should deprive a minority of any clearly-written constitutional right, it might, in a moral point of view, justify revolution; it certainly would, if such right were a vital one. But such is not our case.

All the vital rights of minorities and of individuals are so plainly assured to them by affirmations and negations, guarantees and prohibitions in the Constitution, that controversies never arise concerning them. But no organic law can ever be framed with a provision specifically applicable to every question which may occur in practical administration. No foresight can anticipate, nor any document of reasonable length contain, express provisions for all possible questions. Shall fugitives from labor be surrendered by National or by State authorities? The Constitution does not expressly say. Must Congress protect slavery in the Territories? The Constitution does not expressly say. From questions of this class, spring all our constitutional controversies, and we divide upon them into majorities and minorities.

If the minority will not acquiesce, the majority must, or the Government must cease. There is no alternative for continuing the Government but acquiescence on the one side or the other. If a minority in such a case, will secede rather than acquiesce, they make a precedent which, in turn, will ruin and divide them, for a minority of their own will secede from them whenever a majority refuses to be controlled by such a minority. For instance, why not any portion of a new Confederacy, a year or two hence, arbitrarily secede again, precisely as portions of the present Union now claim to secede from it? All who cherish disunion sentiments are now being educated to the exact temper of doing this. Is there such perfect identity of interests among the States to compose a new Union as to produce harmony only, and prevent renewed secession? Plainly, the central idea of secession is the essence of anarchy.

A majority held in restraint by constitutional check and limitation, and always changing easily with deliberate changes of popular opinions and sentiments, is the only true sovereign of a free people. Whoever rejects it, does, of necessity, fly to anarchy or to despotism. Unanimity is impossible; the rule of a majority, as a permanent arrangement, is wholly inadmissible. So that, rejecting the majority principle, anarchy or despotism, in some form, is all that is left.

I do not forget the position assumed by some that constitutional questions are to be decided by the Supreme Court, nor do I deny that such decisions must be binding in any case upon the parties to a suit, as to the object of that suit, while they are also entitled to a very high respect and consideration in all parallel cases by all other departments of the Government; and while it is obviously possible that such decision may be erroneous in any given case, still the evil effect following it, being limited to that particular case, with the chance that it may be overruled and never become a precedent for other cases, can better be borne than could the evils of a different practice.

At the same time the candid citizen must confess that if the policy of the Government upon the vital questions affecting the whole people is to be irrevocably fixed by the decisions of the Supreme Court, the instant they are made, as in ordinary litigation between parties in personal actions, the people will have ceased to be their own masters, unless having to that extent practically resigned their Government into the hands of that eminent tribunal.

Nor is there in this view any assault upon the Court or the Judges. It is a duty from which they may not shrink, to decide cases properly brought before them; and it is no fault of theirs if others seek to turn their decisions to political purposes. One section of our country believes slavery is right and ought to be extended, while the other believes it is wrong and ought not to be extended ; and this is the only substantial dispute ; and the fugitive slave clause of the Constitution, and the law for the suppression of the foreign slave-trade, are each as well enforced, perhaps, as any law can ever be in a community where the moral sense of the people imperfectly supports the law itself. The great body of the people abide by the dry legal obligation in both cases, and a few break over in each. This, I think, can not be perfectly cured, and it would be worse in both cases after the separation of the sections than before. The foreign slave-trade, now imperfectly suppressed, would be ultimately revived, without restriction, in one section ; while fugitive slaves, now only partially surrendered, would not be surrendered at all by the other.

Physically speaking, we can not separate ; we can not remove our respective sections from each other, nor build an impassable wall between them. A husband and wife may be divorced, and go out of the presence and beyond the reach of each other, but the different parts of our country can not do this. They can not but remain face to face ; and intercourse, either amicable or hostile, must continue between them. Is it possible, then, to make that intercourse more advantageous or more satisfactory after separation than before ? Can aliens make treaties easier than friends can make laws ? Can treaties be more faithfully enforced between aliens than laws can among friends ? Suppose you go to war, you can not fight always; and when, after much loss on both sides, and no gain on either, you cease fighting, the identical questions as to terms of intercourse are again upon you.

This country, with its institutions, belongs to the people who inhabit it. Whenever they shall grow weary of the existing Government, they can exercise their constitutional right of amending, or their revolutionary right to dismember or overthrow it. I can not be ignorant of the fact that many worthy and patriotic citizens are desirous of having the National Constitution amended. While I make no recommendation of amendment, I fully recognize the full authority of the people over the whole subject, to be exercised in either of the modes prescribed in the instrument itself, and I should, under existing circumstances, favor, rather than oppose, a fair opportunity being afforded the people to act upon it.

I will venture to add, that to me the convention mode seems preferable, in that it allows amendments to originate with the people themselves, instead of only permitting them to take or reject propositions originated by others not especially chosen

14   18

for the purpose, and which might not be precisely such as they would wish either to accept or refuse. I understand that a proposed amendment to the Constitution (which amendment, however, I have not seen) has passed Congress, to the effect that the Federal Government shall never interfere with the domestic institutions of States, including that of persons held to service. To avoid misconstruction of what I have said, I depart from my purpose not to speak of particular amendments, so far as to say that, holding such a provision to now be implied constitutional law, I have no objection to its being made express and irrevocable.

The Chief Magistrate derives all his authority from the people, and they have conferred none upon him to fix the terms for the separation of the States. The people themselves, also, can do this if they choose, but the Executive, as such, has nothing to do with it. His duty is to administer the present government as it came to his hands, and to transmit it unimpaired by him to his successor. Why should there not be a patient confidence in the ultimate justice of the people? Is there any better or equal hope in the world? In our present differences is either party without faith of being in the right? If the Almighty Ruler of nations, with his eternal truth and justice, be on your side of the North, or on yours of the South, that truth and that justice will surely prevail by the judgment of this great tribunal, the American people. By the frame of the Government under which we live, this same people have wisely given their public servants but little power for mischief, and have with equal wisdom provided for the return of that little to their own hands at very short intervals. While the people retain their virtue and vigilance, no administration, by any extreme wickedness or folly, can very seriously injure the Government in the short space of four years.

My countrymen, one and all, think calmly and well upon this whole subject. Nothing valuable can be lost by taking time.

If there be an object to hurry any of you, in hot haste, to a step which you would never take deliberately, that object will be frustrated by taking time; but no good object can be frustrated by it.

Such of you as are now dissatisfied still have the old Constitution unimpaired, and on the sensitive point, the laws of your own framing under it; while the new administration will have no immediate power, if it would, to change either.

If it were admitted that you who are dissatisfied hold the right side in the dispute, there is still no single reason for pre cipitate action. Intelligence, patriotism, Christianity, and a firm reliance on Him who has never yet forsaken this favored land, are still competent to adjust, in the best way, all our present difficulties.

In your hands, my dissatisfied fellow-countrymen, and not in mine, is the momentous issue of civil war. The Government will not assail you.

You can have no conflict without being yourselves the aggressors. You have no oath registered in Heaven to destroy the Government; while I shall have the most solemn one to "preserve, protect, and defend" it.

I am loath to close. We are not enemies, but friends. We must not be enemies. Though passion may have strained, it must not break our bonds of affection.

The mystic cords of memory, stretching from every battle-field and patriot grave to every living heart and hearthstone all over this broad land, will yet swell the chorus of the Union, when again touched, as surely they will be, by the better angels of our nature.

Both to the large assemblage that listened to the distinct recital of this address, in tones which made every word audible to the throng, and to loyal men everywhere, as it was brought to them a few minutes or hours later, by the aid of telegraph and printing press, it was a welcome message. The people saw in it an assurance that imbecility, double-dealing, or treachery, no longer had sway in the nation; that the new President was determined to carry out the behests of the people in maintaining the National integrity; and that, while thus faithfully observing his official oath, he would use every lawful and rational means to avert the convulsions of domestic war. He distinctly suggested the holding of a National Constitutional Convention, which would have power to adjust all the questions properly at issue, even including peaceable separation in a lawful manner, by a change of the organic law. He demonstrated unanswerably the utter causelessness of war, and distinctly assured the conspirators that if hostilities were commenced, it must be by them, and not by the Government. He laid down a line of policy which, had it been met in a corresponding spirit on the other side, would inevitably have averted disastrous years of bloodshed and all their consequences. While thus announcing his views, and reaffirming sentiments formerly uttered by himself, as well as those of the political convention which nominated him for the Presidency, he also plainly indicated that the benefits secured by the Constitution to any portion of the people could not be claimed by them while trampling that instrument under foot. He told them plainly that the course he thus marked out was not one to be pursued toward rebels who should plunge the nation in war. He gave them seasonable notice that no immunities could be claimed under the assurances given on this or any other occasion, inconsistent with the changed condition of affairs, should they madly appeal to arms.

The whole address breathes an earnest yearning for an honorable peace. It does not, however, like the unfortunate message of his predecessor, of the previous December, base the desire for peace on a confessed helplessness of the Government or an indisposition to exert its power of self-preservation. A new political era had begun, and true patriots breathed more freely.

One of the first duties of the President was to purge the Government of disloyal or doubtful men in responsible places. Long-continued Democratic precedent justified a general change of civil officers, from highest to lowest, on the ground of political differences alone. But after the treasonable developments of the previous months and years, a thorough sifting of all the Departments became indispensable, from high considerations of duty, on the basis of loyalty and disloyalty, rather than of mere partisanship. No practical measures could be adopted before this change was at least partially accomplished. The magnitude of such a work, to which the President gave the most earnest and unwearying attention for weeks, need not be indicated. The patience with which the "claims" of different candidates for place were weighed, and the kindness (tempered often with a wholesome firmness) which characterized his deportment toward all, usually retained the confidence and esteem of those whom he felt compelled to disappoint.

It was during the days between his arrival in Washington and his inauguration, that the construction of his Cabinet, perhaps substantially settled in his own mind before he left Illinois, was definitely determined. The position occupied by Mr. Seward before the country, was such as to leave no hesitation as to the propriety of offering him the highest place of honor under the Executive, as Secretary of State. This position was, at an early day, placed at Mr. Seward's disposal. The office of Attorney General was, with like promptitude, tendered to Judge Bates, of Missouri, whose leading position as a Southern statesman, with anti-slavery tendencies, of the Clay school, had caused his name to be prominently and widely used in connection with the Presidency before the nomination for that office, made at Chicago. Governor Chase, of Ohio, who had recently been elected to a second term in the Senate, after four years of useful and popular service in the executive chair of his State, perhaps quite as early occurred to the mind of Mr. Lincoln as a man specially fitted to manage the finances of the nation through the troublous times that were felt to be approaching. This difficult post Mr. Chase surrendered his seat in the Senate to accept. Mr. Cameron, of Pennsylvania, selected as Secretary of War; Mr. Welles, of Connecticut, as Secretary of the Navy, and Mr. Montgomery Blair, of Maryland, as Postmaster General, were all leading representatives of the Democratic element of the party which had triumphed in the late election. Mr. Caleb B. Smith, of Indiana, a contemporary of Mr. Lincoln in Congress, and for years one of the most distinguished Whig politicians of the West, was tendered the place of Secretary of the Interior, which he accepted.

It deserves remark here, that John Bell, of Tennessee, who had received a large popular vote at the Presidential election, and whose strength in the electoral college made him the tl ird of four Presidential nominees, was at this time in Washington, and his appointment to a place in the Cabinet, as a loyal Border State man, was desired by many, especially in the West. But Mr. Blair, an avowed Anti-Slavery man, and viewed as one of the most radical of Republicans, was preferred to Mr. Bell, zealous partisan opponent, and one whose unreliable character as developed by his sudden defection to the Rebel cause, President Lincoln was not slow to perceive.

Next to the indispensable and primary duty of securing, in

the places under him, trustworthy men, in sympathy with himself as to the great questions uppermost in the public mind, was that of more directly preparing, at home and abroad, to grapple with the rebellion, now fully organized at Montgomery, and manifestly emerging, with mad haste, into open hostilities. This work involved nice problems of foreign diplomacy, as well as prudent care, at once to avert divisions in the loyal States when the sharp crisis should come, and to place the *onus* of commencing civil war unequivocally upon the secession leaders, if it were to begin. The utmost energy was also needed in so prearranging affairs that means might not be wanting when battle should be forced upon the nation.

In this view, much of the seeming mystery which enveloped the six weeks preceding the attack on Fort Sumter, disappears without inquiring into State secrets, if, at this period, there were such, over which the curtain should still rest.

For several days the inaugural address was quietly working its way among the people, giving heart to the supporters of the Government and startling the conspirators by its calm and telling appeal to thinking men every-where. With the Rebel leaders it became a study to prevent the natural effect of this State paper upon those whom they wished to follow them, not only in the eight Slave States which had, as yet, held back from the fatal step, but even in those States already in insurrection. They scrupled at nothing in their attempts to ward off its influence and to pervert the attitude of the Government. At the same time they were zealous and active in completing the direct preparations for war which had been commenced many months before.

Equally busy, and for a much longer period, had they been in poisoning the public mind of Europe. The diplomatic agents employed by Mr. Buchanan had been, in large proportion, from the Slave States, and of those from the North some were far from manifesting a genuine fidelity to the Government that had accredited them. To change these Foreign Ministers and Consuls, and to instruct their successors, was not the work of a day, nor did a removal of these men from office by any means necessarily involve their retirement from the vantage

ground they had gained.   They had rather been largely reinforced by numerous emissaries sent abroad during the preceding
autumn and winter.

It was the early care of Mr. Lincoln's Administration,
through the polished pen of Mr. Seward, and through the new
diplomats sent abroad, to counteract these influences.   From
this period commenced the gradual formation and concentration
of a public sentiment abroad favorable to the Government.
Yet the change was not immediately apparent, and the work
was a slow and toilsome one.   The aim to convince Foreign
Nations that the malcontents were clearly and wholly in the
wrong, that the intentions of the Government were pacific, and
that there was no revolutionary purpose of overturning Southern society while the dissentients yielded obedience to the
Constitution and the laws, can not have failed of speedy success
with candid and thoughtful men abroad as well as at home.
On whom the whole responsibility of war would rest, should
war come, no longer admitted of doubt.

The Montgomery "Congress," on the 9th of March, passed
an act, pursuant to the recommendation of Mr. Davis, for the
organization of a Confederate army.   Three days later Mr.
Forsyth, of Alabama, and Mr. Crawford, of Georgia, presented
themselves at the State Department in Washington, in the attitude of "Confederate Commissioners," with the pretended
purpose of seeking to negotiate a treaty, on the assumption of
representing "an independent nation *de facto* and *de jure*."
While well knowing, both from the nature of the controversy,
and from the distinct avowals of Mr. Lincoln's inaugural
address, that this preliminary claim, if noticed at all, would be
promptly rejected, and passing over altogether the President's
frank and honorable suggestion of a National Convention, in
which all the States should be represented and all grievances
listened to and constitutionally adjusted, they presumed to
assert that the persons represented by them "earnestly desire
a peaceful solution" of the "great questions" "growing out of
this political separation."   The President declined all recognition of these negotiating parties, and, with a simple "memorandum" of Mr. Seward, apprising them of this fact, was

inclosed a copy of the inaugural address, to which they were referred for the views controlling the Government, and which, in fact, had undoubtedly been carefully perused by them before undertaking this false mission, intended solely for diplomatic effect, both in the loyal States and in Europe.

To the Government this dilatory episode gave a few days of much needed time for the work now in hand. These " Commissioners " at length retired from Washington, discharging their Parthian arrow, in the shape of a final communication to the Secretary of State, on the 9th of April. It was an evidence of that forbearance manifested by Mr. Lincoln through all the earliest stages of this conflict, a forbearance the value of which all the world can now appreciate, however distasteful to more excitable minds at the time, that these defiant rebels were permitted to return to their homes, instead of taking their well-earned place within prison walls.

Five weeks and more had now passed since the inauguration, and the situation of affairs in Fort Sumter, to which the gallant Anderson had transferred his little garrison of seventy men from Fort Moultrie, near the close of the year, portended an approaching crisis. The overt act of war had long since been committed by the Charleston rebels, in firing on the Star of the West as she went to carry relief to that Fort, on which beleaguering batteries, not before unmasked, were already preparing to open. The supply vessel turned back, and though nearly two months had passed before Mr. Buchanan vacated the Presidential chair, his Administration was permitted to expire without an attempt to retrieve that humiliation.

As time wore on, no military preparations, as yet, being visible, Messrs. Forsyth and Crawford being known to be still in Washington, without any thing being positively disclosed as to the character of their intercourse with the State Department, and those persons having been finally permitted to depart, with only the public certainty that they had been denied official recognition, a general uneasiness began to pervade the popular mind. This growing discontent was fanned by the positive assertions of busy quidnuncs that Fort Sumter was to be evacuated in obedience to the demand of the Charleston traitors.

The visit of Mr. Fox to Major Anderson on the 22d day of March, afforded little relief to the current anxiety, so conflicting were the reports as to the purpose of his mission. The visit of still another supposed agent of the Government to Charleston, three days later, was generally construed unfavorably. Sanguine and nervous people were beginning to despond, or to speak openly of "weakness and vacillation" on the part of the President. It was only those who did not thoroughly know Mr. Lincoln who could seriously have doubted him for a moment. And yet, the stranger lingering in the capital during those calm yet dubious days which preceded the outburst of a storm, every moment's delay of which was an incalculable gain to the Government, would almost have pronounced the Administration doomed to ignominious failure, to popular repudiation, such as a counter-revolution of loyal men in the North must inevitably follow, at the very outset of its career.

To omit to record this state of things, vividly impressed as it must be on the mind of every man in Washington, who observed events from the outside, would be to leave out the most striking view in the foreground of the picture. When taken in connection with subsequent events, it would also be as unjust to the fame of President Lincoln, as false to the facts of history.

It was during this period that Mr. Alexander H. Stephens, (who, recreant to the sterling words in which, a few short months earlier, he had denounced this insane attempt to destroy the best Government on earth, for no real grievance whatever, but solely to gratify and revenge the thwarted ambition of defeated politicians, was now enjoying the mimic honors of the "Confederate" Vice Presidency,) delivered a remarkable speech in the city of Savannah, (March 21,) which must also have its permanent place in the annals of the time. The over-crowded audience, the enthusiastic applause, the solemnities of the occasion, and the known, frank, and positive character of the man, all combine to mark this utterance as a genuine reproduction of the thought and purpose of the chief conspirators, and their ready followers, at this hour. Only some of its chief points

19

can be recalled here, as showing both the estimate placed upon Mr. Lincoln's official action hitherto, and the real animus of the rebellion, when relieved of the disguises which Stephens had already stripped off in his anti-secession speech on the 19th of January, in the Georgia Convention.

After proceeding at some length to point out the " Improve ments " he discerned in the Montgomery Constitution over that which the seven "Confederate States" had repudiated. Mr. Stephens said:

But not to be tedious in enumerating the numerous changes for the better, allow me to allude to one other—though last, not least :   The new Constitution has put at rest forever all the agitating questions relating to our peculiar institutions—African slavery as it exists among us—the proper status of the negro in our form of civilization.   This was the immediate cause of the late rupture and present revolution.   Jefferson, in his forecast, had anticipated this, as the rock upon which the old Union would split.   He was right.   What was conjecture with him, is now a realized fact.   But whether he fully comprehended the great truth upon which that rock stood and stands, may be doubted.   The prevailing ideas, *entertained by him and most of the leading statesmen,* at the time of the formation of the old Constitution, were, *that the enslavement of the African was in violation of the laws of nature; that it was* WRONG IN PRINCI-PLE, SOCIALLY, MORALLY AND POLITICALLY.   It was an evil they knew not well how to deal with ; but the general opinion of the men of that day was, *that, somehow or other, in the order of Providence, the institution would be evanescent and pass away.*

Let us pause here, for a moment, to consider this distinct concession—truthful in every word—as to the views of Jeffer-son " and most of the leading statesmen" of the Constitutional era.   How perfectly this agrees with the admission, two months earlier, that under an eminently Southern administration of the Government under the Constitution, for a long period of years, *the South* had no grievance whatever to complain of !   Still more striking is the suggestion which this passage makes of that portion of Mr. Lincoln's celebrated Springfield speech, quoted by the author of the elaborate paper, in imitation of the Declaration of Independence, setting forth the causes of South Carolina's secession, when he says :

Observing the forms of the Constitution, a sectional party has found within that article establishing the Executive Department, the means of subverting the Constitution itself. A geographical line has been drawn across the Union, and all the States north of that line have united in the election of a man to the high office of President of the United States, *whose opinions and purposes are hostile to slavery*. He is to be intrusted with the administration of the common government, because he has declared that that "Government can not endure permanently half slave, half free," and *that the public mind must rest in the belief that slavery is in the course of ultimate extinction*.

Setting aside the special pleading and inaccurate statement of the South Carolinian, how completely is he answered at every point by the Georgian, who had already, beyond a doubt, carefully perused the former's argument! In a word, Stephens fairly and honorably concedes that the exact position held by Jefferson, and most of his contemporary statesmen, in regard to slavery, is precisely that which Mr. Rhett, even in his less candid effusion, attributes to Mr. Lincoln, and both practically unite in bearing testimony to the following clear enunciation of the grand spirit and purpose of the rebellion, as stated in his Savannah speech by Mr. Stephens, after pronouncing these ideas of Jefferson and his contemporaries to be "fundamentally wrong," as resting "upon the assumption of the equality of races :"

Our new Government is founded upon exactly the opposite ideas. Its foundations are laid, *its corner-stone rests*, upon the great truth that the negro is not equal to the white man ; *that slavery, subordination to the superior race, is his natural and normal condition*. This, our new Government, is the first, in the history of the world, BASED UPON *this great physical, philosophical, and moral truth*. * * * * * * It is upon this, as I have stated, our social fabric is firmly planted ; and I can not permit myself to doubt the ultimate success of a full recognition of this principle throughout the civilized and enlightened world. * * * * This stone *which was rejected by the first builders*, " *is become the chief stone of the corner* " *in our new edifice*.

Mr. Stephens, after discussing the ability of the seven States already banded together to go on in their undertaking without the " Border States," and the hopes and wishes entertained in regard to the latter, goes on to discuss the prospect in regard to hostilities with the National Government, as follows :

As to whether we shall have war with our late confederates, or whether all matters of difference between us shall be amicably settled, I can only say that the prospect for a peaceful adjustment *is better, so far as I am informed, than it has been.* The prospect of war is, at least, not so threatening as it has been.   The idea of coercion, shadowed forth in Mr. Lincoln's inaugural, *seems not to be followed up, thus far, so vigorously as was expected.   Fort Sumter, it is believed, will soon be evacuated.* What course will be pursued toward Fort Pickens, and the other forts on the Gulf, is not so well understood.   *It is to be greatly desired that all of them should be surrendered.*   Our object is peace, not only with the North, but with the world. *   *   * The idea of coercing us, or subjugating us, is utterly preposterous.   Whether the intention of evacuating Fort Sumter is to be received as an evidence of a desire for a peaceful solution of our difficulties with the United States, or the result of necessity, I will not undertake to say.   I would fain hope the former.   Rumors are afloat, however, that it is the result of necessity.   All I can say to you, therefore, on that point, is, *keep your armor bright, and your powder dry.*

That Mr. Stephens well understood the impossibility of peace on the only terms he ventured even to hint, is sufficiently manifest, and his reporter further adds, referring to a later part of his speech :

He alluded to the difficulties and embarrassments which seemed to surround the question of a peaceful solution of the controversy with the old Government.   How can it be done? is perplexing many minds.   The President seems to think that he can not recognize our independence, *nor can he, with and by the advice of the Senate, do so.   The Constitution makes no such provision.*   A general convention of all the States has been suggested by some.

He closed without recommending this, or any other practicable method of peace—which, perhaps, for himself he would have consented to—well knowing that quite another policy was predetermined by conspirators older in the work than he, and to whose scheme he had already undoubtedly given his full consent.

The Rebels saw no hope but in war. Any thing short of that would amount only to a brief ebullition, in the States in which insurrection was already dominant. Something was yet needed to " fire the Southern heart." All the initiated knew that the match was soon to be applied to the industriously prepared train. They may have dreamed of the surrender of Sumter or Pickens as a military necessity; but they little understood the purpose of the President, if it was ever thought possible on any other ground. They certainly greatly mistook his intentions, in either event.

It must be remembered that the close of the last Administration found, still in the office of the Adjutant-General of the Army, a man (General Cooper) who now holds a like position in the Confederate service. The Departments and the city were filled with men of like sympathy, whose knowledge of affairs enabled them to communicate immediate information as to every movement inaugurated, and even of the avowed purposes or projects of every high officer of the Government, civil or military. Men deemed entirely trustworthy and faithful, even, were afterward found to have been in complicity with the traitors, and not a few holding military commissions—which could not be revoked without positive grounds—were regarded as doubtful. For a time it was uncertain how far any one— with a few noble exceptions—in responsible places, in Army or Navy, could be relied on for a cordial support of any efficient policy, even of defense. The event has shown how well founded, in numerous instances beside that of General Cooper, was this distrust.

Mr. Lincoln fully appreciated his surroundings. Disloyalty was rampant among the citizens of the capital. In the Departments, or just relieved therefrom, were men who watched every move, and were anxious to aid the rebellion. The sifting process has been steadily going on, yet how impossible was an immediate purification, is manifest. Under all the circumstances of his position, the President had no resource but to keep his own counsel. Inexperienced in military affairs, he had the ready advice and faithful service of the illustrious head of the Army, Lieutenant-General Scott. True and loyal as that veteran General was, however, his political sympathies had never gone with the now dominant party, while his Virginian birth and associations led him to shrink from every appearance of attempted coercion. It is no secret that General Scott openly and earnestly advocated the evacuation of Fort Sumter—on military, if not also on political, grounds. It is believed that he carried over nearly every Cabinet Minister to his views. The President, while adjusting his new agencies, and learning the spirit of the men about him, in the Army and in the Navy, as well as awaiting, with attentive eye, the developments of opinion and action, in both sections, allowed the consideration of this question to be continued, from day to day, without indicating his purpose. The emissaries who waited here on their false diplomatic mission kept duly apprised, through channels easily imaginable after what has since transpired, of the opinions of General Scott and the deliberations thereon. They had constantly communicated with the leaders at home, it being deemed expedient to allow, during all this period, free intercourse by mail and telegraph. The result was a general impression at the South—for which no word of the Chief Executive ever gave any warrant, although he obviously had no occasion to correct any such misconception—that Fort Sumter was to be evacuated, and that no attempt would be made to reinforce Fort Pickens.

The parting missive of these pseudo-diplomats, on the 9th of April, makes the following statement on this point (addressed to Mr. Seward):

The memorandum [of the Secretary of State, before referred to,] is dated March 15, and was not delivered until April 8. Why was it withheld during the intervening twenty-three days? In the postscript to your memorandum you say it "was delayed, as was understood, with their (Messrs. Forsyth and Crawford's) consent." *This is true;* but it is also true that, *on the 15th of March, Messrs. Forsyth and Crawford were assured by a person occu-*

pying a high official position in the Government, and who, as they believed, was speaking by authority, that Fort Sumter would be evacuated within a very few days, and that no measure changing the existing status, prejudicially to the Confederate States, as respects Fort Pickens, was then contemplated, and these assurances were subsequently repeated, with the addition that any contemplated change, as respects Pickens, *would be notified to us.* On the 1st of April we were again informed that there might be an attempt to supply Fort Sumter with provisions, but that Governor Pickens should have previous notice of the attempt. There was no suggestion of reinforcements. The undersigned *did not hesitate to believe that these assurances expressed the intentions* of the Administration at the time, or, at all events, of prominent members of that Administration. This delay was assented to, for the express purpose of attaining the great end of the mission of the undersigned, to-wit: A pacific solution of existing complications. * * * The intervening twenty-three days were employed in active unofficial efforts, the object of which was to smooth the path to a pacific solution, *the distinguished personage alluded to coöperating with the undersigned;* and every step of that effort is recorded in writing, and now in possession of the undersigned and of their Government. * * * * It is proper to add that, during these twenty-three days, two gentlemen of official distinction, *as high as that of the personage hitherto alluded to,* aided the undersigned *as intermediaries in these unofficial negotiations for peace.*

Without stopping to inquire how far the veracity of a document, conceived in such a spirit and designed for immediate effect, North and South, is to be implicitly relied on, it is enough to say that, by its very terms, this paper shows clearly that neither the President, nor any one authorized in any manner to speak for him, ever gave the assurances stated, even in unofficial intercourse. If these conspirators were deceived by " intermediaries," holding responsible places in the Government, yet so abusing the confidence of their superiors as to communicate their military plans to the emissaries of rebels who had already levied war against the Government, and fired upon its flag, it is manifest that neither Mr. Lincoln nor his Constitutional advisers need regret the deception. The President, however, it is proper distinctly to state, never had the slightest knowledge of the communications alleged, if they ever took place.

It should also be definitely stated here, that Mr. Lincoln (whatever military or civil advisers may have imagined) never seriously entertained the purpose of peaceably and voluntarily abandoning any Government fortifications or property. Much less was he prepared to leave the gallant garrisons of Forts Sumter and Pickens to starvation or humiliating surrender.

As early as the 18th of March, General Bragg, then in command of the Confederate forces at Pensacola, issued his order cutting off supplies of every kind from Fort Pickens as well as from the " armed vessels of the United States," then in the harbor—a military step toward the reduction of the fort, in marked contrast with the pacific professions and affected good faith set forth in the Rebel document just quoted from. An intention of precipitating more active hostilities there was plainly indicated by the insurgents, and the necessity of decisive action on the part of the Government was apparent. A small fleet, of eight vessels, was got in readiness with all possible expedition, (including the two sloops-of-war, Pawnee and Powhatan, with transports carrying troops and supplies,) the first of which set sail from the Washington Navy-Yard on the 6th of April, and the remainder during the next three days. The orders were sealed, but the movement could not be altogether a secret. In fact, it seems to have been almost immediately known at the headquarters of secession in the South. While a portion of this fleet paused off Charleston harbor, the remainder saved Fort Pickens by a timely reinforcement.

On the 7th of April, General Beauregard, at Charleston, followed his co-laborer at Pensacola, and issued an order, notice of which was sent to Major Anderson, prohibiting further intercourse between that fort and the city. This was another military step, backed by the rapid concentration of Rebel troops at Charleston, toward compelling the surrender of Fort Sumter. It left no course to the Government short of furnishing supplies to the garrison of that sea-girt fort. And how careful the President was, from the outset, to avoid, so far as was possible, every act that might even unwarrantably provoke a collision of arms, is well illustrated in this instance. On the 8th of April—the day after Beauregard's hostile order—the President caused the parties interested at Charleston to be officially informed that provisions were to be dispatched to Major Anderson by an unarmed vessel. It is easy to see on which side the true pacific purpose lay. The act of war, commenced by firing on the Star of the West, in January, was renewed by Beauregard in the attempt to starve out Major Anderson. This renewal, again, was met by the mere effort to supply, in a peaceable way, the rations of a garrison that could not thus be abandoned.

Beauregard at once communicated the movement, thus officially explained, to the Rebel Secretary of War, and, under special instructions, received April 10th, demanded, on the following day, the surrender of Fort Sumter—the indisputable property of the Federal Government, the right of domain and jurisdiction over which had been expressly and solemnly granted to that Government by the uncancelled vote of South Carolina herself. The demand was courteously refused. Major Anderson was again called on to name a time at which he would evacuate the fort, meanwhile committing no hostile act. That officer replied, on the 12th, that he would, " if provided with the proper and necessary means of transportation, evacuate Fort Sumter by noon on the 15th instant," should he not " receive, prior to that time, controlling instructions" from the Government, " or additional supplies." To this eminently peaceful and reasonable proposition, the reply was returned that the commandant of " the provisional forces of the Confederate States " would open the fire of his batteries on Fort Sumter in one hour from the date of this " pacific " message, "April 12, 1861, 2:30 A. M." This " Confederate" assurance accorded with the result. After enduring the long-continued fire of numerous batteries, Anderson and his garrison of seventy men were compelled to surrender the fort to Beauregard and his seven thousand rebels in arms.

Thus began in dread earnest, by a clearly unwarrantable and unprovoked act, following repeated protestations of a desire for a " peaceable solution" of troubles resulting solely from the constitutional election of a President, confessedly standing on

15

the same platform, in regard to special Southern interests, as Jefferson, and most of the founders of the Government, a civil war, designed to establish a new Government on the chief corner-stone of slavery, and to revolutionize the opinions of the civilized world in regard to that system. Whatever could be done to avert this final step, was patiently, kindly, sincerely done by Abraham Lincoln. All truthful history will record this of him, through all ages, to his lasting praise. No rough passion, no fretful impatience, no revengeful impulse, ever ruffled his spirit during all these days of suspense. But the gauntlet was at length thrown down, and no alternative was left but to meet force with force.

CHAPTER II.

The Loyal Uprising.—The Border Slave States.—Summary of Events. Battle of Bull Run.

THE first effect of the fall of Fort Sumter was to silence, for the time, all opposition to the President in the Free States. One sentiment was uppermost in the minds of all loyal people— that of indignation at the authors of the war, now inaugurated at Charleston, mingled with the purpose of vindicating the National Flag, and of restoring the legitimate authority of the Government in all the States. Wherever a contrary feeling existed, the strong manifestations of popular enthusiasm for the Government caused such treachery to be carefully disguised. For once, the people of the Free States were a unit in action. The demand for vigorous preparation to protect the National Capital, and to suppress the insurrection, was universal. Simultaneously with this development of loyalty, Mr. Lincoln prepared his proclamation of April 15th, calling on the States for their several proportions of an army of seventy-five thousand men. He also, in the same paper, called an extra session of Congress, to commence on the 4th day of July following.

A like unanimity had been hoped by the conspirators in every Slave State. It was, perhaps, chiefly in order to produce this effect, that the responsibility of beginning the war was assumed by the Rebel leaders. As yet the seven States which had originally entered into the Confederacy at Montgomery had received no accessions from the eight remaining States, supposed to have a common interest with them, from a common peculiarity of institutions. On the very next day after that combination was entered into (February 9), the people of Tennessee had voted against secession, by a large majority. On the

1st day of March a similar vote had been taken in Missouri. On the 4th day of April, a secession ordinance had been rejected in the State Convention of Virginia, by a vote of 45 yeas and 89 nays. In Maryland, the firmness and earnest loyalty of Gov. Hicks had defeated all the schemes for assembling a convention in that State to consider the question of secession. Delaware had manifested a decided Union spirit, and the canvass on this question in Arkansas had thus far developed a strong disinclination to embark in the disunion scheme of Davis and his fellow-conspirators. In North Carolina and Kentucky, all the efforts to seduce the people into rebellion appeared to have been of little avail. Thus, with two tiers of Slave States extending from the Atlantic to the Mississippi, two west of the Mississippi, and the two north-east of Virginia, a majority of all, having many interests diverse from those of the Cotton States, now nominally confederated in the crimes of their leaders, the rebellion was manifestly doomed from the outset, if peace and the opportunity for calm deliberation were allowed.

The rebels undoubtedly wished to avoid the lasting odium of bringing on a desolating and destructive civil war. They saw clearly, however, whither the quiet and pacific policy of the Administration was tending. Not another State would join the Secession movement, if that policy were permitted to continue. From the 1st day of February to the fall of Sumter— two months and a half—not a State had joined the movement, and two, on the immediate border of the Cotton States, had deliberately rejected the proposition, although the State Governments of both were in the hands of active Secessionists. The fatal blow—a necessity to the mad project in hand—was accordingly struck. The immediate object was to gain over the remaining Slave States, and naturally, as second only to the preparation for war, the course to be pursued by those States became an object of chief interest.

The necessity of at once gaining over Virginia to the Secession side, in order to the prosecution of their plans, was now manifest to the leading conspirators at Montgomery and Richmond. The Convention of that State, as already seen, had hitherto proved intractable. In electing that body, the people had decided for the Union by a very large majority. What show or pretense of right, even on Secession principles, had these representatives to repudiate alike the clearly expressed wishes of their constituents and their own personal pledges? In the hope of gaining some plausible pretext for such an act of double perfidy, to be used in connection with threats rapidly growing into a reign of terror, a committee of three was appointed by the Convention, just at the time of the impending attack on Fort Sumter, to wait on the President, avowedly to ascertain his intended policy toward the rebellious States. Mr. Lincoln granted this committee an interview on the 13th of April, and gave them the subjoined response:

To Hon. Messrs. PRESTON, STUART and RANDOLPH—*Gentlemen:* As a committee of the Virginia Convention, now in session, you present me a preamble and resolution in these words:

" WHEREAS, In the opinion of this Convention, the uncertainty which prevails in the public mind as to the policy which the Federal Executive intends to pursue toward the seceded States, is extremely injurious to the industrial and commercial interests of the country, tends to keep up an excitement which is unfavorable to the adjustment of the pending difficulties, and threatens a disturbance of the public peace ; therefore,

"*Resolved,* That a committee of three delegates be appointed to wait on the President of the United States, present to him this preamble, and respectfully ask him to communicate to this Convention the policy which the Federal Executive intends to pursue in regard to the Confederate States."

In answer I have to say, that having, at the beginning of my official term, expressed my intended policy as plainly as I was able, it is with deep regret and mortification I now learn there is great and injurious uncertainty in the public mind as to what that policy is, and what course I intend to pursue. Not having as yet seen occasion to change, it is now my purpose to pursue the course marked out in the inaugural address. I commend a careful consideration of the whole document as the best expression I can give to my purposes. As I then and therein said, I now repeat, " The power confided in me will be used to hold, occupy, and possess property and places belonging to the Government, and to collect the duties and imports ; but beyond what is necessary for these objects there will be no invasion, no using of force against or among the people anywhere." By the words "property and places belonging to the Government," I chiefly allude to the military posts and property which were in possession of the Government when it came into my hands. But if, as now appears to be true, in pursuit of a purpose to drive the United States authorities from these places, an unprovoked assault has been made upon Fort Sumter, I shall hold myself at liberty to repossess it, if I can, like places which had been seized before the Government was devolved upon me ; and in any event I shall, to the best of my ability, repel force by force. In case it proves true that Fort Sumter has been assaulted, as is reported, I shall, perhaps, cause the United States mails to be withdrawn from all the States which claim to have seceded, believing that the commencement of actual war against the Government justifies and possibly demands it. I scarcely need to say that I consider the military posts and property situated within the States which claim to have seceded, as yet belonging to the Government of the United States as much as they did before the supposed secession. Whatever else I may do for the purpose, I shall not attempt to collect the duties and imposts by any armed invasion of any part of the country ; not meaning by this, however, that I may not land a force deemed necessary to relieve a fort upon the border of the country. From the fact that I have quoted a part of the inaugural address, it must not be inferred that I repudiate any other part, the whole of which I reaffirm, except so far as what I now say of the mails may be regarded as a modification.

The Governors of Virginia and Kentucky, thoroughly in fellowship with the South Carolina policy from the outset, promptly sent back defiant messages in response to the President's call for troops. "Kentucky will furnish no troops," said Governor Magoffin, "for the wicked purpose of subduing her sister Southern States." "The militia of Virginia," wrote Letcher to Secretary Cameron, "will not be furnished to the powers at Washington for any such use or purpose as they have in view." Similar was the reply of Governor Harris, of Tennessee. Governor Ellis, of North Carolina, with greater moderation in his language, plainly intimated his purpose not to respond to the President's call. On the 17th, the Virginia Convention, yielding at length to the artifices and intimidations of the busy conspirators, in whose service an ignorant mob was conspicuous, passed, in the darkness of a secret conclave, an ordinance of secession. The processes resorted to for the accomplishment of this object were yet insufficient to move many honorable delegates from their fidelity, but the fatal majority was obtained. Although there was still to be, nominally, a vote of the people on this question, on the 23d of May, Union sentiments were no longer tolerated at Richmond. Violence and terror insured a majority for the insurrection in a State which, on a fair vote, would still have pronounced emphatically against secession.

The conspirators in North Carolina also triumphed, as was to be expected after this defection, and Tennessee and Arkansas followed. Thus four States were gained to the "Confederacy"—by no means through a fair or honest vote—as a result of the war begun in Charleston harbor. The desperate efforts to win over Delaware, Maryland, Kentucky and Missouri, utterly failed, as would have been the case with the other four States, just named, had the pacific policy of the Administration been permitted to continue.

The week following the President's proclamation was crowded with important events. Public meetings were held all through the loyal States, and the response to the call for troops was hearty and universal. Companies and regiments were rapidly filled up and started for the National Capital. But a few hours intervened before Massachusetts had one regiment at its rendezvous, and ready for departure. Pennsylvania and New York were on the alert, and a battalion of volunteers, from the former State, were the first to reach Washington, while the New York Seventh was at nearly the same time on its way. The spirit already roused throughout the country was greatly intensified by the attempts of a secession mob in Baltimore to prevent the passage of the Massachusetts Sixth through that city. Here the first blood of Union troops was shed, on an ever memorable anniversary, the 19th day of April. Enlistments followed with such rapidity, that it was soon only a question whose services should be declined, of the tens of thousands offering themselves.

The city of Washington, an object of threatened attack, and

thronged with people, who either openly proclaimed their hostility to the Government, or were of doubtful fidelity, was full of excitement—liable at any moment to an *emeute* or to an irruption of rebel troops already in the field in Virginia. Alexandria was in their possession, or easily accessible at any moment from Richmond. Rumors were current of an immediate intention on the part of the Confederate leaders to occupy Arlington Heights, completely commanding the city, while as yet only a few companies of the regular service, with two or three light field batteries, were in Washington for its defense. To these were added a few hundred volunteer militia, made up chiefly of transient sojourners at the Capital. A few dragoons, with a detachment of artillery, guarded the Long Bridge, and the Navy Yard and other portions of the city had a small guard of extemporized infantry. There was also a single company of sappers and miners, under Lieut. (now General) Weitzel. Thus passed an anxious week, while every exertion was made by the Government and its loyal supporters to assemble an adequate defensive force. How easily the place might have been taken, with not one of the present numerous and strong fortifications, with no army but half a dozen scattered companies of infantry, cavalry and artillery, and with so large a number within ready to rise and give active welcome to the assailing force they so eagerly expected, need not here be discussed. From one extremity of the country to the other, the danger was seen and felt. The few days needful, fortunately were gained.

The 19th of April is further memorable for the proclamation issued on that day, declaring a blockade of every port of the States in insurrection, in the following terms :

WHEREAS, An insurrection against the Government of the United States has broken out in the States of South Carolina, Georgia, Alabama, Florida, Mississippi, Louisiana and Texas, and the laws of the United States for the collection of the revenue can not be efficiently executed therein conformably to that provision of the Constitution which requires duties to be uniform throughout the United States :

AND WHEREAS, A combination of persons, engaged in such

insurrection, have threatened to grant pretended letters of marque to authorize the bearers thereof to commit assaults on the lives, vessels, and property of good citizens of the country lawfully engaged in commerce on the high seas, and in waters of the United States:

AND WHEREAS, An Executive Proclamation has already been issued, requiring the persons engaged in these disorderly proceedings to desist therefrom, calling out a militia force for the purpose of repressing the same, and convening Congress in extraordinary session to deliberate and determine thereon :

Now, therefore, I, Abraham Lincoln, President of the United States, with a view to the same purposes before mentioned, and to the protection of the public peace, and the lives and property of quiet and orderly citizens pursuing their lawful occupations, until Congress shall have assembled and deliberated on the said unlawful proceedings, or until the same shall have ceased, have further deemed it advisable to set on foot a blockade of the ports within the States aforesaid, in pursuance of the laws of the United States, and of the laws of nations in such cases provided. For this purpose a competent force will be posted so as to prevent entrance and exit of vessels from the ports aforesaid. If, therefore, with a view to violate such blockade, a vessel shall approach, or shall attempt to leave any of the said ports, she will be duly warned by the commander of one of the blockading vessels, who will indorse on her register the fact and date of such warning ; and if the same vessel shall again attempt to enter or leave the blockaded port, she will be captured and sent to the nearest convenient port, for such proceedings against her and her cargo as' prize as may be deemed advisable.

And I hereby proclaim and declare, that if any person, under the pretended authority of said States, or under any other pretense, shall molest a vessel of the United States, or the persons or cargo on board of her, such person will be held amenable to the laws of the United States for the prevention and punishment of piracy.

By the President: ABRAHAM LINCOLN.
          WILLIAM H. SEWARD, Secretary of State.
Washington, April 19, 1861.

Intelligence having been received that Virginia troops were marching on Harper's Ferry, to take possession of the important Government property there, the public works were destroyed and the place evacuated by Lieut. Jones, the commandant. Almost simultaneously the Fourth Massachusetts

Regiment, dispatched by wise forethought, arrived at Fortress Monroe (soon after reinforced by the First Vermont, under Col. Phelps), and secured a permanent occupation of that strong position in the Old Dominion, which had now become (without waiting for the consummation of the farce of a popular vote under duress) the eighth State of the Rebel Confederacy.

During this brief period—at the close of a week of unprecedented excitement at Washington and of loyal enthusiasm throughout the country—earnest appeals were made to the President by prominent Marylanders to stop all attempts to transport troops through that State to the National Capital. His prompt reply set all such petitions at rest. The usual thoroughfares, meanwhile, had been obstructed. Treason hoped the work was already accomplished, and relief cut off. Timorous or hesitating men feared that the effort would be useless. But the purpose of Mr. Lincoln was not for an instant shaken. The route by Annapolis was opened by Gen. Butler and his Massachusetts force, and on the 25th of April troops from the North began to pour into Washington, relieving all immediate anxiety. The people had nobly responded. The "great uprising" was an assured event.

Toward the veteran Lieutenant-General of the Army all eyes were turned as the fit organizer and leader of the Government forces. His counsels were potent, necessarily, in the formation of plans suited to the juncture. Compelled to resort to force by armed aggressive rebellion, the foremost purpose was strictly a defensive one. To protect the capital first of all— for in the flush of triumph over the reduction of Fort Sumter, the determination to take Washington, a city surrounded by territory claimed as destined to form part of the Confederacy, was boldly avowed, alike by the Rebel Secretary of War and by the organs of public opinion every-where in the insurrectionary States—was the object aimed at by the President, and energetically undertaken by Gen. Scott. Secondary to this, and a labor for the future, was the reoccupation and re-possession of Federal forts and Federal property already seized by the Rebels, and the retention of such as were threatened, as distinctly promised by the President in his inaugural address—forcibly now, since the peaceable alternative was no longer possible. The blockade by sea, and a defensive campaign by land, were the immediate steps recommended by the General-in-Chief and adopted by the Administration.

On the 27th of April the following announcement of new Military Departments and Commanders was made by Adj.-Gen. Thomas: 1. The Department of Washington, including the District of Columbia, according to its original boundary, Fort Washington and the adjacent country, and the State of Maryland as far as Bladensburgh, inclusive; under the command of Gen. Joseph K. F. Mansfield—headquarters at Washington. 2. The Department of Annapolis, including the country for twenty miles on each side of the railroad from Annapolis to the city of Washington, as far as Bladensburgh; under the command of Gen. B. F. Butler—headquarters at Annapolis. 3. The Department of Pennsylvania, including that State, the State of Delaware, and all of the State of Maryland not embraced within the Departments first named; under command of Gen. Robert Patterson — headquarters at Philadelphia, "or any other point he may temporarily occupy." This organization of Departments indicates the field of contemplated military operations in the East. The Department of Washington extended no further southward than the old limits of the District of Columbia, an extension into Virginia only for the obvious purpose of including Alexandria and Arlington Heights, as essential to the defenses of the capital.

To these Departments were added a fourth, on the 10th day of May, including the States of Ohio, Indiana and Illinois, under the command of Gen. George B. McClellan—headquarters at Cincinnati. This Department was also manifestly organized with a view to the maintenance of a defensive line, on the Ohio river, from Wheeling to Cairo. During the first week succeeding the fall of Fort Sumter, indications were apparent which led the people along this extended line—and particularly at Cincinnati and Cairo, deemed especially vulnerable points—to desire some efficient preparation to repel any Rebel advance. The debatable ground of Kentucky was early coveted as a field for military occupancy by the confident insurgents. The Governor of that State was in open sympathy with the rebellion, and, under the guise of neutrality which even the most loyal of her citizens seemed for a time to acquiesce in as the wisest expedient, was believed to be preparing to subject the State to Rebel domination. Across this middle territory, by the Covington and Lexington Railroad, on the one hand, and by the Mississippi river, from Columbus and Paducah, on the other, an invasion of Ohio or Illinois was reasonably apprehended. That sympathizers and complotters with the Montgomery leaders were eagerly designing and ready to aid such invasion, in both sections of Kentucky, was well understood.

It was from the wish for prompt and decisive action in securing this defensive line, which involved the occupation of all necessary points on the Kentucky side of the river commanding the north bank of the Ohio, just as the possession of the hights south of the Potomac, near Washington, was essential to the defense of that city, that the appointment of Gen. McClellan by Gov. Dennison, of Ohio, as Commander of the Volunteer Militia of that State, was made. This was earnestly desired, especially by influential citizens of Cincinnati, where McClellan had been quietly residing during the previous year or two, charged with responsible duties in the management of an important railroad. It was known that he had a military education and that he was an experienced engineer, which latter quality specially commended him to the favor of those who were anxious for the protection of the city. To render this appointment efficient, by giving him authority to pass the limits of Ohio and to occupy the hights on the Kentucky side of the river, his appointment, by the Federal Government, to a position in the regular army was strenuously urged, and ere long secured. In assigning him so large an area as his Department, its contemplated reorganization at an early day was distinctly announced.

It was also on the 10th day of May that the Rebel Secretary of War issued his order, at Montgomery, directing Gen. Robert E. Lee to assume command of the "forces of the Confederate States in Virginia."

Of the eight Slave States which had stood aloof from the Montgomery Confederacy at the outset, Virginia had nominally entered into an alliance with that pretended Government, as already seen, and practically joined the insurrection, in advance of the promised popular vote. Tennessee and Arkansas followed this example on the 6th of May, and North Carolina (her rulers being previously in practical alliance), on the 20th. Maryland, Missouri and Kentucky, as the event proved, were saved from this suicidal conduct, not without the aid of Federal arms. Delaware remained true.

On the 29th of April the blockade was extended, in accordance with a proclamation of the President, so as to embrace the ports of Virginia and North Carolina, owing to rebellious acts in those States, antecedent to their pretended secession, yet clearly pointing to such an event as practically determined. Jefferson Davis, on the same day, having hastily convened his "Confederate Congress" to make provision for more effective hostilities, submitted his message to that body, containing an elaborate attempt to justify the war that had been precipitated upon the country, appealing to slaveholding interest and prejudice, and instigating a united and zealous prosecution of the war. He recognized, solely, the issue of slavery as the one cause which had led to the outbreak. As to the mode of action pursued by the Rebel leaders, he distinctly claimed that the Constitutional right of secession had been steadily maintained by "the Democratic party of the United States," and urged its pledges "that it would faithfully abide by and uphold" those principles, as they were "laid down in the Kentucky and Virginia Legislatures of 1799," and its adoption of "those principles as constituting one of the main foundations of its political creed." (How vain this appeal, let the prompt and cordial action of such Democrats as Douglas, Andrew Johnson, B. F. Butler, Daniel S. Dickinson, Lewis Cass, and hundreds of other faithful leaders in the ranks of their party testify. The reorganized party, assuming the Democratic name, at a later day, under the auspices of Vallandigham, Richardson, Wood, Cox and their compeers, may perhaps as heartily, though not as openly, indorse this exposition of the "Democratic" faith, as it directly sustains the allegation of Davis that Northern aggressions are the cause of the war.)

The Rebel champion further asserts that these " principles were maintained by overwhelming majorities of the people of all the States of the Union at different elections, especially in the election of Mr. Jefferson, in 1805, Mr. Madison, in 1809, and Mr. Pierce in 1852." Equally veracious are his narratives of the impudent efforts of Crawford and his associates to make an appearance of negotiating for peaceable separation, and of the events immediately preceding the attack on Fort Sumter, with a view to rid himself of the terrible responsibility of in-augurating a war that must consign his name to lasting infamy. He boasts of his attempt to organize piracy on the high seas, by assuming the power of issuing letters of marque and repri-sal, without a shadow of right under international laws, even conceding his claim of a national existence for his pseudo-Con-federacy. He expresses his entire confidence " that, ere you [the 'Confederate Congress '] shall have been many weeks in session, the whole of the Slaveholding States of the late Union will respond to the call of honor and affection. and by uniting their fortune with ours, promote our common interests and secure our common safety." He speaks of " the rapid develop-ment of the purpose of the President of the United States to invade our soil, capture our forts, blockade our ports, and wage war against us," and refers to the report of the " Confederate " Secretary of War " for a full history of the occurrences in Charleston harbor, prior to and including the bombardment and reduction of Fort Sumter, and of the measures subse-quently taken for common defense, on receiving the intelligence of the declaration of war" (so this scrupulous personage chooses to say) " against us by the President of the United States." He gives the number of his troops " now in the field at Charleston, Pensacola, Forts Morgan, Jackson, St. Philip, and Pulaski," as 19,000 men, with 16,000 more " now en route for Virginia." He adds: " It is proposed to organize and hold in readiness for instant action, in view of the present exigences of the country, an army of 100,000 men ;" and declares that volunteers " are constantly tendering their services far in excess of our wants." He does not conclude his extended document without uttering the now familiar words, equally as appropriāte to brigands and pirates as to traitors : "All we ask is, to be let alone."

Partly by way of inciting slaveholders to unite as a body in his unhallowed schemes, and partly to influence public opinion abroad, for the hour, the arch conspirator prepared this skillful, but eminently fallacious, message, and he found the pseudo-Congress he addressed to be willing instruments in organizing the formidable war power he desired.

These preparations at Montgomery and the growing requirements of a service already expanded through so wide a field, made it necessary for Mr. Lincoln to anticipate the extra session of Congress, called for the 4th of July, and to issue, on the 3d of May, a proclamation for 42,000 additional volunteers, for the term of three years, unless sooner discharged, and for eight regiments of infantry, one of cavalry, and one of artillery, numbering 22,714 in the aggregate, to be added to the regular army. A call was also made, in the same proclamation, for 18,000 additional seamen for the naval service. This action, clearly justified by the requirements of the occasion, or rather made obligatory upon him by the necessities of the situation, was confirmed and legalized, without opposition, by Congress at its extra session. It met the universal approval of the loyal men of the country, and the quick response to this call in a few· days more than filled the demand for army volunteers.

Cairo, Illinois, had been occupied by Government forces, under Col. B. M. Prentiss, during the latter part of April. On the Kentucky and Missouri sides of the Mississippi and Ohio rivers, and particularly on each side of the former, at Columbus, Belmont and below, preparations on the part of the insurgents were soon manifest, threatening an aggressive movement, and certainly intended to hold the Mississippi, as a rebel possession, from Cairo to New Orleans. The prompt movement of Illinois volunteers saved the West from invasion. This little army of occupation at Camp Defiance prepared the way for enterprises, enlarging to a magnitude perhaps little imagined at the moment.

At this time, also, Capt. Nathaniel Lyon (subsequently General) was taking prompt measures to protect the United States arms in the Arsenal at St. Louis from seizure by Secessionists, who were scheming to get possession of this prize—of incalculable value to the Union troops then volunteering. The Government now, as for months afterward, though untiring in its efforts, found it no easy task to provide muskets in numbers at all adequate to the emergency. Adroit management secured the very considerable supply at St. Louis to the Department of the Ohio. Like timely action, soon after, broke up a Secession camp forming in the same city, and defeated the plots of a traitorous Governor for betraying the State of Missouri into the hands of the insurgents. Camp Jackson, with a large supply of arms and munitions of war, and several hundred prisoners, were surrendered on the 10th of May—a memorable day for Missouri.

On the 11th of the same month, Gen. W. S. Harney, of the regular army, returning from Richmond, whither he had been taken as a prisoner, captured in Western Virginia, while on his way to Washington, assumed command of the Military Department of the West. His career was a brief one, practically culminating in a compact entered into, on the 21st, with Gen. Sterling Price, acting on behalf of the disloyal Governor of Missouri, to the effect that the whole responsibility and labor of maintaining peace and order in that State should be intrusted to the State authorities; while Gen. Harney, on his part, should make no military movements, and carefully avoid any acts tending to produce jealousy and excitement. It is needless to say that such an engagement never had the sanction of the President. It was definitely set aside by an order of the Adjutant General addressed to Harney, under date of May 27th, and a force was promptly put in the field, under command of Gen. Lyon.

Meanwhile, at Washington, since the free arrival of troops had commenced, the whole country south of the Potomac, except as explored by scouts, was little better than an unknown land. At Alexandria, a secession flag floated in sight of the Capital, while at Manassas Junction a threatening force was gathering. It was not until the morning of the 24th of May that an advance into Virginia, by the forces under Gen. Mansfield, was deemed expedient. This movement, awakening great interest among the people, who had anticipated early and decisive results, and began already to weary of indispensable delay, had no further immediate purpose than the occupancy of Arlington Heights and Alexandria, for the greater security of Washington; for any more extended undertaking, this improvised army, as all now see after three years of war, was entirely inadequate, either in itself or in its appliances. An advance on Manassas Junction, at this time, was indeed discussed in official circles, but military opinions were decidedly against the undertaking, and the Department of Washington was not now enlarged.

This advance into Virginia, early in the morning of the day after the farce of a popular vote for Secession had been enacted, was executed without resistance. Col. Ellsworth, who commanded a regiment ordered to Alexandria, lost his life by the hands of an assassin, in hauling down, with his own hand, the Rebel flag that had, for many days, flaunted defiance toward Washington; otherwise, no serious casualty occurred. To the people of Alexandria this movement was a surprise, and some prisoners fell into the hands of our troops. The number of men who crossed the Potomac, at this time, was about 13,000. They immediately commenced constructing earthworks, where Fort Ellsworth, Fort Corcoran, the defenses of the Long Bridge, and other memorials of like purpose, still attest the labors then entered upon.

Two days later, the Postmaster General issued his order suspending all postal service in the States of Virginia, North Carolina, South Carolina, Georgia, Florida, Alabama, Mississippi, Louisiana, Arkansas and Texas, to take effect on the 31st of May. Tennessee, although in league with the Confederate insurgents, through the State officers, was intentionally omitted in this order. Obvious advantages had resulted from a continuance of the United States mails in all the States hitherto, and it was only when, more active hostilities being imminent, these advantages would be more than counterbalanced, that this order

16 21

was issued. To the leaders and people of the insurgent districts it was no light matter, as at once practically felt, to be deprived of this beneficent intervention of the Federal Government, maintained, as it always had been, in part, by a tax upon the correspondence of the Free States. This order marks the date of the first decisive step toward the enforcement of nonintercourse with the Rebel population, except as their territory might successively fall within the lines of our armies, now rapidly preparing for the field.

A great portion of the army which had been forming under the eye of Gen. McClellan, was to have its first employment, by direction of the President, in sustaining the loyal people of Western Virginia. The force sent into that region was to drive back the Rebel troops which had gone out to destroy the Baltimore and Ohio Railroad, and to subjugate that part of the State, in which a purpose to repudiate secession was already manifested. The order was issued by the General from his headquarters at Cincinnati on the 26th of May, and the First Virginia Regiment of volunteers, under Col. B. F. Kelly, was sent out from Bellaire on the Wheeling branch of the railroad, while the Fourteenth Ohio Regiment of volunteers, under Col. J. B. Steadman, advanced on the Parkersburg branch of the road, toward Grafton.

For several days after this movement commenced, Gen. McClellan remained at Cincinnati. Under the auspices of Gov. Magoffin and his Inspector-General, Simon B. Buckner, a force was organizing in Kentucky, believed to be covertly intended for the Rebel service, and watched with apprehension by loyal people north of the Ohio. During the progress of Buckner's preparations he visited Cincinnati and had a protracted interview with Gen. McClellan, on the 8th of June. In an official report to Gov. Magoffin, made public on the 22d of that month, Buckner set forth in detail what he alleged as a formal agreement between McClellan and himself, the substance of which, after an engagement on the part of Kentucky to maintain "neutrality" between the "United States" and the "Southern States," is contained in the following extract from that document:

Gen. McClellan stipulates that the territory of Kentucky shall be respected on the part of the United States, even though the Southern States should occupy it; but in the latter case he will call upon the authorities of Kentucky to remove the Southern forces from our territory. Should Kentucky fail to accomplish this object in a reasonable time, Gen. McClellan claims the same right of occupancy given to the Southern forces. I have stipulated, in that case, to advise him of the inability of Kentucky to comply with her obligations, and to invite him to dislodge the Southern forces. He stipulates that if he is successful in doing so, he will withdraw his forces from the territory of the State as soon as the Southern forces shall have been removed. This, he assures me, is the policy which he will adopt toward Kentucky.

That this interview took place, is an undisputed fact. That any compact of this nature was entered into, would seem incredible, without other evidence than Buckner's word of honor. But that Gen. McClellan, while commanding the Department of the Ohio, did nothing inconsistent with the alleged terms of agreement, must be conceded. Thus was one controlling purpose in his first appointment by the Governor of Ohio completely defeated. The occupation and defense of the southern bank of the river, near Cincinnati, was voluntarily abandoned—either by reason of this stipulation or without it—by the man specially chosen for that work. Near the same date, Gen. McClellan addressed a letter to the late Mr. Crittenden, expressing regret that some of Gen. Prentiss' men, in making an excursion down the Mississippi, on the 12th of June, had landed on the Kentucky shore and cut down and brought away a Secession flag which they saw flying at Columbus. He disclaimed all responsibility for this intrusion.

Thus cautious was the Commanding General to be no aggressor on the soil of any Slave State, and to wound the sensibilities of neither incipient Rebels nor "neutrals," who were supporters of slave institutions. Even while sending a force to the aid of loyal Western Virginia, at the request of her people, he was careful to assure them:

Notwithstanding all that has been said by the traitors to induce you to believe that our advent among you will be signal ized by interference with your slaves, understand one thing clearly—not only will we abstain from all such interference, but we will, on the contrary, with an iron hand, crush any attempt at insurrection on their part.

The first engagement in Western Virginia was fought at Philippa, on the 2d of June, Gen. Thomas A. Morris, of Indiana, being the officer in actual command of the forces now concentrated at and near Grafton, with headquarters at that place. The arduous and successful expedition thence to Philippa, surprising and breaking up an important camp of Rebels, was under the immediate direction of Col. Dumont, of Indiana.

On the 3d of June, Gen. Patterson issued an address from his headquarters, now at Chambersburg, Pa., to the troops of his Department, promising that they should "soon meet the insurgents." He added: " You must bear in mind you are going for the good of the whole country, and that, while it is your duty to punish sedition, you must protect the loyal, and, should the occasion offer, at once suppress servile insurrection."

It is worthy of note here that Mr. Lincoln, with that magnanimity which would see only an endangered country, had put at the head of three important Military Departments three of the most decided of his political opponents—Patterson, Butler and McClellan. These appointments were made under the earnest conviction—how well justified by the result will presently appear—that these officers possessed the military capacity and skill suited to the wants of the occasion, and that they would heartily sustain the Government in its work of self-preservation. Patterson and McClellan had each been selected by the Republican Executives of their own States. Both had served in Mexico, under the eye of Gen. Scott, and their selection had his approval.

To the voluntary promises made by Patterson and McClellan, that slavery should be upheld by force of arms, if need be, it must be added that a like assurance was given by Butler to the people of Maryland, soon after his occupation of Annapolis.

A few days after the victory at Philippa, Gen. Thomas A. Morris, the General in actual command, on whom, with Gen. W. S. Rosecrans, the direction of the campaign now inaugurated in West Virginia mainly depended, issued his proclamation from headquarters at Grafton, calling on the people to arm for their own protection against the enemies of their "freedom and peace," and to rally in arms to the support of the Constitutional Government. The Convention of loyal Virginia Delegates, held at Wheeling, proclaimed, on the 17th of June, their repudiation of the pretended ordinance of secession by which Virginia was called on "to separate from and wage war against the Government of the United States," and in the name of the people, declared that "the offices of all who adhere to " the Richmond Convention and Gov. Letcher (in the enumerated acts of treason and usurpation perpetrated by them), whether legislative, executive or judicial, are vacated. A new State Government was promptly organized, with Francis H. Pierpont for Governor. In due time a State Legislature was chosen, and Senators and Representatives in Congress were elected. Thus, with the full approbation of President Lincoln, and with his substantial support, was the first step inaugurated toward a restoration of a loyal local Government in the insurgent States. The State Government thus organized was for Virginia in its integrity, and it was sustained by the people, wherever our armies held in check the armed forces of the Rebels.

On the 23d of June, three weeks after the battle of Philippa, Gen. McClellan, having just arrived, issued another proclamation to the people from headquarters at Grafton, announcing that the Army of the Ohio, "headed by Virginia troops, is rapidly occupying all Western Virginia." He reaffirmed the promises of his former proclamation, adding: "Your houses, families, property and all your rights will be religiously respected." He denounced upon guerrillas and marauders the severest penalties of military law. To the soldiers of his Army he issued an order enjoining good conduct, and inspiriting them for the work before them. "We have come here," he said, "to save, not to upturn."

Nearly three weeks later, July 12th (after a skirmish at Laurel Hill, on the 10th), an engagement was had with the Rebels under Col. Pegram, commonly known as the battle of Rich Mountain, resulting in the surrender of that officer and a number of men, officially estimated as "nine hundred or one thousand," as well as in the rout and close pursuit of Gen. Garnett and the forces he was bringing to the support of Pegram, and in the death of Garnett at Carrickford, on the 14th. Without discussing the merits of this brief campaign, in which the number of men engaged on either side may be estimated at rather more than 10,000, it will suffice to quote the final summing up, by the Commanding General, in his dispatch to the War Department, of July 14th, as follows:

HUTTONSVILLE, VA., *July* 14, 1861.

Col. E. D. Townsend, Assistant Adjutant General:

Gen. Garnett and his forces have been routed and his baggage and one gun taken. His army are completely demoralized. Gen. Garnett was killed while attempting to rally his forces at Carrickford, near St. George.

We have completely annihilated the enemy in Western Virginia.

Our loss is but thirteen killed and not more than forty wounded, while the enemy's loss is not far from two hundred killed, and the number of prisoners we have taken will amount to at least one thousand. We have captured seven of the enemy's guns in all.

A portion of Garnett's forces retreated, but I look for their capture by General Hill, who is in hot pursuit.

The troops that Garnett had under his command are said to be the crack regiments of Eastern Virginia, aided by Georgians, Tennesseeans and Carolinians.

Our success is complete, and I firmly believe that secession is killed in this section of the country.

GEORGE B. McCLELLAN, Maj.-Gen. U. S. A.

A similar work was simultaneously going on in Missouri, under the earnest and skillful guidance of Gen. Nathaniel Lyon. Missouri was nearly betrayed by its Secessionist Governor and his subordinates, without the aid of a conspiring Convention, yet she was drifting, under unscrupulous management, in the same direction which Virginia, North Carolina and Tennessee had gone. Gov. Claiborne F. Jackson had defied the popular repudiation of Secession, issued his proclamation, on the 12th, calling out 50,000 militia, to repel "invasion," etc., and immediately organized a further Rebel force at the State Capital, after the breaking up of Camp Jackson, at St. Louis, as already narrated. Gen. Lyon approaching Jefferson City with a moderate force, Jackson evacuated the place on the 14th of June, and the Union forces occupied it on the following day. On the 17th, Gen. Lyon, finding that the Rebel Governor was fortifying at Boonville, forty miles distant (his forces being commanded by Gen. Sterling Price), advanced to that point and gained a complete victory, dispersing the insurgents, who lost heavily in killed, wounded and prisoners. These energetic movements at once secured the possession of a large portion of the State from Rebel interference.

The defeat of the conspirators, first at St. Louis and afterward at Boonville, had been so complete that it was several weeks before any considerable force was rallied to disturb the quiet into which the State was settling down, under the new government of loyal rulers, which was meanwhile forming. On the 31st of July, Hamilton R. Gamble was elected Provisional Governor by the Missouri State Convention, and duly inaugurated, with other loyal officers, chosen at the same time. The future of that State was thus assured.

In Gen. Butler's Department a movement, preparatory to opening the way to Yorktown, was made by a small force, on the 10th of June, resulting in a repulse at Big Bethel. Coming a week after the cheering success at Philippa, under Gen. Morris, the effect of this reverse, unimportant as it may seem, was sadly felt by the country, and placed the Commanding General under a cloud, from which he unfortunately did little to redeem himself, during the time he retained this command.

The fight at Falling Waters, on the 2d of July, was the chief event, which had thus far relieved the general quietude, not to say dullness, prevailing in the Department of Gen. Patterson. This skirmish occurred near Hainesville, Md., in the tardy execution of a long-deferred movement of Patterson's force from Chambersburg, by Williamsport, to Harper's Ferry. The loss was small on either side, yet, as an indication of some approaching activity, it was not without its effect on an already impatient people. With further delays and hesitations, the force of Patterson was at length thrown across the Potomac.

At this time, a considerable Rebel force was believed to have accumulated at Manassas Junction and at Winchester. The popular demand was almost universal that our troops, now so long in arms, the brief term of a large portion of whom was about to expire, should be led against the enemy. Gen. Scott at length decided on a movement upon Manassas—resulting in the battle of Bull Run, with which this first period of the war may be said to have closed.

Gen. Irvin McDowell took command of the troops on the Virginia side of the Potomac, May 27th, three days after they had crossed over. His headquarters were at the Arlington House. On the 31st of May, a company of cavalry, under Lieut. Tompkins, dashed into the village of Fairfax Court House, where several hundred Rebel cavalry were stationed, killing a number of the enemy and capturing five prisoners. His own loss was one killed and five wounded or missing. This may be called the first cavalry raid. As a reconnoissance, this otherwise unimportant affair was of service, the officer in command reporting the presence of Rebel troops at that point to the number of 1,500 men.

After the manifestations, here as well as in the Shenandoah Valley, of a gradual aggressive movement of the insurgents, threatening alike Alexandria, Washington and the upper part of Maryland, the impatience of the people—ignorant as they were of the difficulties in the way of properly equipping a force, even then so much out of proportion to any organized in this country during the last forty years—was natural, when, with only skirmishing along the Potomac, no general movement to thrust back these aggressors had been commenced until the middle of July. That the causes of this delay were beyond the control of the Executive, and that even when commenced the experienced military leaders in command had failed to put their forces in full readiness, is now apparent. The Rebels themselves anticipated an earlier attack, and had prepared for it, awaiting the onset on their chosen ground. Meanwhile batteries began to be erected along the Potomac, at Acquia Creek and elsewhere, threatening a complete blockade of the river. On the 27th of June, Capt. James H. Ward, of the Navy had lost his life in an attack on the obstructions at Matthias Point. The hope and purpose of capturing Washington and subjugating Maryland were clearly shown by the procedure of the Rebels, and not without reason, when we remember their military preparations during a whole year, and the advantages given them by the Administration just closed.

Baltimore, in which there had been, since the 19th of April, constant conspiracies in aid of the rebellion, and which was relied on by the Rebel leaders for important aid in the general scheme of extending their military sway northward to Mason and Dixon's line, had been occupied by Gen. Butler on the 14th of May. Strong works thrown up on Federal Hill, and elsewhere, as well as Fort McHenry, now held the conspirators in check, and their designs were effectually overthrown before Butler's transfer to the new Department of Virginia, a few days later. This Department originally embraced Eastern Virginia to the summit of the Blue Ridge, and the States of North Carolina and South Carolina. Gen. N. P. Banks succeeded to the command at Baltimore, and continued the vigorous measures of his predecessor.

On the 15th of July, Gen. Patterson's army advanced, occupying Bunker Hill, and the Rebel force under J. E. Johnston fell back on Winchester. Patterson was expected at least to occupy the attention of the Rebels, to whose force his own actually was, as believed at the time in Washington, largely superior. Almost simultaneously with this " demonstration" in the Valley, Gen. McDowell issued an order (July 16th) distributing his troops into divisions, and took up the line of march toward Fairfax Court House. This place his advance column occupied on the following day, without resistance. His entire effective force was not far from 50,000 men : the First Division under command of Gen. Daniel Tyler, of Connecticut; the Second under Col. David Hunter, of the Army; the Third under Col. S. P. Heintzelman, of the Army; the Fourth under Gen. Theodore Runyon, of New Jersey, and the Fifth under Col. D. S. Miles, of the Army. The two last divisions were intended to act as the Reserve.

On the 18th, Patterson's force, instead of attacking Johnston at Winchester, was moved on Charlestown—a step which all critics, judging after the event, will agree to have been unfortunate, in consequence of which no effectual coöperation with the Manassas movement was rendered. On the same day, (Thursday) McDowell resumed his march in the direction of Centreville, and a premature engagement was brought on at Blackburn's Ford, by a portion of Gen. Tyler's division. The slight repulse which followed ended an immediate advance, and detained the army, inactive, at and near Centreville, for the next two days.

The plan of battle, as now seen in the published order of Gen. McDowell, for Sunday the 21st, was a good one, but the execution of some of its details was imperfect, and the delay of troops in moving to the scene of action prepared the way for the final disaster, through the arrival of Rebel reënforcements from Johnston, whom Patterson had failed to occupy as ordered. The immediate purpose of giving battle at this time, was to force the enemy from his position commanding the Warrenton road, and to destroy the railroad from Manassas to the Valley of Virginia, preventing communication with the large Rebel force in the latter locality.

The stream named Bull Run passes in a southeasterly direction through the ravine at the foot of the slope beyond Centreville. Three roads lead from the latter place to the South and West—one nearly due south, crossing Bull Run at Blackburn's Ford; a second due west toward Groveton, over the Stone Bridge; and a third, about midway between these two, at an angle of forty-five degrees, to each, extending more directly to Newmarket, (near Manassas Junction), where Beauregard, commanding the Rebel forces, had his headquarters. This last road is known as the Warrenton turnpike. Beyond the run are the Manassas Plains, extending for miles, mostly an open country, like a Western prairie. On the rolling ground near the stream the woods are dense, and there are occasional groves farther away. The Rebel lines extended for a distance of six to ten miles along the right bank of Bull Run, from near Blackburn's Ford to the Stone Bridge, and beyond the Groveton road. The Rebel lines were two or three miles distant, at the nearest point, from Newmarket, and visible from the head-quarters of Beauregard. The number of his men, on Sunday morning, is believed to have been about forty thousand in line, with fifteen or twenty thousand in reserve, exclusive of reën-forcements arriving during the day.

A large portion of Johnston's forces had previously reached Manassas Junction, and that General was present in person, but waiving his seniority of rank, allowed Beauregard to conduct the engagement, his dispositions having already been made.

Leaving part of the division under Miles—two brigades with two batteries—as a reserve at Centreville, together with Rich-ardson's brigade, temporarily assigned to the same division, which was to threaten Blackburn's Ford, covered by the ene-my's right, McDowell ordered Tyler's division to take position on the Warrenton road, menacing the Rebel center. To Hun-ter's division was intrusted the important work of turning the Rebel left, going to the right of the Groveton road, and crossing Bull Run above Sudley's Spring. This force was to be followed by Heintzelman's division, which was to cross lower down, after Hunter had effected his crossing and descended the right bank to a point nearly opposite, driving away any force that might be there to dispute the passage. These two divi-sions were the ones most actively engaged in the ensuing battle. The necessity of strongly guarding against the contingency of a Rebel movement to occupy Centreville, either by Blackburn's Ford or the Warrenton road, was strongly impressed on the mind of the Commanding General. This led to the detach-ment of one of Heintzelman's brigades, after the movement commenced, to be added to the force on our left. The event showed the wisdom of his action in protecting this position, which the Rebel General had deliberately planned to assail, if we may credit his report, written long afterward, and which, but for McDowell's precautions, might have been taken at the close of the battle, to the much more serious discomfiture of our army.

More time was consumed in getting the men in position, on the morning of the 21st, than had been anticipated. Tyler opened with his artillery at half past six o'clock, eliciting no reply. Burnside's brigade, under Hunter, successfully crossed the stream, and emerged from the wooded bank into the open plain beyond. Almost immediately, the head of the column encountered a heavy Rebel force, but Tyler and Heintzelman had each, from their respective positions, succeeded in throwing part of their force across, and presently nearly all but the reserves before mentioned were brought into action. The ground was hotly contested from half past ten o'clock until three. The advantage at the latter hour was clearly on the side of our arms, and the victory seemed assured. That such was the view taken by the Rebel commanders even, is seen from the accounts of the battle from that side.

At this important juncture, a further reënforcement from Johnston's army at Winchester (perhaps, in fact, " the residue" of that army, as supposed by Gen. McDowell) arrived on the field. Our men, who had been up since two o'clock, had marched several miles, and had fought for many hours, were exhausted by the privations they had necessarily undergone, and from the fatigue incident to such labors in an excessively hot day. Most were inexperienced troops. This was their first engagement. The new masses now hurled upon them decided the event. The battle was lost. Panic and pell-mell retreat ensued. Only on reaching Centreville was any degree of order restored, after the first falling back. The official report of Gen. McDowell states his loss as 481 killed, and 1,011 wounded, without an enumeration of prisoners. Beauregard stated his own losses as 269 killed, and 1,438 wounded, and estimated McDowell's entire loss (including prisoners) at over 4,500. The battle field remained in possession of the insurgents, yet, in spite of their superior numbers, they failed to improve their victory by either a destructive pursuit or an early movement upon Washington. The Rebel General confesses, in his official report, that he was intending, before the battle, to attack McDowell, instead of awaiting his farther advance, manifestly hoping, after uniting Johnston's forces and his own, to gain possession of the Federal Capital. The hard-contested field of Bull Run postponed farther attempts to accomplish this purpose, and the prompt and efficient measures taken for the defense of Washington rendered the joint campaign of Johnston and Beauregard as unproductive of material results, as the advance of McDowell, unsustained by Patterson, had been wanting in military success. It was chiefly in its moral effect, at home and abroad, that this battle had any special significance.

CHAPTER III.

Extra Session of Congress.—President Lincoln's Message.—Rebel Affairs at Richmond.

CONGRESS had convened on the 4th of July, in accordance with the President's call in his proclamation of April 15th, and organized by the election of Mr. Grow, of Pennsylvania, as Speaker. Little decisive action had been taken prior to the date to which military events have been traced in the preceding chapter. The President's Message to Congress, at the opening of this extra session, contains a concise statement of the situation of affairs at that time, four months having passed since the delivery of his Inaugural Address, and presents his views as to what was required to be done for the maintenance of the Constitutional Government. With a review of the circumstances under which hostilities were commenced, and with a conclusive exposure of the false pretenses of Secessionism, it also clearly sets forth the acts, motives and purposes of the President. This document is here given at length:

MR. LINCOLN'S FIRST MESSAGE.

FELLOW-CITIZENS OF THE SENATE AND HOUSE OF REPRESENTATIVES: Having been convened on an extraordinary occasion, as authorized by the Constitution, your attention is not called to any ordinary subject of legislation. At the beginning of the present Presidential term, four months ago, the functions of the Federal Government were found to be generally suspended within the several States of South Carolina, Georgia, Alabama, Mississippi, Louisiana and Florida, excepting only those of the Postoffice Department.

Within these States all the Forts, Arsenals, Dock-Yards, Custom-Houses, and the like, including the movable and stationary property in and about them, had been seized, and were held in open hostility to this Government, excepting only

Forts Pickens, Taylor and Jefferson, on and near the Florida coast, and Fort Sumter in Charleston harbor, South Carolina. The forts thus seized had been put in improved condition, new ones had been built, and armed forces had been organized, and were organizing, all avowedly with the same hostile purpose.

The forts remaining in possession of the Federal Government in and near these States were either besieged or menaced by warlike preparations, and especially Fort Sumter was nearly surrounded by well-protected hostile batteries, with guns equal in quality to the best of its own, and outnumbering the latter as, perhaps, ten to one—a disproportionate share of the Federal muskets and rifles had somehow found their way into these States, and had been seized to be used against the Government.

Accumulations of the public revenue lying within them had been seized for the same object. The navy was scattered in distant seas, leaving but a very small part of it within the immediate reach of the Government.

Officers of the Federal Army had resigned in great numbers, and of those resigning a large proportion had taken up arms against the Government.

Simultaneously, and in connection with all this, the purpose to sever the Federal Union was openly avowed. In accordance with this purpose an ordinance had been adopted in each of these States, declaring the States respectively to be separated from the National Union. A formula for instituting a combined Government of those States had been promulgated, and this illegal organization, in the character of the "Confederate States," was already invoking recognition, aid and intervention from foreign powers.

Finding this condition of things, and believing it to be an imperative duty upon the incoming Executive to prevent, if possible, the consummation of such attempt to destroy the Federal Union, a choice of means to that end became indispensable. This choice was made and was declared in the Inaugural Address.

The policy chosen looked to the exhaustion of all peaceful measures before a resort to any stronger ones. It sought only to hold the public places and property not already wrested from the Government, and to collect the revenue, relying for the rest on time, discussion and the ballot-box. It promised a continuance of the mails, at Government expense, to the very people who were resisting the Government, and it gave repeated pledges against any disturbances to any of the people, or any of their rights, of all that which a President might constitutionally and justifiably do in such a case; every thing was forborne, without which it was believed possible to keep the Government on foot.

On the 5th of March, the present incumbent's first full day in office, a letter from Major Anderson, commanding at Fort Sumter, written on the 28th of February, and received at the War Department on the 4th of March, was by that Department placed in his hands. This letter expressed the professional opinion of the writer, that reënforcements could not be thrown into that fort within the time for its relief rendered necessary by the limited supply of provisions, and with a view of holding possession of the same, with a force less than 20,000 good and well-disciplined men. This opinion was concurred in by all the officers of his command, and their memoranda on the subject were made inclosures of Major Anderson's letter. The whole was immediately laid before Lieut. Gen. Scott, who at once concurred with Major Anderson in his opinion. On reflection, however, he took full time, consulting with other officers, both of the Army and Navy, and at the end of four days came reluctantly but decidedly to the same conclusion as before. He also stated at the same time that no such sufficient force was then at the control of the Government, or could be raised and brought to the ground, within the time when the provisions in the fort would be exhausted. In a purely military point of view, this reduced the duty of the Administration in the case to the mere matter of getting the garrison safely out of the fort.

It was believed, however, that to so abandon that position, under the circumstances, would be utterly ruinous; that the necessity under which it was to be done would not be fully understood; that by many it would be construed as a part of a voluntary policy; that at home it would discourage the friends of the Union, embolden its adversaries, and go far to insure to the latter a recognition abroad; that, in fact, it would be our national destruction consummated. This could not be allowed. Starvation was not yet upon the garrison, and ere it would be reached, Fort Pickens might be reënforced. This last would be a clear indication of policy, and would better enable the country to accept the evacuation of Fort Sumter as a military necessity. An order was at once directed to be sent for the landing of the troops from the steamship Brooklyn into Fort Pickens. This order could not go by land, but must take the longer and slower route by sea. The first return news from the order was received just one week before the fall of Sumter. The news itself was that the officer commanding the Sabine, to which vessel the troops had been transferred

from the Brooklyn, acting upon some quasi armistice of the
late Administration, and of the existence of which the present
Administration, up to the time the order was dispatched, had
only too vague and uncertain rumors to fix attention, had refused to land the troops. To now reënforce Fort Pickens before a crisis would be reached at Fort Sumter was impossible,
rendered so by the near exhaustion of provisions at the latter
named fort. In precaution against such a conjuncture the
Government had a few days before commenced preparing an
expedition, as well adapted as might be, to relieve Fort Sumter, which expedition was intended to be ultimately used or
not, according to circumstances. The strongest anticipated
case for using it was now presented, and it was resolved to send
it forward as had been intended. In this contingency it was
also resolved to notify the Governor of South Carolina that he
might expect an attempt would be made to provision the fort,
and that if the attempt should not be resisted there would be
no attempt to throw in men, arms or ammunition, without further notice, or in case of an attack upon the fort. This notice was accordingly given, whereupon the fort was attacked
and bombarded to its fall, without even awaiting the arrival of
the provisioning expedition.

It is thus seen that the assault upon and reduction of
Fort Sumter, was, in no sense, a matter of self-defense on the
part of the assailants. They well knew that the garrison in
the fort could by no possibility commit aggression upon them ;
they knew they were expressly notified that the giving of bread
to the few brave and hungry men of the garrison was all which
would, on that occasion, be attempted, unless themselves, by
resisting so much, should provoke more. They knew that this
Government desired to keep the garrison in the fort, not to
assail them, but merely to maintain visible possession, and thus
to preserve the Union from actual and immediate dissolution ;
trusting, as hereinbefore stated, to time, discussion, and the
ballot-box for final adjustment, and they assailed and reduced
the fort, for precisely the reverse object, to drive out the visible
authority of the Federal Union, and thus force it to immediate
dissolution ; that this was their object the Executive well understood, having said to them in the Inaugural Address, " you can
have no conflict without being yourselves the aggressors." He
took pains not only to keep this declaration good, but also to keep
the case so far from ingenious sophistry as that the world should
not misunderstand it. By the affair at Fort Sumter, with its surrounding circumstances, that point was reached. Then and thereby the assailants of the Government began the conflict of arms—
without a gun in sight, or in expectancy, to return their fire,

- **17**   22

save only the few in the fort sent to that harbor years before, for their own protection, and still ready to give that protection in whatever was lawful. In this act, discarding all else, they have forced upon the country the distinct issue, immediate dissolution or blood, and this issue embraces more than the fate of these United States. It presents to the whole family of man the question whether a Constitutional Republic or Democracy, a Government of the people, by the same people, can or can not maintain its territorial integrity against its own domestic foes. It presents the question whether discontented individuals, too few in numbers to control the Administration according to the organic law in any case, can always, upon the pretenses made in this case, or any other pretenses, or arbitrarily without any pretense, break up their Government, and thus practically put an end to free government upon the earth. It forces us to ask, "Is there in all republics this inherent and fatal weakness?" Must a Government of necessity be too strong for the liberties of its own people, or too weak to maintain its own existence? So viewing the issue, no choice was left but to call out the war power of the Government, and so to resist the force employed for its destruction by force for its preservation. The call was made, and the response of the country was most gratifying, surpassing, in unanimity and spirit, the most sanguine expectation. Yet none of the States, commonly called Slave States, except Delaware, gave a regiment through the regular State organization. A few regiments have been organized within some others of those States by individual enterprise, and received into the Government service. Of course the seceded States, so called, and to which Texas had been joined about the time of the inauguration, gave no troops to the cause of the Union. The Border States, so called, were not uniform in their action, some of them being almost for the Union, while in others, as in Virginia, North Carolina, Tennessee, and Arkansas, the Union sentiment was nearly repressed and silenced. The course taken in Virginia was the most remarkable, perhaps the most important. A Convention, elected by the people of that State to consider this very question of disrupting the Federal Union, was in session at the capital of Virginia when Fort Sumter fell.

To this body the people had chosen a large majority of professed Union men. Almost immediately after the fall of Sumter many members of that majority went over to the original disunion minority, and with them adopted an ordinance for withdrawing the State from the Union. Whether this change was wrought by their great approval of the assault upon Sumter, or their great resentment at the Government's resistance to that assault, is not definitely known. Although they submitted the ordinance for ratification to a vote of the people, to be taken on a day then somewhat more than a month distant, the Convention and the Legislature, which was also in session at the same time and place, with leading men of the State, not members of either, immediately commenced acting as if the State was already out of the Union. They pushed military preparations vigorously forward all over the State. They seized the United States Armory at Harper's Ferry, and the Navy Yard at Gosport, near Norfolk. They received, perhaps invited into their State, large bodies of troops, with their warlike appointments, from the so-called seceded States.

They formally entered into a treaty of temporary alliance with the so-called Confederate States, and sent members to their Congress at Montgomery, and finally they permitted the insurrectionary Government to be transferred to their capitol at Richmond. The people of Virginia have thus allowed this giant insurrection to make its nest within her borders, and this Government has no choice left but to deal with it where it finds it, and it has the less to regret as the loyal citizens have, in due form, claimed its protection. Those loyal citizens this Government is bound to recognize and protect as being in Virginia. In the Border States, so called, in fact the Middle States, there are those who favor a policy which they call armed neutrality, that is, an arming of those States to prevent the Union forces passing one way or the disunion forces the other over their soil. This would be disunion completed. Figuratively speaking, it would be the building of an impassable wall along the line of separation, and yet not quite an impassable one, for under the guise of neutrality it would tie the hands of the Union men, and freely pass supplies from among them to the insurrectionists, which it could not do as an open enemy. At a stroke it would take all the trouble off the hands of secession, except only what proceeds from the external blockade. It would do for the disunionists that which of all things they most desire, feed them well and give them disunion without a struggle of their own. It recognizes no fidelity to the Constitution, no obligation to maintain the Union, and while very many who have favored it are doubtless loyal citizens, it is, nevertheless, very injurious in effect.

Recurring to the action of the Government it may be stated that at first a call was made for 75,000 militia, and rapidly following this a proclamation was issued for closing the ports of the insurrectionary districts by proceedings in the nature of a blockade. So far all was believed to be strictly legal.

At this point the insurrectionists announced their purpose to enter upon the practice of privateering.

Other calls were made for volunteers, to serve three years, unless sooner discharged, and also for large additions to the regular army and navy. These measures, whether strictly legal or not, were ventured upon under what appeared to be a popular demand and a public necessity, trusting then, as now, that Congress would ratify them.

It is believed that nothing has been done beyond the constitutional competency of Congress. Soon after the first call for militia it was considered a duty to authorize the Commanding General, in proper cases, according to his discretion, to suspend the privilege of the writ of habeas corpus; or, in other words, to arrest and detain, without resort to the ordinary processes and forms of law, such individuals as he might deem dangerous to the public safety. This authority has purposely been exercised, but very sparingly. Nevertheless the legality and propriety of what has been done under it are questioned, and the attention of the country has been called to the proposition that one who is sworn to take care that the laws be faithfully executed, should not himself violate them. Of course some consideration was given to the questions of power and propriety before this matter was acted upon. The whole of the laws which were required to be faithfully executed were being resisted, and failing of execution in nearly one-third of the States. Must they be allowed to finally fail of execution, even had it been perfectly clear that, by use of the means necessary to their execution, some single law, made in such extreme tenderness of the citizen's liberty that practically it relieves more of the guilty than the innocent, should, to a very great extent, be violated? To state the question more directly, are all the laws but one to go unexecuted, and the Government itself to go to pieces lest that one be violated? Even in such a case would not the official oath be broken if the Government should be overthrown when it was believed that disregarding the single law would tend to preserve it.

But it was not believed that this question was presented. It was not believed that any law was violated. The provision of the Constitution, that the privilege of the writ of habeas corpus shall not be suspended, unless when, in cases of rebellion or invasion, the public safety may require it, is equivalent to a provision that such privilege may be suspended when, in cases of rebellion or invasion, the public safety does require it. It was decided that we have a case of rebellion, and that the public safety does require the qualified suspension of the privilege of the writ, which was authorized to be made. Now, it is insisted that

Congress, and not the Executive, is vested with this power. But the Constitution itself is silent as to which or who is to exercise the power; and as the provision was plainly made for a dangerous emergency, it can not be believed that the framers of the instrument intended that in every case the danger should run its course until Congress could be called together, the very assembling of which might be prevented, as was intended in this case by the rebellion. No more extended argument is now afforded, as an opinion at some length will probably be presented by the Attorney-General. Whether there shall be any legislation on the subject, and if so, what, is submitted entirely to the better judgment of Congress. The forbearance of this Government had been so extraordinary, and so long continued, as to lead some foreign nations to shape their action as if they supposed the early destruction of our National Union was probable. While this, on discovery, gave the Executive some concern, he is now happy to say that the sovereignty and rights of the United States are now every-where practically respected by foreign Powers, and a general sympathy with the country is manifested throughout the world.

The reports of the Secretaries of the Treasury, War, and the Navy, will give the information, in detail, deemed necessary and convenient for your deliberation and action, while the Executive and all the Departments will stand ready to supply omissions or to communicate new facts considered important for you to know.

It is now recommended that you give the legal means for making this contest a short and decisive one; that you place at the control of the Government for the work at least 400,000 men and $400,000,000; that number of men is about one-tenth of those of proper ages within the regions where apparently all are willing to engage, and the sum is less than a twenty-third part of the money value owned by the men who seem ready to devote the whole. A debt of $600,000,000 now is a less sum per head than was the debt of our Revolution when we came out of that struggle, and the money value in the country bears even a greater proportion to what it was then than does the population. Surely each man has as strong a motive now to preserve our liberties as each had then to establish them.

A right result at this time will be worth more to the world than ten times the men and ten times the money. The evidence reaching us from the country leaves no doubt that the material for the work is abundant, and that it needs only the hand of legislation to give it legal sanction, and the hand of the Executive to give it practical shape and efficiency. One of the greatest perplexities of the Government is to avoid receiving troops faster than it can provide for them; in a word, the people will save their Government if the Government will do its part only indifferently well. It might seem at first thought to be of little difference whether the present movement at the South be called secession or rebellion. The movers, however, well understand the difference. At the beginning they knew that they could never raise their treason to any respectable magnitude by any name which implies violation of law; they knew their people possessed as much of moral sense, as much of devotion to law and order, and as much pride in its reverence for the history and Government of their common country, as any other civilized and patriotic people. They knew they could make no advancement directly in the teeth of these strong and noble sentiments. Accordingly they commenced by an insidious debauching of the public mind; they invented an ingenious sophism, which, if conceded, was followed by perfectly logical steps through all the incidents of the complete destruction of the Union. The sophism itself is that any State of the Union may, consistently with the Nation's Constitution, and therefore lawfully and peacefully, withdraw from the Union without the consent of the Union or of any other State.

The little disguise that the supposed right is to be exercised only for just cause, themselves to be the sole judge of its justice, is too thin to merit any notice with rebellion. Thus sugar-coated, they have been drugging the public mind of their section for more than thirty years, and until at length they have brought many good men to a willingness to take up arms against the Government the day after some assemblage of men have enacted the farcical pretense of taking their State out of the Union, who could have been brought to no such thing the day before. This sophism derives much, perhaps the whole of its currency, from the assumption that there is some omnipotent and sacred supremacy pertaining to a State, to each State of our Federal Union. Our States have neither more nor less power than that reserved to them in the Union by the Constitution, no one of them ever having been a State out of the Union. The original ones passed into the Union before they cast off their British Colonial dependence, and the new ones came into the Union directly from a condition of dependence, excepting Texas, and even Texas, in its temporary independence, was never designated as a State. The new ones only took the designation of States on coming into the Union, while that name was first adopted for the old ones in and by the Declaration of Independence. Therein the United Colonies were declared to be *free* and *independent* States. But even then the object plainly was not to declare their independence of one another of the Union, but directly the contrary, as their mutual pledge and their mutual action before, at the time, and afterward, abundantly show. The express plight of faith by each and all of the original thirteen States in the Articles of Confederation two years later that the Union shall be perpetual, is most conclusive. Having never been States either in substance or in name outside of the Union, whence this magical omnipotence of State rights, asserting a claim of power to lawfully destroy the Union itself. Much is said about the sovereignty of the States, but the word even is not in the National Constitution, nor, as is believed, in any of the State constitutions. What is sovereignty in the political sense of the word? Would it be far wrong to define it a political community without a political superior? Tested by this, no one of our States, except Texas, ever was a sovereignty. And even Texas gave up the character on coming into the Union; by which act, she acknowledged the Constitution of the United States, and the laws and treaties of the United States, made in pursuance of the Constitution, to be, for her, the supreme law of the land. The States have their *status* IN the Union, and they have no other legal *status*. If they break from this they can only do so against law and by revolution. The Union and not themselves separately procured their independence and their liberty by conquest or purchase. The Union gave each of them whatever of independence and liberty it has. The Union is older than any of the States, and, in fact, it created them, as States. Originally, some dependent Colonies made the Union, and in turn the Union threw off their old dependence for them and made them States, such as they are. Not one of them ever had a State constitution independent of the Union. Of course it is not forgotten that all the new States formed their constitutions before they entered the Union; nevertheless, dependent upon, and preparatory to coming into the Union. Unquestionably the States have the powers and rights reserved to them in and by the National Constitution.

But among these surely are not included all conceivable powers, however mischievous or destructive, but at most such only as were known in the world at the time as governmental powers, and certainly a power to destroy the Government itself had never been known as a governmental, as a merely administrative power. This relative matter of National power and State rights as a principle, is no other than the principle of generality and locality. Whatever concerns the whole should be conferred to the whole General Government, while whatever concerns only the State should be left exclusively to the State. This is all there is of original principle about it. Whether the National Constitution, in defining boundaries between the two, has applied the principle with exact accuracy, is not to be questioned. We are all bound by that defining without question. What is now combatted is the position that secession is consistent with the Constitution, is lawful and peaceful. It is not contended that there is any express law for it, and nothing should ever be implied as law which leads to unjust or absurd consequences. The nation purchased with money the countries out of which several of these States were formed. Is it just that they shall go off without leave and without refunding? The nation paid very large sums in the aggregate, I believe nearly a hundred millions, to relieve Florida of the aboriginal tribes. Is it just that she shall now be off without consent, or without any return? The nation is now in debt for money applied to the benefit of these so-called seceding States, in common with the rest. Is it just, either that creditors shall go unpaid, or the remaining States pay the whole? A part of the present National debt was contracted to pay the old debt of Texas. Is it just that she shall leave and pay no part of this herself? Again, if one State may secede so may another, and when all shall have seceded none is left to pay the debts. Is this quite just to creditors? Did we notify them of this sage view of ours when we borrowed their money? If we now recognize this doctrine by allowing the seceders to go in peace, it is difficult to see what we can do if others choose to go, or to extort terms upon which they will promise to remain. The seceders insist that our Constitution admits of secession. They have assumed to make a National Constitution of their own, in which, of necessity, they have either discarded or retained the right of secession, as they insist exists in ours. If they have discarded it, they thereby admit that on principle it ought not to exist in ours; if they have retained it, by their own construction of ours that shows that to be consistent, they must secede from one another whenever they shall find it the easiest way of settling their debts, or effecting any other selfish or unjust object. The principle itself is one of disintegration, and upon which no (Government can possibly endure. If all the States save one should assert the power to drive that one out of the Union, it is presumed the whole class of seceder politicians would at once deny the power, and denounce the act as the greatest outrage upon State rights. But suppose that precisely the same act, instead of being called driving the one out, should be called the seceding of the others from that one, it would be exactly what the Seceders claim to do, unless, indeed, they made the point that the one, because it is a minority, may rightfully do what the others, because they are a majority, may not rightfully do. These politicians are subtle, and profound in the rights of minorities. They are not partial to that power which made the Constitution, and speaks from the preamble, calling itself, "We, the people." It may be well questioned whether there is to-day a majority of the legally qualified voters of any State, except, perhaps, South Carolina, in favor of disunion. There is much reason to believe that the Union men are the majority in many, if not in every one of the so-called seceded States. The contrary has not been demonstrated in any one of them. It is ventured to affirm this, even of Virginia and Tennessee, for the result of an election held in military camps, where the bayonets are all on one side of the question voted upon, can scarcely be considered as demonstrating popular sentiment. At such an election all that large class who are at once for the Union and against coercion would be coerced to vote against the Union. It may be affirmed, without extravagance, that the free institutions we enjoy have developed the powers and improved the condition of our whole people beyond any example in the world. Of this we now have a striking and impressive illustration. So large an army as the Government has now on foot was never before known, without a soldier in it but who has taken his place there of his own free choice. But more than this, there are many single regiments whose members, one and another, possess full practical knowledge of all the arts, sciences, professions, and whatever else, whether useful or elegant, is known in the whole world, and there is scarcely one from which there could not be selected a President, a Cabinet, a Congress, and perhaps a Court, abundantly competent to administer the Government itself. Nor do I say this is not true also in the army of our late friends, now adversaries, in this contest. But it is so much better the reason why the Government which has conferred such benefits on both them and us should not be broken up. Whoever in any section proposes to abandon such a Government, would do well to consider in deference to what principle it is that he does it. What better he is likely to get in its stead, whether the substitute will give, or be intended to give so much of good to the people. There are some foreshadowings on this subject. Our adversaries have adopted some declarations of independence in which, unlike our good old one penned by Jefferson, they omit the words, "all men are created equal." Why? They have adopted a temporary National Constitution, in the preamble of which, unlike our good old one signed by Washington, they omit, "We, the people," and

23

substitute "We, the deputies of the sovereign and independent States." Why? Why this deliberate pressing out of view the rights of men and the authority of the people? This is essentially a people's contest. On the side of the Union it is a struggle for maintaining in the world that form and substance of Government whose leading object is to elevate the condition of men, to lift artificial weights from all shoulders, to clear the paths of laudable pursuit for all, to afford all an unfettered start and a fair chance in the race of life, yielding to partial and temporary departures from necessity. This is the leading object of the Government, for whose existence we contend.

I am most happy to believe that the plain people understand and appreciate this. It is worthy of note that while in this, the Government's hour of trial, large numbers of those in the army and navy who have been favored with the offices, have resigned and proved false to the hand which pampered them, not one common soldier or common sailor is known to have deserted his flag. Great honor is due to those officers who remained true despite the example of their treacherous associates, but the greatest honor and the most important fact of all, is the unanimous firmness of the common soldiers and common sailors. To the last man, so far as known, they have successfully resisted the traitorous efforts of those whose commands but an hour before they obeyed as absolute law. This is the patriotic instinct of plain people. They understand without an argument that the destroying the Government which was made by Washington means no good to them. Our popular Government has often been called an experiment. Two points in it our people have settled: the successful establishing and the successful administering of it. One still remains. Its successful maintenance against a formidable internal attempt to overthrow it. It is now for them to demonstrate to the world that those who can fairly carry an election, can also suppress a rebellion; that ballots are the rightful and peaceful successors of bullets, and that when ballots have fairly and constitutionally decided, there can be no successful appeal back to bullets; that there can be no successful appeal except to ballots themselves at succeeding elections. Such will be a great lesson of peace, teaching men that what they can not take by an election, neither can they take by a war, teaching all the folly of being the beginners of a war.

Lest there be some uneasiness in the minds of candid men as to what is to be the course of the Government toward the Southern States after the rebellion shall have been suppressed, the Executive deems it proper to say it will be his purpose then, as ever, to be guided by the Constitution and the laws, and that he probably will have no different understanding of the powers and duties of the Federal Government relatively to the rights of the States and the people under the Constitution than that expressed in the Inaugural Address. He desires to preserve the Government that it may be administered for all, as it was administered by the men who made it. Loyal citizens every-where have a right to claim this of their Government, and the Government has no right to withhold or neglect it. It is not perceived that in giving it there is any coercion, conquest or subjugation in any sense of these terms.

The Constitution provided, and all the States have accepted the provision, "that the United States shall guarantee to every State in this Union a Republican form of government," but if a State may lawfully go out of the Union, having done so, it may also discard the Republican form of Government. So that to prevent its going out is an indispensable means to the end of maintaining the guarantee mentioned; and when an end is lawful and obligatory, the indispensable means to it are also lawful and obligatory.

It was with the deepest regret that the Executive found the duty of employing the war power. In defense of the Government forced upon him, he could but perform this duty or surrender the existence of the Government. No compromise by public servants could in this case be a cure, not that compromises are not often proper, but that no popular government can long survive a marked precedent, that those who carry an election can only save the Government from immediate destruction by giving up the main point upon which the people gave the election. The people themselves and not their servants can safely reverse their own deliberate decisions.

As a private citizen the Executive could not have consented that these institutions shall perish, much less could he, in betrayal of so vast and so sacred a trust as these free people had confided to him. He felt that he had no moral right to shrink, nor even to count the chances of his own life in what might follow.

In full view of his great responsibility, he has so far done what he has deemed his' duty. You will now, according to your own judgment, perform yours. He sincerely hopes that your views and your actions may so accord with his as to assure all faithful citizens who have been disturbed in their rights, of a certain and speedy restoration to them, under the Constitution and laws, and having thus chosen our cause without guile, and with pure purpose, let us renew our trust in God, and go forward without fear and with manly hearts.

July 4, 1861.   ABRAHAM LINCOLN.

To the recommendation that $400,000,000 be appropriated, and 400,000 men raised, for the prosecution of the war, Congress responded with great unanimity, granting instead $500,-000,000 in money, and calling for 500,000 volunteers for the army. This action was consummated on the 22d of July—the day following the battle of Bull Run. The Senate had passed a bill of similar character on the 10th—five Senators, Messrs. Johnson, of Missouri, Kennedy, Polk, Powell and Saulsbury, voting in favor of an amendment reducing the number of men to 200,000. Otherwise, the measure was unopposed in that body.

On the 22d of July, the House of Representatives passed, with only two dissenting votes, the following resolution, introduced by Mr. Crittenden, of Kentucky:

Resolved, By the House of Representatives of the Congress of the United States, That the present deplorable civil war has been forced upon the country by the Disunionists of the Southern States now in revolt against the Constitutional Government, and in arms around the capital; that in this National emergency Congress, banishing all feeling of mere passion or resentment, will recollect only its duty to the whole country; that this war is not waged on our part in any spirit of oppression, nor for any purpose of conquest or subjugation, nor purpose of overthrowing or interfering with the rights or established institutions of the States, but to defend and maintain the supremacy of the Constitution, and to preserve the Union, with all the dignities, equality and rights of the several States unimpaired; and that as soon as these objects are accomplished the war ought to cease.

On the 10th of July, a bill passed the House of Representatives, authorizing the Secretary of the Treasury to effect a National loan, of not exceeding $250,000,000, on bonds bearing seven per cent. interest, redeemable in twenty years, or in Treasury-notes of a denomination not less than $50, payable in three years, at an interest of seven and three-tenths per cent. Only five Representatives voted in the negative, namely: Messrs. Burnett, Reid, Norton, Vallandigham and Wood. The first three of these, from Kentucky and Missouri, were soon after direct participants in the rebellion, either as civil or military officials. The subsequent course of the other two, living at the North, has been steadily in keeping with this association of their names and acts.

With certain modifications, which need not be particularized, the financial policy thus indicated was ultimately adopted by both houses of Congress, and approved by the President. A new tariff bill, designed to increase the revenue from imports, and a direct tax bill to raise $20,000,000, also became a law on the 2d of August. A confiscation act, moderate in its provisions, was also passed near the close of the session. An act legalizing the official measures of the President, during the recent emergency, received the support of nearly every member of both houses. The extra session closed on the 6th day of August.

On the 20th day of July, the so-called Congress of the Rebel Confederacy assembled at Richmond, the seat of the civil branch of the rebellion having been removed to that city from Montgomery, where the same body had closed its first session on the 21st of May. Eight days after the latter date Davis arrived in Richmond, and his "government" was there put in operation. His message was sent in on the 20th of July. He therein congratulates his friends on the accession of Virginia, North Carolina, Tennessee and Arkansas to the seceding sisterhood, making in all eleven States against twenty-three still loyal. The subjoined extracts will serve to show the general character of the document, giving also an authentic Southern view of the contest down to the day preceding the battle of Manassas :

I deemed it advisable to direct the removal of the several Executive departments, with their archives, to this city, to which you have removed the seat of government. Immediately after your adjournment, the aggressive movements of the enemy required prompt, energetic action. The accumulation of his forces on the Potomac sufficiently demonstrated that his efforts were to be directed against Virginia, and from no point could necessary measures for her defense and protection be so effectively decided as from her own capital. The rapid progress of events for the last few weeks has fully sufficed to lift the vail, behind which the true policy and purposes of the

Government of the United States had been previously concealed. Their odious features now stand fully revealed. The
message of their President, and the action of their Congress
during the present month, confess their intention of the subjugation of these States, by a war by which it is impossible
to attain the proposed result, while its dire calamities, not to
be avoided by us, will fall with double severity on themselves.

Referring to the hearty response of Congress to the recommendation of President Lincoln as to men and means for prosecuting the war begun at Fort Sumter—the responsibility of
which he vainly endeavors, by angry special pleading, to fix
upon the Government—Davis, with a recklessness commensurate with his passion, goes on to say:

These enormous preparations in men and money, for the
conduct of the war, on a scale more grand than any which the
new world ever witnessed, is a distinct avowal, in the eyes of
civilized man, that the United States are engaged in a conflict
with a great and powerful nation. They are at last compelled
to abandon the pretense of being engaged in dispersing rioters
and suppressing insurrections, and are driven to the acknowledgment that the ancient Union has been dissolved. They
recognize the separate existence of these Confederate States,
by an interdictive embargo and blockade of all commerce between them and the United States, not only by sea, but by
land; not only in ships, but in cars; not only with those who
bear arms, but with the entire population of the Confederate
States. Finally, they have repudiated the foolish conceit that
the inhabitants of this Confederacy are still citizens of the
United States; for they are waging an indiscriminate war upon
them all with savage ferocity, unknown in modern civilization.

After a highly-wrought picture of imaginary outrages perpetrated in Virginia by Federal armies that had scarcely begun
to move, except in Western Virginia, where no pretext for such
complaints existed, and by the Government in its adoption of
the policy of non-intercourse, he comes to the case of certain
captured privateersmen who were in close confinement, awaiting
their trial for piracy. No terms for an exchange of prisoners
had yet been agreed upon—the number on either side being
very small, and the civil bearings of the question being yet under consideration. On this subject Davis fiercely remarks.

The prisoners of war taken by the enemy on board the armed schooner Savannah, sailing under our commission, were, as I was credibly advised, treated like common felons, put in irons, confined in a jail usually appropriated to criminals of the worst dye, and threatened with punishment as such. I had made application for the exchange of these prisoners to the commanding officer of the enemy's squadron off Charleston, but that officer had already sent the prisoners to New York when application was made. I therefore deemed it my duty to renew the proposal for the exchange to the constitutional Commander-in-chief of the Army and Navy of the United States, the only officer having control of the prisoners. To this end, I dispatched an officer to him under a flag of truce, and, in making the proposal, I informed President Lincoln of my reso- lute purpose to check all barbarities on prisoners of war by such severity of retaliation on prisoners held by us as should secure the abandonment of the practice. This communication was received and read by an officer in command of the United States forces, and a message was brought from him by the bearer of my communication, that a reply would be returned by President Lincoln as soon as possible. I earnestly hope this promised reply (which has not yet been received) will convey the assurance that prisoners of war will be treated, in this un- happy contest, with that regard for humanity, which has made such conspicuous progress in the conduct of modern warfare. As measures of precaution, however, and until this promised reply is received, I still retain in close custody some officers cap- tured from the enemy, whom it had been my pleasure pre- viously to set at large on parole, and whose fate must neces- sarily depend on that of prisoners held by the enemy.

The bearer of the communication referred to in this extract had come, under a flag of truce, to the headquarters of Gen. McDowell, at the Arlington House, on the 8th of July, causing much speculation, for a brief time, as to the object of his mis- sion. Its real purport, however, was soon known. Capt. Tay- lor, who bore the insolent letter of Davis, reported to the latter on the 10th of July, that the missive had been delivered, and added:

After reading your communication to Mr. Lincoln, Gen. Scott informed me that a reply would be returned by Mr. Lin- coln as soon as possible

It would be more than doubtful, on such equivocal evidence alone, whether any reply was ever " promised," or even remotely suggested by the President. Certain it is that he made neither promise nor reply. At a subsequent date it was decided to put captured privateersmen on the same footing as other prisoners of war.

After persuasive allusions to the Border Slave States, with a palliation of the Kentucky neutrality so unsparingly dealt with by President Lincoln in his message, the Rebel " Executive " proceeds to other topics :

The operations in the field will be greatly extended by reason of the policy which heretofore has been secretly entertained, and is now *avowed* and acted on by us. The forces hitherto raised provide amply for the defense of seven States which originally organized in the Confederacy, as is evidently the fact, since, with the exception of three fortified islands, whose defense is efficiently aided by a preponderating naval force, the enemy has been driven completely out of these stations ; and now, at the expiration of five months from the formation of the Government, not a single hostile foot presses their soil. These forces, however, must necessarily prove inadequate to repel invasion by the half million of men now proposed by the enemy, and a corresponding increase of our forces will become necessary.

To speak of subjugating such a people, so united and determined, is to speak in a language incomprehensible to them ; to resist attack on their rights or their liberties is with them an instinct. Whether this war shall last one, or three, or five years, is a problem they leave to be solved by the enemy alone. It will last till the enemy shall have withdrawn from their borders ; till their political rights, their altars, and their homes are freed from invasion, Then, and then only, will they rest from this struggle to enjoy, in peace, the blessings which, with the favor of Providence, they have secured by the aid of their own strong hearts and steady arms.

It may be added that the chief conspirator found his subordinates of the self-styled Confederate Congress ready to second his wishes, and to act in the spirit of his communication to them. They voted, without stint—in their assumption of authority— men and means for carrying on aggressive as well as defensive war, on the scale planned by their chief.

MR. LINCOLN'S FIRST INAUGURATION. [MARCH 4, 1861.]

18

The issue was now fairly joined. No possible solution remained but one to be achieved by arms, and the most serious stage of the contest seemed to be at hand. On both sides the armies were rapidly filling up, and receiving the necessary organization and discipline under leaders deemed, at the time, best suited for the emergency. From this time onward, the history of Mr. Lincoln's Administration is, to a large extent, merged in that of the war. The most important measures of legislation and all the principal Executive acts and orders, are closely related to, the suppression of a revolt which surpasses, in the magnitude of its proportions and of the final issues involved, any other recorded in authentic annals.

CHAPTER IV.

Military Reorganization.—Resumè of Events to the December Session of Congress.—Action in Regard to "Contrabands" and Slavery.

THE first depression which followed the disaster at Manassas, speedily gave place to an uprising of the loyal sentiment of the nation, surpassing in earnestness and grandeur even that which immediately succeeded the fall of Fort Sumter. For this effect in deepening and strengthening the popular determination, the Rebel cause had received no substantial compensation through its barren victory. The losses were too nearly equal, the ground won was too insignificant, and the fruits which might have been gathered by a Napoleonic general had too completely eluded the grasp of Beauregard and his superior, Davis, (who had come up from Richmond just in time to witness the closing spectacle), to afford real occasion for the exultation universally manifested throughout the territory occupied by the insurgents. Yet, at home and abroad, the immediate effect was auspicious in appearance for the now very sanguine leaders of secession. They looked forward to nothing less than early occupation of Washington, with the subjection of Maryland, Delaware, Kentucky and Missouri, under an armed invasion, and a recognition, throughout the world, of the Rebel Empire.

A prompt reorganization of our armies in front of Washington and in the Shenandoah was ordered by the President. Whatever the merits of McDowell, it was necessary to call another to his place who could better command the public confidence. The ardent dispatches of the young commander in West Virginia were yet fresh in all minds. He had the favoring support of Gen. Scott, and on every side there was a predisposition to hope the most and the best from his assignment to a larger command. If the President erred, it was only in common with the people whose will he had undertaken to execute, and not from favoritism or partiality, political or personal, toward an officer whom he had never seen.

The 25th of July, 1861, is memorable as the day on which Maj. Gen. John C. Fremont arrived in St. Louis, and entered on his command of the Department of the West; as the day on which Maj. Gen. Nathaniel P. Banks (previously in command at Baltimore) reached Harper's Ferry, superseding Gen. Patterson; and as that on which Maj. Gen. George B. McClellan arrived in Washington to take command of the Army of the Potomac. His former place, as commander of the Army in West Virginia, was, by an order issued on the same day, given to the hero of Rich Mountain, Maj. Gen. William S. Rosecrans. At Baltimore, Maj. Gen. John A. Dix assumed command in place of Banks.

For the three months succeeding the battle of Bull Run, the Army of the Potomac, from which the people impatiently awaited worthy deeds to redeem and avenge the former failure, has only the history of rapidly increasing numbers, of improving organization and discipline, and of the needed preparation, in respect to arms, equipments, supplies and experience of camp life. During this period, the number of men under McClellan's command had come to be estimated at about 200,000. It is believed that the effective force, on the 21st of October, when the first movement commenced, fell but little, if any, short of that number. Meanwhile the Potomac had become substantially closed by a Rebel blockade, injurious to many interests, and hazardous in a military point of view. But the prudent General, guarding himself against premature movements, in accordance with the monition which he saw in the result of McDowell's advance, deemed it unwise to risk a general action by coöperating with a naval force, as was desired, to reopen navigation on the river.

On the 18th of August, the command at Fortress Monroe was surrendered to Gen. John E. Wool, by Gen. Butler, who proceeded northward to organize a separate expedition, the destination of which was not disclosed.

In the West stirring events had transpired prior to the arrival of Gen. Fremont at the headquarters of his Department. In Missouri, the Rebel forces had been gradually driven toward the Southwest by the small army under Gens. Lyon and Sigel, with occasional engagements, until finally the insurgents, with greatly increased numbers, had made a stand at a place nine miles beyond Springfield, on Wilson's Creek. Here, on the 10th of August, was fought a memorable battle, which may be termed the second considerable engagement of the war. Gen. Lyon, whose entire force appears to have been less than 6,000, attacked the enemy in camp, reported to be 22,000 strong, now under command of Ben. McCulloch. The advance was made in two columns : one under Lyon himself, moving directly on the enemy ; the other, making a circuit of fifteen miles toward the left, was to turn the enemy's right. This well-planned movement was commenced on the night of the 9th. Gen. Lyon's column, after resting two hours, following the night's march, resumed its course at four o'clock in the morning, and his advance drove in the enemy's pickets an hour later. The camp was soon in full view, extending for three miles along the valley, and the attack was commenced by Blair's Missouri regiment, while Totten's battery began to shell the tents more distant. The Iowa First and two Kansas regiments were also brought up. A cavalry charge of the enemy was met and repulsed. Another attack, about nine o'clock, somewhat staggered our forces, and in placing himself at the head of the Iowa regiment, to lead a bayonet charge, Gen. Lyon, who had already received three wounds that morning, was shot through the breast by a rifle ball and fell dead on the field. The last Rebel advance, made about one o'clock in the afternoon, was repulsed.

The movement under Gen. Sigel was successful at first, and resulted in the destruction of the enemy's tents and entire baggage train, about noon. Sigel's column, however, was obliged at length to give way. Both columns now retired toward Springfield, the entire loss being reported as eight hundred in killed and wounded. The enemy is believed to have suffered heavily, especially from the well-directed fire of our artillery.

He did not pursue our forces, which were led away by Gen. Sigel without confusion or disorder. Although not successful in occupying the enemy's position, yet the partial advantages gained, with so great a disparity of numbers, left a very different moral impression from that of the defeat at Manassas, on the 21st of July.

The loss of Nathaniel Lyon would have been a dear price for the most decided victory. As a General, as a patriot, as a man, his name will remain one of the brightest among those of the memorable heroes of his time.

Gen. Fremont, on his arrival at St. Louis, had set about organizing his forces for an energetic campaign, not only to restore order in Missouri, but also to gain control of the Mississippi river. Volunteers in great numbers sought service under him, his name awakening an enthusiasm, particularly among citizens of German origin, beyond that of any other commander. The operations began under Lyon and Sigel were allowed to continue, substantially following out the plans already formed, while he was carefully fortifying the city of St. Louis, and organizing a gunboat service, afterward to become so important an auxiliary on the Western waters. But a brief time had elapsed, after Fremont's arrival at St. Louis, before the engagement at Wilson's Creek—fought at greatly unequal odds, for which his personal opponents vehemently censured him—and the subsequent retreat, together with the constantly occurring disturbances in various parts of the State, satisfied the commanding General that he had no light task in reëstablishing peace and order in Missouri alone. Before he assumed command, Gen. Pope had already been obliged to resort to energetic measures in the northern part of the State, to suppress the irregular warfare there prevalent, and to quiet the deadly feuds existing between the two parties into which the communities were divided. The necessity of more stringent proceedings throughout the State was daily becoming manifest.

It was under these circumstances that, at length, Gen. Fremont issued his famous order proclaiming martial law, in the following terms:

HEADQUARTERS WESTERN DEPARTMENT, $\Big\}$
ST. LOUIS, August 30, 1861.

Circumstances in my judgment are of sufficient urgency
to render it necessary that the commanding General of this
department should assume the administrative powers of the
State. Its disorganized condition, helplessness of civil authority, and the total insecurity of life, and devastation of
property by bands of murderers and marauders, who infest
nearly every county in the State, and avail themselves of public misfortunes, in the vicinity of a hostile force, to gratify
private and neighborhood vengeance, and who find an enemy
wherever they find plunder, finally demand the severest measures to repress the daily increasing crimes and outrages which
are driving off the inhabitants and ruining the State.

In this condition the public safety and success of our arms
require unity of purpose, without let or hindrance to the
prompt administration of affairs. In order, therefore, to suppress disorders, maintain the public peace, and give security to
the persons and property of loyal citizens, I do hereby extend
and declare established martial law throughout the State of
Missouri. The lines of the army occupation in this State are
for the present declared to extend from Leavenworth, by way
of posts of Jefferson City, Rolla and Ironton, to Cape Girardeau on the Mississippi river. All persons who shall be taken
with arms in their hands within these lines shall be tried by
court-martial, and if found guilty will be shot. Real and personal property of those who shall take up arms against the
United States, or who shall be directly proven to have taken an
active part with their enemies in the field, is declared confiscated to public use, and their slaves, if any they have, are
hereby declared free men.

All persons who shall be proven to have destroyed, after the
publication of this order, railroad tracks, bridges, or telegraph
lines, shall suffer the extreme penalty of the law. All persons
engaged in treasonable correspondence, in giving or procuring
aid to the enemy, in fermenting turmoil, and disturbing public
tranquillity, by creating or circulating false reports, or incendiary documents, are warned that they are exposing themselves.

All persons who have been led away from allegiance,
are required to return to their homes forthwith. Any such
absence, without sufficient cause, will be held to be presump-
tive evidence against them. The object of this declaration is
to place in the hands of military authorities power to give instantaneous effect to the existing laws, and supply such deficiencies as the conditions of the war demand ; but it is not in

tended to suspend the ordinary tribunals of the country, where law will be administered by civil officers in the usual manner, and with their customary authority, while the same can be peaceably administered.

The commanding General will labor vigilantly for the public welfare, and, by his efforts for their safety, hopes to obtain not only acquiescence, but the active support of the people of the country.

J. C. FREMONT,
Major General Commanding.

An order of this character could not fail to become a topic of general discussion throughout the land. The attention of the President was early called to the subject, and the strongest opposition was manifested to the proposed exercise of the military power, by a subordinate commander, for the confiscation of slave property. This sentiment was clearly expressed in a letter to the President, by the Hon. Joseph Holt, under date of September 12th, in which he said:

The late act of Congress providing for the confiscation of the estates of persons in open rebellion against the Government was, as a necessary war measure, accepted and fully approved by the loyal men of the country. It limited the penalty of confiscation to property actually employed in the service of the rebellion with the knowledge and consent of its owners, and, instead of emancipating slaves thus employed, left their status to be determined either by the Courts of the United States or by subsequent legislation. The proclamation, however, of Gen. Fremont, under date of the 30th of August, transcends, and, of course, violates the law in both these particulars, and declares that the property of rebels, whether used in support of the rebellion or not, shall be confiscated, and if consisting in slaves, that they shall be at once manumitted. The act of Congress referred to was believed to embody the conservative policy of your Administration upon this delicate and perplexing question, and hence the loyal men of the Border Slave States have felt relieved of all fears of any attempt on the part of the Government of the United States to liberate suddenly in their midst a population unprepared for freedom, and whose presence could not fail to prove a painful apprehension, if not a terror, to the homes and families of all. You may, therefore, well judge of the alarm and condemnation with which the Union-loving citizens of Kentucky—the State with whose popular sentiment I am best acquainted—have read this proclamation.

The hope is earnestly indulged by them as it is by myself, that this paper was issued under the pressure of military necessity, which Gen. Fremont believed justified the step, but that in the particulars specified it has not your approbation and will not be enforced in derogation of law. The magnitude of the interest at stake, and my extreme desire that by no misapprehension of your sentiments or purposes shall the power and fervor of the loyalty of Kentucky be at this moment abated or chilled, must be my apology for the frankness with which I have addressed you, and for the request I venture to make of an expression of your views upon the points of Gen. Fremont's proclamation on which I have commented.

The President had already written and transmitted the following letter to Gen. Fremont, expressing in definite terms, as a public order, what had been before more privately indicated to him, immediately after that officer's action on this subject was known:

WASHINGTON, D. C., Sept. 11, 1861.

Major General John C. Fremont:

SIR: Yours of the 8th, in answer to mine of the 2d inst., is just received. Assured that you, upon the ground, could better judge of the necessities of your position than I could at this distance, on seeing your proclamation of August 30, I perceived no general objection to it; the particular clause, however, in relation to the confiscation of property and the liberation of slaves appeared to me to be objectionable in its nonconformity to the act of Congress, passed the 6th of last August, upon the same subjects, and hence I wrote you, expressing my wish that that clause should be modified accordingly. Your answer just received expresses the preference on your part that I should make an open order for the modification, which I very cheerfully do. It is, therefore, ordered that the said clause of the said proclamation be so modified, held, and construed as to conform with and not to transcend the provisions on the same subject contained in the act of Congress entitled "An act to confiscate property used for insurrectionary purposes," approved August 6, 1861, and that said act be published at length with this order.

Your obedient servant,

A. LINCOLN.

It will be observed that this modification merely requires the General commanding in the Department of the West "to conform with, and not to transcend, the provisions" of the Confiscation Act in regard to the slaves of Rebels; in other words, it merely required obedience to the law. At the present time, in view of what the President has since done, as Commander-in-chief of the Army, as well as of his sentiments on Slavery clearly set forth, previously, on all proper occasions, no word is needed to prevent misapprehension as to this Executive order.

By a timely movement, anticipating the contemplated advance of Gen. Polk from Hickman and Columbus, Gen. Grant, of Fremont's command, on the 6th of September, occupied Paducah, at the mouth of the Tennessee river—a position virtually flanking that of the Rebel forces on the Mississippi, in Kentucky. Com. A. H. Foote had been ordered, a few days previously, (August 26,) to the command of the naval forces on the Western waters. Price and Jackson were actively engaged in endeavoring to raise a formidable army, and to overrun the State. Their attack on our forces at Lexington had terminated in the surrender of Col. Mulligan and the men under him at that place, on the 12th of September. Fremont at length prepared to take the field in person against the insurgents, in Southwestern Missouri. He collected all the troops which he regarded as properly available for the purpose, and, leaving Jefferson City for Sedalia, on the 8th of October seemed to be energetically commencing a campaign which many thought to have been quite too long deferred. Price's force gradually fell back once more before the National columns, and were finally reported to be preparing to give battle near Springfield. Here Fremont, who was apparently on the point of engaging the enemy, was overtaken by the order relieving him from his command. He was temporarily succeeded by Gen. Hunter, who soon handed over the command to Gen. Halleck.

Gen. Fremont had been created a Major General by the voluntary action of President Lincoln, from a conviction of the fitness of such appointment. When assigned to the command of the Army of the West he was received in that quarter with

24

general enthusiasm, despite the seeming tardiness with which he entered on his work. Of the charges made against him, and of the grounds which seemed to make a change in the command advisable, it is enough to say here that they did not so far influence the mind of Mr. Lincoln against Gen. Fremont, as to prevent his subsequently assigning him a high military trust. The President's action was then, and still may be, to some extent, misconstrued; but no candid person, with the facts before him, will question that honorable and patriotic motives led to an order which was, on mere personal considerations, reluctantly given.

Under Gen. Hunter, our forces retreated without a battle, and the Rebel hordes again advanced over the already devastated country beyond and around Springfield. It was at the latter place, which had been speedily reoccupied by Price, that, on the 25th of October, Fremont's body guard, of three hundred mounted men, under Maj. Zagonyi, charged upon and routed two thousand Rebels, drawn up in line of battle, dispersed them pell-mell, and retired without serious loss—a deed of heroic daring unsurpassed in any war.

In West Virginia, after the departure of McClellan, our army found its labors by no means so completely terminated as that officer had supposed at the date of his glowing dispatch, announcing the victory at Rich Mountain. On the contrary, serious work was still to be done, and there were active enemies to meet, not only under such Brigadiers as Floyd and Wise, but also under Gen. Robert E. Lee. The well-planned schemes of all these Rebel leaders for subjugating the loyal people of that section were foiled by Gen. Rosecrans, but not without his utmost vigilance, and only after labors, hardships and battles, which were by no means unimportant in comparison with those of the earlier summer. On the 10th of September, Floyd was beaten in the battle of Carnifex Ferry, while Lee's attempt to lead a force through Greenbriar County to coöperate in crushing the Ohio forces, which had advanced up the Kanawha and the Gauley, ended at Big Sewell Mountain, in utter failure. It was only on the sudden and final retreat of Floyd, from Gauley Bridge, eluding the grasp of Gen. Benham, to the disappointment of Rosecrans, that, on the 20th of November, West Virginia was substantially freed from armed Rebels, and the campaign in that quarter ended.

During the progress of these events, of the autumn of 1861, two expeditions were in preparation, one under the command of Gen. Butler, and the other under Gen. Burnside. These expeditions, undertaken against the persistent opposition of McClellan, were regarded with interest and hope by the people, who were becoming wearied with the long inaction of the Army of the Potomac, in the presence of an enemy notoriously much inferior in numbers. The fine condition of the roads and the pleasant weather seemed to invite the long-delayed and long-expected advance, which the public had again and again been led to believe, by intimations from headquarters, was about to be commenced. One, at least, of the expeditions named, was for a time believed to be intended to aid McClellan's promised movement, by ascending the Rappahannock or otherwise. Without the slightest detriment, twenty thousand men might have been spared for such a purpose from the already too cumbersome army near Washington. Yet so little did this suit the policy of the commanding General, in whom there was still confidence, that the forces for Butler and Burnside were raised elsewhere, and they were so delayed, in consequence, as in part to thwart their original purpose, and to impair their effectiveness. That under Gen. Butler, acting jointly with a naval force under Com. Stringham, took possession of the Hatteras forts on the 29th of August. The Rebel commandant, Barron, formerly of the United States Navy, after enduring a severe cannonade from the fleet, surrendered the position, with the officers and soldiers under him. This intelligence was received by the country with lively satisfaction, at a time when some reassuring success was specially needed.

In the month of August the Rebels had occupied Munson's Hill, in full view of the capital, and six or seven miles distant in a right line. The force thus advanced was not formidable, and the character of the works thrown up there, as discovered on the voluntary withdrawal of the occupants, clearly showed that their purpose was not serious. They held this position until the 28th of September, on which day a foraging party went out eight miles on the Orange and Alexandria Railroad, without encountering any enemy, or finding any definite trace of his previous presence in that direction. The prompt occupation of Munson's Hill, after its evacuation, by a force which McClellan, with his staff, had accompanied in person, electrified the people with the hope of some decisive action, on the part of the new commander. He shortly returned to Washington, however, and nearly another month passed before there were again visible symptoms of vitality—beyond that of military reviews and rhetorical army orders, or occasional reconnoissances, magnified by admiring correspondents—in the Army of the Potomac.

The movement of Oct. 21st, resulting in the well-known affair at Ball's Bluff, was scarcely less disastrous in its effects than the failure at Bull Run on the 21st of July. Coming after such complete and thorough preparation; following such manifold and inexcusable delays; and transpiring as the first of the weighty manifestations of McClellan's generalship, the consequence could only be mortification to the Administration, and discouragement, mingled with indignation, to the country at large. In this ill-starred fight fell Col. E. D. Baker, of Mexican War fame, the eloquent Senator from Oregon. The loss on our side was officially stated as 150 killed or drowned, 250 wounded, and 500 prisoners. The whole force engaged was given as 2,100. The rebel Gen. Evans, commanding on the other side, states his own loss in killed and wounded as 153. He estimates the Union loss at 1,300 killed, wounded and drowned, and asserts that 710 prisoners were captured, making a total of over 2,000, nearly equal to the whole number actively engaged. This exaggerated claim was not needed to show the destructive character of the engagement. In his general order on this occasion, dated Oct. 25, McClellan gave this version of the disaster:

The gallantry and discipline there displayed deserved a more fortunate result; but situated as these troops were—cut off alike from retreat and reënforcements, and attacked by an overwhelming force—five thousand against one thousand seven hundred—it was not possible that the issue could have been successful.

The fact that Gen. McCall's division was almost simultaneously withdrawn by Gen. McClellan from a position effectually within supporting distance on the Virginia side of the river, instead of being advanced to coöperate in the movement on Leesburg, has not been satisfactorily explained. It is fair to presume, however, that there was no more culpable motive for this than a desire for the presence of McCall's troops at a grand review which was progressing near Lewinsville, while Col. Baker and his men were pushed forward into the jaws of destruction.

With the light thrown on this affair by subsequent investigations, it may well be doubted whether the President should not have viewed this result, after three months of wearisome and unaccountable inaction, as sufficient cause for withdrawing all further confidence from the commanding General. For the time, however, it was made to appear that the blame should rest elsewhere, and Gen. C. P. Stone, the subordinate in the field, became the scapegoat for his superior.

Despite the popular impatience, and all the circumstances favoring prompt action, nothing more was attempted by the commander of the Army of the Potomac—scarcely so much as a picket skirmish disturbed the general stagnation during those calm, dry days—for the next two months.

To Gen. Scott's generous appreciation, perhaps, more than to any other circumstance, was due the confidence extended by President Lincoln, at the outset, to Gen. McClellan, unknown as he was to almost every one else at Washington. His affiliations had formerly been with another class of public men, the principal of whom were now actively engaged in rebellion. With Jefferson Davis in particular, he seems to have been a youthful favorite, as his selection for a place on the Crimean Commission attests. Gen. Scott had formed a favorable opinion of the young Lieutenant in Mexico, and had very essentially aided in securing him credit with the present Administration. Of his subsequent deportment toward Gen. Scott, this is not the place to speak, further than to say that the veteran Lieutenant General, his immediate superior, keenly felt the disrespectful bearing of his subordinate.

Increasing physical infirmity led the Lieutenant General to desire relief from all active duties, and from apparent responsibility for acts in which he really had no share. Directly after the affair at Ball's Bluff, he made known this wish to the President. The request was one which, urged as it was, could not be refused. The following is the President's order on this subject:

EXECUTIVE MANSION, WASHINGTON, Nov. 1, 1861.

On the 1st day of November, A. D. 1861, upon his own application to the President of the United States, Brevet Lieut. Gen. Winfield Scott is ordered to be placed, and hereby is placed, upon the list of retired officers of the Army of the United States, without reduction in his current pay, subsistence or allowances.

The American people will hear with sadness and deep emotion that Gen. Scott has withdrawn from the active control of the army, while the President and the unanimous Cabinet express their own and the nation's sympathy in his personal affliction, and their profound sense of the important public services rendered by him to his country during his long and brilliant career, among which will ever be gratefully distinguished his faithful devotion to the Constitution, the Union and the flag, when assailed by a parricidal rebellion.

ABRAHAM LINCOLN.

This order was read to Gen. Scott, at his residence, by the President, the Cabinet being present. The veteran General replied:

PRESIDENT: This honor overwhelms me. It overpays all services I have attempted to render to my country. If I had any claims before, they are all obliterated by this expression of approval by the President, with the unanimous support of his Cabinet. I know the President and this Cabinet well—I know that the country has placed its interests, in this trying crisis, in safe keeping. Their counsels are wise. Their labors are untiring as they are loyal, and their course is the right one.

President, you must excuse me; I am unable to stand longer to give utterance to the feelings of gratitude which oppress me. In my retirement I shall offer up my prayer to God for this

Administration, and for my country. I shall pray for it with confidence in its success over its enemies, and that speedily.

On Gen. McClellan, who now held the highest rank in the army, the President temporarily devolved the duties of General-in-chief, and that position was assumed in a general order, issued on the day of the Lieutenant General's retirement.

On the 7th of November, an expedition, under the joint command of Com. Dupont and Gen. T. W. Sherman, effected a landing on the South Carolina coast, having achieved a brilliant victory in Port Royal Harbor. In thus approaching a portion of the South densely populated with slaves, it became necessary to define more clearly the policy to be acted upon by our military officers. In doing so, former orders to General Butler, on first entering Virginia, in May, were repeated. The following is the official order to Gen. Sherman :

WAR DEPARTMENT, Oct. 14, 1861.

SIR : In conducting military operations within States declared by the proclamation of the President to be in a state of insurrection, you will govern yourself, so far as persons held to service under the laws of such States are concerned, by the principles of the letters addressed by me to Maj. Gen. Butler, on the 30th of May and the 8th of August, copies of which are herewith furnished to you. As special directions, adapted to special circumstances, can not be given, much must be referred to your own discretion, as Commanding General of the expedition. You will, however, in general, avail yourself of the services of any persons, whether fugitives from labor or not, who may offer them to the National Government ; you will employ such persons in such services as they may be fitted for, either as ordinary employees, or, if special circumstances seem to require it, in any other capacity, with such organization in squads, companies, or otherwise, as you deem most beneficial to the service. This, however, not to mean a general arming of them for military service. You will assure all loyal masters that Congress will provide just compensation to them for the loss of the services of the persons so employed. It is believed that the course thus indicated will best secure the substantial rights of loyal masters, and the benefits to the United States of the services of all disposed to support the Government, while it avoids

all interference with the social systems or local institutions of
every State, beyond that which insurrection makes unavoidable,
and which a restoration of peaceful relations to the Union, under the Constitution, will immediately remove.

Simon Cameron
Secretary of War.

Brig. Gen. T. W. Sherman,
    Commanding Expedition to the Southern Coast.

Gen. Butler having, in his letter of May 27th, apprised the
War Department as to his views and action in regard to fugitive slaves coming within his lines—such " property" being, in
his opinion, *contraband of war*—the Secretary of War had
replied :

Washington, May 30, 1861.

Sir : Your action in respect to the negroes who came within
your lines, from the service of the Rebels, is approved. The
Department is sensible of the embarrassments, which must surround officers conducting military operations in a State, by the
laws of which slavery is sanctioned. The Government can
not recognize the rejection by any State of its Federal obligation, resting upon itself, among these Federal obligations.
However, no one can be more important than that of suppressing and dispersing any combination of the former for the purpose of overthrowing its whole constitutional authority. While,
therefore, you will permit no interference, by persons under
your command, with the relations of persons held to service
under the laws of any State, you will, on the other hand, so
long as any State within which your military operations are
conducted, remain under the control of such armed combinations, refrain from surrendering to alleged masters any persons who come within your lines. You will employ such persons in the services to which they will be best adapted, keeping
an account of the labor by them performed, of the value of it,
and the expenses of their maintenance. The question of their
final disposition will be reserved for future determination.

The other letter to Gen. Butler, referred to above, is in the
following terms :

Washington, August 8, 1861.

General : The important question of the proper disposition to be made of fugitives from service in the States in insur-

MR. LINCOLN'S RESIDENCE, AT SPRINGFIELD, ILLS.

rection against the Federal Government, to which you have again directed my attention, in your letter of July 20, has received my most attentive consideration. It is the desire of the President that all existing rights in all the States be fully respected and maintained. The war now prosecuted on the part of the Federal Government is a war for the Union, for the preservation of all the constitutional rights of the States and the citizens of the States in the Union; hence no question can arise as to fugitives from service within the States and Terri-tories in which the authority of the Union is fully acknowl-edged. The ordinary forms of judicial proceedings must be respected by the military and civil authorities alike for the enforcement of legal forms. But in the States wholly or in part under insurrectionary control, where the laws of the United States are so far opposed and resisted that they can not be effectually enforced, it is obvious that the rights dependent upon the execution of these laws must temporarily fail, and it is equally obvious that the rights dependent on the laws of the States within which military operations are conducted must necessarily be subordinate to the military exigences created by the insurrection, if not wholly forfeited by the treasonable conduct of the parties claiming them. To this the general rule of the right to service forms an exception. The act of Congress approved Aug. 6, 1861, declares that if persons held to service shall be employed in hostility to the United States, the right to their services shall be discharged therefrom. It follows of necessity that no claim can be recognized by the military authority of the Union to the services of such persons when fugitives.

A more difficult question is presented in respect to persons escaping from the service of loyal masters. It is quite apparent that the laws of the State under which only the services of such fugitives can be claimed must needs be wholly or almost wholly superseded, as to the remedies, by the insurrection and the military measures necessitated by it; and it is equally apparent that the substitution of military for judicial measures for the enforcement of such claims must be attended by great inconvenience, embarrassments and injuries. Under these circumstances, it seems quite clear that the substantial rights of loyal masters are still best protected by receiving such fugitives as well as fugitives from disloyal masters, into the service of the United States, and employing them under such organizations and in such occupations as circumstances may suggest or require. Of course a record should be kept showing the names and descriptions of the fugitives, the names and characters, as .oyal or disloyal, of their masters, and such facts as may be

25

19

necessary to a correct understanding of the circumstances of each case.

After tranquillity shall have been restored upon the return of peace, Congress will doubtless properly provide for all the persons thus received into the service of the Union, and for a just compensation to loyal masters. In this way only, it would seem, can the duty and safety of the Government and just rights of all be fully reconciled and harmonized. You will, therefore, consider yourself instructed to govern your future action in respect to fugitives from service by the premises herein stated, and will report from time to time, and at least twice in each month, your action in the premises to this Department. You will, however, neither authorize nor permit any interference by the troops under your command with the servants of peaceable citizens in a house or field, nor will you in any manner encourage such citizens to leave the lawful service of their masters, nor will you, except in cases where the public good may seem to require it, prevent the voluntary return of any fugitive to the service from which he may have escaped. I am, very respectfully, your obedient servant,

SIMON CAMERON,
Secretary of War.

To MAJ. GEN. BUTLER,
Commanding Department of Virginia, Fortress Monroe.

On the 6th of November, a force under Gens. Grant and McClernand left Cairo on transports for the purpose of breaking up a Rebel camp on the Missouri side of the Mississippi river, nearly opposite Columbus, the headquarters of Gen. Polk. The whole number of men engaged in this expedition, including a Chicago battery and two companies of cavalry, was about 3,500. The gunboats Tyler and Lexington accompanied them. The troops effected a landing and were formed in line of battle about eight o'clock the following morning, and at once advanced upon the Rebel works. The Rebels, under Gen. Cheatham, met this attack, but were driven back over the wooded field, fighting from tree to tree, into and through their camp. Twelve guns were captured from the Rebels, their camp burned, and baggage, horses, and many prisoners were taken. Reënforcements from Columbus subsequently crossed to Belmont, compelling the Union forces to return to their transports, under cover of the gunboats. Though a decided success in the early part of the day, the engagement terminated less favorably, and victory was claimed by the Rebels.

About the same time, it is worthy of note, a gunboat reconnoissance was made to Fort Donelson. The movement at Belmont, made by order of Gen. Fremont, perhaps aided another ere long to be undertaken in the latter direction, as well as the advance into Southwestern Missouri, then in progress.

A large force, under Gen. W. T. Sherman, had meanwhile advanced as far as Bowling Green, to meet an invasion of Kentucky under the Rebel Gen. Bragg, while on the left of Sherman, Gen. William Nelson, on the 8th, gained a decisive victory over the Rebels, under Col. Williams, clearing the northeastern part of the State of invaders. Thus the prompt occupation of Paducah by Gen. Grant, the advance of Sherman, and the energy of Nelson, had defeated a well-devised plan of the Rebels for overrunning and subjugating Kentucky. Gen. Buckner, not long after his interview with McClellan at Cincinnati, in June, had thrown off the mask, and was zealously engaged in an attempt to draw Kentucky into the Secession gulf-stream, and to gather a large force of Kentuckians for the Rebel Army. In the latter purpose he was not without success.

On the 10th of November, Gen. H. W. Halleck was appointed to the command of the Department of the West, in the place of Gen. Fremont. At the same date Gen. W. T. Sherman, having lately resigned his command in Kentucky, Gen. D. C. Buell took that General's place.

During the Summer and Autumn, the Navy Department had manifested great energy in collecting the before scattered navy, and in fitting out, equipping and manning for service on the seas and navigable rivers, where available, an adequate force of war vessels, gunboats and transports. A blockade of remarkable stringency, under circumstances so adverse, had been maintained along our immense sea-coast, and numerous prizes had rewarded the vigilance of our naval commanders and seamen. Blockade-running, though frequently attempted, and sometimes too successful, had become hazardous, and communication with foreign countries was but casual. and attended with constant peril. The capture of the forts at Hatteras Inlet effectually closed one avenue of blockade running, and the Port Royal expedition was of like value in sealing another important harbor.

On the 12th of October, the steamer Theodora evaded the blockading fleet off Charleston, and went to sea with two noted Rebel leaders on board, James M. Mason and John Slidell, recently Senators of the United States, now "accredited," respectively, to the Governments of England and France, as Representatives of the Davis Confederacy. Their immediate destination was Cardenas, with the intention of proceeding to Europe by steamer from Havana. At the time of the arrival of these emissaries in Cuba, Com. Wilkes, cruising for the Rebel privateer Sumter, was at Cienfuegos, on the southern coast of that island. Having been notified by Consul Shufeldt, he made all haste to intercept the Theodora on her return, but on arriving at Havana, Oct. 31st, he found she had already gone, and that Mason and Slidell were waiting there, intending to leave for St. Thomas in the British Mail steamer Trent. Com. Wilkes took position with his vessel, the San Jacinto, to intercept the Trent, designing to make prisoners of her two diplomatic passengers. This purpose he accomplished on the 8th of November. The intelligence of this capture, of course, created no little excitement in this country and in Europe. As involving a question of international rights and jurisdiction, the event was widely discussed, while the loyal sentiment of the people undeniably went strongly with Com. Wilkes in his bold action. Secretary Welles promptly congratulated that officer, complimenting him, and his subordinates and crew—fully appreciating the worthy motive, and the energy of the procedure. Meanwhile, Mason and Slidell, having arrived at New York, were transferred to close quarters at Fort Warren, in Boston harbor.

CHAPTER V.

The President's Message, December, 1861.—Proceedings of Congress.—Emancipation.—Confiscation.—Messages and Addresses of Mr. Lincoln.

CONGRESS reassembled on the 2d day of December, 1861. During the last few months public attention had been earnestly directed to the policy of turning to account the great element of Rebel strength or weakness—as it should prove—in shortening a war becoming gigantic in its dimensions and cost. A large portion of the people had come to believe that a proper exercise of the war power would require the slaves of the rebels to be not only withdrawn from producing for the support of the Confederate armies, but also to be actively employed, so far as might be, on the right side. A small class, more radical in their views, insisted on setting aside, by Executive act, all legal or constitutional guarantees of slavery in general, and not merely in so far as they inured to the benefit of Rebels, who had repudiated all laws, and the Constitution itself, by taking up arms against the supreme authority. Had every Slave State joined in the Secession movement, this question would have been free from all embarrassments. But when Mr. Lincoln was inaugurated, only seven of these States had been ranged on the side of the rebellion, while eight remained in an attitude of loyalty. And, in the final event, but four of the remaining eight were drawn into Secession. As the President of an undivided Union, the President had thus far felt compelled, as well in the avowals of his Inaugural Address as in his subsequent action, not to interfere directly with the relations of master and slave. It was only where the slave, in accordance with all the laws of war, could be actually used by military commanders in the field, to subserve military purposes, and not by any general blow at a recognized institution, that he had authorized the relation to be forcibly disturbed.

The existence of this popular agitation, as well as of a similar debate in his own mind, perceptibly appears in the President's annual Message to Congress.

It is likewise to be observed, that the military results, thus far, had not been quite satisfactory, either to the President or to the people. Despite the lavish means provided at the July session of Congress, with a manifest view to energetic aggressive war, little more had been accomplished—and that certainly not a little, however short of expectation—than to protect the National capital, and to save Maryland, West Virginia, Kentucky and Missouri, from being subjugated by Rebel armies. Manassas and Ball's Bluff, in the East, were still unavenged, or but partly compensated by the capture of Hatteras and Port Royal. In the West, large Rebel armies were threatening to overrun Kentucky from Bowling Green and Columbus, and Missouri from the Southwest, as well as holding the Mississippi river to within a few miles of Cairo.

In addition, was the exciting question growing out of the arrest of Mason and Slidell, on board a British ship on the high seas. The popular feeling, on the one hand, seemed to be unanimous in favor of retaining possession of these prisoners, as conspirators and traitors; while on the other, the British Government, in spite of its own precedents, and backed by French influence, seemed determined to regard such action on our part as a cause for war. The juncture was critical. Every sympathizer with rebellion was exultant in the confidence that the Administration would be wrecked upon Scylla or Charybdis—that it would be ruined at home, or involved in a foreign war that must end any further effective effort to put down the rebellion.

The President, fully sensible of the besetting dangers, and mindful of the situation of affairs in these and other respects, submitted to Congress the following views, in a message which was received with great popular favor:

FELLOW-CITIZENS OF THE SENATE AND HOUSE OF REPRESENTATIVES: In the midst of unprecedented political troubles, we have cause of great gratitude to God for unusual good health and most abundant harvests.

You will not be surprised to learn that, in the peculiar exigences of the times, our intercourse with foreign nations has been attended with profound solicitude, chiefly turning upon our own domestic affairs.

A disloyal portion of the American people have, during the whole year, been engaged in an attempt to divide and destroy the Union. A nation which endures factious domestic division, is exposed to disrespect abroad; and one party, if not both, is sure, sooner or later, to invoke foreign intervention.

Nations thus tempted to interfere, are not always able to resist the counsels of seeming expediency and ungenerous ambition, although measures adopted under such influences seldom fail to be unfortunate and injurious to those adopting them.

The disloyal citizens of the United States who have offered the ruin of our country, in return for the aid and comfort which they have invoked abroad, have received less patronage and encouragement than they probably expected. If it were just to suppose, as the insurgents have seemed to assume, that foreign nations, in this case, discarding all moral, social and treaty obligations, would act solely, and selfishly, for the most speedy restoration of commerce, including, especially, the acquisitions of cotton, those nations appear, as yet, not to have seen their way to their object more directly, or clearly, through the destruction than through the preservation of the Union. If we could dare to believe that foreign nations are actuated by no higher principle than this, I am quite sure a sound argument could be made to show them that they can reach their aim more readily and easily by aiding to crush this rebellion than by giving encouragement to it.

The principal lever relied on by the insurgents for exciting foreign nations to hostility against us, as already intimated, is the embarrassment of commerce. Those nations, however, not improbably, saw from the first, that it was the Union which made, as well our foreign, as our domestic commerce. They can scarcely have failed to perceive that the effort for disunion produces the existing difficulty: and that one strong nation promises more durable peace, and a more extensive, valuable and reliable commerce, than can the same nation broken into hostile fragments.

It is not my purpose to review our discussions with foreign States; because whatever might be their wishes or dispositions, the integrity of our country and the stability of our Government mainly depend, not upon them, but on the loyalty, virtue, patriotism and intelligence of the American people. The correspondence itself, with the usual reservations, is herewith submitted.

I venture to hope it will appear that we have practiced prudence and liberality toward foreign powers, averting causes of irritation, and with firmness maintaining our own rights and honor.

Since, however, it is apparent that here, as in every other State, foreign dangers necessarily attend domestic difficulties, I recommend that adequate and ample measures be adopted for maintaining the public defenses on every side. While, under this general recommendation, provision for defending our seacoast line readily occurs to the mind, I also, in the same connection, ask the attention of Congress to our great lakes and rivers. It is believed that some fortifications and depots of arms and munitions, with harbor and navigation improvements, all at well-selected points upon these, would be of great importance to the National defense and preservation. I ask attention to the views of the Secretary of War, expressed in his report, upon the same general subject.

I deem it of importance that the loyal regions of East Tennessee and Western North Carolina should be connected with Kentucky, and other faithful parts of the Union, by railroad. I therefore recommend, as a military measure, that Congress provide for the construction of such road as speedily as possible. Kentucky, no doubt, will coöperate, and, through her Legislature, make the most judicious selection of a line. The northern terminus must connect with some existing railroad; and whether the route shall be from Lexington or Nicholasville to the Cumberland Gap, or from Lebanon to the Tennessee line, in the direction of Knoxville, or on some still different line, can easily be determined. Kentucky and the General Government coöperating, the work can be completed in a very short time; and when done, it will be not only of vast present usefulness, but also a valuable permanent improvement, worth its cost in all the future.

Some treaties, designed chiefly for the interests of commerce, and having no grave political importance, have been negotiated, and will be submitted to the Senate for their consideration.

Although we have failed to induce some of the commercial powers to adopt a desirable melioration of the rigor of maratime war, we have removed all obstructions from the way of this humane reform, except such as are merely of temporary and accidental occurrence.

I invite your attention to the correspondence between Her Britannic Majesty's Minister, accredited to this Government, and the Secretary of State, relative to the detention of the British ship Perthshire, in June last, by the United States steamer Massachusetts, for a supposed breach of the blockade. As this detention was occasioned by an obvious misapprehension of the facts, and as justice requires that we should commit no belligerent act not founded in strict right, as sanctioned by public law, I recommend that an appropriation be made to satisfy the reasonable demand of the owners of the vessel for her detention.

I repeat the recommendation of my predecessor, in his annual message to Congress in December last, in regard to the disposition of the surplus which will probably remain after satisfying the claims of the American citizens against China, pursuant to the awards of the commissioners under the act of the 3d of March, 1859. If, however, it should not be deemed advisable to carry that recommendation into effect, I would suggest that authority be given for investing the principal, over the proceeds of the surplus referred to, in good securities, with a view to the satisfaction of such other just claims of our citizens against China as are not unlikely to arise hereafter in the course of our extensive trade with that empire.

By the act of the 5th of August last, Congress authorized the President to instruct the commanders of suitable vessels to defend themselves against and to capture pirates. This authority has been exercised in a single instance only. For the more effectual protection of our extensive and valuable commerce, in the Eastern seas especially, it seems to me that it would also be advisable to authorize the commanders of sailing vessels to recapture any prizes which pirates may make of United States vessels and their cargoes, and the consular courts, now established by law in Eastern countries, to adjudicate the cases, in the event that this should not be objected to by the local authorities.

If any good reason exists why we should persevere longer in withholding our recognition of the independence and sovereignty of Hayti and Liberia, I am unable to discern it. Unwilling, however, to inaugurate a novel policy in regard to them without the approbation of Congress, I submit for your consideration the expediency of an appropriation for maintaining a charge d'affaires near each of those new States. It does not admit of doubt that important commercial advantages might be secured by favorable treaties with them.

The operations of the treasury during the period which has elapsed since your adjournment have been conducted with signal success. The patriotism of the people has placed at the disposal of the Government the large means demanded by the public exigences. Much of the National loan has been taken by citizens of the industrial classes, whose confidence in their country's faith, and zeal for their country's deliverance from present peril, have induced them to contribute to the support of the Government the whole of their limited acquisitions. This fact imposes peculiar obligations to economy in disbursement and energy in action.

The revenue from all sources, including loans, for the financial year ending on the 30th of June, 1861, was eighty-six million eight hundred and thirty-five thousand nine hundred dollars and twenty-seven cents, and the expenditures for the same period, including payments on account of the public debt, were eighty-four million five hundred and seventy-eight thousand eight hundred and thirty-four dollars and forty-seven cents; leaving a balance in the treasury on the 1st of July of two million two hundred and fifty-seven thousand sixty-five dollars and eighty cents. For the first quarter of the financial year, ending on the 30th of September, 1861, the receipts from all sources, including the balance of the 1st of July, were one hundred and two million five hundred and thirty-two thousand five hundred and nine dollars and twenty-seven cents, and the expenses ninety-eight million two hundred and thirty-nine thousand seven hundred and thirty-three dollars and nine cents; leaving a balance on the 1st of October, 1861, of four million two hundred and ninety-two thousand seven hundred and seventy-six dollars and eighteen cents.

Estimates for the remaining three-quarters of the year, and for the financial year 1863, together with his views of ways and means for meeting the demands contemplated by them, will be submitted to Congress by the Secretary of the Treasury. It is gratifying to know that the expenditures made necessary by the rebellion are not beyond the resources of the loyal people, and to believe that the same patriotism which has thus far sustained the Government will continue to sustain it till peace and Union shall again bless the land.

I respectfully refer to the report of the Secretary of War for information respecting the numerical strength of the Army, and for recommendations having in view an increase of its efficiency and the well being of the various branches of the service intrusted to his care. It is gratifying to know that the patriotism of the people has proved equal to the occasion, and that the number of troops tendered greatly exceeds the force which Congress authorized me to call into the field.

I refer with pleasure to those portions of his report which make allusion to the creditable degree of discipline already attained by our troops, and to the excellent sanitary condition of the entire army.

The recommendation of the Secretary for an organization of the militia upon a uniform basis is a subject of vital importance to the future safety of the country, and is commended to the serious attention of Congress.

The large addition to the regular army, in connection with the defection that has so considerably diminished the number of its officers, gives peculiar importance to his recommendation for increasing the corps of cadets to the greatest capacity of the Military Academy.

By mere omission, I presume, Congress has failed to provide chaplains for hospitals occupied by volunteers. This subject was brought to my notice, and I was induced to draw up the form of a letter, one copy of which, properly addressed, has been delivered to each of the persons, and at the dates respectively named and stated, in a schedule, containing also the form of the letter, marked A, and herewith transmitted.

These gentlemen, I understand, entered upon the duties designated, at the times respectively stated in the schedule, and have labored faithfully therein ever since. I therefore recommend that they be compensated at the same rate as chaplains in the army. I further suggest that general provision be made for chaplains to serve at hospitals, as well as with regiments.

The report of the Secretary of the Navy presents in detail the operations of that branch of the service, the activity and energy which have characterized its administration, and the results of measures to increase its efficiency and power. Such have been the additions, by construction and purchase, that it may almost be said a navy has been created and brought into service since our difficulties commenced.

Besides blockading our extensive coast, squadrons larger than ever before assembled under our flag have been put afloat, and performed deeds which have increased our naval renown.

I would invite special attention to the recommendation of the Secretary for a more perfect organization of the Navy by introducing additional grades in the service.

The present organization is defective and unsatisfactory, and the suggestions submitted by the Department will, it is believed, if adopted, obviate the difficulties alluded to, promote harmony, and increase the efficiency of the navy.

There are three vacancies on the bench of the Supreme Court—two by the decease of Justices Daniel and McLean, and one by the resignation of Justice Campbell. I have so far forborne making nominations to fill these vacancies for reasons which I will now state. Two of the outgoing judges resided within the States now overrun by revolt; so that if successors were appointed in the same localities, they could not now serve upon their circuits; and many of the most competent men there probably would not take the personal hazard of accepting to serve, even here, upon the Supreme Bench. I have been unwilling to throw all the appointments northward, thus disabling myself from doing justice to the South on the return of peace; although I may remark that to transfer to the North one which has heretofore been in the South would not, with reference to territory and population, be unjust.

During the long and brilliant judicial career of Judge McLean his circuit grew into an empire—altogether too large for any one judge to give the courts therein more than a nominal attendance—rising in population from one million four hundred and seventy thousand and eighteen, in 1830, to six million one hundred and fifty-one thousand four hundred and five, in 1860.

Besides this, the country generally has outgrown our present judicial system. If uniformity was at all intended, the system requires that all the States shall be accommodated with circuit courts, attended by supreme judges, while, in fact, Wisconsin, Minnesota, Iowa, Kansas, Florida, Texas, California and Oregon, have never had any such courts. Nor can this well be remedied without a change in the system; because the adding of judges to the Supreme Court, enough for the accommodation of all parts of the country, with circuit courts, would create a court altogether too numerous for a judicial body of any sort. And the evil, if it be one, will increase as new States come into the Union. Circuit courts are useful, or they are not useful; if useful, no State should be denied them; if not useful, no State should have them. Let them be provided for all, or abolished as to all.

Three modifications occur to me, either of which, I think, would be an improvement upon our present system. Let the Supreme Court be of convenient number in every event. Then, first, let the whole country be divided into circuits of convenient size, the supreme judges to serve in a number of them corresponding to their own number, and independent circuit judges be provided for all the rest. Or, secondly, let the supreme judges be relieved from circuit duties, and circuit judges provided for all the circuits. Or, thirdly, dispense with circuit courts altogether, leaving the judicial functions wholly to the district courts, and an independent Supreme Court.

I respectfully recommend to the consideration of Congress the present condition of the statute laws, with the hope that

Congress will be able to find an easy remedy for many of the inconveniencies and evils which constantly embarrass those engaged in the practical administration of them. Since the organization of the Government, Congress has enacted some five thousand acts and joint resolutions, which fill more than six thousand closely printed pages, and are scattered through many volumes. Many of these acts have been drawn in haste and without sufficient caution, so that their provisions are often obscure in themselves, or in conflict with each other, or at least so doubtful as to render it very difficult for even the best informed persons to ascertain precisely what the statute law really is.

It seems to me very important that the statute laws should be made as plain and intelligible as possible, and be reduced to as small a compass as may consist with thefullness and precision of the will of the legislature and the perspicuity of its language. This, well done, would, I think, greatly facilitate the labors of those whose duty it is to assist in the administration of the laws, and would be a lasting benefit to the people, by placing before them, in a more accessible and intelligible form, the laws which so deeply concern their interests and their duties.

I am informed by some whose opinions I respect, that all the acts of Congress now in force, and of a permanent and general nature, might be revised and re-written, so as to be embraced in one volume (or, at most, two volumes,) of ordinary and convenient size. And I respectfully recommend to Congress to consider of the subject, and, if my suggestion be approved, to devise such plan as to their wisdom shall seem most proper for the attainment of the end proposed.

One of the unavoidable consequences of the present insurrection is the entire suppression, in many places, of all the ordinary means of administering civil justice by the officers and in the forms of existing law. This is the case, in whole or in part, in all the insurgent States; and as our armies advance upon and take possession of parts of those States, the practical evil becomes more apparent. There are no courts nor officers to whom the citizens of other States may apply for the enforcement of their lawful claims against citizens of the insurgent States; and there is a vast amount of debt constituting such claims. Some have estimated it as high as two hundred million dollars, due, in large part, from insurgents, in open rebellion, to loyal citizens, who are, even now, making great sacrifices, in the discharge of their patriotic duty, to support the Government.

Under these circumstances, I have been urgently solicited to establish, by military power, courts to administer summary justice in such cases. I have thus far declined to do it, not because I had any doubt that the end proposed—the collection of the debts—was just and right in itself, but because I have been unwilling to go beyond the pressure of necessity in the unusual exercise of power. But the powers of Congress, I suppose, are equal to the anomalous occasion, and therefore I refer the whole matter to Congress, with the hope that a plan may be devised for the administration of justice in all such parts of the insurgent States and Territories as may be under the control of this Government, whether by a voluntary return to allegiance and order, or by the power of our arms. This, however, not to be a permanent institution, but a temporary substitute, and to cease as soon as the ordinary courts can be reëstablished in peace.

It is important that some more convenient means should be provided, if possible, for the adjustment of claims against the Government, especially in view of their increased number by reason of the war. It is as much the duty of Government to render prompt justice against itself, in favor of citizens, as it is to administer the same between private individuals. The investigation and adjudication of claims, in their nature, belong to the judicial department; besides, it is apparent that the attention of Congress will be more than usually engaged for some time to come with great national questions. It was intended, by the organization of the Court of Claims, mainly to remove this branch of business from the halls of Congress; but while the court has proved to be an effective and valuable means of investigation, it in a great degree fails to effect the object of its creation for want of power to make its judgments final.

Fully aware of the delicacy, not to say the danger, of the subject, I commend to your careful consideration whether this power of making judgments final may not properly be given to the court, reserving the right of appeal on questions of law to the Supreme Court, with such other provisions as experience may have shown to be necessary.

I ask attention to the report of the Postmaster General, the following being a summary statement of the condition of the department:

The revenue from all sources during the fiscal year ending June 30, 1861, including the annual permanent appropriation of seven hundred thousand dollars for the transportation of "free mail matter," was nine million forty-nine thousand two hundred and ninety-six dollars and forty cents, being about two per cent. less than the revenue for 1860.

The expenditures were thirteen million six hundred and six thousand seven hundred and fifty-nine dollars and eleven cents, showing a decrease of more than eight per cent. as compared with those of the previous year, and leaving an excess of expenditure over the revenue for the last fiscal year of four million five hundred and fifty-seven thousand four hundred and sixty-two dollars and seventy-one cents.

The gross revenue for the year ending June 30, 1863, is estimated at an increase of four per cent. on that of 1861, making eight million six hundred and eighty-three thousand dollars, to which should be added the earnings of the department in carrying free matter, viz: seven hundred thousand dollars, making nine million three hundred and eighty-three thousand dollars.

The total expenditures for 1863 are estimated at twelve million five hundred and twenty-eight thousand dollars, leaving an estimated deficiency of three million one hundred and forty-five thousand dollars to be supplied from the treasury, in addition to the permanent appropriation.

The present insurrection shows, I think, that the extension of this District across the Potomac river, at the time of establishing the capital here, was eminently wise, and consequently that the relinquishment of that portion of it which lies within the State of Virginia was unwise and dangerous. I submit for your consideration the expediency of regaining that part of the District, and the restoration of the original boundaries thereof, through negotiations with the State of Virginia.

The report of the Secretary of the Interior, with the accompanying documents, exhibits the condition of the several branches of the public business pertaining to that department. The depressing influences of the insurrection have been specially felt in the operations of the Patent and General Land Offices. The cash receipts from the sales of public lands during the past year have exceeded the expenses of our land system only about two hundred thousand dollars. The sales have been entirely suspended in the Southern States, while the interruptions to the business of the country, and the diversions of large numbers of men from labor to military service, have obstructed settlements in the new States and Territories of the Northwest.

The receipts of the Patent Office have declined in nine months about one hundred thousand dollars, rendering a large reduction of the force employed necessary to make it self-sustaining.

The demands upon the Pension Office will be largely increased by the insurrection. Numerous applications for pen sions, based upon the casualties of the existing war, have already been made. There is reason to believe that many who are now upon the pension rolls, and in receipt of the bounty of the Government, are in the ranks of the insurgent army, or giving them aid and comfort. The Secretary of the Interior has directed a suspension of the payment of the pensions of such persons upon the proof of their disloyalty. I recommend that Congress authorize that officer to cause the names of such persons to be stricken from the pension rolls.

The relations of the Government with the Indian tribes have been greatly disturbed by the insurrection, especially in the Southern Superintendency and in that of New Mexico. The Indian country south of Kansas is in the possession of insurgents from Texas and Arkansas. The agents of the United States appointed since the 4th of March for this superintendency have been unable to reach their posts, while the most of those who were in office before that time have espoused the insurrectionary cause, and assume to exercise the powers of agents by virtue of commissions from the insurrectionists. It has been stated in the public press that a portion of those Indians have been organized as a military force, and are attached to the army of the insurgents. Although the Government has no official information upon this subject, letters have been written to the Commissioner of Indian Affairs by several prominent chiefs, giving assurance of their loyalty to the United States, and expressing a wish for the presence of Federal troops to protect them. It is believed that upon the repossession of the country by the Federal forces the Indians will readily cease all hostile demonstrations, and resume their former relations to the Government.

Agriculture, confessedly the largest interest of the nation, has not a department, nor a bureau, but a clerkship only, assigned to it in the Government. While it is fortunate that this great interest is so independent in its nature as to not have demanded and extorted more from the Government, I respectfully ask Congress to consider whether something more can not be given voluntarily with general advantage.

Annual reports exhibiting the condition of our agriculture, commerce and manufactures, would present a fund of information of great practical value to the country. While I make no suggestion as to details, I venture the opinion that an agricultural and statistical bureau might profitably be organized.

The execution of the laws for the suppression of the African slave-trade has been confided to the Department of the Interior. It is a subject of gratulation that the efforts which have been made for the suppression of this inhuman traffic have been recently attended with unusual success. Five vessels being fitted out for the slave-trade have been seized and condemned. Two mates of vessels engaged in the trade, and one person in equipping a vessel as a slaver, have been convicted and subjected to the penalty of fine and imprisonment, and one captain, taken with a cargo of Africans on board his vessel, has been convicted of the highest grade of offense under our laws, the punishment of which is death.

The Territories of Colorado, Dakota, and Nevada, created by the last Congress, have been organized, and civil administration has been inaugurated therein under auspices especially gratifying, when it is considered that the leaven of treason was found existing in some of these new countries when the Federal officers arrived there.

The abundant natural resources of these Territories, with the security and protection afforded by organized government, will doubtless invite to them a large immigration when peace shall restore the business of the country to its accustomed channels. I submit the resolutions of the Legislature of Colorado, which evidence the patriotic spirit of the people of the Territory. So far, the authority of the United States has been upheld in all the Territories, as it is hoped it will be in the future. I commend their interests and defense to the enlightened and generous care of Congress.

I recommend to the favorable consideration of Congress the interests of the District of Columbia. The insurrection has been the cause of much suffering and sacrifice to its inhabitants, and as they have no representative in Congress, that body should not overlook their just claims upon the Government.

At your late session a joint resolution was adopted authorizing the President to take measures for facilitating a proper representation of the industrial interests of the United States at the exhibition of the industry of all nations, to be holden at London in the year 1862. I regret to say I have been unable to give personal attention to this subject—a subject at once so interesting in itself, and so extensively and intimately connected with the material prosperity of the world. Through the Secretaries of State and of the Interior a plan, or system, has been devised, and partly matured, and which will be laid before you.

Under and by virtue of the act of Congress entitled "An act to confiscate property used for insurrectionary purposes," approved August 6, 1861, the legal claims of certain persons to the labor and service of certain other persons have become forfeited; and numbers of the latter, thus liberated, are already dependent on the United States, and must be provided for in some way. Besides this, it is not impossible that some of the States will pass similar enactments for their own benefit respectively, and by operations of which persons of the same class will be thrown upon them for disposal. In such case I recommend that Congress provide for accepting such persons from such States according to some mode of valuation, in lieu, *pro tanto*, of direct taxes, or upon some other plan to be agreed on with such States, respectively; that such persons, on such acceptance by the General Government, be at once deemed free; and that, in any event, steps be taken for colonizing both classes (or the one first mentioned, if the other shall not be brought into existence) at some place or places in a climate congenial to them. It might be well to consider, too, whether the free colored people already in the United States could not, so far as individuals may desire, be included in such colonization.

To carry out the plan of colonization may involve the acquiring of territory, and also the appropriation of money beyond that to be expended in the territorial acquisition. Having practiced the acquisition of territory for nearly sixty years, the question of constitutional power to do so is no longer an open one with us. The power was questioned at first by Mr. Jefferson, who, however, in the purchase of Louisiana, yielded his scruples on the plea of great expediency. If it be said that the only legitimate object of acquiring territory is to furnish homes for white men, this measure effects that object, for the emigration of colored men leaves additional room for white men remaining or coming here. Mr. Jefferson, however, placed the importance of procuring Louisiana more on political and commercial grounds than on providing room for population.

On this whole proposition, including the appropriation of money with the acquisition of territory, does not the expediency amount to absolute necessity—that without which the Government itself can not be perpetuated?

The war continues. In considering the policy to be adopted for suppressing the insurrection, I have been anxious and careful that the inevitable conflict for this purpose shall not degenerate into a violent and remorseless revolutionary struggle. I have, therefore, in every case thought it proper to keep the integrity of the Union prominent as the primary object of the contest on our part, leaving all questions which are not of vital military importance to the more deliberate action of the legislature.

In the exercise of my best discretion, I have adhered to the blockade of the ports held by the insurgents, instead of putting in force, by proclamation, the law of Congress enacted at the late session for closing those ports.

So, also, obeying the dictates of prudence, as well as the obligations of law, instead of transcending, I have adhered to the act of Congress to confiscate property used for insurrectionary purposes. If a new law upon the same subject shall be proposed, its propriety will be duly considered. The Union must be preserved; and hence all indispensable means must be employed. We should not be in haste to determine that radical and extreme measures, which may reach the loyal as well as the disloyal, are indispensable.

The inaugural address at the beginning of the administration, and the message to Congress at the late special session, were both mainly devoted to the domestic controversy out of which the insurrection and consequent war have sprung. Nothing now occurs to add or subtract to or from the principles or general purposes stated and expressed in those documents.

The last ray of hope for preserving the Union peaceably expired at the assault upon Fort Sumter; and a general review of what has occurred since may not be unprofitable. What was painfully uncertain then is much better defined and more distinct now; and the progress of events is plainly in the right direction. The insurgents confidently claimed a strong support from north of Mason and Dixon's line, and the friends of the Union were not free from apprehension on the point. This, however, was soon settled definitely, and on the right side. South of the line, noble little Delaware led off right from the first. Maryland was made to *seem* against the Union. Our soldiers were assaulted, bridges were burned, and railroads torn up within her limits, and we were many days, at one time, without the ability to bring a single regiment over her soil to the capital. Now her bridges and railroads are repaired and open to the Government; she a'ready gives seven regiments to the cause of the Union and none to the enemy; and her people, at a regular election, have sustained the Union by a larger majority and a larger aggregate vote than they ever before gave to any candidate or any question. Kentucky, too, for some time in doubt, is now decidedly, and, I think, unchangeably, ranged on the side of the Union. Missouri is comparatively quiet, and I believe can not again be overrun by the insurrectionists. These three States of Maryland, Kentucky and Missouri, neither of which would promise a single soldier at first, have now an aggregate of not less than forty thousand in the field for the Union; while of their citizens certainly not more than a third of that number, and they of doubtful whereabouts and doubtful existence, are in arms against it. After a somewhat bloody struggle of months, winter closes on the Union people of Western Virginia, leaving them masters of their own country.

An insurgent force of about fifteen hundred, for months dominating the narrow peninsular region, constituting the counties of Accomac and Northampton, and known as the eastern shore of Virginia, together with some contiguous parts of Maryland, have laid down their arms; and the people there have renewed their allegiance to, and accepted the protection of, the old flag. This leaves no armed insurrectionist north of the Potomac or east of the Chesapeake.

Also we have obtained a footing at each of the isolated points, on the southern coast, of Hatteras, Port Royal, Tybee Island, near Savannah, and Ship Island; and we likewise have some general accounts of popular movements, in behalf of the Union, in North Carolina and Tennessee.

These things demonstrate that the cause of the Union is advancing steadily and certainly southward.

Since your last adjournment, Lieut. Gen. Scott has retired from the head of the army. During his long life, the nation has not been unmindful of his merit; yet, on calling to mind how faithfully, ably and brilliantly he has served the country, from a time far back in our history, when few of the now living had been born, and thenceforward continually, I can not but think we are still his debtors. I submit, therefore, for your consideration, what further mark of recognition is due to him, and to ourselves, as a grateful people.

With the retirement of Gen. Scott came the Executive duty of appointing, in his stead, a General-in-chief of the army. It is a fortunate circumstance that neither in council nor country was there, so far as I know, any difference of opinion as to the proper person to be selected. The retiring chief repeatedly expressed his judgment in favor of Gen. McClellan for the position, and in this the nation seemed to give a unanimous concurrence. The designation of Gen. McClellan is, therefore, in considerable degree, the selection of the country as well as of the Executive; and hence there is better reason to hope there will be given him the confidence and cordial support thus, by fair implication, promised, and without which he can not, with so full efficiency, serve the country.

It has been said that one bad General is better than two good ones; and the saying is true, if taken to mean no more than that an army is better directed by a single mind, though inferior, than by two superior ones at variance and cross-purposes with each other.

And the same is true in all joint operations wherein those

engaged *can* have none but a common end in view, and *can* differ only as to the choice of means. In a storm at sea, no one on board *can* wish the ship to sink, and yet, not unfrequently, all go down together because too many will direct and no single mind can be allowed to control.

It continues to develop that the insurrection is largely, if not exclusively, a war upon the first principle of popular government—the rights of the people. Conclusive evidence of this is found in the most grave and maturely-considered public documents, as well as in the general tone of the insurgents. In those documents we find the abridgment of the existing right of suffrage and the denial to the people of all right to participate in the selection of public officers, except the. legislative, boldly advocated, with labored arguments to prove that large control of the people in government is the source of all political evil. Monarchy itself is sometimes hinted at as a possible refuge from the power of the people.

In my present position I could scarcely be justified were I to omit raising a warning voice against this approach of returning despotism.

It is not needed nor fitting here that a general argument should be made in favor of popular institutions; but there is one point, with its connections, not so hackneyed as most others, to which I ask a brief attention. It is the effort to place *capital* on an equal footing with, if not above *labor*, in the structure of government. It is assumed that labor is available only in connection with capital—that nobody labors unless somebody else, owning capital, somehow by the use of it induces him to labor. This assumed, it is next considered whether it is best that capital shall *hire* laborers, and thus induce them to work by their own consent, or *buy* them, and drive them to it without their consent. Having proceeded so far, it is naturally concluded that all laborers are either *hired* laborers, or what we call slaves. And further, it is assumed that whoever is once a hired laborer is fixed in that condition for life.

Now, there is no such relation between capital and labor as assumed; nor is there any such thing as a free man being fixed for life in the condition of a hired laborer. Both these assumptions are false, and all inferences from them are groundless.

Labor is prior to and independent of capital. Capital is only the fruit of labor, and could never have existed if labor had not first existed. Labor is the superior of capital, and deserves much the higher consideration. Capital has its rights, which are as worthy of protection as any other rights. Nor is it denied that there is, and probably always will be, a relation between labor and capital producing mutual benefits. The error is in assuming that the whole labor of community exists within that relation. A few men own capital, and that few avoid labor themselves, and with their capital hire or buy another few to labor for them. A large majority belong to neither class—neither work for others nor have others working for them. In most of the Southern States a majority of the whole people, of all colors, are neither slaves nor masters, while in the Northern a large majority are neither hirers nor hired. Men, with their families—wives, sons, and daughters— work for themselves, on their farms, in their houses, and in their shops, taking the whole product to themselves, and asking no favors of capital, on the one hand, nor of hired laborers or slaves on the other. It is not forgotten that a considerable number of persons mingle their own labor with capital—that is, they labor with their own hands, and also buy or hire others to labor for them; but this is only a mixed, and not a distinct class. No principle stated is disturbed by the existence of this mixed class.

Again, as has already been said, there is not, of necessity, any such thing as the free hired laborer being fixed to that condition for life. Many independent men every-where in these States, a few years back in their lives, were hired laborers. The prudent, penniless beginner in the world, labors for wages awhile, saves a surplus with which to buy tools or land for him- self, then labors on his own account another while, and at length hires another new beginner to help him. This is the just, and generous, and prosperous system, which opens the way to all— gives hope to all, and consequent energy, and progress, and im- provement of condition to all. No men living are more worthy to be trusted than those who toil up from poverty; none less inclined to take or touch aught which they have not honestly earned. Let them beware of surrendering a political power which they already possess, and which, if surrendered, will surely be used to close the door of advancement against such as they, and to fix new disabilities and burdens upon them, till all of liberty shall be lost.

From the first taking of our National Census to the last are seventy years; and we find our population at the end of the period eight times as great as it was at the beginning. The increase of those other things which men deem desirable has been even greater. We thus have at one view what the popu- lar principle, applied to Government through the machinery of the States and the Union, has produced in a given time, and also what it firmly maintained, it promises for the future. There are already among us those who, if the Union be preserved, will live to see it contain two hundred and fifty millions. The struggle *of* to-day is not altogether *for* to-day; it is for a vast future also. With a reliance on Providence all the more firm and earnest, let us proceed in the great task which events have devolved upon us.

ABRAHAM LINCOLN.

WASHINGTON, December 3, 1861.

The organization of an opposition party, taking the Democratic name, had been effected under the auspices of a few anti-war men in Congress, who had occasionally ventured to speak out their dissent at the previous session. This faction, represented in Ohio by Vallandigham, and in Illinois by Richardson, having apparently very little support among the people, began at this session to work in earnest, boldly aspiring to assume control of the House of Representatives to be elected during the coming season. Already, too, plans were formed for carrying the next Presidential election, and there were not wanting sagacious observers, who believed that schemes of this sort had the sympathy of at least one Major General in the army.

At this session of Congress it was early apparent that a great advance had taken place in the public mind on the question of Slavery. Neither Secretary Seward's diplomatic assurances to Governments abroad that no change in Southern institutions was contemplated in any event, nor McClellan's manifesto on this subject to the people of Virginia, nor Halleck's order excluding fugitive slaves from the lines of the Army of the West, nor the 22d of July resolution of Mr. Crittenden, were now satisfactory to the people, who began already to demand that the Rebellion should be attacked in its vital and vulnerable point. On the third day of the session, the Crittenden Resolution was laid on the table, in the popular branch of Congress, by a vote of 71 to 65. The demand of the people for the destruction of Slavery was daily becoming more manifest and more earnest. The President, in his inaugural address, had clearly foreseen a time when, if war should come, the destruction of Slavery must follow. He made no pledge, under such circumstances, not to hasten its destruction by all the means in his power. So soon as the people, whose will he intended faithfully to execute, should sustain him in such a war measure—now beginning to be deemed necessary—he had no dread to strike. A joint committee of both Houses to inquire into the conduct of the war was appointed in the Senate, on the 18th, and in the House on the 19th of December. It is needless to say that this proceeding arose from the general dissatisfaction felt at the inaction of the Army of the Potomac, in the face of a greatly inferior enemy, as well as from the disastrous issue of the only positive movement yet attempted—that at Ball's Bluff. The members of that committee were: Messrs. Wade, Chandler, and Andrew Johnson (whose place was subsequently supplied by Mr. Wright, of Indiana), of the Senate; and Messrs. Gooch, Covode, Julian, and Odell, of the House. The evidence collected by this committee from the best sources of information, including the testimony of the highest Generals, was, from time to time, laid before the President for his consideration, and subsequently given to the public.

The exciting subject of the arrest of Mason and Slidell was early seized upon by the leaders of the Opposition in the House, as one suited to their purpose. An adroitly worded resolution with an elaborate preamble, reciting the complimentary order of the Secretary of the Navy on this arrest, and the unanimous thanks of the House to Com. Wilkes already passed, was offered in the House, calling upon the President not to yield " to any menace or demand of the British Government." This was referred, against the wishes of the mover, to the Committee on Foreign Affairs—ayes 109, nays 16. At a later period, December 30, the President transmitted to Congress the correspondence between Mr. Seward and the authorities of Great Britain on this subject, conceding the illegality of the arrest, though strictly according to English precedent, and offering the proper satisfaction. Mason and Slidell were placed on board a British vessel lying off Boston, to be transported to their original destination. If this decision caused a momentary disappointment, its profound wisdom and prudence were at once apparent. It was to the supporters of Davis, and to the sympathizers with him, the defeat of an ardently cherished hope that so unimportant a matter as the detention or surrender of their two diplomatic friends would involve this country in a foreign war.

A motion in the House, on the 10th of December, involving the question of the "arbitrary arrests" of bold complotters of treason, in the loyal States, showed 108 members in favor of sustaining the President, and 26 in opposition.

At this session, Congress provided for the issue of legal-tender notes, and passed an internal revenue bill, which should largely increase the receipts into the Treasury, insuring a basis for the payment of interest on loans, also authorized, and confidence in the redemption of the National currency. The policy adopted was substantially that recommended and approved by the distinguished head of the Treasury Department, Mr. Chase. Much of the time of Congress was also occupied in considering various bills for confiscating the property of Rebels, and in maturing the measure ultimately passed.

On the 13th of January, 1862, Mr. Cameron resigned his place in the Cabinet as Secretary of War, receiving an appointment as Minister to Russia, and the Hon. Edwin M. Stanton was appointed in his stead.

The message sent by President Lincoln to Congress on the 6th of March, in regard to gradual and compensated emancipation, shows that he had now come to look seriously upon the question of employing some means for the complete eradication of Slavery. He intimates plainly that such a conviction was on his mind when preparing his message of Dec. 3, 1861. His emancipation message is in these words:

FELLOW-CITIZENS OF THE SENATE AND HOUSE OF REPRESENTATIVES: I recommend the adoption of a joint resolution by your honorable bodies, which shall be substantially as follows:

Resolved, That the United States ought to coöperate with any State which may adopt gradual abolishment of slavery, giving to such State pecuniary aid, to be used by such State in its discretion, to compensate for the inconveniences, public and private, produced by such change of system.

If the proposition contained in the resolution does not meet the approval of Congress and the country, there is the end; but if it does command such approval, I deem it of importance

27

that the States and people immediately interested should be at once distinctly notified of the fact, so that they may begin to consider whether to accept or reject it. The Federal Government would find its highest interest in such a measure as one of the most efficient means of self-preservation. The leaders of the existing insurrection entertain the hope that this Government will ultimately be forced to acknowledge the independence of some part of the disaffected region, and that all the Slave States north of such part will then say, "the Union for which we have struggled being already gone, we now choose to go with the southern section." To deprive them of this hope substantially ends the rebellion, and the initiation of emancipation completely deprives them of it as to all the States initiating it. The point is not that *all* the States tolerating slavery would very soon, if at all, initiate emancipation, but that, while the offer is equally made to all, the more northern shall, by such initiation, make it certain to the more southern that in no event will the former ever join the latter in their proposed confederacy. I say "initiation," because, in my judgment, gradual, and not sudden emancipation, is better for all. In the mere financial or pecuniary view, any member of Congress, with the census tables and treasury reports before him, can readily see for himself how very soon the current expenditures of this war would purchase, at fair valuation, all the slaves in any named State. Such a proposition on the part of the General Government sets up no claim of a right by Federal authority to interfere with slavery within State limits, referring, as it does, the absolute control of the subject in each case to the State and its people immediately interested. It is proposed as a matter of perfectly free choice with them.

In the annual message last December I thought fit to say, "the Union must be preserved; and hence all indispensable means must be employed." I said this not hastily, but deliberately. War has been made, and continues to be an indispensable means to this end. A practical reacknowledgment of the National authority would render the war unnecessary, and it would at once cease. If, however, resistance continues, the war must also continue, and it is impossible to foresee all the incidents which may attend and all the ruin which may follow it. Such as may seem indispensable, or may obviously promise great efficiency toward ending the struggle, must and will come.

The proposition now made, though an offer only, I hope it may be esteemed no offense to ask whether the pecuniary consideration tendered would not be of more value to the States and private persons concerned than are the institutions and property in it, in the present aspect of affairs.

While it is true that the adoption of the proposed resolution would be merely initiatory, and not within itself a practical measure, it is recommended in the hope that it would soon lead to important practical results. In full view of my great responsibility to my God and to my country, I earnestly beg the attention of Congress and the people to the subject.

ABRAHAM LINCOLN.

March 6, 1862.

The resolution recommended in the foregoing paper was passed by the House on the 11th of March—ayes 97, noes 36. Only five of the affirmative votes were from the Slave States. The resolution was concurred in by the Senate, with little opposition, and signed by the President on the 10th of April.

Early in April the Senate passed a bill abolishing slavery in the District of Columbia, with compensation to the loyal owners of slaves. This bill passed the House on the 11th of the same month, four days after its transmission—ayes 92, noes 39. In communicating his approval of this measure, the President, departing from the usual practice, sent a message to Congress in the following terms :

FELLOW-CITIZENS OF THE SENATE AND HOUSE OF REPRESENTATIVES : The act entitled " An act for the release of certain persons held to service or labor in the District of Columbia," has this day been approved and signed.

I have never doubted the constitutional authority of Congress to abolish slavery in this District, and I have ever desired to see the National Capital freed from the institution in some satisfactory way. Hence there has never been, in my mind, any question upon the subject except the one of expediency, arising in view of all the circumstances. If there be matters within and about this act which might have taken a course or shape more satisfactory to my judgment, I do not attempt to specify them. I am gratified that the two principles of compensation and colonization are both recognized and practically applied in the act.

In the matter of compensation it is provided that claims may be presented within ninety days from the passage of the act, " but not thereafter," and there is no saving for minors, *femmes-covert*, insane or absent persons. I presume this is an omission by mere oversight, and I recommend that it be supplied by an amendatory or supplemental act.

April 16, 1862.   ABRAHAM LINCOLN.

On the 10th of June, President Lincoln communicated to Congress a copy of a treaty negotiated with Great Britain, having for its design a complete suppression of the African slave-trade.

The Confiscation Act, as finally matured and passed by Congress, with a special provision for conditional pardon and amnesty, received the approval of the Executive on the last day of the session, July 17th. To obviate constitutional objections known to exist in the President's mind, to the measure as at first passed, a supplementary joint resolution had been adopted, limiting the forfeiture of real estate to the lifetime of its rebel owner. His views on this subject were officially set forth in a document, from which the following memorable sentences are quoted :

It is startling to say that Congress can free a slave within a State, and yet were it said that the ownership of a slave had first been transferred to the nation, and that Congress had then liberated him, the difficulty would vanish; and this is the real case. The traitor against the General Government forfeits his slave at least as justly as he does any other property, and he forfeits both to the Government against which he offends. The Government, so far as there can be ownership, owns the forfeited slaves, and the question for Congress in regard to them is, shall they be made free or sold to new masters? I see no objection to Congress deciding in advance that they shall be free.

That those who make a causeless war should be compelled to pay the cost of it, is too obviously just to be called in question. To give Government protection to the property of persons who have abandoned it, and gone on a crusade to overthrow the same Government, is absurd, if considered in the mere light of justice. The severest justice may not always be the best policy.   *   *   I think our military commanders, when, in military phrase, they are within the enemy's country, should, in an orderly manner, seize and keep whatever of real or personal property may be necessary or convenient for their commands, and at the same time preserve in some way the evidence of what they do.

A few days before the adjournment, the President, evidently looking forward to the necessity of a more radical and decisive policy in regard to Slavery, invited the Senators and Representatives of the border Slave States to a conference. The disastrous Peninsular campaign was now over, and depression prevailed throughout the country. The war must somehow be ended, with the rebellion overthrown; and the employment of every effective and legitimate war measure. he felt to be now demanded. He desired the great change to come as lightly as possible on the still loyal Slave States, and it was in this spirit that the interview was solicited by him. Having convened at the Executive Mansion, on the 12th of July, these Representatives were addressed by Mr. Lincoln (reading what he had carefully prepared for the occasion) as follows:

GENTLEMEN: After the adjournment of Congress, now near, I shall have no opportunity of seeing you for several months. Believing that you of the Border States hold more power for good than any other equal number of members, I feel it a duty which I can not justifiably waive to make this appeal to you.

I intend no reproach or complaint when I assure you that, in my opinion, if you all had voted for the resolution in the gradual emancipation message of last March, the war would now be substantially ended. And the plan therein proposed is yet one of the most potent and swift means of ending it. Let the States which are in rebellion see definitely and certainly that in no event will the States you represent ever join their proposed Confederacy, and they can not much longer maintain the contest. But you can not divest them of their hope to ultimately have you with them so long as you show a determination to perpetuate the institution within your own States. Beat them at elections, as you have overwhelmingly done, and, nothing daunted, they still claim you as their own. You and I know what the lever of their power is. Break that lever before their faces, and they can shake you no more forever.

Most of you have treated me with kindness and consideration, and I trust you will not now think I improperly touch what is exclusively your own, when, for the sake of the whole country, I ask, "Can you, for your States, do better than to take the course I urge?" Discarding *punctilio* and maxims adapted to more manageable times, and looking only to the unprecedentedly stern facts of our case. can you do better in any possible event? You prefer that the constitutional relations of the States to the nation shall be practically restored without disturbance of the institution ; and, if this were done, my whole duty in this respect, under the Constitution and my oath of office, would be performed. But it is not done, and we are trying to accomplish it by war. The incidents of the war can not be avoided. If the war continues long, as it must if the object be not sooner attained, the institution in your States will be extinguished by mere friction and abrasion—by the mere incidents of the war. It will be gone, and you will have nothing valuable in lieu of it. Much of its value is gone already. How much better for you and for your people to take the step which at once shortens the war, and secures substantial compensation for that which is sure to be wholly lost in any other event! How much better to thus save the money which else we sink forever in the war! How much better to do it while we can, lest the war, ere long, render us pecuniarily unable to do it! How much better for you, as seller, and the nation, as buyer, to sell out and buy out that without which the war could never have been, than to sink both the thing to be sold and the price of it, in cutting one another's throats !

I do not speak of emancipation at once, but of a decision at once to emancipate gradually. Room in South America for colonization can be obtained cheaply and in abundance, and when numbers shall be large enough to be company and encouragement for one another, the freed people will not be so reluctant to go.

I am pressed with a difficulty not yet mentioned—one which threatens division among those who, united, are none too strong. An instance of it is known to you. General Hunter is an honest man. He was, and I hope still is, my friend. I valued him none the less for his agreeing with me in the general wish that all men every-where could be freed. He proclaimed all men free within certain States, and I repudiated the proclamation. He expected more good and less harm from the measure than I could believe would follow. Yet, in repudiating it, I gave dissatisfaction, if not offense, to many whose support the country can not afford to lose. And this is not the end of it. The pressure in this direction is still upon me, and is increasing. By conceding what I now ask you can relieve me, and, much more, can relieve the country in this important point.

· Upon these considerations, I have again begged your attention to the Message of March last. Before leaving the Capitol, consider and discuss it among yourselves. You are patriots and statesmen, and as such, I pray you consider this proposition, and, at the least, commend it to the consideration of your States and people. As you would perpetuate popular government for the best people in the world, I beseech you that you do in no wise omit this. Our common country is in great peril, demanding the loftiest views and boldest action to bring a speedy relief. Once relieved, its form of government is saved to the world; its beloved history and cherished memories are vindicated, and its happy future fully assured and rendered inconceivably grand. To you, more than to any others, the privilege is given to assure that happiness, and swell that grandeur, and to link your own names therewith forever.

Twenty of the Senators and Representatives thus addressed replied in respectful, but decidedly unfavorable, terms. Nine only made friendly and approving responses.

CHAPTER VI.

Military Events.—Inaction on the Potomac.—Western Campaigns.—
Capture of New Orleans.

THE summary of political events in the preceding chapter
has somewhat outrun the course of military operations.   Gen.
McClellan, as General-in-chief of the entire army, had nominally assumed control alike over Gen. Halleck, commanding in the Department of the West, over Gen. Burnside
and Gen. T. W. Sherman in North and South Carolina, and
over the vast Army of the Potomac.   During the two months
succeeding the retirement of Lieut. Gen. Scott, every day's
delay, while calm skies and dry roads invited to action, added
new weight to the impatience of the people.   But at length
wintry weather put an end to all immediate hope of action.
Opinions as to the General-in-chief were divided.   Ready
excuses on the part of those immediately about him as
to still needed preparations, and lavish promises as to results
when the time of action should come, with frequent intimations of an early movement, satisfied many who would
otherwise have been despondent.   To the President himself,
Gen. McClellan, while reticent as to details, preserved an
air of earnest determination, and held out the prospect of
effective action at no remote day.   An engagement near
Dranesville, Md., under Gen. Ord, favorable to our arms, yet
unimportant in results, had, on the 20th of December,
awakened only to disappoint an expiring hope of some
decisive action before another season.   Some occasional collisions between detachments of the opposing armies were all
that occurred in the Eastern Departments after the successful
landing of the Southern expedition until the opening of spring.

The contrast between this inaction in the East, and the energetic and decisive movements in the West during the same period,
was marked.   Neither this fact, nor the customary mode of

stating the plan of the General-in-chief—which was one of simultaneous movement on all sides—would seem consistent with the supposition that affairs in the West were under any real control of the nominal military head at Washington. His actual relation to these events will in due time appear.

Early in January, Col. Garfield again cleared the eastern border of Kentucky of Rebels, defeating an invading force under Humphrey Marshall, at Middle Creek, near Prestonburg, on the 10th. Gen. George B. Crittenden, at the head of another Rebel force, about 12,000 strong, had issued his proclamation to the people of Kentucky on the 6th, from his headquarters at Mill Spring, a point near the south bank of the Tennessee river, where that stream, making a wide sweep, bends farthest northward into the State. It was in this vicinity that a brilliant victory was gained on the 19th of January, by our forces under command of Gen. George H. Thomas. This achievement, utterly routing the rebel force, with severe loss, including that of Gen. Zollicoffer, killed, and penetrating the extended line of the Rebels opposed to Gen. Buell, was hailed as the promise of more stirring days. On the occasion of receiving this news, the Secretary of War issued the following order:

WAR DEPARTMENT, January 22, 1862.

The President, Commander-in-chief of the Army and Navy, has received information of a brilliant victory achieved by the United States forces over a large body of armed traitors and rebels at Mill Spring, in the State of Kentucky.

He returns thanks to the gallant officers and soldiers who won that victory, and when the official reports shall be received, the military skill and personal valor displayed in battle will be acknowledged and rewarded in a fitting manner.

The courage that encountered and vanquished the greatly superior numbers of the Rebel force, pursued and attacked them in their intrenchments, and paused not until the enemy was completely routed, merits and receives commendation.

The purpose of this war is to attack, pursue and destroy a rebellious enemy, and to deliver the country from danger menaced by traitors. Alacrity, daring, courageous spirit and patriotic zeal, on all occasions and under every circumstance, are expected from the Army of the United States.

21

In the prompt and spirited movements and daring battle of Mill Spring, the nation will realize its hopes, and the people of the United States will rejoice to honor every soldier and officer who proves his courage by charging with the bayonet and storming intrenchments, or in the blaze of the enemy's fire.

By order of the President.

EDWIN M. STANTON,
Secretary of War.

These words of cheer, following acts so successful, reassured despondent hearts, and turned all eyes toward new scenes of hope.

The Rebel line from Columbus, on the Mississippi, to Bowling Green, on Green river, as will be seen from a map of that region, was penetrated by the Cumberland and Tennessee rivers, running in a northerly and nearly parallel direction, about ten miles apart, from the boundary between Kentucky and Tennessee, into the Ohio river, cutting off a triangle comprising seven or eight counties in the south-western part of the former State. To secure their line against the gunboats, which were now making their appearance on the Western rivers, the Rebels had constructed a fort near the State line, on the Tennessee, in the immediate vicinity of Panther Island, called Fort Henry. At a point nearly on the same parallel, on the Cumberland, eastward, near Dover, in Tennessee, was another work named Fort Donelson. These points are about ninety miles distant from the mouths of the respective rivers.

Gen. Grant, almost simultaneously with the movement on Mill Spring, had planned an attack on Fort Henry, with a coöperating gunboat fleet under Com. Foote. This movement was authorized by Gen. Halleck, there being signs of intended reënforcements to the rebel left. Although the roads were in very bad condition, and movements of infantry and artillery were difficult, the high water in the Tennessee was specially favorable for the execution of that portion of the movement under the charge of Com. Foote.

On the 6th of February, the gunboats Essex, Carondelet, Cincinnati, St. Louis, Conestoga, Tyler and Lexington, advanced to the attack on Fort Henry, opening a rapid and heavy fire, replied to by the guns of the fort. After an hour and a quarter the latter were silenced, the fort was surrendered, and Gen. Tilghman, with his staff and sixty men, gave them selves up as prisoners. The remainder of the garrison escaped, the force sent forward by Grant, under Gen. McClernand, owing to the state of the roads or other causes, not having arrived in season to participate in the action. This engagement first thoroughly tested the gunboats, and proved their great value.

Gen. Grant lost no time in dispatching about 15,000 men from Fort Henry, to invest Fort Donelson. The gunboats, meanwhile, had returned to the mouth of the Tennessee, and made their way up the Cumberland, together with sixteen transports loaded with fresh troops, arriving on the 14th. The three divisions engaged were under the command of Gens. C. F. Smith, McClernand, and Lewis Wallace. The infantry and batteries having taken position, the gunboats opened fire on the fort at about two o'clock on that day, with less decisive effect than at Fort Henry. The St. Louis became seriously disabled, and Gen. Grant, making a complete investment of the fort, and strengthening his position, was designing to wait for the gunboats to renew the attack. On the following morning, however, the enemy within the fort, lately heavily reënforced, attacked our extreme right, under McClernand, which rested on Dover, and brought on a general and severe engagement, which had apparently almost resulted in a disastrous repulse of our forces. The right was seasonably reënforced, and after a hardly contested fight, lasting until dark, in which both sides suffered heavily, the Rebels were driven back within their fortifications. Early on the morning of the 16th, a white flag was raised by the Rebel Gen. Buckner, asking an armistice for the purpose of agreeing upon terms of capitulation. In reply, Gen. Grant sent the following memorable note:

HEADQUARTERS ON THE FIELD, FORT DONELSON, }
February 16, 1862. }

To GEN. S. B. BUCKNER—*Sir:* Yours of this date, proposing an armistice and the appointment of commissioners to settle on the terms of capitulation, is just received.   No terms, except unconditional and immediate surrender, can be accepted.

I propose to move immediately on your works.

I am, very respectfully, your obedient servant,

U. S. GRANT,

Brigadier General Commanding.

Gens. Floyd and Pillow, with a portion of the Rebel force, had escaped during the night. Gen. Buckner, and about 15,000 men, were unconditionally surrendered as prisoners of war, and 20,000 stand of arms, with a large amount of stores, fell into the hands of Gen. Grant. A victory so complete and substantial was hailed with joy by the Government and by loyal men every-where, and gave its hero at once a prominent place in the hearts of the people.

Finding his right and left flanks thus completely turned by Thomas and Grant, the enemy evacuated Bowling Green on the 15th, rapidly falling back south of the Cumberland river. Clarksville and Nashville, Tenn., were promptly occupied by our forces. This succession of triumphs, exciting grateful enthusiasm throughout the loyal portion of the nation, caused a corresponding humiliation and despondency in the Rebel States. The border line of the Rebellion, in the West, this side of the Mississippi, was thereby contracted a long distance southward, leaving Kentucky free, and promising a speedy restoration of Tennessee under loyal sway.

The forts on Roanoke Island, on the coast of North Carolina, were captured by a joint expedition under Gen. Burnside and Com. Goldsborough, on the 8th of February, after two days' fighting, in which the losses were comparatively small. Over two thousand prisoners, forty guns, and three thousand small arms, were captured.

In Missouri, Gen. Price had fallen back from point to point, on the approach of our forces under Gen. Curtis. He finally retired from the State, taking up his headquarters at Cross Hollows, in Arkansas, during the latter part of February. On the 23d of that month Gen. Curtis had advanced in pursuit, as far as Fayetteville, Ark., on the White river, in the northwestern part of that State.

The evacuation of Columbus, Kentucky, on the 27th of February, as a necessary result of Grant's capture of Fort Donelson, and the dispersion of the main force of the Rebels in Missouri, invited the attempt to repossess the Mississippi, hitherto blockaded by the Rebels. The importance of this possession, not alone for its commercial consequence to the North-west, but also from military considerations, was too obvious to escape the notice of a Western President. Three Illinois regiments occupied Columbus on the 3d of March, a gunboat fleet having accompanied the transports which conveyed this force. On the same day, an engagement, indecisive in its results, was fought by forces under Gen. Pope, with Rebels, under Gen. Jeff. Thompson, near New Madrid. It soon became evident that, in retreating from Columbus, the Rebels had occupied Island Number Ten, in the Mississippi river, several miles below, and a little distance above New Madrid. This was the beginning of the memorable siege of that place, ultimately captured, with a large number of prisoners and valuable property, on the 8th day of April.

On the 6th, 7th and 8th of March was fought one of the most important engagements of the war at Pea Ridge, in Arkansas, near the Missouri line. Gen. Curtis, as already seen, had driven the Rebels across the Missouri border, and had occupied Fayetteville, Arkansas, on the 23d of February, the opposing forces retiring beyond the Boston Mountains, which divide the valley of White river, on the north, from that of the Arkansas river, in the center of the State. Curtis soon after withdrew toward Missouri, his main force being concentrated at a place called Sugar-creek Hollow, with a rear guard, under Gen. Sigel, at Bentonville.

The forces under Gen. Curtis comprised four divisions— the First under command of Col. Osterhaus, the Second under Gen. Asboth, the Third under Col. Jeff. C. Davis, and the Fourth led by Col. Carr. The Rebel forces were now united under Gen. Earl Van Dorn, who had assumed command of the Trans-Mississippi Department, with his headquarters at Little Rock, on the 29th of January. There were under him in this engagement probably ten thousand Missouri troops, under Gen. Price; from twelve to fifteen thousand men from Arkansas, Louisiana and Texas, under Gen. McCulloch, and about five or six thousand Choctaw, Cherokee, Chickasaw and other Indians, with two white regiments—in all about seven thousand—under Albert Pike. One Rebel account states that Van Dorn's force in this expedition was reckoned as high as thirty-five thousand. The Union force did not much exceed one-third of that number.

Confident in their numerical strength, and believing, as they admitted, that their force was at least double that under Curtis, the Rebels advanced with the hope of annihilating our army. Coming up with Sigel's force at Bentonville, on the morning of the 6th of March, they compelled that General to fall back toward the main army—a movement which he executed with scarcely any loss, having sent forward his trains, while a well-managed battery protected his retreat, inflicting severe injury upon the enemy whenever he approached within shelling distance. A march of ten miles brought Sigel's force to the west end of Pea Ridge, a range of high ground just beyond Sugar Creek, where the main army of Curtis lay. It was now night, and Curtis, who had all day been busily preparing to meet the enemy, made his disposition for the eventful morrow. His force in the hollow had fronted to the south, and Sigel, with Osterhaus' division, now occupied a position about three miles to the west. The Rebel forces crossed the creek still further west, and occupied the higher ground northward and directly in the rear, his two main bodies also separated by about three miles distance—the troops under Price opposite Curtis, and those under McCulloch and McIntosh over against Sigel. A change of front was promptly made, bringing the armies face to face—Curtis commanding the right, now moved to higher ground two miles northward, and Sigel the left.

The enemy attacked our right on the morning of the 7th, and the battle was fiercely maintained throughout the day, with severe loss on both sides. The area fought over did not exceed three-fourths of a mile in diameter. Our right was finally driven back for nearly a mile, the enemy encamping on the field they had thus won. McCulloch, meanwhile, on the left, had in the morning begun a movement south-eastwardly, to form a junction with Price, so as to surround Curtis, and cut off all retreat. Sigel endeavored to check this detected movement by sending forward three pieces of flying artillery, with a cavalry support, to delay McCulloch's advance until his infantry could come up. An overwhelming force of Rebel cavalry bore down upon this detachment, dispersing it and capturing our guns, while McCulloch's infantry gained shelter in a wood beyond a large open field. This wood and field became the scene of a prolonged contest between Osterhaus and McCulloch. The timely arrival of Davis with reënforcements turned the tide, and the enemy was utterly routed, with heavy loss, McCulloch and McIntosh being among the killed.

The position which had been gained by Van Dorn's left was naturally a strong one, cutting off our retreat, and here he concentrated his entire forces. On that chilly night the men of Curtis' army, looking forward to the coming day, might well have been disheartened. Their ultimate defeat must have seemed almost certain. With sunrise the batteries of Price reopened, and with terrible effect on the extreme right, held by Carr's division, and now supported by Davis. The position of the enemy being clearly disclosed, Sigel, with quick insight and prompt action, skillfully disposed his batteries so as to bear directly in the face of the enemy's right, causing great destruction to the latter, with little loss to himself. His thirty pieces silenced battery after battery of the enemy, making terrible havoc. For more than two hours, with admirable tact and unslackened activity, this cannonading was kept up, batteries and infantry approaching nearer and nearer the concentrated foe, until at length Curtis ordered his infantry to charge the enemy in his last shelter of the woods, and, after a short but deadly struggle, the Rebel forces gave way and scattered in confusion and utter rout. The total loss of Curtis, mostly on the 7th, is stated at 1,312 in killed, wounded and missing. The losses of Van Dorn were manifestly much greater, but they are not accurately known.

With this victory, followed six days later by the capture of

New Madrid by Gen. Pope, the conflict in Missouri was substantially brought to an end. The war was now transferred into Arkansas, and from a contest on the part of the Rebels to force an unwilling people into fellowship with a confederacy of traitors, it had now become a movement of the Union armies—ere long to prove successful—for restoring peace, order and law, under the constitutional Government, in a State temporarily overborne by the tide of Secessionism.

Soon after the occupation of Nashville, on the 25th of February, Gen. Buell concentrated his army, for the most part, at and near that city. On the 11th of March, an order of the President placed the forces of Gens. Halleck, Hunter and Buell, under the chief command of Halleck alone, consolidating in one the respective departments of the two first-named commanders, together with so much of that of Gen. Buell "as lies west of a north and south line indefinitely drawn through Knoxville," the whole to be called the Department of the Mississippi. The troops under Buell were mostly from Ohio, Indiana and Kentucky. Among his Generals commanding divisions were A. McD. McCook, George H. Thomas, Ormsby M. Mitchell, Wm. Nelson and Thos. L. Crittenden.

An expedition under Gen. Grant was speedily organized, to proceed up the Tennessee river, the enemy having taken up his defensive line with the Charleston and Memphis Railroad as a base. Grant's new "Army of the Tennessee," was mainly composed of troops from Illinois, Ohio, Indiana and Iowa, with regiments from several other States. Numerous steamboats were employed for the transportation of these forces, which were accompanied by two gunboats. The divisions into which Grant's army was organized, each with its proportion of infantry, cavalry and artillery, were commanded, respectively, by Gens. W. T. Sherman, C. F. Smith, B. M. Prentiss, S. A. Hurlbut, J. A. McClernand and L. Wallace.

On the 5th of March, Gen. Beauregard, having tarried awhile at Richmond, after leaving Centreville about the 1st of February, assumed command of the Rebel "Army of the Mississippi," with his headquarters first at Jackson, Tenn., on the Mobile and Ohio Railroad. The Rebel forces, under the subordinate commands of Bragg, Polk, Cheatham, and others, were chiefly in camp at Corinth, Miss., with detachments at several points on the railroads. This place is at the junction of the Mobile and Ohio and the Memphis and Charleston Railroads, in an uneven country, and not far from the line dividing the States of Tennessee and Mississippi.

Gen. Grant landed his forces at Savannah, Tenn., a small place on the Tennessee river, about one hundred and seventy miles above Fort Henry, and about twenty-five miles from the Mississippi State line. His original force was increased by a considerable body of infantry from Ohio. As many as eighty-two steamers, laden with troops, had arrived at Savannah by the 13th of March. These "invaders" were received with enthusiastic demonstrations of joy by the inhabitants of that part of Tennessee through which they passed.

Soon after the arrival of Gen. Grant in person, the army was advanced seven miles up the river to Pittsburg Landing. Gen. Buell was ordered by Halleck to effect a junction with Grant. Little alacrity, however, was shown by Buell in complying with this order, so manifestly requiring prompt execution in view of the greatly superior Rebel force known to be in front of Grant. It was not until the 28th of March that Buell left Nashville. On the 30th, the rear of his army was at Columbia, but eighty-two miles distant from Savannah. This distance was passed over by leisurely marches, averaging less than twelve miles a day, while Beauregard was putting in execution his well-devised plan for attacking Grant in overwhelming force before Buell should come to his support.

On the 3d of April, Gen. Johnston issued a brief address to the Army of the Mississippi, to inspirit them in executing the purpose formed, "to offer battle to the invaders," and the Rebel forces were put in motion toward Pittsburg Landing. Orders were at the same time issued, dividing the army into three corps, the first to be commanded by Polk, the second by Bragg, and the third by Hardee. John C. Breckinridge was given the command of a reserve division. The chief command seems to have been jointly held by Johnston and Beauregard, until the former fell, early during the first day's engagement

28

Before six o'clock on the morning of Sunday, the 6th day of April, a party of the Rebels attacked Grant's left—that officer being then absent at Savannah, superintending preparations for receiving and crossing over the anxiously-expected forces of Buell. At eight o'clock the enemy advanced in strong force, and captured Gen. Prentiss, with two thousand prisoners. Hurlbut came to the support of the retreating division of Prentiss, and temporarily checked the enemy's advance. Part of Sherman's force, on the right of Prentiss, was routed, and a heavy column was thrown against McClernand's division in the center, which, before noon, was driven backward to the line of Hurlbut. The fight was bravely maintained, and the force attacking McClernand was once temporarily driven back for some distance; but the whole of our army was compelled gradually to give way. Only the most invincible courage of the men, with cool and determined leadership, could save the army now from utter defeat. The division commanded by Gen. W. H. L. Wallace, (in the absence of Gen. C. F. Smith,) on the right, had, with that of Hurlbut on the left, occupied positions next the river, and on these, with one of Sherman's brigades on the extreme left, now fell the weight of the Rebel advance. Four times attempts were made by the Rebels to charge on the gallant forces of Wallace, but each time volleys of musketry and the fire of well-directed artillery, drove back the assailants with terrible slaughter. Hurlbut's division was driven back, at length, from its camp to the shelter of woods beyond. Here, with their raking fire across the open fields, they three times repulsed the advancing enemy. The right of this division was further supported by forces rallied from the broken divisions. Meanwhile Gen. L. Wallace, who was at Crump's Landing, five miles below, was anxiously looked for, in the overwhelming odds against the remaining divisions, but unfortunately, though ordered up, he failed to reach the scene of action until nightfall.

Finally, Hurlbut's division was compelled to retire, and at length that of Wallace, who fell, mortally wounded. The whole army was now compressed into a comparatively small area, near the Landing; many guns had been lost; thousands of prisoners taken; and one more determined attack seemed sufficient to drive the men pell-mell into the river, adequate means for transporting them across the river being wanting. Now it was that the field batteries were collected and skillfully put in position, by Col. Webster, Grant's Chief of Artillery, preparatory to the expected onset. The Rebel advance drew the destructive fire of twenty-two guns, with that of the two gunboats at the mouth of Lick Creek. Staggered by this terrible hail, the enemy were kept in check until night closed upon the bloody field.

Beauregard joyously announced to his superiors at Richmond "a complete victory," with "the loss on both sides heavy, including our commander-in-chief, Albert Sidney Johnston, who fell gallantly leading his troops into the thickest of the fight." As the vaunting author of this dispatch soon learned, however, to his cost, the announcement of victory was premature. Another day entirely changed the face of events.

Before the conflict of Sunday had fairly closed, Gen. Nelson's division of Buell's army appeared on the opposite side of the river, and both those officers in person. During the night, the divisions of Crittenden and McCook also arrived; while Gen. L. Wallace, of Grant's army, took position, about one o'clock in the morning, on the extreme right.

Thus reënforced, Grant assumed the offensive, ordering an advance at dawn. The enemy was now forced back, from point to point, all along his line, the fight continuing without intermission from nine o'clock in the morning until five in the evening. At the latter hour the whole field had been regained, and the defeated Rebels put to flight. Our troops were too weary with the two days' hard conflict to make an effective pursuit. On the next day, Gen. Beauregard sent a flag of truce from his headquarters at Monterey, asking "permission to send a mounted party to the battle-field of Shiloh, for the purpose of giving decent interment" to his dead. To this Gen. Grant replied, on the 9th, saying that, owing to the warmth of the weather, he had deemed it advisable to have all the dead of both parties buried immediately, and that this was "now accomplished."

Gen. Grant estimated his loss in killed and wounded at 5,000. There was the further loss of about 3,000 prisoners taken on Sunday, making a total of 8,000. Gen. Beauregard, in his official report, conceded a Rebel loss of 1,728 killed, 8,012 wounded, and 959 missing—an aggregate of 10,699.

The numbers engaged under Gen. Grant, on the first day, were about 40,000, many of whom were raw troops but recently arrived. Nearly 30,000 fresh troops participated in the battle on the 7th. The Rebel force, consisting of three entire army corps, and a reserve division, may be estimated at not far from 70,000.

Gen. Halleck soon after took the field in person, and prepared for an advance on the enemy's stronghold at Corinth, to which place Beauregard retired with his army, directly after the defeat at Shiloh.

On the 22d of March, the President constituted two new military departments—the first called the Department of the Gulf, comprising all the coast of the Gulf of Mexico west of Pensacola harbor, and so much of the Gulf States as should be occupied by the commander, Maj. Gen. B. F. Butler; and the second, including the States of South Carolina, Georgia and Florida, with the forces heretofore under Gen. T. W. Sherman, to be under the command of Maj. Gen. David Hunter.

A joint expedition under Com. Farragut and Gen. Butler, to capture and occupy New Orleans, and to coöperate thence with the movements from Cairo downward to reopen the Mississippi river, had been organized in the autumn of 1861. Gen. Butler's forces were to rendezvous at Ship Island, for which place the command of Gen. Phelps sailed from Fortress Monroe on the 27th of November, arriving on the 3d of December. During this latter month, two gunboats of Farragut had some skirmishing with Rebel gunboats in Mississippi Sound; and in January another considerable installment of Butler's force arrived at Ship Island. A mortar fleet, under Com. D. D. Porter, was also added to the naval portion of the expedition. Com. Farragut left Hampton Roads in the steamer Hartford, on the 3d of February, to assume command of the squadron which was to operate against New Orleans, and arrived at Ship Island on the 20th. The chief obstacles to his intended advance, after crossing the bar, were Forts St. Philip and Jackson, on the Mississippi river, seventy-five miles below New Orleans. These works were so formidable, and the preparations to receive the "Northern armada" so thorough, that the Rebels were entirely confident of success in repelling all attacks. That part of Farragut's fleet which crossed the bar consisted of the steam sloops Hartford, 24 guns, (flag ship); Richmond, 26; Pensacola, 24; Brooklyn, 24; Mississippi, 12; Iroquois, 9; Oneida, 9; the sailing sloop-of-war Portsmouth, 17; the gunboats Varuna, 12; Cayuga, 9; and eight others of 4 guns each. Com. Porter's mortar fleet consisted of twenty schooners, mounting one large mortar, with two small guns, and was accompanied by the Harriet Lane, (flag ship,) the Miami, and three other steamers carrying five or six guns each. No part of either fleet was iron-clad.

Much time was consumed in getting these vessels over the bar at the mouths of the Mississippi. The bombardment commenced on the 18th of April, the mortar boats leading, supported by the gunboats, which made occasional approaches to the forts, drawing their fire. The bombardment continued for six days with no material result apparent, except the breaking of a heavy rifled gun on Fort St. Philip. By a bold movement, begun at two o'clock on the morning of the 24th, a portion of Farragut's fleet, after a gallant fight, succeeded in overcoming all obstructions and passing the forts. With nine of his vessels, Com. Farragut appeared before New Orleans on the 25th. Forts St. Philip and Jackson capitulated on the 28th. Gen. Butler was at hand with his forces— the Rebel Gen. Lovell made a precipitate retreat into the interior of the State, and the city was surrendered, Gen. Butler taking possession on the 1st day of May.

For a time, the cheering and substantial results recited in this chapter were claimed, by many, as triumphs due to a "grand plan" of the young General-in-chief; while others as confidently pointed out their inconsistency with an alleged scheme which involved "thunder around the whole horizon," when once the spell of silence should be broken. Scarcely the faintest echo, in fact, unless at Roanoke Island, where a victory had been gained in February, responded to the reverberations at Mill Spring, Fort Henry, Fort Donelson, Pea Ridge, Shiloh and New Orleans. All mystery on this subject was dispelled by the subsequent disclosure that, as early as January, the President had substantially revoked the broader authority given to a dilatory General-in-chief, who had caused the Army of the Potomac to waste in idleness six months that had been expected to bring forth a decisive campaign, and who had opposed the movements so brilliantly executed in the West, as well as the Southern expeditions, one of which restored New Orleans and the passes of the Mississippi to the Government. In the West and Southwest, we have seen that ample results, even in the worst season of the year, followed this wise policy of Mr. Lincoln. How the President's order for active movements was carried into effect by the commander of the Army of the Potomac, will appear in the pages immediately following.

CHAPTER VII.

Military Events in the East.—The Peninsular Campaign.

THE fortifications around Washington, commenced by Gen. J. G. Barnard, Chief Engineer under McDowell, and continued by the same officer under McClellan, had been essentially completed before the close of September, 1861. In an order issued on the 30th of that month, the commanding General designated the names by which the thirty-two principal works should be respectively known. From this time onward a large portion of the Army of the Potomac was no longer needed on merely defensive duty. In a communication addressed to the Secretary of War in the latter part of October, Gen. McClellan estimated the number of troops required for the protection of Washington at 35,000, with a further force of 23,000, to be distributed on the Upper and Lower Potomac, and at Baltimore and Annapolis. The main purpose of this vast army, raised, equipped and disciplined at such a cost, was manifestly something quite beyond what 58,000 men alone amply sufficed to accomplish. To destroy the Rebel army before Washington, and to occupy Richmond, were, in the minds alike of military men and civilians, the prime objects to be effected by the Army of the Potomac.

October, November, December, passed without result. The commanding General admits his consciousness of the anxiety no less of the people than of the President for active operations during these pleasant months, on the part of an army sustained at a cost of millions daily. Gen. McClellan's official statement gives his entire force on the 1st of December as 198,213, of whom 169,452 were present for duty, and on the first of January, 1862, as 219,707, of whom 191,480 were "effective." After deducting the 58,000 deemed necessary for defensive purposes—and most of these might also have been employed in a direct movement on Manassas—there thus remained an effective army of 111,452 at the former date, and of 133,480 at the latter, for an aggressive movement. Beauregard, who had his headquarters at Centreville, until he was transferred to another command, on the 30th of January, certainly had at no time a force in McClellan's front exceeding one-half the number of the Army of the Potomac.

Gen. McClellan records no surprising fact, therefore, when he states that "about the middle of January, 1862, upon recovering from a severe illness," he "found that excessive anxiety for an immediate movement of the Army of the Potomac had taken possession of the minds of the Administration."

More than six months having elapsed since the command of this army had devolved upon Gen. McClellan, without the development of either a particular plan or a general purpose of attacking the enemy, under circumstances the most favorable, and an unexpected quiescence having followed his appointment as General-in-chief, the President at length issued his "General War Order, No. 1," as follows:

EXECUTIVE MANSION, WASHINGTON, }
January 27, 1862. }

President's General War Order, No. 1.]

ORDERED, That the 22d day of February, 1862, be the day for a general movement of the land and naval forces of the United States against the insurgent forces.

That especially the Army at and about Fortress Monroe, the Army of the Potomac, the Army of Western Virginia, the Army near Mumfordsville, Kentucky, the Army and Flotilla at Cairo, and a Naval force in the Gulf of Mexico, be ready for a movement on that day.

That all other forces, both land and naval, with their respective commanders, obey existing orders for the time, and be ready to obey additional orders when duly given.

That the Heads of Departments, and especially the Secretaries of War and of the Navy, with all their subordinates, and the General-in-chief, with all other commanders and subordinates of land and naval forces, will severally be held to their strict and full responsibilities for the prompt execution of this order.

ABRAHAM LINCOLN.

This mandate, communicated to high officers immediately

concerned, was not made public until the 11th of March following. In it, the President fully resumed his constitutional position as Commander-in-chief of the Army and Navy, practically dispensing with the services of Gen. McClellan as a "Lieutenant," in the discharge of those high duties, as was more formally announced at a later day, on the publication of this general order.

After thus directing Gen. McClellan's efforts more particularly to the management of the Army of the Potomac, the President soon found it expedient to concentrate that officer's thoughts upon some definite plan—which had evidently been not very clearly before his mind hitherto—for rendering this great force of practical service to the Government. Consequently, four days later, the following order was communicated to McClellan:

EXECUTIVE MANSION, WASHINGTON, ⎱
January 31, 1862. ⎰

ORDERED, That all the disposable force of the Army of the Potomac, after providing safely for the defense of Washington, be formed into an expedition for the immediate object of seizing and occupying a point upon the railroad south-westward of what is known as Manassas Junction; all details to be in the discretion of the Commander-in-chief, and the expedition to move before, or on, the twenty-second day of February next.

ABRAHAM LINCOLN.

Immediately after receiving this order, Gen. McClellan prepared a long letter to Mr. Stanton, (dated January 31, 1862,) in which he set forth his objections to this movement, and vehemently urged the substitution of a plan of advance upon Richmond by the Lower Rappahannock, with Urbana as a base. He insists that a movement by Manassas must be delayed on account of the bad condition of the roads, and that this difficulty would be removed by taking the route he proposes, over a more sandy soil, and in a latitude in which the season is two or three weeks earlier. "This movement, if adopted," he says, "will not at all expose the city of Washington to danger. The total force to be thrown upon the new line would be (according to circumstances) from 110,000 to

22

140,000. I hope to use the latter number by bringing fresh troops into Washington, and still leaving it quite safe." The maximum number here stated would still leave more than 60,000 for the defense of Washington, without additional "fresh troops." Gen. McClellan closes this letter with the following earnest appeal:

In conclusion, I would respectfully but firmly advise that I may be authorized to undertake at once the movement by Urbana. I believe that it can be carried into execution so nearly simultaneously with the final advance of Buell and Halleck, that the columns will support each other. I will stake my life, my reputation, on the result,—more than that, I will stake upon it the success of our cause. I hope but little from the attack on Manassas. My judgment is against it. Foreign complications may entirely change the state of affairs, and render very different plans necessary. In that event, I will be ready to submit to them.

On the 3d of February, President Lincoln addressed to Gen. McClellan the following memorable letter, having reference to the Urbana plan, scarcely more than alluded to by McClellan in his final report, and seemingly as unceremoniously abandoned, after serving a purpose, as it had been zealously improvised:

EXECUTIVE MANSION, WASHINGTON, }
February 3, 1862. }

MY DEAR SIR: You and I have distinct and different plans for a movement of the Army of the Potomac; yours to be done by the Chesapeake, up the Rappahannock to Urbana, and across land to the terminus of the railroad on the York river; mine to move directly to a point on the railroad southwest of Manassas.

If you will give satisfactory answers to the following questions, I shall gladly yield my plan to yours:

1st. Does not your plan involve a greatly larger expenditure of *time* and *money* than mine?

2d. Wherein is a victory *more certain* by your plan than mine?

3d. Wherein is a victory *more valuable* by your plan than mine?

4th. In fact, would it not be *less* valuable in this; that it would break no great line of the enemy's communications, while mine would?

5th. In case of disaster, would not a retreat be more diffi
cult by your plan than mine?

Yours, truly,   A. LINCOLN.

MAJ.-GEN. MCCLELLAN.

These plain test questions were never directly met. In a
ong letter of the same date, however, addressed to the Secretary of War, arguing the merits of the two plans, Gen. McClellan avers that he "substantially answered" the President's
inquiries. The subject remained for some time under consideration, the President's order not withdrawn, but its execution suspended, while McClellan at length proceeded to the
work of opening the Baltimore and Ohio Railroad, under
urgent pressure from his superiors.

On the 26th of February, he announced, from Sandy Hook,
that Loudon and Bolivar Heights, and also Maryland
Heights, had been occupied by our troops, and that G. W.
Smith was expected at Winchester with 15,000 Rebels. After
incurring much cost and delay in the construction of canal
boats to be used in crossing the Upper Potomac, he now
found, on proceeding to use them, a considerable force intended
for Winchester being already under orders, that, as he expressed it in a dispatch to the Secretary of War, Feb. 27th,
"the lift-lock" was "too small" to permit the boats to pass
up to their destination. Mr. Stanton sent this laconic reply,
under the same date: "Gen. McClellan—If the lift-lock is
not big enough, why can not it be made big enough? Please
answer immediately." The response was, that, to do this, the
entire masonry must be destroyed and rebuilt. Consequently,
the boats, long patiently waited for, were summarily dispensed
with, and the marching orders countermanded. At the same
time, for reasons satisfactory to himself, McClellan revoked an
order he had given to Hooker, for a movement toward silencing
the Rebel batteries on the Potomac, which had also been earnestly pressed by the Administration. His plan at Harper's
Ferry, as stated Feb. 28, was chiefly "to occupy Charlestown
and Bunker Hill, so as to cover the rebuilding of the railway,"
making the following objections to the desired advance upon

Winchester and thorough occupation of the Shenandoah Valley: " We could not supply and move to Winchester for many days, and had I moved more troops here, they would have been at a loss for food on the Virginia side." McClellan soon after returned to Washington, and began the movement on Manas. gas, as required by the President's order of January 31st — a full month having now intervened.

Events in the Valley, for some time to come, may here be briefly summed up. Charlestown was occupied in force by Gen. Banks on the 28th of February, and Martinsburg on the 3d of March. Col. Geary occupied Leesburg on the 2d. Stonewall Jackson evacuated Winchester on the 11th, and was pursued by Gen. Shields (who had succeeded the lamented Gen. Lander,) until overtaken near New Market on the 19th, within supporting distance of the Rebel force under Joe Johnston, (who had taken full command, in that quarter, when Beauregard left for the West, the last of January.) Shields retreated rapidly to Winchester, on the 20th. On the 22d, by order of Gen. McClellan, the forces of Gen. Banks, now constituting the Fifth Corps of the Army of the Potomac, were nearly all, with the exception of Shields' division, withdrawn to the vicinity of Manassas. On the same evening, the Rebels, under Jackson and Longstreet, supposed to be 10,000 strong, attacked the place, and were gallantly repulsed by Shields, whose division numbered less than 8,000. After this battle, Gen. Banks, having returned to the Valley, followed up the retreating enemy, successively occupying Strasburg, Woodstock, and (on the 26th of March) Harrisonburg. The Rebel forces now retired from that region, and the Valley was comparatively quiet for nearly two months following.

On the 28th of February, McClellan returned to Washington. The results at Harper's Ferry, as well as the delay in raising the blockade of the Lower Potomac, had been far from satisfactory to the President. The day fixed for a general movement had passed, and the plan of advancing on Richmond by the Chesapeake, if acquiesced in, was manifestly impracticable, unless by the roundabout way of Annapolis, until the Potomac had first been cleared of the Rebel batteries. Meanwhile, as early as the 15th of February, measures had been taken by the Secretary of War to secure with promptness the necessary transportation by water for the forces to be moved. This fact indicates the determination of the Administration to acquiesce in a plan on which the Commanding General was ready to stake so much, rather than to insist on a movement much preferred, yet which could hardly be expected to succeed under the reluctant generalship of one who felt no confidence in its success, and who would show no alacrity in its execution.

With all that had been accomplished in the way of organization, discipline, and general preparation, the Army of the Potomac had still remained without distribution into Army Corps. The President, sustained by the best military authorities and advisers, if not by the universal practice in modern warfare, had desired such organization to be made. This Gen. McClellan had failed to attend to, and it was not until he was on the eve of a movement toward Manassas, with a manifest purpose not to perfect his organization, that President Lincoln issued the following peremptory order:

EXECUTIVE MANSION, WASHINGTON, ⎱
March 8, 1862. ⎰

President's General War Order, No. 2.]

ORDERED, I. That the Major-General commanding the Army of the Potomac proceed forthwith to organize that part of said army destined to enter upon active operations, (including the reserve, but excluding the troops to be left in the fortifications about Washington,) into four army corps, to be commanded according to seniority of rank, as follows:

First Corps, to consist of four divisions, and to be commanded by Maj.-Gen. I. McDowell.

Second Corps, to consist of three divisions, and to be commanded by Brig.-Gen. E. V. Sumner.

Third Corps, to consist of three divisions, and to be commanded by Brig.-Gen. S. P. Heintzelman.

Fourth Corps, to consist of three divisions, and to be commanded by Brig.-Gen. E. D. Keyes.

II. That the divisions now commanded by the officers above assigned to the command of Corps, shall be embraced in and form part of their respective Corps.

III. The forces left for the defense of Washington will be placed in command of Brig.-Gen. James S. Wadsworth, who shall also be Military Governor of the District of Columbia.

IV. That this order be executed with such promptness and dispatch, as not to delay the commencement of the operations already directed to be undertaken by the Army of the Potomac.

V. That the Fifth Army Corps, to be commaded by Maj.-Gen. N. P. Banks, will be formed from his own and Gen. Shields', late Gen. Lander's, division.

ABRAHAM LINCOLN.

To the execution of this order, the Commanding General interposed such obstacles as were in his power, without positive refusal. On the 9th of March, having taken the field, he telegraphed to Secretary Stanton from Hall's Hill, the headquarters of Fitz John Porter, that " in the arrangements for to-morrow it is impossible to carry " the order " into effect," and asks its suspension. The Secretary promptly replied : " I think it is the duty of every officer to obey the President's orders, nor can I see any reason why you should not obey them in the present instance. I must, therefore, decline to suspend them." McClellan, still at Hall's Hill, telegraphs, on the 10th, that he " must suspend movement, or disregard order," alleging "military necessity," and adds : " If you desire it, I will at once countermand " marching orders. To avoid this alternative, consent was granted for a temporary delay, until the impending movement should have been executed. The same day, McClellan informed the Department that the troops were in motion. Centreville was occupied that evening without opposition, and Manassas on the 11th, the only obstacle to movement being that the " roads are horrible."

Before this movement actually commenced, the President, who had reluctantly yielded his preference for such an advance on Richmond as would at the same time cover the National Capital, and who had not been indifferent to the neglect of his wishes in regard to the opening of the Potomac, or to the delays which experience had led him to dread, issued the subjoined general order :

EXECUTIVE MANSION, WASHINGTON, }
March 8, 1862. }

ORDERED, That no change of the base of operations of the Army of the Potomac shall be made without leaving in and about Washington such a force as, in the opinion of the General-in-chief and the commanders of army corps, shall leave said city entirely secure.

That no more than two army corps (about fifty thousand troops) of said Army of the Potomac shall be moved *en route* for a new base of operations until the navigation of the Potomac, from Washington to the Chesapeake Bay, shall be freed from the enemy's batteries, and other obstructions, or until the President shall hereafter give express permission.

That any movement as aforesaid, *en route* for a new base of operations, which may be ordered by the General-in-chief, and which may be intended to move upon Chesapeake Bay, shall begin to move upon the bay as early as the 18th of March, instant, and the General-in-chief shall be responsible that it moves as early as that day.

ORDERED, That the Army and Navy coöperate in an immediate effort to capture the enemy's batteries upon the Potomac between Washington and the Chesapeake Bay.

ABRAHAM LINCOLN.

L. THOMAS, Adjutant-General.

On the 9th of March, the steamer Merrimac, which had been taken possession of by the insurgents at Norfolk, after the abandonment of that post in the spring of 1861, and converted into a formidable iron-clad vessel, re-named the Virginia, attacked and destroyed the Government sailing frigates Cumberland and Congress. The Minnesota, in coming to their assistance, ran aground. For awhile, all the shipping in the harbor seemed at the mercy of the Rebel monster. But the timely arrival of Ericsson's Monitor, just completed, and hitherto regarded as a doubtful experiment, ended the work of destruction, and caused the Merrimac to retire within shelter at Norfolk. These hurried and startling events caused great sensation at the time, both in this country and abroad, and have had a marked influence in regard to naval armaments every-where.

McClellan having now taken the field, so that a supervision of all the armies of the nation was clearly out of his power, the President made public a change that was no secret to the General commanding the Army of the Potomac, through the following order—in which, also, two separate departments were created in the West, to be commanded by Gens. Halleck and Buell, and a third intermediate department, under the command of Gen. Fremont:

EXECUTIVE MANSION, WASHINGTON, }
March 11, 1862. }

President's War Order, No. 3.]

Maj.-Gen. McClellan having personally taken the field at the head of the Army of the Potomac until otherwise ordered, he is relieved from the command of the other military departments, he retaining command of the Department of the Potomac.

ORDERED, FURTHER, That the two departments now under the respective commands of Gens. Halleck and Hunter, together with so much of that under Gen. Buell as lies west of a north and south line indefinitely drawn through Knoxville, Tennessee, be consolidated and designated the Department of the Mississippi, and that until otherwise ordered Maj.-Gen. Halleck have command of said department.

ORDERED, ALSO, That the country west of the Department of the Potomac and east of the Department of the Mississippi be a military department, to be called the Mountain Department, and that the same be commanded by Maj.-Gen. Fremont.

That all the Commanders of Departments, after the receipt of this order by them respectively, report severally and directly to the Secretary of War, and that prompt, full and frequent reports will be expected of all and each of them.

ABRAHAM LINCOLN.

Gen. McClellan telegraphed to the Secretary of War from Fairfax Court House, on the 13th of March, that a council of the commanders of army corps had " unanimously agreed upon a plan of operations," which Gen. McDowell would lay before him. To this the Secretary, on the same day, replied: "Whatever plan has been agreed upon, proceed at once to execute, without losing an hour for any approval."

The plan—which, in answer to a question of Mr. Stanton, Gen. McClellan stated that " the council, together with himself," were unanimous in forming—was given in these words:

HEADQUARTERS ARMY OF THE POTOMAC,
FAIRFAX COURT HOUSE, March 13, 1862.

A council of the Generals commanding army corps, at the headquarters of the Army of the Potomac, were of the opinion—

I. That the enemy having retreated from Manassas to Gordonsville, behind the Rappahannock and Rapidan, it is the opinion of the Generals commanding army corps that the operations to be carried on will be best undertaken from Old Point Comfort, between the York and James rivers : *Provided*,

1st. That the enemy's vessel, Merrimac, can be neutralized.

2d. That the means of transportation, sufficient for an immediate transfer of the force to its new base, can be ready at at Washington and Alexandria to move down the Potomac ; and,

3d. That a naval auxiliary force can be had to silence, or aid in silencing, the enemy's batteries on the York river.

4th. That the force to be left to cover Washington shall be such as to give an entire feeling of security for its safety from menace. (Unanimous.)

II. If the foregoing can not be, the army should then be moved against the enemy, behind the Rappahannock, at the earliest possible moment, and the means for reconstructing bridges, repairing railroads, and stocking them with materials sufficient for supplying the army, should at once be collected, for both the Orange and Alexandria and Acquia and Richmond Railroads. (Unanimous.)

NOTE.—That with the forts on the right bank of the Potomac fully garrisoned; and those on the left bank occupied, a covering force in front of the Virginia line of twenty-five thousand men would suffice. (Keyes, Heintzelman and McDowell.) A total of forty thousand men for the defense of the city would suffice. (Sumner.)

The scheme having been promptly submitted to the President, the following dispatch was immediately returned :

WAR DEPARTMENT, March 13, 1862.

The President having considered the plan of operations agreed upon by yourself and the commanders of army corps, makes no objection to the same, but gives the following directions as to its execution :

1. Leave such force at Manassas Junction as shall make it entirely certain that the enemy shall not repossess himself of that position and line of communication.

2. Leave Washington entirely secure.

3. Move the remainder of the force down the Potomac, choosing a new base at Fortress Monroe, or any-where between

here and there, or, at all eveuts, move such remainder of the army at once in pursuit of the enemy by some route.

EDWIN M. STANTON,
Secretary of War.

Maj.-Gen. GEORGE B. McCLELLAN.

McClellan replied that this would " be at once carried into effect."

Transportation was rapidly provided, under the direction of the War Department, this work having really commenced as early as the middle of February, and the other preparations for departure, on the part of the force intended for the Peninsula, were soon in readiness. The following statement of the numerical strength of this portion of the Army, on the 1st of April, is taken from the official report of the Adjutant General :

First Corps, under General I. McDowell, - -	38,454
Second " " " E. V. Sumner, -	31,037
Third, " " " S. P. Heintzelman,	38,854
Fourth, " " " E. D. Keyes, - -	37,910
Regular Infantry, - - - - - - - - - -	4,765
Regular Cavalry, - - - - - - - - - -	3,141
Artillery Reserve, - - - - - - - - - -	3,116
Provost Guards, U. S. Engineer forces, and Headquarters Cavalry escort, - - - - - - -	1,144
Total, - - - - - - - - - - - -	158,419

From the same authority, it appears that the total force left (according to the intention of Gen. McClellan) under command of Brig.-Gen. James S. Wadsworth, now appointed Military Governor of the District of Washington, was 22,410, of whom less than 20,000 were present for duty. How far this number fell short of all McClellan's previous estimates of the necessary force for the defense of the city, need not be suggested to the reader of the preceding pages. Gen. Wadsworth promptly called the attention of the War Department to this striking deficiency. The plan of the Peninsular movement as submitted for Executive approval, the special order of the President consenting to this plan, on condition that the capital should be rendered secure, and the letter of Gen. Wadsworth on this subject, were referred to Adj.-Gen. Thomas and Maj.-Gen. E. A. Hitchcock, who were required to report whether the President's order, in this matter, had been carried out. Those officers, after full consideration, reported that the force proposed to be left, in execution of that order, was "entirely inadequate." They further said:

In view of the opinion expressed by the council of the commanders of army corps of the force necessary for the capital, though not numerically stated, and of the force represented by Gen. McClellan as left for that purpose, we are of opinion that the requirement of the President that this city shall be left entirely secure, not only in the opinion of the General-in-chief, but that of the commanders of all the army corps, also, has not been fully complied with.

Meanwhile, the movement of troops from Alexandria to Fortress Monroe had commenced. Gen. Hamilton's division, of the Third Corps, embarked on the 17th of March, and was followed by Fitz John Porter's division, of the same corps, on the 22d. Other troops followed at intervals, as transports were ready. Gen. McClellan himself left Alexandria on the 1st of April, and reached Fortress Monroe the next day.

There still remained two army corps which had not yet been transferred to the Peninsula, when the report of Gens. Thomas and Hitchcock was made. The only remedy for McClellan's intended disregard alike of the conditions of his own plan and of the President's requirement, respecting the force to be left at Washington and in its vicinity, was such as the President applied in the first part of the following order, the wisdom of which was soon fully demonstrated:

EXECUTIVE MANSION, WASHINGTON, }
April 3, 1862. }

The Secretary of War will order that one or the other of the corps of Gen. McDowell and Gen. Sumner remain in front of Washington until further orders from the Department, to operate at, or in the direction of, Manassas Junction, or otherwise as the occasion may require; that the other corps, not so ordered to remain, go forward to Gen. McClellan as speedily as possible; that Gen. McClellan commence his forward move-

ments from his new base at once, and that such incidents
modifications as the foregoing may render proper, be also made
ABRAHAM LINCOLN.

On the same day, Gen. McClellan had telegraphed from Fort
ress Monroe: "I expect to move from here to-morrow morning
on Yorktown, where a force of some 15,000 of the Rebels are
in intrenched position, and I think it quite possible they will
attempt to resist us." On the 4th, he said: "Our advance is
at Cockestown, within five miles of Yorktown. . . . I expect to
fight to-morrow, as I shall endeavor to cut the communication
between Yorktown and Richmond." At the same time Gen.
Wool, telegraphing the departure of these forces for Yorktown, expressed a decided opinion that no serious resistance
would be encountered there. It is probable, from the information since obtained, that when the movement commenced, the
Rebel force under Magruder was less than 10,000. It is certain that the intrenchments were by no means so formidable as
to justify the loss of time requisite for a siege, not only wasting precious days, but wearing out as many lives in the
trenches as would have been sacrificed in carrying the works
by assault. Such, at least, appears to have been the opinion
of the President, who did not imagine for a moment, when his
order above quoted was given, that a purpose to sit down before
Yorktown, until the enemy had time to concentrate a strong
force there, was entertained by the Commanding General.

Carrying out the policy of his order of April 3d, the President, as indicated by an order issued from the War Department
on the following day, created two new military departments,
including the spheres of operation and the troops left behind
by McClellan on his withdrawal to the Peninsula. The
Department of the Shenandoah embraced that portion of Virginia and Maryland lying between the Mountain Department
and the Blue Ridge, and was put under the command of Maj.-
Gen. Banks. The Department of the Rappahannock com-.
prised that portion of Virginia east of the Blue Ridge to the
Potomac and the Fredericksburg and Richmond Railroad,
together with the District of Columbia and the country between
the Potomac and the Patuxent. Gen. McDowell was desig-

nated to command this department. The movements of the enemy in the valley, and the exposed condition in which McClellan had been on the point of leaving the National Capital, in disregard of instructions and of the express conditions on which the movement to the Peninsula was permitted, showed the expediency of having a responsible commander in both these localities. The remoteness of Gen. McClellan, and his occupation with other engrossing duties, seemed further to require this change.

If the President had not expected any serious loss of time at Yorktown, it is equally evident, from official dispatches, that such a thought had found no place in the mind of McClellan until about the same date as his official notification of the action of the Administration, just referred to. His dispatch, urging a reconsideration of this action, was prefaced by representations of the numbers and preparations of the enemy, not very closely agreeing with those previously given, yet at least such as to afford cogent reasons for an unhesitating advance. This significant paper is subjoined:

[Received 8.30 A. M., April 6.]

NEAR YORKTOWN, 7½ P. M., April 5.

A. LINCOLN, President: The enemy are in large force along our front, and apparently intend making a determined resistance. A reconnoissance just made by Gen. Barnard shows that their line of works extend across the entire Peninsula from Yorktown to Warwick river. Many of them are very formidable. Deserters say they are being reënforced daily from Richmond and from Norfolk. Under these circumstances, I beg that you will reconsider the order detaching the First Corps from my command. In my deliberate judgment the success of our cause will be imperiled by so greatly reducing my force when it is actually under the fire of the enemy, and active operations have commenced. Two or three of my divisions have been under fire of artillery most of the day. I am now of the opinion that I shall have to fight all the available force of the Rebels not far from here. Do not force me to do so with diminished numbers, but whatever your decision may be I will leave nothing undone to obtain success. If you can not leave me the whole of the First Corps, I urgently ask that I may not lose Franklin and his division.

G. B. McCLELLAN, Major-General.

To this dispatch the following reply was promptly sent:

WAR DEPARTMENT, WASHINGTON CITY, ⎱
April 6, 1862. ⎰

Maj.-Gen. GEO. B. McCLELLAN: The President directs me to say that your dispatch to him has been received. Sumner's corps is on the road to you, and will go forward as fast as possible. Franklin's division is now on the advance toward Manassas. There are no means of transportation here to send it forward in time to be of service in your present operations. Telegraph frequently, and all in the power of the Government shall be done to sustain you as occasion may require.

EDWIN M. STANTON,
Secretary of War.

Magruder, who commanded the Rebel force near Yorktown, fully appreciated the element of time in this campaign, and undoubtedly maneuvered with some skill to put his adversary on a cautious policy. In general orders to be read to his troops, on the 4th of April, he said: "The enemy is before us—our works are strong—our cause is good—we fight for our homes, and must be careful. Every hour we hold out, brings us reënforcements." Instead of availing himself of his overwhelming superiority of numbers, by a resolute attack, McClellan paused to discuss still further the conduct of the Administration as to matters far away from the immediate sphere of his labors, and to beg for reënforcements. On the 6th, he sent the following dispatch, (received in Washington at 3 o'clock P. M.):

HEADQUARTERS ARMY OF THE POTOMAC.

A. LINCOLN, President: The order forming new Departments, if rigidly enforced, deprives me of the power of ordering up wagons and troops absolutely necessary to enable me to advance to Richmond. I have by no means the transportation I must have to move my army even a few miles. I respectfully request that I may not be placed in this position, but that my orders for wagon trains, ammunition, and other material that I have prepared and necessarily left behind, as well as Woodbury's brigade, may at once be complied with. The enemy is strong in my front, and I have a most serious task before me, in the fulfillment of which I need all the aid the

Government can give me. I again repeat the urgent request that Gen. Franklin and his division may be restored to my command.

G. B. McCLELLAN, Major-General.

To this the President replied:

WASHINGTON, April 6, 1862.

Maj.-Gen. McCLELLAN, Fortress Monroe: Yours of 11 A. M. to-day received. The Secretary of War informs me that the forwarding of transportation, ammunition, and Woodbury's brigade, under your orders, is not, and will not be, interfered with. You now have over one hundred thousand troops with you, independent of Gen. Wool's command. I think you had better break the enemy's line from Yorktown to Warwick river at once. They will probably use time as advantageously as you can.

A. LINCOLN.

In disregarding this pointed advice — from one who was entitled to command — a grave, though still not irretrievable, error of the campaign, was committed at the outset. Gen. Burnside had done at Newbern, on the 14th of the previous month, what was incomparably more difficult, in carrying the works of the enemy, when manned by numbers fully equal to his own. His forces, too, were largely made up of raw recruits. The Army of the Potomac, after eight months spent in its formation and discipline, was deemed by its commander inadequate to force its way through the line of fortifications at Yorktown, though so many times more numerous than the enemy. Magruder gained the opportunity which he craved. Davis ordered Johnston and Beauregard to advance from Corinth, on the 3d of April, to crush the army of Grant at Pittsburg Landing— little dreaming then, as may well be supposed, that nearly three months would elapse before their presence would be indispensable at Richmond. The slow processes of a regular siege began in front of the little army of Magruder. Thousands sickened and died in the trenches. The nation grew weary of the same disheartening news, day by day, and week after week. Finally, the siege batteries were prepared to begin; and the enemy, though now strengthened by all the aid that thirty days could bring, was found to have deserted his works the moment an earnest attack was believed to be imminent.

To the President's dispatch of April 6, Gen. McClellan had little else to reply than by extravagant representations of the enemy's strength, with a corresponding disparagement of his own, followed by complaining entreaties for reënforcements that could not be furnished. In this response, he also said: " Under the circumstances that have been developed since we arrived here, I feel fully impressed with the conviction that here is to be fought the great battle that is to decide the existing contest."

So persistent was McClellan in these complaints and demands, that Mr. Lincoln felt constrained to address to him the following frank and kindly letter, plainly rehearsing the facts and reasons of the case, and again pointedly indicating the grand necessity of the hour:

WASHINGTON, April 9, 1862.

MY DEAR SIR: Your dispatches, complaining that you are not properly sustained, while they do not offend me, do pain me very much.

Blenker's division was withdrawn from you before you left here, and you know the pressure under which I did it, and, as I thought, acquiesced in it — certainly not without reluctance.

After you left, I ascertained that less than twenty thousand unorganized men, without a single field battery, were all you designed to be left for the defense of Washington and Manassas Junction, and part of this even was to go to Gen. Hooker's old position. General Banks' corps, once designed for Manassas Junction, was diverted and tied up on the line of Winchester and Strasburgh, and could not leave it without again exposing the Upper Potomac and the Baltimore and Ohio Railroad. This presented, or would present, when McDowell and Sumner should be gone, a great temptation to the enemy to turn back from the Rappahannock and sack Washington. My implicit order that Washington should, by the judgment of all the commanders of army corps, be left entirely secure, had been neglected. It was precisely this that drove me to detain McDowell.

I do not forget that I was satisfied with your arrangement to leave Banks at Manassas Junction: but when that arrangement was broken up, and nothing was substituted for it, of course I was constrained to substitute something for it myself. And allow me to ask, do you really think I should permit the line from Richmond, *via* Manassas Junction, to this city, to be entirely open, except what resistance could be presented by less than twenty thousand unorganized troops? This is a question which the country will not allow me to evade.

There is a curious mystery about the number of troops now with you. When I telegraphed you on the 6th, saying you had over a hundred thousand with you, I had just obtained from the Secretary of War a statement taken, as he said, from your own returns, making one hundred and eight thousand then with you and *en route* to you. You now say you will have but eighty-five thousand when all *en route* to you shall have reached you. How can the discrepancy of twenty-three thousand be accounted for?

As to General Wool's command, I understand it is doing for you precisely what a like number of your own would have to do if that command was away.

I suppose the whole force which has gone forward for you is with you by this time. And if so, I think it is the precise time for you to strike a blow. By delay, the enemy will relatively gain upon you—that is, he will gain faster by fortifications and reënforcements than you can by reënforcements alone. And once more let me tell you, it is indispensable to you that you strike a blow. I am powerless to help this. You will do me the justice to remember I always insisted that going down the bay in search of a field, instead of fighting at or near Manassas, was only shifting, and not surmounting, a difficulty; that we would find the same enemy, and the same or equal intrenchments, at either place. The country will not fail to note, is now noting, that the present hesitation to move upon an intrenched enemy is but the story of Manassas repeated.

I beg to assure you that I have never written you or spoken to you in greater kindness of feeling than now, nor with a fuller purpose to sustain you, so far as, in my most anxious judgment, I consistently can. But you must act.

Yours, very truly,   A. LINCOLN.
Maj.-Gen. McClellan.

Gen. McClellan, in the early part of that report, in which he has given his own rhetorical coloring to his operations, as a military commander, quotes, without contradiction or objection. the following statement of Mr. Tucker, Assistant Secretary of War, showing that he had landed at Fortress Monroe, by the 6th day of April, (having received the final order as early as

23   30

the 28th of February), 121,500 men for McClellan, with a number of wagons and animals manifestly well proportioned to these numbers:

In thirty-seven days from the time I received the order in Washington (and most of it was accomplished in thirty days), these vessels transported from Perryville, Alexandria, and Washington to Fort Monroe (the place of departure having been changed, which caused delay) one hundred and twenty-one thousand five hundred men, fourteen thousand five hundred and ninety-two animals, one thousand one hundred and fifty wagons, forty-four batteries, seventy-four ambulances, besides pontoon bridges, telegraph materials, and the enormous quantity of equipage, etc., required for an army of such magnitude.

And yet McClellan telegraphed to the President on the 7th of April: "My entire force for duty only amounts to 85,000." Six days later, before receiving reënforcements, McClellan himself reported his force (as officially certified by Adj.-Gen. Thomas,) to be 117,721, of whom 100,970 were present for duty. In addition to this was the considerable force of Gen. Wool, on which he was authorized to draw at will. McDowell's command, also, so far as practicable, was put in a position for at once sustaining him and covering Washington.

To Gen. McClellan's earnest appeal for Gen. Franklin's division, on the 10th of April, Secretary Stanton replied on the following day, granting this request. At the same date, McClellan telegraphed: "Nothing is left undone to enable us to attack with the least possible delay. * * There shall not be a moment's unnecessary delay in any of the operations here." On the 12th, he sends thanks for the promised reënforcements, and adds: "I am confident as to results now." On the 13th, he says: "Our work is progressing rapidly. We shall soon be at them, and I am sure of the result." On the 14th: "We are getting up the heavy guns, mortars and ammunition quite rapidly." To the President he telegraphed at the same date: "I have seen Gen. Franklin, and beg to thank you for your kindness and consideration. I now understand the matter, which I did not before."

From day to day, his dispatches continued to hold out the expectation of almost immediate results, yet nothing of consequence occurred for many days, save an unfortunate skirmish at Lee's Mill, on the 16th, in which 35 were killed and 130 wounded, without any advantage gained. McClellan inquiring in regard to the position of McDowell, the President sent the following reply on the 21st: "Your dispatch of the 19th was received that day. Fredericksburg is evacuated and the bridge destroyed by the enemy, and a small part of McDowell's command occupies this side of the Rappahannock opposite the town. He purposes moving his whole force to that point." On the 23d, McClellan reported: "Recent rains have injured the roads and delayed us, but we are making progress all the time." On the 26th, a lunette (of the enemy's works) was carried, and on the 27th, the "first parallel essentially finished without accident," but the roads were "becoming horrid again."

The total number of McClellan's force, on the 30th of April, as officially given by Asst. Adj.-Gen. Townsend, was 130,378, of whom 112,392 are reported as "effective." This includes the division under Gen. Franklin, which had arrived several days before, but still remained on the transports.

Nearly a month had now passed, in the manner indicated by the dispatches above quoted—fair samples of all—when there came a request for additional guns, which drew from the President the following response:

EXECUTIVE MANSION, WASHINGTON, ⎫
May 1, 1862. ⎭

Maj.-Gen. McCLELLAN: Your call for Parrott guns from Washington alarms me—chiefly because it argues indefinite procrastination. Is any thing to be done?

A. LINCOLN.

Two days later, on the night of May 3d, the enemy evacuated his works.

The siege of Yorktown, without a close investment, which was not attempted, if ever contemplated, could have no other than barren results, unless the retreating enemy were promptly pursued. For this, his movement was not soon enough discovered. Here was, indeed, as the President had dreaded, "the story of Manassas repeated"—if that opinion may be hazarded in the face of Gen. McClellan's positive claim of a "brilliant success." His first announcement of the evacuation was in the following dispatch :

HEADQUARTERS ARMY OF THE POTOMAC, }
             May 4, 9 A. M. }

To the Hon. EDWIN M. STANTON, Secretary of War : We have the ramparts. Have guns, ammunition, camp equipage, etc. We hold the entire line of his works, which the engineers report as being very strong. I have thrown all my cavalry and horse-artillery in pursuit, supported by infantry. I move Franklin's division, and as much more as I can transport by water, up to West Point to-day. No time shall be lost. The gunboats have gone up York river. I omitted to state that Gloucester is also in our possession. I shall push the enemy to the wall.

                     G. B. McCLELLAN,
                           Major General.

At 1 o'clock, on the same day, McClellan telegraphed as follows :

Our cavalry and horse-artillery came up with the enemy's rear guard in their intrenchments about two miles this side of Williamsburg. A brisk fight ensued. Just as my aid left, Gen. Smith's division of infantry arrived on the ground, and I presume he carried his works, though I have not yet heard.

The enemy's rear is strong, but I have force enough up there to answer all purposes.

We have thus far seventy-one heavy guns, large amounts of tents, ammunition, etc. All along the lines their works prove to have been most formidable, and I am now fully satisfied of the correctness of the course I have pursued.

The success is brilliant, and you may rest assured its effects will be of the greatest importance. There shall be no delay in following up the enemy. The rebels have been guilty of the most murderous and barbarous conduct in placing torpedoes within the abandoned works, near Mill Springs, near the flag-staffs, magazines, telegraph-offices, in carpet-bags, barrels of flour, etc.

Fortunately we have not lost many men in this manner. Some four or five have been killed and a dozen wounded. I shall make the prisoners remove them at their own peril.

His dispatches of the next day are less joyous in their tone. It is "raining hard," and he pronounces the "roads infamous" and "horrible." An important engagement was fought this day, of which he had apparently gained imperfect knowledge when sending the following dispatch, late in the evening:

> BIVOUAC IN FRONT OF WILLIAMSBURG, }
> May 5, 1862, 10 o'clock P. M. }

Hon. E. M. STANTON, Secretary of War: After arranging for movements up York river, I was urgently sent for here. I find Gen. Joe Johnston in front of me in strong force, probably greater a good deal than my own.

Gen. Hancock has taken two redoubts and repulsed Early's Rebel brigade, by a real charge with the bayonet, taking one Colonel and a hundred and fifty other prisoners, and killing at least two Colonels and many privates. His conduct was brilliant in the extreme.

I do not know our exact loss, but fear that Gen. Hooker has lost considerably on our left.

I learn from the prisoners taken that the Rebels intend to dispute every step to Richmond.

I shall run the risk of at least holding them in check here, while I resume the original plan.

My entire force is undoubtedly inferior to that of the Rebels, who will fight well; but I will do all I can with the force at my disposal.　　　　　　　　G. B. McCLELLAN,
　　　　　　　　　　　　　　　　Major-General Commanding.

Gen. Stoneman had promptly moved his cavalry and horse-artillery, on receiving the order for pursuit, on the morning of the 4th. He first found the enemy within his works, two miles east of Williamsburg, and being unsustained by infantry, was forced to retreat, with some loss, on being attacked by the guns of Fort Magruder. During the afternoon and night, the divisions of Gens. Smith and Hooker arrived on the ground—twelve or fourteen miles distant from Yorktown—as well as the corps commanders, Sumner, Heintzelman and Keyes. No portion of General Sumner's force was yet present, but, as the senior officer, he assumed command, and ordered an attack on the Rebel works, in the evening, by Smith's division. Night, however, came on before the order could be executed. During the night, Sumner posted Hancock's brigade, of that division, in a strong position on the left. Hooker's division, by order of Gen. Heintzelman, had taken position on the Lee's Mill road, coming near Fort Magruder quite early in the morning. At half past 7 o'clock, Hooker began an attack on the works in his front. The enemy gathered in superior force at this point, and the contest continued for hours, Gen. Heintzelman anxiously awaiting the appearance of Kearney's division, which he had sent for in the morning. A heavy rain had commenced the night before, which continued until the following morning, impeding the movement of troops, but not interrupting the determined purpose to carry the enemy's works. Hooker had suffered serious loss, his ammunition was giving out, and his troops were becoming exhausted, when at length, after 3 o'clock, Gen Kearney arrived with his men, and was ordered by Heintzelman at once to attack, which he did so vigorously as to drive the enemy back at all points, and to relieve Hooker, whose left flank was in imminent danger.

On the right, also, the enemy massed troops against Hancock, who kept up a gallant fight to maintain his position, without the reënforcement which Gen. Sumner was unwilling to hazard his center by sending him, until after the arrival of part of Couch's division, at 1 o'clock, which was followed by the remainder during the afternoon, and by Casey's division, so that the entire corps of Gen. Keyes was finally present, on the right and center. Hancock was on the point of being overwhelmed by greatly superior numbers, when the remainder of Smith's division, and Naglee's brigade from Hooker's division, were sent to his support, under the orders of McClellan, who arrived on the ground, as he states in his report, "between 4 and 5 o'clock in the afternoon. Meanwhile, Gen. Hancock, feigning to retreat slowly, drew out the enemy from their position, then turning suddenly, staggered them by volleys of musketry, and completed their rout by a brilliant bayonet charge, with a loss to the enemy of more than five hundred, his own loss being but thirty-one men.

The brunt of the battle had been sustained by the divisions of Hooker and Kearney, under Gen. Heintzelman. The former sustained the principal losses of the day, which were officially stated at 456 killed, 1,400 wounded, and 372 missing. This earnest and gallant battle, fought almost entirely without the knowledge of the commanding General, illustrates what was reasonably expected at the very outset at Yorktown. It seems hardly too much to say that it may have saved another month's siege at Williamsburg, where the position was perhaps even more favorable for defense than that at Yorktown, and where the enemy had a very much greater force than was originally at the latter place. As a result of this battle, the enemy retired from Williamsburg that night, and continued his retreat up the Peninsula. No immediate pursuit was attempted.

Gen. McClellan was exceedingly dissatisfied with Sumner and the other corps commanders for venturing this engagement in his absence. In his first dispatch he notices only the movement of Hancock as a success. He names only Hooker besides, and him merely to refer to his losses. He afterward made some imperfect amends to Gen. Heintzelman and others, under remonstrance, but apparently with grudging reluctance, and even in his final report, after his resentment had ample time to cool, he stops short with the praise of Hancock, giving little credit to those who had done the chief work. On occupying Williamsburg, the next day he announced: "The victory is complete," stating that the enemy lost heavily in killed.

The division under Gen. Franklin had been pushed forward by water to the right bank of the Pamunkey river, opposite West Point, and this movement was sustained by the divisions of Gens. Sedgwick, Porter and Richardson, also transported in steamers. Franklin landed his troops on the morning of the 7th, and Dana's brigade (of Sedgwick's division) arrived soon after. These forces were attacked at 9 o'clock in the morning by a formidable Rebel force, and the battle lasted until 3 o'clock in the afternoon, when the enemy was finally repulsed. Meanwhile, time had been gained for the main Rebel force to retreat unmolested, and with security to its trains. Franklin made a successful defense, only, instead of accomplishing any aggressive results. His total loss is reported as 194, including a large proportion of officers.

Communication between Williamsburg and West Point was

fully opened on the 10th. "Movements were difficult and slow." In the mean time, Norfolk had been taken by Gen. Wool, and the Merrimac finally "neutralized." At this period, the President and Secretary of War—as well as the Secretary of the Treasury, who had accompanied Gen. Wool in his advance on Norfolk—were on a visit at Fortress Monroe. It was while here that the Secretary of War received the following dispatch from Gen. McClellan, dated May 9:

To Hon. E. M. STANTON, Secretary of War: I respectfully ask permission to reorganize the Army Corps. I am not willing to be held responsible for the present arrangement, experience having proved it to be very bad, and it having nearly resulted in a most disastrous defeat. I wish rather to return to the organization by divisions, or else to be authorized to relieve incompetent commanders of Army Corps. Had I been one-half hour later on the field on the 5th, we would have been routed and would have lost every thing. Notwithstanding my positive orders, I was informed of nothing that had occurred, and I went to the field of battle myself upon unofficial information that my presence was needed to avoid defeat. I found there the utmost confusion and incompetency, the utmost discouragement on the part of the men. At least a thousand lives were really sacrificed by the organization into corps. I have too much regard for the lives of my comrades, and too deep an interest in the success of our cause, to hesitate for a moment. I learn that you are equally in earnest, and I therefore again request full and complete authority to relieve from duty with this army, commanders of corps or divisions who find themselves incompetent.   G. B. McCLELLAN,
                                Major-General Commanding.

Secretary Stanton replied, in substance: The President directs me to say that you "may temporarily suspend that organization in the army now under your immediate command, and adopt any you see fit until further orders. He also writes you privately." The President's letter, thus referred to, is as follows:

HEADQUARTERS DEPARTMENT OF VIRGINIA, }
        FORT MONROE, VA., May 9, 1862. }
Maj.-Gen. McCLELLAN—*My Dear Sir:* I have just assisted the Secretary of War in framing the part of a dispatch to you

relating to Army Corps, which dispatch, of course, will have reached you long before this will. I wish to say a few words to you privately on this subject. I ordered the Army Corps organization not only on the unanimous opinion of the twelve generals whom you had selected and assigned as generals of divisions, but also on the unanimous opinion of every *military man* I could get an opinion from, and every modern military book, yourself only excepted. Of course, I did not on my own judgment pretend to understand the subject. I now think it indispensable for you to know how your struggle against it is received in quarters which we can not entirely disregard. It is looked upon as merely an effort to pamper one or two pets, and to persecute and degrade their supposed rivals. I have had no word from Sumner, Heintzelman, or Keyes — the commanders of these corps are, of course, the three highest officers with you : but I am constantly told that you have no consultation or communication with them; that you consult and communicate with nobody but Gen. Fitz John Porter, and perhaps Gen. Franklin. I do not say these complaints are true or just; but at all events, it is proper you should know of their existence. Do the commanders of corps disobey your orders in any thing?

When you relieved Gen. Hamilton of his command the other day, you thereby lost the confidence of at least one of your best friends in the Senate. And here let me say, not as applicable to you personally, that Senators and Representatives speak of *me* in their places as they please without question, and that officers of the army must cease addressing insulting letters to them for taking no greater liberty with *them*.

But to return. Are you strong enough — are you strong enough even with my help—to set your foot upon the necks of Sumner, Heintzelman and Keyes all at once? This is a practical and very serious question to you.

The success of your army and the cause of the country are the same, and of course I only desire the good of the cause.

Yours truly,   A. LINCOLN.

Gen. McClellan did not conclude to make the changes which he had pronounced so indispensable. On the contrary, availing himself of the President's permission, he soon after created two new corps—the " Fifth Provisional Corps," formed of the divisions of Porter and Sykes, the former taken from the corps of Heintzelman, and the latter Regulars, to be commanded by Gen. Fitz John Porter; and the " Sixth Provisional Corps," consisting of Franklin's division, from McDowell's corps, and

Smith's division, from Keyes' corps, to be commanded by Gen. W. B. Franklin.

The headquarters of the Army of the Potomac reached the White House on the 16th of May, and three days later with the corps of Franklin and Fitz John Porter, had advanced to Tunstall's Station, five miles nearer Richmond. Complaints of the roads and requests for reënforcements were not forgotten in the official dispatches of this period ; nor had the President schooled himself to perfect patience with the slow advance up the Peninsula, when he thought that not a moment's unnecessary delay should occur in " pushing the enemy to the wall." On the 14th, Gen. McClellan, being detained by bad roads, took occasion to send a long dispatch, representing his wants and opinions, to which the President, on the 15th, sent the following reply :

Your long dispatch of yesterday is just received. I will answer more fully soon ; will say now that all your dispatches to the Secretary of War have been promptly shown to me. I have done and shall do all I could and can to sustain·you. I hoped that the opening of James river and putting Wool and Burnside in communication with an open road to Richmond or to you, had effected something in that direction. I am still not willing to take all our force off the direct line between Richmond and here.

On the 20th of May, the advance reached the Chickahominy river, and found Bottom's Bridge, across that stream, as well as the railroad bridge, a mile above, destroyed by the enemy. The position was occupied, and the reconstruction of the bridges commenced. The river being fordable at this time, Casey's division was sent across the river and ordered to throw up defenses. Gen. Heintzelman's entire corps was also thrown across, in support. The center and right were advanced to the left bank of the river. On the 24th, the extreme right occupied Mechanicsville, and one of the brigades (Naglee's) of Heintzelman's corps drove the enemy from the Seven Pines, on the Bottom's Bridge road, the left of the army advancing to that position. The distance from the Chickahominy at Bottom's Bridge to Richmond is about twice as great as the distance to Richmond from the same stream at Mechanicsville. The entire line now extended from the latter point to Seven Pines, about half way from the river to Richmond, the Chickahominy flowing between the left and the right and center. This stream, here about forty feet in width, is subject to sudden variations in volume, heavy rains causing it to overflow the bottom-lands on each side, and rendering it impassable except by bridges—all of which, in this vicinity, had been destroyed by the enemy. The Meadow Bridge was north of Richmond, near the Virginia Central railroad, and a short distance above the bridge at Mechanicsville. The third, following down the stream six or seven miles, was called New Bridge, and was a less distance above the York river railroad bridge. Between Bottom's Bridge and Mechanicsville, McClellan determined to construct as many as eleven new bridges.

The Rebel line of defenses, within which the enemy had retired, commenced nearly opposite Drewry's Bluff, on the James river, and bending in a northeasterly direction, across the York river railroad, to the Chickahominy, very nearly followed up the right bank of that stream. The diameter of this semi-circular line was about seven miles, from the center at Richmond. The main body of the enemy, it appears, was encamped on the New Bridge road. Gen. Joseph E. Johnston was still in command.

By instructions from the War Department, issued on the 17th of May, Gen. McDowell, to be reënforced by Shields' division, had been directed to establish a communication, as soon as possible, between his left and McClellan's right. Corresponding directions were sent to Gen. McClellan. A gunboat expedition up the James river had meanwhile been repulsed at Fort Darling, and the attempt to approach Richmond by that means had been effectually abandoned. On the 21st, McClellan telegraphed the following, with many other matters, to the President:

I am not sure that I fully comprehend your orders of the 17th instant, addressed to myself and Gen. McDowell. If a junction is effected before we occupy Richmond, it must necessarily be east of the railroad to Fredericksburg and within my department. This fact, my superior rank, and the express language of the sixty-second article of war, will place his command under my orders, unless it is otherwise specially directed by your Excellency; and I consider that he will be under my command, except that I am not to detach any portion of his forces, or give any orders which can put him out of position to cover Washington. If I err in my construction, I desire to be at once set right. Frankness compels me to say, anxious as I am for an increase of force, that the march of McDowell's column upon Richmond by the shortest route will, in my opinion, uncover Washington, as to any interposition by it, as completely as its movement by water. The enemy can not advance by Fredericksburg on Washington. Should they attempt a movement, which to me seems utterly improbable, their route would be by Gordonsville and Manassas.

The President replied as follows, under date of May 22 :

Your long dispatch of yesterday is just received. You will have just such control of Gen. McDowell and his forces as you therein indicate. McDowell can reach you by land sooner than he could get aboard of boats, if the boats were ready at Fredericksburg, unless his march shall be resisted, in which case the force resisting him will certainly not be confronting you at Richmond. By land he can reach you in five days after starting; whereas by water he would not reach you in two weeks, judging by past experience. Franklin's single division did not reach you in ten days after I ordered it.   A. LINCOLN.

How the purpose above indicated came necessarily to be changed, will best appear from the two following dispatches :

MAY 24, 1862.

I left Gen. McDowell's camp at dark last evening. Shields' command is there, but it is so worn that he can not move before Monday morning, the 26th. We have so thinned our line to get troops for other places, that it was broken yesterday at Front Royal, with a probable loss to us of one regiment infantry, two companies cavalry, putting Gen. Banks in some peril.

The enemy's forces, under Gen. Anderson, now opposing Gen. McDowell's advance, have, as their line of supply and retreat, the road to Richmond.

If, in conjunction with McDowell's movement against Anderson, you could send a force from your right to cut off the enemy's supplies from Ricnmond, preserve the railroad bridge across the two forks of the Pamunkey and intercept the enemy's retreat, you will prevent the army now opposed to you from receiving an accession of numbers of nearly 15,000 men; and if you succeed in saving the bridges, you will secure a line of railroad for supplies in addition to the one you now have. Can you not do this almost as well as not, while you are building the Chickahominy bridges? McDowell and Shields both say they can, and positively will, move Monday morning. I wish you to move cautiously and safely.

You will have command of McDowell, after he joins you, precisely as you indicated in your long dispatch to us of the 21st.   A. LINCOLN.

Maj.-Gen. G. B. McCLELLAN.

McClellan, in his report, erroneously gives a later dispatch (dated May 24) as the President's response on this occasion.

Intelligence received at a later hour on the same day, caused the President to suspend the order in regard to Gen. McDowell's movement, as the subjoined dispatch indicated to McClellan:

MAY 24, 1862.

In consequence of Gen. Banks' critical position, I have been compelled to suspend Gen. McDowell's movements to join you. The enemy are making a desperate push upon Harper's Ferry, and we are trying to throw Gen. Fremont's force and part of Gen. McDowell's in their rear.   A. LINCOLN.

To this, Gen. McClellan replied: " I will make my calculations accordingly."

The next dispatch clearly sets forth the situation of affairs at the time:

WASHINGTON, May 25, 1862.

Your dispatch received. Gen. Banks was at Strasburg with about six thousand men, Shields having been taken from him to swell a column for McDowell to aid you at Richmond, and the rest of his force scattered at various places. On the 23d, a Rebel force of seven to ten thousand fell upon one regiment and two companies guarding the bridge at Port Royal, destroying it entirely; crossed the Shenandoah, and on the 24th, yesterday, pushed on to get north of Banks on the road to Winchester. Gen. Banks ran a race with them, beating them into Winchester yesterday evening. This morning a battle ensued between the two forces, in which Gen. Banks was beaten back into full retreat toward Martinsburg, and probably is broken up into a total rout. Geary, on the Manassas Gap railroad, just now reports that Jackson is now near Front Royal with ten thousand troops, following up and supporting, as I understand, the force now pursuing Banks. Also, that another force of ten thousand is near Orleans, following on in the same direction. Stripped bare, as we are here, I will do all we can to prevent them crossing the Potomac at Harper's Ferry or above. McDowell has about twenty thousand of his forces moving back to the vicinity of Port Royal; and Fremont, who was at Franklin, is moving to Harrisonburg; both these movements intended to get in the enemy's rear.

One more of McDowell's brigades is ordered through here to Harper's Ferry; the rest of his forces remain for the present at Fredericksburg. We are sending such regiments and dribs from here and Baltimore as we can spare to Harper's Ferry, supplying their places in some sort, calling in militia from the adjacent States. We also have eighteen cannon on the road to Harper's Ferry, of which arm there is not a single one at that point. This is now our situation.

If McDowell's force was now beyond our reach, we should be entirely helpless. Apprehensions of something like this, and no unwillingness to sustain you, has always been my reason for withholding McDowell's forces from you.

Please understand this, and do the best you can with the forces you have. A. LINCOLN.

Maj.-Gen. McCLELLAN.

Later, on the same day, the President sent the following:

WASHINGTON, May 25, 1862.

Maj.-Gen. McCLELLAN: The enemy is moving north in sufficient force to drive Banks before him—in precisely what force we can not tell. He is also threatening Leesburg and Geary on the Manassas Gap railroad, from both north and south, in precisely what force we can not tell. I think the movement is a general and concerted one, such as could not be if he was acting upon the purpose of a very desperate defense of Richmond. I think the time is near when you must either attack Richmond or give up the job, and come to the defense of Washington. Let me hear from you instantly. A. LINCOLN.

On the same day, McClellan replied: "Telegram received. Independently of it, the time is very near when I shall attack Richmond. The object of the movement is probably to prevent reënforcements being sent to me. . . . . I have two corps across the Chickahominy, within six miles of Richmond; the others on this side at other crossings within the same distance, and ready to cross when bridges are completed."

Gen. Stoneman was sent out with a small cavalry force to cut the Virginia Central railroad between the Chickahominy and Hanover Court House. This is the eastern one of two lines of railroad from Richmond, both of which meet at Hanover Junction, several miles beyond the Court House. The other extends nearly due north from Richmond to Fredericksburg and Acquia Creek. Both roads cross the South Anna river a few miles south of their junction, and at no great distance apart. To have destroyed both the South Anna bridges of these roads would have cut the enemy's direct communications with the forces in the Valley, and with those resisting McDowell's advance southward. In cutting only one of these roads, several miles south of the South Anna, very little was effected. The President anxiously telegraphed, on the 26th: "Can you not cut the Acquia Creek railroad also? What impression have you as to the intrenched works for you to contend with in front of Richmond? Can you get near enough to throw shells into the city?" McClellan replied (on the same day) that he had "cut the Virginia Central railroad in three places, between Hanover Court House and the Chickahominy," and would "try to cut the other." To the other questions of the President, he replied: "I do not think Richmond intrenchments formidable; but am not certain. Hope very soon to be within shelling distance. Have railroad in operation from White House to Chickahominy. Hope to have Chickahominy bridge repaired to-night. Nothing of interest to-day." Later, he telegraphed as follows:

CAMP NEAR NEW BRIDGE, }
May 26, 1862, 7.30 P. M. }

Have arranged to carry out your last orders. We are quietly closing in upon the enemy, preparatory to the last struggle. Situated as I am, I feel forced to take every possible precaution against disaster, and to secure my flanks against the probably superior force in front of me. My arrangements for to-morrow are very important, and if successful, will leave me free to strike on the return of the force detached.

G. B. McCLELLAN, Major-General.

His Excellency, A. LINCOLN, President.

On the 27th, Fitz John Porter, with the Fifth Corps, was sent to disperse a Rebel force near Hanover Court House, threatening the communications of our army, and in a position to reënforce Jackson or to interfere with any southward movement of McDowell. This force was Branch's division, estimated to have been about nine thousand strong. Porter's corps, without needing the aid of Sykes' division of Regulars, sent to his support on the 28th, broke up the Rebel camp, and dispersed Branch's force. The result was thus announced by the Commanding General:

Porter's action of yesterday was truly a glorious victory; too much credit can not be given to his magnificent division and its accomplished leader. The rout of the rebels was complete; not a defeat, but a complete rout. Prisoners are constantly coming in; two companies have this moment arrived with excellent arms.

The President, after receiving this and other glowing dispatches on the subject, as well as repeated demands for reënforcements on the ground that all the Rebel forces were concentrating at Richmond, sent the following:

WASHINGTON, May 28, 1862.

I am very glad of Gen. F. J. Porter's victory; still, if it was a total rout of the enemy, I am puzzled to know why the Richmond and Fredericksburg railroad was not seized again, as you say you have all the railroads but the Richmond and Fredericksburg. I am puzzled to see how, lacking that, you can have any, except the scrap from Richmond to West Point. The scrap of the Virginia Central, from Richmond to Hanover Junction, without more, is simply nothing. That the whole of the enemy is concentrating on Richmond, I think, can not be certainly known to you or me. Saxton, at Harper's Ferry, informs us that large forces, supposed to be Jackson's and Ewell's, forced his advance from Charlestown to-day. Gen. King telegraphs us from Fredericksburg that contrabands give certain information that fifteen thousand left Hanover Junc-

tion Monday morning to reënforce Jackson. I am painfully impressed with the importance of the struggle before you, and shall aid you all I can consist. ıtly with my view of due regard to all points.   A. LINCOLN.
Maj.-Gen. McCLELLAN.

On the 29th, Gen. Marcy (chief of McClellan's staff) sent the following dispatch to the Secretary of War:

A detachment from Gen. F. J. Porter's command, under Major Williams, Sixth Cavalry, destroyed the South Anna railroad bridge at about 9 A. M. to-day; a large quantity of Confederate public property was also destroyed at Ashland this morning.

The President replied:

WASHINGTON, May 29, 1862.
Your dispatch as to the South Anna and Ashland being seized by our forces this morning is received. Understanding these points to be on the Richmond and Fredericksburg railroad, I heartily congratulate the country, and thank Gen. McClellan and his army for their seizure.
                                          A. LINCOLN.
Gen. R. B. MARCY.

The President had previously telegraphed to Gen. McDowell, on the 28th: "If Porter effects a lodgment on both railroads, near Hanover Court House, consider whether your force in Fredericksburg should not push through and join him."

It is difficult to conceive any collateral operation which, at this juncture, could have had more positive results, than a thorough breaking of the enemy's communication with Jackson, by destroying the South Anna bridges and otherwise. After receiving the President's congratulations, however, on the supposed accomplishment of this object, the Commanding General telegraphed as follows — clearly implying that Porter's movement had really effected little in that direction, as the event proved:

HEADQUARTERS ARMY OF THE POTOMAC, }
                    May 30, 1862. }
From the tone of your dispatches, and the President's, I do
24

not think you at all appreciate the value and magnitude of Porter's victory. It has entirely relieved my right flank, which was seriously threatened; routed and demoralized a considerable portion of the Rebel forces; taken over seven hundred and fifty prisoners; killed and wounded large numbers; one gun, many small arms, and much baggage taken. It was one of the handsomest things in the war, both in itself and in its results. Porter has returned, and my army is again well in hand. Another day will make the probable field of battle passable for artillery. It is quite certain that there is nothing in front of McDowell at Fredericksburg. I regard the burning of South Anna bridges as the least important result of Porter's movement.

G. B. McCLELLAN, Major-General.

Hon. E. M. STANTON, Secretary of War.

On the 29th, Mr. Lincoln had telegraphed: "I think we shall be able, within three days, to tell you certainly whether any considerable force of the enemy, Jackson or any one else, is moving on Harper's Ferry or vicinity. Take this expected development into your calculation." On the 31st, McClellan said in a dispatch: "A contraband reports that Beauregard arrived in Richmond day before yesterday with troops, and amid great excitement. . . . . Roads again frightful. Need more ambulances." At the same date, the President sent the following important information:

A circle whose circumference shall pass through Harper's Ferry, Front Royal and Strasburg, and whose center shall be a little north-east of Winchester, almost certainly has within it this morning the forces of Jackson, Ewell and Edward Johnson; quite certainly they were within it two days ago. Some part of their forces attacked Harper's Ferry at dark last evening. Shields, with McDowell's advance, retook Front Royal at 11 A. M. yesterday, with a dozen of our own prisoners taken there a week ago, one hundred and fifty of the enemy, etc. . . Shields at Front Royal reports a rumor of still an additional force of the enemy, supposed to be Anderson's, having entered the Valley of Virginia. This last may or may not be true. Corinth is certainly in the hands of Gen. Halleck.

The Army of the Potomac, as officially reported on the 31st of May, numbered 127,166, of which force 98,008 were present for duty. To this was added the force of Gen. Wool, now put under Gen. McClellan's command, numbering 14,007 in the aggregate, 11,514 being "effective." Total, 141,173, with 109,522 present for duty. Gen. Sigel was also ordered to report, with his command, to Gen. McClellan; but the order was subsequently countermanded, and this force sent to Harper's Ferry. McCall's division was ordered to him on the 6th of June, and he received many other regiments from time to time.

An order of the War Department, June 1, extended the Department of Virginia to include that part of the State south of the Rappahannock and east of the railroad from Fredericksburg to Richmond, Petersburg, and Weldon, under command of Maj.-Gen. McClellan. Gen. Wool was assigned to the command of the Middle Department, succeeding Gen. Butler, with directions to report to Gen. McClellan for orders.

Despite the diversion of a portion of his force for operations in the Valley, the Rebel General in command at Richmond now boldly assumed the aggressive against McClellan.

Taking advantage of a sudden rise of the Chickahominy, before the entire completion of the bridges, Johnston attacked our left in heavy force near Seven Pines and Fair Oaks, on the 31st of May, having skillfully made his combinations with a view to cut off the corps of Heintzelman and Keyes. The attack commenced about 1 o'clock in the afternoon. Casey's division, in the advance, was driven backward, after stoutly contesting the field for hours, while Heintzelman's two divisions were brought up in support. The enemy, attempting to force his way between these troops and Bottom's Bridge, was kept in check until about 6 o'clock. Gen. Sumner came up at that hour with Sedgwick's division, followed by Richardson's, having crossed on the imperfect bridge which they had constructed, and appeared suddenly on the left flank of Johnston's force, opening a destructive fire with his batteries, which stopped the enemy's advance. Then, by a gallant bayonet charge, led by Sumner in person, the Rebels were driven back with great slaughter, beyond Fair Oaks Station. What had been almost a crushing defeat, would have been turned into a brilliant victory, had our remaining troops been brought into action, and might probably have given us possession of Richmond.

This great opportunity escaped the Commanding General. As Prince de Joinville, his friend and volunteer aid during this campaign, informs us: "It was not until 7 o'clock in the evening that the idea of securing all the bridges without delay, and causing the whole army to cross at daybreak to the right bank of the Chickahominy, was entertained. It was now too late. Four hours had been lost, and the opportunity — that moment so fleeting, in war as in other circumstances — had gone."

The river rose rapidly during the night, sweeping away all the bridges. The enemy renewed the attack in the morning, knowing that our left and center were now completely isolated from the remainder of their comrades, the corps of Porter and Franklin. The troops of Sumner, Heintzelman and Keyes fought with desperate courage, sustaining themselves against the concentrated strength of the enemy, until nearly noon, when the latter retired, leaving his dead unburied, and many of his wounded on the field. Both sides had suffered severely in the battles of Saturday and Sunday. The Government loss is stated as about 5,000 and the Rebel loss about 8,000.

The situation of the Army of the Potomac was now full of interest—its opportunities clearly to be seen. The whole force which could be sent against it from Richmond had been beaten by one-half of this army. Jackson, with a force estimated at 25,000, was now fighting with Banks, and Fremont and McDowell were endeavoring to close in about him. In relation to reported reënforcements to Johnston, McClellan telegraphed, on the 3d: "I am satisfied that Beauregard is not here." At the same time, he was fully aware that the forces of Beauregard and Bragg had evacuated Corinth on the 30th of May, and were now partly disposable for active service wherever they were most needed. Every day's delay was now an advantage to the enemy. To wait for reënforcements was to wait for his adversary to gather in every scattered regiment, and to hasten the arrival of Jackson and Beauregard. To pause for pleasant weather and good roads, was to postpone action indefinitely. He was already almost within shelling distance of Richmond. His supplies came with regularity by water to White House. and thence by railroad to his lines. And yet, with almost daily dispatches about rains and bad roads, with continual appeals for more men, which he knew could not be granted to any great extent, and with repeated assurances of what he was just going to do, nearly an entire month wore away, at this critical and most favorable juncture, without result.

On the 3d of June, he says : " The next leap will be the last one." The Government and the country expected it to be taken at once. But on the 5th, comes an argument for more troops. Five new regiments, and McCall's division, from McDowell's command, are promptly granted him. On the 8th, he says : " I shall be in perfect readiness to move forward to take Richmond the moment McCall reaches here, and the ground will admit the passage of artillery." On the same day, McDowell informs him : " For the third time I am ordered to join you, and this time I hope to get through." Having thus the long-sought forces of McDowell apparently within his grasp, he improves the occasion to call for more, telegraphing as follows, on the 11th : " I have again information that Beauregard has arrived, and that some of his troops are to follow him." He asks, therefore, that reënforcements may be sent him from Halleck's army. He laments that he is the victim of an " abnormal season," and adds : " I am completely checked by the weather." At the same date (despite the weather) he reports that " McCall's troops have commenced arriving."

On the 12th, he reports : " Another good day. All quiet this morning. I move headquarters to-day across the river." On the 14th : " I hope two days more will make the ground practicable." On the 15th : " Another rain set in about 3 P. M. to-day." On the 18th he thinks reënforcements for Jackson* had gone from Richmond. Mr. Lincoln replies, stating

---

* The battles of Cross Keys and Port Republic, in which Gen. Fremont failed to arrest the retreat of Stonewall Jackson, had been fought on the 8th and 9th of June.

circumstances by which this opinion is "corroborated," adding: "If this is true, it is as good as a re-enforcement to you of an equal force. I could better dispose of things, if I could know about what day you can attack Richmond." McClellan replies, the same day: "A general engagement may take place any hour. . . . . We shall await only a favorable condition of the earth and sky, and the completion of some necessary preliminaries."

On the 19th, the President suggests that the reported re-enforcement of Jackson may be a mere ruse. McClellan replies, on the 20th: "I have no doubt that Jackson has been re-enforced from here. There is reason to believe that Gen. R. S. Ripley has recently joined Lee's army,* with a brigade or division from Charleston. Troops have arrived recently from Goldsboro. There is not the slightest reason to suppose the enemy intends evacuating Richmond. He is daily increasing his defenses. . . . . I would be glad to have permission to lay before your Excellency, by letter or telegraph, my views as to the present state of military affairs throughout the whole country. In the mean time, I would be pleased to learn the disposition, as to numbers and position, of the troops not under my command, in Virginia and elsewhere."

To this singular dispatch, the President sent the following reply:

WASHINGTON, June 21, 1862, 6 P. M.

Your dispatch of yesterday, 2 P. M., was received this morning. If it would not divert too much of your time and attention from the army under your immediate command, I would be glad to have your views as to the present state of military affairs throughout the whole country, as you say you would be glad to give them. I would rather it should be by letter than by telegraph, because of the better chance of secrecy. As to the numbers and positions of the troops not under your command, in Virginia and elsewhere, even if I could do it with accuracy, which I can not, I would rather not transmit either by telegraph or letter, because of the chances

---

*Gen. Robert E. Lee had been assigned to the command of the Rebel forces at Richmond, on the 3d of June, superseding Johnston, who had been wounded at Fair Oaks.

of its reaching the enemy. I would be very glad to talk with you, but you can not leave your camp, and I can not well leave here. A. LINCOLN, President.

Maj.-Gen. GEORGE B. McCLELLAN.

In his final report, Gen. McClellan makes the following statement: "All the information I could obtain, previous to the 24th of June, regarding the movements of Gen. Jackson, led to the belief that he was at Gordonsville, where he was receiving re-enforcements from Richmond *via* Lynchburg and Staunton; but what his purposes were, did not appear until the date specified," etc. Entertaining this opinion, it may well be asked, in passing, how happened it that he so vehemently urged, again and again, the withdrawal of all troops from before Washington, leaving an entirely inadequate garrison within the city itself, in order to transfer all to the Peninsula? Such, on the one hand, is his confession ; such, on the other, was his demand. That Jackson was prepared for any "purpose" that best suited the occasion — that he would have attacked Washington had McDowell's army been withdrawn, as McClellan desired, or that he would have invaded Maryland by way of the Valley, as Lee has since done—can admit of no rational doubt. Both those movements were defeated by the wise forecast of the President, and by his persistence in adhering to the policy so clearly marked out, with the approval of all the leading generals, at the outset of the Peninsular movement. When McClellan admits his inability to discern the intentions of Jackson, more than a month after the latter left Richmond, he at once puts at rest all cavils in regard to the opinions of those who assumed some other purpose possible than that finally developed. But what solution can be given of his own inaction during all this period of Jackson's known absence? And how will he even give a plausible look to his eagerness to withdraw McDowell, and to leave to Jackson an unobstructed route to the National Capital?

But the "purposes" of Jackson, hitherto so uncertain, were discovered on the 24th of June, and thus reported :

HEADQUARTERS ARMY OF THE POTOMAC, }
June 24, 1862, 12 P. M. }

A very peculiar case of desertion has just occurred from the enemy. The party states that he left Jackson, Whiting, and Ewell, (fifteen brigades,) at Gordonsville, on the 21st; that they were moving to Frederickshall, and that it was intended to attack my rear on the 28th. I would be glad to learn, at your earliest convenience, the most exact information you have as to the position and movements of Jackson, as well as the sources from which your information is derived, that I may the better compare it with what I have.

G. B. McCLELLAN, Major-General.

The reply was as follows:

WASHINGTON, June 25, 1862.

We have no definite information as to the numbers or position of Jackson's force. Gen. King yesterday reported a deserter's statement that Jackson's force was, nine days ago, forty thousand men. Some reports place ten thousand Rebels under Jackson, at Gordonsville; others, that his force is at Port Republic, Harrisonburg, and Luray. Fremont yesterday reported rumors that Western Virginia was threatened; and Gen. Kelley, that Ewell was advancing to New Creek, where Fremont has his depots. The last telegram from Fremont contradicts this rumor. The last telegram from Banks says the enemy's pickets are strong in advance at Luray; the people decline to give any information of his whereabouts. Within the last two days the evidence is strong that for some purpose the enemy is circulating rumors of Jackson's advance in various directions, with a view to conceal the real point of attack. Neither McDowell, who is at Manassas, nor Banks and Fremont, who are at Middletown, appear to have any accurate knowledge of the subject.

A letter transmitted to the department yesterday, purported to be dated at Gordonsville on the 14th instant, stated that the actual attack was designed for Washington and Baltimore, as soon as you attacked Richmond, but that the report was to be circulated that Jackson had gone to Richmond, in order to mislead. This letter looked very much like a blind, and induces me to suspect that Jackson's real movement is now toward Richmond. It came from Alexandria, and is certainly designed, like the numerous rumors put afloat, to mislead. I think, therefore, that while the warning of the deserter to you may also be a blind, that it could not safely be disregarded. I will transmit to you any further information on this subject that may be received here.

Edwin M. Stanton, Secretary of War.

Maj.-Gen. McClellan.

On the 25th, McClellan began to advance his left, preparatory, he says, to a general forward movement. In the evening of the same day, he reported: " The affair is over, and we have gained our point fully, and with but little loss, notwithstanding the strong opposition." An hour and a half earlier, he had telegraphed: "On our right, Porter has silenced the enemy's batteries in his front."

The blow which the wily deserter had announced to be struck by Jackson on the 28th, fell two days earlier. Only an hour after announcing the success of his preliminary movement on the 25th, McClellan reported that he had "information confirming the supposition that Jackson's advance is at or near Hanover Court House, and that Beauregard arrived, with strong reënforcements, in Richmond yesterday." The desponding side of his temper, and an impulse to protect himself from the extreme effects of an apprehended fall, appear in the following paragraph of this dispatch:

I regret my great inferiority in numbers, but feel that I am in no way responsible for it, as I have not failed to represent repeatedly the necessity of re-enforcements, that this was the decisive point, and that all the available means of the Government should be concentrated here. I will do all that a general can do with the splendid army I have the honor to command, and, if it is destroyed by overwhelming numbers, can at least die with it and share its fate. But if the result of the action which will probably occur to-morrow, or within a short time, is a disaster, the responsibility can not be thrown on my shoulders; it must rest where it belongs.

Secretary Stanton replied:

Washington, June 25, 1862, 11.20 P. M.

Your telegram of fifteen minutes past 6 has just been received. The circumstances that have hitherto rendered it impossible for the Government to send you any more reënforcements than has been done, have been so distinctly stated to you by the President, that it is needless for me to repeat them.

32

Every effort has been made by the President and myself to strengthen you. King's division has reached Falmouth; Shield's division and Ricketts' division are at Manassas. The President designs to send a part of that force to aid you as speedily as it can be done.

E. M. STANTON, Secretary of War.

Maj.-Gen. G. B. McCLELLAN.

The President sent the following dispatch on the same subject:

WASHINGTON, June 26, 1862.

Maj.-Gen. McCLELLAN: Your three dispatches of yesterday in relation to the affair, ending with the statement that you completely succeeded in making your point, are very gratifying.

The later one, of 6.15 P. M., suggesting the probability of your being overwhelmed by two hundred thousand, and talking of where the responsibility will belong, pains me very much. I give you all I can, and act on the presumption that you will do the best you can with what you have, while you continue, ungenerously I think, to assume that I could give you more if I would. I have omitted, and shall omit, no opportunity to send you reënforcements whenever I possibly can.

A. LINCOLN.

P. S. Gen. Pope thinks if you fall back, it would be much better toward York river than toward the James. As Pope now has charge of the Capitol, please confer with him through the telegraph.   A. LINCOLN.

The aggregate number of the Army of the Potomac, on the 20th of June, was 156,838. The campaign had now extended into the season when disease could not fail to be prevalent, in the low, swampy region now occupied by the Government troops. The effective men numbered 115,102.

From the evening of the 26th, when Jackson attacked his right, and threatened his communications by the Pamunkey river, Gen. McClellan states that "every energy of the army was bent" to the end of "an immediate change of base across the Peninsula." The Rebel Gen. D. H. Hill had gone out from Richmond with his command that day, over Meadow Bridge, to form a junction with Jackson, who was approaching by way of Ashland and Hanover Court House. At about 3 o'clock P. M., Hill attacked McCall, at Mechanicsville, and was finally repulsed, with great loss. Gen. McClellan telegraphed: "Victory to-day complete, and against great odds. I almost begin to think we are invincible." During the night, the baggage of the Fifth Corps (Porter's) was sent across to the west side of the Chickahominy, and preparations were made to start the trains next day, for James river. Orders were at the same time sent to the White House for the removal of all the stores possible from that vicinity, by water, up the James river, to meet the retreating army, and to destroy whatever supplies could not be thus reshipped. These orders were promptly executed. Gen. Stoneman, with his cavalry force, having been cut off, made a successful retreat to the White House.

McCall was to fall back and unite with the rest of Porter's corps, on the east bank of the Chickahominy, to hold the bridges at Gaines' Mill, giving time for the main army to execute its intended movement. This position was to have been maintained until the night of the 27th, when Porter's force was to cross, destroying the bridges. Hill, however, attacked McCall at dawn with great vigor, compelling him to retire further down the stream, leaving the bridge at Mechanicsville to the enemy. A large part of the Rebel force was now on the left bank of the river, and expeditiously concentrated for the destruction of Porter's forces at Gaines' Mill, near the New Bridge. Porter's left at length gave way, under the fierce and overwhelming onset of the enemy, and the center was thrown into confusion, with imminent danger of utter rout. Reënforcements were hurried across from the south bank of the river, and saved the day. Meagher's Irish brigade, fighting with unsurpassed gallantry, and French's brigade, with like heroic conduct, came to the support of Porter's broken divisions, and held the enemy in check until night closed the conflict. This battle was one of the most sanguinary of the campaign, resulting in defeat, but it gained time for starting the trains and troops through White Oak Swamp. It had also drawn out Lee's forces from Richmond, so as to prevent any immediate interference with the retreat from that quarter.

It was not until the 28th, that Lee became fully aware of

the purpose of McClellan to withdraw his army to the James river. The single road by which this movement was to be made was exposed, at different points, to an advance of the enemy from Richmond, by the several roads leading from the city. There was no degree of security until the rear had passed through the Swamp, and on emerging therefrom the danger would be soon renewed. The corps of Sumner and Franklin were stationed at Fair Oaks on Sunday, the 29th, (Heintzelman meanwhile retiring,) and having protected the trains, which were now well on their way, (a large amount of property which could not be transferred having been destroyed,) began to fall back. The enemy, perceiving the movement, promptly attacked the retiring forces, about 2 o'clock P. M., and they made a stand not far from Savage's Station. The Rebel masses, brought up within a short distance of our artillery, now in position, were repulsed with great loss, and their repeated attacks were successfully repelled. During the night, Sumner and Franklin fell back to the White Oak Swamp bridge. On the morning of the 30th, the last of the troops had followed the trains across that bridge. Franklin remained to dispute the passage of the Rebels at this point, while Heintzelman, with the four divisions of Hooker, Sedgwick, Kearney and McCall, took position at Charles City Cross Roads, where several roads leading from Richmond intersect. Jackson's corps crossed the Chickahominy early on Monday morning, following up the retreating army by the Williamsburg road. The forces of Longstreet, A. P. Hill, Magruder and Huger went out the Charles City road with the expectation of intercepting our forces at that point. Jackson had come close upon the position held by Franklin at the White Oak Swamp, a little before noon; but the rear of our army had already crossed and destroyed the bridge. An artillery engagement followed, lasting until night, with severe losses on both sides. Two brigades of Sumner's corps participated in this action. Further pursuit from this direction was not attempted.

Toward night, on the same day, the forces of Longstreet and others (commanded by Gen. A. P. Hill, the former being absent,) attacked the force under Heintzelman, who was aided by part of Sumner's corps. The enemy was repulsed with great slaughter and thrown into confusion. In vain were fresh troops massed against the well-managed batteries and heavy musketry fire of our forces. After a desperate conflict, in which the fate of the whole Army of the Potomac was at stake, and with all the strength the Rebels could bring upon the field, a decisive victory was gained for the Government. This has been called the battle of Glendale.

The corps of Keyes and Porter had meanwhile moved forward, in advance of the remaining troops, toward James river, near Turkey Bend, to open communication with the gunboats. The rear of the trains had reached Malvern Hill while the action at Glendale was going on. The transports from the White House arrived almost simultaneously. During the night, the corps of Sumner, Heintzelman and Franklin fell back to the vicinity of this point. Here was an elevated open table-land, a mile and a half in length by three-fourths of a mile in breadth, crossed by several intersecting roads. The troops were massed on this hill for a final encounter, most of the artillery being placed in position—including ten siege guns at the very summit. Porter's corps held the left, Heintzelman and Sumner the center, and Keyes the right, the line curving backward nearly to the river. The left flank was protected by the gunboats under command of Com. Rodgers, which took part in the action, and on the right the roads were barricaded.

Thus disposed, after the losses incurred during a wearisome retreat of seventeen miles, fighting by day and marching by night, the Army of the Potomac was compelled to grapple with the collected forces of the enemy. Before 10 o'clock in the morning, Rebel skirmishers, with artillery, appeared all along the left wing. About 2 o'clock a column was seen in front of Heintzelman, beyond the range of his artillery, moving toward the right, but it disappeared without making an attack. An hour later, the divisions of Kearney and Couch, on the left center, were fiercely assailed with artillery and musketry. The fire was returned with such effect as to drive back the assailants in disorder, our forces advancing several hundred yards to a stronger position. This action occupied about an hour. The enemy renewed the attack on the left about six o'clock, with artillery, advancing his infantry columns to storm the hill. These were swept away by our batteries, and each successive attacking party shared the same fate, until the field was covered with the wounded and dead. Not only artillery fire, but also volleys of musketry and bayonet charges, met the persistent assailants, who advanced, column after column, only to be crushed and scattered. Night ended the terrible struggle—the Stars and Stripes floating in grand triumph over the field made ghastly with the Rebel masses, fallen in the vain attempt to overwhelm a gallant army that six days before had seemed their easy prey.

Instead of improving the advantage gained, to drive into Richmond an enemy whose strength, as now shown by repeated trials, had been greatly overrated, and who was disheartened by continued defeat, the commanding General withdrew his forces from their strong position, retiring to Harrison's Landing. This was effected during the next two days, with no serious attempt at molestation from the enemy. Gen. McClellan states the entire number of his killed, wounded and missing during these seven days, at 15,249.

Thus ended the Peninsular campaign—adding three disastrous months of unmasterly activity to the eight months of dreamy indecision before Washington. It was no fault of the army. It was from no lack of support by the Government. It was due to no combination of untoward events. The positive successes at Williamsburg, at Fair Oaks, at Savage's Station, at Glendale, and at Malvern Hill, show that the Army of the Potomac could win victories, even against great supposed odds in numbers and in position, when courageously led to the fight.   •

In adopting a route to Richmond by the Lower Chesapeake, against the better judgment of the President, Gen. McClellan had expressed his readiness to stake his reputation, his life, and the cause itself, on the success of his plan. He was furnished all needful means, and every available man, consistently with *his own* opinions as to the necessary security of Washington, and with the express conditions agreed to by himself in undertaking the work. He sadly failed in his efforts to employ those men and means to the accomplishment of the end desired.

The military record of the campaign has a singular sameness. When occasionally his roads are good, he can not move without reënforcements. When his reënforcements come, he has to wait for better roads. Thus time passes—the month of April, before an army originally one-eighth as large as his own; much of May and June by the sickly Chickahominy, his men not unfit for duty engaged in throwing up intrenchments, to be abandoned on the first attack. Day after day, he is only waiting for something just on the point of being gained, when his final advance and assault are to commence. But perfect readiness never comes; and at last, the enemy, concentrating all his strength, himself attacks, and puts upon its defense, an army that was confidently led forth for aggressive war.

A month wasted at Yorktown, without plausible palliation; tardy pursuit, after the unintended battle, resulting in victory at Williamsburg; unaccountable hesitation and slackness on the Chickahominy; utter neglect to use the known absence of Jackson, or to anticipate the arrival of Beauregard after the evacuation of Corinth; insured an otherwise impossible discomfiture. Never did the result of a campaign more bitterly disappoint public hope. The worst that Mr. Lincoln had foreseen from the adoption of the Peninsular plan had happened, and even a loss of the entire army was now dreaded. Every advantage supposed by Gen. McClellan to be attainable by this route to Richmond had been thrown away. The cause had suffered a vastly greater blow than at Bull Run. The nation was more depressed; the Administration more painfully embarrassed, than by any previous calamity. The worst effects upon the cause, abroad and at home, were to be apprehended from this unfortunate issue of a grand military plan.

CHAPTER VIII.

Campaign of the Army of Virginia.—Withdrawal of the Army of the Potomac from the Peninsula.—First Invasion of Maryland.—McClellan Superseded.

GEN. FREMONT, commanding the Mountain Department, and Gen. Banks, commanding the Department of the Shenandoah, having failed to coöperate effectively in carrying out the President's order intended to entrap Jackson in his bold operations in the Valley, and the subsequent movements of Gen. McDowell, in command of the Department of the Rappahannock, having also been unable to render decisive aid in this work, it became manifest that a reorganization of the forces in question, under one head, had become necessary. Some time before the final catastrophe at Richmond, it had also become apparent that the Army of the Potomac, instead of accomplishing its object, was rather in danger of being itself sacrificed. Meanwhile, the capture of New Madrid, the occupation of Corinth, and the rapid advance of our forces down the Mississippi, taking possession of Fort Pillow on the 5th of June, and of Memphis on the 6th, and passing with little opposition to Vicksburg, (before which our fleet appeared on the 25th,) had not only secured substantial results, but had also awakened a desire for similar leadership in the East.

Few events of the war, thus far, had evinced better generalship than the operations at New Madrid and Island Number Ten, in which Maj.-Gen. John Pope was the hero. Aside from Gen. Grant, still needed with the Army of the Tennessee, no other general, at this time, was more emphatically a rising man in the army. The President accordingly determined to call Gen. Pope to Washington, where he arrived about the 20th of June. After full consultation and deliberation, the President having visited Gen. Scott at West Point, on the 24th, it was decided to consolidate the three departments specified above, and to organize a new campaign. In pursuance of this purpose, the President issued his order, on the 26th of June, creating the Army of Virginia, under the command of Gen. Pope, the forces under Gen. Fremont to constitute the First Army Corps, those of Gen. Banks the Second Corps, and those under Gen. McDowell the Third Corps, each to be commanded by those officers respectively. At the time of this action, the critical condition of McClellan's army seemed to impose the necessity of positive measures for protecting Washington and holding the approach into Maryland and Pennsylvania by the Shenandoah Valley, from the first foreseen, as since demonstrated, to be an important element of the military position.

On the 27th, Gen. Fremont asked to be relieved from his command. This request was granted, and his connection with the army, in any active command, has never since been resumed. Gen. Francis Sigel was soon after put in command of the First Corps of the Army of Virginia in his stead.

Maj.-Gen. Halleck was also called to Washington. It may be safely assumed that the appointment of this officer as General-in-chief of the army was one of the subjects in regard to which the President had anxiously desired the counsel of Gen. Scott, and about which there was a free interchange of views, on the memorable visit of the 24th of June. The appointment of Gen. Halleck as General-in-chief was officially announced on the 11th of July.

On the 28th of June, the Governors of seventeen States united in an address to the President, expressing their belief in the readiness of the people to respond to a call for more troops, and in the popular desire for prompt and vigorous measures to end the rebellion. In response, the following circular was sent to each of the Governors uniting in this suggestion, and the call for three hundred thousand additional troops was at once published :

EXECUTIVE MANSION, WASHINGTON, }
July 1, 1862. }

GENTLEMEN: Fully concurring in the wisdom of the views expressed to me in so patriotic a manner by you in the com-

25   33

munication of the 28th day of June, I have decided to call
into the service an additional force of three hundred thousand
men.

I suggest and recommend that the troops should be chiefly
of infantry. The quota of your State would be ———. I trust
that they may be enrolled without delay, so as to bring this
unnecessary and injurious civil war to a speedy and satisfactory
conclusion.

An order fixing the quotas of the respective States will be
issued by the War Department to-morrow.

ABRAHAM LINCOLN.

Gen. Pope at once entered on the work of preparation for
the far from welcome duties assigned him. On ascertaining
the condition of the forces placed at his command, he was painfully conscious of the great disproportion of the means at his
disposal to the ends that were desired. In addition to the
troops within the intrenchments around Washington, the
whole effective force at his disposal was as follows: First Corps,
11,500; Second Corps, (as reported,) 14,500; and Third Corps,
18,400—making in all, 44,400. Gen. Pope states, however,
that the Second Corps really numbered but about 8,000, so that
the total was barely 38,000. With this force, the new Commanding General had the triple task of defending Washington,
holding the Shenandoah Valley, and creating a diversion in
favor of the army at Harrison's Landing.

At the first intelligence of Jackson's onset upon the Army
of the Potomac by way of Hanover Court House, on the 26th,
Gen. Pope had earnestly and repeatedly urged the impolicy of
a retreat to the James river, still further away from re-enforcements, but advised, instead, that McClellan should make his
way northward, where effective support could be rendered him
by the remaining troops in Virginia. This policy of concentration may have been impracticable, under the circumstances;
and at all events, it was little regarded by McClellan, except
upon conditions that would expose to the enemy all the approaches to Washington and the Valley. The necessity of cordial coöperation between the little army left for the defense of
these positions, and the remnant of McClellan's force, at Harrison's Landing, was obvious. The utter impossibility of send

ing to the latter point any re-enforcements drawn from the former, hardly needs to be stated, and yet it was for precisely the reason that this was not done, that Gen. McClellan, after his disastrous battle at Gaines' Mill, on the 28th, wrote the following letter—which, but for his deliberate reproduction of it in his final report, might have been charitably dismissed as a mere hasty ebullition—received with a forbearance which, perhaps, such unamiable weakness had long since ceased to deserve :

> HEADQUARTERS ARMY OF THE POTOMAC, }
> SAVAGE'S STATION, June 28, 1862, 12.20 A. M. }
>
> I now know the full history of the day. On this side of the river (the right bank) we repulsed several strong attacks. On the left bank our men did all that men could do, all that soldiers could accomplish, but they were overwhelmed by vastly superior numbers, even after I brought my last reserves into action. The loss on both sides is terrible. I believe it will prove to be the most desperate battle of the war. The sad remnants of my men behave as men. Those battalions who fought most bravely, and suffered most, are still in the best order. My regulars were superb; and I count upon what are left to turn another battle, in company with their gallant comrades of the volunteers. Had I twenty thousand or even ten thousand fresh troops to use to-morrow, I could take Richmond; but I have not a man in reserve, and shall be glad to cover my retreat and save the material and *personnel* of the army.
>
> If we have lost the day, we have yet preserved our honor, and no one need blush for the Army of the Potomac. I have lost this battle because my force was too small.
>
> I again repeat that I am not responsible for this, and I say it with the earnestness of a general who feels in his heart the loss of every brave man who has been needlessly sacrificed to-day. I still hope to retrieve our fortunes; but to do this the Government must view the matter in the same earnest light that I do. You must send me very large re-enforcements, and send them at once. I shall draw back to this side of the Chickahominy, and think I can withdraw all our material. Please understand that in this battle we have lost nothing but men, and those the best we have.
>
> In addition to what I have already said, I only wish to say to the President that I think he is wrong in regarding me as ungenerous when I said that my force was too weak. I merely

intimated a truth which to-day has been too plainly proved. If, at this instant, I could dispose of ten thousand fresh men, I could gain the victory to-morrow.

I know that a few thousand more men would have changed this battle from a defeat to a victory. As it is, the Government must not and can not hold me responsible for the result.

I feel too earnestly to-night. I have seen too many dead and wounded comrades to feel otherwise than that the Government has not sustained this army. If you do not so now, the game is lost.

If I save this army now, I tell you plainly that I owe no thanks to you, or to any other persons in Washington.

You have done your best to sacrifice this army.

G. B. McCLELLAN.

Hon. E. M. STANTON.

Further communication with this officer was interrupted until, after his arrival at Harrison's Landing, the following dispatch was sent in reply:

WASHINGTON, July 1, 1862, 3.30 P. M.

It is impossible to re-enforce you for your present emergency. If we had a million of men, we could not get them to you in time. We have not the men to send. If you are not strong enough to face the enemy, you must find a place of security, and wait, rest, and repair. Maintain your ground if you can, but save the army at all events, even if you fall back to Fort Monroe. We still have strength enough in the country, and will bring it out. A. LINCOLN.

Maj.-Gen. G. B. McCLELLAN.

Obviously, the chief concern in regard to this army was now to preserve it from further loss—there having been, in fact, apprehensions through the country that its entire surrender would be the ultimate result, even after it had reached its present comparatively secure position. Indeed, had the numbers under Lee at all corresponded with McClellan's estimate, this danger was still imminent. The enemy held one bank of the James river, the chief security to our communications being in the fleet of gunboats under Commodore Rodgers.

It was under these circumstances that Gen. Pope, having unsuccessfully appealed to the chief authorities at Washington to relieve him from a command from which so little was to be hoped, and in which his high military reputation was staked at fearful odds, issued an energetic address to his army, with the vigorous orders so offensive to his adversaries, and proceeded earnestly to the performance of the three-fold duties already indicated, drawing almost the entire army of Lee away from Richmond.

One of Pope's first movements was the sending out of cavalry detachments from Fredericksburg, to cut the Virginia Central railroad at several points. This having been duly accomplished, orders were given to Gen. Banks, on the 14th of July, to send forward all his cavalry, with an infantry support, to occupy Culpepper Court House, and to advance from thence to Gordonsville, destroying the railroad for ten or fifteen miles eastward from that place. The cavalry commander failed to execute the latter part of the order, going only as far as Madison Court House—a failure which cost him his command. Jackson's advance, under Ewell, reached Gordonsville on the 16th. Gen. Pope took the field in person on the 29th, and the main portion of his infantry and artillery was placed in position, by the 7th of August, along the turnpike road from Sperryville to Culpepper. Gen. Buford, who had been assigned to the command of the cavalry in Banks' corps, was posted at Madison Court House with five regiments, his pickets extending along the Rapidan, from Burnett's Ford to the Blue Ridge. Gen. Sigel was directed to send a brigade of infantry and a battery of artillery, in support of Buford, to Robertson's river. Gen. Bayard, with four cavalry regiments, was posted near Rapidan Station, his pickets extending eastward along the Rapidan to Raccoon Ford, and westward to meet those of Buford at Burnett's Ford. Cavalry pickets were also stationed along the Rapidan from Raccoon Ford to the confluence of that river with the Rappahannock, while King's division of infantry remained opposite Fredericksburg, substantially completing the line to the Potomac.

On the 8th, the enemy was reported in force in front of both Bayard and Buford, the former slowly falling back toward Culpepper. Crawford's brigade, of Banks' corps, was sent toward Cedar mountain, to support Bayard, and to aid in ascertaining

25

the numbers and intentions of the enemy. On the 9th, Banks was ordered, with the remainder of his corps, to join the brigade under Crawford—Sigel having failed, for some reason, to arrive from Sperryville, to participate in this movement as intended. Ricketts' division, of McDowell's corps, was posted three miles in the rear of Banks, so as to be available for his support, or to be thrown toward Sperryville, whither Buford was retreating, reporting a heavy Rebel force advancing toward Culpepper from Madison Court House.

During the day, on the 9th, and down to five o'clock, the enemy did not appear before Banks, in any considerable force, which led that officer, contrary to the intentions of the commanding General, who merely desired the enemy at this point to be kept in check, to advance two miles to attack. In reality, he encountered a superior force in a strong position, his troops fighting bravely. The action lasted less than two hours, the Government forces being gradually driven back to their former position, with considerable loss. Ricketts' division now came up to their aid, with Gen. Pope at its head. A brisk artillery fire was soon after commenced, driving back the enemy to his former shelter in the woods.

Sigel having arrived, his corps was now advanced and that of Banks withdrawn toward Culpepper, to be put in condition after its fatigues and losses. King had been telegraphed for at Fredericksburg on the 8th, and arrived on the night of the 11th, which day had been spent by both parties in burying the dead. Pope, now having numbers about equal to those of the enemy, determined to bring on a battle, by falling on his line of communications at daybreak. But, during the night, Jackson retired hurriedly across the Rapidan, toward Gordonsville, leaving behind many of his dead and wounded. Gen. Pope reports a loss of about 1,800 men, in killed, wounded and prisoners.

A cavalry force, under Buford and Bayard, followed the enemy to the Rapidan, capturing many stragglers. Thereupon the cavalry resumed its former position, on the line of the Rapidan, from Raccoon Ford to the Blue Ridge.

On the 14th, Pope had an accession to his strength, by the

arrival of Gen. Reno, with 8,000 men from the forces of Gen. Burnside (Ninth Corps), which had arrived at Falmouth. The army was then advanced, taking a favorable position, with its right, under Sigel, resting on Robertson's river; the center, under McDowell, occupying both flanks of Cedar mountain, and the left, under Reno, taking position near Raccoon Ford, covering the road thence to Stevensburg and Culpepper Court House. The cavalry, meanwhile, continued to operate on the communications of the enemy, who was receiving heavy reënforcements from Richmond. A cavalry expedition sent toward Louisa Court House, on the 16th, captured the Adjutant General of Stuart, and, among other papers, an autograph letter from Gen. Robert E. Lee to the latter, showing the plans of the enemy to mass an overwhelming force in Pope's front, and to fall upon him before he could be reënforced from the Army of the Potomac. Despairing of such assistance in holding his present strong position, Pope made the best dispositions in his power for withdrawing behind the Rappahannock, which movement was executed with great skill and expedition, on the night of the 18th, and during the day of the 19th.

It now becomes necessary to return to the Army of the Potomac, the presence and coöperation of which had become so essential to success at this critical juncture.

During the first days of July, Gen. McClellan had been endeavoring to render his new position as secure as possible. It was early manifest that a withdrawal of his force, to aid in the operations before Washington, did not accord with his individual views. To the last, he was extremely loath to abandon the Peninsula. On the 4th of July, McClellan had said, in a dispatch to the President: "Our communications by the James river are not secure. There are points where the enemy can establish themselves with cannon or musketry and command the river, and where it is not certain that our gunboats can drive them out." At the same date, before receiving the dispatch just quoted from, the President, still anxious in regard to the preservation of McClellan's remaining force, and without having definitely determined on the course to be pursued with regard to it, wrote him as follows:

WAR DEPARTMENT, }
WASHINGTON CITY, D. C., July 4, 1862. }

I understand your position as stated in your letter, and by Gen. Marcy. To re-enforce you so as to enable you to resume the offensive within a month, or even six weeks, is impossible. In addition to that arrived and now arriving from the Potomac, (about ten thousand men, I suppose), and about ten thousand I hope you will have from Burnside very soon, and about five thousand from Hunter a little later, I do not see how I can send you another man within a month. Under these circumstances, the defensive, for the present, must be your only care. Save the army, first, where you are, if you *can*, and, secondly, by removal, if you must. You, on the ground, must be the judge as to which you will attempt, and of the means for effecting it. I but give it as my opinion, that with the aid of the gunboats and the re-enforcements mentioned above, you can hold your present position; provided, and so long as you can keep the James river open below you. If you are not tolerably confident you can keep the James river open, you had better remove as soon as possible. I do not remember that you have expressed any apprehension as to the danger of having your communications cut on the river below you, yet I do not suppose it can have escaped your attention.

Yours, very truly,   A. LINCOLN.
Maj.-Gen. McCLELLAN.

P. S.—If at any time you feel able to take the offensive, you are not restrained from doing so.   A. L.

McClellan replied, on the 7th: "My position is very strong, and daily becoming more so. If not attacked to-day, I shall laugh at them. I have been anxious about my communications. . . . . Alarm yourself as little as possible about me, and don't lose confidence in this army." At the same date, he wrote a long letter to the President, volunteering a statement of his "general views concerning the existing state of the rebellion." He reminds Mr. Lincoln that "the Rebel army is in the front, with the purpose of overwhelming us by attacking our positions or reducing us by blocking our river communications." He "can not but regard" his "condition as critical." The singularity of one sitting down, under such circumstances, to write a political disquisition, as if he were the veriest gentleman of leisure, is more striking than any thing in the document itself. Two or three paragraphs in this letter (dated July 7, 1862, and published at length in the writer's last official report) will serve to show its quality:

Our cause must never be abandoned; it is the cause of free institutions and self-government. The Constitution and the Union must be preserved, whatever may be the cost in time, treasure, and blood. If secession is successful, other dissolutions are clearly to be seen in the future. Let neither military disaster, political faction, nor foreign war shake your settled purpose to enforce the equal operation of the laws of the United States upon the people of every State. The time has come when the Government must determine upon a civil and military policy, covering the whole ground of our National trouble. . . . .

This rebellion has assumed the character of a war; as such it should be regarded, and it should be conducted upon the highest principles known to Christian civilization. It should not be a war looking to the subjugation of the people of any State, in any event. It should not be at all a war upon population, but against armed forces and political organizations. Neither confiscation of property, political executions of persons, territorial organization of States, or forcible abolition of slavery should be contemplated for a moment. . . .

Unless the principles governing the future conduct of our struggle shall be made known and approved, the effort to obtain requisite forces will be almost hopeless. A declaration of radical views, especially upon slavery, will rapidly disintegrate our present armies. The policy of the Government must be supported by concentrations of military power. The National forces should not be dispersed in expeditions, posts of occupation, and numerous armies, but should be mainly collected into masses, and brought to bear upon the armies of the Confederate States. Those armies thoroughly defeated, the political structure which they support would soon cease to exist.

From time to time, Gen. McClellan continued to urge the policy of preparing his army to advance on Richmond from its present position. He called for reënforcements, asking a concentration under his command of " every thing we can possibly spare from less important points, to make sure of crushing the enemy at Richmond, which seems clearly to be the most important point in rebeldom." The President visited Harrison's Landing on the 8th of July, and in company with the Commanding General, reviewed the Army of the Potomac. For an entire month, scarcely so much as a reconnoissance in force occurred to break the monotony of life in that unhealthy locality. On the 30th, Gen. Halleck suggested that the enemy at Richmond be pressed, to ascertain the strength of his force there. Finally, on the 4th of August, one day after being ordered to prepare for a prompt withdrawal to Acquia Creek, the divisions of Hooker and Sedgwick, by order of Gen. McClellan, advanced and turned Malvern Hill, causing the Rebel force which had occupied that position to retreat toward Richmond. Col. Averill, on the evening of the 5th, returned from a cavalry reconnoissance in the direction of Savage's Station, and McClellan announced: "Our troops have advanced twelve miles in one direction, and seventeen in another, toward Richmond to-day." Meanwhile, he had commenced sending off his sick and disabled soldiers, as directed by Gen. Halleck, on the 30th of July—the order being repeated, with emphasis, on the 2d of August. On the 6th, he was ordered to send, "immediately," a regiment of cavalry and several batteries of artillery to Burnside's command at Acquia Creek. Instead of promptly complying with this order, Gen. McClellan returned a dispatch offering reasons for non-compliance, and promising to "obey the order as soon as circumstances per- mit." It was partly complied with a day or two later.

From the 3d of August, when he was directed to take "immediate measures" for withdrawing his army from the Peninsula, Gen. McClellan earnestly resisted this order, until, on the 6th, he was definitively informed: "The order will not be rescinded, and you will be expected to execute it with all possible promptness." Gen. Halleck, who had not determined on this course, until he had visited Gen. McClellan in camp, respectfully considered the views presented against it, and wrote him at length, assigning the following, among other reasons, for the policy adopted:

You and your officers at our interview estimated the enemy's forces in and around Richmond at 200,000 men. Since then, you and others report that they have received, and are receiving, large re-enforcements from the South. Gen. Pope's army, covering Washington, is only about 40,000. Your effective force is only about 90,000. You are thirty miles from Richmond, and Gen. Pope, eighty or ninety, with the enemy directly between you, ready to fall with his superior numbers upon one or the other, as he may elect; neither can re-enforce the other in case of such an attack.

If Gen. Pope's army be diminished to re-enforce you, Washington, Maryland and Pennsylvania would be left uncovered and exposed. If your force be reduced to strengthen Pope, you would be too weak to even hold the position you now occupy, should the enemy turn round and attack you in full force. In other words, the old Army of the Potomac is split into two parts, with the entire force of the enemy directly between them. They can not be united by land without exposing both to destruction, and yet they must be united. To send Pope's forces by water to the Peninsula is, under present circumstances, a military impossibility. The only alternative is to send the forces on the Peninsula to some point by water, say Fredericksburg, where the two armies can be united. * *

But you will reply, why not re-enforce me here, so that I can strike Richmond from my present position? To do this, you said, at our interview, that you required 30,000 additional troops. I told you that it was impossible to give you so many. You finally thought you would have some chance of success with 20,000. But you afterward telegraphed me that you would require 35,000, as the enemy was being largely re-enforced.

If your estimate of the enemy's strength was correct, your requisition was perfectly reasonable; but it was utterly impossible to fill it until new troops could be enlisted and organized, which would require several weeks.

To keep your army in its present position until it could be so re-enforced, would almost destroy it in that climate.

The months of August and September are almost fatal to whites who live on that part of James river; and even after you received the re-enforcements asked for, you admitted that you must reduce Fort Darling and the river batteries before you could advance on Richmond.

It is by no means certain that the reduction of these fortifications would not require considerable time—perhaps as much as those at Yorktown.

This delay might not only be fatal to the health of your army, but in the mean time Gen. Pope's forces would be exposed to the heavy blows of the enemy without the slightest hope of assistance from you.

In regard to the demoralizing effect of a withdrawal from

the Peninsula to the Rappahannock, I must remark that a large number of your highest officers, indeed a majority of those whose opinions have been reported to me, are decidedly in favor of the movement. Even several of those who originally advocated the line of the Peninsula, now advise its abandonment.

This final decision was telegraphed to McClellan on the 6th. Pope's situation on the Rapidan, as already seen, was becoming critical, and yet, on the 9th, Gen. Halleck found occasion to telegraph as follows :

WASHINGTON, August 9, 1862, 12.45 P. M.

I am of the opinion that the enemy is massing his forces in front of Gens. Pope and Burnside, and that he expects to crush them and move forward to the Potomac.

You must send re-enforcements instantly to Acquia Creek.

Considering the amount of transportation at your disposal, your delay is not satisfactory. You must move with all possible celerity.   H. W. HALLECK,
                                                                Major-General.
Maj.-Gen. G. B. McCLELLAN.

He received in reply : "There has been no unnecessary delay, as you assert—not an hour's—but every thing has been and is being pushed as rapidly as possible to carry out your orders." On the 10th, a full week after the original order, Gen. Halleck again telegraphed : "The enemy is crossing the Rapidan in large force. They are fighting Gen. Pope to-day. There must be no further delay in your movements. That which has already occurred was entirely unexpected, and must be satisfactorily explained." The chief excuse for this delay was the want of sufficient transportation. He had not yet disposed of even the sick—a work required to be at once proceeded with, as early as the 30th of July. But even this imperfect explanation is set aside by Gen. Halleck in the following reply, (August 12th) : "The Quartermaster General informs me that nearly every available steam vessel in the country is now under your control. . . . . Burnside moved nearly 13,000 troops to Acquia Creek in less than two days, and his transports were immediately sent back to you. All the vessels in the James river and the Chesapeake Bay were placed at your disposal and it was supposed that eight or ten thousand of your men could be transported daily. . . . . There has been, and is, the most urgent necessity for dispatch, and not a single moment must be lost in getting additional troops in front of Washington." Gen. McClellan again asseverates, in reply, that he is doing all he can, and actually says, (August 12th), nine days after the order to move : " If Washington is in danger now, this army can scarcely arrive in time to save it; it is in much better position to do so from here than from Acquia."

Two or three days later, in a dispatch dated August 14, 11 P. M., McClellan at length announced : " Movement has commenced by land and water. All sick will be away to-morrow night " — the " movement " referred to being, as he states in his final report, that " of the main army." At noon on the 15th, we find him saying : " Two of my army corps marched last night and this morning *en route* for Yorktown — one *via* Jones' Bridge, and the other *via* Barrett's Ferry, where we have a pontoon bridge. The other corps will be pushed forward as fast as the roads are clear; and I hope before to-morrow morning to have the entire army in motion." In a word, under the most urgent orders to hasten to Washington, at a time of imminent danger, *nearly two weeks* expire before the march is commenced. The remainder of the movement was executed in accordance with this beginning.

On the 21st, eighteen days after the order to move was given, Gen. Halleck sends the following to McClellan, then at Fortress Monroe : " The forces of Burnside and Pope are hard pushed, and require aid as rapidly as you can send it. Come yourself as soon as you can. By all means, see that the troops sent have plenty of ammunition. We have no time here to supply them. Moreover, they may have to fight as soon as they land." McClellan replied : " I have ample supplies of ammunition for infantry and artillery, and will have it up in time. I can supply any deficiency that may exist in Gen. Pope's army." Leaving the corps of Gen. Keyes to occupy Yorktown, and Sumner's corps waiting for transportation, the remainder of the troops having at length embarked, McClellan sailed from Fortress Monroe for Acquia Creek on the evening of August 23, and reported from that place on the morning of the 24th. On the 27th, he reached Alexandria.

Gen. Pope, having promptly executed his retrograde movement, had his men in a strong position on the Rappahannock line, with the following dispositions on the 20th August: The right, under Sigel, was posted three miles above Rappahannock Station, on the left bank of the river, and connecting closely with McDowell in the center, near that point, and the left keeping open the connection with Fredericksburg, whence reënforcements from the Army of the Potomac were partly to come. Repeated calls were made from Washington for additional forces to cover his right, which could not be further extended without exposing this necessary connection on the left, and which was strongly threatened by the enemy. Ample time had passed, since the order of August 3, for the arrival of the requisite force for this purpose from the Peninsula, but the tardy movement of McClellan had rendered this reënforcement, reasonably expected, as yet impossible. The enemy, now in strong force, confronted Pope from Kelly's Ford, to a point beyond his extreme right. On the 21st and 22d, attempts were made by the Rebels to cross the river at several points, but in every instance they were repulsed. Pope was urged to make every exertion to hold out for two days longer, when it was believed his line would be adequately strengthened. But up to the 25th, the only forces that had arrived in his vicinity, except the detachment under Reno, from Burnside's corps, were 2,500 of the Pennsylvania Reserves, under Gen. Reynolds, which reached Kelly's Ford, and Kearney's division, 4,500 strong, at Warrenton Junction. The evident movements of the enemy to turn his right, caused the Commanding General much uneasiness, but the necessity of maintaining his communication on the left was still imperative. Sigel was instructed to stand firm, allowing the enemy to cross at Sulphur Springs, and move toward Warrenton, when Pope determined to mass his force to the right for the purpose of falling upon the enemy's advance. All of the cavalry, under Buford and Bayard, were pushed to the right of Sigel, toward Fayetteville and Sulphur Springs, to picket the river and to watch the enemy's movements. On the night of the 22d, a small cavalry force made an attack on our army trains at Catlett's Station, doing no great damage. The right of Pope being still heavily threatened, while a strong force was massed in his front at Rappahannock Station, he formed the bold plan of concentrating his force, recrossing the Rappahannock, and assailing the flank and rear of the opposing army. On the morning of the 23d, his forces were collected for this purpose near Rappahannock Station. The river had meanwhile suddenly risen, and finding that a crossing could not be effected in less than thirty-six hours, the plan was changed. Sigel's corps, supported by those of Banks and Reno, were ordered to Sulphur Springs, to attack any force fallen in with, and to advance to Waterloo Bridge. McDowell, to whose command the reënforcements under Reynolds were attached, was moved directly upon Warrenton, to unite with Sigel, if occasion should require, on the road from thence to Sulphur Springs or Waterloo Bridge.

It was ascertained that, on the afternoon of the 24th, the whole force of the enemy was extended along the river, from Rappahannock Station to Waterloo Bridge, his center being near Sulphur Springs. During the day, a large Rebel force moved rapidly northward toward Rectortown, west of Bull Run Mountains, (which are crossed by the Manassas railroad at Thoroughfare Gap.) This movement clearly evinced a purpose to turn the right of Pope's army by way of White Plains and Thoroughfare Gap. Gen. Pope, feeling bound, as he says, by his instructions to maintain his communication with Fredericksburg, and having assurances that 30,000 men were to be sent forward that day, or the next morning, did not immediately change his position to meet that emergency. The main force of the enemy steadily tending in the same direction as the advance, he determined, on the night of the 25th, to abandon the lower fords of the Rappahannock, and directed McDowell, with his own corps and that of Sigel, to hold Warrenton, while Reno was pushed forward three miles on the Warrenton turnpike, and Fitz John Porter, who had now reported to him from near Bealton Station, was ordered to join Reno. Heintzelman's corps was left at Warrenton Junction, with the intention of being sent, at the proper time, to Greenwich, intermediate between Warrenton and Gainesville. It was requested of Gen. Halleck that Franklin's corps should be hastened to Gainesville, and that a strong division of the Peninsular troops should be posted at Manassas Junction. All the cavalry at that place was ordered to be sent forward to Thoroughfare Gap, for observation. Gen. Kearney was directed to post strong guards all along the railroad in his rear, from Warrenton Junction southward, while Gen. Sturgis was charged with the performance of a like duty from Manassas Junction to Catlett's Station. It was confidently expected by Gen. Pope that these several dispositions would have been completed by the afternoon of the 26th.

Jackson advanced through Thoroughfare Gap, as anticipated, and at 8 o'clock P. M., on the 26th, he had cut the railroad six miles east of Warrenton Junction, near Kettle Run. A sharp action ensued on the 27th between Hooker and Ewell, near Bristow, in which the latter was beaten. No report had been made by the cavalry sent to watch the enemy's movement, and it now became manifest to the commanding General that the re-enforcements so confidently expected on the assurances given, had failed to come to his support. His plans, otherwise likely to have been successful in stopping Jackson's advance, were thus foiled. He determined to throw the forces he had upon the enemy, moving toward Manassas and Gainesville, and getting between Lee's army and Bull Run. His entire force, much of which was greatly exhausted by continual marching or fighting, during the last nine days, now numbered about 54,000. On the morning of the 27th he proceeded to execute the purpose just indicated.

McDowell reached Gainesville during the night of the 27th, as directed, and Kearney and Reno took position at Greenwich, according to orders, communicating with McDowell. This force was thus successfully interposed between the main army of Lee, still west of the Bull Run Mountains, near White Plains, and the forces of Jackson, Ewell, and A. P. Hill, now south of the Warrenton turnpike, in the immediate vicinity of Manassas Junction. It was now that Gen. Pope, feeling that Jackson was completely in his power, ordered Fitz John Porter, with his command of fresh troops, to move at 1 o'clock the next morning to Bristow Station, with a view to complete the work of inclosing and crushing Jackson. This order was defiantly disregarded, as charged by Gen. Pope, and as subsequently proved to the full satisfaction of a court-martial, by whose verdict Porter, for this and other acts during the two or three days ensuing, was ignominiously dismissed from the service. Kearney, having been moved to Bristow Station, was sent thence, followed by Hooker, (whose command, notwithstanding the orders of Gen. Halleck, and the lavish promises of McClellan in reply, was almost entirely destitute of ammunition), in pursuit of Ewell toward Manassas. Porter's corps did not arrive at Bristow until half past 10 o'clock in the morning of the 28th. Meanwhile, Jackson had evacuated Manassas Junction, very early that morning. Sigel's corps, in the advance at Gainesville, had also failed to move on Manassas as expeditiously as was intended, otherwise the retreat of Jackson would have been intercepted before he reached Bull Run. The commanding General reached Manassas Junction, with Reno's corps and Kearney's division, within an hour after Jackson in person had left for Centreville. Hooker, Kearney and Reno were immediately sent forward toward the latter place, and Porter was ordered to bring up his corps. McDowell was also apprised of the state of affairs, and ordered to recall his troops advancing on Manassas, (as directed before Jackson's retreat was begun,) and to move out the road from Gainesville toward Centreville. Near night, Gen. Kearney drove Jackson's rear-guard out of the latter place, occupying it about dark, with his advance a little beyond. McDowell, who had with him Sigel's corps and Reynolds' division, in addition to his own corps, (from which the division of Ricketts had been detached in the direction of Thoroughfare Gap), encountered the advance of Jackson about 6 o'clock in the evening, and a conflict ensued, lasting until dark, when each force held its ground. Contrary to expectation, however, King's division, which had sustained the principal part in this action, withdrew during the night, and Ricketts had been driven back from the Gap, retiring upon Bristow

26 34

Station. The party assailing Ricketts was the advance of Longstreet, sent to re-enforce Jackson.

Gen. Sigel, supported by Reynolds, was directed to attack Jackson on the 29th, and Gen. Heintzelman, with the divisions of Hooker and Kearney, was ordered forward from Centreville to attack the enemy in the rear. Orders were sent to McDowell and Porter to move forward, with their two corps, to Gainesville, with all haste, to participate in the battle. Sigel began the attack at daylight, (on the 29th), a mile or two east of Groveton, where he was soon joined by Hooker and Kearney. Jackson at first attempted to avoid an engagement by falling back, but was compelled to take a stand, having his right a little south of the Warrenton turnpike, and his left near Sudley Springs. His line was covered by an old railroad grade, extending from Gainesville toward Leesburg. The engagement was a severe and protracted one. Porter having entirely failed to bring his men into action as ordered, Jackson, though his forces were badly cut up, was able to hold out until Longstreet, with the advance of Lee's main army, near night came up to his support.

The losses were very heavy on both sides, Gen. Pope estimating his killed and wounded at six or eight thousand. That of the enemy was very much greater.

The battle of the 30th, the enemy being thus re-enforced, was fought under great disadvantages, near the old battleground of Bull Run. The Government troops fought with great bravery, maintaining their position with remarkable firmness amidst heavy losses, though the left was gradually forced back. Pope had boldly attacked, in the morning, to anticipate the arrival of further re-enforcements to the enemy by Thoroughfare Gap. It was not until dark that this sanguinary engagement ceased, when our left had receded nearly three-fourths of a mile, though with unbroken ranks and in good order, the turnpike in the rear, which the enemy had endeavored to occupy, being still well covered. The losses on both sides were very heavy.

Gen. Pope's army was not only exhausted with hard work before the commencement of this day's fight, but was also becoming destitute of supplies. To an urgent request on the 28th for rations and forage, to be promptly forwarded, he received the following reply on the morning of the 30th:

TO THE COMMANDING OFFICER AT CENTREVILLE: I have been instructed by Gen. McClellan to inform you that he will have all the available wagons at Alexandria loaded with rations for your troops, and all the cars also, as soon as you will send in a cavalry escort to Alexandria as a guard to the train.
Respectfully,   W. B. FRANKLIN,
Major-General commanding Sixth Corps.

"Such a letter," says Gen. Pope, "when we were fighting the enemy, and Alexandria was swarming with troops, needs no comment." Neither Sumner's corps nor Franklin's had as yet been advanced to render any aid in a military crisis, which urgently demanded the presence of every available man at the scene of action. Another corps, commanded by McClellan's chief favorite, Fitz John Porter, though close at hand, had been found equally wanting at Groveton, through the deliberate disobedience of its commander, though it took part in the battle of the 30th. Gen. McClellan was, meanwhile, quietly waiting at Alexandria, having been ordered by Gen. Halleck, on the 27th, to "take entire direction of the sending out of the troops from Alexandria;" and having also been told on the same day, that "Franklin's corps should march" to Manassas "as soon as possible." On the previous day, the 26th, Sumner's corps commenced disembarking at Acquia Creek. While thus leisurely waiting, charged with the duty of promptly sending indispensable re-enforcements to Pope, yet neglecting to send even the needed supplies to the troops he already had, McClellan was sending such suggestions to Washington as the following:

I am clear that one of two courses should be adopted: First, to concentrate all our available forces to open communications with Pope; Second, to leave Pope to get out of his scrape, and at once use all our means to make the Capital perfectly safe.

To this the President replied:

WASHINGTON, August 29, 1862, 4.10 P. M.

Yours of to-day just received.   I think your first alternative, to-wit. : "to concentrate all our available forces to open communication with Pope," is the right one, but I wish not to control.   That I now leave to Gen. Halleck, aided by your counsels.   A. LINCOLN.

Maj.-Gen. McCLELLAN.

After the battle of the 30th, and the opening of free communication for the enemy at Thoroughfare Gap, through which the main army of Lee was now pouring in great numbers, it only remained for Gen. Pope to withdraw his army, as best he could, toward Washington.   All the troops were withdrawn to Centreville in good order, where they were rested during the day, on the 31st, receiving supplies and ammunition.   Here he was joined by Sumner and Franklin, with an aggregate re-enforcement of 19,000 men.   On the 1st of September, the enemy was found moving toward Fairfax Court House, endangering Pope's right.   Due precautions had been taken, so that when the right was attacked at sunset, the enemy was met by McDowell, Reno, Hooker, and Kearney.   A sharp conflict followed, at Chantilly, in the midst of a thunder-storm, terminating soon after dark.   The Rebels were handsomely repulsed. Maj.-Gen. Kearney and Brig.-Gen. Stevens were among our killed.

On the 2d, the forces under Gen. Pope were ordered to be withdrawn within the intrenchments around Washington, which movement was executed in good order.   Directly after, Gen. Pope was relieved, and appointed to the command of the Department of the Northwest.

Gen. McClellan, on the 1st of September, was orally directed by Gen. Halleck to take command of the defenses of Washington.   He immediately entered on the work, his command, however, being still limited to the Army of the Potomac, and no new jurisdiction being assigned to him outside of the fortifications.   It was without any formal extension of this authority that he went out to meet the enemy in Maryland, where Lee next assumed a threatening position, having gone out by Lees burg and crossed the Upper Potomac.

Proceeding cautiously, until the purpose of the enemy was definitely developed, the advance of Gen. McClellan's forces, on the 14th of September, came up with and defeated the rear-guard of Lee at South Mountain. This was a gallant action, in which Gen. Burnside and his corps took a conspicuous part, and in which Gen. Reno lost his life. On the side of the Government, about 30,000 men were engaged, at various points, including the forces under Gen. Meade. The Commanding General reports his losses as 312 killed, 1,234 wounded, and 22 missing. About 1,500 prisoners were taken from the enemy, whose losses in killed and wounded were estimated to have largely exceeded those of the Government forces.

Meanwhile, Gen. Franklin had been executing a movement on the left, by Crampton's Gap, where he had a sharp engagement. He was directed to relieve Harper's Ferry, where Col. Miles, with a force of nearly 14,000 men, was in imminent danger. Before Franklin came to his aid, though within sound of his guns, Miles (who was soon after killed) had surrendered his position, his munitions of war, and his entire force of infantry and artillery. His cavalry, numbering about 2,000, cut its way out on the night of the 14th, under the command of Col. Davis, capturing, on its route to the Government lines, the train of Longstreet and over one hundred prisoners.

McClellan's forces were soon through the mountain passes, and a prompt engagement with the enemy was expected, with a view to prevent his return across the Potomac, without a crushing defeat. The circumstances now seemed favorable to this result, the forces of McClellan being massed in the immediate vicinity of the Rebel army, which was now contending merely for a secure retreat—in itself a concession of decided inferiority.

On the 15th, the enemy made a stand on the hights beyond Antietam Creek, in the vicinity of Sharpsburg. McClellan, seeing the formidable position thus occupied, deemed it advisable to prepare with great deliberation, for the attack he had intended to make at once. The 15th and most of the 16th were accordingly employed in this preparation, during which time the enemy also made new dispositions, some artillery firing going on during both days. Meanwhile, Jackson's forces returned from the capture of Harper's Ferry. The corps of Sumner and Hooker (the latter of whom had taken the place of Heintzelman, assigned to duty within the fortifications at Washington) were posted on the right, near Keedyville, on both sides of the Sharpsburg turnpike. Franklin's corps and Couch's division were placed in front of Brownsville, in Pleasant Valley. Burnside's corps occupied a position on the left. Heavy artillery was massed in the center, behind which, in the low ground, Porter's corps was held in reserve. The right, center and left, were each, respectively, near three stone bridges across Antietam Creek, the one on the right being about three and a half miles from that on the left.

In the evening of the 16th, Hooker's corps advanced across the stream, by the upper bridge and by a ford near it, with orders to endeavor to turn the enemy's left. After a short engagement, the opposing force was driven back, and Hooker encamped for the night on the ground thus gained. Sumner's corps crossed at the same point, and was followed by the corps of Gen. Mansfield (the Twelfth, consisting of the divisions of Gens. Williams and Green.)

At an early hour on the morning of the 17th, Hooker made an attack on the enemy's left—his whole corps being soon engaged, as well as the remaining troops that had crossed over, on the right. Franklin's corps and other forces were also brought into action. The contest was a severe one, the enemy having evidently moved a heavy force to the support of his left—his right not having been engaged by Burnside, until after the heaviest of this fighting was over. Gen. Mansfield fell mortally wounded. Gen. Hooker was early so severely wounded as to be compelled to leave the field. Gen. Hartsuff, of Hooker's corps, was also badly wounded, as were Gens. Sedgwick and Dana, and many other officers. On both sides, there was heavy slaughter. The enemy was finally driven backward some distance, and our right held the position gained.

Gen. Burnside's advance, on the left, was not commenced until hours after Hooker had brought on the action on the right. About 8 o'clock in the morning, he was ordered by the Commanding General to carry the bridge before him, and to occupy the hights beyond, advancing along their summit toward Sharpsburg. The bridge was not carried until 1 o'clock, and a halt was again made until 3, the hights being finally carried in a gallant manner. Burnside earnestly asked, but failed to receive reënforcements from the heavy reserve under Porter, which remained inactive through the day. The enemy, as night approached, heavily reënforced his right, compelling Burnside to fall back to a lower range of hills than that he had gained.

On the whole, our forces had gained a substantial advantage, and had inflicted the heaviest damage on the enemy, in killed and wounded.

Instead of renewing the engagement, next morning, as a less prudent general would undoubtedly have done, Gen. McClellan spent the 18th "in collecting the dispersed, giving rest to the fatigued, removing the wounded, burying the dead, and the necessary preparations for a renewal of the battle." During the night of the 18th, Lee's entire army retreated across the Potomac. "As their line was but a short distance from the river," Gen. McClellan says in his final report, "the evacuation presented but little difficulty, and was effected before daylight." His dispatches of the 19th, show that he regarded these matters somewhat differently at the time. In fact, several hours elapsed, before the Commanding General appears to have understood how completely the enemy had eluded his grasp.

In his official dispatch of Sept. 29, Gen. McClellan says, in summing up his estimate of the Rebel losses:

As nearly as can be determined at this time, the number of prisoners taken by our troops in the two battles will, at the lowest estimate, amount to 5,000. The full returns will no doubt show a larger number. Of these about 1,200 are wounded. This gives the Rebel loss in killed, wounded and prisoners, 25,542. It will be observed that this does not include their stragglers, the number of whom is said by citizens here to be large. It may be safely concluded, therefore, that the Rebel army lost at least 30,000 of their best troops during their campaign in Maryland.

In his last report, Gen. McClellan states his own losses during the same period as amounting, in the aggregate, to 15,520.

It was not until the 20th, that Maryland Hights were occupied by the corps of Gen. Williams. On the 22d, Gen. Sumner was advanced to Harper's Ferry. On the 23d, Gen. McClellan regarded the enemy as still remaining in front of him, with "indications of an advance of reënforcements," and accordingly proceeded to act on a defensive policy. On the 27th, he believes "the main body of the enemy is concentrated not far from Martinsburg," and extending "toward our right and beyond it." All efforts to induce a vigorous pursuit of an enemy lately represented as completely routed and panic-stricken, proved of no avail.

On the 1st of October, the President visited the army, (the headquarters of which were still on the Maryland side of the Potomac) and passed over the battle-fields of South Mountain and Antietam, in company with Gen. McClellan. It is not too much to say that this visit was made, in part, from the extreme anxiety felt by Mr. Lincoln on account of the protracted delay in moving the army, and from a desire to ascertain, by personal observation, how far this inaction was necessary or reasonable. On the President's return, the following dispatch was sent by Gen. Halleck to Gen. McClellan:

WASHINGTON, D. C., October 6, 1862.

I am instructed to telegraph you as follows: The President directs that you cross the Potomac and give battle to the enemy, or drive him south. Your army must move now, while the roads are good. If you cross the river between the enemy and Washington, and cover the latter by your operation, you can be reënforced with thirty thousand men. If you move up the valley of the Shenandoah, not more than twelve or fifteen thousand can be sent you. The President advises the interior line between Washington and the enemy, but does not order it. He is very desirous that your army move as soon as possible. You will immediately report what line you adopt, and when you intend to cross the river; also to what point the reënforcements are to be sent. It is necessary that the plan of your operations be positively determined on, before orders are given for building bridges and repairing railroads. I am directed to add, that the Secretary of War and the General-in-chief fully concur with the President in these instructions.

Under various dilatory pleas, this peremptory order was effectually disregarded. After fifteen days, during which various supplies were asked and furnished, and an appearance of being on the eve of moving was kept up, McClellan sent Gen. Halleck a dispatch, on the 21st, complaining of a want of horses, as an excuse for further delay, and begging "leave to ask whether the President desires" him "to march at once, or to await the reception of the new horses, every possible step having been taken to insure their prompt arrival." The General-in-chief immediately replied : "Your telegram of 12 M. has been submitted to the President. He directs me to say that *he has no change to make in his order of the 6th inst.* . . . The President does not expect impossibilities; but he is very anxious that all this good weather should not be wasted in inactivity." A full investigation of the facts is believed to have justified the following conclusion, stated by Gen. Halleck to the Secretary of War, on the 28th of October : "In my opinion, there has been no such want of supplies in the army under Gen. McClellan as to prevent his compliance with my order to advance against the enemy. Had he moved his army to the south side of the Potomac, he could have received his supplies almost as readily as by remaining inactive on the north side."

During the last days of October and the earlier days of November, the Army of the Potomac was put in motion After weeks of fine weather had passed unimproved, it is not surprising that "heavy rains delayed the movement considerably in the beginning." The army advanced along the southern base of the Blue Ridge, by Lovettsville, Snicker's Gap, and Rectortown, until the several corps were massed in the vicinity of Warrenton. The main army of Lee at the same time fell back on Gordonsville.

On the night of the 7th, a dispatch from President Lincoln reached Gen. McClellan, at his headquarters near Rectortown, relieving him from the command of the Army of the Potomac. Maj.-Gen. Ambrose E. Burnside was designated as his successor. This transfer of the command was promptly carried into effect, and Gen. McClellan, on the 10th, took his final leave of the army.

35

CHAPTER IX.

A New Era Inaugurated.—Emancipation.—Message of the President.—Last Session of the Thirty-seventh Congress.

THE elections, prior to the autumn of 1862, had shown large majorities for the Administration. Brilliant successes had been won by its armies in the West, until, in June, the tide of victory paused before Vicksburg. In the East, military inefficiency had culminated on the Peninsula and before Washington. Lee had invaded Maryland, and leisurely retired, unpursued. Political defeat followed military disaster. Ohio and Pennsylvania gave small majorities against the Administration in October. New York, in the next month, followed the example. The lower House of the next Congress was already claimed as secured by the Opposition. Popular discontent and despondency were every-where manifest. Opposition politicians held the President responsible before the people for the non-action of their favorite General, whom they did not cease to lament when removed. Peace Democrats rallied behind banners inscribed, "For a more vigorous prosecution of the war;" yet their repre entative man was the one who, evading orders of the Administration, and thwarting the President's wishes, had wasted lavish preparations and abundant military forces, during a whole year, in organizing failure.

Long before this disheartening epoch, however, President Lincoln, as seen in previous pages, had earnestly directed his thoughts to the proper mode of dealing with slavery, in its necessary relations to the war. His final speech to the Border State men on compensated emancipation, as we have seen, plainly indicated that, as early as July, his mind was made up to wrest this element of military power from the support of the Rebellion.

In the month of May, 1862, Gen. Hunter, then commanding the Department of the South, issued an unauthorized order, in

LIFE OF ABRAHAM LINCOLN. **411**

which he attempted, by logical deduction from the premise of Secession, to establish the conclusion that, in his military department, all slaves had become manumitted. As a result of this logical exercise, he declared such persons to be " forever free." This order, like the rhapsody on Slavery and Romanism, issued by Gen. Phelps, in his proclamation at Ship Island, might have been suffered to pass without public notice by the Executive, had it not emanated from a commanding general in whose department were two of the States in which slaves were the most numerous, and had it not the appearance of an authentic announcement of a new policy, which Gen. Hunter had lately been sent out to put in operation. The President felt constrained to set aside this order, which he did in the following well-considered proclamation:

WHEREAS, There appears in the public prints what purports to be a proclamation of Major General Hunter, in the words and figures following, to wit:

HEADQUARTERS DEPARTMENT OF THE SOUTH, ⎫
HILTON HEAD, S. C., May 9, 1862. ⎰
General Orders No. 11.]

The three States of Georgia, Florida, and South Carolina, comprising the Military Department of the South, having deliberately declared themselves no longer under the protection of the United States of America, and having taken up arms against the said United States, it becomes a military necessity to declare them under martial law. This was accordingly done on the twenty-fifth day of April, 1862. Slavery and martial law in a free country are altogether incompatible. The persons in these three States, Georgia, Florida, and South Carolina, heretofore held as slaves, are therefore declared forever free.

DAVID HUNTER,
Major General Commanding.

Official: ED. W. SMITH, Acting Assistant Adjutant General.

AND WHEREAS, The same is producing some excitement and misunderstanding,

Therefore, I, Abraham Lincoln, President of the United States, proclaim and declare that the Government of the United States had no knowledge or belief of an intention, on the part of Gen. Hunter, to issue such a proclamation, nor has it yet any authentic information that the document is genuine; and, further, that neither Gen. Hunter nor any other commander, or person, has been authorized by the Government of the United States to make proclamation declaring the slaves of any State free, and that the supposed proclamation now in question, whether genuine or false, is altogether void, so far as respects such declaration.

I further make known that, whether it be competent for me, as Commander-in-chief of the Army and Navy, to declare the slaves of any State or States free, and whether, at any time, or in any case, it shall have become a necessity indispensable to the maintenance of the Government to exercise such supposed power, are questions which, under my responsibility, I reserve to myself, and which I can not feel justified in leaving to the decision of commanders in the field. These are totally different questions from those of police regulations in armies and camps.

On the sixth day of March last, by a special message, I recommended to Congress the adoption of a joint resolution, to be substantially as follows:

" *Resolved*, That the United States ought to coöperate with any State which may adopt a gradual abolishment of slavery, giving to such State in its discretion to compensate for the inconveniences, public and private, produced by such change of system."

The resolution, in the language above quoted, was adopted by large majorities in both branches of Congress, and now stands an authentic, definite, and solemn proposal of the nation to the States and people most immediately interested in the subject matter. To the people of these States I now earnestly appeal. I do not argue; I beseech you to make the arguments for yourselves. You can not, if you would, be blind to the signs of the times. I beg of you a calm and enlarged consideration of them, ranging, if it may be, far above personal and partisan politics. This proposal makes common cause for a common object, casting no reproaches upon any. It acts not the Pharisee. The change it contemplates would come gently as the dews of Heaven, not rending or wrecking any thing. Will you not embrace it? So much good has not been done by one effort in all past time, as, in the Providence of God, it is now your high privilege to do. May the vast future not have to lament that you have neglected it.

In witness whereof, I have hereunto set my hand and caused the seal of the United States to be affixed.

Done at the city of Washington, this nineteenth day of May, in the year of our Lord one thousand eight hundred and sixty-two, and of the Independence of the United States the eighty-sixth. ABRAHAM LINCOLN.

The policy on which the Government had been acting, in the Slave districts, was substantially that repeated in an Executive order, under date of July 22, 1862 :

That military and naval commanders shall employ as laborers, within and from said States, so many persons of African descent as can be advantageously used for military or naval purposes, giving them reasonable wages for their labor.

That, as to both property, and persons of African descent, accounts shall be kept sufficiently accurate and in detail to show quantities and amounts, and from whom both property and such persons shall have come, as a basis upon which compensation can be made in proper cases ; and the several departments of this Government shall attend to and perform their appropriate parts toward the execution of these orders.

In August, Mr. Greeley, of New York, published in his Journal, the *Tribune*, an editorial article on this subject, in the form of a letter addressed to the President, severely criticising his action, and complaining, in no very gentle terms, of various matters, wherein the Administration had, in his opinion, fallen short of the just expectations of "twenty millions" of loyal people. The whole letter proceeded from the mistaken assumption that the President had not, all along, reflected as earnestly, and felt as deeply, in regard to the question of emancipation, as any man living. It was written in ignorance of the fact that the President had already fully matured and resolved upon a definite policy in regard to Slavery, and was only awaiting the fitting moment for its announcement.

Mr. Lincoln thought proper to address Mr. Greeley the following letter, in reply to his complaints :

EXECUTIVE MANSION, WASHINGTON, ⎱
August 22, 1862. ⎰

Hon. HORACE GREELEY—*Dear Sir :* I have just read yours of the 19th, addressed to myself through the New York *Tribune*. If there be in it any statements or assumptions of fact which I may know to be erroneous, I do not now and here controvert them. If there be in it any inferences which I may believe to be falsely drawn, I do not now and here argue against them. If there be perceptible in it an impatient and dictatorial tone, I waive it in deference to an old friend, whose heart I have always supposed to be right.

As to the policy I " seem to be pursuing," as you say, I have not meant to leave any one in doubt.

I would save the Union. I would save it the shortest way under the Constitution. The sooner the National authority can be restored, the nearer the Union will be " the Union as it was." If there be those who would not save the Union unless they could at the same time *save* Slavery, I do not agree with them. If there be those who would not save the Union unless they could at the same time *destroy* Slavery, I do not agree with them. My paramount object in this struggle *is* to save the Union, and is *not* either to save or destroy Slavery. If I could save the Union without freeing *any* slave, I would do it; and if I could save it by freeing *all* the slaves, I would do it; and if I could do it by freeing some and leaving others alone, I would also do that. What I do about Slavery and the colored race, I do because I believe it helps to save this Union; and what I forbear, I forbear because I do *not* believe it would help to save the Union. I shall do *less* whenever I shall believe what I am doing hurts the cause, and I shall do *more* whenever I shall believe doing more will help the cause. I shall try to correct errors when shown to be errors; and I shall adopt new views so fast as they shall appear to be true views. I have here stated my purpose according to my view of *official* duty, and I intend no modification of my oft-expressed *personal* wish that all men, every-where, could be free.

Yours,   A. LINCOLN.

Although the proclamation of Emancipation had been prepared sometime before this letter was written—in fact as early as July—it was not deemed a fitting occasion to announce this great measure, when our army was recoiling from before Richmond, or when our Capital itself was threatened and Maryland invaded. The battle of Antietam, followed by the withdrawal of Lee's army into Virginia, occurred on the 17th day of September. The President, five days later, issued the following

PROCLAMATION OF EMANCIPATION.

I, Abraham Lincoln, President of the United States, and Commander-in-chief of the Army and Navy thereof, do hereby proclaim and declare that hereafter, as heretofore, the war will be prosecuted for the object of practically restoring the constitutional relation between the United States and the people thereof in those States in which that relation is, or may be, suspended or disturbed; that it is my purpose upon the next meeting of Congress to again recommend the adoption of a practical measure tendering pecuniary aid to the free acceptance or rejection of all the Slave States, so-called, the people whereof may not then be in rebellion against the United States, and which States may then have voluntarily adopted, or thereafter may voluntarily adopt, the immediate or gradual abolishment of Slavery within their respective limits, and that the effort to colonize persons of African descent, with their consent, upon the continent or elsewhere, with the previously obtained consent of the government existing there, will be continued; that on the first day of January, in the year of our Lord one thousand eight hundred and sixty-three, all persons held as slaves within any State, or any designated part of a State, the people whereof shall then be in rebellion against the United States, SHALL BE THEN, THENCEFORWARD AND FOREVER, FREE; and the military and naval authority thereof will recognize and maintain the freedom of such persons, and will do no act or acts to repress such persons, or any of them, in any efforts they may make for actual freedom; that the Executive will, on the first day of January aforesaid, by proclamation, designate the States and parts of States, if any, in which the people thereof respectively shall then be in rebellion against the United States; and the fact that any State, or the people thereof, shall on that day be in good faith represented in the Congress of the United States by members chosen thereto, at elections wherein a majority of the qualified voters of such State shall have participated, shall, in the absence of strong countervailing testimony, be deemed conclusive evidence that such State and the people thereof have not been in rebellion against the United States.

Your attention is hereby called to an act of Congress entitled, "An act to make an additional article of war," approved March 13, 1862, and which act is in the words and figures following:

"*Be it enacted by the Senate and House of Representatives of the United States of America, in Congress assembled*, That hereafter the following shall be promulgated as an additional article of war for the government of the Army of the United States, and shall be observed and obeyed as such:

"ARTICLE —. All officers or persons of the military or naval service of the United States are prohibited from employing any of the forces under their respective commands for the purpose of returning fugitives from service or labor who may have escaped from any persons to whom such service or labor is claimed to be due, and any officer who shall be found guilty by a court-martial of violating this article, shall be dismissed from the service.

"SEC. 2. And be it further enacted, that this act shall take effect from and after its passage."

Also to the ninth and tenth sections of an act entitled, "An act to suppress insurrection, to punish treason and rebellion, to seize and confiscate property of Rebels, and for other purposes," approved July 17, 1862, and which sections are in the words and figures following :

"SEC. 9. And be it further enacted, that all slaves of persons who shall hereafter be engaged in rebellion against the Government of the United States, or who shall in any way give aid or comfort thereto, escaping from such persons and taking refuge within the lines of the army; and all slaves captured from such persons or deserted by them, and coming under the control of the Government of the United States, and all slaves of such persons found on (or being within) any place occupied by Rebel forces and afterward occupied by the forces of the United States, shall be deemed captives of war, and shall be forever free of their servitude and not again held as slaves.

"SEC. 10. And be it further enacted, that no slave escaping into any State, Territory or the District of Columbia, from any of the States, shall be delivered up, or in any way impeded or hindered of his liberty, except for crime, or some offense against the laws, unless the person claiming said fugitive shall first make oath that the person to whom the labor or service of such fugitive is alleged to be due, is his lawful owner, and has not been in arms against the United States in the present rebellion, nor in any way given aid or comfort thereto ; and no person engaged in the military or naval service of the United States shall, under any pretense whatever, assume to decide on the validity of the claim of any person to the service or labor of any other person, or surrender up any such person to the claimant, on pain of being dismissed from the service."

And I do hereby enjoin upon, and order all persons engaged in the military and naval service of the United States to observe, obey and enforce within their respective spheres of service the act and sections above recited.

And the Executive will, in due time, recommend that all citizens of the United States who shall have remained loyal thereto throughout the rebellion, shall (upon the restoration of the constitutional relation between the United States and their respective States and people, if the relation shall have been suspended or disturbed) be compensated for all losses by acts of the United States, including the loss of slaves.

In witness whereof, I have hereunto set my hand and caused the seal of the United States to be affixed.

Done at the city of Washington, this twenty-second day of September, in the year of our Lord one thousand eight hundred and sixty-two, and of the Independence of the United States the eighty-seventh.

By the President: ABRAHAM LINCOLN.
WM. H. SEWARD, Secretary of State.

This proclamation, inaugurating a new era in the progress of the war, and constituting a landmark in the nation's history for all time, was received with great satisfaction throughout the loyal States, reassuring the faith and reviving the confidence of those who now saw the only hope of a complete overthrow of the slaveholders' conspiracy, in the utter eradication of its mischievous and immoral cause. This decree flashed a new light across the Atlantic, and gave cheer to the friends of American republicanism abroad, affording them a firm foothold among the nations of the Old World, so many of whose ruling men had manifested a positive affinity for Davis and the inhuman revolt against freedom and civilization which he had inaugurated. From this time onward, that portion of the European population in sympathy with the constitutional government of this nation began steadily to advance, until its power has come to be strongly felt, and its influence controlling. In Europe, the line was now distinctly drawn between the grand principles of universal freedom and the usurpations of slaveholding barbarism; between legitimate authority on the side of liberty, and organized revolt to perpetuate oppression.

On the 1st day of January, the expected proclamation, completing this great work and giving it actual vitality, was promulgated in the following terms:

WHEREAS, On the twenty-second day of September, in the year of our Lord one thousand eight hundred and sixty-two, a proclamation was issued by the President of the United States, containing, among other things, the following, to-wit:

That on the first day of January, in the year of our Lord one thousand eight hundred and sixty-three, all persons held as slaves within any State, or any designated part of a State, the people whereof shall then be in rebellion against the

27

United States, shall be thenceforward and forever free, and the Executive Government of the United States, including the military and naval authority thereof, will recognize and maintain the freedom of such persons, and will do no act or acts to repress such persons, or any of them, in any efforts they may make for their actual freedom:

That the Executive will, on the first day of January aforesaid, by proclamation, designate the States and parts of States, if any, in which the people thereof respectively shall then be in rebellion against the United States, and the fact that any State, or the people thereof, shall on that day be in good faith represented in the Congress of the United States by members chosen thereto at elections wherein a majority of the qualified voters of such State shall have participated, shall, in the absence of strong countervailing testimony, be deemed conclusive evidence that such State and the people thereof are not then in rebellion against the United States:

Now, therefore, I, Abraham Lincoln, President of the United States, by virtue of the power in me vested as Commander-in-chief of the Army and Navy of the United States, in time of actual armed rebellion against the authority and Government of the United States, and as a fit and necessary war measure for repressing said rebellion, do, on this first day of January, in the year of our Lord one thousand eight hundred and sixty-three, and in accordance with my purpose so to do, publicly proclaimed for the full period of one hundred days from the day of the first above-mentioned order, and designate, as the States and parts of States wherein the people thereof respectively are this day in rebellion against the United States, the following, to-wit. : Arkansas, Texas, Louisiana, except the parishes of St. Bernard, Plaquemines, Jefferson, St. John, St. Charles, St. James, Ascension, Assumption, Terre Bonne, Lafourche, St. Mary, St. Martin, and Orleans, including the city of New Orleans, Mississippi, Alabama, Florida, Georgia, South Carolina, North Carolina, and Virginia, except the forty-eight counties designated as West Virginia, and also the counties of Berkeley, Accomac, Northampton, Elizabeth City, York, Princess Ann, and Norfolk, including the cities of Norfolk and Portsmouth, and which excepted parts are, for the present, left precisely as if this proclamation were not issued.

And by virtue of the power and for the purpose aforesaid, I do order and declare that all persons held as slaves within said designated States and parts of States are, and henceforward shall be free; and that the Executive Government of the United States, including the military and naval authorities thereof, will recognize and maintain the freedom of said persons.

And I hereby enjoin upon the people so declared to be free, to abstain from all violence, unless in necessary self-defense, and I recommend to them, that in all cases, when allowed, they labor faithfully for reasonable wages.

And I further declare and make known that such persons of suitable condition will be received into the armed service of the United States to garrison forts, positions, stations, and other places, and to man vessels of all sorts in said service.

And upon this, sincerely believed to be an act of justice, warranted by the Constitution, upon military necessity, I invoke the considerate judgment of mankind and the gracious favor of Almighty God.

In witness whereof, I have hereunto set my hand and caused the seal of the United States to be affixed.

[L. S.] Done at the city of Washington, this first day of January, in the year of our Lord one thousand eight hundred and sixty-three, and of the Independence of the United States of America the eighty-seventh.

By the President: ABRAHAM LINCOLN.
WILLIAM H. SEWARD, Secretary of State.

The power exercised by President Lincoln in suspending the writ of habeas corpus, in certain cases, gave some uneasiness to a class of men whose efforts to obstruct the Government in putting down the rebellion had been pursued under the assumption that they would escape punishment on a formal trial, for the treason of which they were morally guilty. The people, however, fully sustained this course of the Executive, in a time of great public peril, and his prompt action therein tended materially to strengthen the Government. His proclamation on this subject, issued on the 24th day of September, 1862, contained the following orders:

That during the existing insurrection, and as a necessary measure for suppressing the same, all Rebels and insurgents, their aiders and abettors, within the United States, and all persons discouraging volunteer enlistments, resisting militia drafts, or guilty of any disloyal practice affording aid and comfort to the Rebels against the authority of the United States, shall be subject to martial law, and liable to trial and punishment by courts-martial or military commissions.

That the writ of habeas corpus is suspended in respect to all persons arrested, or who are now, or hereafter during the rebellion shall be, imprisoned in any fort, camp, arsenal, military prison, or other place of confinement, by any military authority, or by the sentence of any court-martial or military commission.

In noticing these measures, which have occupied so large a place in the public mind, it is fitting also to mention the order issued by President Lincoln, in response to an appeal made to him by many Christian men, in regard to the better observance of Sunday as a day of rest and religious devotion. "In revolutionary times," this reverence for the day can seldom be maintained in that strictness which is required even by human laws; but that a great improvement in this respect was practicable, could not be denied. The President's order on this subject, issued on the 16th of November, 1862, is one which deserves a perpetual remembrance. It is here subjoined :

The President, Commander-in-chief of the Army and Navy, desires and enjoins the orderly observance of the Sabbath, by the officers and men in the military and naval service. The importance, for man and beast, of the prescribed weekly rest, the sacred rights of Christian soldiers and sailors, a becoming deference to the best sentiment of a Christian people, and a due regard for the Divine will, demand that Sunday labor in the army and navy be reduced to the measure of strict necessity.
The discipline and character of the National forces should not suffer, nor the cause they defend be imperiled, by the profanation of the day or name of the Most High. "At this time of public distress," adopting the words of Washington in 1776, "men may find enough to do in the service of God and their country, without abandoning themselves to vice and immorality." The first general order issued by the Father of his Country, after the Declaration of Independence, indicates the spirit in which our institutions were founded and should ever be defended: "The General hopes and trusts that every officer and man will endeavor to live and act as becomes a Christian soldier defending the dearest rights and liberties of his country."   ABRAHAM LINCOLN.

The Thirty-seventh Congress convened, for its last session, on the first day of December, 1862. The annual message of the President was transmitted to both Houses on that day. In view of the marked events of the preceding season, this document was looked for with unusual interest; nor was its favorable reception disproportioned to the public expectation. The material portions of this State paper are as follows:

MR. LINCOLN'S ANNUAL MESSAGE, 1862.

FELLOW-CITIZENS OF THE SENATE AND HOUSE OF REPRESENTATIVES: Since your last annual assembling, another year of health and bountiful harvests has passed. And, while it has not pleased the Almighty to bless us with a return of peace, we can but press on, guided by the best light He gives us, trusting that, in His own good time, and wise way, all will yet be well. . . . .

If the condition of our relations with other nations is less gratifying than it has usually been at former periods, it is certainly more satisfactory than a nation so unhappily distracted as we are, might reasonably have apprehended. In the month of June last there were some grounds to expect that the maritime powers which, at the beginning of our domestic difficulties, so unwisely and unnecessarily, as we think, recognized the insurgents as a belligerent, would soon recede from that position, which has proved only less injurious to themselves than to our own country. But the temporary reverses which afterward befell the National arms, and which were exaggerated by our own disloyal citizens abroad, have hitherto delayed that act of simple justice.

The civil war, which has so radically changed, for the moment, the occupations and habits of the American people, has necessarily disturbed the social condition, and affected very deeply the prosperity of the nations with which we have carried on a commerce that has been steadily increasing throughout a period of half a century. It has, at the same time, excited political ambitions and apprehensions which have produced a profound agitation throughout the civilized world. In this unusual agitation we have forborne from taking part in any controversy between foreign States, and between parties or factions in such States. We have attempted no propagandism, and acknowledged no revolution. But we have left to every nation the exclusive conduct and management of its own affairs. Our struggle has been, of course, contemplated by foreign nations with reference less to its own merits, than to its supposed, and often exaggerated, effects and consequences resulting to those nations themselves. Nevertheless, complaint on the part of this Government, even if it were just, would certainly be unwise.

The treaty with Great Britain for the suppression of the slave-trade has been put into operation, with a good prospect of complete success. It is an occasion of special pleasure to acknowledge that the execution of it, on the part of Her Majesty's Government, has been marked with a jealous respect for the authority of the United States, and the rights of their moral and loyal citizens. . . . .

Applications have been made to me by many free Americans of African descent to favor their emigration, with a view to such colonization, as was contemplated in recent acts of Congress. Other parties, at home and abroad—some from interested motives, others upon patriotic considerations, and still others influenced by philanthropic sentiments—have suggested similar measures; while, on the other hand, several of the Spanish-American republics have protested against the sending of such colonies to their respective territories. Under these circumstances, I have declined to move any such colony to any State, without first obtaining the consent of its Government, with an agreement on its part to receive and protect such emigrants in all the rights of freemen; and I have, at the same time, offered to the several States situated within the tropics, or having colonies there, to negotiate with them, subject to the advice and consent of the Senate, to favor the voluntary emigration of persons of that class to their respective territories, upon conditions which shall be equal, just and humane. Liberia and Hayti are, as yet, the only countries to which colonists of African descent from here, could go with certainty of being received and adopted as citizens; and I regret to say such persons, contemplating colonization, do not seem so willing to migrate to those countries, as to some others, nor so willing as I think their interest demands. I believe, however, opinion among them in this respect, is improving; and that, ere long, there will be an augmented and considerable migration to both these countries, from the United States. . . . . .

I have favored the project for connecting the United States with Europe by an Atlantic telegraph, and a similar project to extend the telegraph from San Francisco, to connect by a Pacific telegraph with the line which is being extended across the Russian Empire.

The Territories of the United States, with unimportant exceptions, have remained undisturbed by the civil war; and they are exhibiting such evidence of prosperity as justifies an expectation that some of them will soon be in a condition to be organized as States, and be constitutionally admitted into the Federal Union.

The immense mineral resources of some of those Territories ought to be developed as rapidly as possible. Every step in that direction would have a tendency to improve the revenues of the Government, and diminish the burdens of the people. It is worthy of your serious consideration whether some extraordinary measures to promote that end can not be adopted. The means which suggest itself as most likely to be effective, is a scientific exploration of the mineral regions in those Territories, with a view to the publication of its results at home and in foreign countries—results which can not fail to be auspicious.

The condition of the finances will claim your most diligent consideration. The vast expenditures incident to the military and naval operations required for the suppression of the rebellion, have hitherto been met with a promptitude and certainty unusual in similar circumstances ; and the public credit has been fully maintained. The continuance of the war, however, and the increased disbursements made necessary by the augmented forces now in the field, demand your best reflections as to the best modes of providing the necessary revenue, without injury to business, and with the least possible burdens upon labor.

The suspension of specie payments by the banks, soon after the commencement of your last session, made large issues of United States notes unavoidable. In no other way could the payment of the troops, and the satisfaction of other just demands, be so economically, or so well provided for. The judicious legislation of Congress, securing the receivability of these notes for loans and internal duties, and making them a legal tender for other debts, has made them an universal currency ; and has satisfied, partially, at least, and for the time, the long felt want of an uniform circulating medium, saving thereby to the people immense sums in discounts and exchanges.

A return to specie payments, however, at the earliest period compatible with due regard to all interests concerned, should ever be kept in view. Fluctuations in the value of currency are always injurious, and to reduce these fluctuations to the lowest possible point will always be a leading purpose in wise legislation. Convertibility, prompt and certain convertibility into coin, is generally acknowledged to be the best and the surest safeguard against them ; and it is extremely doubtful whether a circulation of United States notes, payable in coin, and sufficiently large for the wants of the people, can be permanently, usefully and safely maintained.

Is there, then, any other mode in which the necessary provision for the public wants can be made, and the great advantages of a safe and uniform currency secured?

. I know of none which promises so certain results, and is, at the same time, so unobjectionable, as the organization of banking associations, under a general act of Congress, well guarded in its provisions. To such associations the Government might furnish circulating notes, on the security of the United States bonds deposited in the treasury. These notes, prepared under the supervision of proper officers, being uniform in appearance ar.d security, and convertible always into coin, would at once protect labor against the evils of a vicious currency, and facilitate commerce by cheap and safe exchanges.

A moderate reservation from the interest on the bonds would compensate the United States for the preparation and distribution of the notes, and a general supervision of the system, and would lighten the burden of that part of the public debt employed as securities. The public credit, moreover, would be greatly improved, and the negotiation of new loans greatly facilitated by the steady market demand for Government bonds which the adoption of the proposed system would create.

It is an additional recommendation of the measure of considerable weight, in my judgment, that it would reconcile, as far as possible, all existing interests, by the opportunity offered to existing institutions to reorganize under the act, substituting only the secured uniform national circulation for the local and various circulation, secured and unsecured, now issued by them.

The receipts into the treasury, from all sources, including loans, and balance from the preceding year, for the fiscal year ending on the 30th June, 1862, were $583,885,247 06, of which sum $49,056,397 62 were derived from customs; $1,795,331 73 from the direct tax; from public lands $152,203 77; from miscellaneous sources, $931,787 64; from loans in all forms, $529,692,460 50. The remainder, $2,257,065 80, was the balance from last year.

The disbursements during the same period were for congressional, executive, and judicial purposes, $5,939,009 29; for foreign intercourse, $1,339,710 35; for miscellaneous expenses, including the mints, loans, post office deficiencies, collection of revenue, and other like charges, $14,129,771 50; for expenses under the Interior Department, $3,102,985 52; under the War Department, $394,368,407 36; under the Navy Department, $42,674,569 69; for interest on public debt, $13,190,324 45; and for payment of public debt, including reimbursement of temporary loan, and redemptions, $96,096,922 09; making an aggregate of $570,841,700 25, and leaving a balance in the treasury on the first day of July, 1862, of $13,043,546 81.

It should be observed that the sum of $96,096,922 09, expended for reimbursements and redemption of public debt, being included also in the loans made, may be properly deducted, both from receipts and expenditures, leaving the actual receipts for the year, $487,788,324 97 ; and the expenditures, $474,744,778 16. . . . .

On the 22d day of September last a proclamation was issued by the Executive, a copy of which is herewith submitted.

In accordance with the purpose expressed in the second paragraph of that paper, I now respectfully recall your attention to what may be called "compensated emancipation."

A nation may be said to consist of its territory, its people and its laws. The territory is the only part which is of certain durability. "One generation passeth away and another generation cometh, but the earth abideth forever." It is of the first importance to duly consider, and estimate, this ever-enduring part. That portion of the earth's surface which is owned and inhabited by the people of the United States, is well adapted to be the home of one national family ; and it is not well adapted for two, or more. Its vast extent, and its variety of climate and productions, are of advantage, in this age, for one people, whatever they might have been in former ages. Steam, telegraphs and intelligence have brought these to be an advantageous combination for one united people.

In the inaugural address I briefly pointed out the total inadequacy of disunion, as a remedy for the differences between the people of the two sections. I did so in language which I can not improve, and which, therefore, I beg to repeat :

"One section of our country believes Slavery is *right*, and ought to be extended, while the other believes it is *wrong*, and ought not to be extended. This is the only substantial dispute. The fugitive slave clause of the Constitution, and the law for the suppression of the foreign slave-trade, are each as well enforced, perhaps, as any law can ever be in a community where the moral sense of the people imperfectly supports the law itself. The great body of the people abide by the dry legal obligation in both cases, and a few break over in each. This, I think, can not be perfectly cured ; and it would be worse in both cases *after* the separation of the sections, than before. The foreign slave-trade, now imperfectly suppressed, would be ultimately revived without restriction in one section ; while fugitive slaves, now only partially surrendered, would not be surrendered at all by the other.

"Physically speaking, we can not separate. We can not remove our respective sections from each other, nor build an impassable wall between them. A husband and wife may be divorced, and go out of the presence, and beyond the reach of each other ; but the different parts of our country can not do this. They can not but remain face to face ; and intercourse, either amicable or hostile, must continue between them. Is it

36

possible, then, to make that intercourse more advantageous, or more satisfactory, *after* separation than *before?* Can aliens make treaties easier than friends can make laws? Can treaties be more faithfully enforced between aliens, than laws can among friends? Suppose you go to war, you can not fight always; and when, after much loss on both sides, and no gain on either, you cease fighting, the identical old questions, as to terms of intercourse, are again upon you."

There is no line, straight or crooked, suitable for a National boundary, upon which to divide. Trace through, from east to west, upon the line between the free and slave country, and we shall find a little more than one-third of its length are rivers, easy to be crossed, and populated, or soon to be populated, thickly, upon both sides; while nearly all its remaining length are merely surveyors' lines, over which people may walk back and forth without any consciousness of their presence. No part of this line can be made any more difficult to pass, by writing it down on paper, or parchment, as a national boundary. The fact of separation, if it comes, gives up, on the part of the seceding section, the fugitive slave clause, along with all other constitutional obligations upon the section seceded from, while I should expect no treaty stipulation would ever be made to take its place.

But there is another difficulty. The great interior region, bounded east by the Alleghanies, north by the British Dominions, west by the Rocky Mountains, and south by the line along which the culture of corn and cotton meets, and which includes part of Virginia, part of Tennessee, all of Kentucky, Ohio, Indiana, Michigan, Wisconsin, Illinois, Missouri, Kansas, Iowa, Minnesota, and the Territories of Dakotah, Nebraska, and part of Colorado, already has above ten millions of people, and will have fifty millions within fifty years, if not prevented by any political folly or mistake. It contains more than one-third of the country owned by the United States—certainly more than one million of square miles. Once half as populous as Massachusetts already is, it would have more than seventy-five millions of people. A glance at the map shows that, territorially speaking, it is the great body of the Republic. The other parts are but marginal borders to it; the magnificent region sloping west from the Rocky Mountains to the Pacific, being the deepest, and also the richest, in undeveloped resources. In the production of provisions, grains, grasses, and all which proceed from them, this great interior region is naturally one of the most important in the world. Ascertain from the statistics the small proportion of the region which has, as yet, been brought into cultivation, and also the large and rapidly increasing amount of its products, and we shall be overwhelmed with the magnitude of the prospect presented. And yet this region has no sea-coast, touches no ocean any-where. As part of one nation, its people now find, and may forever find, their way to Europe by New York, to South America and Africa by New Orleans, and to Asia by San Francisco. But separate our common country into two nations, as designed by the present rebellion, and every man of this great interior region is thereby cut off from some one or more of these outlets, not, perhaps, by a physical barrier, but by embarrassing and onerous trade regulations.

And this is true, *wherever* a dividing or boundary line may be fixed. Place it between the now free and slave country, or place it south of Kentucky, or north of Ohio, and still the truth remains, that none south of it can trade to any port or place north of it, and none north of it can trade to any port or place south of it, except upon terms dictated by a government foreign to them. These outlets, east, west, and south, are indispensable to the well-being of the people inhabiting, and to inhabit, this vast interior region. *Which* of the three may be the best, is no proper question. All are better than either; and all, of right, belong to that people, and to their successors forever. True to themselves, they will not ask *where* a line of separation shall be, but will vow, rather, that there shall be no such line. Nor are the marginal regions less interested in these communications to, and through them, to the great outside world. They, too, and each of them, must have access to this Egypt of the West, without paying toll at the crossing of any national boundary.

Our National strife springs not from our permanent part; not from the land we inhabit; not from our National homestead. There is no possible severing of this, but would multiply, and not mitigate, evils among us. In all its adaptations and aptitudes, it demands union, and abhors separation. In fact, it would, ere long, force reunion, however much of blood and treasure the separation might have cost.

Our strife pertains to ourselves—to the passing generations of men; and it can, without convulsion, be hushed forever with the passing of one generation.

In this view, I recommend the adoption of the following resolution and articles amendatory to the Constitution of the United States:

"*Resolved by the Senate and House of Representatives of the United States of America in Congress assembled,* (two-thirds of both Houses concurring,) That the following articles be proposed to the Legislatures (or conventions) of the several States as amendments to the Constitution of the United States, all or any of which articles, when ratified by three-fourths of the said Legislatures (or conventions), to be valid as part or parts of the said Constitution, viz.:

"ARTICLE —. Every State, wherein slavery now exists, which shall abolish the same therein, at any time, or times, before the first day of January, in the year of our Lord one thousand and nine hundred, shall receive compensation from the United States as follows, to-wit:

" The President of the United States shall deliver, to every such State, bonds of the United States, bearing interest at the rate of —— per cent. per annum, to an amount equal to the aggregate sum of   for each slave shown to have been therein, by the eighth census of the United States, said bonds to be delivered to such State by installments, or in one parcel, at the completion of the abolishment, accordingly as the same shall have been gradual, or at one time, within such State; and interest shall begin to run upon any such bond, only from the proper time of its delivery as aforesaid. Any State, having received bonds as aforesaid, and afterward re-introducing or tolerating slavery therein, shall refund to the United States the bonds so received, or the value thereof, and all interest paid thereon.

"ARTICLE —. All slaves who shall have enjoyed actual freedom by the chances of the war, at any time before the end of the rebellion, shall be forever free; but all owners of such, who shall not have been disloyal, shall be compensated for them, at the same rates as is provided for States adopting abolishment of slavery, but in such way, that no slave shall be twice accounted for.

"ARTICLE —. Congress may appropriate money, and otherwise provide for colonizing free colored persons, with their own consent, at any place or places without the United States."

I beg indulgence to discuss these proposed articles at some length. Without slavery, the rebellion could never have existed; without slavery, it could not continue.

Among the friends of the Union, there is great diversity of sentiment, and of policy, in regard to slavery, and the African race among us. Some would perpetuate slavery; some would abolish it suddenly, and without compensation; some would abolish it gradually, and with compensation; some would remove the freed people from us, and some would retain them with us; and there are yet other minor diversities. Because of these diversities, we waste much strength in struggles among ourselves. By mutual concession we should harmonize, and act together. This would be compromise; but it would be compromise among the friends, and not with the enemies of the Union. These articles are intended to embody a plan of such mutual concessions. If the plan shall be adopted, it is assumed that emancipation will follow, at least in several of the States.

As to the first article, the main points are: first, the emancipation; secondly, the length of time for consummating it—thirty-seven years; and, thirdly, the compensation.

The emancipation will be unsatisfactory to the advocates of perpetual slavery; but the length of time should greatly mitigate their dissatisfaction. The time spares both races from the evils of sudden derangement—in fact, from the necessity of any derangement—while most of those whose habitual course of thought will be disturbed by the measure, will have passed away before its consummation. They will never see it. Another class will hail the prospect of emancipation, but will deprecate the length of time. They will feel that it gives too little to the now living slaves. But it really gives them much. It saves them from the vagrant destitution which must largely attend immediate emancipation in localities where their numbers are very great; and it gives the inspiring assurance that their posterity shall be free forever. The plan leaves to each State, choosing to act under it, to abolish slavery now, or at the end of the century, or at any intermediate time, or by degrees, extending over the whole or any part of the period; and it obliges no two States to proceed alike. It also provides for compensation, and, generally, the mode of making it. This, it would seem, must further mitigate the dissatisfaction of those who favor perpetual slavery, and especially of those who are to receive the compensation. Doubtless, some of those who are to pay, and not to receive, will object. Yet the measure is both just and economical. In a certain sense, the liberation of slaves is the destruction of property—property acquired by descent, or by purchase, the same as any other property. It is no less true for having been often said, that the people of the South are not more responsible for the original introduction of this property, than are the people of the North; and when it is remembered how unhesitatingly we all use cotton and sugar, and share the profits of dealing in them, it may not be quite safe to say, that the South has been more responsible than the North for its continuance. If, then, for a common object, this property is to be sacrificed, is it not just that it be done at a common charge?

And if, with less money, or money more easily paid, we can preserve the benefits of the Union by this means, than we can by the war alone, is it not also economical to do it? Let us

consider it then.   Let us ascertain the sum we have expended
in the war since compensated emancipation was proposed last
March, and consider whether, if that measure had been
promptly accepted, by even some of the slave States, the same
sum would not have done more to close the war, than has been
otherwise done.   If so, the measure would save money, and, in
that view, would be a prudent and economical measure.   Certainly it is not so easy to pay *something* as it is to pay *nothing ;*
but it is easier to pay a *large* sum, than it is to pay a *larger* one.
And it is easier to pay any sum *when* we are able, than it is to
pay it *before* we are able.   The war requires large sums, and
requires them at once.   The aggregate sum necessary for compensated emancipation, of course, would be large.   But it would
require no ready cash; nor the bonds even, any faster than the
emancipation progresses.   This might not, and probably would
not, close before the end of the thirty-seven years.   At that
time we shall probably have a hundred millions of people to
share the burden, instead of thirty-one millions, as now.   And
not only so, but the increase of our population may be expected
to continue for a long time after that period, as rapidly as
before; because our territory will not have become full.   I do
not state this inconsiderately.   At the same, ratio of increase
which we have maintained, on an average, from our first National census, in 1790, until that of 1860, we should, in 1900,
have a population of 103,208,415.   And why may we not continue that ratio far beyond that period ?   Our abundant room—
our broad National homestead—is our ample resource.   Were
our territory as limited as are the British Isles, very certainly
our population could not expand as stated.   Instead of receiving the foreign born, as now, we should be compelled to send
part of the native born away.   But such is not our condition.
We have two millions nine hundred and sixty-three thousand
square miles.   Europe has three millions and eight hundred
thousand, with a population averaging seventy-three and one-
third persons to the square mile.   Why may not our country,
at some time, average as many ?   Is it less fertile ?   Has it
more waste surface, by mountains, rivers, lakes, deserts, or other
causes ?   Is it inferior to Europe in any natural advantage ?
If, then, we are, at some time, to be as populous as Europe,
how soon ?   As to when this *may* be, we can judge by the past
and the present; as to when it *will* be, if ever, depends much
on whether we maintain the Union.   Several of our States are
already above the average of Europe — seventy-three and a
third to the square mile.   Massachusetts has 157; Rhode
Island, 133; Connecticut, 99; New York and New Jersey,
each, 80.   Also two other great States, Pennsylvania and Ohio,

are not far below, the former having 63 and the latter 59. The States already above the European average, except New York, have increased in as rapid a ratio, since passing that point, as ever before; while no one of them is equal to some other parts of our country, in natural capacity for sustaining a dense population.

Taking the nation in the aggregate, and we find its population and ratio of increase, for the several decennial periods, to be as follows:

1790............	3,929,827		
1800............	5,305,937	35.02 per cent. ratio of increase.	
1810............	7,239,814	36.45 "	"
1820............	9,638,131	33.13 "	"
1830............	12,866,020	33.49 "	"
1840............	17,069,453	32.67 "	"
1850............	23,191,876	35.87 "	"
1860............	31,443,790	35.58 "	"

This shows an average decennial increase of 34.60 per cent. in population through the seventy years from our first, to our last census yet taken. It is seen that the ratio of increase, at no one of these seven periods, is either two per cent. below, or two per cent. above, the average, thus showing how inflexible, and, consequently, how reliable, the law of increase, in our case, is. Assuming that it will continue, gives the following results:

1870...	42,323,341
1880...	56,967,216
1890...	76,677,872
1900...	103,208,415
1910...	138,918,526
1920...	186,984,335
1930...	251,680,914

These figures show that our country *may* be as populous as Europe now is, at some point between 1920 and 1930 — say about 1925 — our territory, at seventy-three and a third persons to the square mile, being the capacity to contain 217,186,000.

And we *will* reach this, too, if we do not ourselves relinquish the chance, by the folly and evils of disunion, or by long and exhausting war, springing from the only great element of National discord among us. While it can not be foreseen exactly how much one huge example of secession, breeding lesser ones indefinitely, would retard population, civilization, and prosperity, no one can doubt that the extent of it would be very great and injurious.

The proposed emancipation would shorten the war, perpetuate peace, insure this increase of population, and proportionately the wealth of the country. With these, we should pay all the emancipation would cost, together with our other debt, easier than we should pay our other debt, without it. If we had allowed our old National debt to run at six per cent. per annum, simple interest, from the end of our Revolutionary struggle until to-day, without paying any thing on either principal or interest, each man of us would owe less upon that debt now, than each man owed upon it then; and this because our increase of men, through the whole period, has been greater than six per cent.; has run faster than the interest upon the debt. Thus, time alone relieves a debtor nation, so long as its population increases faster than unpaid interest accumulates on its debt.

This fact would be no excuse for delaying payment of what is justly due; but it shows the great importance of time in this connection—the great advantage of a policy by which we shall not have to pay until we number a hundred millions, what, by a different policy, we would have to pay now, when we number but thirty-one millions. In a word, it shows that a dollar will be much harder to pay for the war, than will be a dollar for emancipation on the proposed plan. And then the latter will cost no blood, no precious life. It will be a saving of both.

As to the second article, I think it would be impracticable to return to bondage the class of persons therein contemplated. Some of them, doubtless, in the property sense, belong to loyal owners; and hence, provision is made in this article for compensating such.

The third article relates to the future of the freed people. It does not oblige, but merely authorizes, Congress to aid in colonizing such as may consent. This ought not to be regarded as objectionable, on the one hand, or on the other, in so much as it comes to nothing, unless by the mutual consent of the people to be deported, and the American voters, through their representatives in Congress.

I can not make it better known than it already is, that I strongly favor colonization. And yet I wish to say there is an objection urged against free colored persons remaining in the country, which is largely imaginary, if not sometimes malicious.

It is insisted that their presence would injure, and displace white labor and white laborers. If there ever could be a proper time for mere catch arguments, that time surely is not now. In times like the present, men should utter nothing for which they would not willingly be responsible through time and in eternity. Is it true, then, that colored people can displace any more white labor by being free, than by remaining slaves? If they stay in their old places, they jostle no white laborers; if they leave their old places, they leave them open to white laborers. Logically, there is neither more nor less of it. Emancipation, even without deportation, would probably enhance the wages of white labor, and, very surely, would not reduce them. Thus, the customary amount of labor would still have to be performed; the freed people would surely not do more than their old proportion of it, and very probably, for a time, would do less, leaving an increased part to white laborers, bringing their labor into greater demand, and, consequently, enhancing the wages of it. With deportation, even to a limited extent, enhanced wages to white labor is mathematically certain. Labor is like any other commodity in the market—increase the demand for it, and you increase the price of it. Reduce the supply of black labor, by colonizing the black laborer out of the country, and, by precisely so much, you increase the demand for, and wages of, white labor.

But it is dreaded that the freed people will swarm forth, and cover the whole land? Are they not already in the land? Will liberation make them any more numerous? Equally distributed among the whites of the whole country, and there would be but one colored to seven whites. Could the one, in any way, greatly disturb the seven? There are many communities now, having more than one free colored person to seven whites; and this without any apparent consciousness of evil from it. The District of Columbia, and the States of Maryland and Delaware, are all in this condition. The District has more than one free colored to six whites; and yet, in its frequent petitions to Congress, I believe it has never presented the presence of free colored persons as one of its grievances. But why should emancipation South send the freed people North? People, of any color, seldom run, unless there be something to run from. *Heretofore*, colored people, to some extent, have fled North from bondage; and *now*, perhaps, from both bondage and destitution. But if gradual emancipation and deportation be adopted, they will have neither to flee from. Their old masters will give them wages, at least until new laborers can be procured; and the freed men, in turn, will gladly give their labor for the wages, till new homes can be found for them, in congenial climes, and with people of their own blood and race. This proposition can be trusted on the mutual interests involved. And, in any event, can not the North decide for itself, whether to receive them?

Again, as practice proves more than theory, in any case, has

37

there been any irruption of colored people northward, because of the abolishment of slavery in this District last spring?

What I have said of the proportion of free colored persons to the whites, in the District, is from the census of 1860, having no reference to persons called contrabands, nor to those made free by the act of Congress abolishing slavery here.

The plan consisting of these articles is recommended, not but that a restoration of the National authority would be accepted without its adoption.

Nor will the war, nor proceedings under the proclamation of September 22, 1862, be stayed because of the *recommendation* of this plan. Its timely *adoption*, I doubt not, would bring restoration, and thereby stay both.

And, notwithstanding this plan, the recommendation that Congress provide by law for compensating any State which may adopt emancipation, before this plan shall have been acted upon, is hereby earnestly renewed. Such would be only an advance part of the plan, and the same arguments apply to both.

This plan is recommended as a means, not in exclusion of, but in addition to, all others for restoring and preserving the National authority throughout the Union. The subject is presented exclusively in its economical aspect. The plan would, I am confident, secure peace more speedily, and maintain it more permanently, than can be done by force alone; while all it would cost, considering amounts, and manner of payment, and times of payment, would be easier paid than will be the additional cost of the war, if we rely solely upon force. It is much—very much—that it would cost no blood at all.

The plan is proposed as permanent constitutional law. It can not become such without the concurrence of, first, two-thirds of Congress, and, afterward, three-fourths of the States. The requisite three-fourths of the States will necessarily include seven of the slave States. Their concurrence, if obtained, will give assurance of their severally adopting emancipation, at no very distant day, upon the new constitutional terms. This assurance would end the struggle now, and save the Union forever.

I do not forget the gravity which should characterize a paper addressed to the Congress of the nation, by the Chief Magistrate of the nation. Nor do I forget that some of you are my seniors; nor that many of you have more experience than I in the conduct of public affairs. Yet I trust that, in view of the great responsibility resting upon me, you will perceive no want of respect to yourselves, in any undue earnestness I may seem to display.

Is it doubted, then, that the plan I propose, if adopted, would shorten the war, and thus lessen its expenditure of money and of blood? Is it doubted that it would restore the National authority and National prosperity, and perpetuate both indefinitely? Is it doubted that we here—Congress and Executive—can secure its adoption? Will not the good people respond to a united and earnest appeal from us? Can we, can they, by any other means, so certainly, or so speedily, assure these vital objects? We can succeed only by concert. It is not, "Can *any* of us *imagine* better?" but, "Can we *all* do better?" Object whatsoever is possible, still the question recurs, "Can we do better?" The dogmas of the quiet past are inadequate to the stormy present. The occasion is piled high with difficulty, and we must rise with the occasion. As our case is new, so we must think anew, and act anew. We must disinthrall ourselves, and then we shall save our country.

Fellow-citizens, *we* can not escape history. We, of this Congress and this Administration, will be remembered in spite of ourselves. No personal significance, or insignificance, can spare one or another of us. The fiery trial through which we pass, will light us down, in honor or dishonor, to the latest generation. We *say* we are for the Union. The world will not forget that we say this. We know how to save the Union. The world knows we do know how to save it. We—even *we here*—hold the power, and bear the responsibility. In *giving* freedom to the *slave*, we *assure* freedom to the *free*—honorable alike in what we give, and what we preserve. We shall nobly save, or meanly lose, the last best hope of earth. Other means may succeed; this could not fail. The way is plain, peaceful, generous, just—a way which, if followed, the world will forever applaud, and God must forever bless.

ABRAHAM LINCOLN.

DECEMBER 1, 1862.

During the session, the Opposition leaders, elated with their recent successes in the elections, assumed a greater boldness of hostility to the Administration, some of them defiantly avowing their desire that further resistance to armed rebellion should cease. Throughout the country, the mask under which so many Congressional districts had lately been carried, began to be gradually withdrawn.

Among the principal transactions of this session, aside from the necessary appropriations, were: The admission of the new State of West Virginia, by an act approved Dec. 31, 1862; the organization of the new territory of Arizona, Feb. 24, 1863; the passage of a stringent act to prevent and punish frauds upon the Government, March 2, 1863; the enactment of a law for enrolling and calling out the National forces (sometimes called the "conscription act;") an authorization of the issue of letters of marque and reprisal; the organization of the new territory of Idaho; and the passage of an act to provide for the collection of abandoned property in insurrectionary districts; the last four measures having been approved on the 3d of March, 1863, when the session closed.

Soon after the adjournment of Congress, a closely contested election occurred in New Hampshire, in which the Opposition spared no exertion to secure a popular verdict against the Administration. It was soon manifest, however, that a change was taking place in the public mind—a strong reaction from that tone of sentiment which brought political defeat in the preceding autumn. The election had a highly favorable result. Connecticut and Rhode Island, also, in the following month, emphatically indorsed President Lincoln and his policy. The most trying period had passed.

CHAPTER X.

Summary of Military Movements in the West.—Army of the Potomac.—Gen. Hooker Superseded.—Gen. Meade takes Command.—Battle of Gettysburg.

AFTER the occupation of Corinth, the armies, respectively commanded by Gens. Grant and Buell, had separated for different undertakings. Grant was to advance southward, occupying the military positions captured along the banks of the Mississippi, as possession of that river was gradually recovered, and coöperating in the work, as occasion was presented. Buell was to move on Chattanooga and to attempt the relief of East Tennessee, occupying that stronghold and cutting the Rebel communications by that great thoroughfare.

In carrying out this policy, Buell gradually moved his army to the vicinity of Chattanooga, on the north side of the river, but soon found himself in a critical position, on account of the weakness of so long a line of communication with his base of supplies. Bragg, who had now assumed command of the opposing Rebel army, had the two corps of Hardee and Polk at Chattanooga, and that of Kirby Smith at Knoxville—having reached the former place in advance of Buell, after the evacuation of Corinth. Gen. Geo. W. Morgan, with a considerable Government force, had meanwhile occupied Cumberland Gap, which he held for weeks, but was finally flanked by Kirby Smith, and retreated across the country to the Ohio river. This exposed the left of Buell, and Morgan's failure was fatal to the campaign.

While Smith pursued his course toward Lexington, a portion of Bragg's force, on the 21st of August, crossed the Tennessee river, at Harrison, a short distance above Chattanooga, and turned the left of Buell, moving up the Sequatchie, while another detachment moved on McMinnville. A junction of the three Rebel corps was to be effected in the interior of Kentucky.

An advance force of the Rebels appeared before Munfordsville, on the 13th of September. The enemy were repulsed, on

the 14th, by the small force there, under command of Col.
Wilder, but the place was surrendered on the 17th. Buell
meanwhile moved with celerity, and, approaching Louisville,
compelled the enemy to turn aside from his movement on that
city, to open communication with the remainder of his forces,
at Lexington and elsewhere. On the 18th, Bragg issued a
proclamation at Glasgow, calling upon the people of Kentucky
to rally to his support. On the 4th of October, Buell arrived
at Bardstown, on his way to meet the enemy. On the same
day, a Rebel "Provisional Governor" of Kentucky was proclaimed at Frankfort, a portion of Bragg's forces having possession of the State Capital.

During the hurrying to and fro of these opposing armies, not
a little excitement prevailed at Cincinnati and Louisville, in
view of the apparent danger impending. Both cities were
almost entirely undefended; and now might be seen the full
significance of the memorable Buckner-McClellan compact.
The Kentucky hights opposite the city, instead of being held
and fortified, were open to scarcely disputed occupancy by the
invaders. Works were speedily thrown up before Cincinnati,
and Gen. Wallace, who was assigned to the command of this
post, soon found a large number of men at his disposal, many
thousands of the people of Ohio and Indiana having rallied at the
call of the State authorities. The events of this invasion and
"siege" will long have a prominent place in local tradition
and history.

On the 6th, Gen. Buell's advance reached Springfield, sixty
miles from Louisville, between Danville and Bardstown. His
army at this time was organized into three corps, respectively
commanded by Gens. Gilbert, Crittenden and McCook. Learning that a considerable Rebel force was at Perryville, a few
miles distant, on the 7th, Buell formed the plan of surrounding the portion of the enemy there, bringing each of his corps
into action. Gen. Crittenden, however, failed to come up in
time, and Bragg, learning this fact, determined to fall upon
McCook and Gilbert, recalling Hardee's corps to Perryville for
that purpose, after he was already on his retreat. On the 8th,
the battle was fought, McCook's force suffering heavily before

reënforcements from Gilbert arrived, after 3 o'clock P. M. The conflict continued until dark, the Government forces falling back. Crittenden's corps came up that night, and Bragg retreated without renewing the engagement.

Buell's loss in this engagement, including Brig. Gens. Jackson and Terrill, is stated at 466 killed, 1,463 wounded, and 160 missing—a total of 2,089. The Rebel loss was estimated at about the same.

Bragg succeeded in making his escape with a large amount of spoils, consisting mainly of various supplies, of which his army was greatly in need. He retired by way of Stanford and Mount Vernon, where pursuit ceased, and from whence Buell fell back on the line of Nashville and Louisville. Here he was superseded by Gen. Rosecrans, under the President's order of the 25th of October.

Gen. Grant having sent reënforcements to Buell during this period of marching and countermarching in Kentucky, the enemy began to assume a threatening attitude in front of his line, which extended from Corinth to Tuscumbia. The second brigade of Gen. Stanley's division fell back from the latter place, which it had held under command of Col. Murphy, to Iuka, on the 10th of September, and the Ohio brigade, holding that place, withdrew, on the 11th, to Corinth, leaving Murphy's command to hold the post. A sudden dash of Rebel cavalry put Murphy's force to rout, and secured a large amount of booty which that officer, completely surprised, neglected to destroy.

Gen. Rosecrans, who had succeeded to the command surrendered by Gen. Pope on going to Virginia, took prompt measures to meet the emergency. The force under Price appears to have been sent forward for the purpose of either coöperating with Bragg, or of drawing away troops from Corinth, to facilitate its capture by Van Dorn. The movement was met by an attempt of Gen. Grant to cut off the retreat of Price, and to force him to surrender his army, numbering, as reported, about 15,000 men. A force of about 5,000 men, under Gen. Ord, (who was accompanied by Gen. Grant in person,) was to move toward Burnsville, to attack in front, while Gen

Rosecrans was to take part of his command by Jacinto to at tack the flank of Price's army. The execution of this plan commenced on the 18th of September. Rosecrans, advancing by rapid marches, in a heavy rain, fell in with the Rebel pickets on the following day, seven miles from Iuka, and a skirmish ensued, the force encountered falling back toward that village. The forces of Rosecrans were now concentrated at Barnett's, and after waiting two hours for the expected sound of Ord's cannon, a dispatch from Gen. Grant, on the other side of Iuka, was received, saying that he was waiting for Rosecrans to open on the enemy. The force was then moved up from Barnett's to within two miles of Iuka, where the Rebels were found in strong position on a commanding ridge. A hot engagement immediately commenced, which lasted more than two hours, closing at nightfall.

Gen. Hamilton's division bore the brunt of this conflict, aided by the Eleventh Ohio Battery, which, in half an hour of the thickest of the fight, lost 72 men in killed and wounded. The Fifth Iowa Regiment lost 116 men in killed and wounded, and the Eleventh Missouri, 76. The fiercest contest was over the Ohio battery, twice captured by the Rebels, twice retaken at the point of the bayonet. During the night, Price escaped, retiring to Bay Spring. Grant and Ord had not been able, it appears, to engage the enemy, or to prevent his flight. The road by which he withdrew was one unknown to the commanding General. The loss of Rosecrans was 148 killed, 570 wounded, and 94 missing—a total of 812. He took several hundred prisoners from Price, whose other losses were believed to be greater than those of Rosecrans, including two or three generals killed.

This battle had the effect of preventing Price from rendering any direct aid to Bragg, in his incursion through Kentucky, one apprehended purpose of this movement. The retreating column was pursued for some distance, and its loss in arms and other property was large.

On the 26th of September, Gen. Rosecrans took command at Corinth, Gen. Grant proceeding to Jackson, and Gen. Ord to Bolivar—both on the Mobile and Ohio railroad, north of

Grand Junction. Price, continuing his retreat to Baldwin, Mississippi, moved to Dumas, fifteen miles northwest, and effected a junction with Van Dorn. He was afterward joined by Mansfield Lovell at Pocahontas, Van Dorn having chief command of the concentrated force. Gen. Rosecrans anticipated an attack on Corinth, and prepared accordingly. The position was regarded as a strong one, Gen. Halleck having much improved the defensive works of the place, after its evacuation by Beauregard.

The forces under Van Dorn's command having concentrated at Ripley, crossed the Hatchie river and occupied the railroad north of Corinth, on which they advanced on the 2d of October, cutting off direct communication with Bolivar and Jackson. A force was sent by Gen. Grant, however, under command of McPherson, which seasonably arrived at Corinth by a circuitous route. Of the four divisions of Rosecrans at Corinth, three, under Gens. Hamilton, Davies and McKean, were drawn up in line of battle near the outer intrenchments, while the other division remained in the town as a reserve. Heavy skirmishing was kept up through the day on the 3d. On the morning of the 4th, two dense assaulting columns approached, about 9 o'clock—one on the right, under the lead of Price; the other on the left, under Van Dorn. The movement was intended to be simultaneous, but Price, having a less obstructed route, first forced his way, under the destructive fire of numerous heavy guns, quite within the outer intrenchments. For a moment, the division of Davies fell back, and all seemed lost. Rosecrans in person rallied his men, however, and under the gallant conduct of the Fifty-sixth Illinois Regiment, which delivered an effective fire of musketry and advanced with a resolute charge of bayonets, the enemy was driven back, and scattered with terrible havoc. This brilliant affair was well over, when Van Dorn, approaching in a similar manner, found himself confronted by Hamilton's division—the Ohio brigade, under Col. Fuller, and the Eleventh Missouri Regiment, bearing the brunt of the fight, on the part of the infantry force. The batteries on this side of the town, also, did frightful execution, and Van Dorn's column failed to gain a foothold within the intrenchments. He was driven back with great slaughter, the guns sweeping away the retreating masses with unsparing fury.

The Rebel force outnumbered that on the Government side, two to one, but from the character of the fight their losses were greatly disproportionate. Those of Van Dorn were 1,423 killed, and, by the usual estimate, 5,692 wounded. He also lost 2,265 prisoners—making a total of 9,380. In small arms, cannon, ammunition, and other property, his loss was also large. Further damage was inflicted by the forces sent out in pursuit. Rosecrans had 315 killed, 1,812 wounded, and 230 taken prisoners or missing—in all, 2,357. This was one of the most decisive victories of the war.

On the 24th of October, an attempt was made by Breckinridge to recover Baton Rouge, which was occupied by a Government force under Gen. Williams, (who lost his life in the engagement,) but the attempt was defeated, by a decisive victory over the assailants.

The stronghold of Vicksburg had as yet proved an insuperable obstacle to the recovery of full possession of the Mississippi river. It had become manifest that a strong land force was required to coöperate in the reduction of the place. An expedition for this purpose was accordingly organized at Cairo and Memphis, under Gen. W. T. Sherman, to proceed down the Mississippi in transports, and to approach the city in the rear from the Yazoo river. It was also intended that Gen. Grant, commanding the department within which these operations were to be, should advance southward by the Mississippi Central railroad, coming in with his forces by Jackson, Miss., to aid Sherman in this undertaking. Gen. Hovey's division of 7,000 men, was sent by Gen. Curtis from Helena, Ark., now occupied by a Government force, to cut the railroad beyond the Tallahatchie, intercepting the Rebels in their retreat. This having been accomplished, the detachment returned to Arkansas. Its appearance, however, had served to alarm the enemy, leading to an overestimate of the strength of Grant's column. Gen. Pemberton, commanding a Rebel force at Grenada, consequently fell back toward Canton. Grant's advance, under

Hamilton, occupied Holly Springs on the 29th of November. On the 4th of December, Grant established his headquarters at Oxford, and was preparing to advance on Grenada. The withdrawal of Hovey's force, however, becoming known to Van Dorn, he sent out an expedition, which made a rapid advance on Holly Springs, in Grant's rear, defeating the garrison there on the 20th, through the culpable neglect of Col. Murphy, in command of the post, and destroying the Government stores, collected in large quantity at that place. A similar attack at Davis' Mills, further north, was gallantly repulsed by the garrison under command of Col. W. H. Morgan. A body of Rebel cavalry under Forrest, at nearly the same time, made an attack on Jackson, in Tennessee, destroying the railroad for some distance; the town of Humboldt, on the same road, further north, was occupied; Trenton was surrendered by Col. Fry, the officer in command, much property being destroyed; and other points on the road were captured. Though Forrest was soon after utterly routed, these combined disasters, but especially that at Holly Springs, led Gen. Grant to fall back, abandoning the intended movement further southward. As the event proved, this turn of affairs was fortunate, for the subsequent unusual rise in the rivers of that country would have cut off alike his communications and his line of retreat, seriously imperiling his whole force.

Gen. Sherman's expedition took its departure down the river, from Memphis, on the 20th of December, over one hundred transports conveying his troops. In the night of the 24th, having arrived at Milliken's Bend, a detachment under Gen. Morgan L. Smith landed on the west bank of the Mississippi, and destroyed a section of the Vicksburg and Texas railroad, ten miles from the river, returning to the main army. Christmas having been passed at Milliken's Bend, the expedition proceeded up the Yazoo river, and on the morning of the 27th, the troops disembarked, the right at the plantation of the late Gen. Albert Sidney Johnston, and the center and left extending along Lake's plantation, to within two or three miles of Haines' Bluff, where a Rebel battery and force prevented a further advance up the river. The line was extended about six miles along the Yazoo.

A gunboat fleet on the Mississippi meanwhile coöperated, assaulting the place from the opposite side, with no material success, and receiving not a little damage.

The face of the country, for the eight or ten miles intervening between this position and the high ground on which the city of Vicksburg stands, is first low and marshy, with lagoons, sandbars and bayous, and then peculiarly rough, deep ravines alternating with precipitous bluffs, mostly wooded, or covered with cane-brake and rank undergrowth. Among these natural defenses there nestled masked batteries and rifle pits, manned by an ample force gathered to meet this expected assault upon the rear of Vicksburg.

On attempting to advance, determined resistance was encountered from the enemy, who was gradually driven back, during eight hours of hard fighting, closing at night. On the 28th, the conflict was early renewed, continuing with varying success, but with little permanent change of position, through the day. On the following morning, a general assault on the Rebel works was every-where repulsed, with heavy loss. The 30th was mostly spent in burying the dead and transferring the wounded to the transports. The undertaking was now abandoned. The forces of Sherman, reëmbarking, returned to Milliken's Bend, and there went into camp, at the beginning of the new year.

Gen. Burnside, on assuming command of the Army of the Potomac, determined on an advance toward Richmond by way of Fredericksburg, instead of executing another plan of advance preferred (without being ordered) by the President and Gen. Halleck. A force occupied Acquia Creek, and commenced repairing the railroad which had been destroyed by the Rebels. Pontoons were ordered, to be in readiness for a rapid movement, Burnside being nearer than the enemy to Falmouth, where the crossing was to be made, and no considerable force then occupying Fredericksburg. Chiefly through a mortifying dilatoriness on the part of the proper officer at Washington, in forwarding the pontoons, Lee gained time to move his force and to take the position he desired for meeting the intended advance. The principal battle resulting from this movement occurred on the 13th of December, when Burnside's forces endeavored to carry the enemy's strong position on Fredericksburg hights, by assault. After a hard-fought contest, through the day, attended by partial successes—Gen. Meade having temporarily carried a portion of the enemy's works—night found the army still unsuccessful, and suffering heavy losses. The position held in town and across the Rappahannock was retained by Burnside during the next two days, but the morning of the 16th found the whole army safely withdrawn to the Falmouth side, without any loss or interruption in this retrograde movement.

The losses in Gen. Sumner's grand division (the Second and Ninth Corps,) on the right, were 473 killed, 4,090 wounded, 748 missing; in Gen. Hooker's grand division (the Third and Fifth Corps,) in the center, 326 killed, 2,468 wounded, 754 missing; and in Gen. Franklin's grand division (the First and Sixth Corps,) on the left, 339 killed, 2,547 wounded, and 576 missing—a total of 12,321.

The army now went into winter quarters, little being done until Gen. Burnside was relieved, and Gen. Joseph Hooker appointed in his place, assuming command of the Army of the Potomac on the 26th of January. At the same time, Gens. Franklin and Sumner were relieved, being presently assigned to other commands.

Gen. Rosecrans arrived at Nashville on the 10th of November, and proceeded to reorganize the Army of the Cumberland, which was increased by new levies and put in excellent condition, and to restore the railroad communication between Louisville and Nashville. The Rebel army, on the other hand, now under command of Gen. Joseph E. Johnston, was concentrating at Murfreesboro and vicinity, prepared to contest any advance of the Government forces. Supposing, from the information he had, that Rosecrans would go into winter quarters at Nashville, Johnston detached the cavalry force under Forrest, which was to cut the railroad in West Tennessee, in Grant's rear, and another body of cavalry under Morgan to make a raid into Kentucky, to perform a like service in the rear of Rosecrans. Instead of helplessly calling for reënforcements, Rosecrans improved the opportunity afforded by this weakening of Johnston's army, to strike an effective blow. He began to move on the enemy on the 26th of December. McCook, with three divisions, advanced on Triune to attack Hardee, whose corps was believed to be between that place and Eagleville; but it had retreated on McCook's approach, and was pursued until it was found that he had gone to Murfreesboro, where Polk and Kirby Smith's forces were. Thomas and Crittenden also advanced on Nolinsville, Stewart's Creek, and Lavergne. Polk's corps and Wheeler's brigade of cavalry had been stationed at the last-named place, but retired before Crittenden's advance.

On the 28th, being Sunday, the troops, for the most part, rested. Meanwhile, the Rebel purpose of concentrating near Stone River was developed. The enemy's right, under Polk, consisting of the three divisions of Cheatham, Buckner and Breckinridge, rested on the Lebanon pike—the center, under Kirby Smith, extended westward, and the left, commanded by Hardee, rested on the Murfreesboro and Franklin road. On the 29th, the Government forces moved up nearer to the Rebel line, taking position preparatory to assuming the offensive. On the 30th, McCook, on the right, finding his position in danger of being turned by Hardee, advanced his line, under fire from the enemy, to avoid this result. On the 31st, early in the morning, the Rebels suddenly made an attack in heavy force along the entire line of McCook. His forces were driven back with the loss of many prisoners, but the ground was well contested by the division of Davis, especially, and the purpose of turning the right of Rosecrans failed.

The right having thus fallen back, Gen. Rosecrans prepared for an advance of the enemy upon his center and left, by massing his artillery at the anticipated point of assault, and sent forward Negley's division, sustained by that of Rousseau, to support the broken forces of McCook. This movement stopped further pursuit in that quarter. The Rebels were driven back in turn, with the loss of many prisoners. The forces of Negley and Rousseau, acting under orders, retreated on meeting another wave of battle, and the Rebels advanced in dense numbers, exulting in their supposed victory, until brought within the deadly fire of the newly-placed batteries of Rosecrans, not hitherto discovered. Leaving immense numbers of dead and wounded on the field, the Rebel forces now turned and fled in confusion, not to be rallied again until much later in the day. The right of Rosecrans had been forced backward more than two miles, and his line was now formed anew, the flanks having better protection.

The Rebels renewed the engagement, about 3 o'clock P. M., by an attack on the center and left of our army. A sharp and destructive conflict continued for two hours, with no advantage to the assailants. Gen. Rosecrans, who was personally in the thick of the fight, had shown rare skill and energy in handling his troops, after his right had been doubled back upon his left. A change of front was successfully accomplished under fire, and a seemingly sure defeat turned into a substantial victory.

The two armies confronted each other during the next three days, without becoming actively engaged. On the 4th of January, Johnston was found to have retreated, and Murfreesboro was promptly occupied by our forces. The Government loss, in killed and wounded, was 8,778, and about 2,800 in prisoners. The Rebel loss is computed by Gen. Rosecrans at 14,560.

This summary of military events, in the East and in the West, embraces what is deemed most important down to the eve of the campaigns of 1863, rendered illustrious by the great victories at Vicksburg, Port Hudson, Gettysburg, and Chattanooga. The first two years of the war, with varying successes in detail, had resulted, on the whole, in decided advantages to the Government arms. Commencing their "Confederacy" with seven States, the conspirators had determined, by intrigue and by the force of arms, to wrest the remaining eight slaveholding States the Indian Territory, New Mexico, and Arizona, from their allegiance to the Government, and to add this immense region, with its population, to the side of the Davis usurpation. The vigorous campaign of Gen. Canby, in New Mexico, and the victory at Fort Craig, in 1862, hurled back the invaders in that quarter into Texas, while the grand Rebel defeat at Pea

Ridge, Ark., under Gen. Curtis, in March of the same year, had put an end to all hopes of any Rebel acquisition in the Territories of the United States. The four slave States of Virginia, North Carolina, Tennessee, and Arkansas, had been swept into the Secession rebellion at the very outset. All the determined efforts to extend the Rebel boundary beyond these States, had proved abortive. On the contrary, the spring of 1863 found Arkansas substantially reclaimed; New Orleans and a large portion of Louisiana, (including the State capital,) restored to the Government; the Mississippi river reconquered during its entire length, except the comparatively short distance from Vicksburg to Port Hudson, inclusive; the capital of Tennessee, and most of the western and middle parts of the State, occupied by Government garrisons; the western half of Virginia reorganized under a loyal government, and much of Eastern Virginia firmly held; a permanent foothold gained on the coasts of North Carolina, South Carolina, and Florida; Northern Alabama returning to sentiments of loyalty, under the supporting presence of Government troops; a blockade, under the active operations of our formidable Navy, pressing heavily upon the rebellious States; and the power of slavery materially crippled, under the effects of the Emancipation Proclamation of the President, deranging the productive interests of the rebellion, and adding a new element of increasing strength to our arms.

To save their waning cause, the Rebels were now putting forth every energy to hold their trans-Mississippi communications, the Red river country and Texas being among their most abundant sources of supplies. To this end, it was necessary to keep their strongholds at Vicksburg and Port Hudson. A land force under Gen. Banks (who had succeeded Gen. Butler as commander of the Department of the Gulf,) and the fleet of Admiral Farragut, began the work of reducing the latter post, on the 8th of May. After severe engagements on land and water, during the next two months, the place being closely invested, Port Hudson was unconditionally surrendered on the 8th of July, with its garrison, numbering 6,223. This event, however, was preceded by the fall of Vicksburg, and may be regarded as partly the result of the brief and brilliant campaign of Gen. Grant, which terminated in the surrender of that more important stronghold, on the 4th of July.

Running transports past the batteries at Vicksburg, and crossing the river near the mouth of the Big Black, on the 30th of April, with about 40,000 men, Gen. Grant occupied Grand Gulf, which had been forced by Admiral Porter to surrender, after a vigorous bombardment; defeated the enemy near Port Gibson, on the 1st of May; moved rapidly northward to interpose his force between the covering army of Johnston and the troops of Pemberton, advancing from Vicksburg; gained decisive victories at Raymond, on the 12th; at Jackson, the State capital, on the 14th; at Baker's Creek, and at Champion Hill, on the 16th, and at Black River Bridge, on the 17th; finally driving the enemy within his works at Vicksburg. The fact that Johnston was in his rear, with the prospect of his being heavily reënforced, led Grant to make two attempts to carry the place by storm, on the 19th and on the 22d, but without success. The siege lasted until the 4th of July, when Pemberton capitulated, and Grant occupied the place, taking over 30,000 prisoners. This great victory opened the Mississippi to the Gulf, cutting off the territory west of that river from its connection with the remainder of the "Confederacy"—a practical loss of nearly one-half of the Rebel territory.

In Eastern Virginia, Hooker fought Lee at Chancellorsville, on the 2d and 3d of May, and was repulsed, with heavy losses on both sides, retiring across the Rappahannock. Among the Rebel losses was that of Stonewall Jackson, mortally wounded. Lee now assumed the offensive, advancing through Maryland into Pennsylvania. Gen. Hooker, moving on an interior line, covered Washington and kept his forces in an attitude to strike the enemy with effect. During these movements, Hooker was superseded, on the 28th of June, by Gen. George G. Meade. The battle of Gettysburg was fought on the 1st, 2d and 3d days of July, in which an important victory was gained over Lee, who retreated in all possible haste over the Potomac, glad to escape with the remnant of his army. He had lost heavily, in killed, wounded and prisoners, the latter numbering 13,621.

29 38

He left 28,178 small arms on the field. His entire loss dur.ng this invasion, including numerous desertions, must have approached, if it did not equal, 40,000 men. Meade's total losses, in killed, wounded and missing, numbered 23,186.

The operations before Charleston and other points, attended wit ı less success than was for a time promised, were not without favorable results.

Another disaster to the Rebel cause, and one of the greatest magnitude, followed the advance of Gen. Rosecrans on Chattanooga, and of Gen. Burnside upon Knoxville, in the latter part of August. With no very severe fighting, Burnside occupied Knoxville on the 1st of September, and Cumberland Gap on the 9th. Rosecrans, after the unfavorable battle of Chickamauga, took possession of Chattanooga, on the 21st of September. East Tennessee was thus completely in our possession, and a line of communication of the greatest importance to the enemy was finally severed. On the 19th of October, Gen. Grant, by the President's order, assumed command of the united armies of the Tennessee, the Cumberland, and the Ohio. The subsequent victories of Lookout Mountain and Missionary Ridge, on the 24th and 25th of November, and the decisive defeat of Longstreet in his bold attempt to recover Knoxville, made this great acquisition entirely secure. The way was thus prepared for assuming the offensive, by an advance into the heart of Georgia.

The rebellion seemed now to have been brought to the verge of final overthrow.

CHAPTER XI.

The Popular Voice in 1863.—First Session of the Thirty-eighth Congress.—Amnesty Proclamation.—Message.—Orders, Letters and Addresses.—Popular Sentiment in 1864.—Appointment of Lieutenant General Grant.—Opening of the Military Campaigns of 1864.—Conclusion.

THE great popular reaction in favor of the Administration of Mr. Lincoln, indicated by the spring elections, was fully apparent in the verdict of every loyal State i: the autumn of 1863. In Ohio, the so-called Democratic organization, which had prevailed in that State by a small majority in October, 1862, put forward, as its candidate for Governor, a notorious Peace Democrat named Vallandigham, whose action, while a member of the previous Congress, had been in strict conformity with his avowed motto: "Not a man or a dollar for the war." To such an extent was his support of the rebellion carried, by haranguing his followers, and all who would hear him, against the Government and the measures it had adopted in the prosecution of the war, that he had been arrested by Gen. Burnside, then in command of the Department including Ohio, tried for his treasonable practices, convicted, and ordered to be sent through the lines of our army to his friends at the South. The proceedings under which he was thus condemned, were fully reviewed before the United States District Court at Cincinnati, on a motion for a writ of *habeas corpus*, and sustained by the decision of Judge Leavitt. It may be added that this action was further confirmed, several months later, on a hearing before the Supreme Court of the United States. Hon. John Brough, the Administration candidate, was chosen Governor of Ohio, after a protracted and earnest canvass, by more than 100,000 majority over Vallandigham.

In Pennsylvania, the Republican candidate for Governor, Hon. Andrew G. Curtin, was reëlected by a large majority over

Judge Woodward, another Peace Democrat. In New York, where the most violent opposition was made to "conscription," resulting in a barbarous riot in New York city, the Administration ticket for sundry State officers had a very large majority over the candidates of the Seymour and Wood Democracy. Notwithstanding the utmost efforts of the Opposition, and the fact that hundreds of thousands of soldiers had been lately called into the field, every other loyal State, except New Jersey, (in which there were Administration gains,) gave similarly decided majorities for the supporters of Mr. Lincoln.

During the earlier, as well as the later, elections of this year, a prominent issue before the people was the course of the Administration in regard to Emancipation. Both at home and abroad, this policy had proved an element of great strength in shaping public opinion favorably to Mr. Lincoln. It identified his Administration, from the day this great step was taken, with not only a most effective means for suppressing the rebellion, but also with a measure in accordance with the high behests of justice, and the clearest interests of civilization and humanity. At the beginning of the year, the President received a gratifying testimonial of sympathy and confidence from the workingmen of Manchester, in England, and of their warm appreciation, especially, of his action in issuing the Proclamation of Emancipation. To this address, Mr. Lincoln sent the following reply:

EXECUTIVE MANSION, }
WASHINGTON, January 19, 1863. }

TO THE WORKINGMEN OF MANCHESTER : I have the honor to acknowledge the receipt of the address and resolutions which you sent me on the eve of the new year.

When I came, on the 4th of March, 1861, through a free and constitutional election, to preside in the Government of the United States, the country was found at the verge of civil war. Whatever might have been the cause, or whosesoever the fault, one duty, paramount to all others, was before me, namely, to maintain and preserve at once the Constitution and the integrity of the Federal Republic. A conscientious purpose to perform this duty is the key to all the measures of administration which have been, and to all which will hereafter be pursued. Under our frame of government and my official oath, I could not depart from this purpose if I would. It is not always in the power of governments to enlarge or restrict the scope of moral results which follow the policies that they may deem it necessary, for the public safety, from time to time to adopt.

I have understood well that the duty of self-preservation rests solely with the American people. But I have, at the same time, been aware that the favor or disfavor of foreign nations might have a material influence in enlarging and prolonging the struggle with disloyal men in which the country is engaged. A fair examination of history has seemed to authorize a belief that the past action and influences of the United States were generally regarded as having been beneficial toward mankind. I have, therefore, reckoned upon the forbearance of nations. Circumstances—to some of which you kindly allude—induced me especially to expect that, if justice and good faith should be practiced by the United States, they would encounter no hostile influence on the part of Great Britain. It is now a pleasant duty to acknowledge the demonstration you have given of your desire that a spirit of peace and amity toward this country may prevail in the councils of your Queen, who is respected and esteemed in your own country only more than she is by the kindred nation which has its home on this side of the Atlantic.

I know, and deeply deplore, the sufferings which the workingmen at Manchester, and in all Europe, are called to endure in this crisis. It has been often and studiously represented that the attempt to overthrow this Government, which was built upon the foundation of human rights, and to substitute for it one which should rest exclusively on the basis of human slavery, was likely to obtain the favor of Europe. Through the action of our disloyal citizens, the workingmen of Europe have been subjected to severe trial, for the purpose of forcing their sanction to that attempt. Under these circumstances, I can not but regard your decisive utterances upon the question as an instance of sublime Christian heroism, which has not been surpassed in any age or in any country. It is indeed an energetic and reinspiring assurance of the inherent power of truth, and of the ultimate and universal triumph of justice, humanity, and freedom. I do not doubt that the sentiments you have expressed will be sustained by your great nation; and, on the other hand, I have no hesitation in assuring you that they will excite admiration, esteem, and the most reciprocal feelings of friendship among the American people. I hail this interchange of sentiment, therefore, as an augury that, whatever else may happen, whatever misfortune may befall your country or my own, the peace and friendship which now exist between the two nations will be, as it shall be my desire to make them, perpetual.   ABRAHAM LINCOLN.

Later in the season, Mr. Lincoln was invited to revisit his home in Springfield, on the occasion of a mass meeting of the people of Illinois, who were unconditionally for the Union, to be held at that place. The letter addressed by him, in reply, to the chairman of the Committee of Invitation, an esteemed personal friend, was published at the time, and received with satisfaction by the loyal people of the country. The subject of Emancipation is again treated therein, after discussing the possible terms of peace, and the issue brought directly home to the minds of the people, with pointed force and sunlike clearness. The letter is in these words:

EXECUTIVE MANSION, WASHINGTON, ⎰
August 26, 1863. ⎱

MY DEAR SIR: Your letter inviting me to attend a mass meeting of unconditional Union men, to be held at the capital of Illinois on the 3d day of September, has been received. It would be very agreeable to me thus to meet my old friends at my own home; but I can not just now be absent from this city so long as a visit there would require.

The meeting is to be of all those who maintain uncondi-tional devotion to the Union; and I am sure that my old politi-cal friends will thank me for tendering, as I do, the nation's gratitude to those other noble men whom no partisan malice or partisan hope can make false to the nation's life. There are those who are dissatisfied with me. To such I would say: You desire peace, and you blame me that we do not have it. But how can we attain it? There are but three conceivable ways: First, to suppress the rebellion by force of arms. This I am trying to do. Are you for it? If you are, so far we are agreed. If you are not for it, a second way is to give up the Union. I am against this. If you are, you should say so, plainly. If you are not for force, nor yet for dissolution, there only remains some imaginable compromise.

I do not believe that any compromise embracing the mainte-nance of the Union is now possible. All that I learn leads to a directly opposite belief. The strength of the rebellion is its military—its army. That army dominates all the country and all the people within its range. Any offer of any terms made by any man or men within that range in opposition to that army, is simply nothing for the present, because such man or men have no power whatever to enforce their side of a compromise, if one were made with them. To illustrate: Suppose refugees from the South and peace men of the North get together in convention, and frame and proclaim a compromise embracing the restoration of the Union. In what way can that compromise be used to keep Gen. Lee's army out of Pennsylvania? Gen. Meade's army can keep Lee's army out of Pennsylvania, and I think can ultimately drive it out of existence. But no paper compromise to which the controllers of Gen. Lee's army are not agreed, can at all affect that army. In an effort at such compromise we would waste time, which the enemy would improve to our disadvantage, and that would be all. A compromise, to be effective, must be made either with those who control the Rebel army, or with the people, first liberated from the domination of that army by the success of our army. Now, allow me to assure you that no word or intimation from the Rebel army, or from any of the men controlling it, in relation to any peace compromise, has ever come to my knowledge or belief. All charges and intimations to the contrary are deceptive and groundless. And I promise you that if any such proposition shall hereafter come, it shall not be rejected and kept secret from you. I freely acknowledge myself to be the servant of the people, according to the bond of service, the United States Constitution; and that, as such, I am responsible to them.

But, to be plain. You are dissatisfied with me about the negro. Quite likely there is a difference of opinion between you and myself upon that subject. I certainly wish that all men could be free, while you, I suppose, do not. Yet I have neither adopted nor proposed any measure which is not consistent with even your view, provided you are for the Union. I suggested compensated emancipation, to which you replied that you wished not to be taxed to buy negroes. But I have not asked you to be taxed to buy negroes, except in such way as to save you from greater taxation, to save the Union exclusively by other means.

You dislike the Emancipation Proclamation, and perhaps would have it retracted. You say it is unconstitutional. I think differently. I think that the Constitution invests its Commander-in-chief with the law of war in the time of war. The most that can be said, if so much, is, that the slaves are property. Is there, has there ever been, any question that by the law of war, property, both of enemies and friends, may be taken when needed? And is it not needed whenever taking it helps us or hurts the enemy? Armies, the world over, destroy enemies' property when they can not use it; and even destroy their own to keep it from the enemy. Civilized belligerents do all in their power to help themselves or hurt the enemy, except a few things regarded as barbarous or cruel. Among the exceptions are the massacre of vanquished foes and non-combatants, male and female. But the proclamation, as law, is valid or is not valid. If it is not valid, it needs no retraction. If it is valid, it can not be retracted, any more than the dead can be brought to life. Some of you profess to think that its retraction would operate favorably for the Union. Why better after the retraction than before the issue? There was more than a year and a half of trial to suppress the rebellion before the proclamation was issued, the last one hundred days of which passed under an explicit notice, that it was coming unless averted by those in revolt returning to their allegiance. The war has certainly progressed as favorably for us since the issue of the proclamation as before. I know as fully as one can know the opinions of others, that some of the commanders of our armies in the field, who have given us our most important victories, believe the emancipation policy and the aid of colored troops constitute the heaviest blows yet dealt to the rebellion, and that at least one of those important successes could not have been achieved when it was but for the aid of black soldiers. Among the commanders holding these views are some who have never had any affinity with what is called abolitionism, or with "republican party politics," but who hold them purely as military opinions. I submit their opinions as being entitled to some weight against the objections often urged that emancipation and arming the blacks are unwise as military measures, and were not adopted as such in good faith.

You say that you will not fight to free negroes. Some of them seem to be willing to fight for you—but no matter. Fight you, then, exclusively to save the Union. I issued the proclamation on purpose to aid you in saving the Union. Whenever you shall have conquered all resistance to the Union, if I shall urge you to continue fighting, it will be an apt time then for you to declare that you will not fight to free negroes. I thought that, in your struggle for the Union, to whatever extent the negroes should cease helping the enemy, to that extent it weakened the enemy in his resistance to you. Do you think differently? I thought that whatever negroes can be got to do as soldiers, leaves just so much less for white soldiers to do in saving the Union. Does it appear otherwise to you? But negroes, like other people, act upon motives. Why should they do any thing for us if we will do nothing for them? If they stake their lives for us, they must be prompted by the strongest motive, even the promise of freedom. And the promise, being made, must be kept.

The signs look better. The Father of Waters again goes unvexed to the sea. Thanks to the great North-west for it. Nor yet wholly to them. Three hundred miles up they met New England, Empire, Keystone, and Jersey, hewing their way right and left. The sunny South, too, in more colors than one, also lent a hand. On the spot their part of the history was jotted down in black and white. The job was a great National one, and let none be banned who bore an honorable part in it; and, while those who have cleared the great river may well be proud, even that is not all. It is hard to say that any thing has been more bravely and better done than at Antietam, Murfreesboro, Gettysburg, and on many fields of less note. Nor must Uncle Sam's web-feet be forgotten. At all the waters' margins they have been present: not only on the deep sea, the broad bay and the rapid river, but also up the narrow, muddy bayou; and wherever the ground was a little damp, they have been and made their tracks. Thanks to all. For the great Republic—for the principles by which it lives and keeps alive—for man's vast future—thanks to all. Peace does not appear so far distant as it did. I hope it will come soon, and come to stay: and so come as to be worth the keeping in all future time. It will then have been proved that among freemen there can be no successful appeal from the ballot to the bullet, and that they who take such appeal are sure to lose their case and pay the cost. And then there will be some black men who can remember that, with silent tongue, and clenched teeth, and steady eye, and well poised bayonet, they have helped mankind on to this great consummation; while I fear that there will be some white men unable to forget that, with malignant heart and deceitful speech, they have striven to hinder it.

Still, let us not be over-sanguine of a speedy final triumph. Let us be quite sober. Let us diligently apply the means, never doubting that a just God, in His own good time, will give us the rightful result.

Yours, very truly,   A. Lincoln.

James C. Conkling, Esq.

Mr. Lincoln, whose gratitude to the gallant soldiers who have rallied at the call of their country, and whose proud satisfaction in their heroic conduct on so many battle-fields, have been constantly manifested, was unwilling to decline the invitation to be present on the solemn occasion of consecrating

39

a National Cemetery at Gettysburg, for the fallen in the san-guinary conflicts at that place, in July, 1863. No truer or tenderer sympathy than his, for the brave dead and for their surviving friends, ever had place in any human breast. The elaborate eloquence of our most accomplished orator, Edward Everett, and the presence of an innumerable multitude of people, added a solemn grandeur to the ceremonies of the day. But no fitter or more touching words were spoken than these of Mr. Lincoln:

ADDRESS AT GETTYSBURG, NOV. 19, 1863.

Fourscore and seven years ago our fathers brought forth upon this continent a new nation, conceived in Liberty, and dedicated to the proposition that all men are created equal. Now we are engaged in a great civil war, testing whether that nation, or any nation so conceived and so dedicated, can long endure. We are met on a great battle-field of that war. We are met to dedicate a portion of it as the final resting-place of those who here gave their lives that that nation might live. It is altogether fitting and proper that we should do this.

But, in a larger sense, we can not dedicate, we can not consecrate, we can not hallow this ground. The brave men, living and dead, who struggled here, have consecrated it far above our power to add or detract. The world will little note, nor long remember, what we say here, but it can never forget what they did here. It is for us, the living, rather, to be dedicated here to the unfinished work that they have thus far so nobly carried on. It is rather for us to be here dedicated to the great task remaining before us—that from these honored dead we take increased devotion to the cause for which they here gave the last full measure of devotion—that we here highly resolve that the dead shall not have died in vain—that the nation shall, under God, have a new birth of freedom, and that the Government of the people, by the people, and for the people, shall not perish from the earth.

The concluding elections for the Thirty-eighth Congress bitterly disappointed the expectations previously entertained by the Opposition. They were so favorable to the Administration as to insure it a decided majority in the House of Representatives—a result which had not happened for many years in the choice of the second Congress during any Presidential term.

On the assembling of the Thirty-eighth Congress, on the 7th

day of December, 1863, the Hon. Schuyler Colfax, of Indiana, (the Administration candidate,) was elected Speaker of the House of Representatives, on the first ballot, receiving one hundred and one votes, against eighty-one for all others—a majority of twenty. The Opposition votes were scattered upon half a dozen different candidates. The Hon. Edward McPherson, of Pennsylvania, was chosen Clerk of the House, by a vote of one hundred and two to sixty-nine for Emerson Etheridge, whom the Republicans had chosen to that position in the previous House, and who had since gone over to the Democratic side. A still more striking indication of the present tone of National sentiment was perhaps to be found in the fact that the Rev. William Henry Channing, whose extreme views on the great questions of the day are well known, was elected Chaplain of the House, the principal Opposition vote being cast for Bishop Hopkins, of Vermont, a noted apologist for slavery.

After the decisive advantages gained by our arms, the rebellion being substantially at an end in the States of Louisiana, Tennessee and Arkansas, and movements for their reorganization under loyal local governments already under consideration by the people of those States, some indication of the President's policy for restoring order and law, in the territory reconquered from armed Rebels, was naturally expected by the people. Mr. Lincoln, as the meeting of Congress approached, had given his earnest attention to this difficult subject—now become one of the highest practical moment. By an act approved July 17, 1862, Congress had provided :

That the President is hereby authorized, at any time hereafter, by proclamation, to extend to persons who may have participated in the existing rebellion in any State or part thereof, pardon and amnesty, with such exceptions, and at such time, and on such conditions, as he may deem expedient for the public welfare.

In the judgment of Mr. Lincoln, the fitting time had now come for exercising this power. Among the "conditions" which he was authorized to prescribe, very clearly, good faith and consistency required him to include an effective one for carrying out his policy of Emancipation. This and other considerations also made it indispensable that he should indicate—without inflexibly prescribing, as he did not—an acceptable mode of reorganizing loyal State Governments. The result of his deliberations was set forth simultaneously with the publication of his annual message, in the celebrated paper following :

A PROCLAMATION.

WHEREAS, In and by the Constitution of the United States it is provided that the President " shall have power to grant reprieves and pardons for offenses against the United States, except in cases of impeachment;" and whereas, a rebellion now exists whereby the loyal State Governments of several States have for a long time been subverted, and many persons have committed and are now guilty of treason against the United States; and whereas, with reference to said rebellion and treason, laws have been enacted by Congress declaring forfeitures and confiscation of property and liberation of slaves, all upon terms and conditions therein stated ; and also declaring that the President was thereby authorized at any time thereafter, by proclamation, to extend to persons who may have participated in the existing rebellion, in any State or part thereof, pardon and amnesty, with such exceptions and at such times and on such conditions as he may deem expedient for the public welfare ; and whereas, the Congressional declaration for limited and conditional pardon accords with well-established judicial exposition of the pardoning power ; and whereas, with reference to said rebellion, the President of the United States has issued several proclamations, with provisions in regard to the liberation of slaves ; and whereas, it is now desired by some persons heretofore engaged in said rebellion, to resume their allegiance to the United States, and to reinaugurate loyal State Governments within and for their respective States ; therefore,

I, Abraham Lincoln, President of the United States, do proclaim, declare, and make known to all persons who have, directly or by implication, participated in the existing rebellion, except as hereinafter excepted, that a full pardon is hereby granted to them and each of them, with restoration of all rights of property, except as to slaves, and in property cases where rights of third parties shall have intervened, and upon the condition that every such person shall take and subscribe an oath, and thenceforward keep and maintain said oath inviolate; and which oath shall be registered for permanent preservation, and shall be of the tenor and effect following, to-wit:

" I, —— ——, do solemnly swear, in presence of Almighty

God, that I will henceforth faithfully support, protect and defend the Constitution of the United States, and the Union of the States thereunder; and that I will, in like manner, abide by and faithfully support all acts of Congress passed during the existing rebellion with reference to slaves, so long and so far as not repealed, modified, or held void by Congress, or by decision of the Supreme Court; and that I will, in like manner, abide by and faithfully support all proclamations of the President made during the existing rebellion having reference to slaves, so long and so far as not modified or declared void by decision of the Supreme Court. So help me God."

The persons excepted from the benefits of the foregoing provisions are all who are, or shall have been, civil or diplomatic officers or agents of the so-called Confederate Government; all who have left judicial stations under the United States to aid the rebellion; all who are, or shall have been, military or naval officers of the said so-called Confederate Government, above the rank of colonel in the army, or of lieutenant in the navy; all who left seats in the United States Congress to aid the rebellion; all who resigned commissions in the Army or Navy of the United States, and afterward aided the rebellion; and all who have engaged in any way in treating colored persons, or white persons in charge of such, otherwise than lawfully as prisoners of war, and which persons may have been found in the United States service as soldiers, seamen, or in any other capacity.

And I do further proclaim, declare, and make known, that whenever, in any of the States of Arkansas, Texas, Louisiana, Mississippi, Tennessee, Alabama, Georgia, Florida, South Carolina, and North Carolina, a number of persons, not less than one-tenth in number of the votes cast in such State at the Presidential election of the year of our Lord 1860, each having taken the oath aforesaid, and not having since violated it, and being a qualified voter by the election law of the State existing immediately before the so-called act of secession, and excluding all others, shall re-establish a State Government which shall be republican, and in nowise contravening said oath, such shall be recognized as the true Government of the State, and the State shall receive thereunder the benefits of the constitutional provision which declares that "the United States shall guarantee to every State in this Union a republican form of government, and shall protect each of them against invasion; and on application of the Legislature, or the Executive, (when the Legislature can not be convened,) against domestic violence."

And I do further proclaim, declare, and make known that

any provision which may be adopted by such State Government in relation to the freed people of such State, which shall recognize and declare their permanent freedom, provide for their education, and which may yet be consistent, as a temporary arrangement, with their present condition as a laboring, landless, and homeless class, will not be objected to by the National Executive. And it is suggested as not improper, that in constructing a loyal State Government in any State, the name of the State, the boundary, the subdivisions, the Constitution, and the general code of laws, as before the rebellion, be maintained, subject only to the modifications made necessary by the conditions hereinbefore stated, and such others, if any, not contravening said conditions, and which may be deemed expedient by those framing the new State Government.

To avoid misunderstanding, it may be proper to say that this proclamation, so far as it relates to State Governments, has no reference to States wherein loyal State Governments have all the while been maintained. And for the same reason, it may be proper to further say that whether members sent to Congress from any State shall be admitted to seats constitutionally, rests exclusively with the respective Houses, and not to any extent with the Executive. And still further, that this proclamation is intended to present the people of the States wherein the National authority has been suspended, and loyal State Governments have been subverted, a mode in and by which the National authority and loyal State Governments may be re-established within said States, or in any of them; and, while the mode presented is the best the Executive can suggest, with his present impressions, it must not be understood that no other possible mode would be acceptable.

Given under my hand at the city of Washington, the 8th day of December, A. D. 1863, and of the Independence of the United States of America the eighty-eighth.   ABRAHAM LINCOLN.

[L. S.]

Mr. Lincoln's Annual Message was sent in to Congress on the 9th day of December. This document — omitting only portions of less abiding interest—is as follows:

MR. LINCOLN'S ANNUAL MESSAGE.

FELLOW-CITIZENS OF THE SENATE AND HOUSE OF REPRESENTATIVES: Another year of health and sufficiently abundant harvests, has passed. For these, and especially for the improved condition of our National affairs, our renewed and profoundest gratitude to God is due.

We remain in peace and friendship with foreign powers.

The efforts of disloyal citizens of the United States to involve us in foreign wars, to aid an inexcusable insurrection, have been unavailing. Her Britannic Majesty's Government, as was justly expected, have exercised their authority to prevent the departure of new hostile expeditions from British ports. The Emperor of France has, by a like proceeding, promptly vindicated the neutrality which he proclaimed at the beginning of the contest. Questions of great intricacy and importance have arisen, out of the blockade and other belligerent operations, between the Government and several of the maritime powers, but they have been discussed, and, as far as was possible, accommodated in a spirit of frankness, justice, and mutual good will. It is especially gratifying that our prize courts, by the impartiality of their adjudications, have commanded the respect and confidence of maritime powers.

The supplemental treaty between the United States and Great Britain for the suppression of the African slave-trade, made on the 17th day of February last, has been duly ratified, and carried into execution. It is believed that, so far as American ports and American citizens are concerned, that inhuman and odious traffic has been brought to an end. . . .

Incidents occurring in the progress of our civil war have forced upon my attention the uncertain state of international questions touching the rights of foreigners in this country and of United States citizens abroad. In regard to some Governments, these rights are at least partially defined by treaties. In no instance, however, is it expressly stipulated that, in the event of civil war, a foreigner residing in this country, within the lines of the insurgents, is to be exempted from the rule which classes him as a belligerent, in whose behalf the Government of his country can not expect any privileges or immunities distinct from that character. I regret to say, however, that such claims have been put forward, and, in some instances, in behalf of foreigners who have lived in the United States the greater part of their lives.

There is reason to believe that many persons born in foreign countries, who have declared their intention to become citizens, or who have been fully naturalized, have evaded the military duty required of them by denying the fact, and thereby throwing upon the Government the burden of proof. It has been found difficult or impracticable to obtain this proof, from the want of guides to the proper sources of information. These might be supplied by requiring clerks of courts, where declarations of intention may be made or naturalizations effected, to send, periodically, lists of the names of the persons naturalized.

or declaring their intention to become citizens, to the Secretary of the Interior, in whose Department those names might be arranged and printed for general information.

There is also reason to believe that foreigners frequently become citizens of the United States for the sole purpose of evading duties imposed by the laws of their native countries, to which, on becoming naturalized here, they at once repair, and, though never returning to the United States, they still claim the interposition of this Government as citizens. Many altercations and great prejudices have heretofore arisen out of this abuse. It is, therefore, submitted to your serious consideration. It might be advisable to fix a limit, beyond which no citizen of the United States residing abroad may claim the interposition of his Government.

The right of suffrage has often been assumed and exercised by aliens, under pretenses of naturalization, which they have disavowed when drafted into the military service. .I submit the expediency of such an amendment of the law as will make the fact of voting an estoppel against any plea of exemption from military service, or other civil obligation, on the ground of alienage. . . . . .

The condition of the several organized Territories is generally satisfactory, although Indian disturbances in New Mexico have not been entirely suppressed. The mineral resources of Colorado, Nevada, Idaho, New Mexico, and Arizona are proving far richer than has been heretofore understood. I lay before you a communication on this subject from the Governor of New Mexico. I again submit to your consideration the expediency of establishing a system for the encouragement of immigration. Although this source of National wealth and strength is again flowing with greater freedom than for several years before the insurrection occurred, there is still a great deficiency of laborers in every field of industry, especially in agriculture and in our mines, as well of iron and coal as of the precious metals. While the demand for labor is thus increased here, tens of thousands of persons, destitute of remunerative occupation, are thronging our foreign consulates, and offering to emigrate to the United States if essential, but very cheap, assistance can be afforded them. It is easy to see that, under the sharp discipline of civil war, the nation is beginning a new life. This noble effort demands the aid, and ought to receive the attention and support, of the Government.

Injuries, unforeseen by the Government and unintended, may, in some cases, have been inflicted on the subjects or citizens of foreign countries, both at sea and on land, by persons in the service of the United States. As this Government expects redress from other Powers when similar injuries are inflicted by persons in their service upon citizens of the United States, we must be prepared to do justice to foreigners. If the existing judicial tribunals are inadequate to this purpose, a special court may be authorized, with power to hear and decide such claims of the character referred to as may have arisen under treaties and the public law. Conventions for adjusting the claims by joint commission have been proposed to some Governments, but no definite answer to the proposition has yet been received from any.

In the course of the session, I shall probably have occasion to request you to provide indemnification to claimants where decrees of restitution have been rendered and damages awarded by admiralty courts, and in other cases, where this Government may be acknowledged to be liable in principle, and where the amount of that liability has been ascertained by an informal arbitration.

The proper officers of the Treasury have deemed themselves required, by the law of the United States upon the subject, to demand a tax upon the incomes of foreign consuls in this country. While such demand may not, in strictness, be in derogation of public law, or perhaps of any existing treaty between the United States and a foreign country, the expediency of so far modifying the act as to exempt from tax the income of such consuls as are not citizens of the United States, derived from the emoluments of their office, or from property not situated in the United States, is submitted to your serious consideration. I make this suggestion upon the ground that a comity which ought to be reciprocated exempts our consuls, in all other countries, from taxation to the extent thus indicated. The United States, I think, ought not to be exceptionably illiberal to international trade and commerce.

The operations of the Treasury during the last year have been successfully conducted. The enactment by Congress of a National Banking Law has proved a valuable support of the public credit; and the general legislation in relation to loans has fully answered the expectations of its favorers. Some amendments may be required to perfect existing laws; but no change in their principles or general scope is believed to be needed.

Since these measures have been in operation, all demands on the Treasury, including the pay of the Army and Navy, have been promptly met and fully satisfied. No considerable body of troops, it is believed, were ever more amply provided, and more liberally and punctually paid; and it may be added that by no people were the burdens incident to a great war ever more cheerfully borne.

The receipts during the year from all sources, including loans and the balance in the Treasury at its commencement, were $901,125,674 86, and the aggregate disbursements, $895,796,630 65, leaving a balance on the 1st of July, 1863, of $5,329,044 21. Of the receipts there were derived from customs $69,059,642 40; from internal revenue, $37,640,787 95; from direct tax, $1,485,103 61; from lands, $167,617 17; from miscellaneous sources, $3,046,615 35; and from loans, $776,682,361 57; making the aggregate, $901,125,674 86. Of the disbursements, there were, for the civil service, $23,253,922 08; for pensions and Indians, $4,216,520 79; for interest on public debt, $24,729,846 51; for the War Department, $599,298,600 83; for the Navy Department, $63,211,105 27; for payment of funded and temporary debt, $181,086,635 07; making the aggregate, $895,796,630 65; and leaving the balance of $5,329,044 21. But the payment of funded and temporary debt, having been made from moneys borrowed during the year, must be regarded as merely nominal payments, and the moneys borrowed to make them as merely nominal receipts; and their amount, $181,086,635 07, should therefore be deducted both from receipts and disbursements. This being done, there remain, as actual receipts, $720,039,039 79; and the actual disbursements, $714,709,995 58, leaving the balance as already stated.

The actual receipts and disbursements for the first quarter, and the estimated receipts and disbursements for the remaining three quarters, of the current fiscal year 1864, will be shown in detail by the report of the Secretary of the Treasury, to which I invite your attention. It is sufficient to say here that it is not believed that actual results will exhibit a state of the finances less favorable to the country than the estimates of that officer heretofore submitted; while it is confidently expected that at the close of the year both disbursements and debt will be found very considerably less than has been anticipated.

The report of the Secretary of War is a document of great interest. It consists of—

1. The military operations of the year, detailed in the report of the General-in-Chief.

2. The organization of colored persons into the war service.

3. The exchange of prisoners, fully set forth in the letter of General Hitchcock.

4. The operations under the act for enrolling and calling out

the National forces, detailed in the report of the Provost Marshal General.

5. The organization of the invalid corps; and

6. The operation of the several departments of the Quartermaster General, Commissary General, Paymaster General, Chief of Engineers, Chief of Ordnance, and Surgeon General.

It has appeared impossible to make a valuable summary of this report, except such as would be too extended for this place, and hence I content myself by asking your careful attention to the report itself.

The duties devolving on the naval branch of the service during the year, and throughout the whole of this unhappy contest, have been discharged with fidelity and eminent success. The extensive blockade has been constantly increasing in efficiency, and the Navy has expanded; yet on so long a line it has so far been impossible to entirely suppress illicit trade. From returns received at the Navy Department, it appears that more than one thousand vessels have been captured since the blockade was instituted, and that the value of prizes already sent in for adjudication, amounts to over thirteen million dollars.

The naval force of the United States consists, at this time, of five hundred and eighty-eight vessels, completed and in the course of completion, and of these seventy-five are iron-clad or armored steamers. The events of the war give an increased interest and importance to the Navy, which will probably extend beyond the war itself.

The armored vessels in our Navy, completed and in service, or which are under contract and approaching completion, are believed to exceed in number those of any other Power. But while these may be relied upon for harbor defense and coast service, others, of greater strength and capacity, will be necessary for cruising purposes, and to maintain our rightful position on the ocean.

The change that has taken place in naval vessels and naval warfare since the introduction of steam as a motive power for ships-of-war, demands either a corresponding change in some of our existing navy-yards, or the establishment of new ones, for the construction and necessary repair of modern naval vessels. No inconsiderable embarrassment, delay, and public injury have been experienced from the want of such Governmental establishments. The necessity of such a navy-yard, so furnished, at some suitable place upon the Atlantic seaboard, has, on repeated occasions, been brought to the attention of Congress by the Navy Department, and is again presented in the report of the Secretary which accompanies this communication.

I think it my duty to invite your special attention to this subject, and also to that of establishing a yard and depot for naval purposes upon one of the Western rivers. A naval force has been created on those interior waters, and under many disadvantages, within little more than two years, exceeding in numbers the whole naval force of the country at the commencement of the present Administration. Satisfactory and important as have been the performances of the heroic men of the Navy at this interesting period, they are scarcely more wonderful than the success of our mechanics and artisans in the production of war vessels, which has created a new form of naval power.

Our country has advantages superior to any other nation in our resources of iron and timber, with inexhaustible quantities of fuel in the immediate vicinity of both, and all available and in close proximity to navigable waters. Without the advantage of public works, the resources of the nation have been developed, and its power displayed, in the construction of a navy of such magnitude, which has, at the very period of its creation, rendered signal service to the Union.

The increase of the number of seamen in the public service, from seven thousand five hundred men in the spring of 1861, to about thirty-four thousand at the present time, has been accomplished without special legislation or extraordinary bounties to promote that increase. It has been found, however, that the operation of the draft, with the high bounties paid for army recruits, is beginning to affect injuriously the naval service, and will, if not corrected, be likely to impair its efficiency, by detaching seamen from their proper vocation and inducing them to enter the army. I therefore respectfully suggest that Congress might aid both the army and naval services by a definite provision on this subject, which would at the same time be equitable to the communities more especially interested.

I commend to your consideration the suggestions of the Secretary of the Navy in regard to the policy of fostering and training seamen, and also the education of officers and engineers for the naval service. The Naval Academy is rendering signal service in preparing midshipmen for the highly responsible duties which in after-life they will be required to perform. In order that the country should not be deprived of the proper quota of educated officers for which legal provision has been made at the Naval School, the vacancies caused by the neglect or omission to make nominations from the States in insurrection have been filled by the Secretary of the Navy. The school is now more fu'l and complete than at any former period, and in every respect entitled to the favorable consideration of Congress.

During the past fiscal year the financial condition of the Post Office Department has been one of increasing prosperity, and I am gratified in being able to state that the actual postal revenue has nearly equaled the entire expenditures; the latter amounting to $11,314,206 84, and the former to $11,163,789 59, leaving a deficiency of but $150,417 25. In 1860, the year immediately preceding the rebellion, the deficiency amounted to $5,656,705 49, the postal receipts of that year being $2,645,722 19 less than those of 1863. The decrease since 1860 in the annual amount of transportation has been only about 25 per cent., but the annual expenditure on account of the same has been reduced 35 per cent. It is manifest, therefore, that the Post Office Department may become self-sustaining in a few years, even with the restoration of the whole service. . . . . .

The quantity of land disposed of during the last and the first quarter of the present fiscal years was 3,841,549 acres, of which 161,911 acres were sold for cash, 1,456,514 acres were taken up under the homestead law, and the residue disposed of under laws granting lands for military bounties, for railroad and other purposes. It also appears that the sale of the public lands is largely on the increase.

It has long been a cherished opinion of some of our wisest statesmen that the people of the United States had a higher and more enduring interest in the early settlement and substantial cultivation of the public lands than in the amount of direct revenue to be derived from the sale of them. This opinion has had a controlling influence in shaping legislation upon the subject of our National domain. I may cite, as evidence of this, the liberal measures adopted in reference to actual settlers; the grants to the States of the overflowed lands within their limits, in order to their being reclaimed and rendered fit for cultivation; the grants to railway companies of alternate sections of land upon the contemplated lines of their roads, which, when completed, will so largely multiply the facilities for reaching our distant possessions. This policy has received its most signal and beneficent illustration in the recent enactment granting homesteads to actual settlers. Since the 1st day of January last, the before-mentioned quantity of 1,456,514 acres of land have been taken up under its provisions. This fact and the amount of sales furnish gratifying evidence of increasing settlement upon the public lands, notwithstanding the great struggle in which the energies of the Nation have been engaged, and which has required so large a withdrawal of our citizens from their accustomed pursuits. . . . . .

The measures provided at your last session for the removal of certain Indian tribes, have been carried into effect. Sundry treaties have been negotiated which will, in due time, be submitted for the constitutional action of the Senate. They contain stipulations for extinguishing the possessory rights of the Indians to large and valuable tracts of lands. It is hoped that the effect of these treaties will result in the establishment of permanent friendly relations with such of these tribes as have been brought into frequent and bloody collision with our outlying settlements and emigrants. Sound policy and our imperative duty to these wards of the Government demand our anxious and constant attention to their material well-being, to their progress in the arts of civilization, and above all, to that moral training which, under the blessing of Divine Providence, will confer upon them the elevated and sanctifying influences, the hopes and consolations of the Christian faith. . . . . .

When Congress assembled a year ago, the war had already lasted nearly twenty months; and there had been many conflicts on both land and sea, with varying results. The rebellion had been pressed back into reduced limits; yet the tone of public feeling and opinion, at home and abroad, was not satisfactory. With other signs, the popular elections, then just past, indicated uneasiness among ourselves, while, amid much that was cold and menacing, the kindest words coming from Europe were uttered in accents of pity that we were too blind to surrender a hopeless cause. Our commerce was suffering greatly by a few armed vessels built upon and furnished from foreign shores; and we were threatened with such additions from the same quarter as would sweep our trade from the sea and raise our blockade. We had failed to elicit from European Governments any thing hopeful upon this subject. The preliminary Emancipation Proclamation, issued in September, was running its assigned period to the beginning of the new year. A month later the final proclamation came, including the announcement that colored men of suitable condition would be received into the war service. The policy of emancipation, and of employing black soldiers, gave to the future a new aspect, about which hope and fear and doubt contended in uncertain conflict. According to our political system, as a matter of civil administration, the General Government had no lawful power to effect emancipation in any State; and for a long time it had been hoped that the rebellion could be suppressed without resorting to it as a military measure. It was all the while deemed possible that the necessity for it might come, and that, if it should, the crisis of the contest would then be presented. It came, and as was anticipated, it was followed by dark and doubtful days. Eleven months having now passed, we are permitted to take another review. The Rebel borders are pressed still further back, and by the complete opening of the Mississippi the country dominated by the rebellion is divided into distinct parts, with no practical communication between them. Tennessee and Arkansas have been substantially cleared of insurgent control, and influential citizens in each, owners of slaves and advocates of slavery at the beginning of the rebellion, now declare openly for emancipation in their respective States. Of those States not included in the Emancipation Proclamation, Maryland and Missouri, neither of which, three years ago, would tolerate any restraint upon the extension of slavery into new Territories, only dispute now as to the best mode of removing it within their own limits.

Of those who were slaves at the beginning of the rebellion, full one hundred thousand are now in the United States military service, about one-half of which number actually bear arms in the ranks; thus giving the double advantage of taking so much labor from the insurgent cause, and supplying the places which otherwise must be filled with so many white men. So far as tested, it is difficult to say they are not as good soldiers as any. No servile insurrection, or tendency to violence or cruelty, has marked the measures of emancipation and arming the blacks. These measures have been much discussed in foreign countries, and contemporary with such discussion the tone of public sentiment there is much improved. At home the same measures have been fully discussed, supported, criticised, and denounced, and the annual elections following are highly encouraging to those whose official duty it is to bear the country through this great trial. Thus we have the new reckoning. The crisis which threatened to divide the friends of the Union is past.

Looking now to the present and future, and with reference to a resumption of the National authority within the States wherein that authority has been suspended, I have thought fit to issue a proclamation, a copy of which is herewith transmitted. On examination of this proclamation it will appear, as is believed, that nothing is attempted beyond what is amply justified by the Constitution. True, the form of an oath is given, but no man is coerced to take it. The man is only promised a pardon in case he voluntarily takes the oath. The Constitution authorizes the Executive to grant or withhold the pardon at his own absolute discretion; and this includes the power to grant on terms, as is fully established by judicial and other authorities.

It is also proffered that if, in any of the States named, a State Government shall be, in the mode prescribed, set up, such Government shall be recognized and guaranteed by the United States, and that under it the State shall, on the constitutional conditions, be protected against invasion and domestic violence. The constitutional obligation of the United States to guarantee to every State in the Union a republican form of government, and to protect the State, in the cases stated, is explicit and full. But why tender the benefits of this provision only to a State Government set up in this particular way? This section of the Constitution contemplates a case wherein the element within a State favorable to republican government, in the Union, may be too feeble for an opposite and hostile element external to or even within the State ; and such are precisely the cases with which we are now dealing.

An attempt to guarantee and protect a revived State Government, constructed in whole, or in preponderating part, from the very element against whose hostility and violence it is to be protected, is simply absurd. There must be a test by which to separate the opposing element, so as to build only from the sound ; and that test is a sufficiently liberal one, which accepts as sound whoever will make a sworn recantation of his former unsoundness.

But if it be proper to require, as a test of admission to the political body, an oath of allegiance to the Constitution of the United States, and to the Union under it, why also to the laws and proclamations in regard to slavery? Those laws and proclamations were enacted and put forth for the purpose of aiding in the suppression of the rebellion. To give them their fullest effect, there had to be a pledge for their maintenance. In my judgment they have aided, and will further aid, the cause for which they were intended. To now abandon them would be not only to relinquish a lever of power, but would also be a cruel and an astounding breach of faith. I may add at this point that, while I remain in my present position, I shall not attempt to retract or modify the Emancipation Proclamation ; nor shall I return to slavery any person who is free by the terms of that proclamation, or by any of the acts of Congress. For these and other reasons, it is thought best that support of these measures shall be included in the oath ; and it is believed the Executive may lawfully claim it in return for pardon and restoration of forfeited rights, which he has clear constitutional power to withhold altogether, or grant upon the terms which he shall deem wisest for the public interest. It should be observed, also, that this part of the oath is subject to the modifying and abrogating power of legislation and supreme judicial decision.

The proposed acquiescence of the National Executive in any reasonable temporary State arrangement for the freed people, is made with the view of possibly modifying the confusion and destitution which must, at best, attend all classes by a total revolution of labor throughout whole States. It is hoped that the already deeply afflicted people in those States may be somewhat more ready to give up the cause of their affliction, if, to this extent, this vital matter be left to themselves; while no power of the National Executive to prevent an abuse, is abridged by the proposition.

The suggestion in the proclamation as to maintaining the political framework of the States on what is called reconstruction, is made in the hope that it may do good without danger of harm. It will save labor, and avoid great confusion.

But why any proclamation now upon this subject? This question is beset with the conflicting views that the step might be delayed too long or be taken too soon. In some States the elements for resumption seem ready for action, but remain inactive, apparently for want of a rallying point—a plan of action. Why shall A adopt the plan of B, rather than B that of A? And if A and B should agree, how can they know but that the General Government here will reject their plan? By the proclamation a plan is presented which may be accepted by them as a rallying point, and which they are assured in advance will not be rejected here. This may bring them to act sooner than they otherwise would.

The objection to a premature presentation of a plan by the National Executive consists in the danger of committals on points which could be more safely left to further developments. Care has been taken to so shape the document as to avoid embarrassments from this source. Saying that, on certain terms, certain classes will be pardoned, with rights restored, it is not said that other classes or other terms will never be included. Saying that reconstruction will be accepted, if presented in a specified way, it is not said it will never be accepted in any other way.

The movements, by State action, for emancipation in several of the States, not included in the Emancipation Proclamation, are matters of profound gratulation. And while I do not repeat in detail what I have heretofore so earnestly urged upon this subject, my general views and feelings remain unchanged; and I trust that Congress will omit no fair opportunity of aiding these important steps to a great consummation.

40

In the midst of other cares, however important, we must not lose sight of the fact that the war power is still our main reliance. To that power alone can we look, yet for a time, to give confidence to the people in the contested regions that the insurgent power will not again overrun them. Until that confidence shall be established, little can be done any-where for what is called reconstruction. Hence our chiefest care must still be directed to the Army and Navy, who have thus far borne their harder part so nobly and well. And it may be esteemed fortunate that in giving the greatest efficiency to these indispensable arms, we do also honorably recognize the gallant men, from commander to sentinel, who compose them, and to whom, more than to others, the world must stand indebted for the home of freedom disinthralled, regenerated, enlarged, and perpetuated.

ABRAHAM LINCOLN.

DECEMBER 8, 1863.

During its first session, the President found in this Congress the ready coöperation he needed in all measures for the prosecution of the war. A system of direct taxation, affording a firm basis for all Government securities, and insuring against financial disaster, was carefully matured and passed. The enactments required to carry out the policy of the distinguished Secretary of the Treasury, and to sustain his earnest efforts, hitherto successful, to meet all the pressing demands upon the National exchequer, received the necessary attention. A controlling desire to further the energetic exertions of the Government in preparing for the grand struggle with rebellion in its last desperate campaign, as hoped, was so manifested in the action of both Houses as to inspire the country with confidence in a speedy and favorable issue of the war.

The improved temper of the House of Representatives, as compared even with that of the preceding one, was seen in its severe and indignant censure of the Secessionist, Harris, of Maryland, (whose expulsion was voted by a decided majority of the members, failing of the requisite two-thirds only by the recusancy of Democrats professedly loyal,) and of his sympathizing coadjutor, Alexander Long, of Ohio, both declared " unworthy members " of that body. It will be borne in mind that Vallandigham, of whom Long was but a docile disciple, habitually belched his treasonable sentiments in the previous

House without official rebuke ; and that traitors, like Burnett, of Kentucky, and Reid, of Missouri, retained their seats therein through the extra session, going directly after into the Rebel military or civil service. Toleration to treason in utterance was now no longer a virtue.

On the first day of the session, Mr. Washburne, of Illinois, offered a joint resolution, reviving the rank of Lieutenant General in the army. This resolution was adopted by both Houses in the last days of February, and was approved by the President. All eyes were now turned upon Gen. Ulysses S. Grant, the hero of so many victories, who was seen to be, if not the most earnest and the most unselfish, at least the most successful, commander in a war, in which so many officers had won a high place in popular regard, as the fit person to receive this chief honor, with its immense responsibilities. The President immediately nominated Gen. Grant as Lieutenant General, and he was unanimously confirmed, on the 2d day of March, by the Senate. Having been called to Washington without delay, he received his commission with a rare modesty, and at once proceeded to organize a grand campaign, embracing the armies of the East and the West in a combined effort for their closing work.

In intrusting this great power to Lieut.-Gen. Grant, the direction of military affairs was limited by no hampering conditions. The entire forces of the country, with such subordinates and such preparations as he chose to ask, were freely placed at his disposal.

The Lieutenant General had not only heartily supported the Administration in its endeavors to put down, by vigorous attacks, a wantonly wicked insurrection, but he had emphatically expressed, in his correspondence, his personal approval of the President's policy of emancipation and of enrolling colored soldiers in the armies of the Government.

Earlier movements in Florida and in Louisiana, already undertaken, afforded no very auspicious opening to the cam paigning season ; Fort Pillow on the Mississippi and Plymouth in North Carolina were captured by the Rebels, followed by massacres unparalleled in barbarism by the acts of any professedly civilized people since the darkest ages; but the grand armies of Eastern Tennessee and in Virginia, heavily increased in strength by new levies and by the withdrawal of troops from positions in which their action could not be effective in executing the intended advance upon the great central points of the rebellion, were put in condition for striking the last mortal blows upon a tottering conspiracy, too long suffered to gather hope from the delay of retribution on its crimes.

The following speech, delivered by Mr. Lincoln on the 18th of April, 1864, at a fair held in Baltimore for the benefit of the United States Sanitary Commission, is particularly suggestive, in regard to the date, place, and occasion of its delivery. On his way to Washington, in February, 1861, he passed through the city of Baltimore *incognito*, to escape from a plot of assassination, of which he had been forewarned. On the 19th of April, in the same year, the blood of loyal soldiers, on marching to protect the National Capital, had flowed in the streets of that city. He now stood before an immense throng in the same city, on the anniversary eve of the assault upon those soldiers, at the fair in aid of an organization for the benefit of Union soldiers every-where. He spoke, too, of slavery, and was loudly cheered when he referred to the practically accomplished annihilation of that institution in Maryland. He even took this opportunity—the first public occasion presented—to announce his determined purpose of enforcing retaliation (long before enjoined on the army by special orders) for the crime, then just perpetrated, of massacreing the colored garrison of Fort Pillow, refusing quarter.

The report of this speech, as it appeared in the Baltimore journals at the time, is here given:

After the cheering had ended, and after, with great exertions, order had been secured—every body being anxious to see the President—he said, substantially:

LADIES AND GENTLEMEN: Calling it to mind that we are in Baltimore, we can not fail to note that the world moves. [Applause.] Looking upon the many people I see assembled here to serve as they best may the soldiers of the Union, it occurs to me that three years ago those soldiers could not pass through Baltimore. I would say, blessings upon the men who have wrought these changes, and the ladies who have assisted them. [Applause.] This change which has taken place in Baltimore, is part only of a far wider change that is taking place all over the country.

When the war commenced, three years ago, no one expected that it would last this long, and no one supposed that the institution of slavery would be materially affected by it. But here we are. The war is not yet ended, and slavery has been very materially affected or interfered with. [Loud applause.] So true is it that man proposes and God disposes.

The world is in want of a good definition of the word liberty. We all declare ourselves to be for liberty, but we do not all mean the same thing. Some mean that a man can do as he pleases with himself and his property. With others, it means that some men can do as they please with other men and other men's labor. Each of these things are called liberty, although they are entirely different. To give an illustration: A shepherd drives the wolf from the throat of his sheep when attacked by him, and the sheep, of course, thanks the shepherd for the preservation of his life; but the wolf denounces him as despoiling the sheep of his liberty—especially if it be a black sheep. [Applause.]

This same difference of opinion prevails among some of the people of the North. But the people of Maryland have recently been doing something to properly define the meaning of the word, and I thank them from the bottom of my heart for what they have done and are doing. [Applause.]

It is not very becoming for a President to make a speech at great length, but there is a painful rumor afloat in the country, in reference to which a few words shall be said. It is reported that there has been a wanton massacre of some hundreds of colored soldiers at Fort Pillow, Tennessee, during a recent engagement there, and it is fit to explain some facts in relation to the affair. It is said by some persons that the Government is not, in this matter, doing its duty. At the commencement of the war, it was doubtful whether black men would be used as soldiers or not. The matter was examined into very carefully, and after mature deliberation, the whole matter resting as it were with himself, he, in his judgment, decided that they should. [Applause.]

He was responsible for the act to the American people, to a Christian nation, to the future historian, and, above all, to his God, to whom he would have, one day, to render an account of his stewardship. He would now say that in his opinion the black soldier should have the same protection as the white soldier, and he would have it. [Applause.] It was an error to say that the Government was not acting in the matter. The Government has no direct evidence to confirm the reports in existence relative to this massacre, but he himself believed the facts in relation to it to be as stated. When the Government does know the facts from official sources, and they prove to substantiate the reports, retribution will be surely given. [Applause.]

A month earlier, Mr. Lincoln had made the following happy response to a call of the assembled multitude at a fair, for similar objects, held in Washington:

LADIES AND GENTLEMEN: I appear, to say but a word. This extraordinary war in which we are engaged falls heavily upon all classes of people, but the most heavily upon the soldier. For it has been said, all that a man hath will he give for his life; and, while all contribute of their substance, the soldier puts his life at stake, and often yields it up in his country's cause. The highest merit, then, is due to the soldier.

In this extraordinary war, extraordinary developments have manifested themselves, such as have not been seen in former wars; and among these manifestations nothing has been more remarkable than these fairs for the relief of suffering soldiers and their families. And the chief agents in these fairs are the women of America. I am not accustomed to the use of the language of eulogy; I have never studied the art of paying compliments to women; but I must say that, if all that has been said by orators and poets, since the creation of the world, in praise of women, were applied to the women of America, it would not do them justice for their conduct during this war. I will close by saying, God bless the women of America! [Great applause.]

The spring elections of 1864, in New Hampshire, Connecticut and Rhode Island, showed still more decidedly than those of the previous year, that the Administration had become strong in the confidence and affection of the people. That this gratifying result had a direct relation to Mr. Lincoln in person, is seen in the fact that the Administration party in each of those States, had committed itself, without dissent, in favor of his reëlection, making this a distinct issue of the canvass. In twelve other States, nearly at the same time, the popular voice, as declared through State Conventions or Legislatures, demanded, with like unanimity and enthusiasm, that Mr. Lincoln should continue in the Presidency for another term. A similar current of opinion was seen to exist in every other loyal State. Since the celebrated "era of good feeling," in the days of President Monroe, this manifestation of popular sentiment has had no parallel. Abroad, too, no less than at home, the true friends of our Government have almost universally looked upon the reëlection of Mr. Lincoln, under the present circumstances of the country, as the manifest interest and duty of the American people.

The policy of Mr. Lincoln's Administration has been fully set forth in his own words. No dissembling, no insincerity, gives the least false tinge to any of his public papers or addresses. This outspoken, frank, confiding way of his, has given him a hold upon the popular heart, and upon the love of all true men, such as few statesmen have ever had. "Honesty" is the word which has been commonly used in speaking of this trait—coupled with a sterling integrity that excludes all selfish and sinister ends; yet it is something more, as the Golden Rule has a wider scope than simple justice. He not only really believes in the right and the true as infinitely preferable to the wrong and the false, both in means and in end, but he is also sure that the people have the same pure faith, and will judge him with that degree of candor which he uses in unfolding to them his purposes and his thoughts. The spirit of that Diplomacy which conceals, and feigns, and doubles, and deceives, never for a moment darkened his mind.

Of necessity, the questions relating to slavery and the African element of our population, have occupied the foremost ground during all this great struggle, in which Mr. Lincoln has been called to lead the organized action of the nation. His whole policy on this general subject, and a concise history of his action and of the processes of his mind thereon, are set forth, with admirable frankness and precision, in the following letter to a gentleman in Kentucky:

EXECUTIVE MANSION,
WASHINGTON, April 4, 1864.

A. G. HODGES, Esq., Frankfort, Ky.—*My Dear Sir:* You ask me to put in writing the substance of what I verbally said, the other day, in your presence, to Gov. Bramlette and Senator Dixon. It was about as follows :

I am naturally anti-slavery. If slavery is not wrong, nothing is wrong. I can not remember when I did not so think and feel. And yet, I have never understood that the Presidency conferred upon me an unrestricted right to act officially upon this judgment and feeling. It was in the oath I took, that I would, to the best of my ability, preserve, protect, and defend the Constitution of the United States. I could not take the office without taking the oath. Nor was it my view, that I might take an oath to get power, and break the oath in using the power. I understood, too, that, in ordinary civil administration, this oath even forbade me to practically indulge my primary, abstract judgment, on the moral question of slavery. I had publicly declared this many times, and in many ways. And I aver that, to this day, I have done no official act in mere deference to my abstract judgment and feeling on slavery.

I did understand, however, that my oath to preserve the Constitution to the best of my ability, imposed upon me the duty of preserving, by every indispensable means, that Government—that Nation—of which that Constitution was the organic law. Was it possible to lose the Nation, and yet preserve the Constitution?

By general law, life and limb must be protected ; yet often a limb must be amputated to save a life ; but a life is never wisely given to save a limb. I feel that measures, otherwise unconstitutional, might become lawful, by becoming indispensable to the preservation of the Constitution, through the preservation of the Nation. Right or wrong, I assumed this ground, and now avow it. I could not feel that to the best of my ability I had even tried to preserve the Constitution, if to save slavery or any minor matter, I should permit the wreck of Government, Country and Constitution, all together. When early in the war, Gen. Fremont attempted military emancipation, I forbade it, because I did not then think it an indispensable necessity. When a little later, Gen. Cameron, then Secretary of War, suggested the arming of the blacks, I objected, because I did not yet think it an indispensable necessity. When, still later, Gen. Hunter attempted military emancipation, I again forbade it, because I did not yet think the indispensable necessity had come.

When, in March, and May, and July, 1862, I made earnest and successive appeals to the Border States to favor compensated emancipation, I believed the indispensable necessity for military emancipation and arming the blacks would come unless averted by that measure. They declined the proposition, and I was, in my best judgment, driven to the alternative of either surrendering the Union, and with it the Constitution, or of laying strong hand upon the colored element. I chose the latter. In choosing it, I hoped for greater gain than loss; but of this I was not entirely confident. More than a year of trial now shows no loss by it, in our foreign relations; none in our home popular sentiment: none in our white military force—no loss by it anyhow or any-where. On the contrary, it shows a gain of quite a hundred and thirty thousand soldiers, seamen, and laborers. These are palpable facts, about which, as facts, there can be no caviling. We have the men, and we could not have had them without the measure.

And now let any Union man who complains of the measure, test himself, by writing down in one line that he is for subduing the rebellion by force of arms, and in the next that he is for taking these 130,000 men from the Union side, and placing them where they would be, but for the measure he condemns. If he can not face his cause so stated, it is only because he can not face the truth.

I add a word, which was not in the verbal conversation. In telling this tale, I attempt no compliment to my own sagacity. I claim not to have controlled events, but confess plainly that events have controlled me. Now, at the end of three years' struggle, the Nation's condition is not what either party or any man devised or expected. God alone can claim it. Whither it is tending, seems plain. If God now wills the removal of a great wrong, and wills also that we of the North, as well as you of the South, shall pay fairly for our complicity in that wrong, impartial history will find therein new cause to attest and revere the justice and goodness of God.

Yours, truly,   A. LINCOLN.

When Mr. Lincoln's determination to employ negro soldiers first became publicly known, it encountered "conservative" opposition in the loyal States. To many, even, who hoped success from this movement, it was a doubtful experiment. The results shown in the foregoing letter, leave this no longer an open question. Prejudice has given way before demonstrated fact, until soldiers in the field and citizens at home now welcome the aid of this immense power, wrested from the enemy and added to the loyal armies.

The arch conspirator at Richmond had the sagacity to see that serious consequences were involved in this policy. Resorting to the methods so long potent with the men of his class, and

31   41

seemingly forgetful, for the moment, that they were not still equally available, he fulminated a threatening edict, designed to arrest this work by intimidation. It was plainly indicated that neither black soldiers nor their white officers need claim any of the immunities recognized under the laws of war. This was emphatically met by the President, in the only possible way, by orders for retaliation, issued to our armies.

General Order, No. 100, under date of April 24, 1863, promulgating general instructions for the government of our armies, " previously approved by the President," contain the following directions, specially enjoining the protection of colored troops:

The law of nations knows of no distinction of color, and if an enemy of the United States should enslave and sell any captured persons of their army, it would be a case for the severest retaliation, if not redressed upon complaint. The United States can not retaliate by enslavement; therefore, death must be the retaliation for this crime against the law of nations.

All troops of the enemy known or discovered to give no quarter in general, or to any portion of the army, receive none.

Mr. Lincoln made these instructions more explicit and direct, in the following order issued by himself as Commander-in-Chief, and communicated to the entire Army, referring to this subject alone :

EXECUTIVE MANSION, }
WASHINGTON, July 30, 1863. }

It is the duty of every Government to give protection to its citizens, of whatever class, color or condition, and especially to those who are duly organized as soldiers in the public service. The law of Nations, and the usages and customs of war, as carried on by civilized powers, permit no distinction as to color in the treatment of prisoners of war as public enemies. To sell or enslave any captured person, on account of his color, and for no offense against the laws of war, is a relapse into barbarism, and a crime against the civilization of the age.

The Government of the United States will give the same protection to all its soldiers; and if the enemy shall sell or enslave any one because of his color, the offense shall be punished by retaliation upon the enemy's prisoners in our possession.

It is therefore ordered, that for every soldier of the United States killed in violation of the laws of war, a Rebel soldier shall be executed ; and for every one enslaved by the enemy or sold into slavery, a Rebel soldier shall be placed at hard labor on the public works, and continued at such labor until the other shall be released and receive the treatment due to a prisoner of war. ABRAHAM LINCOLN.

How completely the Administration has been able, under the often critical and complicated situations resulting from an extended blockade of our coast, from a premature concession of belligerent rights to armed Rebels by leading powers of Europe, from the constant and crafty efforts of Secession emissaries to secure a recognition of the so-called Confederacy by those powers, and from all the incidents of an unprecedented civil war, necessarily affecting our foreign relations in various ways, to maintain peace with other nations, can not be lost sight of in the excitement of military events at home. The value of this successful pacific policy—which has been attended by an increase rather than a diminution of respect abroad—can not be too highly estimated.

Not less conspicuous is the success which has attended the financial policy of the Government. This is, indeed, a marvel which would have hardly been credited in advance as possible, with the prospect of a war lengthened out beyond the period of three years, and calling into the service a million and a half of men, with all the attendant expenditures. To-day, however, Government securities are firm; no one doubts the full payment of every dollar of the public indebtedness; every new loan is speedily taken; and no adjusted claim has long to await liquidation.

The operations of the Army and Navy, related in only the merest summary of the more prominent events, and necessarily excluding more than an allusion to much that would have required volumes to detail at large, have engrossed a great portion of the preceding pages. Could exact justice be done in such a narrative, as affecting both these branches of the service, it would clearly appear that neither has been wanting in efficient executive management, or in its proper share of the great work already accomplished. On these two strong arms of war, now so organized by the President as to secure universal confidence, must mainly depend the future issues of the great conflict.

PART III.

CHAPTER I.

A new Epoch of the War.—Lieutenant-General Grant in the East.—Campaign of the Army of the Potomac from the Rapidan to Petersburg.—The Wilderness.—Spottsylvania Court House.—The North Anna.—Cold Harbor.—Across the James—Sheridan's Grand Raid.—Sigel and Hunter in the Shenandoah Valley.—The Army of the James.—Averill and Crook in South-western Virginia.—Combined Armies before Petersburg.

THE epoch with which the third and last period of the life of Abraham Lincoln opens, in these pages, was one of grave interest to the nation. To the leaders of the rebellion, and to its friends at home and abroad, it was a time of hope. To the true men of the nation, the trust in an ultimate and signal triumph was shadowed by the dread of a more wearisome protraction of the sanguinary strife than was earlier looked for. The President, firm as ever in faith, earnest as ever in effort, anxiously watched the reorganization and remarshaling of the hundreds of thousands of brave men now placed under the control of the new general-in-chief. Not presuming to hope for an easy triumph in the coming renewal of battle, he took care that Grant should lack nothing he required, whether men or materials of war, in order that, without hindrance of any sort, he might be able to inflict mortal blows upon armed treason. A new call for two hundred thousand men had been made on the 15th of March, and the hearty response of the several States was already furnishing constant accessions to swell the Union armies.

The main campaigns of the year 1864 were to be made by the two grand armies in the East and the West, under the respective commands of Maj.-Gens. Meade and Sherman. It was with the latter of these armies that the Lieutenant-Gen-

485

eral, prior to his last promotion, had exclusively served. He now joined the Army of the Potomac, giving special direction to its movements, while controlling the entire combinations of the various national forces. Widely separated as was the one main Army from the other, their advance was to be nearly simultaneous, and their movements were to be co-operative and convergent.

The chief work to be accomplished, manifestly, was the destruction of the veteran insurgent army under Lee. This army, sometimes successful, sometimes beaten, constantly renewed and skillfully commanded, had with its friends a brilliant prestige. It was the main stay of the rebellion, the chief hope of the Richmond conspirators. Twice it had driven in the Union forces of the East upon the national capital. Twice 'it had invaded the States of Maryland and Pennsylvania, plundering and destroying; retiring with only such losses as were readily repaired. And after three years of severe conflict, it still held, in perhaps more formidable power than ever, the south bank of the Rapidan and the lower Rappahannock. With his headquarters at Orange Court House, and his army behind the defenses of Mine Run, Lee tenaciously held, on the 1st of May, the position from which Gen. Meade had vainly advanced to dislodge him on the 1st of December previous, prior to going into winter quarters at Stevensburg.

During the month of April, Gen. Grant was occupied with the work of augmenting and reorganizing the Army of the Potomac, and of making the necessary preparations for an active campaign. If Lee had contemplated an aggressive movement northward, his purpose was anticipated by the prompt action of the new commander confronting him. The Ninth Army Corps, under Gen. Burnside, including several colored regiments, had rendezvoused at Annapolis, as if intended for some separate movement southward. During the last week of April, this force was expeditiously marched through Washington—where it was reviewed by the President as it passed—to swell the main body now lying between the upper Rappahannock and the Rapidan. This large corps had as yet hardly reached the front, when the general advance commenced in earnest. In a stirring order of the 4th of May, as the movement began, Gen. Meade said to the army:

You have been reorganized, strengthened and fully equipped in every respect. You form a part of the several armies of your country, the whole under the direction of an able and distinguished general who enjoys the confidence of the Government, the people and the army.

Your movement being in co-operation with others, it is of the utmost importance that no effort should be left unspared to make it successful.

Soldiers, the eyes of the whole country are looking with anxious hope to the blow you are about to strike in the most sacred cause that ever called men to arms! Remember your homes, your wives and children, and bear in mind that the sooner your enemies are conquered, the sooner you will be returned to enjoy the benefits and blessings of peace!

Bear with patience the hardships and sacrifices you will be called upon to endure. Have confidence in your officers and in each other. Keep your ranks on the march and on the battle-field, and let each man earnestly implore God's blessing, and endeavor by his thoughts and actions to render himself worthy the favor he seeks.

The main army, as reorganized after the appointment of Lieut.-Gen. Grant, consisted of the Second, Fifth and Sixth Army Corps, respectively commanded by Maj.-Gens. Hancock, Warren and Sedgwick. Among the division commanders were, in the Second Corps, Gens. Barlow, Gibbons, Birney, and (at a later date) R. O. Tyler. The four divisions of the Fifth Corps were respectively commanded by Gens. Griffin, Ayres, Wadsworth (who was succeeded by Gen. Crawford), and Cutler. In the Sixth Corps, Gens. Wright (subsequently corps commander), Getty and Ricketts commanded divisions. The Ninth Corps was afterward formally attached to the Army of the Potomac. There was also a large cavalry force, in excellent condition, under the command of Maj.-Gen. Sheridan, which was to prove a most valuable arm of the service in the coming campaign. The total was not less than 25,000 men.

The three corps first named were encamped within the triangular area lying between the Rappahannock and the Rapidan, on two sides, and the Orange and Alexandria railroad on the third, which crosses these rivers about twenty-five miles west and north-west from the point of their confluence. The north bank of the Rapidan was held by Union pickets. There was likewise a small army at Winchester, in the Shenandoah Valley, under command of Maj.-Gen. Sigel—which might be called an outpost of the same army, though nominally belonging to another military department—and a cavalry force under Maj.-Gen. Averill, which was to operate beyond Lynchburg, and to support Sigel, as occasion required.

The Rebel army of Lee, occupying the position already indicated, south of the Rapidan, had been strengthened during the winter, probably, in part, at the expense of the army under Johnston, in Georgia, as well as from other sources, but was still somewhat inferior in numbers, it is believed, to that which had now passed under the immediate supervision of Gen. Grant.

Gen. Hancock's command, the Second Corps, crossed the Rapidan on the 4th of May, at Ely's Ford, not far above the point of junction between that river and the Rappahannock, and advanced on the direct road toward Chancellorsville. The Fifth Corps crossed on the same day, at Germanna Ford, a few miles further up the stream, proceeding out the road toward Todd's tavern, crossing that from Fredericksburg to Orange Court House, some distance west of Chancellorsville. The Sixth Corps, occupying the right, was the last to cross. The cavalry division, under Gen. Wilson, advanced on the right of Warren's corps, pushing on toward the enemy's works on Mine Run. No serious opposition was made to the crossing of any portion of these forces. On the following day, May 5th, the march was continued, the course of the army lying through the wide extent of forest known as the Wilderness. Wilson's cavalry, having gone out by the plank road, had encamped near Mine Run on the night of the 4th. Resuming their march on the next morning, they arrived, during the forenoon, in the vicinity of Shady Grove Church, some miles to the south-west of Todd's Tavern, to which the Fifth Corps was now approaching. The Second Corps was moving up as rapidly as possible, extending its right to form a junction with the

Fifth. This connection, but for a prompt movement of the enemy, would have been effected at Shady Grove Church, giving possession of an important pike before nightfall.

Toward noon, a lively cannonading announced that the cavalry advance had encountered an opposing force. An attack of Rebel cavalry, of Wade Hampton's division, compelled Wilson to fall back gradually, after a sharp engagement, toward Warren's column, which advanced in support. The principal fighting occurred near Parker's Store, Ewell's corps having come up to oppose Warren. The purpose of Lee to crush the central column, and to interpose a heavy force between our right and left, was now clearly disclosed. The attack was made by Ewell with great impetuosity and persistence. He was supported by the corps of A. P. Hill, which afterward came up by the plank road. The plan was well conceived by the Rebel commander, and the danger of its success was imminent. Griffin's division first encountered the Rebel force, fighting with great bravery (the nature of the country permitting only the use of musketry), and at length, sustained by the other divisions of the same corps, forcing back the enemy, though with severe losses.

The next effort of the Rebel general was to prevent the execution of the movement which Hancock was making, as already described. From half-past two o'clock until after dark, a furious attack was kept up on the divisions of Birney and Gibbons, the entire Second Corps being more or less engaged. The assailants were finally repulsed, but no decisive advantage was gained, beyond the maintenance of the positions already occupied.

Thus closed Thursday, the 5th of May, after well-planned, persistent, and concentrated attacks on the moving and separated columns of our army, which was fortunately so well directed, as not to be altogether out of mutually supporting distance. Both sides seriously suffered. The opening was by no means disastrous, nor yet was it auspicious. The coming day could not but be looked forward to with anxiety, the enemy having manifestly the advantage in position and in knowledge of the country, which was to be the battle-field.

From such a scene of action, so difficult for the movement of troops, so beset with the intricacies and entanglements of wild woods but imperfectly known, it may be that other commanders, at an earlier stage of the war, would have thought themselves fortunate in accomplishing a safe retreat. No such thought was now entertained.

Combined with the movement thus commenced by Grant, and an essential element of the situation, was the landing of a considerable army under Butler at Bermuda Hundred, directly threatening Richmond. The army of the Potomac was so advancing as to cover Washington. Lee might now have retired on Lynchburg as his base and assumed the aggressive—and such was not improbably his earlier purpose; but the formidable movement south of Richmond, which he was to defend at all hazards, left him no such alternative. It was on the 5th of May that the new army of the James, under Maj.-Gen B. F. Butler, occupied Bermuda Hundred. This command consisted of the 10th and 18th Army Corps, respectively under Maj-Gens. Q. A. Gilmore and W. F. Smith. The communications south of Richmond were immediately threatened, while a fleet of gunboats, under Rear Admiral S. P. Lee, was ready to advance up the river toward that city. This combined movement below the Rebel capital apparently determined the course of Lee in his present relations to the army which had boldly crossed the Rapidan, threatening the flank of his formidably entrenched forces.

Failing in his efforts to crush our advancing columns, which he had allowed to cross the Rapidan unopposed, Lee now found, on the morning of the 6th, that it was too late, even to retreat at once upon Richmond, his adversary being too close upon his flank. At the same time, he could not abandon that city to its fate, threatened as he now knew it was, and fall back on Lynchburg. He accordingly determined to give battle, resuming the aggressive, availing himself of his advantages over the Union army, from the nature of the ground, for rapidly concentrating his men at whatever point he chose. On the morning of the 6th his troops were early in motion.

" The Wilderness " will ever be memorable as one of the

bloodiest fields of the war. The character of the country is much the same as that on which the battle of Chancellorsville was fought, the battle-field being in fact, a portion of the same forest. The ill success of the advance, which ended with that engagement, undoubtedly emboldened the Rebel army to hope a like result on the present occasion, and led to that bravery and persistence in assault, which, from the nature of the conflict, necessarily produced an almost unprecedented harvest of carnage and agony.

In the forenoon of Friday, the 6th of May, Hancock's corps, reinforced by Wadsworth's division of the Fifth Corps, L. A. Grant's brigade from Getty's division of the Sixth Corps, and other forces, advanced on our left, steadily pushing back the enemy (at first apparently only A. P. Hill's Corps), for the distance of about two miles and occupying their front line of breastworks. Hancock held the position gained, until, soon after noon, he was impetuously attacked by heavily massed forces of the enemy, including the corps of Longstreet (who was severely wounded in this action), and in turn forced back, with serious loss to his former position, of the morning. In like manner, Sedgwick, on the right drove the Rebel forces in his front, but was compelled to yield before the assaults of their reinforced column, giving up all the ground he had gained. Following up their temporary success, the Rebel troops pressed on until the right flank of our army was partly turned, and the danger of fatal disaster seemed imminent. The coolness of Sedgwick, and the well-tried valor of the Sixth Corps, saved the day. In addition to his other losses, however, was that of a considerable number of prisoners, including two commanders of brigades, Gens. Shaler and Seymour. A stampede among the teams in the rear of this corps had commenced just at night, and general confusion was menaced. But the incipient panic, which had not extended to the men in line, was fortunately stayed. During the night, all transportation wagons, and ambulances, were kept in orderly motion toward Chancellorsville. Some even retired beyond that place, to Ely's Ford, but were promptly recalled in the morning—an advance being intended, and not a retreat. If there had been a thought, in the minds of any one, of returning north of the Rapidan, the Lieutenant-General himself entertained no such design for a moment.

The Rebel assailants closed the day's work by a night attack, still later than that just spoken of, upon the center, breaking through Warren's lines, forcing him backward for a considerable distance, and compelling Sedgwick's corps to hasten its withdrawal rearward and to the left, to prevent being cut off from the remainder of the army. A stand was ere long made by the Fifth, however, and the final success of this overwhelming attack averted. The rout of the Union army, and its precipitate flight across the Rapidan, which Lee had seemed on the point of accomplishing, was completely foiled. His efforts to that end had cost more heavily than he could afford, without the anticipated success.

The persistent bravery and good conduct of our men, no less than the gallantry of our generals and other officers, were conspicuous in the actions of these two days. Few armies would have stood against such odds. It is a wonder—as the study of this battle will more and more disclose—that any army so situated and so assailed should have escaped annihilation. By his peculiar advantages of communication, Lee was enabled, by his command of roads in the rear of the Wilderness, as we have seen, to precipitate the mass of his army first on our left, repelling the temporarily successful advance of Hancock; then upon the right, forcing Sedgwick backward, after a destructive resistance, ultimately flanking him, partially doubling up his force, and making important captures; and finally piercing the center, being seemingly on the point of driving Warren's corps pellmell, until by reinforcements and skillful dispositions, the latter was enabled to meet the shock.

A portion of Burnside's Corps, which crossed the Rapidan on the 5th, participated in the engagement, and aided to save the day.

The total losses on each side have been variously estimated, but probably fell little short of 18,000 (killed, wounded and prisoners), during the two days. Among the killed was the much lamented Gen. James S. Wadsworth, commander of a division in the Fifth Corps—a gentleman of large estate, and of large heart, who bravely sacrificed all for his country.

While the two days' fighting has many of the aspects of a drawn battle, and was by no means decisive in result, it may be observed that Grant maintained his purpose of drawing out Lee and establishing himself beyond the Rapidan; while Lee, on the contrary, vainly exhausted all his efforts, with a loss believed to be relatively (though not actually) greater than Grant's, to force the latter to retrace his steps. The next movement, as will be seen, was, with Grant, a bold advance, and, with Lee, a prompt retreat. The latter had discovered, on the morning of the 7th, the march of our cavalry under Wilson and Gregg toward Spottsylvania Court House, with indications of a general movement in that direction. He immediately began to fall back. His whole line of works on Mine Run was abandoned, and his intrenchments in the Wilderness were only held by a rear guard, while the work of burying his own dead, caring for his wounded and securing the prisoners he had captured, received hurried attention. An attempt appears to have been made to embarrass Hancock on the left, and a claim was put forth by the Rebels that he had, for a time, been driven. There can have been little more than some harassing of his flank, soon obviated by the support which Burnside rendered.

While the Rebel army was moving southward, to take up its new position on the Po river, beyond Spottsylvania Court House, the National forces were executing a nearly unobstructed movement toward the left, by Chancellorsville and beyond Fredericksburg—a substantial pursuit, in the guise of a threatened turning of the enemy's right. Many of our dead and wounded in the Wilderness were unfortunately left on parts of the field that had been crossed and recrossed, remaining in hostile possession. In spite of extraordinary exertions, and a care quite unusual in the midst of movements so engrossing, there were many whose sufferings remained unalleviated for days, or who experienced the added torture of listening helplessly to approaching fires, which ran through the woods, and from which, if they were not actually intended to dc this cruel work, the Rebels at least took no pains to rescue the wounded and dying. Some were saved after remaining for days in these wild and bloody thickets, and there are those still surviving, no doubt, who can repeat the tale of the sufferings, though never adequately describe the horrors that followed the great contests of the Wilderness.

The march of the rear of our army from the position held by the Fifth Corps, at the close of the conflict on the night of the 6th, to Chancellorsville, nine miles distant, was completed on the 9th of May. On the previous day the main army was well up to the banks of the Ny, near Spottsylvania Court-House, about fifteen miles south-east of Chancellorsville. The former place had already been entered by Custer's cavalry, and temporarily held, but this force was soon withdrawn. Grant's headquarters were twenty miles south-eastward from the battle-field of the 6th, as early as noon on the 8th. Our forces speedily occupied Fredericksburg, which was made a depot for the wounded, a large number of the houses of that city being taken for temporary hospitals. The movement in this direction—a small force clearing the way for the transportation of the wounded, while the main army advanced toward Spottsylvania—was heralded in Richmond prints: "Grant retreats towards Fredericksburg." In similar style, it had been announced, at an earlier day, that he was "falling back on Vicksburg," while driving Pemberton into that city, preparatory to the capture of his whole army. Communication with the Potomac, by way of Fredericksburg and Belle Plain, was an essential auxiliary to his movement on Richmond, and marked a rapid advance in that direction.

The news of the unchecked progress of Grant, thus far, pressing Lee forward or drawing him on by flank movements, gave an assurance of the firm footing our forces had gained in a greatly advanced position, and of a determination of purpose, which, in spite of all losses, occasioned a general satisfaction more positive than the true history of the case, bating all exaggerations of the moment, would, perhaps, fully warrant. President Lincoln, moderately and justly estimating the results attained, and soberly appreciating the grave task yet before him, issued at this time the following proclamation:

EXECUTIVE MANSION, WASHINGTON,
May 9, 1864.

To THE FRIENDS OF UNION AND LIBERTY: Enough is known of army operations within the last five days to claim our special gratitude to God; while what remains undone demands our most sincere prayers to and reliance upon Him, without whom all human effort is vain.

I recommend that all patriots, at their homes, in their places of public worship, and wherever they may be, unite in common thanksgiving and prayer to Almighty God.

ABRAHAM LINCOLN.

Gen. Sheridan, directly after the days of the Wilderness, had started on an extensive cavalry expedition around and beyond the army of Lee, toward Richmond. The forces under his command had been brought to a high degree of strength and efficiency, and were prepared to test the vaunted superior-ity of the cavalry battalions of the enemy. Sheridan proceeded by way of Fredericksburg, to near the Po river, encountering and defeating Stuart's cavalry in a sharp engagement, on the 9th of May. The evening of the same day found Sheridan near Beaver Dam Station, on the Virginia Central (Gordonsville) railroad, where he stopped for the night. During the next five days, the expedition continued on its course across the North and South Anna rivers, to Ashland Station, and onward to the immediate vicinity of Richmond, destroying railroad tracks, bridges and public property. On the 11th, a battle was fought at Yellow Tavern, in which Sheridan gained another victory over Stuart. The latter was mortally wounded in this fight, and died on the following day, having lived to see his boasted arm of the Rebel service not only repeatedly beaten, but permanently surpassed by the cavalry of Sheridan. Continuing his course, the latter encamped at Mechanicsville on the night of the 13th, and was at Bottom's Bridge, on the Chickahominy, the day following. He penetrated the outer fortifications at Richmond, retiring safely, and finally communicated with the Army of the James. These brilliant operations between Lee and Richmond, for a time seriously interfered with that general's communications, and created no small excitement at the Rebel capital. This famous raid demonstrated, also, the present decided superiority of the Union cavalry, and marked a positive decline in that of the enemy, from which it never recovered.

During the movement of the main army to the Ny, and while the different corps were taking position and intrenching, there was occasional fighting with the enemy. There was a sharp conflict, on the afternoon of the 8th, between Warren and Longstreet's corps, now temporarily under Anderson, its commander being disabled by the wounds he had received on the 6th. It was during the same day that Maj.-Gen. Sedgwick, while personally aiding to put in position a battery of his own corps, was instantly killed by a Rebel sharpshooter; a loss which occasioned universal sorrow through the army and nation. Maj.-Gen. Wright succeeded to the command of the Sixth Corps, and Gen. Russell was advanced to the head of the First Division.

On the 9th, skirmishing was continued on different portions of the extended lines. A more serious engagement took place on the 10th, Grant having ordered an attack on the enemy's works. The Second and Ninth Corps were in the severest part of the action, which prevailed more or less along the whole line. The wings of Lee were forced backward, and a large number of prisoners captured. Here, as on the previous days, the forces engaged were mostly in the woods, permitting only an occasional use of artillery. The results were not decisive, though favorable to our arms. The fighting on the following day was comparatively slight. The 12th, the two armies still occupying nearly the same position as before, is memorable for one of the severest contests of the campaign— the grand culmination of battle in this neighborhood.

At daylight, on the 12th, the combined forces of Hancock and Burnside, on the left, advanced on the enemy's lines. A brilliant bayonet charge was made on the right and center of Lee's intrenchments, driving him back for miles, capturing several thousand prisoners, with their general officers, and thirty pieces of artillery. Most of the noted "Stonewall" brigade, of Ewell's corps, was taken in this brilliant affair. Our victorious forces then advanced upon Early's division, but without equal success. Much of the Fifth Corps was also actively engaged. The Sixth, later in the forenoon, came to the aid of the Second and Ninth, against which a heavy Rebel force was now massed. The enemy fought with great desperation, after his first reverses, and the slaughter on both sides was great. The decided advantages gained in the early part of the day were not counterbalanced by any subsequent results. Though not a decisive victory, properly speaking, it was a substantial triumph for our arms. While the enemy was not ultimately dislodged from his defensive lines, his losses were relatively greater. His prestige was permanently impaired. And yet this close and deadly grapple had also taught Gen. Grant that, while he had wisely determined persistently to "fight it out on this line," and to aim steadily at the destruction of Lee's army, no less than at the capture of Richmond, he had serious work before him, and a sacrifice of life which he, no less than President Lincoln, would gladly have avoided, were not the sacrifice now a certain gain for the future, and a positive economy in the dread losses inseparable from the war which traitors had forced upon the country. It does not appear that even the most unscrupulous Rebel leaders ever claimed a victory in this terrible battle of the 12th. Their losses in prisoners alone were such as they could ill afford, apart from the many thousands killed or wounded. From this day, it is manifest, the army of Lee was seriously crippled, never fully regaining its wonted strength and spirit. Grant, on the other hand, ere long saw his losses fully repaired, and was in good condition to resume his advance—again by flank, in preference to trying further the enemy's continued series of works in the direct line to Richmond. In the absence of official reports, it is hazardous to attempt definite estimates of the losses in these battles at Spottsylvania. The total aggregate, on the Union side, can hardly have fallen short of 15,000. That of the Rebels, including prisoners, undoubtedly exceeded that number. Many valuable Union officers gave their lives with the noble patriots in the ranks who fell in the glorious cause.

After burying his dead and duly caring for the wounded, during the 13th, Grant advanced a little by the left flank toward the south-east, to a position nearer the Richmond and Fredericksburg railroad. From portions of the lines of his army, Spottsylvania Court House was seen in clear prospect through the trees—in a region more open than that through which the men had marched and fought for the last ten days, yet still divided between cultivated inclosures and unbroken forests. The Rebels were strongly fortified near the village, numerous batteries jealously watching any further advance of the "invader," and an ample series of earth-works evidencing the determination to stay any onward sweep of the waves of assault. On this new ground, Burnside, with his corps of mingled white regiments and black, held the extreme right. The Fifth Corps, with its veteran regulars, and its well-tried volunteers, commanded by the youthful Warren, was next in order toward the left. Then came Wright's corps (the Sixth), lamenting its noble commander, Sedgwick, who had added his own life to the many sacrifices of his heroic followers. On the extreme left was Hancock, worthy leader of a corps renowned for its brilliant achievements, and destined to new honors in the conflicts to come.

Some fighting occured, on the 14th, the Rebels attacking the Fifth Corps in heavy force, but recoiling, with severe loss, from its well-matured intrenchments. Ayres' division then made a gallant charge upon the rear of the retreating enemy, capturing a battery and a number of prisoners. Grant's headquarters were now established on the south bank of the Ny river, Lee's line being about two miles beyond, on the Po. The position of the latter, which it was impracticable to turn, was a strong one, and he indicated a purpose of persistently maintaining his ground. No material change in the position of the armies occurred until the 18th.

Meanwhile, the subsidiary operations under Butler, between Petersburg and Richmond ; those under Sigel in the Shenandoah Valley, and under Crook and Averill in South-western

Virginia, during these two eventful weeks, had become note-worthy elements of the Eastern Campaign. The two corps constituting the Army of the James, made up of 18,000 men at and near Fortress Monroe, and 20,000 withdrawn from the seaboard of North and South Carolina, had, as before stated, landed near the mouth of the Appomattox, on the 5th of May. This army took up, and fortified, a position at Bermuda Hun dred and westward, its lines extending from the James to the Appomattox, and to a point within about twelve miles of Rich-mond. The Rebel force opposed to this army was under the command of Beauregard.

Butler, while securely intrenching himself, and during the first surprise which followed his startling and admirably execuetd movement, demonstrated on the roads between Rich-mond and Petersburg, threatening each of those cities. Still farther to weaken the force opposing Grant, and to divert attention from the cavalry raids of Sheridan and Kautz, (the latter of whom had been sent out by Butler to cut the Danville road) a vigorous demonstration was made on Fort Darling, on the 13th of May, and continued during the two following days, ending in a sally by Beauregard and a battle on the 16th, and in the retirement of Butler within his lines at Bermuda Hun-dred on the 17th. His losses were somewhat serious, including many prisoners. This advance on Richmond followed the panic created there by the near approach of Sheridan's cavalry on the 11th, when alarm bells were rung, and the greatest excitement prevailed, every available man being put under arms for the defense of the city. On the 12th, Sheridan had penetrated the outer fortifications, and attacked the second line of batteries on the Mechanicsville road. Had the battles of the 10th and 12th at Spottsylvania terminated in the decisive victories hoped for by Grant, his advance would have followed closely upon the adventurous steps of Sheridan, bringing his main army to the James above Mechanicsville—cooping up Lee within his capital, should he continue to retreat thither— while Butler should advance on the south side of the James, forming a junction with Grant, and closing around the doomed city. If such were the plan entertained, as all the movements would indicate, the Rebel forces, on the inside of the circle, were so skillfully handled, and so obstinately fought as to postpone, if not wholly defeat this purpose. The Army of the Potomac had thus far, though not defeated, been kept in check, with its triumphs chastened, and its anticipations deferred. The movements of Butler and Sheridan had thus but the secondary importance of subsidiary operations, instead of constituent parts of the grand design.

The advance of Sigel up the Valley of the Shenandoah, and of Crook and Averill into the salt regions, and on the railroad in South-western Virginia, manifestly had but this secondary object, of destroying communications and supplies, and weakening the well concentrated force of the enemy by drawing his attention to the circumference. Gen. Sigel had met with but feeble opposition as he moved toward Staunton, breaking lines of transportation and destroying depots of supplies, until he encountered a more formidable force under Breckinridge at New Market, on the 15th of May. The battle was lost, the enemy capturing from him five pieces of artillery and fifty prisoners ; and his killed and wounded numbering six hundred or more. Sigel manifested his customary skill in effecting a retreat across the Shenandoah, without further loss, his force reaching Strasburg in good order.

The operations in South-western Virginia were more successful. On the 10th, Gen. Averill's cavalry attacked the Rebel forces under Jones at Wytheville, routing him, and advancing to the destruction of the railroad, in the direction of Lynchburg. Simultaneous with this movement was that of the raiding party under Gen. Crook, who struck the railroad near New river, still farther eastward. He fought the Rebel guarding force near Newbern, on the 10th, capturing seven guns and a number of prisoners, and destroyed the valuable bridge across New river.

These successes were vigorously followed up, inflicting serious damage on the railroads and government works in the south-western portion of Virginia. Gen. Hunter was soon after placed in command of the Department of West Virginia, including the Shenandoah Valley, and immediately assumed the direction of all the forces hitherto under Sigel, Crook and Averill, and speedily organized a movement upon Lynchburg, which created no little alarm at that important strategic point and depot, drawing away a considerable force from the vicinity of Richmond. The advance of Hunter, however, did not commence until some days later than the date to which the operations under the immediate supervision of Grant have been brought down.

On the 19th of May, at about six o'clock in the evening, a sudden and furious attack was made by Ewell, on Grant's rear-guard, this side of Spottsylvania, with the purpose of capturing his transportation train, and, by a flank movement, interposing a force between the National army and Fredericksburg. This assault was promptly met by the divisions of Birney and Tyler, aided by a portion of the Fifth Corps. The assailants were repulsed, leaving their killed and wounded on the field, and with a loss of about three hundred prisoners. The total Union loss was about seven hundred and fifty.

During the week intervening since the severe battle of the 12th, Grant had been receiving heavy reinforcements and putting his army into good condition for the work still before it. More than twenty-five thousand veterans had been sent him since the commencement of the campaign, including a large force from the Department of Washington under Gen. Augur. As the present movement covered the national capital, a large force could thus be spared from the defenses of Washington, without endangering its safety. Mr. Lincoln had earnestly pointed out this advantage in the first campaign against Richmond, but his advice had been disregarded by the commander who, on that occasion, led the army of the Potomac to defeat and disaster. The native sagacity of Grant had led him to adopt this course at last, without dictation, however, or counsel from the President. This is not the only occasion during the campaign of 1864, in which the intuitive military judgment or President Lincoln was vindicated, and the fatal errors of his first subordinate general-in-chief, when differing in his opinions, were demonstrated. To reach the fortifications of Richmond without loss, and there to encounter the Rebel army not only

unharmed, but trebly intrenched, concentrated, and strengthened, was evidently no gain. The enemy was to be encountered, and his strength broken, sooner or later. While this
must necessarily cost heavily, the plan of campaign pursued by
Grant was such that his losses could be readily supplied and
his numbers kept up, while the army of his opponent was
crumbling away under constant attrition. The protraction of
the struggle between the Rapidan and Richmond was thus telling no less positively on the final result—but rather the
reverse—than a lengthened siege of Richmond. The test of
comparative strength and resources might as well come here as
elsewhere. It was thus no mere bravado, but the expression
of sound practical wisdom, when Grant declared it to be his
purpose to "fight it out on this line," though it should "take
all the summer." It was for a campaign against Lee and
Richmond, fought out in this resolute spirit, with no postponement or evasion of the struggle that must inevitably come at
last, that the country had long been waiting. It was nothing
less than this that could bring the war to a close. People had
occasional misgivings. The loss of life was felt to be fearful.
But, through all, there remained an abiding faith in the course
pursued, and a conviction that unwise economy, even of life,
at this juncture, could only end in more terrible sacrifices in
the final aggregate.

On the evening of the 20th, Grant began the new advance
which he had been preparing for, to Guiney's Station, on the
Richmond and Fredericksburg Railroad, and southward,
flanking the enemy's strong lines at Spottsylvania. The movement was handsomely executed without opposition. The Rebel
commander discovering what was transpiring, Longstreet's
corps was started southward late the same night. Ewell's
corps followed on Saturday, the 21st. The whole force of Lee
made haste to get in a position, apparently heretofore fortified,
between the North and South Anna, the rapid marches of
Grant threatening an interception of his progress toward that
stronghold. The Union army, on the other hand, proceeding
by Guiney's Station and Bowling Green, reached Milford Station, the advance crossing the Mattapony, by the morning of

the 22d. Warren's corps had the lead, following the telegraph road southward from Guiney's Station, and capturing some prisoners in occasional skirmishes with the rear of Ewell's corps. Hancock had the advance on the Bowling Green road, and remained at Milford until the afternoon of the 22d, when his corps moved on and took position next day on the left of Warren, who had now crossed the Mattapony and advanced to the North Anna. The enemy's rear, under Ewell, was found intrenched on both banks of that river. Skirmishing began the same evening. The batteries in the center of Hancock's corps, on the left, commenced shelling the enemy at 4 o'clock, while Birney's division, charging through storms of bullets from the rifle pits, and of shells from the batteries on the opposite bank of the river, drove the enemy across the bridge and secured its possession. At 5 o'clock, Warren, who had proceeded out a road leading to Jericho Ford, a mile or two farther up the stream, threw a force across to the south bank of the river, which immediately intrenched itself, and successfully resisted a heavy assault of the enemy on the same evening, repulsing the assailants with serious loss, who left their killed and wounded on the field. At dark, the corps of Burnside arrived, and took its place between the Second and Fifth Corps, preparatory to the general advance intended for the next morning. Wright took position near the Fifth Corps, having crossed at the same ford as Warren. The Union losses in these spirited engagements were comparatively light, probably not exceeding seven hundred in the aggregate of killed and wounded. The Rebel loss was hardly less, exclusive of a number of prisoners taken by Birney.

Early on the morning of the 24th a general advance was made to the south side of the river, when the fact was disclosed that the enemy had retired from his works, and no opposition was made. The impression, at first, prevailed that Lee was retiring beyond the South Anna, and hastening toward the Rebel capital. An order from Lee to Ewell directing him to fall back rapidly within the defenses of Richmond was found on the person of a captured orderly of the former general, but this appears to have been a *ruse de guerre*. In truth, Lee had

now taken up a stronger position than any he had held heretofore, since leaving Mine Run, and he desired Grant's entire
force to cross the North Anna, to meet the unexpected reception which was thought to have been prepared for him.

The lines of Grant now extended from the Richmond and
Fredericksburg railroad, near Chesterfield Station, westward
some miles, to Jericho Ford of the North Anna. Three miles
south of the point at which the railroads cross this stream, is
Sexton's Junction, where the Fredericksburg and Gordonsville
roads intersect each other. The latter road runs nearly parallel with the river, about three miles southward therefrom, for
the distance of fifteen or twenty miles. Directly south of the
Gordonsville railroad, again, is a stream called Little river,
much of the way only two or three miles distant, though growing more remote as it approaches the point where the Fredericksburg railroad crosses. Further eastward it is crossed by
the Gordonsville road, just before entering the North Anna,
three or four miles above its junction with the South Anna, to
form the Pamunkey. The complication of railroads and rivers
in this vicinity is peculiar, remarkably well adapting this country between the Annas for defensive operations.

On the 25th, the firing between the two armies was chiefly
by artillery. The enemy held his advance works north of the
Little river quietly, for the most part, not caring to hasten an
engagement—choosing, probably, in fact, to maintain the appearance of having only a feeble rear-guard left behind to delay pursuit. It was ascertained, however, by reconnoissances
made beyond the Gordonsville road, that the three corps of
Longstreet, Hill and Ewell were yet at hand. Meanwhile, the
time was busily employed by detachments in destroying the
Gordonsville road for several miles westward.

It now became manifest to Grant, if such had not from the
first been his conviction, that an attempt to force the passage
of fortifications and positions of such strength and complication, would involve too great a disadvantage to his army, and
was to be avoided by drawing his opponent upon more equal
ground. Under the cover of skillful demonstrations to the
right and left, therefore, Grant withdrew the main portion of

his army, and began a new flanking movement, which had nearly surprised Lee. On the night of the 26th, the Union forces recrossed to the north side of the North Anna, crossed over the Mattapony, and with that stream, and subsequently the Pamunkey, between itself and the enemy, marched rapidly southward, in nearly the reverse order of the advance from Spottsylvania, Hancock's corps bringing up the rear, and Wright's taking the van. The movement was directed toward Hanovertown, where the entire force was to cross the Pamunkey, and move forward to Richmond, which is about eighteen miles distant from the river at this point. Sheridan, with the First and Second Divisions of his cavalry, took possession of the Hanover Ferry at nine o'clock on the morning of the 27th, and the First Division of Wright's corps arrived an hour later, and held the place until the remainder of the army came up.

In throwing his vast army across the Rapidan, Grant broke altogether his communications with Washington by the Orange and Alexandria railroad. The communication was first reopened by way of Belle Plain and Fredericksburg, while the army remained in Spottsylvania county, and its base of supplies was next transferred to Port Royal, on the Rappahannock, as the advance was made to the North Anna. The new and adroit movement to the Pamunkey made a still further transfer necessary, the communication being now resumed by the York and Pamunkey rivers, with such railway helps as a further advance toward Richmond rendered practicable. The sick and wounded were all removed from the vicinities of Fredericksburg and Port Royal, and the large number of prisoners in our possession were taken to Point Lookout, Maryland, and elsewhere. Grant thus secured, whenever he moved, a secure base, with the least possible embarrassment and loss in the matter of transportation and movable property—showing a great improvement in the art of making war since the first disastrous campaign on the Peninsula, to which locality the Army of the Potomac had again arrived. Our forces were now in full strength and excellent spirit, and the immediate work in hand was again renewed, with such mortal injuries already inflicted on the opposing army as it had no means to recover from with

43

corresponding promptitude and perfection. It may, in fact, be said, in view of the results now known, that the crisis in the fate of the rebellion was reached, and the fatal blows given during the month of May, 1864. Grant had fought out the issue on his chosen line, and the final victory is a decisive demonstration of the mistake of those who maintained that his present position might have been equally as well gained without loss, by water transportation—involving, first, a great diminution of his strength, by leaving a defensive force of 60,000 for the protection of Washington, which he had steadily covered during every step of his course; and, secondly, the full, unimpaired, concentrated strength of Lee's army, had he chosen to rush to Richmond, foregoing an almost invited invasion of Maryland, Pennsylvania, West Virginia, or even Ohio.

Rapid as was the execution of this last movement by the left flank, Lee, having the inner line, was apprised of it in season to prevent any serious interruption of his retreat upon the lines about Richmond. He hastily abandoned his formidable works on and before the South Anna, from which he had apparently expected so much, and fell back, with little intermediate skirmishing, Grant's movement having for the moment widely separated the main portions of the two armies, toward his last defenses. At the same time, he saw his communications seriously impaired or imminently endangered. Hunter was moving on Lynchburg. Kautz had already cut the Danville road. The Gordonsville and Fredericksburg roads were now rendered entirely useless, and whether they should so continue through the season depended on events which he could hardly hope to control. He had still, however, the James river canal, extending westward, and the Richmond and Petersburg road, continued by the Weldon and other roads southward. It became of the last importance to him to maintain these lines of transportation intact, and to reopen the Danville and other routes with the utmost possible expedition, preventing the close siege at which the Union general appeared to be aiming.

Hanovertown, on the south bank of the Pamunkey, is twelve miles distant from Meadow Bridge across the Chickahominy, as also from Mechanicsville, east of that locality, a little distant from the river, and about twenty miles from the new base of supplies, White House—places already made familiar by the campaign of 1862. In order to carry out what seems to have been part of his original purpose, it was now necessary for Grant to cross the Chickahominy at or near Meadow Bridge, or further up the stream, and to proceed across the two railroads leading northward from Richmond, to the left bank of the James, above the city. How far the details of his plan had come to be modified by the delays interposed by the enemy's obstinate resistance, and by the results of subsidiary movements elsewhere, need not be conjectured here. The first operations, however, after reaching the Pamunkey, appear to have looked toward the cutting of the Gordonsville and Fredericksburg railroads, just north of Richmond, and its close investment by the aid of the Army of the James.

On Friday, the 27th, Meade's headquarters were at Mongohick Church, ten miles north of Hanovertown. The cavalry advance which had crossed the Pamunkey in the morning, was pressing forward, and the entire force under Sheridan, which had rejoined the army on the 25th, was busily occupied in its appropriate work. Before night, on Saturday, the whole army was across the Pamunkey, elated with the prospect before them, and in good condition for immediate action. It was soon apparent, from the cavalry reconnoissances, that Lee had promptly occupied Hanover Court House, five miles south of the South Anna, and fifteen miles north-west of Hanovertown, and was swinging around to confront the forces of Grant. Breckinridge's command, fresh from its victory over Sigel, was in the van, with the support of the cavalry of Lomax and Wickham. To ascertain more definitely whether the enemy was extending his line from Hanover Court House, or abandoning that place to move on Richmond in full force, the cavalry divisions of Torbert and Gregg were sent out by the road on the north of Tolopotamoy creek. They became briskly engaged with Rebel cavalry under Hampton and Fitzhugh Lee, about noon of Saturday, near Hawes' store, six or eight miles south-west of Hanovertown. After a conflict of over two hours, the enemy was defeated, and retired, leaving the field in possession of our forces, with part of his killed and wounded. The total casualties on each side numbered about four hundred. Wilson's division of cavalry was meanwhile continuing the destruction of the railroads west and north of Sexton's Junction.

On the 29th, the main army was in position about three miles from Hanovertown, looking south-westward. Its movements were now deliberate, a possible attack from Lee being regarded as imminent. By careful reconnoissances it was at length found that the main rebel force was lying a few miles distant beyond Tolopotamoy creek, the right resting on Mechanicsville and Shady Grove Church, the right center near Atlee's Station, on the Gordonsville Railroad, and the left still covering Hanover Court House. Tolopotamoy creek is a small sluggish stream, first running south-east, passing nearly opposite Atlee's Station, for a distance of about five miles, then turning at right angles and running north-eastwardly, falling into the Pamunkey four or five miles below Hanovertown. Atlee's Station is six miles from Mechanicsville, by a road running nearly parallel with the first named portion of the creek and with the Gordonsville Railroad, intermediate between them. Hanover Court House is eight miles further north. It it will thus be seen that the line was long, and, with Lee's force, rather attenuated—there being an apparent anxiety to protect the railroads, and to prevent a flanking movement around the Rebel left. This position was somewhat modified on the 30th, as officially stated, though the extremes were still Shady Grove Church as its right, and Hanover Court House as its left.

In the Union line, Wright's Corps held the extreme right, extending toward Hanover Court House (part of Getty's division having moved on that place on the 29th, and to Pease Station on the 30th), Hancock's corps the right center, on the Shady Grove road, Warren's the left center, on the Mechanicsville road, and Burnside's the extreme left, a little to the rear, and threatening an advance on Richmond. The right and rear were covered by the Third Cavalry Division, under Wilson, while the Divisions of Gregg and Torbert were moved out beyond the left. The latter held the cross roads at

Bethesda Church, six miles north of Cold Harbor, two squadrons doing picket duty on the road leading from the former place to the latter. About noon on the 30th, these pickets were driven in, when a spirited engagement followed, the brigades of Devins, Merritt and Custer coming into action before the enemy was finally driven back toward Cold Harbor, averting his intended raid around our left. The loss hardly reached one hundred men on the Union side.

The Fifth corps, also, while moving to the left by the Mechanicsville road, was attacked by Ewell, about five o'clock on the same day, Rhodes' division being supported in this assault by two brigades of cavalry. Crawford's division, holding the advance, was forced back, and this success of the enemy was so vigorously followed up, that the corps of Warren was in danger of being flanked. Reënforcements averted this disaster, and the enemy was compelled, after a brisk contest, to fall back in the direction of Cold Harbor, on a road nearly parallel with that down which Torbert had driven his assailants. While the engagement of Warren with Ewell was going on, General Meade ordered an attack along the entire line. Only Hancock received the order in time to execute it before dark. Dashing upon the skirmish line of his adversary, he captured the Rebel rifle pits, and kept them through the night, despite a midnight attempt to dislodge him. Warren meanwhile held his ground near Mechanicsville, seven or eight miles from Richmond, while the enemy was hurrying troops in that direction to save his right. Burnside, at the same time, moved forward to the support of Warren.

On Tuesday afternoon, the 31st, at five o'clock, Sheridan attacked a force of Rebel cavalry, under Fitzhugh Lee, near Cold Harbor, and, after a sharp battle, routed Lee, together with a brigade of infantry that had come to his support, and carried the position assailed. Sheridan was directed to hold his ground, and Wright's corps withdrawn from the extreme right, was sent to occupy the place. Wilson, the same evening, encountered and routed a brigade of Rebel cavalry near Hanover Court House.

Cold Harbor, as the place of junction of several roads, and

from its proximity to the Chickahominy, was a place of great military importance, in the movements now going on. The attempt to make this a sallying point for the interruption of our communication with the White House, or for cutting off reënforcements from the army of the James, had thus far been foiled. Meanwhile it was not actually in our possession, and the enemy was moving large forces in that direction, on the 1st of June, as if determined to prevent its permanent occupation by our troops. A corresponding movement on our side showed that an important battle was soon to be fought in that neighborhood.

In obedience to an order of the Lieutenant-General, a force of seventeen thousand men, under command of Gen. W. F. Smith, was withdrawn from Butler's command at Bermuda Hundred, to reënforce the army of the Potomac. Setting out on the 29th of May, Smith effected a junction with Wright's corps, now moving to the left, on the 1st of June, in good season to take part in the impending engagement. The aid thus brought was most opportune.

The Sixth Corps, instead of finding Cold Harbor merely awaiting occupation, as appears to have been first anticipated by the commanding general, from the report he had received, soon learned that the position was to be contended for with desperation by the enemy. Wright attacked the enemy's works there, as ordered, at five o'clock in the afternoon of June 1st, while the forces under Smith, Hancock, Burnside and Warren, were prepared to advance on their respective fronts at the word of command. The enemy's works on the right of the Sixth Corps, were carried, and the first line in front of Smith's, after severe fighting, which lasted until dark. Smith, however, found the position he had gained untenable. While these operations were going on, the enemy repeatedly attacked each corps not engaged in the assault at the left, but was constantly repulsed with loss. Several hundred prisoners were taken from the Rebels, and their loss in killed and wounded must have been very considerable. During the night, they lost still further by several ineffectual attempts to regain what the Sixth Corps had taken from them.

On the 2d, in the afternoon, there was a spirited action near Bethesda Church, in which the Ninth Corps was engaged, and some skirmishing took place at other points during the day, the two armies now concentrating for a more determined strug. gle, for the possession of Cold Harbor. The Rebel movements threatened, as we have seen, the maintenance of unobstructed communication with White House, and opposed the advance of our forces on the left to the Chickahominy, the hither side of which Lee was endeavoring to defend. To Gen. Grant it seemed essential to hold this ground, and the struggle in this vicinity was one of the most desperate of the campaign. Destructive as had been the engagements in the Wilderness and at Spottsylvania, the mortality of the four days, from the 31st of May to the close of the 3d of June, was, perhaps, unsurpassed by that of any like period during the war. Nor were the ten days immediately following unattended with serious losses.

Between the Fifth Corps, on the Mechanicsville road, and the Sixth, which had carried a portion of the enemy's work's before Cold Harbor, the Eighteenth Corps, under Smith, had intrenched itself, closing up the line. Part of the corps was deployed along the road, on the night of the 2d, to patrol the transportation trains of the Fifth.

At five o'clock on the morning of the 3d of June, the 10th Massachusetts Light Battery fired the signal gun, which notified the waiting lines that the moment had come for a simultaneous advance to the general attack which had been ordered. Every corps in the front, promptly and cheerily responded to the call. The works in front of the Second Corps were too formidable to be carried, though bravely assailed, and our forces retired at length with serious loss. Some of the troops, coming within fifty or a hundred yards of the enemy's position, halted, and intrenched, commencing a "siege," instead of returning under a destructive fire. Even here, the Rebel sharpshooters picked off many men. Griffin's division of the Fifth Corps, charged across an open field, in spite of a deadly artillery fire, driving the enemy from the woods, and occupying his first line of works. This position was persistently held by our forces, under a galling fire, until dark. The remainder of the corps was chiefly engaged with similar results. The Ninth Corps charged bravely up to the enemy's works, intrenching, in portions of its line, within less than a hundred yards of the Rebel works, which were found too formidable to be successfully assaulted. The infantry and artillery of this corps were warmly engaged during the entire day. The Eighteenth Corps again made a courageous and persistent attack on the Rebel lines in its front, under a terrible fire of musketry and artillery but only gained an advanced line of rifle pits, after severe losses. The Sixth Corps continued to hold the works it had taken on the 1st, and was to-day less actively engaged.

During the night, the enemy violently assaulted different portions of our lines, but was unable to dislodge any portion of the Union army from its position, and paid dearly for the attempt. Under cover of this attack, it is probable that a withdrawal had already been commenced by those parts of the Rebel forces in front of the Fifth, Ninth and Eighteenth Corps. In the morning, at least, they were found to have retired to new ground. Lee was not yet prepared to fall back beyond the Chickahominy, but still showed a determined purpose to cover Mechanicsville and the railroads and canal, running northward and westward. Both parties might naturally claim a victory. Each had prevented his adversary from accomplishing his main purpose, and each had inflicted serious loss on the other. The prestige, however, was clearly with the Union army, which had compelled its opponent to take up a new position, and had evinced that unconquerable determination which actuated its great leader, showing conclusively that the purpose in hand would never be abandoned.

On the following evening an attack was made on the Second Corps, and on a portion of the Sixth, but was repulsed ; and though again and again renewed, each assault was attended with severe slaughter to the enemy. These conflicts were renewed, more or less, during several days following, with similar results, the Union losses being comparatively slight. Our forces were engaged in mining approaches to the Rebel lines, while neither side abandoned any part of its works.

After the succession of desperate conflicts, ending with the 3d of June, however, Gen. Grant had decided on another movement by the left flank, more startling than any that had preceded. This purpose was so well concealed from the Rebel commander, that he knew nothing of it until the entire army of Grant was found, one morning, to be gone. Nor was this tardy information accompanied by any clue to the place toward which the new movement was tending. It appears, in fact, that Lee at first surmised an approach to Richmond by Malvern Hill as the design of his opponent, and lost no time in a transfer of his army to meet that false expectation, to which countenance was given by a covering advance in that direction, on the part of a small Union force.

On the evening of the 12th of June, every thing having been prepared for this change during the preceding days, a general movement to the south side of the James was commenced. The Eighteenth Corps marched directly to the White House, embarking thence on transports for Bermuda Landing, where they arrived on Tuesday, the 14th. Gen. Grant in person reached the headquarters of Gen. Butler on the same day. The Second and Fifth Corps advanced by the way of Long Bridge, below the White Oak Swamp, across the Chickahominy, to Wilcox's Landing, on the James river. The Sixth and Ninth Corps crossed the Chickahominy at Jones' Bridge, two miles farther down the river, and moved directly south by Charles City Court House to the James. The entire movement was executed with celerity and in excellent order, no casualty of any kind having occurred during the march. The wounded had been previously removed, and the government property on the Pamunkey secured. On the 14th the troops commenced crossing the James, and arrived promptly on the south bank, while the enemy, apparently preparing for an attack on Richmond from the north side, by way of Malvern Hill, immediately moved in that direction, without dispatching any troops southward from the city toward Petersburg, now actually threatened in heavy force.

While these operations were going on near the Rebel capital, Hunter was advancing up the Shenandoah Valley, sweeping

33

before him the little force now left in his front. At Staunton, prior to the 13th, after a decisive victory at Piedmont, he had taken possession, and destroyed, several valuable factories and founderies engaged in furnishing supplies to the Rebel armies. The amount of property destroyed was estimated at three millions of dollars. An expedition had been sent out to Waynesboro, on the railroad leading to Gordonsville, which destroyed bridges and tore up the track for miles. Over one thousand prisoners, from Imboden's and other Rebel commands, were sent backward by Buffalo Gap and Huttonsville, to be transferred to Washington. On the 13th, Hunter again moved his forces, advancing rapidly toward Lynchburg, to the defense of which Lee was obliged to detach part of the troops now operating with him at Richmond.

The bold attempt to capture Petersburg, which now had a slender defense, aside from the hastily organized militia of the town, and some not very important works on the south side, not heretofore menaced, seemed on the point of success. So well assured, apparently, was the result, that the very winds were charged with the tale, and rumor proclaimed it through the land as an accomplished fact.

Early on the morning of the 9th of June, soon after midnight, a cavalry column, under Gen. Kautz, of Gillmore's corps (the Tenth), with a battery, set out for a reconnoissance south of Petersburg. After a toilsome march of twenty-five miles, by winding routes, this force reached the outer picket lines, three miles from the city, and drove the outposts within the outer intrenchments, a mile distant. After a lively contest for half an hour, these intrenchments were captured, the enemy again retiring to their inner line. The object of this dash having been accomplished, and the force being manifestly inadequate to take the place, which was now astir with preparations for defense, Kautz promptly returned again to his camp near Point of Rocks, arriving the next day. An immediate advance of Gillmore's corps, had that been possible, might, perhaps, have secured possession of the city, before sufficient reënforcements could arrive. But the position of Bermuda Hundred could not be abandoned. Without such an advance, the alarm now given must have been injurious rather than otherwise.

On the 16th, the Army of the Potomac being now well up in the vicinity of City Point, and the enemy having abandoned his works in front of our lines at Bermuda Hundred, Gen. Butler ordered an advance on the Richmond and Petersburg railroad, with a view to cut the communications between the two cities. After destroying two miles of the track, however, this force (a portion of Gillmore's corps), was obliged to retire to its former position, the advance of Lee's army having now come up, on the way from its position at Cold Harbor, to the rescue of Petersburg.

Meanwhile, on the 14th, Gen. Smith, with fifteen thousand men, including Wilde's colored division, had begun to move on Petersburg on the south, and Hancock was to follow as rapidly as possible with his corps. The city of Petersburg, on the south bank of the Appomattox river, is about twelve miles south-west from City Point, at the confluence of that river with the James. The two places are connected by railway, running along the left bank of the Appomattox—part of the way at some distance from the river. The city is about twenty-six miles from Richmond, by railroad, and its position is strategically important with reference to the latter place, from the fact that three of the principal railroads running southward radiate from this point, leaving only the Danville railroad (not fully completed until since the commencement of the rebellion), as the only one southward connecting directly with Richmond, or available after the occupation of Petersburg. It was not without reason, therefore, that this place was regarded as substantially the key to the Rebel capital.

Gen. Smith appeared before the defenses of Petersburg on the morning of the 15th. The enemy's works had now been greatly strengthened, and were well manned. Smith carried a line of works at Beatty's House, the colored troops leading the assault with great intrepidity, and driving the enemy from the rifle pits. Their gallantry was specially commended by their commanding general. There was a heavy fire of Rebel artillery, and the main lines of the enemy were obstinately held till the close of the day. At about half-past seven o'clock, in the evening, our forces attacked and succeeded in carrying the principal line of intrenchments, taking thirteen cannon, and over three hundred prisoners from the command of Beauregard. The line thus taken was two miles from the city. Hancock, through an unforeseen delay, having encamped for the night, on the 14th, a short distance from the James, did not get up until three o'clock in the morning of the 16th, when he formed his line of battle on Smith's left. At sunrise, before the Second Corps had thrown up any intrenchments, the enemy opened a terrific fire on our men, who were in an open field about five hundred yards from the Rebel batteries. Skirmishers were subsequently thrown out, and the batteries quieted, while the corps was intrenching itself. In the evening, a charge was made on the enemy's works, and one line carried, but the assailing party was unable to advance further. The Eighteenth Corps gained no decided advantage during the day.

The opportunity for the capture of Petersburg by surprise ended with the reconnoitering expedition under Kautz. There still remained, apparently, the chance for getting into the city before any considerable portion of Lee's army could come up. This was to have been attempted by the corps of Smith and Hancock, on the 15th. As demonstrated by the movement under Gillmore to cut the Richmond and Petersburg railroad, on the 16th, Lee's army was close at hand on that day, and thereafter the whole power of the enemy, under Lee and Beauregard combined, was to be met, and once more in strongly intrenched positions. The loss of the twenty-four hours, between the mornings of the 15th and 16th, postponed the final result for many wearisome months, and greatly disheartened the many in whose anticipations Petersburg was already taken by shrewd strategy, and with little loss. Smith's corps was promptly on the ground, all that fateful day. Hancock's corps, also expected, was absent until the following morning. This is said, not in censure, but as a historical fact, which at the time was a source of popular regret, and which seems to be the hinging point of the new campaign now about to open.

The combined Armies of the Potomac and the James now

assumed once more the attitude of what has been popularly, though inaccurately, termed a "siege." The Tenth Corps held its fortified position at Bermuda Hundred, on the north side of the Appomattox. The right of the Eighteenth Corps, in the position it had gained on the 15th, extended near that river. Our Navy forces commanded the mouth of that river, and the space intervening between these two corps was practically occupied. The Second Corps, as we have seen, had taken position on the immediate left of the Eighteenth, on the morning of the 16th. The Ninth Corps arrived on the left of the Second, in the evening of the same day, and made a successful charge, on the 17th, gaining a position deemed of special value, and taking two redoubts. The Fifth and Sixth Corps came into position on the 17th, still further to the left. All these forces were at once busily engaged in fortifying, with occasional skirmishes or assaults during several days following.

Thus had passed six weeks of great activity, of constant marching or fighting, of severe losses, and of apparently indecisive results. But Lee, for the first time, had thus far been kept exclusively on the defensive. The country had hoped, under the generalship of Grant, an early capture of Richmond, with the destruction of Lee's grand army. There was a feeling of uncomplaining, and mostly unexpressed, disappointment. The President, trusting the well-tested military qualities of the Lieutenant-General, confident in the valor of our soldiers, instant in providing that the necessary reënforcements and supplies should not be lacking, had less sanguine expectations, at the outset of this movement, and an unshaken faith always in the great cause, and in the strong hand to which the guidance of our armies had been specially intrusted. He felt this no less with the army at bay before Petersburg, than when it defiantly crossed the Rapidan. And, in truth, this campaign was the one which, tardily though the result may be thought to have appeared, yet actually turned the crisis of the war.

CHAPTER II.

The Campaign in Georgia.—From Chattanooga to Marietta.—Early
Movements of Sherman and Thomas.—Capture of Dalton.—Battle
of Resacca.—Retreat of Johnston.—Slight Engagements.—Occupation of Kingston.—Destruction of Rebel Works at Rome.—Advance to Cassville.—Battle near Dallas and Powder Spring.—Occupation of Acworth and Big Shanty.—Attempts on Sherman's line
of Communications.—Kenesaw Mountain.—Battle of Nickojack
Creek.—Pause at Marietta.—Louisiana and Arkansas.—Another
Invasion of Kentucky.—Movements of the Navy.

ON the promotion of Gen. Grant to the chief command of
all the armies of the United States, the direction and control
of the main army of the West, at and beyond Chattanooga,
devolved upon Maj.-Gen. William T. Sherman. This officer
had borne a conspicuous part in most of the military movements of Grant in the West, from the field of Shiloh, on which
his services were invaluable, to the movement from Port Gibson, ending in the siege and capture of Vicksburg; and, at a
later period, had succeeded him as commander of the Army of
the Tennessee, on the consolidation of the Western armies under Grant, after the capture of Chattanooga. The grand army
now placed under command of Sherman, originally comprised
the Army of the Tennessee, to the command of which Maj.-
Gen. James B. McPherson succeeded; the Army of the Cumberland, under Maj.-Gen. George H. Thomas; and the Army
of the Ohio, under Maj.-Gen. John M. Schofield. This
army was strengthened, in preparation for a campaign into
Georgia, by the addition of the Twentieth Army Corps, under
Maj.-Gen. Joseph Hooker, comprising the consolidated Eleventh
and Twelfth Corps, transferred from the East, and attached to
the Army of the Cumberland; and by troops newly raised in
several Western States. A large cavalry force had also been
gathered and well equipped, under Gens. Stoneman, Rousseau,
Garrard, Kilpatrick, and others. In numbers, organization,

and condition, this army was hardly surpassed by any as yet brought into the field during the war.

After the capture of Lookout Mountain and Mission Ridge, near the close of November, giving entire security to the communications of the army, previously threatened, no material advance southward had been attempted during the winter. The close of February, 1864, found Sherman returned, with the portion of the army then under his command, to Vicksburg, after a bold movement eastward from that place to Meridian, occupying three weeks. For the want of successful coöperation on the part of the cavalry force which was to sustain him, or from other causes, his purpose, whatever it may have been, was substantially defeated, and it was now his first work to return with dispatch to the main army. This he successfully accomplished. Meanwhile, on the 21st of February, a force under Gen. Palmer had been advanced by Grant to Ringgold, eighteen miles south of Chattanooga, permanently occupying that place. Tunnel Hill having been taken on the 26th, after severe skirmishing, Thomas moved, on the 1st of March, toward Dalton, a town situated about twenty miles south-east from Ringgold, at the point where the East Tennessee railroad crosses the Georgia State road, as well as the point of junction of that branch of the railroad extending to Chattanooga with the former road. As this advance was manifestly coöperative with that of Sherman eastward from Vicksburg toward Alabama, the abandonment of the latter expedition was speedily followed by the withdrawal of Thomas from beyond Tunnel Hill to Ringgold, which was accomplished on the 7th of March. The Army of the Ohio, in the command of which Gen. Schofield had succeeded Gen. Foster, had been, during the winter, in East Tennessee, but advanced to take part in the concentrated movement into Georgia, which was now to be made by the grand army of Sherman.

The primary objective point of the campaign, in regard to which, and other military plans, Grant made a visit to Chattanooga, after assuming the duties of general-in-chief at Washington, was Atlanta. This was one of the most thriving cities in Georgia prior to the war, being a prominent point in the railroad system of the Southern States, and a place of great use to the rebellion, no less for its manufactures than as a depot of supplies. To capture Atlanta, and to break up the railroad communications there centering, was to strike a blow, not only at the heart of the Empire State of the South, but also at whatever of " Confederate " vitality now remained between the Savannah river and the Mississippi. The occupation of this point also looked directly toward ulterior objects still more important than the capture of a place which it seemed likely to cost as much to hold as to take.

During the month of April, the final preparations for the advance were completed. On the last few days of the month, concentrating movements were made, and the various commands were in readiness for the order to march. The First Division of the Twentieth Corps, under Gen. Williams, had been doing duty along the line of the Nashville and Chattanooga railroad; the Second (Geary's) had been stationed at Bridgeport, Alabama; and the Third (Butterfield's) at Lookout Valley. All united at the latter point, on the 3d of May, and the whole corps began its march on the same day, crossing Lookout Mountain, and encamping for the night in Chattanooga Valley, two miles south-eastward from the town of Chattanooga; while McPherson, with the Army of the Tennessee, was executing a movement still further to the right, by Snake Creek Gap, with a view to flank the enemy in his defensive line before Dalton. Hooker advanced on the 4th and 5th, by Gordon s Mills, to the foot of the north-western slope of Taylor's Ridge, at a point twelve miles south-west from Ringgold. His corps encamped here during the next day, reducing its transportation train to the minimum, and advanced across Taylor's Ridge on the 7th, at Nickojack trace, five miles south-westward from the last camping ground. On completing this movement, the enemy was found in a very strong position at Buzzard's Roost, directly in front. The corps remained here in position, three or four miles from the enemy's works, until the morning of the 10th.

Meanwhile, Thomas, in the center, from his advanced position at Ringgold, had marched to Tunnel Hill, dislodging the enemy, with no great difficulty, and occupying the place on the 6th of May. Schofield held the left, advancing by way of Cleveland and the line of the East Tennessee and Georgia railroad, encountering Wheeler's Rebel cavalry on the 9th, the advance being temporarily interrupted, with the loss of a small number of prisoners. The enemy, however, was repulsed without any severe fighting. As our forces advanced, both the railroads were put in repair. Thomas advanced from Tunnel Hill, and appeared before the enemy's position north of Dalton, supported by Schofield's forces on the left, and by Hooker's corps on the right, May 9th; McPherson, meantime, was executing his important movement on the extreme right. The Rebel position on Rocky-face Ridge, and at Buzzard's Roost, was of the most formidable character, and was apparently thought by the enemy sufficiently impregnable to withstand a siege, and to delay further movements into Georgia, if not altogether to arrest them. Here they first seriously contested the advance of Sherman.

The Rebel army in Georgia was now commanded by Gen. Joseph E. Johnston, who had succeeded Bragg after his fatal failure which gave our armies possession of East Tennessee, and a foothold on the border of Georgia. His leading generals were Hood, Polk and Hardee, each in command of an army corps. He had also a large cavalry force under Gens. Wheeler, Forrest, Rhoddy, and other commanders. The enemy's great advantage in position, in knowledge of the country, and in the fact that every mile's advance by Sherman added a new difficulty and hazard to his communications, was partly balanced by the superiority of numbers on the Union side. The result of this advance was regarded by President Lincoln rather with hope than with any assured expectation. The Rebel leaders, on the other hand, affected a consciousness of entire security, so utterly impracticable did they pronounce the advance of so large an army so far away from its base, with such force to encounter as that now confronting Sherman. In fact, serious difficulty had for a time been experienced in keeping up the line from Nashville to Chattanooga, without its further prolongation. The accumulation of supplies at the latter

44

place, however, rendered it practically a new base, for the time, and more especially since the enemy had been almost entirely driven out from East Tennessee.

While the several movements on the left and center, just indicated, were taking place, McPherson, with the Army of the Tennessee, moving by the road to Lafayette, on the extreme right, had passed through Snake Creek Gap, turning the Rebel position. Hooker's corps, moving south about twelve miles from its location in front of the enemy's lines, where it had remained since crossing Taylor's Ridge, on the 7th, passed through Snake Creek Gap on the 10th and 11th, effecting a junction with McPherson. On discovering this completely successful flanking movement in heavy force, the Rebel general ordered a retreat to Resacca, which commenced on the 10th. Sherman occupied Dalton on the 12th, having at once secured an important point, and dislodged the enemy from a position of great strength, without any more serious engagement than had attended his steady pressure on the front of the enemy's position north of Dalton.

Resacca is an important railroad station, about fifteen miles south of Dalton, and some distance north of the Oostenaula river. The new position taken by the enemy near this point was on a commanding ridge, densely covered with woods and thickets, and both naturally and artificially of great strength. On the 13th, Hooker's corps moved toward the front of the enemy's position, and skirmishers were thrown out, who became partially engaged with the opposing skirmish line, without bringing on any serious fighting. On the same day, McPherson's command advanced, a force sent out by him striking the railroad and capturing nine trains with supplies, retiring from Dalton. On the 14th, Howard's corps (the Fourth), now on the left of Hooker, became heavily engaged with the enemy at Resacca, and in the afternoon was forced back for some distance, when the First and Second Divisions of the Twentieth Corps were moved up in support. These re-enforcements arrived at nightfall, and the enemy's column was checked and forced back, the Union forces sleeping on their arms. Early in the morning, a reconnoissance was sent out to discover the enemy's position, and soon after noon, the Third Division of Hooker's corps having in the meantime been brought up, a combined attack, in which the latter division led the way, was made upon the enemy's works, which forced him to abandon his outer line. Wood's brigade, of Butterfield's division, also captured one of the inner forts, with a battery of five guns, but being exposed to a concentrated fire, was obliged to withdraw. Still strong in his inner intrenchments, the enemy made three successive sallies, in heavy masses, but was repulsed each time with severe loss. Darkness closing upon the field, our men again lay down in line of battle, with their arms at their side. Before daylight on the next morning, our skirmishers discovered that Johnston had hastily retreated, leaving his dead unburied, and his wounded on the field. Thus terminated the battle of Resacca, the first heavy engagement of the campaign. The losses were considerable on each side, those of the Union forces being somewhat the most severe in killed and wounded (estimated at 3,600). Gens. Hooker, Willich, Kilpatrick and Manson were wounded; the three latter seriously. The Rebel corps of Polk and Hardee lost several hundred prisoners, and the killed and wounded on that side were estimated at 2,000. Seven pieces of artillery were captured from the enemy, and three of his general officers were reported killed.

Pursuit was commenced on the morning of the 16th, Howard leading the advance in the center, but the main army of Johnston was not overtaken during the next three days. If we except a little unimportant skirmishing with his rear guard, near the close of that day, some fighting at Adairsville on the railroad, about ten miles north of Kingston, and a brief engagement with Newton's division of the Fourth Corps, on the 17th, three miles beyond Calhoun, the enemy made no stand until he had reached Cassville. Near this place, toward night, on the 19th of May, an attack on Hooker's foremost division, advancing on the right center, was made by Hardee's corps, and some skirmishing followed, but a general engagement was avoided, the remainder of Hooker's corps not having come up. Our advanced forces intrenched themselves in front of the enemy's lines at Cassville, but the morning of the 20th again found Johnston's army gone. Here, as before Dalton, a retreat without giving earnest battle had been compelled by a rapid advance of McPherson on the right, threatening Johnston's left flank. Cassville, not far from the Etowah river, is a few miles beyond Kingston, the point from which a branch railroad diverges westward to the important manufacturing town of Rome, at the junction of the Oostenaula and Etowah, forming the Coosa river. Kingston and Rome were occupied on the 20th of May, Howard's corps first entering the former town, while the Twentieth and the Twenty-third Corps, moving forward on the left, entered Cassville the same day. A large portion of the army remained encamped at these places for the three days following, while McPherson demolished the Rebel manufactories at Rome, and prepared to continue his effective movements southward—steadily threatening the enemy's flank, and pressing on with all convenient speed toward the Chattahoochee. The railroad was, meanwhile, put in running order to Cassville, and the telegraph lines were extended with Sherman's advance.

Continuing the march on the 23d of May, Hooker crossed the Etowah river, his entire corps encamping at night on the south side of that stream. On the 24th and 25th, his corps was crossing over the Allatoona Mountains, while Sherman's center occupied Dallas. This movement to turn Allatoona drew out the enemy, who attacked Hooker's First Division near Pumpkin Vine Creek, about three miles from Dallas, on the 25th. A general action ensued, sometimes designated as the battle of New Hope Church. The enemy was driven back three miles, and at nightfall had been forced within his inner line of intrenchments. The new position taken up by Johnston was a strong one at the fork of the roads to Marietta and Atlanta, in a thickly wooded and broken country, with scarcely any roads, among the Etowah mountains. The center of Sherman's army was now about three miles north of Dallas, his right being at that place. This situation, with occasional sharp conflicts, was maintained for several days.

McPherson's flanking column, meanwhile, moving forward

from Rome, by a wide circuit to the right, had passed beyond Dallas, toward the Chattahoochee river. At Powder Spring, a dozen miles north of Sandtown, on the Chattahoochee, McPherson encountered a considerable force of the enemy, a sharp engagement following, in which the Rebels were driven toward Marietta, with the loss of 2,500 killed and wounded left on the field, and about 300 prisoners. The total Union loss did not exceed 300, as officially stated. After this victory, it appears that a cavalry force advanced to the Chattahoochee, at Sandtown, but was subsequently withdrawn.

On the 1st of June, a movement was commenced by the Army of the Tennessee toward the left, Sherman concentrating his forces for the purpose of flanking, by a general advance to the left, the enemy's position, from which he could, with great difficulty, be dislodged. His works were firmly held during several days, in which more or less fighting occurred. The approaches to the Chattahoochee by our right were especially guarded against, and McPherson's advance in that direction was suspended. On the 5th, the enemy was again found to have withdrawn, to avoid the new menace, now on their right, toward the railroad, and Sherman advanced his army to Acworth, on the railroad, north of the Kenesaw Mountain, about fifteen miles from Marietta. Headquarters remained at this place during the next five days, while supplies were brought up, and preparations made for a further advance. On the morning of the 11th, Big Shanty was occupied, the Army of the Tennessee proceeding southward on the railroad, until within sight of the enemy's lines at a point called the Peach Orchard, when our forces formed in line of battle, throwing up intrenchments at the edge of an open field. The enemy's left now rested on Lost Mountain, and his right on Kenesaw. From this point the army gradually advanced by the usual slow approaches toward the opposing intrenchments, with some losses, until the 19th, when Johnston was found to have fallen back. During this period (on the 14th of June) Gen. Polk was killed. Sherman at once ordered an advance toward Marietta, in the hope of occupying that place without further serious opposition.

The enemy had now also put in motion a cavalry column to strike the railroad northward, and to break Sherman's communications with his base. Wheeler made his appearance at Calhoun on the 10th of June, cut the railroad and seized a train of cars laden with grain, which was on its way to the army. A train going northward was telegraphed and stopped at Adairsville, about twelve miles below, when Gen. Hovey, who was on board, collected a battalion of two hundred convalescent soldiers, who proceeded with the train, moving cautiously on. About half way to Calhoun, a torpedo exploded under the train, throwing the locomotive from the track, and demolishing four cars—no person on board being seriously injured. On reaching Calhoun, the enemy was found to have retreated, and the train passed on uninterruptedly to Resacca. Wheeler appeared again the same evening, destroying the track below Calhoun. This raid, however, only delayed the trains for two or three days. Meanwhile, there were reports of a much more formidable expedition under Forrest, aiming at the communications farther north, and, perhaps, across the Tennessee. Early in the month of June a large cavalry force, under Gen. Grierson, had set out eastward from Memphis, with the evident purpose of watching Forrest and keeping him in check.

A campaign, undertaken by the Rebel Gen. Pillow, with all the confidence of a Burgoyne, to force Sherman into hasty retreat, prematurely ended in his mortifying repulse, with severe loss, before Lafayette, on the 24th of June.

Instead of continuing his retreat, on the 19th, Johnston had established his lines in a position of great strength upon the crest of Kenesaw, defying assault and arresting a further advance. Sherman intrenched again, and remained in this position, with only occasional skirmishing, until the 27th of June, when an attempt was made to carry the enemy's lines by assault. The battle of this day, in which our losses were somewhat severe, resulted in a repulse at all the intrenched points attacked. Schofield, however, with the Army of the Ohio, succeeded in flanking the enemy, driving a column of Rebel cavalry before him. On the 3d of July, Johnston's forces evacuated their works on Kenesaw Mountain, and fell back to a position designed to cover the crossing of the Chattahoochee. On the morning of the 4th, McPherson's column crossed Nickojack Creek, at Ruff's Mills, and forming on the south bank, assailed the enemy, who retired within his intrenchments. During the day our forces constructed rifle pits, and, just at dark, a brilliant charge, made by the 39th and 27th Ohio Regiments, grandly carried the enemy's works. So complete a success, in a direct assault upon formidable works, had rarely, if ever, occurred during the war. It cost many losses in killed and wounded. Among the latter was Col. Noyes, of the 39th, who lost a foot.

The army now advanced on the right, pressing closely upon the lines of the enemy, the right and left of which rested on the Chattahoochee. Marietta was now securely in the possession of Sherman, who had driven back the enemy from one stronghold after another, with a steadily lengthening line of communication, for the distance of one hundred and twenty-five miles, during a campaign of two months. Many were the complaints of Rebel observers, and great the discontent manifested at Richmond. by reason of the repeated evacuations and retreats of Johnston's army, from positions of almost unparalleled strength. It is not to be denied that, on the other hand, there was some anxiety among loyal men, as the season wore on, and the difficulties in Sherman's path were apparently increasing, instead of his achieving the prompt capture of Atlanta, which the too sanguine had anticipated. So much as this is now manifest: Johnston handled his army with great skill, making the most of his resources—wisely, no doubt, determining to avoid any desperate stake or heavy losses until Sherman should have advanced far into the interior, when his communications could be effectively assailed, and his further advance indefinitely prolonged by elaborate fortifications, at last desperately defended, near the Rebel base. The arrival of our army at Marietta, confronting the enemy, resolutely defending the north bank of the Chattahoochee, terminates one distinct period of this campaign. The rough mountains, the gorges, creeks and forests were passed. A large river was now to be crossed, and only a brief space of gently rolling and open country lay beyond, between our victorious troops and the elaborate fortifications of Atlanta.

To maintain his communication with Chattanooga, and thence to Nashville; to force his way across the Chattahoochee, in spite of all the resistance his adversary could make, and to carry at last the manifold lines protecting Atlanta, without the possibility of establishing a close siege : such were the important problems which Sherman must solve. To fail in one of them was to ruin all. To succeed in each, could only be accomplished by the highest order of generalship. President Lincoln, while entertaining an exalted opinion of the military skill of the general commanding in Georgia, with a due appreciation of what he had thus far accomplished, had also such a conception of the obstacles still to be overcome, that he never spoke, without a degree of moderation bordering on apprehension, at this stage, of the probable issue of the advance on Atlanta.

If the campaign in Georgia, no less than that in Eastern Virginia, had, as yet, failed fully to satisfy the popular hope, the disasters which had attended the Red river expedition under General Banks still weighed with depressing effect upon the public heart. The returning steps of our army in Louisiana, and the work of extricating the fleet under Admiral Porter, were watched with an anxiety dreading further defeat, and not with any hope of redeeming success. By an effort of skill which will ever be memorable, Colonel Bailey had built his dam across the falls of the Red river, above Alexandria, and our gunboats and transports were thus relieved, on the 9th of May. General Canby, succeeding Banks, reached the mouth of Red river on the 14th, intending to coöperate with the latter in securing a safe withdrawal of his force, but no assistance was required. In moving from Alexandria to the Mississippi, Banks had two engagements with the enemy, first at Mansuna, then at Yellow Bayou, repulsing his assailants in both instances.

The dangers which threatened affairs in Arkansas, after the advance of General Steele toward Shreveport, and the failure of Banks to support the intended converging movement, were averted by the bravery of our soldiers and by the skill of their general. When Banks and Porter had completed their withdrawal from the Red river, Steele had also made secure his possession of Little Rock, having gallantly fought his way backward in the face of the Rebel forces of Marmaduke and Price.

Another invasion of Kentucky, by the Rebel Morgan, was commenced on the 7th of June. After plundering Lexington, and proceeding as far as the Lexington and Covington Railroad at Cynthiana, which place was taken, the brief campaign was brought to an inglorious termination, by the capture or dispersion of nearly his entire force, as a result of the prompt measures taken by General Burbridge. By the 17th of June, this menacing raid was over, and pursuit of the raiders at an end, with little damage to the invaded district, and with the humiliating discomfiture of Morgan.

During the period over which the events of this chapter extend, there was a formidable naval expedition fitted out, which ere long put to sea, under the command of Admiral Farragut, and was subsequently heard of in connection with movements against Mobile. The blockading squadron was faithfully performing its work, with a success that left little to desire, save in regard to the port of Wilmington, where, from the nature of the coast, and the strong defenses commanding the entrance to Cape Fear river, the profitable contraband traffic with Nassau, and other ports, was still stealthily carried on to an extent that afforded substantial aid to the rebellion. The Government was earnestly considering by what means this deficiency in a blockade, otherwise unusually thorough and stringent, might best be remedied. The fruits of these deliberations were to appear at no distant day. Occasional attempts of guerrilla parties to obstruct the navigation of the Mississippi served to show at once the high estimate placed upon the possession of the great "inland sea," and the impotence of such efforts as could be spared, despite former boasts, for the interruption of transportation thereon.

A memorable naval victory was gained off the French port of Cherbourg, on the 19th of June, by which a pest of the

seas, the Rebel piratical vessel Alabama, was defeated and
sunk by the United States ship Kearsarge, under the command
of Commodore John A. Winslow. The Rebel commander—
Semmes—escaped in the yacht of an Englishman, to the
embrace of English friends. The enthusiasm with which the
destruction of his vessel was received in America and by her
friends everywhere, was scarcely excelled by the sympathy
displayed by British blockade-runners and republic-haters for
the ingloriously defeated champion of Rebel piracy. To
unfriendly eyes in Europe, assuredly, the success of our Government in the subjugation of treason seemed as remote as in
the beginning, and the rebellion still in the ruddy glow of
health and the robustness of insuperable vigor.

CHAPTER III.

Mr. Lincoln's Administration in issue before the People.—Disadvantages of the Hour.—Opposition in Official Quarters, and on the Union side in Congress.—The "Radical" Movement.—Recapitulation of the Administration Policy in regard to Virginia and Missouri.—Mr. Lincoln's Method with the Insurrectionary States.—Gen. Fremont's Military Administration in Missouri.—His Removal.—Personality of the Missouri Feud.—How Mr. Lincoln Regarded it.—His Letter to Gen. Schofield.—His Reply to the Demands of the "Radical" Committee.—The Situation in Louisiana.—Military Governorship in Tennessee.—State Reorganization in Arkansas.—Factious Opposition.—Uprising of the People for Mr. Lincoln.—The Baltimore Convention.—The Nominations.—Responses of Mr. Lincoln.—Address of the Methodist General Conference.—The President's Reply.

As the time approached at which nominations were to be made for the offices of President and Vice-President for the ensuing Presidential term, it naturally happened that the public acts and personal character of Abraham Lincoln came to receive more particular consideration among the people in all parts of the nation, and also in the countries of Europe, than at any previous period during his administration. His policy was freely discussed, his conduct of affairs, domestic and foreign, was canvassed with the unrestricted freedom which accords with the genius of republican institutions; and it soon became evident that the coming election, whatever its other results, was at least to determine the popular verdict upon Mr. Lincoln's management of affairs thus far, and upon his fitness for completing the work in progress. The brief summary of the events of the war heretofore given has failed clearly to present the exact position of the great struggle, if it is not manifest to the reader that the moment when the preliminary decision was to be had, by representatives of the dominant party, "fresh from the people," in national convention, was not so specially favorable as to insure an indorsement of the President from a merely temporary bias or caprice.

President Lincoln himself was not deceived, however gratified he might have been with such successes as had been first gained, as to the desperation with which the military campaigns of this season were to be contested. His customary moderation of tone, and his habitual confidence in the cause, appear in the following speech in response to a serenade, on the night of May 9th, after the Wilderness battles :

FELLOW-CITIZENS: I am very much obliged to you for the compliment of this call, though I apprehend it is owing more to the good news received to-day from the army than to a desire to see me. I am, indeed, very grateful to the brave men who have been struggling with the enemy in the field, to their noble commanders who have directed them, and especially to our Maker. Our commanders are following up their victories resolutely and successfully. I think, without knowing the particulars of the plans of Gen. Grant, that what has been accomplished is of more importance than at first appears. I believe I know (and am especially grateful to know), that Gen. Grant has not been jostled in his purposes ; that he has made all his points ; and to-day he is on his line, as he purposed before he moved his armies. I will volunteer to say that I am very glad at what has happened ; but there is a great deal still to be done. While we are grateful to all the brave men and officers for the events of the past few days, we should, above all, be very grateful to Almighty God, who gives us victory.

There is enough yet before us requiring all loyal men and patriots to perform their share of the labor and follow the example of the modest General at the head of our armies, and sink all personal considerations for the sake of the country. I commend you to keep yourselves in the same tranquil mood that is characteristic of that brave and loyal man. I have said more than I expected when I came before you; repeating my thanks for this call, I bid you good bye. [Cheers.]

A month later, the public heart was less exultant. The war had dragged wearily on, to a great extent disappointing the popular hope. The "short, sharp, decisive" battles once promised were found to be partly too real, partly illusive. An almost unlimited vista of bloodshed and devastation still opened before the eye directed to the future.   The past had its palpable triumphs, but the spirit of the rebellion was apparently still as rampant as ever.   Nor, as will have been observed from the two preceding chapters, had the grand coöperative campaigns, from which early and decisive results had been too sanguinely anticipated, culminated in any conclusive triumphs, even far on into midsummer.   There were, then, it may be undoubtingly said, few adventitious circumstances to conduce to a prejudiced judgment in Mr. Lincoln's favor.

It may, indeed, be affirmed that there was a vantage-ground in the possession of the chief executive power and its patronage; but never, probably, were officers of the Government so closely and exclusively occupied with their immediate duties, or so little attentive to any supposed interest in the succession. Scarcely any one of them certainly took an active part in any organized efforts to influence the Presidential nomination, except in behalf of other candidates.   Thus, whatever personal adherents were gained by the possession of the Presidential office, must have been more than counterbalanced by the inevitable alienations resulting from the disappointment of expectants, and by the adverse efforts of many in place.

Mr. Lincoln had, further, the disadvantage of an active and perhaps increasing party in Congress, from whom he might at least have expected a partisan support, who manifested on all occasions a zealous personal opposition.   To such an extent was this opposition carried, in fact, now upon one ground and now upon another, that it was even doubtful whether, in the Spring of 1864, a majority of either branch of Congress could be relied on for the support of distinctively Administration measures. A " Radical " movement was organized, with its central club in Washington and an extensive correspondence throughout the country, with the earnest purpose of bringing forward a leading member of the Cabinet as the next Presidential candidate.   Whatever thorough organization and energetic political management could do to bring forward a new man, under the " Radical " party cry, was done.   And after the refusal of the Secretary of the Treasury to allow a further use of his name as a rallying point, there was still a resolute remnant who joined their

fortunes to the cause of Gen. Fremont, on whose behalf an independent convention was called, in opposition to the Republican Union organization.

A proper devotion to " the truth of history " would seem to
require an effort to understand the exact meaning of this
"Radical" movement, and the justice of its opposition to Mr.
Lincoln.   For this end, it will be necessary to go backward a
little, to consider the state of affairs in Missouri, out of which
this division arose, and in Louisiana, where further material
was furnished to the growing flame.

The early policy of the Administration in regard to the restoration of loyal State Governments, in place of those in complicity with the rebellion, received the explicit sanction of Congress and the people, as illustrated in the case of Virginia, in
1861.   It was held that the loyal people of that State, in dis-
owning the authority of officers in rebellion, and in establishing, through a State Convention, a new government, at the head
of which was Gov. Pierpoint, were to be sustained by the
United States, under the guarantees of the Constitution.   Practically, it mattered little as to the relative numbers of the loyal
and disloyal in any State thus to be rescued from treasonable
sway.   It was only expedient that the numbers, in general
terms, should be such as to justify the attempt to maintain
their ascendency, with such aids as could be reasonably given
by the National Government.   The disloyal inhabitants, having
forfeited their rights as citizens by joining the rebellion, were
not entitled to be regarded, in re-constituting loyal State
governments.   Their pleasure was not to be consulted.   The
fact that they might be a majority, abated nothing from the
rights of a loyal minority to be sustained in organizing a legitimate government.   The carrying out of this principle—so
obvious that at the outset it was scarcely controverted, except
by undisguised traitors—led to the emphatic recognition of the
government established at Wheeling in 1861, in the name of
the whole State of Virginia.   A National force was sent into
Western Virginia, to prevent the armed intervention of the
Rebel Government to defeat this purpose.   The Pierpoint
Government was distinctly recognized by every branch of the

National Government, and Senators and Representatives from Virginia took their seats in Congress, from Eastern no less than from Western Virginia, under no other tenure of office than such as the new State Government, recognized by Congress as the only legitimate government in that State, gave these members, by virtue of legislative and popular elections. Virginia was subsequently divided, as could only have been done constitutionally on the fullest recognition of this policy, and the new State of West Virginia created, the Pierpoint Government still maintaining its jurisdiction over Virginia proper—the remainder of the State.

In Missouri, no pretense of secession had been consummated. The people represented in State convention, had distinctly refused to join hands with the traitors of South Carolina and Mississippi. Yet the Governor of Missouri, defying the loyal majority of the people of that State, openly levied war against the National Government, and endeavored to coerce his State into the movement, which its people had emphatically repudiated. Gov. Jackson's organized forces were captured or driven out, and he himself ere long fled from the State, leaving no loyal successor entitled to assume his functions. The State Convention, whose loyalty had already been demonstrated, reorganized the State Government, with Gov. Gamble at its head. This Government, too—and the principle of its establishment was the same, though the circumstances differed, as that applied in the case of Virginia—was recognized at Washington, and the State fully represented in Congress. In both States, a system of emancipation had been adopted, which was nominally gradual, instead of being unconditional and immediate. This action was originated by the people of those States, not forced upon them by the National Government. Unhappily, Gen. Fremont, during his brief military administration in Missouri, had been less successful in restoring order than had Gen. Rosecrans in Western Virginia. Fremont had been appointed a Major-General among the very first after the outbreak of war, by Mr. Lincoln, of his own motion, with only the support and approval, as may now, without impropriety, be stated, of a single Cabinet officer, Mr. Blair. This former Republican standard-bearer had the President's fullest confidence. And when Gen. Fremont, assuming what only the President as Comman-der-in-Chief could do, issued his not only unauthorized but positively illegal order concerning slaves, the President merely " modified " his subordinate's action, by requiring it to con-form to the law affecting that subject, then just passed by Con-gress. The only portion of this once famous order * which relates in any manner to slavery, is this single sentence : " Real and personal property of those who shall take up arms against the United States, or who shall be directly proven to have taken an active part with their enemies in the field, is declared confiscated to public use, *and their slaves, if any they have, are hereby declared free men."* The President's order† that the clause here given in italics, " be so modified, held and con-strued as to conform with and not to transcend the provisions on the same subject, contained in the act of Congress entitled ' an act to confiscate property used for insurrectionary purposes,' approved August 6th, 1861," can not certainly be regarded as any sensible starting-point for the formation of a new party. As a matter of fact, however, it would seem to have been occasionally perverted to the purpose of fostering a misappre-hension and prejudice, which interested parties were cautiously nursing, respecting President Lincoln. It was even alleged, with an equal misapprehension of the truth, that the councils of pro-slavery Border-State men had a controlling influence with him—a singular reversal of relations, gaining a certain popular currency for a while, but effectively disposed of by subsequent realities too palpable to be mistaken.

When Gen. Fremont was subsequently relieved from his com-mand in Missouri, during which, by his misfortune or other-wise, disorder and commotion had been but too prevalent, and the Rebel army under Jackson and Price, had gathered strength, the Blairs were known to have cast their influence against him, while Judge Bates, in the Cabinet, and Gov. Gam-ble, at home, were also held responsible as advisers of the change. The name of Fremont, which was identified with

---

* Given at length on pp. 278-9 *ante.*

† *Ante,* p. 280.

the Republican organization in the canvass of 1856, had become, in the minds of many, a symbol of a sacred cause. When he was displaced from his command in Missouri, it was easy to associate this action with causes on which it never, in the remotest degree, depended. The true reasons were strictly military and administrative; the fancied ones were political. The act itself, which few can have recently doubted to be wise, may have hastened a party division. Missouri "Radicalism" desired to deal promptly and finally with slavery, and organized for that end at home, in the exercise of the prerogative of "popular sovereignty." The State Convention, loyal but "conservative," adopted a more quiet and gradual process of disposing of the great evil. Perhaps something too much of personal feeling entered into the hostility toward the late Gov. Gamble. Certain it is, that Att'y.-Gen. Bates—years before a practical emancipationist, while one of his leading "Radical" enemies was actually enriching himself by the slave-trade—was either greatly misjudged, or wantonly maligned. The "Conservative" party had the disadvantage in reputation, whatever the gain in votes, of attracting to its support many of those whose loyalty was doubtful, or whose treason was indisputable. Yet the masses of the two parties really differed less in principle than in personal feeling The attempt to expand this local strife into a National division of parties appears to have been thought of by no one, until a comparatively late day. To Mr. Lincoln, the feud was one too deeply regretted for either side to gain his confidence. He thought both should adhere to the Government against its enemies, their own as well, and settle their disagreements, when both so nearly meant the same thing—personalities excepted.

Precisely how Mr. Lincoln regarded this matter, may best be shown by his own words, addressed to Gen. Schofield when the quarrel was still local, ere the plan of National diffusion had been invented:

EXECUTIVE MANSION,   }
WASHINGTON, May 27, 1863.   }

Gen. J. M. SCHOFIELD—*Dear Sir:* Having removed Gen. Curtis, and assigned you to the command of the Department of

the Missouri, I think it may be of some advantage to me to
state to you why I did it.   I did not remove Gen. Curtis because of my full conviction that he had done wrong by commission or omission.   I did it because of a conviction in my
mind that the Union men of Missouri, constituting, when united,
a vast majority of the people, have entered into a pestilent, factious quarrel among themselves, Gen. Curtis, perhaps not of
choice, being the head of one faction, and Gov. Gamble that
of the other.   After months of labor to reconcile the difficulty,
it seemed to grow worse and worse, until I felt it my duty to
break it up somehow, and as I could not remove Gov. Gamble,
I had to remove Gen. Curtis.   Now that you are in the position, I wish you to undo nothing merely because Gen. Curtis or
Gov. Gamble did it, but to exercise your own judgment, and do
right for the public interest.   Let your military measures be
strong enough to repel the invaders and keep the peace, and not
so strong as to unnecessarily harass and persecute the people.
It is a difficult *role*, and so much greater will be the honor if
you perform it well.   If both factions, or neither, shall abuse
you, you will probably be about right.   Beware of being assailed by one and praised by the other.

Yours, truly,   A. LINCOLN.

The two concluding sentences of this characteristic letter
afford a key to the course of Mr. Lincoln himself, in dealing
with a difficulty to him so unpleasant, until partly as a result
of his policy, affairs assumed a more satisfactory phase.

In the Autumn of 1863, a committee representing the "Radical" wing in Missouri, waited on President Lincoln to urge the
removal of Gen. Schofield, who, whether justly or not, seemed
to have become as much the special object of attack as a "Conservative," as had Gen. Curtis for his identification with the
opposite side.   The letter addressed to Gen. Schofield, on the
1st of October, the day after the formal petition of this committee had been presented, shows the attitude in which that
officer now stood in the eyes of President Lincoln, and the
policy of the latter, as exhibited in his communications with
the one whom the "Radicals" were now chiefly opposing.   The
letter is as follows :

EXECUTIVE MANSION, }
WASHINGTON, D. C., October 1, 1863. }

Gen. JOHN M. SCHOFIELD : There is no organized military
force in avowed opposition to the General Government now in

Missouri, and if any shall reappear, your duty in regard to it will be too plain to require any special instruction. Still, the condition of things, both there and elsewhere, is such as to render it indispensable to maintain, for a time, the United States military establishment in that State, as well as to rely upon it for a fair contribution of support to that establishment generally. Your immediate duty in regard to Missouri now is, to advance the efficiency of that establishment, and to so use it, as far as practicable, to compel the excited people there to let one another alone.

Under your recent order, which I have approved, you will only arrest individuals, and suppress assemblies or newspapers, when they may be working *palpable* injury to the military in your charge; and in no other case will you interfere with the expression of opinion in any form, or allow it to be interfered with violently by others. In this you have a discretion to exercise with great caution, calmness and forbearance.

With the matter of removing the inhabitants of certain counties *en masse*, and of removing certain individuals from time to time, who are supposed to be mischievous, I am not now interfering, but am leaving it to your own discretion.

Nor am I interfering with what may still seem to you to be necessary restrictions upon trade and intercourse. I think proper, however, to enjoin upon you the following: Allow no part of the military under your command to be engaged in either returning fugitive slaves, or in forcing or enticing slaves from their homes; and, so far as practicable, enforce the same forbearance upon the people.

Report to me your opinion upon the availability for good of the enrolled militia of the State. Allow no one to enlist colored troops, except upon orders from you, or from here through you.

Allow no one to assume the functions of confiscating property, under the law of Congress, or otherwise, except upon orders from here.

At elections, see that those, and only those, are allowed to vote, who are entitled to do so by the laws of Missouri, including as of those laws the restrictions laid by the Missouri Convention upon those who may have participated in the rebellion.

So far as practicable, you will, by means of your military force, expel guerrillas, marauders, and murderers, and all who are known to harbor, aid, or abet them. But, in like manner, you will repress assumptions of unauthorized individuals to perform the same service, because, under, pretense of doing this, they become marauders and murderers themselves.

To now restore peace, let the military obey orders; and those not of the military leave each other alone, thus not breaking the peace themselves.

In giving the above directions, it is not intended to restrain you in other expedient and necessary matters, not falling within their range.   Your obedient servant,   A. LINCOLN.

In this letter of instructions, an attempt was made to insure practical remedies for all the evils camplained of that seemed to have a substantial ground, yet without the removal of Gen. Schofield, as asked.   In other words, it was the aim to cure real grievances, without granting the complainants a merely personal triumph.   To the latter party he replied more at length, and his words are worthy of careful reading, as showing, better than any other language can do, Mr. Lincoln's actual opinions and policy regarding the matters at issue.   The letter is in these words:

EXECUTIVE MANSION,
WASHINGTON, October 5, 1863.

Hon. CHAS. D. DRAKE and others, Committee—*Gentlemen :* Your original address, presented on the 30th ult., and the four supplementary ones presented on the 3d inst., have been carefully considered.   I hope you will regard the other duties claiming my attention, together with the great length and importance of these documents, as constituting a sufficient apology for my not having responded sooner.'

These papers, framed for a common object, consist of the things demanded, and the reasons for demanding them.

The things demanded are :

1st. That Gen. Schofield shall be relieved, and Gen. Butler be appointed as Commander of the Military Department of Missouri ;

2d. That the system of enrolled militia in Missouri may be broken up, and National forces be substituted for it ; and

3d. That at elections persons may not be allowed to vote who are not entitled by law to do so.

Among the reasons given, enough of suffering and wrong to Union men, is certainly, and I suppose truly stated.   Yet the whole case, as presented, fails to convince me that Gen. Schofield, or the enrolled militia, is responsible for that suffering and wrong.   The whole can be explained on a more charitable, and, as I think, a more rational hypothesis.

We are in a civil war.   In such cases there always is a main question ; but in this case that question is a perplexing compound—Union and Slavery.   It thus becomes a question not of two sides merely, but of at least four sides, even among those who are for the Union, saying nothing of those who are against it. Thus, those who are for the Union *with*, but not *without slavery*—those for it *without*, but not *with*—those for it *with* or *without*, but prefer it *with*, and those for it *with* or *without*, but prefer it *without*.

Among these, again, is a subdivision of those who are for *gradual*, but not for *immediate*, and those who are for *immediate*, but not for *gradual* extinction of slavery.

It is easy to conceive that all these shades of opinion, and even more, may be sincerely entertained by honest and truthful men. Yet, all being for the Union, by reason of these differences, each will prefer a different way of sustaining the Union. At once, sincerity is questioned, and motives are assailed. Actual war coming, blood grows hot, and blood is spilled. Thought is forced from old channels into confusion. Deception breeds and thrives. Confidence dies, and universal suspicion reigns. Each man feels an impulse to kill his neighbor, lest he be killed by him. Revenge and retaliation follow. And all this, as before said, may be among honest men only. But this is not all. Every foul bird comes abroad, and every dirty reptile rises up. These add crime to confusion. Strong measures deemed indispensable, but harsh at best, such men make worse by maladministration. Murders for old grudges, and murders for pelf, proceed under any cloak that will best serve for the occasion.

These causes amply account for what has occurred in Missouri, without ascribing it to the weakness or wickedness of any general. The newspaper files, those chroniclers of current events, will show that the evils now complained of, were quite as prevalent under Fremont, Hunter, Halleck, and Curtis, as under Schofield. If the former had greater force opposed to them, they also had greater force with which to meet it. When the organized rebel army left the State, the main Federal force had to go also, leaving the Department Commander at home, relatively no stronger than before. Without disparaging any, I affirm with confidence, that no Commander of that Department has, in proportion to his means, done better than Gen. Schofield.

The first specific charge against Gen. Schofield is, that the enrolled militia was placed under his command, whereas it had not been placed under the command of Gen. Curtis. The fact is, I believe, true; but you do not point out, nor can I conceive how that did, or could, injure loyal men or the Union cause.

You charge that Gen. Curtis being, superseded by Gen.

Schofield, Franklin A. Dick was superseded by James O. Broadhead as Provost-Marshal General. No very specific showing is made as to how this did or could injure the Union cause. It recalls, however, the condition of things, as presented to me, which led to a change of commander of that department.

To restrain contraband intelligence and trade, a system of searches, seizures, permits and passes, had been introduced, I think, by Gen. Fremont. When Gen. Halleck came, he found and continued the system, and added an order, applicable to some parts of the State, to levy and collect contributions from noted rebels, to compensate losses, and relieve destitution caused by the rebellion. The action of Gen. Fremont and Gen. Halleck, as stated, constituted a sort of system which Gen. Curtis found in full operation when he took command of the department. That there was a necessity for something of the sort was clear ; but that it could only be justified by stern necessity, and that it was liable to great abuse in administration, was equally clear. Agents to execute it, contrary to the great prayer, were led into temptation. Some might, while others would not resist that temptation. It was not possible to hold any to a very strict accountability ; and those yielding to the temptation, would sell permits and passes to those who would pay most, and most readily for them ; and would seize property and collect levies in the aptest way to fill their own pockets. Money being the object, the man having money, whether loyal or disloyal, would be a victim. This practice, doubtless, existed to some extent, and it was a real additional evil, that it could be, and was plausibly charged to exist in greater extent than it did.

When Gen. Curtis took command of the department, Mr. Dick, against whom I never knew any thing to allege, had general charge of this system. A controversy in regard to it rapidly grew into almost unmanageable proportions. One side ignored the *necessity* and magnified the evils of the system, while the other ignored the evils and magnified the necessity ; and each bitterly assailed the other. I could not fail to see that the controversy enlarged in the same proportion as the professed Union men there distinctly took sides in two opposing political parties. I exhausted my wits, and very nearly my patience also, in efforts to convince both that the evils they charged on each other were inherent in the case, and could not be cured by giving either party a victory over the other.

Plainly, the irritating system was not to be perpetual ; and it was plausibly urged that it could be modified at once with advantage. The case could scarcely be worse, and whether it could be made better could only be determined by a trial. In this view, and not to ban, or brand Gen. Curtis, or to give a victory to any party, I made the change of commander for the department. I now learn that soon after this change, Mr. Dick was removed, and that Mr. Broadhead, a gentleman of no less good character, was put in the place. The mere fact of this change is more distinctly complained of than is any conduct of the new officer, or other consequence of the change.

I gave the new commander no instructions as to the administration of the system mentioned, beyond what is contained in the private letter afterward surreptitiously published, in which I directd him to act solely for the public good, and independently of both parties. Neither any thing you have presented me, nor any thing I have otherwise learned, has convinced me that he has been unfaithful to this charge.

Imbecility is urged as one cause for removing Gen. Schofield, and the late massacre at Lawrence, Kansas, is pressed as evidence of that imbecility. To my mind, that fact scarcely tends to prove the proposition. That massacre is only an example of what Grierson, John Morgan, and many others, might have repeatedly done on their respective raids, had they chosen to incur the personal hazard, and possessed the fiendish hearts to do it.

The charge is made that Gen. Schofield, on purpose to protect the Lawrence murderers, would not allow them to be pursued into Missouri. While no punishment could be too sudden or too severe for those murderers, I am well satisfied that the preventing of the threatened remedial raid into Missouri was the only way to avoid an indiscriminate massacre there, including probably more innocent than guilty. Instead of condemning, I therefore approve what I understand Gen. Schofield did in that respect.

The charge that Gen. Schofield has purposely withheld protection from loyal people, and purposely facilitated the objects of the disloyal, are altogether beyond my power of belief. I do not arraign the veracity of gentlemen as to the facts complained of; but I do more than question the judgment which would infer that these facts occurred in accordance with the purposes of Gen. Schofield.

With my present views, I must decline to remove Gen. Schofield. In this I decide nothing against Gen. Butler. I sincerely wish it were convenient to assign him a suitable command.

In order to meet some existing evils, I have addressed a letter of instruction to Gen. Schofield, a copy of which I inclose to you. As to the " Enrolled Militia," I shall endeavor to ascertain, better than I now know, what is its exact value. Let me say now, however, that your proposal to substitute National force for the "Enrolled Militia," implies that, in your judgment, the latter is doing something which needs to be done; and if so, the proposition to throw that force away, and to supply its place by bringing other forces from the field, where they are urgently needed, seems to me very extraordinary. Whence shall they come? Shall they be withdrawn from Banks, or Grant, or Steele, or Rosecrans?

Few things have been so grateful to my anxious feelings, as when in June last, the local force in Missouri aided General Schofield to so promptly send a large general force to the relief of Gen. Grant, then investing Vicksburg, and menaced from without by Gen. Johnston. Was this all wrong? Should the Enrolled Militia then have been broken up, and Gen. Heron kept from Grant, to police Missouri? So far from finding cause to object, I confess to. a sympathy for whatever relieves our general force in Missouri, and allows it to serve elsewhere.

I therefore, as at present advised, can not attempt the destruction of the Enrolled Militia of Missouri. I may add, that the force being under the National military control, it is also within the proclamation with regard to the *habeas corpus*.

I concur in the propriety of your request in regard to elections, and have, as you see, directed Gen. Schofield accordingly. I do not feel justified to enter upon the broad field you present in regard to the political differences betwen Radicals and Conservatives. From time to time I have done and said what appeared to me proper to do and say. The public knows it well. It obliges nobody to follow me, and I trust it obliges me to follow nobody. The Radicals and Conservatives each agree with me in some things and disagree in others. I could wish both to agree with me in all things; for then they would agree with each other, and would be too strong for any foe from any quarter. They, however, choose to do otherwise, and I do not question their right. I, too, shall do what seems to be my duty. I hold whoever commands in Missouri, or elsewhere, responsible to me, and not to either Radicals or Conservatives. It is my duty to hear all; but at last I must, within my sphere, judge what to do and what to forbear.

Your obedient servant,   A. LINCOLN.

How any Chief Magistrate, consistently with duty, to say nothing of the dignity becoming his office, could make himself a partisan of either side in a petty local conflict, mainly personal in its origin, or what more befitting attitude could have been taken, than was done in the closing paragraph of this letter, it is not easy to discover. Some of the leading "Radical" men in fact, who had most vehemently urged the removal of Gen. Schofield, and among them Senator Lane of Kansas (for that State, then included in the same military department, had also been heard on this occasion by its representatives), so clearly recognized the propriety of the President's position, and so well understood his views on all matters of principle to harmonize essentially with theirs, that they became his earnest adherents. The attempt to make an issue with Mr. Lincoln on this matter, and to arraign him before the nation, only convicted the movers of the scheme of utterly misconceiving alike, the person whom they accused, and the people before whom the issue was to be tried. The Missouri squabble could not be nationalized. Mr. Lincoln could not be proscribed for adhesion to the one side or the other.

The condition of affairs in Louisiana, on the capture of New Orleans, in 1862, had been materially different from that in Virginia and Missouri. The restoration of order seemed to require a temporary pupilage under a military governor. The proportion of loyal inhabitants was not such as to justify, in the opinion of the Government, an immediate attempt to restore civil authority in the State. So large a portion of its territory was yet in disloyal hands, and so small a number of its people of tested fidelity as to require the continued presence of armies and the prolonged ascendency of military jurisdiction. Even then, however, the popular branch of Congress had generously recognized and admitted Representatives from two of the districts of Louisiana. In due time, the state of affairs had so changed that the formation of a loyal civil government, repudiating slavery, as well as all the acts consequent upon pretended secession, was favored by the National Government, and by the military commander, Gen. Banks, under directions from President Lincoln.

Tennessee had early been placed under a military governor, in the person of Gen. Andrew Johnson, who had resigned his seat in the Senate, and accepted a military commission, in order the better to further the great work of redeeming his State and

35 46

restoring a legitimate civil authority. Arkansas, less exposed to military invasions, and apparently weary of a rebellion reluctantly joined, resumed almost at once the civil functions of a State, abolishing slavery, and repudiating secession.

The national Executive was ready to extend his cordial support to the movements thus diversely organized, according to the circumstances, in these three States, as he had done to those in Virginia and Missouri. All were proceeding on the same substantial principle, yet Congress, through the opposition of a sufficient number of Republican Union members to break the Administration majority, turned back from its former policy, and disappointed the hopes which the President, adhering to the course heretofore approved, had properly encouraged. It is not strange that this opposition should come to be regarded as either factious or visionary. Different reasons were assigned for this conduct. Honest differences of opinion undeniably existed. It is also manifest that a positive element of this opposition, which endeavored to find a nucleus in the local "Radicalism" of Missouri, and materials for coalescence in every kind of discontent existing among adherents of the dominant party was something aside from mere zealous patriotism.

An issue was raised in the House of Representatives on the Monroe doctrine, by a "Radical" member who very well knew that Mr. Lincoln's views of Maximilian's usurpation were no less emphatic than his own. The surrender of Arguelles to the punishment due the crime and infamy of the slave-trader, though not absolutely required by any treaty of extradition, was bitterly denounced by some of the "Radicals," while the great majority of those thus designating themselves, would have still more vehemently demurred at the "Conservatism" which could for a moment hesitate to give up the criminal. Some affecting "Radicalism" even joined the Opposition cry against military trials, the suppression of treasonable papers, summary arrests, and the silencing of orators endeavoring to demoralize the army and to incite insurrection in a time of great national peril. In some instances, beyond doubt, the same parties who made these proceedings a ground of complaint against Mr. Lincoln, would have declaimed against him for a want of vigor, had he been less zealous to preserve the nation, by the exercise of the war power as necessity required.

Much of the newspaper correspondence, as if some secret influence were working to pervert the utterances of the hour, as in the case of the army correspondence in the days of the Peninsula campaign, was made up with less regard for scrupulous veracity than for the opportunity of starting a new prejudice, or of confirming an old one, to the injury of the President. An important feature would be wanting, were this fact ignored. Paragraphs were constantly appearing in the spirit of the following, taken from the Washington dispatches to the New York *Tribune*, under date of May 24, 1864:

Mr. Chase on Arbitrary Arrests.—The subject of arbitrary arrests was incidentally discussed in Cabinet council to-day. Mr. Chase manfully denounced them. The suppression of the New York papers, and extradition of Arguelles were both condemned by him as devoid of policy and wanting law. The defense of these measures was more irritable than logical and assured.

It is unimportant to contradict any such statements, except to illustrate the wantonness of this apparently organized system for undermining the popular attachment to Mr. Lincoln. But, in fact, this dispatch was sheer fiction throughout. No such matter was discussed at the Cabinet council named, nor was Mr. Chase himself present, having for months habitually absented himself from such meetings. It may be doubted, even, whether he entertained the views thus attributed to him, or was grateful for this apparent attempt to commend him to the good will of "Copperhead" malignants. But where abuse and perversion were demanded of professional correspondents, the columns waiting for such material would not be empty.

It was in spite of all these disadvantages, of the military situation, of partizan intrigue, of Congressional disaffection, and of manifold personal discontents among influential men who were personally passed by, or whose counsels had not been implicitly regarded in the dispensation of patronage, that the people, almost by a spontaneous uprising, demanded the re-nomination of Mr. Lincoln as the Union candidate for the

Presidency. In disregard of passionate appeals, through circulars, letters, central clubs, and peripatetic agents, the popular current set with unmistakable preponderance in one direction. Secretary Chase declined a further use of his name as a Presidential candidate. As a last resort, many voices clamored for a postponement of the national convention. This body had been called to meet at Baltimore on the 7th day of June, 1864, three weeks later than the date at which the like convention had assembled in 1860. There was not even a plausible reason for wishing a later day, unless from the hope of a change in the popular current. The efforts to secure a postponement having failed, the now dwindling remnant of "Radical" opposition decided to meet at Cleveland one week *earlier*, and to present nominations in advance of those to be made at Baltimore. This they did, using the name so familiarized by the canvass of 1856. But that was no longer a name to conjure by. The Cleveland convention, which threatened for an hour to secure a Democratic success, scarcely produced a ripple on the surface of national politics.

As indicated in previous pages, fourteen States had declared, either through their legislatures or popular conventions, a decided preference for Mr. Lincoln's re-nomination. Before the assembling of the convention, the popular will was too clear to admit of any doubt as to the result on that point. The call for the national convention was addressed to "all qualified voters who desire the unconditional maintenance of the Union, the supremacy of the Constitution, and the complete suppression of the existing rebellion, with the cause thereof, by vigorous war, and all apt and efficient means," inviting their participation in the choice of delegates. Each State was to be represented by a number equal to twice its electoral vote.

The key-note of the convention may be said to have been given by the Rev. Dr. R. J. Breckinridge, of Kentucky, who was selected as the temporary presiding officer. This distinguished gentleman had been chosen as a delegate by the Kentucky State convention, after assuring that body that he would only accept the trust on condition of being instructed to vote "first, last, and all the time for Abraham Lincoln."

Dr. Breckinridge's declaration of his life-long conviction of the evil and wrong of slavery, and his earnest desire for its extinction throughout the land, was received with such applause as showed an entire harmony of feeling in regard to eradicating the "cause" of the rebellion. But scarcely less emphatic was the applause which had previously greeted him when he said:

In the first place, nothing can be more plain than the fact that you are here as the representatives of a great nation—voluntary representatives chosen without forms of law, but as really representing the feelings, the principles, and if you choose, the prejudices of the American people, as if it were written in laws and already passed by votes—for the man that you will nominate here for the Presidency of the United States, and ruler of a great people in a great crisis, is just as certain, I suppose, to become that ruler, as anything under heaven is certain before it is done. And, moreover, you will allow me to say—though, perhaps, it is hardly strictly proper that I should—but as far as I know your opinions, I suppose it is just as certain now, before you utter it, whose name you will utter, and which will be responded to from one end to the other of this nation, as it will be after it has been uttered and recorded by your secretary. Does any man doubt that this convention intends to say that Abraham Lincoln shall be the nominee? [Great applause.]

Ex-Governor William Dennison, of Ohio, was chosen permanent President of the Convention. Delegates were admitted from such of the Territories as had sent them, and from the District of Columbia. Questions arose in regard to the admission of delegates from Tennessee, Louisiana, Arkansas and Virginia; (West Virginia was duly represented;) and there were two contesting delegations from Missouri, representing the two parties there, already referred to. The Convention admitted the "Radical" delegation, with almost entire unanimity. The delegates from Tennessee, Louisiana and Arkansas were cordially received. The Virginia delegation was excluded.

On the ballot for the Presidential candidate, Mr. Lincoln received every vote in the convention, with the single exception of the delegation from Missouri, whose vote was changed, making the nomination unanimous. The joyous demonstrations with which this announcement was received in the veritable city of Baltimore, only three years before so hostile, and not yet free from slavery, were in keeping with the general satisfaction felt throughout the country, at the consummation of this expected result.

The ballot on the nomination of Vice President stood, before any changes, as follows: Andrew Johnson, of Tennessee, 200; Hannibal Hamlin, of Maine, 145; Daniel S. Dickinson, of New York, 113; B. F. Butler, of Massachusetts, 28; Lovell H. Rousseau, of Kentucky, 21; all others, 12. The States of Ohio, Indiana, Iowa, Tennessee, Arkansas, West Virginia, Delaware and Connecticut, voted unitedly for Gov. Johnson. A majority of the votes of New York and Vermont were also cast in the same direction. A sufficient number of votes were at once changed to give a majority to Andrew Johnson, and he was unanimously declared the nominee for Vice President.

The following resolutions were adopted by the convention:

THE BALTIMORE PLATFORM, 1864.

Resolved, That it is the highest duty of every American citizen to maintain against all their enemies the integrity of the Union and the paramount authority of the Constitution and the laws of the United States; and that, laying aside all differences and political opinions, we pledge ourselves as Union men, animated by a common sentiment, and aiming at a common object, to do everything in our power to aid the Government in quelling, by force of arms, the rebellion now raging against its authority, and in bringing to the punishment, due to their crimes, the rebels and traitors arrayed against it.

Resolved, That we approve the determination of the Government of the United States not to compromise with rebels, or to offer them any terms of peace except such as may be based upon an " unconditional surrender " of their hostility and a return to their just allegiance to the Constitution and the laws of the United States; and that we call upon the Government to maintain this position and to prosecute the war with the utmost possible vigor to the complete suppression of the rebellion, in full reliance upon the self-sacrifices, the patriotism, the heroic valor, and the undying devotion of the American people to their country and its free institutions.

Resolved, That as Slavery was the cause and now constitutes the strength of this rebellion, and as it must be always and everywhere hostile to the principles of republican government,

justice and the national safety demand its utter and complete
extirpation from the soil of the Republic, and that we uphold
and maintain the acts and proclamations by which the Government, in its own defense, has aimed a death-blow at this gigantic evil. We are in favor, furthermore, of such an amendment
to the Constitution, to be made by the people in conformity
with its provisions, as shall terminate and forever prohibit the
existence of slavery within the limits or the jurisdiction of the
United States.

Resolved, That the thanks of the American people are due
to the soldiers and sailors of the army and the navy, who have
periled their lives in defense of their country, and in vindication of the honor of the flag; that the nation owes to them
some permanent recognition of their patriotism and their valor,
and ample and permanent provision for those of their survivors
who have received disabling and honorable wounds in the service of the country; and that the memories of those who have
fallen in its defense shall be held in grateful and everlasting
remembrance.

Resolved, That we approve and applaud the practical wisdom,
the unselfish patriotism and unswerving fidelity to the Constitution and the principles of American Liberty with which
Abraham Lincoln has discharged, under circumstances of
unparalleled difficulty, the great duties and responsibilities of the
Presidential office; that we approve and indorse, as demanded
by the emergency and essential to the preservation of the
nation, and as within the Constitution, the measures and acts
which he has adopted to defend the nation against its open and
secret foes; that we approve especially the Proclamation of
Emancipation, and the employment as Union soldiers of men
heretofore held in slavery; and that we have full confidence in
his determination to carry these and all other constitutional
measures essential to the salvation of the country into full and
complete effect.

Resolved, That we deem it essential to the general welfare
that harmony should prevail in the national councils, and we
regard as worthy of public confidence and official trust those
only who cordially indorse the principles proclaimed in these
resolutions, and which should characterize the administration
of the Government.

Resolved, That the Government owes to all men employed
in its armies, without regard to distinction of color, the full
protection of the laws of war, and that any violations of these
laws or of the usages of civilized nations in the times of war by
the rebels now in arms should be made the subject of full and
prompt redress.

Resolved, That the foreign immigration which in the past has added so much to the wealth and development of resources and increase of power to this nation, the asylum of the oppressed of all nations, should be fostered and encóuraged by a liberal and just policy.

Resolved, That we are in favor of the speedy construction of the railroad to the Pacific.

Resolved, That the national faith pledged for the redemption of the public debt must be kept inviolate, and that for this purpose we recommend economy and rigid responsibility in the public expenditures, and a vigorous and just system of taxation; that it is the duty of any loyal State to sustain the credit and promote the use of the national currency.

Resolved, That we approve the position taken by the Government that the people of the United States can never regard with indifference the attempt of any European power to overthrow by force or to supplant by fraud the institutions of any republican government on the Western Continent, and that they will view with extreme jealousy, as menacing to the peace and independence of this, our country, the efforts of any such power to obtain new footholds for monarchical governments, sustained by a foreign military force in near proximity to the United States.

Immediately after the Convention, a committee of one from each State represented therein, waited on the President, orally communicating the fact of his re-nomination, and presenting a copy of the foregoing resolutions. Responding to the address of their Chairman, Mr. Lincoln said:

MR. CHAIRMAN AND GENTLEMEN OF THE COMMITTEE: I will neither conceal my gratification nor restrain the expression of my gratitude that the Union people through their convention, in the continued effort to save and advance the nation, have deemed me not unworthy to remain in my present position.

I know no reason to doubt that I shall accept the nomination tendered; and yet, perhaps, I should not declare definitely before reading and considering what is called the platform.

I will say now, however, I approve the declaration in favor of so amending the Constitution as to prohibit slavery throughout the nation. When the people in revolt, with a hundred days of explicit notice that they could within those days resume their allegiance without the overthrow of their institutions, and that they could not resume it afterward, elected to stand out, such amendments to the Constitution as is now proposed became a fitting and necessary conclusion to the final success of the Union cause. Such alone can meet and cover all cavils. Now, the unconditional Union men, North and South, perceive its importance, and embrace it. In the joint names of Liberty and Union, let us labor to give it legal form and practical effect.

In response to a call from the Ohio delegation in the Baltimore Convention, accompanied by Menter's band, of Cincinnati, the President remarked:

GENTLEMEN: I am very much obliged to you for this compliment. I have just been saying, and as I have just said it, I will repeat it: The hardest of all speeches which I have to answer is a serenade. I never know what to say on such occasions. I suppose that you have done me this kindness in connection with the action of the Baltimore Convention which has recently taken place, and with which, of course, I am very well satisfied. [Laughter and applause]. What we want still more than Baltimore Conventions or Presidential elections is success under General Grant. [Cries of " Good," and applause.] I propose that you constantly bear in mind that the support you owe to the brave officers and soldiers in the field is of the very first importance, and we should therefore bend all our energies to that point. Now, without detaining you any longer, I propose that you help me to close up what I am now saying with three rousing cheers for General Grant and the officers and soldiers under his command.

In an interview with a delegation of the National Union League, in the East Room, he used substantially the following language—the homely illustrations at the close (and the manner of presenting it), exciting prolonged laughter and applause :

GENTLEMEN: I can only say in response to the kind remarks of your Chairman, as I suppose, that I am very grateful for the renewed confidence which has been accorded to me both by the Convention and by the National League. I am not insensible at all to the personal compliment there is in this, and yet I do not allow myself to believe that any but a small portion of it is to be appropriated as a personal compliment. That really the Convention and the Union League assembled with a higher view—that of taking care of the interests of the country for the present and the great future— and that the part I am entitled to appropriate as a compliment is only that part which I may lay hold of as being the opinion of the Convention and of the League, that I am not entirely unworthy to be entrusted with the place which I have occupied for the last three years. But I do not allow myself to suppose that either the Convention or the League have concluded to decide that I am either the greatest or best man in America, but rather they have concluded that it is not best to swap horses while crossing the river, and have further concluded that I am not so poor a horse that they might not make a botch of it in trying to swap.

The Committee to notify President Lincoln of his re-nomination subsequently transmitted to him a letter, formally announcing the choice of the Convention, in the course of which they said :

We believe, sir, that the honest will of the Union men of the country was never more truly represented than in this Convention. Their purpose we believe to be the overthrow of armed rebels in the field, and the security of permanent peace and union, by liberty and justice under the Constitution. That these results are to be achieved amid cruel perplexities, they are fully aware. That they are to be reached only by cordial unanimity of counsel, is undeniable. That good men may sometimes differ as to the means and the time, they know. That in the conduct of all human affairs the highest duty is to determine, in the angry conflict of passion, how much good may be practically accomplished, is their sincere persuasions. They have watched your official course, therefore, with unflagging attention ; and amid the bitter taunts of eager friends and the fierce denunciation of enemies, now moving too fast for some, now too slowly for others, they have seen you throughout this tremendous contest patient, sagacious, faithful, just ; leaning upon the heart of the great mass of the people, and satisfied to be moved by its mighty pulsations.

It is for this reason that, long before the Convention met, the popular instinct had plainly indicated you as its candidate ; and the Convention, therefore, merely recorded the popular will. Your character and career prove your unswerving fidelity to the cardinal principles of American Liberty and of the American Constitution. In the name of that Liberty and

Constitution, sir, we earnestly request your acceptance of this nomination.

To this letter, Mr. Lincoln replied in the following words:

EXECUTIVE MANSION, ⎰
WASHINGTON, June 27, 1864. ⎱

Hon. WILLIAM DENNISON and others, a Committee of the Union National Convention: *Gentlemen*—Your letter of the 14th instant, formally notifying me that I have been nominated by the Convention you represent for the Presidency of the United States, for four years from the 4th of March next, has been received. The nomination is gratefully accepted, as the resolutions of the Convention—called the platform—are heartily approved.

While the resolution in regard to the supplanting of republican government upon the Western Continent is fully concurred in, there might be misunderstanding were I not to say that the position of the Government in relation to the action of France and Mexico, as assumed through the State Department, and indorsed by the Convention, among the measures and acts of the Executive, will be faithfully maintained so long as the state of facts shall leave that position pertinent and applicable.

I am especially gratified that the soldier and the seamen were not forgotten by the Convention, as they forever must and will be remembered by the grateful country for whose salvation they devote their lives.

Thanking you for the kind and complimentary terms in which you have communicated the nomination and other proceedings of the Convention, I subscribe myself

Your obedient servant,

ABRAHAM LINCOLN.

Every-where through the loyal States, and not less among our heroic armies fighting for the Republic on disloyal soil, and among our brave forces afloat on gunboats and men-of-war, the nomination of Abraham Lincoln for a second term was received with joy, and ratified with hearty good will. More than thirty years had passed since any President of the United States had received the honor of a reëlection. Never, as yet, had any President from the North been chosen for a second term, although every Southern President, elected as such, until the time of Mr. Polk, had served for eight years. Aside from merely personal considerations, there was undoubtedly a feeling that the policy of the Administration, being satisfactory, should not be materially changed at this important juncture, and that the name associated with the policy of emancipation, in its inception, should be connected with its ultimate triumph.

There was also a certain earnest devotion in President Lincoln's calm faith in the guidance and aid of Divine Providence, which strongly impressed all sober minds—a religious trust which became more and more his support in the severe trials of his official station. This trait of his character, and the confidence reposed in him by the churches, can not be better illustrated than by giving the following address of sympathy and loyal attachment which belongs to this period, although of somewhat earlier date than the President's re-nomination—presented in person by a delegation of distinguished clergymen, headed by Bishop Ames, on behalf of the General Conference of Methodist Episcopal churches, together with the brief, unpremeditated reply made on that occasion.

To His Excellency Abraham Lincoln, President of the United States : The General Conference of the Methodist Episcopal Church, now in session in the city of Philadelphia, representing nearly seven thousand ministers, and nearly a million of members, mindful of their duty as Christian citizens, takes the earliest opportunity to express to you the assurance of the loyalty of the Church, her earnest devotion to the interests of the country, and her sympathy with you in the great responsibilities of your high position in this trying hour.

With exultation we point to the record of our Church as having never been tarnished by disloyalty. She was the first of the churches to express, by a deputation of her most distinguished ministers, the promise of support to the Government in the days of Washington. In her Articles of Religion she has enjoined loyalty as a duty, and has ever given to the Government her most decided support.

In this present struggle for the nation's life, many thousands of her members, and a large number of her ministers, have rushed to arms to maintain the cause of God and humanity. They have sealed their devotion to the country with their blood, on every battle-field of this terrible war.

We regard this dreadful scourge now desolating our land and

wasting the nation's life, as the result of a most unnatural utterly unjustifiable rebellion ; involving the crime of treason against the best of human governments, and sin against God. It required our Government to submit to its own dismemberment and destruction, leaving it no alternative but to preserve the national integrity by the use of the national resources. If the Government had failed to use its power to preserve the unity of the nation, and maintain its authority, it would have been justly exposed to the wrath of Heaven, and to the reproach and scorn of the civilized world.

Our earnest and constant prayer is, that this cruel and wicked rebellion may be speedily suppressed; and we pledge you our hearty coöperation in all appropriate means to secure this object.

Loyal and hopeful in national adversity, in prosperity thankful, we most heartily congratulate you on the glorious victories recently gained, and rejoice in the belief that our complete triumph is near.

We believe that our national sorrows and calamities have resulted, in a great degree, from our forgetfulness of God, and oppression of our fellow-men. Chastened by affliction, may the nation humbly repent of her sins, lay aside her haughty pride, honor God in all future legislation, and render justice to all who have been wronged.

We honor you for your proclamations of liberty, and rejoice in all the acts of the Government designed to secure freedom to the enslaved.

We trust that when military usages and necessities shall justify interference with established institutions, and the removal of wrongs sanctioned by law, the occasion will be improved, not merely to injure our foes and increase the national resources, but, also, as an opportunity to recognize our obligations to God, and to honor His law. We pray that the time may speedily come when this shall be truly a republican and free country, in no part of which, either State or Territory, shall slavery be known.

The prayers of millions of Christians, with an earnestness never manifested for rulers before, daily ascend to Heaven, that you may be endued with all needed wisdom and power. Actuated by the sentiments of the loftiest and purest patriotism, our prayer shall be continually for the preservation of our country undivided, for the triumph of our cause, and for a permanent peace, gained by the sacrifice of no moral principles, but founded on the Word of God, and securing, in righteousness, liberty and equal rights to all.

Signed, in behalf of the General Conference of the Methodist Episcopal Church.

PHILADELPHIA, May 14, 1864.

President Lincoln replied in the following words:

GENTLEMEN: In response to your address, allow me to attest the accuracy of its historical statements, indorse the sentiments it expresses, and thank you, in the nation's name, for the sure promise it gives.

Nobly sustained, as the Government has been by all the churches, I would utter nothing which might in the least appear invidious against any. Yet, without this, it may fairly be said that the Methodist Episcopal Church, not less devoted than the best, is, by its greater numbers, the most important of all. It is no fault in others that the Methodist Church sends more soldiers to the field, more nurses to the hospitals, and more prayers to heaven than any. God bless the Methodist Church; bless all the churches; and blessed be God, who, in this our great trial, giveth us the churches.

There was some corresponding action on the part of nearly or quite all the general ecclesiastical bodies of the United States. "All the churches," without regard to sectarian difference, not only confided in his high character, but also received from him a reciprocation of kindly feeling and thankfulness.

The first stage of the Presidential canvass was now passed. The nominations were made. The Administration platform was before the people. It now remained to be determined whether the Republican Union party should continue in the ascendant—whether a majority of the people of the nation, entitled to a voice on the question, should fully confirm and ratify what the party itself had with such cordial unanimity agreed upon, or should intrust the power of the nation to new men, on an entirely different basis of public policy.

CHAPTER IV.

Congress.—The Constitutional Amendment prohibiting Slavery.—Its Defeat in the House.—Repeal of the Fugitive Slave Laws.—New Bureaus Established.—Other Important Legislation.—" Reconstruction."—Opposition to the President's Policy.—The Davis Bill.— Disagreement of the two Houses Thereon.—Its Final Passage.— The President withholds his Signature.—His Proclamation on the Subject.—The Wade-Davis Manifesto.—Letters of Mr. Lincoln in regard to Matters in New Orleans and St. Louis.—President Lincoln's Speech at the Philadelphia Fair.—A Democratic National Convention Called and Postponed.—Clay, Thompson and other Conspirators in Canada.—The Greeley Negotiations with them.—President Lincoln's Action in the Case.—North-western Conspiracy.— The Chicago Nominations and Platform, 1864.

THE first session of the Thirty-eighth Congress terminated on the 4th day of July, 1864. On the 10th day of February, Mr. Trumbull, in the Senate, had reported from the Committee on the Judiciary a joint resolution proposing to the legislatures of the several States (to become valid when ratified by three-fourths of the same) the following article as an amendment to the Constitution of the United States:

ARTICLE XIII.—*Section* 1. Neither slavery nor involuntary servitude, except as a punishment for crime, whereof the party shall have been duly convicted, shall exist within the United States, or any place subject to their jurisdiction.

Section 2. Congress shall have power to enforce this article by appropriate legislation.

This resolution passed the Senate on the 8th of April, by a vote of 38 to 6 (the negative votes being given by Messrs. Davis and Powell, of Kentucky, Riddle and Salisbury, of Delaware, Hendricks, of Indiana, and McDougall, of California). The resolution having been transmitted to the House of Representatives, was taken up on the 31st of May, when, Mr

Holman, of Indiana, having objected to its second reading, that body was brought to a direct vote on its rejection, which stood, yeas 55, nays 76, the Democratic opposition voting unanimously against any consideration of the question. On the 15th of June, the resolution was directly voted on, and rejected for want of the requisite two-thirds vote—the yeas being 95, and the nays 66. Mr. Ashley, of Ohio, having voted in the negative, with a view to secure a reconsideration of the vote at the next session, entered a motion to that effect on the same day. Thus a great measure of vital consequence to the nation for all time, was defeated by the Democratic opposition, still unwilling to cut loose from the doomed institution, and still apparently hopeful of renewing a Southern bondage which had been so long the basis of their political power. On the other hand, the Republican Union party had adopted this measure in its platform, as a vital issue of the time, and supported it with entire unanimity in both branches of Congress. President Lincoln himself had already given his hearty approval to this method for the utter and final extinction of slavery wherever the jurisdiction of the United States extends.

The time had now come when the odious legislation for returning to bondage the slaves who had asserted their natural right to freedom by escaping into free territory, should cease to have a place among the laws of a free republic. Various attempts had been made to this end, both in the Senate and in the House of Representatives, during this and the previous sessions of Congress, without final effect, until, on the 13th of June, 1864, Mr. Morris, of New York, from the Committee on the Judiciary, reported an act repealing the fugitive slave act of 1850, and the third and fourth sections of that of 1793. This repealing act passed by nearly a strict party vote—yeas 86, nays 60—the Administration members, save Mr. Smithers, of Delaware, voting unitedly for the repeal, and the Opposition members, except Mr. Griswold, of New York, voting in the negative. This bill passed the Senate on the 22d day of June, and received the approval of the Executive on the 28th.

The Bureau of National Currency, in the Treasury Department, was created at this session, and Hon. Hugh McCulloch, of Indiana, appointed to the office of Comptroller of the Currency. In the War Department, the Bureau of Military Justice was established, at the head of which Hon. Joseph Holt, of Kentucky, was appointed, as Judge Advocate General, with the rank of brigadier-general. An additional loan of $400,000,000 was authorized; the enrollment act was materially modified, by repealing the commutation clause (releasing any drafted man on the payment of three hundred dollars), and otherwise rendering it more efficient; important amendments were made in the pension laws; and acts were passed for the punishment of guerrillas, for increasing the efficiency of the navy, and in aid of the proposed international telegraph by British and Russian America to Asia.

In his annual message, with the accompanying proclamation of amnesty, President Lincoln had, somewhat at length and in detail, given his views as to the best means of restoring practical relations between the insurrectionary States and the National Government. These views were in accord with those hitherto acted upon, and approved by every branch of the Government, although, coupled as they were with proffers of amnesty, they were extended to embrace particular suggestions not before presented. The methods of reorganization proposed were recommendations merely, properly guarded, and the purpose of prescribing any invariable rule of action in the premises, was distinctly disavowed. As already seen,* the President, in this proclamation of amnesty with certain conditions, was not only exercising the prerogative belonging to the pardoning power conferred on him by the Constitution, but was also carrying out the formally expressed will of Congress. Early in the session (December 15, 1863), Mr. Davis, of Maryland, moved the reference of so much of the President's message as related to this subject to a committee of nine, which was agreed to, the mover being appointed chairman. On the 4th of May following, a bill and preamble were reported by Mr. Davis, embodying a fixed and elaborate plan of "reconstruction." It provided for the appointment of a Provisional

---

* *Ante* page 459

36

Governor by the President, in each State declared to be in rebellion, to serve until a State government should have been organized and recognized by the National Government. On the suppression of military resistance to the authority of the United States in any such State, an enrollment of white male citizens was to be made, and a convention was to be called, when a *majority* of them should have taken the oath of allegiance, to act upon the reëstablishment of a State government. All persons having held any office in the Rebel service, civil or military, State or Confederate, and all those having voluntarily borne arms in such service, were to be prohibited from voting for or being elected as delegates to the State convention. The convention was required, by the bill, to insert in the new constitution to be framed by it, provisions (1st) disfranchising those who have " held or exercised any civil or military office (except offices merely ministerial, and military offices below a colonel), State or Confederate, under the usurping power; " (2d), prohibiting slavery ; and (3d), repudiating all debts created by or under sanction of " the usurping power," "State or Confederate." The State government thus created was to be recognized by the President, after obtaining the assent of Congress, and only after such recognition, the State to be represented in Congress, and in the electoral college. Slavery was further formally declared to be abolished in all the States in question, with remedies and penalties to give this declaration effect. Those Rebels holding any civil or military office, with the conditions above stated, after this bill should become a law, were declared not to be citizens of the United States.

This bill passed the House on the day it was reported, yeas 74, nays 66. Among the latter were several Administration members. The preamble, giving a key-note to the spirit and purpose of the bill, was in these words :

WHEREAS, The so-called Confederate States are a public enemy, waging an unjust war, whose injustice is so glaring that they have no right to claim the mitigation of the extreme rights of war which are accorded by modern usage to an enemy who has a right to consider the war a just one ; and whereas none of the States which, by a regularly recorded majority of its citizens, have joined the so-called Southern Confederacy, can be considered and treated as entitled to be represented in Congress, or to take any part in the political government of the Union.

This was rejected, ayes 57, nays 75.

In the Senate, on the 1st of July, Mr. Brown, of Missouri, moved the following substitute for the entire bill which was carried, yeas 20, nays 13:

That when the inhabitants of any State have been declared in a state of insurrection against the United States, by proclamation of the President, by force and virtue of the act entitled " An act to provide for the collection of duties on imports, and for other purposes," approved July 13, 1861, they shall be, and are hereby declared to be, incapable of casting any vote for electors of President or Vice President of the United States, or of electing Senators or Representatives in Congress, until said insurrection in said State is suppressed or abandoned, and said inhabitants have returned to their obedience to the Government of the United States, nor until such return to obedience shall be declared by proclamation of the President, issued by virtue of an act of Congress, hereafter to be passed, authorizing the same.

The bill having been returned to the House, as thus amended, the amendment was non-concurred in. The Senate ultimately receded from its amendment, yeas 18, nays 14, thus concurring in the passage of the bill as it first came from the House. It is manifest, from the action taken on this bill, that it was not unobjectionable to the majority of the Senate, and that, on free discussion of its prominent details, it could not certainly command a majority in the House on a full vote. That it could ever have received a two-thirds vote in both houses, had it been returned by the Executive with objections, probably its most zealous supporter never imagined. It so happened that the bill, passed just at the close of the session, only reached the President about an hour before the actual adjournment, when numerous other bills were awaiting his signature, allowing him hardly time to even read it with care, much less to prepare a veto message. Much of it he fully approved. Other parts he thought seriously objectionable. Committed, too, as he

already had been, publicly, to the recognition of the new State
governments of Louisiana and Arkansas, he could not, in good
faith, repudiate his promises to the people of those States, as
would have been done by approving the Davis bill. Only a
dictatorial and factious spirit could call in question the President's unrestricted right to withhold his signature, or the purity
of the motive which led him to do so. Not less evidently was
it proper for him to publish the bill, with a statement of his
reasons for the course he had taken, and to give it a place with
his own suggestions made in the amnesty proclamation, reserving his former action in regard to Louisiana and Arkansas, and
declining to make compliance with the terms of this bill indispensable in any case. He had long before appointed military
governors in Tennessee and North Carolina. The power to do
so clearly belonged to him, as Commander-in-chief of the Army
and Navy. But it was questionable, to say the least, whether
Congress could constitutionally exercise any " provisional "
local jurisdiction in the States, as proposed.

On the 8th of July, 1864, President Lincoln issued the
following proclamation, on the subject, accompanied by the
Davis Reconstruction bill :

WHEREAS, At the late session, Congress passed a bill " to
guarantee to certain States, whose governments have been
usurped or overthrown, a republican form of government," a
copy of which is hereunto annexed :

AND WHEREAS, The said bill was presented to the President
of the United States for his approval less than one hour before
the *sine die* adjournment of said session, and was not signed by
him :

AND WHEREAS, The said bill contains, among other things,
a plan for restoring the States in rebellion to their proper practical relation in the Union, which plan expresses the sense of
Congress upon that subject, and which plan it is now thought
fit to lay before the people for their consideration :

Now, therefore, I, Abraham Lincoln, President of the United
States, do proclaim, declare, and make known, that, while I am
(as I was in December last, when by proclamation I propounded a plan for restoration) unprepared, by a formal
approval of this bill, to be inflexibly committed to any single
plan of restoration ; and, while I am also unprepared to declare
that the free State constitutions and governments already

adopted and installed in Arkansas and Louisiana shall be set aside and held for nought, thereby repelling and discouraging the loyal citizens who have set up the same as to further effort, or to declare a constitutional competency in Congress to abolish slavery in States, but am at the same time sincerely hoping and expecting that a constitutional amendment abolishing slavery throughout the nation may be adopted, nevertheless I am fully satisfied with the system for restoration contained in the bill as one very proper plan for the loyal people of any State choosing to adopt it, and that I am, and at all times shall be, prepared to give the Executive aid and assistance to any such people, so soon as the military resistance to the United States shall have been suppressed in any such State, and the people thereof shall have sufficiently returned to their obedience to the Constitution and laws of the United States, in which cases Military Governors will be appointed, with directions to proceed according to the bill.

It was not unnatural that the mover of this bill should be unpleasantly affected by its failure to become a law. He had matured, to his own entire satisfaction, a method of "reconstruction"—the vexed question which had been so much and so prematurely discussed—and it had received the indorsement of both Houses of Congress. He could not doubt its perfect sufficiency as a solution of the problem; yet his work had become of no effect for the lack of the President's signature.

Mr. Davis, however, was mistaken in supposing that the people attached any special value to his scheme, or that any appeal he could make to them would avert their ready and intuitive conclusion that he, rather than President Lincoln, was in the wrong. Such an appeal was, nevertheless, determined upon. At a moment when the country was growing impatient and apprehensive over severe losses in the field, without the decisive victories hoped for, when the Opposition was exultant in the prospect of a Presidential triumph in November, and when all cordial supporters of the Baltimore nominations were earnest and united in their efforts to avoid a possible defeat of the cause, Mr. Davis' arraignment of the President was issued. The paper was published on the 5th of August; Senator Wade also giving it his signature. In its imputation of bad motives, in its sweeping denunciations and in its angry

uncharitableness of temper, it was more remarkable than in
the weight of its arguments or in the accuracy of its representations.* The *New York Tribune*, which was chosen as the
medium for laying this address before the people, although
unfriendly to Mr. Lincoln's renomination, and although its
chief editor, at a later day, was concerned in a secret movement
to bring about his withdrawal, promptly expressed its approval
of the President's action in withholding his signature from the
measure in question. The principal effect to be anticipated
from this manifesto was a weakening of public confidence in
the Government, and an embarrassment of the Administration
party at the most critical period of the political canvass. The

---

* I have not deemed it worth while to copy, in the text, from a passionate effusion so speedily forgotten by the public, and which its
author would, perhaps, gladly forget. The following brief extracts will
suffice to justify what I have said as to its general character:

The President, by preventing this bill from becoming a law, *holds
the electoral votes* of the Rebel States *at the dictation of his personal
ambition* . . . . . The President's proclamation . . . . . *discards the
authority of the Supreme Court,* and strides headlong *toward the anarchy* his proclamation of the 8th of December *inaugurated* . . . . . A
more studied outrage *on the legislative authority* of the people has never
been perpetrated . . . . . He has already exercised *this dictatorial
usurpation* in Louisiana, and he *defeated the bill to prevent its limitation.*

Bearing in mind that the President has a qualified veto power, by
the Constitution, in regard to all legislation; and, further, that the
Davis bill was opposed by a considerable minority of "Union men"
in both Houses, the accuracy of the following extract from the same
paper, will be fully appreciated:

But he must understand that our support is of a cause and not
of a man; that *the authority of Congress is paramount* and must be
respected; that *the whole body of the Union men of Congress* will not
submit to be impeached by him of rash and unconstitutional legislation; and if he wishes our support, *he must confine himself to his executive duties—to obey and execute, not make the laws*—to suppress by
arms armed rebellion, and leave political reorganization to Congress.
If the supporters of the Government fail to insist on this, they
become responsible for the *usurpations which they fail to rebuke,* and are
justly liable to the indignation of the people whose rights and security,
committed to their keeping, *they sacrifice.*
Let them consider the remedy for these usurpations, and, having
found it, fearlessly execute it.

event showed, however, that its influence with the people was inconsiderable.

As illustrating President Lincoln's views in regard to the deportment of Southern Union men in the early part of the struggle, and his mode of dealing with the people of Louisiana in particular, a characteristic letter of his, written in 1862, is subjoined. A Mr. Durant had written to the President, through Mr. Bullitt, a gentleman known to him, and a former resident of Kentucky, manifesting dissatisfaction with the policy pursued by the Government at New Orleans, after the capture of that city. Among other things complained of, was the alleged protection given to escaping slaves, and their retention from their masters. It was also urged as a grievance, that men choosing to avail themselves of the benefits of the reëstablished Government were required to take the oath of allegiance, and that trade with the Rebels was prohibited. The President replied to this singular appeal as follows:

WASHINGTON, D. C., July 28, 1862.

Sir: The copy of a letter, addressed to yourself by Mr. Thomas J. Durant, has been shown to me. The writer appears to be an able, a dispassionate, and an entirely sincere man. The first part of the letter is devoted to an effort to show that the secession ordinance of Louisiana was adopted against the will of a majority of the people. This is probably true, and in that fact may be found some instruction. Why did they allow the ordinance to go into effect? Why did they not exert themselves? Why stand passive and allow themselves to be trodden down by a minority? Why did they not hold popular meetings, and have a convention of their own to express and enforce the true sentiments of the State. If preorganization was against them, then why not do this now, that the United States army is present to protect them? The paralyzer—the dead palsy—of the Government in the whole struggle is, that this class of men will do nothing for the Government—nothing for themselves, except demanding that the Government shall not strike its enemies, lest they be struck by accident.

Mr. Durant complains that, in various ways, the relation of master and slave is disturbed by the presence of our army; and he considers it particularly vexatious that this, in part, is done under cover of an act of Congress, while constitutional guarantees are superadded on the plea of military necessity The truth is, that what is done and omitted about slaves is done and omitted on the same military necessity. It is a military necessity to have men and money; and we can not get either, in sufficient numbers or amounts, if we keep from or drive from our lines slaves coming to them.

Mr. Durant can not be ignorant of the pressure in this direction, nor of my efforts to hold it within bounds, till he, and such as he, shall have time to help themselves.

I am not posted to speak understandingly on the public regulations of which Mr. Durant complains. If experience shows any of them to be wrong, let them be set right. I think I can perceive in the freedom of trade which Mr. Durant urges, that he would relieve both friends and enemies from the pressure of the blockade. By this he would serve the enemy more effectively than the enemy is able to serve himself.

I do not say or believe that to serve the enemy is the purpose of Mr. Durant, or that he is conscious of any purposes other than national and patriotic ones. Still, if there were a class of men, who, having no choice of sides in the contest, were anxious only to have quiet and comfort for themselves while it rages, and to fall in with the victorious side at the end of it, without loss to themselves, their advice as to the mode of conducting the contest would be precisely such as his.

He speaks of no duty, apparently thinks of none, resting upon Union men. He even thinks it injurious to the Union cause that they should be restrained in trade and passage, without taking sides. They are to touch neither a sail nor a pump—live merely passengers (" dead heads " at that)—to be carried snug and dry throughout the storm and safely landed right side up. Nay, more—even a mutineer is to go untouched, lest these sacred passengers receive an accidental wound.

Of course, the rebellion will never be suppressed in Louisiana, if the professed Union men there will neither help to do it, nor permit the Government to do without their help.

Now, I think the true remedy is very different from what is suggested by Mr. Durant. It does not lie in rounding the rough angles of the war, but in removing the necessity for the war. The people of Louisiana, who wish protection to person and property, have but to reach forth their hands and take it. Let them in good faith reinaugurate the national authority, and set up a State Government conforming thereto under the Constitution. They know how to do it, and can have the protection of the army while doing it. The army will be withdrawn so soon as such Government can dispense with its presence, and the people of the State can then, upon the old terms, govern themselves to their own liking. This is very simple and easy.

If they will not do this—if they prefer to hazard all for the sake of destroying the Government—it is for them to consider whether it is probable I will surrender the Government to save them from losing all. If they decline what I suggest, you scarcely need to ask what I will do.

What would you do in my position? Would you drop the war where it is, or would you prosecute it in future with elder-stalk squirts, charged with rosewater? Would you deal lighter blows, rather than heavier ones? Would you give up the contest, leaving every available means unapplied?

I am in no boastful mood. I shall not do more than I can, but I shall do all I can to save the Government, which is my sworn duty as well as my personal inclination. I shall do nothing in malice. What I deal with is too vast for malicious dealing.

Yours, very truly,   A. LINCOLN.

The following response to a petition in behalf of a secessionist clergyman in St. Louis, will afford an example of President Lincoln's mode of disposing of impudent pretensions set up by rebellious people in the Border States, and is otherwise memorable:

EXECUTIVE MANSION,
WASHINGTON, December 23, 1863.

I have just looked over a petition signed by some three dozen citizens of St. Louis, and their accompanying letters, one by yourself, one by a Mr. Nathan Ranney, and one by a Mr. John D. Coalter, the whole relating to the Rev. Dr. McPheeters. The petition prays, in the name of justice and mercy, that I will restore Dr. McPheeters to all his ecclesiastical rights.

This gives no intimation as to what ecclesiastical rights are withdrawn. Your letter states that Provost Marshal Dick, about a year ago, ordered the arrest of Dr. McPheeters, pastor of the Vine-street Church, prohibited him from officiating, and placed the management of affairs of the church out of the control of the chosen trustees; and near the close you state that a certain course " would insure his release." Mr. Ranney's letter says : " Dr. Samuel McPheeters is enjoying all the rights of a civilian, but can not preach the gospel!" Mr. Coalter, in his letter, asks : " Is it not a strange illustration of the condition of things, that the question who shall be allowed to preach in a church in St. Louis shall be decided by the President of the United States?"

Now, all this sounds very strangely; and, withal, a little as if you gentlemen making the application do not understand the case alike—one affirming that this doctor is enjoying all the rights of a civilian, and another pointing out to me what will secure his *release!* On the 2d of January last, I wrote to Gen. Curtis in relation to Mr. Dick's order upon Dr. McPheeter's; and, as I suppose the Doctor is enjoying all the rights of a civilian, I only quote that part of my letter which relates to the church. It was as follows: "But I must add that the United States Government must not, as by this order, undertake to run the churches. When an individual, in a church or out of it, becomes dangerous to the public interest, he must be checked; but the churches, as such, must take care of themselves. It will not do for the United States to appoint trustees, supervisors, or other agents for the churches."

This letter going to Gen. Curtis, then in command, I supposed, of course, it was obeyed, especially as I heard no further complaint from Dr. Mc. or his friends for nearly an entire year. I have never interfered, nor thought of interfering, as to who shall or shall not preach in any church; nor have I knowingly or believingly tolerated any one else to interfere by my authority. If any one is so interfering by color of my authority, I would like to have it specially made known to me.

If, after all, what is now sought is to have me put Dr. Mc. back over the heads of a majority of his own congregation, that, too, will be declined. I will not have control of any church or any side.　　　A. LINCOLN.

On the 16th of June, President Lincoln, by invitation, attended the great Fair, for the benefit of the Sanitary Commission, at Philadelphia. His reception was such as to leave no doubt that he had the cordial affection of the people of that city. After two or three hours spent by him (Mrs. Lincoln being also present), in passing through the rooms of the fair, which contained rare works of art and varieties of objects attractive to the intellectual taste, he was conducted to the supper-room, where Edward Everett and other distinguished guests joined him at the table. His health having been proposed, the President made the following remarks:

War, at the best, is terrible, and this war of ours, in its magnitude and duration, is one of the most terrible. It has deranged business, totally in some locations, and partially in all locations. It has produced a national debt and taxation unprecedented, at least, in this country. It has carried mourning to almost every home, until it may almost be said that "the heavens are hung with black."

Yet the war continues, and several relieving coincidents have accompanied it from the beginning, which have not been known, as I understand it, in former wars in the history of the world. The Sanitary Commission, with all its benevolent labors; the Christian Commission, with all its benevolent and Christian labors, and the various places, arrangements, institutions, so to speak, that have contributed to the comfort and relief of the soldier. You have two of these places in your city: the Cooper Shop and the Union Volunteer Refreshment Saloons; and, lastly, these fairs, which, I believe, began only in last August, if I mistake not, at Chicago, then at Boston, at Cincinnati, at Brooklyn, at New York, at Baltimore, and at the present at St. Louis, Pittsburg, Philadelphia, and, perhaps, at some other places which I do not remember.

The motives and objects that lie at the bottom of all these are the most worthy; for, say what you will, after all, the most is due to the soldier, who takes his life in his hand, and goes to fight the battles of his country. [Loud cheering.] In what is contributed to his comfort as he passes to and fro, from city to city; in what is contributed to him when he is sick and wounded; in whatever shape it comes, whether from the fair hand of woman, or from whatever source it may, it is much, very much. But I think that there is still that which is of much value to him, in the continual reminders he sees in the newspapers, that while he is absent he is yet remembered by the loved ones at home. [Cheers.]

Another view of these various institutions, if I may so call them, is worthy of consideration, I think. They are voluntary contributions, given zealously and earnestly, on top of all the disturbances of business, of all the disorders, of all the taxations, and of all the burdens that the war has imposed upon us, giving proof that the national resources are not at all exhausted; that the national spirit of patriotism is even firmer and stronger than at the commencement of the war.

It is a pertinent question, often asked in the mind privately, and from one to another, when is the war to end? Surely I feel as great an interest in this question as any other can. But I do not wish to name the day, or the month, or the year with which it is to end. I do not wish to run the risk of seeing the time come without our being ready for the end, for fear of disappointment, because the time had come and not the end.

We accepted this war; we did not begin it. But we accepted the war for an object, a worthy object, and the war will end when that object is attained, and I hope under God it never will without. [Tumultuous cheering.] Speaking of the present campaign, Gen. Grant is reported to have said: "I am going through on this line if it takes all summer." This war has taken three years. It was begun or accepted on the line of restoring the national authority over all the national domain. And for the American people, as far as my knowledge enables me to speak, I say we are going through on this line if it takes three years more. [Great cheering].

My friends, I did not know but that I might be called upon to say a few words before I got away from here; but I did not know it was coming just here. [Laughter.] I have never been in the habit of making predictions in regard to the war, but I am almost tempted to make one. If I were to hazard it, it is this: That Grant is this evening, with Gen. Meade and Gen. Hancock, of Pennsylvania, and the brave officers and soldiers with him, in a position where he will never be dislodged until Richmond is taken. And I have but one single proposition further to put now, and perhaps I can best put it in the form of an interrogatory.

If I shall discover that Gen. Grant, and the noble officers and men under him, can be greatly facilitated in their work by a sudden pouring forth of armed men to their assistance, will you give them to me? [Cries of "yes." and cheers.] Are you ready to march? Then, I say, stand ready, for I am watching for the chance. [Merriment, and applause.] I thank you, gentlemen.

It will be remembered that Gen. Grant, at the date of this speech, had just advanced beyond the James and appeared before Petersburg. The details of this movement were then but imperfectly known, but the President's prediction—a cautious one, by no means over sanguine, yet distinct and definite—was strictly fulfilled. It well illustrates the firm confidence, without extravagant anticipations, which he reposed in the Lieutenant-General and the brave men under his command.

The Opposition party, styling itself Democratic, had early in the season called a National Convention, to be assembled at Chicago on the 4th of July, for the purpose of nominating candidates for President and Vice-President of the United States. As the time approached, however, the Democratic leaders, perhaps unable to determine whether it were better to adopt a war or a peace basis, perhaps anxious for the Union of the various elements of opposition to Mr. Lincoln, and certainly willing to afford the fullest scope for the development and strengthening of divisions on the Administration side, by deferring to present any definite opponent or issue, decided to postpone their Convention until the 29th of August.

It was somewhat earlier in the season, that a band of Rebel leaders, including Jacob Thompson, Buchanan's Secretary of the Interior, Clement C. Clay, once a Senator from Alabama, J. P. Holcombe, of Virginia, and George N. Sanders, a renegade New Yorker of notorious worthlessness, ran the blockade, safely reaching Bermuda, and embarked from thence to Canada, being, as they subsequently represented, " in the *confidential employment*" of Jefferson Davis. At the time, their mission was supposed to have more immediate reference to political movements in the loyal States, with a view to a change of the Administration by the election of Peace Democratic candidates. It was then hardly suspected that their purposes extended to such desperate and infamous measures in behalf of the " Confederacy " as have since been associated with their names. These persons, with the exception of Thompson, who appears to have divided his time chiefly between Montreal and Toronto, soon made their appearance at Niagara Falls, whither leading Democrats were reported to be resorting, to hold with them confidential conferences. Sanders, on whose suggestion is not known, addressed a note to the Hon. Horace Greeley, on the 12th of July, suggesting that Clay, Holcombe, himself " and one other," not named by him, would like " to go at once to Washington, upon complete and unqualified protection being given, either by the President or Secretary of War." No object is assigned for the proposed journey. Mr. Greeley assumed that the purpose was to talk of negotiations for peace, an assumption scarcely warranted by the facts then known, and much less in the light of information since disclosed. In a communication written not long after, Mr. Greeley thus refers to this note and its results :

As I saw no reason why the Opposition should be the sole recipients of these gentlemen's overtures, if such there were (and it is stated that Mr. Clay aforesaid is preparing or to prepare an important letter to the Chicago Convention), I wrote the President, urging him to invite the Rebel gentlemen aforesaid to Washington, there to open their budget. I stated expressly that I knew not what they would propose if so invited, but I could imagine no offer that might be made by them which would not conduce, in one way or another, to a restoration of the integrity and just authority of the Union.

The President ultimately acquiesced in this view so far as to consent that the Rebel agents should visit Washington, but directed that *I* should proceed to Niagara and accompany them thence to the capital. This service I most reluctantly undertook, feeling deeply, and observing that almost any one else might better have been sent on this errand. But time seemed precious, and I immediately started.

In his notes to Clay and others, written after reaching the Falls, Mr. Greeley more clearly indicates the understanding upon which President Lincoln consented that the parties should be thus escorted to Washington. The ingenious efforts of Mr. Greeley to throw into the background the writer who opened the correspondence are noticeable, as well as the insertion of Thompson's name, without any warrant, so far as publicly appears :

NIAGARA FALLS, N. Y., July 17, 1864

GENTLEMEN : I am informed that you are duly accredited from Richmond, as the bearers of propositions looking to the establishment of peace ; that you desire to visit Washington in the fulfillment of your mission, and that you farther desire that Mr. George N. Sanders shall accompany you. If my information be thus far substantially correct, I am authorized by the President of the United States to tender you his safe conduct on the journey proposed, and to accompany you at the earliest time that will be agreeable to you. I have the honor to be, gentlemen, yours, HORACE GREELEY.

To Messrs. CLEMENT C. CLAY, JACOB THOMPSON, JAMES P. HOLCOMBE, Clifton House, C. W.

On the next day, Messrs. Holcombe and Clay replied :

The safe conduct of the President of the United States has

been tendered us, we regret to state, under some misapprehension of facts. We have not been accredited to him from Richmond as the bearers of propositions looking to the establishment of peace. We are, however in the confidential employ ment of our Government, and are entirely familiar with its wishes and opinions on that subject; and we feel authorized to declare that, if the circumstances disclosed in this correspond ence were communicated to Richmond, we would be at once invested with the authority to which your letter refers; or other gentlemen, clothed with full powers, would be immediately sent to Washington with the view of hastening a consummation so much to be desired, and terminating at the earliest possible moment the calamities of the war. We respectfully solicit, through your intervention, a safe conduct to Washingington, ,and thence, by any route which may be designated, through your lines, to Richmond. We would be gratified if Mr. George N. Sanders was embraced in this privilege.

To which Mr. Greeley, after acknowledging their note, rejoins :

The state of facts therein presented being materially different from that which was understood to exist by the President when he intrusted me with the safe conduct required, it seems to me on every account advisable that I should communicate with him by telegraph, and solicit fresh instructions, which I shall at once proceed to do. I hope to be able to transmit the result this afternoon; and at all events I shall do so at the earliest moment.

This last application for a safe conduct for Rebel emissaries to visit Washington, was met by the following memorable passport in President Lincoln's own handwriting:

EXECUTIVE MANSION, ⎱
WASHINGTON, July 18, 1864.⎰

To whom it may concern :

Any proposition which embraces the restoration of peace, the integrity of the whole Union, and the abandonment of slavery, and which comes by and with an authority that can control the armies now at war against the United States, will be received and considered by the Executive Government of the United States, and will be met by liberal terms on substantial and collateral points; and the bearer thereof shal have safe conduct both ways.   ABRAHAM LINCOLN

The indispensable conditions mentioned in this paper were such as to put an end to all further trifling on the part of self-constituted, irresponsible or insincere negotiators. Many would have preferred that no occasion had been presented requiring Mr. Lincoln to connect himself in the remotest manner with an affair of this sort. Yet if he were to speak, good faith and plain dealing admitted of no less than was actually said. The fact was definitely recognized, that the vital force of the rebellion was in "the armies now at war against the United States," and peace agitators on both sides were given to understand, once for all, that only when those armies were vanquished, or disbanded, and the Emancipation policy, to which the Government had plighted its faith, was accepted as a finality, could peace be expected. As the event proved, it may be well that these issues, "the abandonment of slavery" included, were thus directly presented to the people in the Presidential canvass.

While this pacific exterior was maintained by the Rebel emissaries in Canada, a monster conspiracy was becoming revealed in the North-west, the object of which was a counter-revolution in the loyal States, in concert with the Rebellion. In the latter part of June, important facts in regard to the secret combinations to this end were made public by Gen. Carrington, and several of the leaders were arrested in Indiana. The enormity and extent of the schemes disclosed on the subsequent trials surpassed the worst suspicions at first entertained, involving crimes of the darkest shade, and evincing a depth of disloyal hate not unworthy of the arch-fiends in Milton's Pandemonium. Premature outbreaks occurred in Coles County, Illinois, and elsewhere in the North-west; soldiers were murdered; enrolling officers waylaid and shot; and arms were secretly distributed for the equipment of men who had other purposes than the service of their country. The discovery of this plot was timely, and the prevention of its fuller consummation most fortunate. The full connection of these men with leaders of the Rebellion admits of no doubt, and it is known that a day had been fixed—and nearly reached at the date of the arrests—for a concerted and general outbreak.

Two months passed after the Baltimore nominations, and the third month was well on toward completion, before the so-called Democratic Opposition began to contemplate in earnest the work of preparation for the canvass. Faction and discontent were doubtless hoped to be doing more for the defeat of Lincoln and Johnson, than could be accomplished by direct and energetic opposition. Fremont was still a candidate. The German Republican voters were reported to be every-where hostile to Mr. Lincoln. Grant was still before Petersburg, after fruitless mining and disappointing losses. Farragut had captured Fort Gaines, but Mobile still held out against both Navy and Army. Sherman was still at bay before Atlanta. What remained now but for an exultant Democracy—with its Vallandigham returned from across the border, and his place in Canada supplied by a bevy of Confederates giving aid and comfort—to name its candidates, make up its issues, and stride directly to the high places of power? Emboldened by the seeming divisions of the Republicans, cheered by the lack of decisive and final Union victories, to reconcile the country to heavy losses of life and treasure, the Peace Democrats were growing more and more determined in asserting the prerogative of leaders and dictators. Their compact organization and the favoritism of the multitude for the " victims " who had suffered for defiant attempts to arrest the war, gave them an advantage over the probably more numerous leaders who not only believed the war should be sustained, but also thought the nominations and platform should, from policy, have a decided leaning toward " coercion."

The Democratic Convention met on the day last fixed— August 29. It presented the name of George B. McClellan for President, and of George H. Pendleton for Vice-President. The former nomination was esteemed so decided a concession to the War Democracy—having encountered some opposition from such " Democrats " as B. G. Harris, the " unworthy " Congressman from Maryland, a delegate to the Convention— that the nomination for Vice-President was conferred upon an unequivocal Peace Democrat, and the resolutions, or platform, were made very explicit on the " failure " of the war, and in

37   49

demanding "that immediate efforts be made for a cessation of hostilities." The entire "Chicago Platform," (Democratic, 1864,) is as follows :

Resolved, That in the future, as in the past, we will adhere with unswerving fidelity to the Union under the Constitution, as the only solid foundation of our strength, security, and happiness as a people, and as a framework of government equally conducive to the welfare and prosperity of all the States, both Northern and Southern.

Resolved, That this Convention does explicitly declare, as the sense of the American People, that, after four years of failure to restore the Union by the experiment of war, during which, under the pretense of a military necessity of a war power higher than the Constitution, the Constitution itself has been disregarded in every part, and public liberty and private right alike trodden down, and the material prosperity of the country essentially impaired, justice, humanity, liberty, and the public welfare, demand that immediate efforts be made for a cessation of hostilities, with a view to an ultimate Convention of all the States, or other peaceable means to the end that at the earliest practicable moment peace may be restored on the basis of the Federal Union of the States.

Resolved, That the direct interference of the military authority of the United States in the recent elections held in Kentucky, Maryland, Missouri and Delaware, was a shameful violation of the Constitution, and the repetition of such acts in the approaching election will be held as revolutionary, and resisted with all the means and power under our control.

Resolved, That the aim and object of the Democratic party is to preserve the Federal Union and the rights of the States unimpaired; and they hereby declare that they consider the administrative usurpation of extraordinary and dangerous powers not granted by the Constitution, the subversion of the civil by military law in States not in insurrection, the arbitrary military arrest, imprisonment trial and sentence of American citizens in States where civil law exists in full force, the suppression of freedom of speech and of the press, the denial of the right of asylum, the open and avowed disregard of State rights, the employment of unusual test-oaths, and the interference with and denial of the right of the people to bear arms, as calculated to prevent a restoration of the Union and the perpetuation of a government deriving its just powers from the consent of the governed.

Resolved, That the shameful disregard of the Administration to its duty in respect to our fellow-citizens who now and long have been prisoners of war in a suffering condition, deserves the severest reprobation, on the score alike of public interest and common humanity.

Resolved, That the sympathy of the Democratic party is heartily and earnestly extended to the soldiery of our army, who are and have been in the field under the flag of our country; and in the event of our attaining power, they will receive all the care and protection, regard and kindness, that the brave soldiers of the Republic have so nobly earned.

The nomination of Gen. McClellan had been a foregone conclusion from the first. There were dreams, for a time, that Gen. Fremont, or an active War Democrat, like Gen. Dix, might be taken as the candidate, for the sake of uniting all elements of opposition in a grand effort to defeat Mr. Lincoln. But the visionary notion was not entertained for a moment by Belmont and his associates. Their hopes were firmly fixed on McClellan. Democrats like the New York Woods, denouncing the war altogether, manifested delicate scruples in regard to " epauletted gentlemen ;" and Maryland Secessionists indignantly remembered the " arbitrary arrests " made in their State by the Peninsular hero ; but it was not doubted that these objections would promptly enough disappear before the magic power of a regular nomination. And so it was. Mutterings of discontent were momentarily heard, only in quarters where such responses were preferable to warm support. Candidates and platform were accepted by the united Democracy, and the canvass at length actually opened.

On the Administration side, the issue was joined, with prospects immediately brightened. There was now an organized opponent to meet; and he had presented himself in an attitude that promised an advantage to the supporters of Mr. Lincoln. Dissension, and factious opposition speedily disappeared. More cheering news began to come from our armies, and the affectionate confidence of the great majority of the loyal people in Abraham Lincoln manifested itself more and more clearly as the day of election approached.

The action of the Border States in adapting themselves to the new order of things, never failed to interest the President·

who, at an earlier day, had earnestly endeavored to impress upon the Representatives of those States, the expediency of prompt measures in preparation for the inevitable event of emancipation. It was not many days after the adjournment of the Baltimore Convention, that the delegates of the people of Maryland decided upon abolishing slavery in that State; subject only to the test of a popular vote, to be taken a few months later. The State Convention of Maryland consummated this action, bringing the issue directly before the people for their full deliberation and ultimate action, on the 24th day of June.

In the State of Louisiana, a new Constitution prohibiting slavery was adopted by a State Convention, duly chosen by the loyal people, on the 22d day of July.

All the great champions of freedom were near to the affections of Mr. Lincoln, but no one of them was, perhaps, more personally endeared to him than the late Owen Lovejoy, his intimate friend for many years. No one, on the other hand, had a more earnest, loving confidence in the President during all his trials, and not the least when he was assailed by men who questioned his "radicalism." In one of the last speeches ever made by Mr. Lovejoy to any public assembly, not many months before his death, he defended the President from such attacks, and warmed into a heartfelt eulogy of his friend, such as brought tears to many eyes, and will long be remembered by those who listened. All complaint, for the time, was henceforth silenced. "On a recent occasion," said Mr Lovejoy, illustrating the high and unselfish motives which controlled all the President's actions, "I ventured, in the freedom of our private intercourse, to speak of the temptations besetting a man in his exalted position, with such patronage and power in his hands, and to counsel him to rise above all regard to or thought of perpetuating his power by a reëlection, adhering firmly to the higher plane of simple duty. With characteristic earnestness of tone and expression, the President replied: 'If I know my own heart, Mr. Lovejoy, I can assure you that it does not cost me an effort so to do.' That answer, gentlemen, I firmly believe to have been given in honest truth. That great heart is incorruptible, and constantly lives in the pure, high region into which false motive and selfish scheming never come."

The death of Mr. Lovejoy was mourned by Mr. Lincoln as that of a dear friend. When a meeting was to be held in the former home of the deceased veteran in the cause of liberty, to take measures for the erection of a monument to his memory, the President was invited to be present. This being impossible, he sent the following letter:

EXECUTIVE MANSION, }
WASHINGTON, May 30, 1864. }

HON. JOHN H. BRYANT.—*My Dear Sir:* Yours of the 14th inst., inclosing a card of invitation to a preliminary meeting contemplating the erection of a monument to the memory of Hon. Owen Lovejoy, was duly received. As you anticipate, it will be out of my power to attend. Many of you have known Mr. Lovejoy longer than I have, and are better able than I to do his memory justice. My personal acquaintance with him commenced only about ten years ago, since when it has been quite intimate; and every step in it has been one of increasing respect and esteem, ending with his life, in no less affection on my part. It can be truly said of him, that, while he was personally ambitious, he bravely endured the obscurity which the unpopularity of his principles imposed, and never accepted official honors until those honors were ready to admit his principles with him. Throughout my heavy and perplexing responsibilities here to the day of his death, it would scarcely wrong any other to say he was my most generous friend. Let him have the marble monument, along with the well-assured and more endearing one in the hearts of those who love liberty unselfishly for all men.

Yours, truly,   A. LINCOLN.

From the time Mr. Stanton succeeded Mr. Cameron as Secretary of War, on the 11th of January, 1862, until this summer, only one change had occurred in the Cabinet of President Lincoln—that occasioned by the appointment of Secretary Smith as Judge of the District Court of Indiana, who was succeeded by Hon. John P. Usher, of the same State, on the 8th of January, 1863. Several months previous, on account of opposition manifested by a number of Senators, Mr. Seward had tendered his resignation as Secretary of State, and Mr. Chase had, at the same time, proposed to withdraw from the Secretaryship of the Treasury. Both these resignations, the President peremptorily refused to accept.

On the 30th of June, 1864, Secretary Chase, for personal reasons, again tendered his resignation, which Mr. Lincoln deemed it expedient to accept. A want of cordiality on the part of Mr. Chase toward the President had been noticed for a good while previous, and his attendance on Cabinet meetings had been irregular, or, in fact, practically intermitted altogether. The occasion of his final resignation—the acceptance was perhaps not confidently anticipated—was a disagreement with the President in regard to an important appointment for New York City. There was, perhaps, no period during the war when the financial condition of the country was deemed more critical than at this date and during the few weeks succeeding prior to the 1st of September. The place thus made vacant was first tendered to Ex-Gov. David Tod, of Ohio, who declined the appointment. Senator Wm. P. Fessenden, of Maine, was afterward appointed, and entered upon the duties of the office on the 5th of July.

In the midst of a Presidential canvass, while the people were becoming weary over hopes deferred and indecisive campaigns, it may well be supposed that an executive who was studying the chances of a reëlection would have long hesitated to call for five hundred thousand more men for the army, to be made good by a draft, after a very short period, if not previously filled by volunteers. But the success of our arms demanded it, and President Lincoln promptly determined to do what duty required. The following proclamation was accordingly issued:

WHEREAS, By the act approved July 4, 1864, entitled "An act further to regulate and provide for the enrolling and calling out the national forces, and for other purposes," it is provided that the President of the United States may, " at his discretion, at any time hereafter, call for any number of men as volunteers, for the respective terms of one, two, and three years, for military service," and " that in case the quota of any part thereof, or any town, township, ward of a city, precinct, or election district, or of a county not so subdivided, shall not be filled within the space of fifty days after such call, then the President shall immediately order a draft for one year to fill such quota, or any part thereof, which may be unfilled;"

AND WHEREAS, The new enrollment heretofore ordered is so far completed as that the aforementioned act of Congress may now be put in operation for recruiting and keeping up the strength of the armies in the field, for garrisons and such military operations as may be required for the purpose of suppressing the rebellion and restoring the authority of the United States Government in the insurgent States;

Now, therefore, I, Abraham Lincoln, President of the United States, do issue this my call for five hundred thousand volunteers for the military service: Provided, nevertheless, that this call shall be reduced by all credits which may be established under section eight of the aforesaid act, on account of persons who have entered the naval service during the present rebellion, and by credits for men furnished to the military service in excess of calls heretofore made.

Volunteers will be accepted under this call for one, two, or three years, as they may elect, and will be entitled to the bounty provided by law for the period of service for which they enlist.

And I hereby proclaim, order, and direct, that immediately after the fifth day of September, 1864, being fifty days from the date of this call, a draft for troops, to serve for one year, shall be had in every town, township, ward of a city, precinct, or election district, or county not so subdivided, to fill the quota which shall be assigned to it under this call, or any part thereof which may be unfilled by volunteers on the said fifth day of September, 1864.

In testimony whereof, I have hereunto set my hand and caused the seal of the United States to be affixed.

Done at the city of Washington this eighteenth day of July, in the year of our Lord one thousand eight hundred

[L. S.] and sixty-four, and of the independence of the United States the eighty-ninth.

ABRAHAM LINCOLN.

By the President:

WILLIAM H. SEWARD, Secretary of State.

The governments of the several loyal States at once set about the work of filling their quotas by volunteering, and the response showed an alacrity and confidence among the people which disappointed alike those who had hoped our armies could not again be replenished, and those who feared disaffection to the cause from the heavy sacrifices demanded. No disheartening circumstances could shake the people from their firm purpose of wrenching from the hands of treason its weapons of revolt. No hour was so dark that loyal eyes could not clearly see the duty of keeping up our armies, and of steadily pressing forward to ultimate and decisive victory, however long deferred the consummation.

CHAPTER V.

Military Operations before Petersburg and Richmond, from June to November, 1864.—Gen. Hunter's Campaign.—Movements in the Shenandoah Valley.—Early's Invasion of Maryland.—His Demonstration against Washington.—His Retreat up the Valley, and Second Advance to the Potomac.—Burning of Chambersburg.—Successes of Gen. Averill.—Battle of Moorfield.—Gen. Sheridan takes Command in the Valley.—Admiral Farragut before Mobile.—Brilliant Naval Victories.—Movements of Sheridan.—Important Successes in the Valley.—Thanksgiving Proclamation of President Lincoln.

AFTER it had become apparent that Petersburg was not at once to be taken, and the several army corps had intrenched themselves in the positions indicated in a previous chapter, it next became an object to work all practicable damage on the Rebel communications. Of the three railroads leading southward from Petersburg, the Suffolk road alone was yet in Grant's possession. This, extending south-eastward, connects with another at Suffolk, leading from Norfolk to Weldon, having no military value to the enemy, while Norfolk and Portsmouth are in our hands and the junction within easy command. The Weldon road, running due south, was at this time the one most immediately important of all; yet its loss was by no means a fatal one, with the Danville road, extending south-west from Burkesville, still open, and the Southside road (to Lynchburg) still occupied by the Rebels, from Petersburg to Burkesville. To extend the Union lines across the Weldon and Southside roads, without cutting loose from the base at City Point, was not at once practicable. It only remained, with the present force, to endeavor to reach and hold the Weldon road, and to rely upon cavalry raids for the remainder of the work of breaking up the Rebel communications.

President Lincoln visited the army in its new position, south of Petersburg, on the 21st of June, and was warmly greeted by the soldiers as he rode along the lines. On the 22d, he visited Butler's command on the right, meeting with a like hearty reception from the soldiers and their commanders.

Gen. Sheridan had gained a victory at Trevillian Station, on the Virginia railroad, near Gordonsville, on the 11th of June, after having materially injured the Rebel communications northward from Richmond by a sweeping raid, commenced before Grant's movement from Cold Harbor to the south of the James. On the 13th, he recrossed the North Anna, and aided in covering the movements then in progress. The cavalry of Hampton and Fitzhugh Lee, on the 20th, recalled Sheridan, by attacking the small force under Gen. Abercrombie, at the White House, endeavoring to cut off the former's communications and supplies. This assault was repulsed without severe loss. Sheridan maintained his position at the White House against all attacks, until, on the 25th, he rejoined Grant, after accomplishing the purpose for which he remained north of the James.

Movements had now been commenced on the Weldon and Southside railroads, by the cavalry forces under Gens. Wilson and Kautz. As the former moved out on the Weldon road, the Second and Sixth Corps were transferred to the left, for the purpose of extending the line across that road. This movement had been anticipated by Lee, and when the Second Corps was near the Jerusalem plank road, it was met by the Rebel corps of Hill, about two o'clock, on the 22d, and an engagement of some severity followed. The Sixth Corps had advanced still further on the left, and a portion of the Fifth Corps was within supporting distance of the Second, on its right. Lee assumed the offensive, with considerable vigor, capturing a battery in the advance, turning the flank of Barlow's division, taking several hundred prisoners and driving back our men, for the time, in some confusion. The Union lines were speedily re-formed, after which the repeated assaults of the enemy were repulsed. Skirmishing was kept up along the whole line during the night, and about midnight the musketry firing and cannonading in front of the Ninth Corps, which held the Prince George county road, were particularly heavy. The results were unimportant. The locality of the principal action was only three or four miles distant from the Weldon road. On the following day, an unsuccessful attempt was made to extend the lines across that road, resulting in considerable loss.

Wilson's cavalry had struck the railroad at Reams' Station, ten or twelve miles south of Petersburg, and advanced southward, destroying the track and bridges. On the 22d, Kautz struck the Danville road (or rather its connecting route between Petersburg and Burkesville Junction), at Ford's Station, capturing two trains, and inflicting other important damage. He advanced upon Burkesville on the 23d, destroying the station there, and further injuring the enemy's communications. On the 24th, the work of destruction was continued for a distance of about eighteen miles, when a heavy Rebel force was encountered, and the Union cavalry repulsed. On the 28th, the forces of Kautz and Wilson had another engagement at Stony Creek, on the Weldon railroad, about thirty miles south of Petersburg. In the night they effected their retreat to Reams' Station, where, on the 29th, they encountered a heavy force of the enemy, and were defeated, with a loss exceeding 1,000. The Sixth Corps were advanced to the support of the cavalry, but did not arrive in season to take an active part in the battle. On the following day, the force under Kautz reached Grant's lines. Wilson's main force came in on the 1st of July, having lost most of its artillery and trains, the wounded falling into the hands of the enemy. The horses were much jaded, and the men greatly exhausted by this expedition, which was one of the boldest yet undertaken. It had inflicted serious injury, though but temporary, on all the remaining communications from Richmond and Petersburg southward. As one result of this series of movements, our forces effected a secure lodgment on the Weldon road, about four miles from Petersburg.

In the meantime, Hunter had pressed forward with his command, including the forces under Crook and Averill, and appeared near Lynchburg on the 18th of June. The defenses of this place had been greatly strengthened, and a heavy force had been sent thither from Richmond. Hunter found it necessary to retire, and, having exhausted his ammunition, his utmost skill was required to extricate himself from his dangerous position. He accomplished this by marching rapidly to Gauley Bridge, his men suffering not a little from the privations and hardships to which, during two or three days, they were necessarily subjected. It may have been possible for him, by a more prompt attack, to have occupied Lynchburg—a point too important to the Rebels for him to be permitted to hold it for any time without a much larger army ; but even this is doubtful. Situated as he was, he acted wisely in retreating, but to return down the Valley, pursued by a greatly superior force, was clearly impracticable. His retreat into Western Virginia, unfortunately, left open the gateway into Maryland and Pennsylvania, excepting only the small garrisons at the the outposts of Winchester, Martinsburg and Harper's Ferry.

A critical point in the Eastern campaign had now been reached. Sheridan's raid on the Virginia Central railroad, and the less successful expeditions of Wilson and Kautz, had left our cavalry much weakened, and illy prepared for immediate movements on any extensive scale. The main army was apparently at a dead-lock before Petersburg. Part of the army of the James was thrown across the James river, on the 21st, taking position at Deep Bottom, and threatening a movement on Richmond, while our fleet, under Admiral Lee, was not inactive. In spite of all the operations and menacing demonstrations of our armies on the Appomattox and the James, however, a large force, probably about thirty thousand men, was dispatched by Lee to Lynchburg and the Shenandoah Valley. The purpose of this expedition was, evidently, not merely the protection of Lynchburg, but also an offensive movement which would divert Grant's attention, and perhaps gain important advantages, including even the capture of the national capital, no longer covered by the main Union army, or adequately garrisoned. By means of transports, however, a very considerable force could be transferred from City Point to Washington, as presently seen, in twenty-four hours—a movement more rapid than Lee could make in that direction, though under cover of the greatest practicable secrecy.

The invading force was under the immediate command of the Rebel Gen. Early, comprising infantry (the main portion of the army), cavalry and horse artillery. Among the general officers under him were Breckinridge, Rhodes, Ramseur, Wharton and Gordon. After pursuing Hunter, as he retreated westward, until all hope of inflicting serious damage was found to be vain, a cavalry force was advanced down the Valley, to capture the Union supplies at Staunton, or on their way thither, and ultimately to strike the Baltimore and Ohio railroad. The remaining force followed with little delay. While the people were still anxiously looking for definite news of the safety of Hunter, this Rebel expeditionary force was stealthily moving toward the Potomac, and preparing to surprise the often disturbed border with another invasion.

Martinsburg was evacuated on the 2d of July, by the small Union force which occupied it. Sigel fell back from Winchester to Harper's Ferry, on the 3d, the former place being promptly occupied by Early, and the running of trains on the Baltimore and Ohio railroad being suspended. Sigel, with the forces that had retreated to Harper's Ferry, occupied Maryland Heights, on the opposite side of the Potomac, and prepared to hold the place. The tide steadily coming on, and flowing over into Maryland, Hagerstown was evacuated on the 6th.

Gen. Wallace, in command of the Department invaded, having his headquarters at Baltimore, made such preparations as were in his power to stay the progress of the enemy, and to protect the points threatened. He sent out a reconnoitering force beyond Frederick City to Middletown, on the 7th of July, and finding the invaders too strong for the body of troops at his command, he evacuated Frederick on the 8th. Early's Rebels entered the place on the same day, plundering the citizens, as had previously been done at Hagerstown. Wallace took position at Monocacy, on the 9th of July, with such troops as he could collect, mostly new levies, having been also reënforced by the Third Division of the Sixth Corps, under Gen. Ricketts. The scene of this engagement is nearly equidistant (about forty miles) from Baltimore and Washington. The remainder of the Sixth Corps was soon to arrive from before Petersburg, and the day gained by Wallace's defense at Monocacy, though he was obliged at last to yield, was of great value to the capital, the road to which was immediately taken by Early's main force. He sent out raiding parties of cavalry, however, through Maryland, plundering and destroying. On the 9th, Westminster was entered by Rebel cavalry. On the 10th, the Northern Central railroad was struck at Cockeysville and elsewhere, and depredations were committed at various points in the country. On the 11th, a raiding party reached the Philadelphia, Wilmington and Baltimore railroad at Magnolia Station, captured two trains, robbed the passengers, burning the cars, and setting fire to the Gunpowder Bridge.

Early reached Rockville on the 10th, and on the morning of the 11th his main army was in the immediate vicinity of the outer fortifications of Washington on the north side, having established his headquarters at Silver Spring, the residence of Francis P. Blair, sr. The house of Postmaster General Blair, a little distance farther from the city, was burned to the ground. The main demonstration was made in front of Fort Stevens, out the Seventh street road. Forces appeared, however, before the works near Tennallytown on the west, and near Fort Lincoln, eastward from the city. A small portion of the Sixth Corps reached Washington on Sunday evening, the 10th. The main arrival was not until the following day. The garrisons of the various forts, and most of the troops within the city, prior to the evening of the 11th, were either inexperienced "hundred days' men," or new militia from the departments or workshops. By a vigorous assault, with a considerable sacrifice of life, Early might not improbably have entered the capital, had he not lost a day at Monocacy, or even had he not hesitated for a number of hours after his arrival. There was constant skirmishing during Monday and Tuesday, until finally, in the afternoon of the latter day (the 12th), a sally was made by a portion of the Sixth Corps, beyond Fort Stevens, and, after a brief engagement, the Rebels were driven back, leaving a number of killed and wounded on the ground. The President was a witness of this fight, from Fort Stevens. During the following night, Early hastily retired, passing through Rockville, and hastening his flight across the Potomac. For want of a sufficient cavalry force, little more was immediately accomplished in the way of pursuit than the capture of stragglers, and a small portion of the rear-guard. A considerable quantity of stock, plundered in Maryland, estimated at five thousand neat cattle, and fifteen hundred horses, was taken safely into Virginia. Early's line of retreat was through Loudoun county, and by Snicker's Gap into the Shenandoah Valley. The Sixth Corps was promptly moved out to follow the retreating army.

During this time, Hunter's forces had not remained inactive, but, having been transferred as rapidly as possible, by rail, after reaching the Baltimore and Ohio road, were already in the lower part of the Valley, while General Couch, with a militia force chiefly, reoccupied Hagerstown. Part of the Rebel plunder was recaptured at Snickers' Gap, where a portion of the enemy was encountered and beaten. Early was again driven back from Winchester, on the 20th, by the forces under Averill, with serious losses. The Rebels now appearing to have withdrawn once more from the Valley, the Sixth Corps came back to the vicinity of Georgetown, with the apparent purpose of returning to the main army before Petersburg. Averill was now joined by the infantry of Crook, who had been worsted in a fight with Breckinridge's command, at Island Ford, two days before.

Pursuit of the Rebels was resumed, and on the 23d our cavalry was repulsed at Kernstown, four miles beyond Winchester, and fell back upon the main force. On the next day, Early, having been now reënforced, sent his cavalry again to the attack, and drove the Union cavalry in confusion and rout through Winchester down the Valley. Crook had formed in line of battle, having about 10,000 men, consisting of the cavalry under Averill and Duffie, and two divisions of infantry. The retreat of the cavalry left his wings exposed, and he was outflanked, right and left, and driven back from point to point by the superior numbers of the enemy. Such was the character of the fight, lasting from noon until night, along the pike to Bunker Hill, Early's main body resting five miles north of Winchester, while his cavalry closely pursued our forces as far as Martinsburg. The Union losses were about 1,200 in the aggregate. Among the killed was Colonel Mulligan, in command of the rear brigade covering the retreat. Thus again our forces in that department passed through the "Valley of humiliation."

Some fighting occurred at Martinsburg on the 25th, the Union commander desiring to get off his trains, which he succeeded in doing, and crossed into Maryland on the following day, without interruption by the enemy. Excitement was now again prevalent in Maryland and over the Pennsylvania border, a more formidable invasion than the previous one being dreaded. The Rebels held the right bank of the Potomac, from Shepherdstown to Williamsport, during two or three succeeding days, without clearly developing their plan. On the morning of the 30th, a cavalry force under the Rebel Gen. McCausland, entered Chambersburg, and, after plundering the citizens, burned the town. About two hundred and fifty buildings were destroyed, at an estimated loss exceeding one million of dollars. McCausland had just withdrawn from Chambersburg, about 11 o'clock in the forenoon, when Averill entered the town, passing directly on in pursuit toward the west. It was near night when he overtook the enemy's rear, eight miles beyond McConnellsburgh. McCausland continued his flight on the following day, and withdrew toward Cumberland. The men and the horses of Averill's command being jaded by long marches, in addition to their severe labors during the earlier part of the campaign, he gained no immediate material advantages over the enemy. Early still retained possession of fords across the Potomac, and particularly at Duffield, within six miles of Harper's Ferry, while inferior cavalry squadrons made incursions into Maryland, spreading a general panic. There was no little excitement also in Pennsylvania, and a special session of the State Legislature was called by Gov. Curtin, to meet on the 9th of August, to take such action as the occasion might seem to require. A movement westward toward Pittsburgh was at one time thought imminent, and Gen Couch made dispositions of the militia forces accordingly.

The Sixth Corps was permitted little rest in its camp near Georgetown. They set forward for the Valley once more, on the 26th of July, after receiving news of Crook's disaster, marching by way of Rockville, Monocacy and Frederick, to Halltown, near Harper's Ferry, arriving on the 6th of August. A portion of the Nineteenth Corps, returned from the Department of the Gulf, was advanced to the same vicinity, meeting there, also, the infantry of Hunter's command, under Crook. This was the day before the burning of Chambersburg. The combined force was ordered out to meet a reported advance of Early into Pennsylvania, but the falsity of the rumor was speedily disproved and the movement recalled. The reported occupation of Hagerstown by a Rebel infantry force proved to be unfounded, and our cavalry occupied the place on the 7th. In fact, no Rebel infantry crossed the Potomac on this second "invasion." On the same day, Averill gained a victory over the Rebel cavalry at Moorfield, capturing all the enemy's artillery, five hundred prisoners, and many wagons and small arms, and driving the remainder of his force to the mountains.

A new era in the affairs of the Valley dates from the 7th day of August, when Maj.-Gen. Philip H. Sheridan, pursuant to orders of the War Department (after a conference with Gen. Grant, in Washington, on the 5th), assumed command of the Middle Military Division, comprising the Middle Department, Department of the Susquehanna, and Department of West Virginia, with headquarters, at first, at Harper's Ferry. In addition to the troops already operating in his district, large reënforcements of cavalry (Torbert's division, and later, Wilson's) were brought up from before Petersburg and Richmond. Lowell's brigade of cavalry was also added, from the Department of Washington, and Devin's brigade. The infantry force consisted of the former Army of the Kanawha, under Crook, the Sixth, the Eighth, and part of the Nineteenth Corps.

Before Petersburg, the army remained comparatively quiet, during the period that had now elapsed since the occupation of the Weldon railroad. The heat and dust were patiently endured by the soldiers, and there was no unusual degree of sickness in camp. The hostile lines nearly approached each

38   50

other, both sides having fortified their positions in the strongest manner. More or less skirmishing and artillery firing was kept up, without material results. A movement was made across the James on the 27th and 28th of July, by the divisions of Barlow and Abbott, of the Second Corps—a battery of the enemy being captured by the former division, nearly opposite Jones' Neck. The whole force soon returned to its former position. The movement was occasioned by an advance of the enemy to meet an anticipated attack on Richmond by way of Malvern Hill.

For some time past, a mining operation had been silently going on, with the purpose of blowing up a formidable Rebel fort in front of the Second Division of the Ninth Corps. This work had been contrived, and its execution conducted by Lieut.-Col. Henry Pleasants, of the 48th regiment of Pennsylvania Volunteers. The skill displayed in laying out and constructing this work, and the severe labors of the officers and men of the regiment in its execution, were specially commended in an order of Gen. Meade. The explosion of this mine took place on the 30th of July, when it was intended to pierce the enemy's lines through the breach thus made, and to carry his position by an assault in force.

The mine itself was an entire success. The fort was blown up, with the South Carolina troops manning it, and wide consternation was produced among the forces of the enemy, of which proper advantage was not taken. The tardy assault of Ledlie's division, insufficiently sustained, resulted in an ultimate repulse, a destructive fire having been opened on his column from adjoining Rebel works. Our losses were severe, amounting in the aggregate to about 5,000. The Rebel loss is stated at 1,200. No substantial benefit was gained. The disheartening effect of this failure—at a moment when the capture of Petersburg was apparently within our power—was manifest through the country. Most of the losses fell upon the Ninth Corps, and were fully shared by the colored regiments. The Second and Fifth Corps took little part in either of the two unsuccessful assaults. Evidently, " some one had blundered." and the responsibility appears to have been divided to some extent between subordinate generals. Gen. Burnside was soon after relieved from his command of the Ninth Corps, being temporarily succeeded by Gen. Wilcox, and more permanently, at a later day, by Gen. Parke.

On the 9th of August, Gen. Butler commenced the construction of a canal across the peninsula at Dutch Gap, a work which occupied a large number of men for several months, without any definite advantage to strictly military or naval operations. If completed, it would have made the distance to Richmond a few miles shorter for the fleet, and enabled it to avoid certain Rebel defenses; but no positive purpose of attempting to pass Fort Darling, a short distance above, had yet been manifested by Admiral Lee, to whom the numerous obstructions no doubt appeared too formidable to be encountered.

The fleet under Rear-Admiral Farragut, which had some time earlier sailed for the Gulf, appeared, in due course of events, off the entrance to the Bay of Mobile. On the 5th of August, Farragut compelled the evacuation of Fort Powell by the Rebel garrison, its commander blowing up the fort. On the morning of that day, seventeen of our vessels passed Fort Morgan, the Tecumseh, a Union monitor, having been sunk by the guns of that fort. The Rebel vessel, the Tennessee, was surrendered, after a sharp engagement, by its commander, Buchanan, who was severely wounded. The Selma was captured from the enemy; and the Gaines, another Rebel vessel, was beached. Fort Powell had been attacked during nearly the entire day, before it was abandoned by the Rebel officer in command.

On the 7th, Farragut opened heavily on Fort Gaines, a strong work which had been provisioned for six months, and had a garrison of six hundred men. On the morning of the 8th the fort was surrendered by Col. Anderson, against the wishes of Gen. Page, the Rebel commander of the defenses of Mobile, who soon saw, to his chagrin, the stars and stripes waving over this stronghold, gallantly conquered and "repossessed" by rightful authority. These brilliant successes were hailed with universal joy, reanimating the popular heart, which was becoming depressed at the long delay of the decisive victories so eagerly hoped.

These advantages were vigorously followed up, by a coöperating land force under Gen. Granger, until Fort Morgan was surrendered on the 23d of August, leaving the entrance to the bay completely within the control of our navy. These successes utterly closed one more port against all hope of blockade-running, and accomplished what was really the main object in view in fitting out the fleet under the Rear-Admiral.

In the Shenandoah Valley, active operations were speedily resumed, after Sheridan had taken the command. Early's rearguard withdrew from Martinsburg, up the Valley, on the 9th, and at 4 o'clock, in the afternoon of the 10th, the advance of Sheridan's forces, moving out in pursuit at sunrise that day, began skirmishing with the enemy, within ten miles of Winchester. The infantry bivouacked near Berryville, having marched fifteen miles. Advancing on the 11th, Custer's cavalry brigade fell in with the enemy in considerable force near Sulphur Springs bridge, three miles from Winchester. An engagement followed, lasting nearly two hours, Custer having one battery, and the enemy no artillery. Our forces were driven back with slight loss. Another cavalry force, under Devin, moved by a circuitous route by White Post, toward Newtown, with the purpose of flanking the Rebel column retreating by the Strasburg pike. The advance regiment soon became engaged with a Rebel skirmishing party, near White Post, and a general action followed, on the part of Devin's command, lasting about three hours, the enemy retiring some distance in the direction of Newtown. Crook's infantry at length came up, and the further pursuit of the enemy by the cavalry brigade of Gibbs, led to further fighting before Newtown, which Early succeeded in holding. Our infantry encamped for the night about six miles beyond (and south-west of) Winchester.

On the next day (the 12th), our forces advanced, the enemy continuing his retreat. About noon, a force of the enemy was discovered on a hill before Strasburg, from which our cavalry skirmishers were shelled and driven back. The infantry now came up, and both armies formed their line of battle, with Cedar Creek between them, about three miles north of Strasburg. There was lively skirmishing through the day. No general engagement followed. During the night, Early had decamped, retiring beyond the town, which our skirmishers entered on the morning of the 13th. They soon after withdrew, however, the enemy re-appearing, and our main army, which had begun to advance, was recalled to Cedar Creek, remaining mostly inactive there until the 15th, while the enemy retained possession of Strasburg, his works on Fisher's Hill, beyond, commanding the town.

In going up the Valley, Sheridan's army had passed the several gaps on its left, so well known in guerrilla operations, and before so successfully used by the enemy in his operations in that region. These gaps had been incautiously left unguarded. On the 13th, an inconsiderable partisan force under Mosby passed through Snicker's Gap, and surprised Sheridan's supply train at Berryville, putting the guard to flight in a panic, destroying a large number of wagons and capturing several hundred horses and mules, with many beef cattle and other supplies. These disasters led to the report that Longstreet's corps was coming up in the rear to cut off Sheridan's army. Late in the evening, of Monday, the 15th, a retreat was commenced, and the whole army fell back to Charlestown.

After the affair of July 30th the army before Petersburg was comparatively quiet for several days. On Friday evening, the 5th of August, the enemy exploded a mine in front of the Eighteenth Corps, without inflicting any serious injury, the work having failed to reach the point intended. Considerable fighting followed, without severe losses or important results on either side.

There was some activity on the north side of the James, on the 14th and 15th of August, and skirmishing with the enemy. On the 16th, there was a considerable engagement near Deep Bottom. The forces moved out for the apparent purpose of turning the left of the Rebel fortifications before Richmond encountered superior numbers, and were obliged to retire, though without heavy losses.

On the 18th of August, an advance was made on the Weldon railroad, to a point near the Yellow Tavern. The enemy stoutly resisted the movement, and temporarily drove back our forces, but the ground lost was retaken, fortified and held during the night. On the 19th, the Rebels renewed the attack, and succeeded in breaking the Union lines, both on the right and on the left, and formed in the rear of Meade's position. In this battle there was a loss of 3,000 men, a large proportion of whom were taken prisoners. Another vigorous effort to dislodge our forces from the Weldon road, at this point, was made on the 21st of August, but the enemy was repulsed, with severe loss. Our men, now fighting behind strong intrenchments, suffered but slightly in comparison. The Rebel forces were now withdrawn from before the Fifth and Ninth Corps, on the Weldon road, to their lines within two or three miles of Petersburg. Hancock's corps now occupied Reams' Station, a few miles south of the scene of the late engagements. This position was furiously assailed by the enemy in heavy force, on the 25th of August, with a persistent purpose of turning the Union left. A severe and prolonged contest followed, both sides fighting desperately. Hancock finally withdrew from Reams' Station, with a loss of 3,000 in killed, wounded and prisoners, and of nine guns. The Rebel loss in killed and wounded alone was 1,500. Considering the number of men engaged, this was one of the severest battles of the campaign. The result was to give the enemy possession of the railroad from Yellow Tavern, six miles from Petersburg, southward. The road had, however, been thoroughly destroyed from a point three or four miles beyond Reams' Station to within three miles of Petersburg.

Our guns were now continually sending shell into Petersburg, while skirmishing was kept up along the lines. On the 2d of September, Gen. Gregg, who had succeeded Sheridan in command of the cavalry corps, made a reconnoissance toward the Boydton plank road, by which route it was ascertained that the enemy was hauling his supplies, after reaching the break in the railroad beyond Reams' Station. He found the enemy well fortified, and had some skirmishing with his cavalry, but no important engagement. Our picket line was extended across the plank road on the 10th of September, and the main lines advanced half a mile in the same direction. During the next two or three weeks, the position of affairs on the Appomattox and the James remained without material change. On the 28th, the Rebels made a night assault on our lines in front of Hancock, on the Jerusalem plank road, and were repulsed. On the 30th, Warren advanced two miles to Poplar Grove Church, attacked and carried the first line of the enemy's works, at Peeble's Farm. Following up this success, a charge was made upon the second line of Rebel defenses, and the position carried. The Ninth Corps had in the mean time advanced beyond the Fifth, and, encountering a heavy force, in strong works, was driven back in confusion, losing 1,500 prisoners, and 500 killed and wounded. Griffin's division of the Fifth Corps came to the support of the Ninth, now heavily pressed, and the combined forces repelled the enemy, who suffered a serious loss. The new position gained by the Fifth Corps was maintained and fortified. On the 2d of October, the Rebels again fell back from Warren's front, to their main lines, from the Petersburg Lead Works to the Southside railroad. No further important change of position took place in this vicinity, until near the close of the month.

A new movement to the left was commenced by Grant on the 26th of October, toward Hatcher's Run, the object of which, apparently, was to extend our lines to the Southside railroad. The enemy was prepared for this advance, and was encountered in strong force, on the 27th, near the Boydton plank road. A severe engagement followed, in which the Union losses are stated as amounting to 3,000, while those of the Rebels were considerably less. The forces engaged in this movement returned on the next day, resuming nearly their former position. The two armies remained comparatively quiet until, on the 5th of November (three days before the Presidential election), the Rebels made an attack on Fort Sedgwick, near the Jerusalem plank road, being handsomely repulsed. These attempts were renewed elsewhere, a purpose being manifested of piercing the center of the Union lines, with the hope of gaining a substantial advantage that would damage the Government at this special juncture, and weaken its cause in the loyal States. All these efforts were fortunately foiled.

While affairs were thus indecisive around Petersburg, attention had been directed, at first anxiously—for misfortune had there followed misfortune—to the Shenandoah Valley. The first movement under the new commander, Sheridan, had seemingly terminated little better than previous operations in that quarter. He had assumed command on the 7th of August, with an army formidable in numbers and tried in the service; had advanced to Strasburg, and had hastily retreated to Charlestown. Here he still remained, at the beginning of September. On the 3d day of that month, Sheridan's army was again put in motion, and marched about ten miles, encamping near Berryville. Here a line of battle was formed, and intrenchments thrown up. Before the entire army had reached this point, Gen. Crook's command repulsed a spirited attack of the enemy. It was not until the 19th that the movement was resumed, and a new position taken up, three or four miles east of Winchester. On the day previous, Gen. Averill had driven a Rebel force from Martinsburg up the Valley. The enemy was found in position at Winchester, skirmishers were advanced about 10 o'clock, on the 19th, and at noon, the action became general, lasting until 5 o'clock, when the enemy was forced to retreat, and was sent "whirling up the Valley" by Sheridan's vigorous pursuit. Early lost seriously in killed and wounded, and 5,000 prisoners and five guns were captured from him.

On the 20th, Sheridan's infantry marched sixteen miles, to the vicinity of Strasburg. On the 21st, the army remained quiet on Cedar Creek, the enemy occupying a strong position on Fisher's Hill. Before daylight on the 22d, the Union troops were in motion, and a flanking column speedily appeared in the rear of the enemy, and a general charge along his lines drove him in great confusion from his works, securing another brilliant victory. Among the Rebel losses on this memorable day were 1,100 prisoners, and sixteen guns. Pursuit was continued through the night, the enemy retiring beyond Mount Jackson, the terminus of the railroad. On the 25th, Sheridan's forces were at Harrisonburg, a portion of them having marched fifty miles in two days. The remnant of Early's army retired by Cross Keys and Port Republic, toward Charlottesville, going through Brown's Gap, on the 26th, where the Rebel rear-guard arrested the pursuit made by Gen. Merritt's cavalry.

General Wilson's division of cavalry advanced to Staunton on the 27th, destroying the railroad depot at that place, with a large amount of supplies; and on the 28th visited Waynesboro, destroying an important railroad bridge and other property. A cavalry force, supported by the Sixth and Nineteenth Corps, was at the same time advanced from Harrisonburg to Mount Crawford, ten miles distant, destroying mills, granaries and other Rebel stores and sources of supply. Wilson retired to the same point from Waynesboro, and all returned to Harrisonburg on the 29th. As a military necessity, the country was " desolated " for a circuit of several miles around.

Having driven the enemy from the Valley and deprived him, to a great degree, of the fruits of his late harvestings in that region, as well as of the means of support in any future advance, Sheridan leisurely returned down the valley, reaching New Market on the 6th of October, and Strasburg on the 8th. The main army went into camp on the north-east side of Cedar Creek, in the vicinity of Middletown, on the 10th, and there intrenched

On the 8th of October, the cavalry under Merritt and Custer gained a decisive victory over the Rebel cavalry divisions of Rosser and Lomax, in the battle of Thom's Brook, driving the enemy twenty miles, and capturing a number of prisoners, as well as several pieces of artillery.

The enemy, anxious to retrieve the misfortunes he had suffered under the vigorous hand of Sheridan, had promptly dispatched large reënforcements of infantry and cavalry, the former from Longstreet's corps, the latter under a new commander, Rosser, to operate in the valley. This was done with all the stealth which strategic skill and the peculiar character of the country, favorable to secrecy of movement, could command. Rosser was fallen in with at an early day, however, as already seen, and severely chastised. The presence of Longstreet's men was more carefully concealed until the moment arrived for the intended decisive blow. This was struck during the temporary absence of Sheridan in Washington.

On the morning of the 19th of October, just as the army, in its position at Cedar Creek, was preparing breakfast, the Rebels suddenly attacked the Eighth Corps, on the left of the line, completely surprising the men, and driving them in great confusion from their camp. Pursuit was continued for nearly four miles, flanking the position of the main army, and communicating the panic to other parts of the line. The Sixth and Nineteenth Corps were almost hopelessly endeavoring to stem the tide of defeat, when Sheridan, who had hastened to the front, arrived in time to throw the inspiring influence of his presence into the scale, and to save the day by his guidance. He speedily made new dispositions of his forces, and by vigorous flank attacks, succeeded in repulsing the enemy and driving him back in utter rout. The victory was even more signal than that gained a month before at Winchester. The enemy lost about fifty guns, a large number of killed and wounded, and thousands of prisoners. The pursuit was continued that night to Fisher's Hill, and on the following day, the cavalry pursued the flying battalions as far as Mount Jackson. Returning, the army re-occupied its old camp between Middleton and Cedar Creek. Among the deeply lamented losses in this famous battle, was that of Col. Lowell, a gallant officer of the cavalry.

These important victories in the Shenandoah Valley gave unbounded joy to loyal hearts throughout the nation. They gratified the popular thirst for military success, and awakened a true enthusiasm for the heroic commander who had redeemed the history of the Valley. General Sheridan was promoted, by the President, to be a Major-General of the Regular Army, in place of Gen. George B. McClellan, immediately after the latter had tendered his resignation, taking effect on the 8th of November.

On the day following the memorable victory at Cedar Creek, the President issued the following proclamation, for a day of national thanksgiving:

A PROCLAMATION.

It has pleased Almighty God to prolong our national life another year, defending us with his guardian care against unfriendly designs from abroad, and vouchsafing to us in His mercy many and signal victories over the enemy, who is of our own household. It has also pleased our Heavenly Father to favor as well our citizens in their homes as our soldiers in their camps, and our sailors on the rivers and seas, with unusual health. He has largely augmented our free population by emancipation and by immigration, while He has opened to us new sources of wealth, and has crowned the labor of our workingmen in every department of industry with abundant rewards. Moreover, He has been pleased to animate and inspire our minds and hearts with fortitude, courage, and resolution sufficient for the great trial of civil war into which we have been brought by our adherence as a nation to the cause of freedom and humanity, and to afford to us reasonable hopes of an ultimate and happy deliverance from all our dangers and afflictions.

Now, therefore, I, Abraham Lincoln, President of the United States, do hereby appoint and set apart the last Thursday of November next as a day which I desire to be observed by all my fellow-citizens, wherever they may be, as a day of thanksgiving and praise to Almighty God, the beneficent Creator and Ruler of the Universe. And I do further recommend to my fellow-citizens aforesaid, that, on that occasion, they do reverently humble themselves in the dust, and from thence offer up penitent and fervent prayers and supplications to the Great Disposer of events for a return of the inestimable blessings of peace, union, and harmony throughout the land which it has pleased Him to assign as a dwelling-place for ourselves and our posterity throughout all generations.

In testimony whereof, I have hereunto set my hand and caused the seal of the United States to be affixed.

Done at the city of Washington this twentieth day of October, in the year of our Lord one thousand eight hundred [L. S.] and sixty-four, and of the independence of the United States the eighty-ninth.

ABRAHAM LINCOLN.

By the President:
WILLIAM H. SEWARD, Secretary of State.

CHAPTER VI.

Gen. Sherman s Campaign in Georgia.—From Marietta to Atlanta.—
Passage of the Chattahoochee.—Rousseau's Raid.—Battles before
Atlanta.—Heavy losses of the Rebels after Hood succeeds Johnston.—Cavalry expeditions under Stoneman and McCook.—Their
Failure.—Operations around Atlanta.—Kilpatrick's Raid.—Sherman's Army on the Macon Railroad.—Battle of Jonesboro.—
Capture of Atlanta.—Rebel Raids.—Hood's operations in Sherman's rear.—Price's Invasion of Missouri.—General Results of
the South-western Campaigns.

On retiring from Kenesaw Mountain, the Rebel commander
in Georgia had taken up a strong position on the further bank
of the Chattahoochee, having succeeded in effecting the crossing without interruption.   He had previously provided a strong
tete de pont covering his communication across the stream, and
an advanced line of intrenchments on the hither side, crossing
the railroad at Smyrna, five miles south of Marietta.   These
works had secured his safe retreat.   The river is one of such
depth and rapidity of current as not to be fordable, except at
one or two points.   A reconnoissance made on the 5th of July
showed that Johnston's position could not be turned except by
crossing this stream.   General Sherman accordingly made his
dispositions to effect this object with the least possible delay.

General Schofield was ordered up to Smyrna, from his position on the right, and directed to throw a force across the
river, near the mouth of Soap's Creek.   This he satisfactorily
effected on the 7th of July, surprising the guard, and laying
secure bridges.   The place he occupied was on advantageous
ground, commanding roads leading eastward.   Gen. Garrard's
cavalry division, operating with the Army of the Tennessee,
was hastening forward to Roswell, where there were factories
which had long been engaged in manufacturing cloth for the
Rebel armies.   After destroying these factories, Garrard took

possession of the ford across the Chattahoochee, near by, and McPherson's army was speedily transferred from the right, to this position on the extreme left. In the mean time General Howard had succeeded in throwing a bridge across the river at Powers' Ferry, two miles below where the Army of the Ohio had crossed, and had taken position on the right of the latter. These important advantages having been gained by Gen. Sherman, Johnston destroyed his bridge on the 10th of July, and left the right bank of the Chattahoochee to the Union armies without further contest.

During the next six days, the main army rested in camp, while supplies were accumulated at Marietta and Vining's Station (near the Chattahoochee), and the garrisons and guards along the railroad were strengthened. It was now, too, that the word was given for the setting out of an important cavalry expedition, under Gen. Rousseau, to break Johnston's railroad communications, in Alabama, on the main thoroughfare between Atlanta and the South-west, running from Opelika Junction to Montgomery. The force intended for this purpose had been for some time past gathering at Decatur, in Northern Alabama, and numbered, at the time of starting, but little more than two thousand men. The movement began on the 10th of July, and continued, with only occasional interruptions, to destroy stores accumulated by impressment for the Rebel army, or to chastise a guerrilla party, until the river Coosa was reached, near Ashville, on the evening of the 13th. The First Brigade crossed the river, while the Second remained on the north bank, and on the next day the forces began their march down the stream, a brigade on each side, until the ford was reached where Jackson crossed in 1814, and defeated the Creek Indians. Here, as the Second Brigade began to pass over, they were fired upon from the shelter of rocks and thickets by a considerable Rebel force under Clanton, mostly dismounted cavalry. The Second Brigade speedily found a favorable position from which the fire was returned with effect. The First Brigade charged upon Clanton's men, completely routing them. Gen. Rousseau then resumed his march, reaching Talladega late the same evening, and driving in the enemy's pickets. Entering the town in the morning, he destroyed the commissary stores found there, and continued his march. On the evening of the 16th, the Tallapoosa river was crossed at Smith's Ford, near Youngville, about thirty-five miles from Montgomery. On the 17th, the railroad was struck at Loccopaca, one hundred and thirty-five miles south-west of Atlanta, and on the following day the work of destruction was earnestly commenced. The column which proceeded toward Montgomery was attacked near Chewa Station, by a much superior force sent down from Montgomery, but being reënforced by the main body under Rousseau in person, our men defeated and drove back the enemy, destroying an important trestle work about twelve miles from the city. Rousseau's forces then proceeded eastward to Opelika, destroying the road as they went. On the 19th they entered Opelika and burned " Confederate " storehouses, railroad depots, and army supplies of various kinds. A large Rebel force approaching from West Point, Rousseau turned aside from the railroad toward Lafayette. The march was continued on the next two days in the direction of Sherman's lines,which were reached on the morning of the 22d of July. The expedition had traveled 450 miles, losing less than thirty men, and fully accomplishing its purpose.

Preparatory to an intended advance, Gen. Sherman had also sent the cavalry of Gens. Stoneman and McCook down the Chattahoochee river, scouting far to the right, and diverting the enemy's attention. On the 17th of July, a general advance commenced, the army of Thomas crossing at the bridges built by Howard, and marching toward Atlanta by way of Buckhead ; Schofield, already over, proceeding by Cross Keys ; and McPherson moving directly toward a point near Stone Mountain, on the Augusta railroad, east of Decatur. A general line was formed along the Old Peach Tree road. McPherson reached the Augusta road, seven miles east of Decatur, on the 18th, and destroyed the track for a distance of four miles Schofield, on the same day, entered the town of Decatur. On the 19th, the lines were contracted from the left, McPherson marching into Decatur, and Schofield advancing some distance by one of the roads (passing the Howard House), from that place to Atlanta. Thomas meanwhile crossed Peach Tree Creek, under fire from the enemy's well intrenched lines on the south bank. Each of these three columns encountered opposition, and skirmished on its way. On the 20th all were closed in, converging upon Atlanta. About 4 o'clock in the afternoon of that day, the enemy suddenly sallied from his works, and heavily attacked Sherman's right center, engaging Hooker's corps, and portions of Howard's and Palmer's corps. The Twentieth Corps was entirely unprotected by fortifications, and Newton's division of the Fourth Corps, which was first assailed, was only partially covered by hastily constructed lines of rail piles. The enemy, notwithstanding these advantages, was repulsed with great loss, leaving over 500 dead on the field, about 1,000 severely wounded, and many prisoners—in the aggregate not far from 5,000 men. The total casualties on the side of the Government were estimated by the commanding general at not exceeding 1,500, mostly in Hooker's corps. The battle of Peach Tree Creek, resulting in so depressing a defeat of the Rebels, had almost immediately followed a change of commanders— Gen. Hood having succeeded Johnston, after the latter's failure to hold the line of the Chattahochee.

By a reconnoissance on the next day, the enemy's intrenched lines were found to be on commanding hights beyond Peach Tree Creek, extending across the Augusta road, on the east, to near Turner's Ferry, on the Chattahoochee, at a distance of about four miles from Atlanta. On the 22d, to the surprise of Gen. Sherman, this strong line was found to be abandoned. But Atlanta was not yet to be surrendered. The new Rebel general had determined on a change of strategy, of which the battle of the 20th afforded the first illustration. The Union army passed over the deserted works of Hood, advancing until the lines were approached to within a general distance of two miles from the city. The enemy had now taken shelter behind a line of redoubts built a year before, and was busily engaged in connecting and strengthening these by the usual works. The Army of the Tennessee, in advancing from Decatur, had substantially followed the railroad, Logan's Corps (the Fifteenth) and Blair's (the Seventeenth) on the left, and Dodge's (the Sixteenth) on the right. In contracting the arc, the Fifteenth Corps had connected directly with the left of Schofield, near the Howard House, leaving the Sixteenth Corps out of line. Blair's corps, on the extreme left, after a severe fight, had gained possession of a high hill, giving a view into the heart of the town. Dodge was ordered to the support of the left in this position, and was moving by a diagonal path for that purpose, when the enemy moved out, soon after noon, on the 22d of July, to attack that part of the lines. Gen. McPherson, while passing by a narrow road, leading by the rear, through wooded ground, from Dodge's corps to the division on the extreme left of Blair, was killed by Rebel sharpshooters—a death deeply lamented. Maj.-Gen. John A. Logan temporarily succeeded to his command. A severe engagement had already begun. Hardee's corps assailed and enveloped Blair's left flank, while Stewart's corps attacked in front. The two divisions of Generals Giles A. Smith and Leggett, of the Seventeenth Corps, maintained the fight with desperate valor, while the moving column of Gen. Dodge speedily closed up the line holding the enemy in check, and driving him back with destructive blows. The battle raged over this part of the ground until about 4 o'clock, when there was a brief lull, followed by a desperate attempt of the enemy to break through the lines where they had been weakened by the withdrawal of Martin's brigade of the Fifteenth Corps, to reënforce the left. This attack, after partial success, was finally repulsed, and the corps regained all the ground lost, with all the guns captured by the enemy, but two.

The Union loss in this battle of Atlanta was 3,722, in killed, wounded and prisoners. Gen. Sherman estimates the enemy's total loss as certainly not less than 8,000 men, while Gen. Logan reported the number as at least 10,000. Of his dead, 2,200 were actually counted on the field. His aggregate losses in the two battles of the 20th and 22d, probably exceeded 15,000.

On the 21st, Garrard's division of cavalry had been dispatched to Covington, forty-two miles east of Atlanta, on the

Augusta railroad, to destroy two important bridges in that vicinity. During Garrard's absence, Wheeler had attempted to destroy the wagon trains of the Army of the Tennessee, left behind at Decatur; but they were protected and safely withdrawn, by the management of Col. (afterward Gen.) Sprague, and the three regiments under his command. On the 23d, Garrard returned, having fully accomplished his purpose, and bringing in a number of prisoners and horses, with the loss of but two men.

The Rebel commander was now reduced to the Macon railroad exclusively, for the transportation of his supplies. To reach this road, therefore, became an important object to Gen. Sherman. Two expeditionary forces of cavalry were accordingly organized for this purpose—one numbering not less than 5,000, placed under the command of Gen. Stoneman, and the other numbering about 4,000, under Gen McCook; the former to move by the left beyond Atlanta, to McDonough, and the latter by the right to Fayetteville—the two bodies acting in concert, to meet at a given time and place on the Macon railroad. This joint expedition, which seemed to promise complete success, and was to have been followed by an attempt to release the Union prisoners at Andersonville, resulted in disaster, Gen. Stoneman himself having been taken prisoner, with 700 of his men, near Macon. It appears that he had attempted a sudden descent on Andersonville, before completing the contemplated work in conjunction with McCook. The latter officer proceeded at the same time to execute his part of the plan of operations, crossing the Chattahoochee near Rivertown, and moving rapidly to the West Point railroad, near Palmetto Station, where he broke up the road; and thence to Fayetteville, destroying 500 wagons and various supplies for the army found there. He then struck the Macon Railroad at Lovejoy's, on the night of the 29th of July, as appointed. Failing to hear from Stoneman, and being heavily pressed, he withdrew to Newman, on the West Point road, where he fell in with a considerable infantry force, moving from Mississippi to Atlanta, which had been stopped there by the break which McCook had just previously made at Palmetto. He was speedily hemmed in and

39

forced to give battle. He succeeded in cutting his way out, with a loss of about 500 men, and reached Marietta without further interruption. The serious losses from this raid were not compensated by any material advantages—the slight damage done to the railroads beyond East Point being easily repaired by the enemy.

Gen. Sherman had determined to withdraw the Army of the Tennessee from its position on the left, and move it around, by the rear of Schofield and Thomas, to the right, extending the Union lines below Proctor's Creek, while Schofield extended his forces to the Augusta railroad. This change was commenced on the night of the 26th of July, and the Army of the Tennessee (Gen. O. O. Howard having now succeeded to the command), was in its new position on the 28th, and speedily threw up the temporary covering works which our troops had accustomed themselves to construct. The enemy, hoping to find Howard's troops still in motion and unprepared to receive an attack, repeated the attempt which had cost him so heavily on the 20th and 22d. A series of assaults (on some points as many as seven), were made, chiefly on Logan's corps, and each time repulsed, with comparatively little loss on the Union side. The Rebel loss in killed and wounded was not less than 5,000. Of Rebel dead left on the field, 642 were counted by our men, who buried them. The aggregate Union loss was reported at less than 500. This battle, so disastrous to the assailants, terminated Hood's efforts of this sort, the three actions fought within little more than a week having cost him over 20,000 men, without profit, and with only a proportionately very small reduction of the strength of our armies. Henceforward the enemy remained on the defensive, and endeavored, by strong works, to prevent a further extension of Sherman's lines southward toward the railroad below East Point.

Gen. Schofield's army was subsequently transferred to the right of Howard, and also Gen. Palmer's corps, of the Army of the Cumberland. The latter corps moved into position below Utoy Creek, on the 1st of August, and Schofield, going still farther to the right, extended the line to a location near East Point. These changes were made without interruption from Hood. The extension of the right was continued by Gen. Sherman, with demonstrations along the whole line, until the 5th.

On the promotion of Gen. Howard to the command of the Army of the Tennessee, Maj.-Gen. D. S. Stanley succeeded him as commander of the Fourth Corps. Gen. J. C. Davis, nearly at the same time, was appointed to the command of the Fourteenth Corps, in place of Gen. Palmer, resigned. Gen. Hooker, dissatisfied at not being appointed to succeed Gen. McPherson, asked to be relieved from the command of the Twentieth Corps, and was succeeded by Gen. H. W. Slocum, as soon as the latter could arrive from Vicksburg, where he had been in command.

It appears that the Rebel general had now received large accessions of militia, and other reënforcements, so that he was able to maintain a defensive line stretching from near Decatur to a point below East Point, a distance of about fifteen miles. An attempt was made by a brigade of Gen. Cox's division of Schofield's army to break through the hostile lines at a point below Utoy Creek, on the 5th of August, but the assault failed, with a loss of 400 men. On the 6th, this position was turned by Gen. Hascall, but without succeeding in reaching the Macon railroad, or that to West Point. To cut these roads, and particularly that to Macon—the failure of Stoneman and McCook being now known—was a necessary work which the main army must somehow perform. Sherman ordered four heavy siege guns from Chattanooga, which were put in position on the 10th, and were kept constantly at work, night and day, for some time, doing considerable damage in the city, without affecting the pertinacity with which the enemy maintained his defensive lines. Gen. Sherman consequently decided on a new movement to get possession of the Macon road, and to compel the evacuation of Atlanta. So quietly had it been planned, that his own men were puzzled, and the enemy mystified when its execution was actually commenced. This was nothing less than a withdrawal from the works before the city, and an ultimate movement of the army by the right flank, crossing the

West Point railroad, and striking the Macon road some distance south of Atlanta.

As the movement was about to have begun on the 18th of August, information was received that Hood had dispatched a cavalry expedition, numbering from 6,000 to 10,000 men, under Wheeler, to cut Gen. Sherman's communications by the single railroad northward to Chattanooga. This force had struck Adairsville, capturing 900 beef cattle, and had torn up the railroad track near Calhoun. Nothing could have happened more opportunely for Sherman's purpose. Gen. Kilpatrick, with 5,000 cavalry, advanced to the right on the night of the 18th, thoroughly broke the West Point railroad, near Fairborn, and then struck the Macon road near Jonesboro, engaging and defeating a cavalry force under Ross, and holding the road for five hours, doing such damage to it as he was able. He was, however, compelled to retire—an overwhelming force of infantry and cavalry assailing him—and, making a circuit, again came upon the railroad near Lovejoy's Station, but was again so heavily menaced that, after a charge upon the Rebel cavalry, capturing a number of prisoners, and four guns, he withdrew to Decatur, arriving on the 22d of August. Gen. Sherman, hoping that Kilpatrick's raid would accomplish his purpose, without the aid of the main army, had postponed the general movement ordered for the 18th. It now became manifest that the Macon road had not been sufficiently broken to interrupt the trains for many days, and the original plan of " taking the field with our main force, and using it against the communications of Atlanta, instead of against its intrenchments," was resumed.

On the night of the 25th, the Fourth Corps (Stanley's) withdrew from the extreme left, and marched below Proctor's Creek, on the right. The Twentieth Corps (temporarily commanded by Gen. Williams) at the same time moved back to the Chattahoochee river. On the night of the 26th, the armies of the Tennessee and the Cumberland drew out of their lines and moved on to the right, the former army advancing circuitously, and approaching Sandtown. The next move brought Howard's army upon the West Point railroad, above Fairborn and Thomas's army near Red Oak—Schofield, who had hitherto remained in his former position, now bringing up the rear. The entire day was spent, on the 28th, in destroying the West Point railroad, more than twelve miles of the track being thoroughly broken up. On the 29th, the armies moved eastward by several roads, Howard advancing, on the right, toward Jonesboro, Thomas, in the center, by Shoal Creek Church to Couch's, and Schofield, on the left, toward Morrow's Mills. The position thus aimed at was deemed so decidedly advantageous, that Gen. Sherman was anxious to secure it at the earliest moment. Thomas reached his assigned place early in the afternoon, without much opposition. Schofield moved in a circuit around East Point, which the enemy still tenaciously held, and came into the position intended, toward Rough-and-Ready Station. Gen. Howard had the greatest distance to move, and was more or less delayed by skirmishing with cavalry of the enemy, supported by artillery, at different points on the way. He continued his march, however, until within half a mile of Jonesboro, when darkness prevented his further advance, and he encamped for the night. In the morning (August 31st) he found a heavy Rebel force in his front, and made his dispositions accordingly. Gen. Sherman, who was with the center, immediately gave directions for strengthening both Howard and Schofield, and ordered the latter at once to strike the Macon railroad near Rough-and-Ready. Meanwhile, the enemy came out from his works at Jonesboro, and attacked Howard's forces, which were now in a good situation to receive their assailants. The assault was made by Hardee's and Lee's corps. The conflict lasted for more than two hours, when the enemy withdrew, leaving over 400 dead on the field, and having about 2,500 wounded. The Union losses were comparatively light. The movements ordered on the left and center were entirely successful, and the work of destruction was soon going on with vigor, all along the line. The troops were ordered, in the afternoon, to concentrate around Jonesboro, while Kilpatrick's cavalry was sent to attack or menace the railroad below that place. The various corps having closed in as ordered, Davis attacked the enemy's lines about 4 o'clock in the afternoon of the 1st of September, charging across open fields, and carrying the works in a brilliant manner. The corps of Schofield and Stanley had been unable to get up until night on account of the difficult nature of the country to be traversed, and the enemy effected his escape southward. Pursuit was made next day as far as Lovejoy's Station, where the Rebel forces were found in a strongly intrenched position, covering the McDonough and Fayetteville road.

On the night of September 1st, Hood began the evacuation of Atlanta, blowing up seven trains of cars, and destroying other property. Gen. Slocum, who had now assumed command of the Twentieth Corps, left on the Chattahoochee, took possession of the place on the 2d of September. The work of destroying the railroad ceased when these facts became known to Gen. Sherman, and the entire forces south of Atlanta were gradually withdrawn to that place, the grand objective point of the campaign being now gained.

The news of the fall of Atlanta gave exuberant joy to the friends of the Government every-where. It created a corresponding depression among the adherents of the "Confederacy." It was a brilliant triumph, nobly earned by officers and men. It remained to be seen whether the place could be securely held, with a single line of communication so extended, to be maintained, and with an army of 100,000 men to be supported. But enough for the moment was the delight of victory. This was no time to doubt that our gallant generals and armies would take care of the rest, and turn the triumph to good account.

The raid of Wheeler's cavalry, on Sherman's line of railroad communication with Chattanooga, accomplished far less than might have been reasonably expected. Care had been taken, however, in guarding the road, and in garrisoning important points; and under the efficient and skillful direction of Col. Wright, in charge of construction and repairs, the temporary damage done at different points was so speedily repaired as to occasion no real inconvenience to the main army, which continued to be amply supplied. After breaking the road and destroying property at Adairsville and Calhoun, Wheeler, on the 14th of August, appeared before Dalton, where there was a garrison of less than 500 men under Col. Laibold, and, after surrounding the place, demanded its surrender. The gallant officer laconically replied: "I have been placed here to defend this post, and not to surrender it." And he performed that duty, withstanding a severe and long-continued attack, in the hope of being reënforced in season to hold the place. This expectation was not disappointed. Gen. Steadman arrived next morning with fresh troops, and Wheeler was driven off. His next movement was into Tennessee, where he appéars ultimately to have met Forrest, after his capture of Athens, part of the coöperating forces moving northward, crossing the Holston and the Clinch rivers, near Strawberry Plains and Clinton, and going around · by the Sequatchee Valley, into middle Tennessee. Other raiders approached Nashville at Lebanon, Murfreesboro and Franklin. These parties, which were apparently aiming to effect a junction at Tullahoma, were driven toward Florence, and finally out of the State, by the forces under Generals Rousseau, Steadman and Granger. Near Murfreesboro, on the 1st of September, Rousseau had an engagement with the invading forces, driving them back three miles, and on the 3d, they were further chastised. On the 4th, the notorious John Morgan was surprised and killed by General Gillem, at Greenville, in East Tennessee, and his forces captured or dispersed. On the 8th, the Rebel Jessie and 100 of his men were captured at Ghent, in Kentucky. The attempts to create an invasion excitement like that which had formerly led Gen. Buell into hasty retreat were all foiled. Not a little damage in several localities was done by guerrilla parties, and by the larger expeditions of Wheeler and Forrest, but on the general military situation, all these affairs combined had no perceptable effect.

After the loss of Atlanta, Hood withdrew to Macon. Here he was visited by his chief, Jefferson Davis, who, appalled at the disaster which had undoubtedly been hastened by his removal of Johnston, was eager to avert the furthei misfortunes impending in that quarter. The Governor of Georgia, on the other hand, had almost immediately recalled fifteen thousand of the militia of that State, in undisguised rage at the central management of military affairs, and in manifest contempt for Hood. Consequent upon this visit of Davis to Macon, a new military scheme was entered upon, such as the situation in fact not unnaturally invited, for compelling Gen. Sherman to release his hold upon Georgia. This scheme was simply that of an aggressive movement, in mass, upon the communications of the Union commander, with an invasion of the territory in his rear. The raids of Wheeler, Forrest and other cavalry leaders had indeed foreshadowed this movement, but merely as an incident, not as the main purpose, of a campaign. And it was quite another matter to move the main army of infantry on so long an expedition, abandoning the country in front of the invading force.

Hood's main force was soon moved in a westward direction, turning Sherman's right, by a circuitous march. For some days following the 29th of September, telegraphic and other communication between Atlanta and Chattanooga was interrupted. The purpose of Hood was now fully disclosed, and he proceeded to execute it with his accustomed vigor. On the 3d of October, Gen. Sherman, leaving Gen. Slocum in command at Atlanta, with only the Twentieth Corps as a garrison, re-crossed the Chattahoochee with the main army, which was provided with fifteen days' rations. General Thomas was on the same day dispatched to Chattanooga. Hood gained possession of Big Shanty and Acworth on the 5th, and destroyed several miles of the railroad. On the 6th, he appeared before Alatoona, but was repulsed by its brave garrison with severe loss. The approach of Gen. Sherman caused him to retire from that vicinity on the 9th, when he fell back upon Cedartown, some distance west of Alatoona, and south of Rome. Sherman's forces moved up the railroad, which was rapidly repaired, and were concentrated about Rome on the 12th of the month. About the same time Hood, having moved in advance of Sherman on the left, struck the railroad again at Resacca, which place our forces reached on the 14th. Hood retired across Taylor's Bridge, obstructing Snake Creek Gap, which was quickly again made passable for the army and trains.

On the 16th, Sherman took possession of Shipp's Gap, in the same mountain range, capturing some Rebel prisoners. The rear of Hood's army left Lafayette at daylight on the morning of the 17th, retiring south-westwardly into a mountainous and uncultivated region of Alabama, were prolonged pursuit was impracticable. Our advance stopped at Gaylesville in that State. Hood had carefully avoided giving battle, since his disastrous repulse at Allatoona, but had succeeded in destroying the railroad for about twenty miles between Resaca and Tunnel Hill, and for considerable distances at other points. All this damage was repaired, however, with remarkable rapidity, and the supplies at Atlanta were ample for the intermediate period. On the 29th, the main portion of the army moved back toward Atlanta. For several days, the headquarters remained at Kingston, a portion of the army having advanced as far as Marietta on the 5th of November. An attack on the outposts of Atlanta was made by Rebel militia under Iverson on the 9th, and repulsed by Gen. Slocum.

A new campaign was announced in general orders issued at Kingston on the 7th of November, and the final preparations were made for its commencement.

A well-organized and somewhat formidable invasion of Missouri was undertaken this season, under the leading auspices of the Rebel Price. This was doubtless but a fragment of a broken scheme of general aggressive warfare, transferring the seat of war into the loyal States, which had been devised at Richmond, and with the execution of which Lieut.-Gen. Grant had early and persistently interfered. The *debris* of this grand plan could be discerned all along the border line, eastward and in the center; but in Missouri and the far Southwest, the parts assigned appear to have been undertaken substantially, as at first intended. With such means as could reasonably be placed at his disposal, Gen. Rosecrans energetically combatted the earlier guerrilla movements in his department, and the later well-matured expedition of Price. Gen. Curtis, commanding in Kansas, also bore his part in repelling a movement which threatened his own district, as well as the Department of the Missouri.

52

The situation of affairs in many parts of Missouri was indeed deplorable, prior to the operations under the larger bands of Price and Shelby. In an address to the people of that State, issued on the 28th of June, 1864, Gen. Rosecrans said: "With a great and populous State, a fertile soil, vast mineral wealth, supplied with outlets by water and railroad, for all your productions, no actual war within your borders for the last two years, and yet plundering, robbery and arson, have prevailed every where to a certain extent, except at points garrisoned by troops, and some few strictly loyal sections of the State." Earnestly appealing to the people to unite with him in his efforts to put down these disorders, and to respond to the arrangement made with the Governor of the State for calling out a portion of the enrolled militia, Gen. Rosecrans gave his earnest attention—with the best results, as ultimately appeared—to the difficult work before him. These duties occupied the forces in his Department—the details of their operations being too minute and disconnected for any summary recital—until the appearance of considerable invading forces from across the border, with the manifest purpose of attempting to overrun and re-conquer the State.

With a force estimated at 10,000 men, Price crossed the White River at Salina, Arkansas, on the 14th of September, on his way through the north-eastern portion of Arkansas into Missouri. His advance, under Shelby, reached the little town of Bloomfield, in Stoddard County, Missouri, in the south-eastern corner of the State, on the 23d of the month. He appears to have ranged through the country with very little opposition, depredating and "conscripting" at will. On the 26th, Gen. Rosecrans issued another stirring order, calling on the people to prepare a fitting reception for the invader; and Gov. Gamble took prompt measures for putting a militia force in the field. Gen. Rosecrans authorized the formation of a Veteran Brigade at St. Louis, under Col. Laibold (of Dalton memory) "for the defense of the city, and to punish Price, Shelby and their companions, as well as the traitors at home who are waiting to join them, and who have aided and supplied them with horses, stolen from their neighbors during the last few weeks, and sent South."

A brigade of Gen. A. J. Smith's command, under Gen. Ewing, was sent out to operate against Price's column, and occupied the town of Pilot-knob on the 25th of September; anticipating the movement of the enemy, who appeared before that place on the 26th. Price proceeded at once to attack our lines, but was repulsed in all his attempts, suffering serious loss. Ewing's position was, however, subsequently made untenable by Price's occupation of Shepherd's Mountain. He accordingly blew up his magazine, and retired to Harrison's Station, where he made a stand behind intrenchments previously erected by a militia force that had occupied the place. Price closely followed him, breaking the railroad on each side of Ewing, and putting his smaller force in imminent danger. But the latter soon extricated himself from the enemy's toils, brought his command, with little loss, to Rolla, which was a fortified post occupied by Gen. McNeil.

Gen. Steele, having been reinforced by troops drawn from Memphis and other points, despatched a force under .Gen. Mower from Brownsville, Arkansas, on the 17th of September, in pursuit of Price. This column reached Cape Girardeau on or about the 6th of October, without falling in with any hostile force. Price, in the meantime, after feigning an advance on St. Louis, where Gen. Rosecrans had concentrated considerable forces, moved off toward the interior of the State, threatening Jefferson City. Mower's forces speedily embarked on transports at Cape Girardeau for St. Louis, and from thence proceeded up the Missouri River to Jefferson City. Gen. Rosecrans left St. Louis for the front on the 13th of October, and took the field in person on the 19th. The various Union forces in the State were concentrating about the scene of Price's operations, Gen. Curtis advancing from Kansas, and Gen. Pleasanton leading the forces that moved out from St. Louis, where he had been in command of the defenses of the city.

Glasgow, on the north side of the Missouri River, was taken by the Rebel Clark on the 15th, and a large amount of property destroyed, while the guerrilla parties were active in various parts of northern Missouri, from which section a large number of recruits were obtained for Price. About this time, Shelby crossed the river at Booneville, with 2,000 cavalry, and started on a circuit north and west.

After remaining some time in the vicinity of Jefferson City, on which he hesitated to make his threatened attack, Price had retired westward, destroying the La Mine bridge, on the Pacific railroad, and hovering about Booneville, in some of the earlier days of October, Gen. Sanborn harassing the enemy's flanks and rear. Jeff. Thompson defeated the militia garrison at Sedalia, and entered that town on the 16th of October. Price got possession of Lexington on the 17th. Curtis drove a Rebel force from Independence on the 16th, and advanced toward Lexington, while the forces of Rosecrans moved rapidly up from the East. Price quickly abandoned the latter place, and fell back toward the Kansas border, sending off his long wagon train toward the South-west, while his raiders in northern Missouri re-crossed the river. Price was defeated at the Little Blue River, on the 22d of October, and driven to the Big Blue. Shelby gained a temporary advantage at Westport, on the 23d, but was afterward beaten, on the same day, by our main army. On the 25th, Price was again attacked, on the Fort Scott road, and beaten with serious loss. Still more decisive victories were gained over him at Mine Creek, on the 26th, when his Generals, Marmaduke and Cabell, were captured, with a large number of their men; on the 27th, at Marais des Cygnes (in Kansas); and again at Newtonia on the 28th.

The invasion of Missouri was now at an end. The residue of Price's men—including the fresh recruits, whose departure was not disadvantageous to the peace and civilized order of the State—were but too glad to escape without a further contest.

With a grasp upon Georgia that could not be shaken off, with an utter dispersion of the invading expedition of Price in Missouri, with Mobile Bay commanded by our Navy, and with firm possession, despite occasional raids, of all the territory thus far regained west of the Alleghany range, the President, in the early days of November, looked with gladdened sight upon a military situation portending a near approach of the end. With the taking of Atlanta—as the event has fully proved—all the Rebel territory between the Savannah and the Mississippi, embracing three of the most important Gulf States, had been practically conquered and reclaimed, as the result of the season's work. Texas was long since isolated. Arkansas was still held by Gen. Steele. The Mississippi river was not seriously obstructed by the persistent attempts to interrupt navigation on its waters. Tennessee could not be wrested from the firm hand of the military Governor, Andrew Johnson. Practically, the area of the Rebellion was now narrowed to the limits of the Carolinas and South-eastern Virginia, with the flash of loyal bayonets and the thunder of "Lincoln gun-boats" all along the sea-board of each.

CHAPTER VII.

THE actual opening of the Presidential canvass was marked by the subsidence of all opposition to Mr. Lincoln within the Republican Union party. Those who had reluctantly come into his support, did not covet the position of leaders without any following. Those who had tested the futile scheme for bringing about his withdrawal, speedily learned that the people had no inclination for such trifling. Gen. Fremont, who had begged an instantaneous acceptance of his resignation as a Major-General, that he might use the more freedom in the letter of acceptance, which he was in haste to write, now (not too graciously) recalled that acceptance. Mr. Chase, hitherto, silently awaiting the turn of events, no longer hesitated to take the stump for Lincoln and Johnson. Radicals and Conservatives heartily united in the common cause, and all minor divisions were forgotten.

The Democratic National Convention, in its platform, as well as in its nominations, had shown a singular misapprehension of the strong current of loyal opinion. It pronounced the fatal words, "four years of failure to restore the Union by the experiment of war," which vexed the ears of the heroic soldiers and of the faithful citizens alike. More untimely and infatuated still, was the "demand that immediate efforts be made for the cessation of hostilities," at the moment when our brave soldiers were entering Atlanta. Recreant leaders sealed the doom of their party on the moment of these strange utterances. Vain was McClellan's attempted change of base, in his letter of acceptance. Unavailing was Pendleton's abstinence of speech. There was nothing in the record of either, to their misfortune, that neutralized the effect of these significant words.

If by these grave mistakes, the Opposition had thrown itself into a hopelessly defensive attitude, scarcely less maladroit were its aggressive attempts. Issues were raised, so transparently false, as to offend the plainest common sense. Arbitrary arrests, interference with liberty of speech, ambitious despotism, and a general infraction of the Constitution, were resolutely charged upon Mr. Lincoln's administration. The people were told that their rights were recklessly trampled under foot. In fact, the Chicago Democratic platform—in anti-climatic eagerness—averred that " the Constitution itself has been disregarded *in every part*, and public liberty and private right alike trodden down, and the material prosperity of the country essentially impaired." By a curious infelicity, complaint was made of an alleged " direct interference of the military authority of the United States in the recent elections held in Kentucky, Maryland, Missouri, and Delaware," coupled with a threat of resistance by force of arms. Was it supposed that the people had so soon forgotten the military interference of the Opposition candidate, in arresting a whole legislature in Maryland, and forcibly preventing the intended steps toward ·' secession "? Or that this action—the brightest in his career —was heartily approved by public opinion throughout the country? To deny the right of preventing the consummation of plotted treason, was only to claim immunity for treason, itself. And such was, throughout, the spirit of this platform. It lamented restraints upon the liberties of traitors and their abettors; it arraigned the exercise of the war power, in meeting a war begun by rebels; it denounced the refusal of " the right of asylum " to a foreign slave-pirate ; it grew indignant at "the employment of unusual test oaths," from which no loyal nerve ever suffered a twingle ; and grieved over the strangely asserted

" denial of the right of the people to bear arms "—meaning the refusal of permission to a secret order of conspirators in Indiana, and elsewhere, which had already been exposed, to arm and organize in private for the direct coöperation with the Southern Rebel forces.*

It is not surprising that Thompson and Sanders, those arch Rebels " in the confidential employment " of Jefferson Davis in Canada, promptly telegraphed their agent in Halifax, on the conclusion of this Chicago conclave, in the following terms: "Platform and Vice President satisfactory ; speeches very satisfactory." Subsequent disclosures throw a lurid glare over these historic words. Humiliating enough it certainly was, for men not utterly lost to all sense of loyalty, and to all love of country, to receive such an indorsement from known traitors ; but from traitors plotting the unparalleled iniquities which time was erelong to reveal, what could be more lastingly iniquitous than this approbation? In this view, some of the " very satisfactory " speeches become too strangely significant to be passed over as they might otherwise deserve. The reports to be quoted from appeared in the Chicago *Times*, a party organ of the opposition, and the speeches were made by delegates, either actually in the Convention, or at popular meetings outside, on that occasion.

A delegate—certainly not a " Senator " in Congress, as the reporter intimated ; can it have been the identical Samuel S. Cox, of Ohio, who, two years before, when greatly in need of Republican votes to secure his election to Congress, called on his auditors in a strongly loyal county to give "three cheers for Abraham Lincoln"? A delegate to the Chicago Democratic National Convention was thus reported by the party organ on that occasion :

Senator Cox being introduced, said he did not want to use any harsh language toward Old Abe [cries of "give it to him"]. He had attempted in his own city, a few weeks since, to show, in a very quiet way, that Abraham Lincoln had deluged the country with blood, created a debt of four thou-

---

* For the Chicago Democratic Platform, entire, see page 578.

sand millions of dollars, sacrificed two millions of human lives, and filled the land with grief and mourning.

For less offenses than Mr. Lincoln had been guilty of, the English people had chopped off the head of the first Charles. In his opinion, Lincoln and Davis ought to be brought to the same block together. The other day they arrested a friend of his, a member of Congress from Missouri, for saying, in private conversation, that Lincoln was no better than Jeff. Davis. He was ready to say the same here now in Chicago.

Another Democratic orator and delegate, H. Clay Dean, of Iowa, is represented as follows in the same journal's report:

He said in the presence of the force of Camp Douglas, and all the satraps of Lincoln, that the American people were ruled by felons. Lincoln had never turned a dishonest man out of office or kept an honest one in. [A voice—" What have you to say of Jeff. Davis?"] I have nothing to say about him. Lincoln is engaged in a controversy with him, and I never interfere between black dogs. * * * *

And still the monster usurper wanted more men for his slaughter-pens. [Loud cries of " he shan't have more."] The careful husbandman, in deadening the forest, was always careful in preserving the young growth of timber; and in selecting his swine for the slaughter, he preserved the younger ones for future use. But the tyrant and despot who ruled this people to destruction paid no regard to age or condition. He desired to double the widowhood and duplicate the orphans. He blushed that such a felon should occupy the highest place in the gift of the people. Perjury and larceny were written over him as often as was " one dollar " on the one dollar bills of the Bank of the State of Indiana. [Cries of " the old villain."]

Ever since the usurper, traitor and tyrant had occupied the Presidential chair, the Republican party had shouted war to the knife, and the knife to the hilt. Blood had flowed in torrents, and yet the thirst of the old monster was not quenched. His cry was for more blood.

A delegate named Benjamin Allen, of New York, is reported in the same journal, to have said:

The people will soon rise, and if they can not put Lincoln out of power by the ballot they will by the bullet. [Loud cheers.]

40 53

These examples will suffice to show the spirit of the speeches made at the Chicago Democratic Convention, which were so "very satisfactory" to the men "in the confidential employment" of the "Confederate Government." Such was, to a great extent, the character of the opposition made to Mr. Lincoln, during the canvass of 1864. That "Confederate" funds were used in sustaining the secret organization which so largely influenced this convention, or that these conspirators were in constant communication and full accord with those malignants who were already hatching their terrible brood of crimes, across the Canada border, has since been placed beyond reasonable doubt.

The exposure of the "privy conspiracy and rebellion" in Indiana, and the trial of some of the leaders concerned therein, was not without effect upon the canvass. At first incredulous, the whole country was speedily startled by damning proofs of the reality of this treasonable secret order, and of the existence of designs even more reckless and wicked than were originally surmised. In an elaborate report, made on the 8th of October, Judge Advocate General Holt stated at length the purposes of this infamous order, as thus far shown by undoubted testimony, under the following heads:

1. Aiding soldiers to desert, and harboring and protecting deserters.

2. Discouraging enlistments, and resisting the draft.

3. Circulation of disloyal and treasonable publications.

4. Communicating with and giving intelligence to the enemy.

5. Aiding the enemy by recruiting for them, or assisting them to recruit, within our lines.

6. Furnishing the Rebels with arms, ammunition, etc.

7. Co-operating with the enemy in raids and invasions.

8. Destruction of Government property.

9. Destruction of private property and persecution of Union men.

10. Assassination and murder.

11. Establishment of a North-western Confederacy.

In concluding his report, Judge Holt said:

But, although the treason of the Order has been thoroughly exposed, and although its capacity for fatal mischief has, by means of the arrest of its leaders, the seizure of its arms, and the other vigorous means which have been pursued, been seriously impaired, it is still busied with its secret plottings against the Government, and with its perfidious designs in aid of the Southern rebellion. It is reported to have recently issued new signs and passwords, and its members assert that foul means will be used to prevent the success of the Administration at the coming election; and threaten an extended revolt in the event of the reëlection of President Lincoln.

In the presence of the rebellion and this secret Order—which is but its echo and faithful ally—we can not but be amazed at the utter and wide-spread profligacy, personal and political, which these movements against the Government disclose. The guilty men engaged in them, after casting aside their allegiance, seem to have trodden under foot every sentiment of honor and every restraint of law, human and Divine. Judea produced but one Judas Iscariot, and Rome, from the sinks of her demoralization, produced but one Cataline, and yet, as events prove, there has arisen together in our land an entire brood of such traitors, all animated by the same parricidal spirit, and all struggling with the same relentless malignity for the dismemberment of our Union. Of this extraordinary phenomenon—not paralleled, it is believed, in the world's history—there can be but one explanation, and all these blackened and fetid streams of crime may well be traced to the same common fountain. So fiercely intolerant and imperious was the temper engendered by slavery, that when the Southern people, after having controlled the national councils for half a century, were beaten at an election, their leaders turned upon the Government with the insolent fury with which they would have drawn their revolvers on a rebellious slave in one of their negro quarters ; and they have continued since to prosecute their warfare, amid all the barbarisms and atrocities naturally and necessarily inspired by the infernal institution in whose interests they are sacrificing alike themselves and their country. Many of these conspirators, as is well known, were fed, clothed, and educated at the expense of the nation, and were loaded with its honors at the very moment they struck at its life with the horrid criminality of a son stabbing the bosom of his own mother while impressing kisses on his cheeks. The leaders of the traitors in the loyal States, who so completely fraternize with these conspirators, and whose machinations are now unmasked, it is as clearly the duty of the Administration to prosecute and punish, as it is its duty to subjugate the Rebels who are openly in arms against the Government. In the performance of this duty, it is entitled to expect, and will doubtless receive, the zealous coöperation of true men everywhere, who, in crushing the truculent foe ambushed in the haunts of this secret Order, should rival in courage and faithfulness the armies which are so nobly sustaining our flag on the battle-fields of the South.

The deadly spirit of hatred to the Government, and of affinity with treason, thus forcibly and truthfully described, had been more or less exhibited in the North from the beginning of the rebellion. Vallandigham, fitly chosen as the head of this organization, had defiantly affirmed, before war actually began, that he would resist any attempt to coerce the Seceders—that any armed force going from his district to subjugate the South should "march over his dead body" before they left the State.* His conduct was accordant with this promise of aid to the Rebel cause. In the course of his efforts of this nature, as mentioned in previous pages, he had been arrested, subjected to a military trial, refused a writ of habeas corpus, on appeal to the civil courts, and sent through the lines of the Rebel army. Escaping on a blockade-runner, he had arrived in Canada, somewhat in advance of Thompson, Clay and Sanders. From thence he escaped in the summer of 1864, after the latter traitors "in the confidential employment" of the Richmond "government" had become fully installed at Montreal, Niagara Falls, and Toronto.

It was in behalf of this Vallandigham and such precious patriots as he, that the great outcry concerning arbitrary arrests and the suspension of the habeas corpus was made. In May, 1863, a "Democratic" meeting held at Albany, had seen fit to pass resolutions on this subject, and to inclose them to President Lincoln. His reply is an exhaustive one, and may fitly be reproduced here, as a masterly and unanswerable vindication of the Administration from every assault of this character, no less than as a clear exposition of constitutional law that will have a lasting remembrance and authority.

* This statement is made on evidence which the writer had at the very time, and which, despite a subsequent denial, was definitely proved by witnesses of unquestioned veracity.

EXECUTIVE MANSION, }
WASHINGTON, June 13, 1863. }

HON. ERASTUS CORNING and others—*Gentlemen :* Your letter of May 19th, inclosing the resolutions of a public meeting held at Albany, New York, on the 16th of the same month, was received several days ago.

The resolutions, as I understand them, are resolvable into two propositions—first, the expression of a purpose to sustain the cause of the Union, to secure peace through victory, and to support the Administration in every constitutional and lawful measure to suppress the rebellion ; and, secondly, a declaration of censure upon the Administration for supposed unconstitutional action, such as the making of military arrests. And from the two propositions a third is deduced, which is, that the gentlemen composing the meeting are resolved on doing their part to maintain our common Government and country, despite the folly or wickedness, as they may conceive, of any Administration. This position is eminently patriotic, and as such I thank the meeting and congratulate the nation for it. My own purpose is the same, so that the meeting and myself have a common object, and can have no difference, except in the choice of means or measures for effecting that object.

And here I ought to close this paper, and would close it, if there were no apprehension that more injurious consequences than any merely personal to myself might follow the censures systematically cast upon me for doing what, in my view of duty, I could not forbear. The resolutions promise to support me in every constitutional and lawful measure to suppress the rebellion, and I have not knowingly employed, nor shall knowingly employ any other. But the meeting, by their resolutions, assert and argue that certain military arrests, and proceedings following them, for which I am ultimately responsible, are unconstitutional. I think they are not. The resolutions quote from the Constitution the definition of treason, and also the limiting safeguards and guarantees therein provided for the citizen on trial for treason, and on his being held to answer for capital, or otherwise infamous crimes, and in criminal prosecutions, his right to a speedy and public trial by an impartial jury. They proceed to resolve, " that these safeguards of the rights of the citizen against the pretensions of arbitrary power were intended more *especially,* for his protection in times of civil commotion."

And, apparently to demonstrate the proposition, the resolutions proceed : " They were secured substantially to the English people *after* years of protracted civil war, and were adopted into our Constitution at the *close* of the Revolution." Would not the demonstration have been better if it could have been truly said that these safeguards had been adopted and applied *during* the civil wars and *during* our Revolution, instead of *after* the one and at the *close* of the other ? I, too, am devotedly for them *after* civil war, and *before* civil war, and at all times, " except when, in cases of rebellion or invasion, the public safety may require " their suspension. The resolutions proceed to tell us that these safeguards " have stood the test of seventy-six years of trial, under our republican system, under circumstances which show that, while they constitute the foundation of all free government, they are the elements of the enduring stability of the Republic." No one denies that they have so stood the test up to the beginning of the present rebellion, if we except a certain occurrence at New Orleans ; nor does any one question that they will stand the same test much longer after the rebellion closes. But these provisions of the Constitution have no application to the case we have in hand, because the arrests complained of were not made for treason— that is, not for *the* treason defined in the Constitution, and upon conviction of which the punishment is death—nor yet were they made to hold persons to answer for any capital or otherwise infamous crimes ; nor were the proceedings following, in any constitutional or legal sense, " criminal prosecutions." The arrests were made on totally different grounds, and the proceedings following accorded with the grounds of the arrest. Let us consider the real case with which we are dealing, and apply to it the parts of the Constitution plainly made for such cases.

Prior to my installation here, it had been inculcated that any State had a lawful right to secede from the National Union, and that it would be expedient to exercise the right whenever the devotees of the doctrine should fail to elect a President to their own liking. I was elected contrary to their liking, and accordingly, so far as it was legally possible, they had taken seven States out of the Union, and had seized many of the United States forts, and had fired upon the United States flag, all before I was inaugurated, and, of course, before I had done any official act whatever. The rebellion thus began, soon ran into the present civil war ; and, in certain respects, it began on very unequal terms between the parties. The insurgents had been preparing for it more than thirty years, while the Government had taken no steps to resist them. The former had carefully considered all the means which could be turned to their account. It undoubtedly was a well-pondered reliance with them that, in their own unrestricted efforts to destroy Union, Constitution, and law altogether, the Government would, in great degree, be restrained by the same Constitution and law from arresting their progress. Their sympathizers pervaded all departments of the Government, and nearly all communities of the people. From this material, under cover of "liberty of speech," "liberty of the press," and "*habeas corpus*," they hoped to keep on foot among us a most efficient corps of spies, informers, suppliers, and aiders and abettors of their cause in a thousand ways. They knew that in times such as they were inaugurating, by the Constitution itself, the "*habeas corpus*" might be suspended ; but they also knew they had friends who would make a question as to *who* was to suspend it; meanwhile, their spies and others might remain at large to help on their cause. Or if, as has happened, the Executive should suspend the writ, without ruinous waste of time, instances of arresting innocent persons might occur, as are always likely to occur in such cases, and then a clamor could be raised in regard to this which might be, at least, of some service to the insurgent cause. It needed no very keen perception to discover this part of the enemy's programme, so soon as, by open hostilities, their machinery was put fairly in motion. Yet, thoroughly imbued with a reverence for the guarranteed rights of individuals, I was slow to adopt the strong measures which by degrees I have been forced to regard as being within the exceptions of the Constitution, and as indispensable to the public safety. Nothing is better known to history than that courts of justice are utterly incompetent in such cases. Civil courts are organized chiefly for trials of individuals, or at most, a few individuals acting in concert, and this in quiet times, and on charges of crimes well-defined in the law. Even in times of peace, bands of horse-thieves and robbers frequently grow too numerous and powerful for the ordinary courts of justice. But what comparison, in numbers, have such bands ever borne to the insurgent sympathizers even in many of the loyal States? Again, a jury too frequently has at least one member more ready to hang the panel than to hang the traitor. And yet, again, he who dissuades one man from volunteering, or induces one soldier to desert, weakens the Union cause as much as he who kills a Union soldier in battle. Yet this dissuasion or inducement may be so conducted as to be no defined crime of which any civil court would take cognizance.

Ours is a case of rebellion—so called by the resolutions before me—in fact a clear, fragrant and gigantic case of rebellion ; and the provision of the Constitution that " the privilege of the writ of *habeas corpus* shall not be suspended unless when, in cases of rebellion or invasion, the public safety may require it," is *the* provision which specially applies to our present case. This provision plainly attests the understanding of those who made the Constitution, that ordinary courts of justice are inadequate to "cases of rebellion"—attests their purpose that, in such cases, men may be held in custody whom the courts, acting on ordinary rules, would discharge. *Habeas corpus* does not discharge men who are proved to be guilty of defined crime; and its suspension is allowed by the Constitution on purpose that men may be arrested and held who can not be proved to be guilty of defined crime, "when, in cases of rebellion or invasion, the public safety may require it." This is precisely our present case—a case of rebellion, wherein the public safety *does* require the suspension. Indeed, arrests by process of courts, and arrests in cases of rebellion, do not proceed altogether upon the same basis. The former is directed at the small percentage of ordinary and continuous perpetration of crime ; while the latter is directed at sudden and extensive uprisings against the Government, which at most will succeed or fail in no great length of time. In the latter case arrests are made, not so much for what has been done as for what probably would be done. The latter is more for the preventive and less for the vindictive than the former. In such cases the purposes of men are much more easily understood than in cases of ordinary crime. The man who stands by and says nothing when the peril of his Government is discussed, can not be misunderstood. If not hindered, he is sure to help the enemy ; much more, if he talks ambiguously—talks for his country with "buts," and "ifs" and "ands." Of how little value the constitutional provisions I have quoted will be rendered, if arrests shall never be made until defined crimes shall have been committed, may be illustrated by a few notable examples. Gen. John C. Breckinridge, Gen. Robert E. Lee, Gen. Joseph E. Johnston, Gen. John B. Magruder, Gen. William B. Preston, Gen. Simon B. Buckner, and Commodore Franklin Buchanan, now occupying the very highest places in the rebel war service, were all within the power of the Government since the rebellion began, and were nearly as well known to the traitors then as now. Unquestionably, if we had siezed and held them, the insurgent cause would be much weaker. But no one of them had then committed any crime defined by law. Every one of them, if arrested, would have been discharged on *habeas corpus*, were the writ allowed to operate. In view of these, and similar cases, I think the time not unlikely to come when I shall be blamed for having made too few arrests rather than too many.

By the third resolution, the meeting indicate their opinion that military arrests may be constitutional in localities where rebellion actually exists, but that such arrests are unconstitutional in localities where rebellion or insurrection does *not* actually exist. They insist that such arrests shall not be made "outside of the lines of necessary military occupation and the scenes of insurrection." Inasmuch, however, as the Constitution itself makes no such distinction, I am unable to believe that there *is* any such constitutional distinction, I concede that the class of arrests complained of can be constitutional only when, in cases of rebellion or invasion, the public safety may require them; and I insist that in such cases they are constitutional *wherever* the public safety does require them; as well in places to which they may prevent the rebellion extending, as in those where it may be already prevailing, as well where they may restrain mischievous interference with the raising and supplying of armies to suppress the rebellion, as where the rebellion may actually be; as well where they may restrain the enticing men out of the army, as where they would prevent mutiny in the army; equally constitutional at all places where they will conduce to the public safety, as against the dangers of rebellion or invasion. Take the particular case mentioned by the meeting. It is asserted, in substance, that Mr. Vallandigham was, by a military commander, siezed and tried "for no other reason than words addressed to a public meeting, in criticism of the course of the Administration, and in condemnation of the military orders of the general." Now, if there be no mistake about this—if this assertion is the truth and the whole truth—if there was no other reason for the arrest, then I concede that the arrest was wrong. But the arrest, as I understand, was made for a very different reason. Mr. Vallandigham avows his hostility to the war on the part of the Union; and his arrest was made because he was laboring, with some effect, to prevent the raising of troops; to encourage desertion from the army, and to leave the rebellion without an adequate military force to suppress it. He was not arrested because he was damaging the political prospects of the Administration, or the personal interests of the commanding general, but because he was damaging the army, upon the existence and vigor of which the life of the nation depends. He was warring upon the military, and this gave the military constitutional jurisdiction to lay hands upon him. If Mr. Vallandigham was not damaging the military power of the country, then his arrest was made on

mistake of fact, which I would be glad to correct on reason
ably satisfactory evidence.

I understand the meeting whose resolutions I am considering
to be in favor of suppressing the rebellion by military force—
by armies. Long experience has shown that armies can not be
maintained unless desertions shall be punished by the severe
penalty of death. The case requires, and the law and the Constitution sanction, this punishment. Must I shoot a simple-
minded soldier boy who deserts, while I must not touch a hair
of a wily agitator who induces him to desert ? This is none the
less injurious when effected by getting a father, or brother, or
friend, into a public meeting, and there working upon his feelings till he is persuaded to write the soldier boy that he is fighting in a bad cause, for a wicked Administration of a contempt-
ible Government, too weak to arrest and punish him if he shall
desert. I think that in such a case to silence the agitator and
save the boy is not only constitutional, but withal a great mercy.

If I be wrong on this question of constitutional power, my
error lies in believing that certain proceedings are constitutional when, in cases of rebellion or invasion, the public safety
requires them, which would not be constitutional when, in the
absence of rebellion or invasion, the public safety does *not*
require them ; in other words, that the Constitution is not, in
its application, in all respects the same—in cases of rebellion
or invasion involving the public safety, as it is in time of profound peace and public security. The Constitution itself makes
the distinction ; and I can no more be persuaded that the Government can constitutionally take no strong measures in time
of rebellion, because it can be shown that the same could not
be lawfully taken in time of peace, than I can be persuaded
that a particular drug is not good medicine for a sick man,
because it can be shown not to be good food for a well one.
Nor am I able to appreciate the danger apprehended by the
meeting, that the American people will, by means of military
arrests during the rebellion, lose the right of public discussion,
the liberty of speech and the press, the law of evidence, trial
by jury, and *habeas corpus*, throughout the indefinite peaceful
future, which I trust lies before them, any more than I am able
to believe that a man could contract so strong an appetite for
emetics, during temporary illness, as to persist in feeding upon
them during the remainder of his healthful life.

In giving the resolutions that earnest consideration which
you request of me, I can not overlook the fact that the meeting
speak as "Democrats." Nor can I, with full respect for their
known intelligence, and the fairly presumed deliberation with
which they prepared their resolutions, be permitted to suppose

that this occurred by accident, or in any way other than that they preferred to designate themselves "Democrats" rather than "American Citizens." In this time of National peril, I would have preferred to meet you on a level one step higher than any party platform; because I am sure that, from such more elevated position, we could do better battle for the country we all love, than we possibly can from those lower ones where, from the force of habit, the prejudices of the past, and selfish hopes of the future, we are sure to expend much of our ingenuity and strength in finding fault with and aiming blows at each other. But, since you have denied me this, I will yet be thankful, for the country's sake, that not all Democrats have done so. He on whose discretionary judgment Mr. Vallandigham was arrested and tried is a Democrat, having no old party affinity with me; and the judge who rejected the constitutional view expressed in these resolutions, by refusing to discharge Mr. Vallandigham on *habeas corpus*, is a Democrat of better days than these, having received his judicial mantle at the hands of President Jackson. And still more, of all those Democrats who are nobly exposing their lives and shedding their blood on the battle-field, I have learned that many approve the course taken with Mr. Vallandigham, while I have not heard of a single one condemning it. I can not assert that there are none such.

And the name of Jackson recalls an incident of pertinent history: After the battle of New Orleans, and while the fact that the treaty of peace had been concluded was well known in the city, but before official knowledge of it had arrived, Gen. Jackson still maintained martial or military law. Now that it could be said the war was over, the clamor against martial law, which had existed from the first grew more furious. Among other things, a Mr. Louiallier published a denunciatory newspaper article. Gen. Jackson arrested him. A lawyer by the name of Morrel procured the United States Judge Hall to issue a writ of *habeas corpus* to relieve Mr. Louiallier. Gen. Jackson arrested both the lawyer and the Judge. A Mr. Hollander ventured to say of some part of the matter that "it was a dirty trick." Gen. Jackson arrested him. When the officer undertook to serve the writ of *habeas corpus*, Gen. Jackson took it from him, and sent him away with a copy. Holding the judge in custody a few days, the General sent him beyond the limits of his encampment, and set him at liberty, with an order to remain till the ratification of peace should be regularly announced, or until the British should have left the Southern coast. A day or two more elapsed, the ratification of a treaty of peace was regularly announced, and the judge and others were fully liberated. A few days more and the judge called Gen. Jackson into court and fined him $1,000 for having arrested him and the others named. The General paid the fine, and there the matter rested for nearly thirty years, when Congress refunded principal and interest. The late Senator Douglas, then in the House of Representatives, took a leading part in the debates, in which the Constitutional question was much discussed. I am not prepared to say whom the journals would show to have voted for the measure.

It may be remarked: First, that we had the same Constitution then as now; secondly, that we then had a case of invasion, and now we have a case of rebellion; and, thirdly, that the permanent right of the people to public discussion, the liberty of speech and of the press, the trial by jury, the law of evidence, and the *habeas corpus*, suffered no detriment whatever by that conduct of General Jackson, or its subsequent approval by the American Congress.

And yet, let me say that, in my own discretion, I do not know whether I would have ordered the arrest of Mr. Vallandigham. While I can not shift the responsibility from myself, I hold that, as a general rule, the commander in the field is the better judge of the necessity in any particular case. Of course, I must practice a general directory and revisory power in the matter.

One of the resolutions expresses the opinion of the meeting that arbitrary arrests will have the effect to divide and distract those who should be united in suppressing the rebellion, and I am specifically called on to discharge Mr. Vallandigham. I regard this as, at least, a fair appeal to me on the expediency of exercising a constitutional power which I think exists. In response to such appeal, I have to say, it gave me pain when I learned that Mr. Vallandigham had been arrested—that is, I was pained that there should have seemed to be a necessity for arresting him—and that it will afford me great pleasure to discharge him as soon as I can, by any means believe the public safety will not suffer by it. I further say that, as the war progresses, it appears to me, opinion and action which were in great confusion at first, take shape and fall into more regular channels, so that the necessity for strong dealing with them gradually decreases. I have every reason to desire that it should cease altogether; and far from the least is my regard for the opinions and wishes of those who, like the meeting at Albany, declare their purpose to sustain the Government in every constitutional and lawful measure to suppress the rebellion. Still, I must continue to do so much as may seem to be required by public safety. A. LINCOLN.

A fortnight after this letter was written, a committee of Ohio Democrats waited upon President Lincoln, presenting resolutions of their State Convention, which had seen fit to nominate Vallandigham for Governor, demanding his release from the sentence of exile. The committee backed their appeal by such arguments as the occasion suggested to them. The reply of Mr. Lincoln is a proper pendant to the foregoing letter :

THE PRESIDENT'S REPLY TO THE COMMITTEE FROM OHIO URGING THE RECALL OF MR. VALLANDIGHAM.

WASHINGTON, June 29, 1863.

GENTLEMEN : The resolutions of the Ohio Democratic State Convention, which you present me, together with your introductory and closing remarks, being, in position and argument, mainly the same as the resolutions of the Democratic meeting at Albany, New York, I refer you to my response to the latter as meeting most of the points in the former.

This response you evidently used in preparing your remarks, and I desire no more than that it be used with accuracy. In a single reading of your remarks, I only discovered one inaccuracy in matter which I suppose you took from that paper. It is where you say, " The undersigned are unable to agree with you in the opinion you have expressed that the Constitution is different in time of insurrection or invasion from what it is in time of peace and public security."

A recurrence to the paper will show you that I have not expressed the opinion you suppose. I expressed the opinion that the Constitution is different *in its application* in cases of rebellion or invasion involving the public safety, from what it is in times of profound peace and public security. And this opinion I adhere to, simply because, by the Constitution itself, things may be done in the one case which may not be done in the other.

I dislike to waste a word on a merely personal point, but I must respectfully assure you that you will find yourselves at fault should you ever seek for evidence to prove your assumption that I " opposed, in discussions before the people, the policy of the Mexican War."

You say : " Expunge from the Constitution this limitation upon the power of Congress to suspend the writ of *habeas corpus,* and yet the other guarantees of personal liberty would remain unchanged." Doubtless, if this clause of the Constitution, improperly called, as I think, a limitation upon the power of Congress, were expunged, the other guarantees would remain the same; but the question is, not how those guarantees would stand with that clause *out* of the Constitution, but how they stand with that clause remaining in it, in case of rebellion or invasion involving the public safety. If the liberty could be indulged, in expunging that clause, letter and spirit, I really think the constitutional argument would be with you.

My general view on this question was stated in the Albany response, and hence I do not state it now. I only add that, as seems to me, the benefit of the writ of *habeas corpus* is the great means through which the guarantees of personal liberty are conserved and made available in the last resort; and corroborative of this view is the fact that Mr. Vallandigham, in the very case in question, under the advice of able lawyers, saw not where else to go but to the *habeas corpus*. But by the Constitution, the benefit of the writ of *habeas corpus* itself may be suspended, when, in case of rebellion or invasion, the public safety may require it.

You ask, in substance, whether I really claim that I may override all the guaranteed rights of individuals, on the plea of conserving the public safety—when I may choose to say the public safety requires it. This question, divested of the phraseology calculated to represent me as struggling for an arbitrary personal prerogative, is either simply a question *who* shall decide, or an affirmation that *nobody* shall decide, what the public safety does require in cases of rebellion or invasion. The Constitution contemplates the question as likely to occur for decision, but it does not expressly declare who is to decide it. By necessary implication, when rebellion, or invasion comes, the decision is to be made from time to time; and I think the man whom, for the time, the people have, under the Constitution, made their Commander-in-chief of the Army and Navy, is the man who holds the power and bears the responsibility of making it. If he uses the power justly, the same people will probably justify him; if he abuses it, he is in their hands, to be dealt with by all the modes they have reserved to themselves in the Constitution.

The earnestness with which you insist that persons can only, in times of rebellion, be lawfully dealt with in accordance with the rules for criminal trials and punishments in times of peace, induces me to add a word to what I said on that point in the Albany response. You claim that men may, if they choose, embarrass those whose duty it is to combat a giant rebellion, and then be dealt with only in turn as if there were no rebellion. The Constitution itself rejects this view. The military arrests and detentions which have been made, including those of Mr. Vallandigham, which are not different in principle from the other, have been for *prevention*, and not for *punishment*— as injunctions to stay injury, as proceedings to keep the peace— and hence, like proceedings in such cases and for like reasons, they have not been accompanied with indictments, or trial by juries, nor in a single case by any punishment whatever beyond what is purely incidental to the prevention. The original sentence of imprisonment in Mr. Vallandigham's case was to prevent injury to the military service only, and the modification of it was made as a less disagreeable mode to him of securing the same prevention.

I am unable to perceive an insult to Ohio in the case of Mr. Vallandigham. Quite surely nothing of this sort was or is intended. I was wholly unaware that Mr. Vallandigham was, at the time of his arrest, a candidate for the Democratic nomination for Governor, until so informed by your reading to me the resolutions of the convention. I am grateful to the State of Ohio for many things, especially for the brave soldiers and officers she has given, in the present National trial, to the armies of the Union.

You claim, as I understand, that, according to my own position in the Albany response, Mr. Vallandigham should be released; and this because, as you claim, he has not damaged the military service by discouraging enlistments, encouraging desertions, or otherwise; and that if he had, he should have been turned over to the civil authorities under the recent act of Congress. I certainly do not *know* that Mr. Vallandigham has specifically and by direct language advised against enlistments and in favor of desertions and resistance to drafting. We all know that combinations, armed, in some instances, to resist the arrest of deserters, began several months ago; that more recently the like has appeared in resistance to the enrollment preparatory to a draft; and that quite a number of assassinations have occurred from the same animus. These had to be met by military force, and this again has led to bloodshed and death. And now, under a sense of responsibility more weighty and enduring than any which is merely official, I solemnly declare my belief that this hindrance of the military, including maiming and murder, is due to the cause in which Mr. Vallandigham has been engaged, in a greater degree than to any other cause; and it is due to him personally in a greater degree than to any other man.

These things have been notorious, known to all, and of course known to Mr. Vallandigham. Perhaps I would not be wrong to say they originated with his especial friends and adherents. With perfect knowledge of them he has frequently, if not constantly, made speeches in Congress and before popular assemblies; and if it can be shown that, with these things staring him in the face, he has ever uttered a word of rebuke or counsel against them, it will be a fact greatly in his favor with me, and one of which, as yet, I am totally ignorant. When it is known that the whole burden of his speeches has been to stir up men against the prosecution of the war, and that in the midst of resistance to it, he has not been known in any instance to counsel against such resistance, it is next to impossible to repel the inference that he has counseled directly in favor of it.

With all this before their eyes, the convention you represent have nominated Mr. Vallandigham for governor of Ohio, and both they and you have declared the purpose to sustain the National Union by all constitutional means, but, of course, they and you, in common, reserve to yourselves to decide what are constitutional means, and, unlike the Albany meeting, you omit to state or intimate that, in your opinion, an army is a constitutional means of saving the Union against a rebellion, or even to intimate that you are conscious of an existing rebellion being in progress with the avowed object of destroying that very Union. At the same time, your nominee for governor, in whose behalf you appeal, is known to you, and to the world, to declare against the use of an army to suppress the rebellion. Your own attitude, therefore, encourages desertion, resistance to the draft, and the like, because it teaches those who incline to desert and to escape the draft to believe it is your purpose to protect them, and the hope that you will become strong enough to do so.

After a personal intercourse with you, gentlemen of the committee, I can not say I think you desire this effect to follow your attitude; but I assure you that both friends and enemies of the Union look upon it in this light. It is a substantial hope, and by consequence, a real strength to the enemy. If it is a false hope, and one which you would willingly dispel, I will make the way exceedingly easy. I send you duplicates of this letter, in order that you, or a majority of you, may, if you choose, indorse your names upon one of them, and return it thus indorsed to me, with the understanding that those signing are thereby committed to the following propositions, and to nothing else:

1. That there is now a rebellion in the United States, the object and tendency of which is to destroy the National Union; and that, in your opinion, an army and navy are constitutional means for suppressing that rebellion.

2. That no one of you will do any thing which, in his own judgment, will tend to hinder the increase, or favor the decrease, or lessen the efficiency of the Army and Navy, while engaged in the effort to suppress that rebellion; and—

3. That each of you will in his sphere, do all he can to have the officers, soldiers, and seamen of the Army and Navy, while engaged in the effort to suppress the rebellion, paid, fed, clad, and otherwise well provided and supported.

And with the further understanding that upon receiving the letter and names thus indorsed, I will cause them to be published, which publication shall be, within itself, a revocation of the order in relation to Mr. Vallandigham.

It will not escape observation that I consent to the release of Mr. Vallandigham upon terms not embracing any pledge from him or from others as to what he will or will not do. I do this because he is not present to speak for himself, or to authorize others to speak for him; and hence I shall expect that on returning he would not put himself practically in antagonism with the position of his friends. But I do it chiefly because I thereby prevail on other influential gentlemen of Ohio to so define their position as to be of immense value to the army—thus more than compensating for the consequences of any mistake in allowing Mr. Vallandigham to return, so that, on the whole, the public safety will not have suffered by it. Still, in regard to Mr. Vallandigham and all others, I must hereafter, as heretofore, do so much as the public service may seem to require.

I have the honor to be, respectfully, yours, etc.,

ABRAHAM LINCOLN.

The gentlemen addressed, many of whom were members elect of the Thirty-eighth Congress, were quite indisposed to comply with the easy terms proposed by the President as a condition for the release of their chosen leader. They allowed him still to pine in exile, over the border, and apparently hoped to turn his "cruel wrongs" to political account. In this, however, they were greatly miscalculating the intelligence and loyalty of the people, who saw nothing to admire in such a political character. The verdict of Ohio, in the following October, repudiating Vallandigham by more than one hundred thousand majority, was sufficient to show the popular judgment on this question. Why, then, renew the issue in the

Presidential canvass of 1864? This infatuation only aided their gravitation toward defeat.

Vallandigham had suddenly appeared at a district convention held in Butler county, Ohio, on the 15th of June, 1864. After more than a year's absence, he defiantly released himself, and probably counted upon promised resistance by organized force, on his anticipated re-arrest, as the act which was to fire the secretly-prepared train of revolution in the North-west. He was chosen a delegate to the Chicago convention, and "instructed to favor the nomination of no man who is either directly or indirectly committed to the further prosecution of this war." The resolutions of this local convention, in the same spirit, declared "that the history of the past three years has already demonstrated the utter hopelessness, as well as the gigantic wrong, of a further continuance of the present conflict." Had Sanders himself appeared on the scene, the budget of resolutions could not have been more acceptable to Jefferson Davis. But any serious danger from Vallandigham's influence was no longer to be dreaded. He had already suffered a year's exile. He had been repudiated by the people of his own State. No notice was taken of his escape at Washington. Henceforth he had entire freedom of locomotion, and liberty of speech.

A more potent influence from Canada was that of the Rebel funds dispensed at the will of Jacob Thompson. Three days before the Chicago convention, he had procured $250,000 in "greenback" notes, obviously for use in the loyal States. Evidence was given, on the trial of the Indiana conspirators, going to show that money for arming their secret Order was obtained from the same source. Later in the season, as the Opposition cause became more desperate, the Rebel funds under the control of Thompson, as purser, were employed in furthering schemes too fiendish for belief, were they not definitely and clearly proved. The seizure of steamboats on Lake Erie; the release of prisoners at Johnson's Island, Camp Chase, and elsewhere; attacks upon border towns, to be attended with conflagrations, pillage and murder; and robberies of banks, plunderings of villages, and massacres of non-belligerents, were among the gentler plans of these men in Canada, whose mission was, a little earlier, so gratuitously assumed by innocent philanthropists to be one of peace and brotherly kindness. Compared with the dark-hued purposes afterward developed, even these malicious projects—which could have no possible effect in aid of the Rebel cause, and which were devised in bitter hatred and rage at the prospect of Mr. Lincoln's reëlection—fade into venial dimness of shade.

The active canvass was to be short, and the first election after the "Democratic" nominations and platform were announced—that occurring in the State of Vermont, where there was little room to improve on previous elections, and every effort was made by the Opposition to insure an Administration loss—was regarded with anxious interest, as indicating the direction of the popular current. The result gratified the friends of the Administration, and disheartened its enemies, there being a decided increase of the Union majority of the previous year, and the vote being more than two to one for the Administration ticket. Maine soon followed, with a large majority on the same side. It was no longer doubtful that the Republican Union party was united and true in the support of Lincoln and Johnson. On the second Tuesday in October, Pennsylvania, Ohio and Indiana were to hold their State elections. The results would be conclusive as to the Presidential election. In Ohio and Indiana the Administration majorities were unprecedentedly large—54,751 in the former, and 20,883 in the latter—and in Pennsylvania, where there was no general ticket, the Union aggregate majority for members of Congress, though small, was decisive. These elections settled the political character of the next Congress. In the previous House of Representatives, Ohio had but five Administration members, to fourteen Opposition. At this election, seventeen Administration Representatives were chosen, and two Opposition. In Indiana, where a Democratic Legislature had refused to the soldiers in the field the right of voting, eight Administration Representatives were returned, and three Opposition, against four Administration and seven Opposition members in the previous House. In Pennsylvania, sixteen Admin istration members and eight Opposition were elected, against fourteen Administration and ten Opposition in the previous Congress. In the three States, the Administration had a majority of twenty-eight members in the new Congress—the Opposition a majority of eight members in the last—making a net gain of thirty-six.

The State elections disclosed very clearly, what the Opposition had hitherto earnestly disputed, that our gallant soldiers in the field were so firmly attached to Abraham Lincoln, and regarded him as so fully the representative of the cause on behalf of which they were breasting the bayonets and bullets of the Rebels in the field, that no devotion to a military commander—least of all to one who had only led his army to defeat or to indecisive victory—could seduce them into the support of a party whose success was earnestly desired by the enemy they were fighting. With a unanimity which the exceptions only rendered more emphatic, they supported the administration tickets, while winning victories that doubly helped the Union cause—in their front and in the rear.

No one more deeply and sincerely felt the unbounded obligations of the country to the men of the Army and Navy, or was more ready on all occasions to recognize their services than did President Lincoln. In a note to the Postmaster General, early in the summer, he expressed his wish that a preference should be given, in his appointments, so far as practicable, to the men who had thus proved their devotion to the Republic. There was no topic to which he recurred more naturally, or on which he spoke with more emotion, on public occasions, than the heroic sacrifices made by our soldiers and seamen. He was tenderly conscious of the kind sentiments manifested by them, in so many ways, toward himself personally. To have been reëlected without their hearty support, or in spite of their votes for another, would have poorly compensated the loss, to his heart, of their sympathy and preference.

An important service was rendered, during the season, by a portion of the militia force of several Western States, who were called out for a term of one hundred days, mainly during the interval between the expiration of the time of a large number of enlistments and the incoming of new levies. Ohio furnished the largest number of "hundred-days' men," who served mainly in the Eastern Departments. Many of these last were reviewed by the President at the close of their service, and were thanked and complimented by him in person. The following order, relating to the other Western militia thus serving, in another quarter, shows the feeling entertained toward all:

EXECUTIVE MANSION,
WASHINGTON CITY, October 1, 1864.

Special Executive Order, returning thanks to the volunteers for one hundred days from the States of Indiana, Illinois, Iowa, and Wisconsin.—The term of one hundred days, for which volunteers from the States of Indiana, Illinois, Iowa, and Wisconsin volunteered, under the call of their respective Governors, in the months of May and June, to aid in the recent campaign of General Sherman, having expired, the President directs an official acknowledgment to be made of their patriotic service. It was their good fortune to render effective service in the brilliant operations in the South-west, and to contribute to the victories of the national arms over the Rebel forces in Georgia, under the command of Johnston and Hood. On all occasions, and in every service to which they were assigned, their duty, as patriotic volunteers, was performed with alacrity and courage, for which they are entitled, and are hereby tendered, the national thanks, through the Governors of their respective States.

The Secretary of War is directed to transmit a copy of this order to the Governors of Indiana, Illinois, Iowa, and Wisconsin, and to cause a certificate of this honorable service to be delivered to the officers and soldiers of the States above named, who recently served in the military forces of the United States, as volunteers for one hundred days.

A. LINCOLN.

On the 12th of October, the day following the elections, a vote was taken by the people of Maryland on the New State Constitution adopted by their convention, in regard to which the main issue was the section providing for immediate and unconditional emancipation. The result made Maryland forever a free State. The contest had been an earnest one. In the strongly Secession counties, the pro-slavery vote was unexpectedly large, many disregarding the prescribed oath intended to exclude those who had actually participated in the Rebellion, or taking that oath under the advice of an eminent counsellor, that no "moral injunction" was violated in so doing, because the convention had no right to require such a qualification for voting. When it is recollected that this oath related to the past record of the party taking it, not to his present sentiments of loyalty, it may be inferred that the casuistry on which such advice was based had regard rather to legal technicality than to the moral sentiments or to religious sanctions. Despite all efforts of the friends of the old order, however, the Constitution was adopted, and became the organic law of the State.

In honor of this great event, when the result was finally ascertained, a party of loyal Marylanders, with accessions to their number from other residents in Washington, serenaded President Lincoln at the Executive Mansion, on the evening of October 19th. In reply to this call, Mr. Lincoln said:

Friends and Fellow Citizens: I am notified that this is a compliment paid me by the loyal Marylanders resident in this District. I infer that the adoption of the new Constitution for that State furnishes the occasion, and that in your view the extirpation of slavery constitutes the chief merit of the new Constitution. Most heartily do I congratulate you and Maryland and the nation, and the world upon the event. I regret that it did not occur two years sooner, which I am sure would have saved to the nation more money than would have met all the private loss incident to the measure. But it has come at last, and I sincerely hope its friends may fully realize all their anticipations of good from it, and that its opponents may by its effect be agreeably and profitably disappointed.

A word upon another subject. Something was said by the Secretary of State, in his recent speech at Auburn, which has been construed by some into a threat that if I should be beaten at the election, I will, between then and the end of my constitutional term, do what I may be able to ruin the Government. Others regard the fact that the Chicago Convention adjourned, not *sine die*, but to meet again if called to do so by a particular individual, as the intimation of a purpose that if their nominee shall be elected he will at once seize control of the Government.

I hope the good people will permit themselves to suffer no uneasiness on either point. I am struggling to maintain the Government; not to overthrow it. I am struggling especially to prevent others from overthrowing it, and I therefore say, that if I shall live, I shall remain President until the 4th of next March, and that whoever shall be constitutionally elected thereto in November, shall be duly installed as President on the 4th of March, and that in the meantime I shall do my utmost, that whoever is to hold the helm for the next voyage shall start with the best possible chance to save the ship. This is due to the people, both on principle and under the Constitution. Their will, constitutionally expressed, is the ultimate law for all.

If they should deliberately resolve to have immediate peace, even at the loss of their country and their liberties, I know not the power or the right to resist them. It is their own business, and they must do as they please with their own. I believe, however, they are still resolved to preserve their country and their liberty, and in this, in office or out of it, I am resolved to stand by them.

I may add that in this purpose, to save the country and its liberties, no classes of people seem so nearly unanimous as the soldiers in the field and the seamen afloat. Do they not have the hardest of it? Who should quail while they do not?

God bless the soldiers and seamen, with all their brave commanders.

It is now known that communication was kept up between the Rebel cabal in Canada and the men at Richmond, in whose " confidential employment " they were, by means of special messengers passing through the States. Directly after the October elections, a dispatch in cipher, which has since come into the possession of the Government, was sent from Canada to headquarters, found to contain the following language, under date of October 13th, 1864:

We again urge our gaining immediate advantages. Strain every nerve for victory. We now look upon the reëlection of Lincoln as certain, and we need to whip the hirelings to prevent it. Besides, with Lincoln reëlected, and his armies victorious, we need not hope even for recognition, much less the help mentioned in our last. Holcombe will explain this. Our friend shall be immediately set to work as you direct.

Perhaps Professor Holcombe alone can now fully explain the exact "work" referred to, or who was the "friend" that was to take it in hand. The enterprise may have been the piratical seizure of steamers on the lakes; the descent upon St. Albans, or the contemplated, but never executed, attack on Ogdensburgh and Buffalo. Possibly, as the feeling of desperation increased, the plots had already reached a more fiendish stage, and the "friend" may have been Beall or Kennedy, about to undertake the conflagration of New York, with an indiscriminate destruction of the lives of men, women and children. These schemes, and more infernal ones than these, were already beginning to be discussed, during the months of October and November. "Secretary" Benjamin returned a reply to this missive, on the 19th of October, which being decyphered, reads on this wise:

"Your letter of the 13th inst., is at hand. There is yet time enough to colonize many voters before November. A blow will shortly be stricken here. It is not quite time. Gen. Longstreet is to attack Sheridan without delay, and then move north, as far as practicable, toward unprotected points. This will be made instead of the movements before mentioned. He will endeavor to assist the Republicans in the collection of their ballots. Be watchful, and assist him."

"Plaquemine" days hopefully revive in the memory of trusty Benjamin. Votes for McClellan must be "colonized." May we not at least carry New York, and save Governor Seymour to the cause? Grant is shortly to be attacked (as it has already been seen he was, a little after this date—with poor results to the attacking party). Longstreet is to attack Gen. Sheridan at once—as he or Early did this very day, at Cedar Creek with what result we know. It was not to be the fortune of Longstreet—near as the object seemed to be, for a few hours on that memorable 19th of October—to collect Republican ballots. Sheridan the rather, before night closed upon them, was busy in collecting his enemy's standards, his small arms, his two or three score of cannon, his scattering host. But Longstreet had at least gallantly done his best for McClellan and Pendleton. Benjamin must rely solely, now, but upon the process of "colonizing voters," while Purser Thompson, dispenses his funds with a liberal hand.

The Baltimore Convention, which expressed the will of the people, but without the power conferred upon their earlier elected Representatives in Congress, had recognized Tennessee as a loyal State, not only by admitting her delegation with full powers, but also by nominating one of her heroic sons to the office of Vice President. It was not strange that the people of this State should consequently desire to vote. To guard this sacred privilege from desecration by traitors, Governor Johnson, at the request of a State Convention, had prescribed certain regulations to govern the election, such as his own experience, and his knowledge of the people led him to adopt. A McClellan electoral ticket had already been nominated, and the gentlemen whose names appeared thereon felt aggrieved that Rebels, sympathizing with their candidates and platform, should find any obstacles in the way of their voting. These candidates for electors consequently waited upon President Lincoln, with a memorial on the supject. Fully appreciating, as he did, the real frivolousness of their complaints, and that their zeal to make political capital for their friends in other States, by this very paper, was quite equal to their concern about carrying the vote of Tennessee, the validity of which was at least doubtful, and which in fact was not ultimately received, Mr. Lincoln bestowed no great amount of time on the petitioners. Their interruption of his more important business with such a paper, no doubt seemed to him a little impertinent. Soon after, however, he addressed to this delegation, and furnished to the public press, a reply containing their memorial at length, the proclamation of Governor Johnson complained of, and a few characteristic words of his own, disposing of the whole matter. This document, omitting certain unimportant portions as indicated, is in the following words:

EXECUTIVE MANSION, }
WASHINGTON, October 22, 1864. }

Messrs. Wm. B. Campbell, Thos. A. R. Nelson, James T. B. Carter, John Williams, A. Blizzard, Henry Cooper, Bailie Peyton, John Lellyett, Em. Etheridge. John D. Perryman:

55

GENTLEMEN :   On the 15th day of this month, as I remem
ber, a printed paper, with a few manuscript interlineations,
called a protest, with your names appended thereto, and
accompanied by another printed paper purporting to be a proclamation by Andrew Johnson, Military Governor of Tennessee,
and also a manuscript paper purporting to be extracts from
the Code of Tennessee, was laid before me.   The Protest,
Proclamation and Extracts are respectively as follows :

*To his Excellency, Abraham Lincoln, President of the United
     States :*
   SIR :   The undersigned, loyal citizens of the United States
and of the State of Tennessee, on our own behalf and on behalf
of the loyal people of our State, ask leave to submit this Protest against the Proclamation of his Excellency Andrew Johnson, Military Governor, ordering an election to be held for
President and Vice President, under certain regulations and
restrictions therein set forth.   A printed copy of said proclamation is herewith inclosed.
   The Constitution of the United States provides that " Each
State shall appoint, *in such manner as the Legislature thereof
may direct,* a number of electors," etc.   Under this provision of
the Federal Constitution, the Legislature of Tennessee, years
before the present rebellion, prescribed the mode of election to
be observed, which will be found to differ essentially from the
mode prescribed by the Military Governor.   We herewith
inclose a copy of the law of Tennessee governing the holding
of said election.
   The Military Governor expressly assumes, by virtue of
authority derived from the President, to so alter and amend
the election law of Tennessee, (enacted under authority of the
Constitution of the United States, as above set forth), as to
make the same conform to his own edict as set forth in the
proclamation aforesaid.
   He assumes so to modify our law as to admit persons to vote
at the said election who are not entitled to vote under the law
and the Constitution of Tennessee.   Instance this : our Constitution and law require that each voter shall be "a citizen of
the county wherein he may offer his vote, for six months next
preceding the day of election ;" while the Governor's order
only requires that he shall (with other qualifications named)
be a citizen of Tennessee for six months, etc.   This provision
would admit to vote many persons not entiled by law.
   We will, for the sake of brevity, pass over some less important points of conflict between the proclamation and the law,
but will instance in this place another.   By our law it is pro-

vided that the polls shall be opened in every civil district, in each county in the State; but the proclamation provides only for their being opened at one place in each county. This provision would put it out of the power of many legal voters to exercise the elective franchise.

We solemnly protest against these infringements of our law, conflicting as they do with the very letter of the Federal Constitution, because they are without authority, and because they will prevent a free, fair, and true expression of the will of the loyal people of Tennessee.

But we protest still more emphatically against the most unusual and impracticable test oath which it is proposed to require of all citizen voters in Tennessee. A citizen qualified to vote, and whose loyalty can not be " disproved by other testimony," is to be required to swear, first, that he ".will henceforth support the Constitution of the United States and defend it against all enemies." This obligation we are willing to renew daily; but this is not yet deemed a sufficient test of loyalty. He is required to make oath and subscribe to a mass of vair repetitions concerning his activity as a friend of the Union and the enemy of its enemies—concerning his desires, his hopes and fears—and that he finds it in his heart to rejoice over the scenes of blood, and of wounds, of anguish and death, wherein his friends, his kindred, his loved ones are slain, or maimed, or made prisoners of war—whereby the land of his birth or adoption is made desolate, and lamentation and mourning are spread over the whole nation. While all the civilized world stands aghast in contemplation of the unequaled horrors of our tremendous strife, the citizen of Tennessee is called upon by her military Governor, under your authority, to swear that in these things he finds occasion to *rejoice!* As if this were still not enough, the citizen is further required to swear to the indefinite prolongation of this war, as follows: " That I will cordially oppose all armistices or *negotiations for peace with rebels in arms*, until the Constitution of the United States, and all laws and proclamations made in pursuance thereof, shall be established over all the people of every State and Territory embraced within the National Union;" until (in brief) the war shall be at an end. Now, we freely avow to your Excellency, and to the world, that we earnestly desire the return of peace and good-will to our now unhappy country—that we seek neither pleasure, profit, nor honor in the perpetuation of war—that we should feel bound, as Christians, as patriots and as civilized men—that we are bound by the oaths we have taken—to countenance and encourage any negotiations which may be entered into by the proper authorities, with the intent to restore peace and union under the Constitution we have sworn to support and defend. We should be traitors to our country, false to our oaths—false, indeed, to the primary clause of the oath we are now discussing, to oppose such negotiations. We can not consent to swear at the ballot-box a war of extermination against our countrymen and kindred, or to prolong by our opposition, for a single day after it can be brought to an honorable and lawful conclusion, a contest the most sanguinary and ruinous that has scourged mankind.

You will not have forgotten, that in the month of July last, you issued the following proclamation:

"EXECUTIVE MANSION, }
WASHINGTON, July 8, 1864. }

" *To whom it may concern :*

"Any proposition which embraces the restoration of peace, the integrity of the whole Union, and the abandonment of slavery, and which comes by and with an authority that can control the armies now at war against the United States, will be received and considered by the Executive Government of the United States, and will be met by liberal terms on other substantial and collateral points; and the bearer or bearers thereof shall have safe conduct both ways.

"ABRAHAM LINCOLN."

This is certainly a proposition to treat with Rebels in arms—with their chiefs. Are we now to understand by this proclamation of one acting under your authority, and himself a candidate with you for the second office, that even the above proposition is withdrawn—that you will henceforth have no negotiations upon any terms, but unrelenting war to the bitter end? Or, are we to understand, that while you hold this proposition open, or yourself free to act as your judgment may dictate, we, the citizens of Tennessee, shall *swear* to OPPOSE your negotiations?

In the next breath, the voter who has been thus *qualified*, is required to swear that he will "heartily aid and assist the loyal people *in whatever measures may be adopted* for the attainment of these ends." Adopted by whom? The oath does not say. We can not tell what measures may be adopted. We can not comment upon the absurdity of the obligation here imposed, without danger of departing from that respectful propriety of language which we desire to preserve in addressing the Chief Magistrate of the American people. But this is the clause of an oath which the candidate for the Vice Presidency requires at the lips of the loyal and qualified voters of Tennessee, before these citizens shall be allowed to vote for or against you and himself at the coming election?

For these reasons, and others, which, for the sake of brevity, we omit, we solemnly protest against the interference of the Military Governor with the freedom of the elective franchise in Tennessee. We deny his authority and yours, to alter, amend, or annul any law of Tennessee. We demand that Tennessee be allowed to appoint her Electors, as expressly provided by the Federal Constitution, which you have sworn to support, protect, and defend, in the manner which the Legislature thereof has prescribed. And to that end, we respectfully demand of you, as the principal under whose authority this order has been issued, that the same shall be revoked. We ask that all military interference shall be withdrawn so far as to allow the loyal men of Tennessee a full and free election. By the loyal men of Tennessee we mean those who have not participated in the rebellion, or given it aid and comfort; or who may have complied with such terms of amnesty as have been offered them under your authority.

On the 8th day of December, 1863, you, as President, issued a proclamation, declaring that "a full pardon is hereby granted, with restoration of all rights of property," &c., to each of our citizens having participated, directly or by implication, in the existing rebellion, (with certain exceptions,) "upon the condition that every such person shall take and subscribe an oath, and thenceforward keep and maintain said oath inviolate." And it is further provided in the Proclamation aforesaid, that in the contingency of the re-organization of a State Government in Tennessee, or certain other States named, the persons having taken the oath referred to, being otherwise qualified by the election law of the State, shall be entitled to vote. The undersigned would state, that many of our citizens have complied, in good faith, with the terms of amnesty proposed in your proclamation aforesaid, and are, therefore, by reason of the full pardon granted them, fully entitled to vote and exercise all other rights belonging to loyal citizens, without let or hindrance; and we respectfully appeal to you as President of the United States, to make good your promise of pardon to these citizens, by the removal of all other and further hindrance to the exercise of the elective franchise.

But if it be claimed upon the plea of military necessity, that guards and restrictions shall be thrown around the ballot-box in Tennessee, we still ask the withdrawal of the Proclamation of the Military Governor, because the conditions thereby imposed upon the loyal men of Tennessee as a qualification for voting are irrelevant, unreasonable, and not in any sense a test of loyalty. But they pledge the citizen to oppose the lawful authorities in the discharge of their duty. The oath required is only calculated to keep legal and rightful voters from the poles. We suggest that no oath be required but such as is prescribed by law. Our people will not hesitate, however, to take the usual oath of loyalty—for example, in the language of the primary clause of the oath in question—"That I will henceforth support the Constitution of the United States, and defend it against the assaults of its enemies." Denying your right to make any departure from the law in the case, we shall, however, feel no hardship in this.

The convention to which Gov. Johnson refers was a mere partisan meeting, having no authority, and not representing the loyal men of Tennessee, in any sense.

The names of the signers of this protest have been placed before the people of Tennessee as candidates for Electors, who, if chosen, are expected to cast the electoral vote of Tennessee for George B. McClellan for President, and George H. Pendleton for Vice President. By virtue of such position, it becomes our province especially to appear before you in the attitude we do. We are aware that grave questions may arise, in any event, with regard to the regularity of the vote in Tennessee, in consequence of the partially disorganized condition of the State. The friends of your re-election, however, announced an electoral ticket; and the public became aware that preparations were being made for the holding of the election, leaving that matter no longer a question. Some time thereafter, our electoral ticket was placed before the public, and within a few days followed the proclamation complained of. We, for ourselves and those we represent, are willing to leave all questions involving the right of Tennessee to participate in the election to the decision of competent authority.

[Here follow the names of the ten signers as given at the beginning of this letter.]

PROCLAMATION.

BY THE GOVERNOR.

STATE OF TENNESSEE, }
EXECUTIVE DEPARTMENT, }
NASHVILLE, TENN., Sept. 30th, 1864. }

WHEREAS, A respectable portion of the loyal people of Tennessee, representing a large number of the counties of the State, and supposed to reflect the will of the Union men in their respective counties, recently held a convention in the city of Nashville, in which, among other things touching the re-organization of the State, they with great unanimity adopted the following resolutions:

2. *Resolved,* That the people of Tennessee, who are now and have been attached to the National Union, do hold an election for President and Vice-President in the ensuing election in November.

3. That the electors shall be the following and no others; the same being free white men, twenty-one years of age, Citizens of the United States, and for six months previous to the election, citizens of the State of Tennessee—

1st. And who have voluntarily borne arms in the service of the United States during the present war, and who are either in the service or have been honorably discharged.

2d. All the known active friends of the Government of the United States in each county.

4. *Resolved,* That the citizen electors designated in the fore-going resolutions shall, at least fifteen days before the election, register their names with an agent to be appointed for that purpose, and no citizen not thus registered shall be allowed to vote. Such registration shall be open to the public for inspection, and to be executed according to such regulations as may hereafter be prescribed: Provided that the officers of the election, in the discharge of their duty, may reject any party so registered on proof of disloyalty.

5. *Resolved,* That, as means for ascertaining the qualifications of the voters, the registers and officers holding the election may examine the parties on oath touching any matter of fact. And each voter, before depositing his vote, shall be required to take and subscribe the following oath, viz:

I solemnly swear, that I will henceforth support the Constitution of the United States, and defend it against the assaults of all enemies; that I am an active friend of the Government of the United States, and the enemy of the so-called Confederate States; that I ardently desire the suppression of the present rebellion against the Government of the United States; that I sincerely rejoice in the triumph of the armies and navies of the United States, and in the defeat and overthrow of the armies, navies and of all armed combination in the interest of the so-called Confederate States; that I will cordially oppose all armistices or negotiations for peace with rebels in arms, until the Constitution of the United States and all laws and proclamations made in pursuance thereof, shall be established over all the people of every State and Territory embraced within the National Union, and that I will heartily aid and assist the loyal people in whatever measures may be adopted for the attainment of these ends; and further that I take this oath freely and voluntarily, and without mental reservation. So help me God.

Said oath being *prima facie* evidence, subject to be disapproved by other testimony.

6. *Resolved,* That the polls be opened at the county seat, or some other suitable place in each county, and the ballot-box be so guarded and protected as to secure to electors a free, fair, and impartial election, and that polls also be opened for the convenience of the soldiers, at such places as may be accessible to them.

And whereas, it further appears from the proceedings of said Convention, "That the Military Governor of the State of Tennessee is requested to execute the foregoing resolutions in such manner as he may think best subserves the interests of the Government."

And whereas I, Andrew Johnson, Military Governor of the State of Tennessee, being anxious to co-operate with the loyal people of the State, and to encourage them in all laudable efforts to restore the State to law and order again, and to secure the ballot-box against the contamination of treason by every reasonable restraint that can be thrown around it, I do therefore order and direct that an election for President and Vice-President of the United States of America be opened and held at the county seat, or other suitable place in every county in the State of Tennessee, upon the first Tuesday after the first Monday in the month of November next, at which all citizens and soldiers, being free white men, twenty-one years of age, citizens of the United States, and for six months prior to the election citizens of the State of Tennessee, who qualified themselves by registration, and who take the oath prescribed in the foregoing resolutions, shall be entitled to vote, unless said oath shall be disproved by other testimony, for the candidates for President and Vice-President of the United States.

And to the end that the foregoing resolutions, which are made part of this proclamation, may be faithfully executed, and the loyal citizens of the State, and none others, be permitted to exercise the right of suffrage I do hereby appoint the several gentlemen whose names are affixed to this proclamation, to aid in said election and superintend the registration of the loyal voters in their respective counties, as provided by the fourth resolution above quoted.

But as the day of election is near at hand, and there may

be a difficulty in completing the registration within the time limited, it is not intended that the registration be an indispensable pre-requisite to the qualification of the voter; and in such cases, where it is impracticable, and where the voter is of known and established loyalty, he shall be entitled to vote, notwithstanding he may not have registered his name as required by the foregoing resolution.

The election shall be opened, conducted, returns made, etc., in all respects as provided by the 4th chapter of the "Code of Tennessee," except so far as the same is modified by this proclamation.

But in cases where the County Court fail or neglect to appoint inspectors or judges of election, and there is no Sheriff or other civil officer in the county qualified by law to open and hold said election, the registrating agents, hereto appended, may act in his stead, and in all respects discharge the duties imposed in such cases upon sheriffs.

In like manner it is declared the duty of the military officers commanding Tennessee regiments, battalions, or detached squads, and surgeons in charge of the hospitals of Tennessee soldiers to open and hold elections on the day aforesaid, under the same rules and regulations hereinbefore prescribed, and at such suitable places as will be convenient to the soldiers who are hereby declared entitled to vote without registration.

In testimony whereof, I, Andrew Johnson, Military Governor of the State of Tennessee do hereunto set [L. S.] my hand, and have caused the great seal of the State to be affixed at this Department, on the 30th day of September, A. D. 1864.

By the Governor: ANDREW JOHNSON.
EDWARD H. EAST, Secretary of State.

[The names of superintendents of election in the several counties, and the extracts from the Tennessee code are omitted here.]

At the time these papers were presented as before stated, I had never seen either of them, nor heard of the subject to which they relate, except in a general way, only one day previously. Up to the present moment nothing whatever upon the subject has passed between Governor Johnson, or any one else connected with the proclamation and myself. Since receiving the papers as stated, I have given the subject such brief consideration as I have been able to do in the midst of so many pressing public duties. My conclusion is that I can have nothing to do with the matter, either to sustain the plan as the Convention and Governor Johnson have initiated it, or to revoke or modify it as you demand. By the Constitution and laws, the President is charged with no duty in the conduct of a presidential election in any State; nor do I, in this case, perceive any military reason for his interference in the matter. The movement set on foot by the Convention and Governor Johnson does not, as seems to be assumed by you, emanate from the National Executive. In no proper sense can it be considered other than as an independent movement of at least a portion of the loyal people of East Tennessee. I do not perceive in the plan any menace of violence or coercion toward any one. Governor Johnson like any other loyal citizen of Tennessee, has the right to favor any political plan he chooses, and, as Military Governor, it is his duty to keep the peace among and for the loyal people of the State. I can not discern that by this plan he purposes any more. But you object to the plan. Leaving it alone will be your perfect security against it. It is not proposed to force you into it. Do as you please on your own account peacefully and loyally, and Gov. Johnson will not molest you; but will protect you against violence so far as in his power.

I presume that the conducting of a Presidential election in Tennessee in strict accordance with the old code of the State is not now a possibility. It is scarcely necessary to add that if any election shall be held, and any votes shall be cast in the State of Tennessee for President and Vice-President of the United States, it will belong, not to the military agents nor yet to the Executive Department, but exclusively to another department of the Government, to determine whether they are entitled to be counted; in conformity with the Constitution and laws of the United States. Except it be to give protection against violence, I decline to interfere in any way with any Presidential election.

ABRAHAM LINCOLN.

However important this question might be regarded by either side, on general grounds, it was already sufficiently manifest that it had no practical bearing on the grand result of the Presidential election. It might well be doubted how far, in a close contest, it would have been expedient or just to insist on an electoral majority, obtained by throwing into either scale the votes of States in the condition of Tennessee, Louisiana and Arkansas; but, that the loyal people of those States should be protected in their purpose of presenting their votes for the acceptance or rejection of the two Houses of Congress, manifestly follows from the measures already taken to secure to them the enjoyment of a loyal republican State government; and, to any fair exercise of this privilege of voting, it is difficult to see how they could have dispensed with safeguards like those proposed by Governor Johnson. The McClellan ticket was, however, declared to be withdrawn, and and the opponents of the Administration in Tennessee mostly abstained from voting.

Great exertions were made by the Opposition to carry the State of New York for McClellan, and to re-elect Governor Seymour. The Rebel Benjamin's project of "colonizing voters" from Canada, may or may not have been actually undertaken. Certain it is, that a gigantic fraud was attempted, under the peculiar law of New York, in regard to the voting of soldiers by proxy—a fraud requiring no small expenditure of money for its execution. The parties convicted of this crime were manifestly but the tools of others unknown, from whom they received the means and the incitement. There is reason to believe that, but for the discovery of this enormity before the plot was fully carried out, the actual voice of the people of New York would have been annulled, and a false majority returned. It is not uncommon for charges of fraud or unfairness in elections to be loosely made on both sides. It would certainly be unjust to hold any party, as such, responsible for all that designing individuals may do in its behalf. But the statements made in this instance are based on definite proof, and the facts fall in, not unnaturally, with the conduct of many of the men who were zealously striving for the defeat of Mr. Lincoln.

On the 8th day of November, the people expressed their sovereign will in regard to the Presidency and Vice-Presidency for another term. In the midst of the struggle with a powerful rebellion, at the close of a canvass in which the party administering the government, had been assailed in the most violent and threatening terms, and at a time when on-looking nations might naturally expect ruinous convulsions and a lapse into anarchy or despotism, the election in every city, village, and precinct of the loyal States, proceeded with an order and decorum scarcely equalled in the most peaceful times. Even the soldier who was just going into battle remembered the day, and was careful to exercise the right of a freeman. The spectacle was impressive. Its lesson could nowhere be mistaken.

In 1860, Mr. Lincoln had received the electoral votes of seventeen States, (that of New Jersey being divided,) in all 180 votes, and an aggregate popular vote of 1,866,452. In 1864, the number of States that voted for him was twenty-two,* having a total electoral vote of 213, while he received an aggregate popular vote of 2,203,831. The whole number of votes cast for Mr. Lincoln in 1860, in the slave-holding States was 26,430. In 1864, he received in those States (including Maryland, West Virginia and Missouri, which became non-slaveholding during his administration) an aggregate vote of 169,728. These several statements do not include Tennessee, Louisiana or Arkansas, the votes of which were excluded in the official canvass by Congress.

Only three States voted for Gen. McClellan, namely : New Jersey, Delaware and Kentucky, giving an aggregate electoral vote of 21. Mr. Lincoln thus received more than ten to one in the electoral college. The total popular vote for McClellan was 1,797,019. The majority for Mr. Lincoln on the popular vote was 406,812.   .

---

* This includes the States of Kansas and Nevada, admitted into the Union since 1860, and of West Virginia, formed by the division of the State of Virginia.

The vote of the several States may be seen in the following table :

STATES.	POPULAR VOTE.		ELECTORAL VOTE.	
	Lincoln	M'Clellan	Lincoln	M'Clellan
Maine..................................	61,803	44,211	7	
New Hampshire....................	36,400	32,871	5	
Vermont..............................	42,419	13,321	5	
Massachusetts......................	126,742	48,745	12	
Rhode Island.......................	13,692	8,470	4	
Connecticut.........................	44,691	42,285	6	
New York............................	368,735	361,986	33	
New Jersey..........................	60,723	68,024		7
Pennsylvania........................	296,391	276,316	26	
Delaware.............................	8,155	8,767		3
Maryland.............................	40,153	32,739	7	
Kentucky.............................	26,592	61,478		11
Ohio...................................	264,975	205,557	21	
Indiana.......................	150,238	130,233	13	
Illinois................................	189,496	158,730	16	
Missouri..............................	71,676	31,626	11	
Michigan.............................	85,352	67,370	8	
Wisconsin..............	83,458	65,884	8	
Iowa...................................	89,075	49,596	8	
California............................	58,698	42,255	5	
Minnesota...........................	25,060	17,375	4	
Oregon................................	9,888	8,457	3	
Kansas................................	16,441	3,691	3	
West Virginia......................	23,152	10,438	5	
Nevada................................	9,826	6,504	3*	
Total............................	2,203,831	1,797,019	213	21

On the evening of November 10th, a procession, with music, banners and transparencies, marched to the White House to pay their compliments to President Lincoln. A national salute was fired, and cheers, prolonged and earnest, greeted the appearance of the President at the window from which he was accustomed to speak when thus called out by his friends. On this joyous occasion, free from any manifestations of merely

---

*The official report of the Canvassing Committee, on the second Wednesday in February, as printed in the Globe, gives but two electoral votes for Nevada, and a total for Mr. Lincoln of 212.

personal or even partisan triumph, he made the following memorable speech :

FRIENDS AND FELLOW CITIZENS : It has long been a grave question whether any government not *too* strong for the liberties of its people can be strong *enough* to maintain its own existence in great emergencies. On this point the present Rebellion brought our Republic to a severe test; and a Presidential election, occurring in regular course during the Rebellion, added not a little to the strain.

If the loyal people *united* were put to the utmost of their strength by the rebellion, must they not fall when *divided* and partially paralyzed by a political war among themselves?

But the election was a necessity. We can not have free government without elections; and if the rebellion could force us to forego or postpone a national election, it might fairly claim to have already conquered and ruined us. The strife of the election is but human nature practically applied to the facts of the case. What has occurred in this case, must ever recur in similar cases. Human nature will not change. In any future great national trial, compared with the men of this, we shall have as weak and as strong, as silly and as wise, as bad and as good.

Let us, therefore, study the incidents of this, as philosophy to learn wisdom from, and none of them as wrongs to be revenged.

But the election, along with its incidental and undesirable strife, has done good too. It has demonstrated that a people's government can sustain a national election in the midst of a great civil war. [Enthusiastic cheers.] Until now, it has not been known to the world that this was a possibility. It shows, also, how sound and how strong we still are. It shows that, even among candidates of the same party, he who is most devoted to the Union, and most opposed to treason, can receive most of the people's votes. [Long-continued applause.] It shows, also, to the extent yet known, that we have more men now than we had when the war began. Gold is good in its place, but living, brave, patriotic men, are better than gold. [Applause.]

But the rebellion continues; and now that the election is over, may not all, having a common interest, re-unite in a common effort to save our common country? [Cries of "Yes," "Good."] For my own part, I have striven, and will strive, to avoid placing any obstacle in the way. So long as I have been here, I have not willingly planted a thorn in any man's bosom.

While I am deeply sensible to the high compliment of a reëlection, and duly grateful, as I trust, to Almighty God, for having directed my countrymen to a right conclusion, as I think, for their own good, it adds nothing to my satisfaction that any other man may be disappointed or pained by the result. [Applause.]

May I ask those who have not differed with me to join with me in the same spirit toward those who have?

And now, let me close by asking three hearty cheers for our brave soldiers and seamen, and their gallant and skillful commanders.

The cheers were given with hearty good-will in response to the President's call. A venerable Democrat in the crowd remarked, with feeling: "God is good to us. He has again given us as a ruler, that sublime specimen of His noblest work, an honest man."

The result of the election becoming known to the army, Lieut.-Gen. Grant sent the following congratulatory dispatch to the Secretary of War:

CITY POINT, Nov. 10, 1864—10.30 P. M.

Hon. Edwin M. Stanton, Secretary of War:

Enough now seems to be known to say who is to hold the reins of Government for the next four years.

Congratulate the President for me for this double victory.

The election having passed off quietly, no bloodshed or riot throughout the land, is a victory worth more to the country than a battle won.

Rebeldom and Europe will construe it so.

U. S. GRANT, Lieutenant General.

The election had, in fact, demonstrated to the Rebels, and to the world, that the people were determined to sustain our armies, and to keep their ranks filled with new levies, so long as needed, until the last vestige of armed opposition to the Government should disappear. To the soldier, and to the citizen ready to become a soldier—should he be wanted—the result was alike gratifying. The assertion of the Chicago platform, that the war was a failure, was branded as false. The impudent demand for a cessation of hostilities, in the midst of the full tide of success, was emphatically rebuked

The recreant intrigues with a cabal of traitors in Canada, were condemned to the infamy they deserved. The malignant calumnies against the noblest and truest of rulers were summarily repudiated. Every man who had any thing at stake, of whatever party, breathed freer for the demonstrated stability of our Government. Better days already dawned on the Republic.

CHAPTER VIII.

Second Session of the Thirty-Eighth Congress.—President Lincoln's last Annual Message.—Cabinet Changes.—Mr. Blair withdraws, and Gov. Dennison becomes Postmaster-General.—Mr. Speed Succeeds Judge Bates, as Attorney-General.—Death of Chief Justice Taney.—Mr. Chase his Successor.—Our Relations with Canada.— The Reciprocity Treaty to Terminate.—Call for 300,000 more Soldiers.—Amendment of the Constitution, Prohibiting Slavery, Concurred in by the House.—Popular Rejoicing.—The Rebel Treatment of Union Prisoners.—Retaliation Discussed in the Senate, but Repugnant to Public Sentiment.—The Wharncliffe Correspondence.— Testimony of Goldwin Smith.—Peace Memorial from Great Britain.—Correspondence Thereon.—Congratulatory Address of the Workingmen of Great Britain.—Speech of Mr. Lincoln in Reply to the Swedish Minister.—Speech of Mr. Lincoln on the Death of Edward Everett.—Political affairs in Tennessee, Louisiana and Arkansas.—Abortive Peace Negotiations.—Full Details of the Hampton Roads Conference.—Rebel Accounts of the Same.—Affairs in Richmond.—Close of the Thirty-Eighth Congress.—Creation of the Bureau of Freedmen, and other Legislation.

The second session of the Thirty-eighth Congress commenced on the 5th of December, 1864. On the next day, President Lincoln transmitted to the two houses his annual message—exhibiting with brevity and force the general progress of events, and the present condition of national affairs—as follows:

Fellow-Citizens of the Senate and House of Representatives:—Again the blessings of health and abundant harvests claim our profoundest gratitude to Almighty God.

The condition of our foreign affairs is reasonably satisfactory.

Mexico continues to be a theater of civil war. While our political relations with that country have undergone no change, we have, at the same time, strictly maintained neutrality between the belligerents.

56

At the request of the States of Costa Rica and Nicaragua, a competent engineer has been authorized to make a survey of the river San Juan and the port of San Juan. It is a source of much satisfaction that the difficulties which for a moment excited some political apprehensions, and caused a closing of the inter-oceanic transit route, have been amicably adjusted, and that there is a good prospect that the route will soon be re-opened with an increase of capacity and adaptation. We could not exaggerate either the commercial or the political importance of that great improvement.

It would be doing injustice to an important South American State not to acknowledge the directness, frankness, and cordiality with which the United States of Colombia have entered into intimate relations with this Government. A claims convention has been constituted to complete the unfinished work of the one which closed its session in 1861.

The new liberal constitution of Venezuela having gone into effect with the universal acquiescence of the people, the Government under it has been recognized, and diplomatic intercourse with it has opened in a cordial and friendly spirit. The long-deferred Aves Island claim has been satisfactorily paid and discharged.

Mutual payments have been made of the claims awarded by the late joint commission for the settlement of claims between the United States and Peru. An earnest and cordial friendship continues to exist between the two countries, and such efforts as were in my power have been used to remove misunderstanding and avert a threatened war between Peru and Spain.

Our relations are of the most friendly nature with Chili, the Argentine Republic, Bolivia, Costa Rica, Paraguay, San Salvador, and Hayti.

During the past year no differences of any kind have arisen with any of those republics, and, on the other hand, their sympathies with the United States are constantly expressed with cordiality and earnestness.

The claim arising from the seizure of the cargo of the brig Macedonian in 1821 has been paid in full by the Government of Chili.

Civil war continues in the Spanish part of San Domingo, apparently without prospect of an early close.

Official correspondence has been freely opened with Liberia, and it gives us a pleasing view of social and political progress in that republic. It may be expected to derive new vigor from American influence, improved by the rapid disappearance of slavery in the United States.

I solicit your authority to furnish to the republic a gunboat at moderate cost, to be reimbursed to the United States by installments. Such a vessel is needed for the safety of that State against the native African races; and in Liberian hands it would be more effective in arresting the African slave trade than a squadron in our own hands. The possession of the least organized naval force would stimulate a generous ambition in the republic, and the confidence which we should manifest by furnishing it would win forbearance and favor toward the colony from all civilized nations.

The proposed overland telegraph between America and Europe, by the way of Behring's Straits and Asiatic Russia, which was sanctioned by Congress at the last session, has been undertaken, under very favorable circumstances, by an association of American citizens, with the cordial good-will and support as well of this Government as of those of Great Britain and Russia. Assurances have been received from most of the South American States of their high appreciation of the enterprise, and their readiness to coöperate in constructing lines tributary to that world-encircling communication. I learn with much satisfaction that the noble design of a telegraphic communication between the eastern coast of America and Great Britain has been renewed with full expectation of its early accomplishment.

Thus it is hoped that with the return of domestic peace the country will be able to resume with energy and advantage its former high career of commerce and civilization.

Our very popular and estimable representative in Egypt died in April last. An unpleasant altercation which arose between the temporary incumbent of the office and the Government of the Pasha resulted in a suspension of intercourse. The evil was promptly corrected on the arrival of the successor to the consulate, and our relations with Egypt, as well as our relations with the Barbary Powers, are entirely satisfactory.

The rebellion which has so long been flagrant in China, has at last been suppressed, with the coöperating good offices of this Government, and of the other western commercial States. The judicial consular establishment there has become very difficult and onorous, and it will need legislative revision to adapt it to the extension of our commerce, and to the more intimate intercourse which has been instituted with the Government and people of that vast empire. China seems to be accepting with hearty good-will the conventional laws which regulate commercial and social intercourse among the western nations.

Owing to the peculiar situation of Japan, and the anomalous

form of its government, the action of that empire in performing treaty stipulations is inconstant and capricious. Nevertheless, good progress has been effected by the western Powers, moving with enlightened concert. Our own pecuniary claims have been allowed, or put in course of settlement, and the inland sea has been re-opened to commerce. There is reason also to believe that these proceedings have increased rather than diminished the friendship of Japan toward the United States.

The ports of Norfolk, Fernandina, and Pensacola have been opened by proclamation. It is hoped that foreign merchants will now consider whether it is not safer, and more profitable to themselves, as well as just to the United States, to resort to these and other open ports, than it is to pursue, through many hazards, and at vast cost, a contraband trade with the other ports which are closed, if not by actual military occupation, at least by a lawful and effective blockade.

For myself, I have no doubt of the power and duty of the Executive, under the law of nations, to exclude enemies of the human race from an asylum in the United States. If Congress should think that proceedings in such cases lack the authority of law, or ought to be further regulated by it, I recommend that provision be made for effectually preventing foreign slave traders from acquiring domicile and facilities for their criminal occupation in our country.

It is possible that, if it were a new and open question, the maritime Powers, with the lights they now enjoy, would not concede the privileges of a naval belligerent to the insurgents of the United States, destitute, as they are, and always have been, equally of ships-of-war and of port and harbors. Disloyal emmissaries have been neither less assiduous nor more successful during the last year than they were before that time in their efforts, under favor of that privilege, to embroil our country in foreign wars. The desire and determination of the governments of the maritime States to defeat that design are believed to be as sincere as, and can not be more earnest than our own. Nevertheless, unforseen political difficulties have arisen, especially in Brazilian and British ports, and on the northern boundary of the United States, which have required, and are likely to continue to require, the practice of constant vigilance, and a just and conciliatory spirit on the part of the United States, as well as of the nations concerned and their governments.

Commissioners have been appointed under the treaty with Great Britain on the adjustment of the claims of the Hudson's Bay and Puget Sound Agricultural Companies, in Oregon, and are now proceeding to the execution of the trust assigned to them.

In view of the insecurity of life and property in the region adjacent to the Canadian border, by reason of recent assaults and depredations, committed by inimical and desperate persons who are harbored there, it has been thought proper to give notice that after the expiration of six months, the period conditionally stipulated in the existing arrangements with Great Britain, the United States must hold themselves at liberty to increase their naval armament upon the lakes if they shall find that proceeding necessary. The condition of the border will necessarily come into consideration in connection with the question of continuing or modifying the rights of transit from Canada, through the United States, as well as the regulation of imposts, which were temporarily established by the reciprocity treaty of the 5th June, 1854.

I desire, however, to be understood, while making this statement, that the colonial authorities of Canada are not deemed to be intentionally unjust or unfriendly toward the United States; but, on the contrary, there is every reason to expect that, with the approval of the imperial Government, they will take the necessary measures to prevent new incursions across the border.

The act passed at the last session for the encouragement of emigration, has, so far as was possible been put into operation. It seems to need amendment which will enable the officers of the Government to prevent the practice of frauds against the immigrants while on their way, and on their arrival in the ports, so as to secure them here a free choice of avocations and places of settlement. A liberal disposition toward this great national policy is manifested by most of the European States, and ought to be reciprocated on our part by giving the immigrants effective national protection. I regard our emigrants as one of the principle replenishing streams which are appointed by Providence to repair the ravages of internal war, and its wastes of national strength and health. All that is necessary, is to secure the flow of that stream in its present fullness, and to that end the Government must, in every way, make it manifest that it neither needs nor designs to impose involuntarily military service upon those who come from other lands to cast their lot in our country.

The financial affairs of the Government have been successfully administered during the last year. The legislation of the last session of Congress has beneficially affected the revenues, although sufficient time has not yet elapsed to experience the full effect of several of the provisions of the acts of Congress imposing increased taxation.

The receipts during the year, from all sources, upon the basis of warrants signed by the Secretary of the Treasury, including loans and the balance in the Treasury on the 1st day of July, 1863, were $1,394,796,007 62; and the aggregate disbursements, upon the same basis, were $1,298,056,101 89, leaving a balance in the Treasury, as shown by warrants, of $96,839,905 73.

Deduct from these amounts the amount of the principal of the public debt redeemed, and the amount of issues in substitution therefor, and the actual cash operations of the Treasury were: receipts, $884,076,646, 57; disbursements, $865,234,-087 86; which leaves a cash balance in the Treasury of $18,-842,558 71.

Of the receipts, there were derived from customs $102,316,-152 99; from lands, $588,333 29; from direct taxes, $475,648 96; from internal revenue, $109,741,134 10; from miscellaneous sources, $47,511,448 10; and from loans applied to actual expenditures, including former balance, $623,443,-929 13.

There were disbursed, for the civil service, $27,505,599 46; for pensions and Indians, $7,517,930 97; for the War Department, $690,791,842 97; for the Navy Department, $85,733,-292 77; for interest of the public debt, $53,685,421 69—making an aggregate of $865,234,087 86, and leaving a balance in the Treasury of $18,842,558 71, as before stated.

For the actual receipts and disbursements for the first quarter, and the estimated receipts and disbursements for the three remaining quarters of the current fiscal year, and the general operations of the Treasury in detail, I refer you to the report of the Secretary of the Treasury. I concur with him in the opinion that the proportion of moneys required to meet the expenses consequent upon the war derived from taxation should be still further increased; and I earnestly invite your attention to this subject, to the end that there may be such additional legislation as shall be required to meet the just expectations of the Secretary.

The public debt on the 1st day of July last, as appears by the books of the Treasury, amounted to $1,740,690,489 49. Probably, should the war continue for another year, that amount may be increased by not far from $500,000,000. Held as it is, for the most part, by our own people, it has become a substantial branch of national, though private, property. For obvious reasons, the more nearly this property can be distributed among all the people the better. To favor such genera. distribution, greater inducements to become owners might, perhaps, with good effect and without injury, be presented to persons of limited means. With this view, I suggest whether it might not be both competent and expedient for Congress to provide that a limited amount of some future issue of public securities might be held by any *bona fide* purchaser exempt from taxation and from seizure for debt, under such restrictions and limitations as might be necessary to guard against abuse of so important a privilege. This would enable every prudent person to set aside a small annuity against a possible day of want.

Privileges like these would render the possession of such securities, to the amount limited, most desirable to every person of small means who might be able to save enough for the purpose. The great advantage of citizens being creditors as well as debtors, with relation to the public debt, is obvious. Men readily perceive that they can not be much oppressed by a debt which they owe to themselves.

The public debt on the 1st day of July last, although somewhat exceeding the estimate of the Secretary of the Treasury made to Congress at the commencement of the last session, falls short of the estimate of that officer made in the preceding December, as to its probable amount at the beginning of this year, by the sum of $3,995,097 31. This fact exhibits a satisfactory condition and conduct of the operations of the Treasury.

The national banking system is proving to be acceptable to capitalists and to the people. On the 25th day of November, five hundred and eighty-four national banks had been organized, a considerable number of which were conversions from State banks. Changes from State systems to the national system are rapidly taking place, and it is hoped that very soon there will be in the United States no banks of issue not authorized by Congress, and no bank-note circulation not secured by the Government. That the Government and the people will derive great benefit from this change in the banking systems of the country can hardly be questioned. The national system will create a reliable and permanent influence in support of the national credit, and protect the people against losses in the use of paper money. Whether or not any further legislation is advisable for the suppression of State bank issues, it will be for Congress to determine. It seems quite clear that the Treasury can not be satisfactorily conducted unless the Government can exercise a restraining power over the bank-note circulation of the country.

The report of the Secretary of War, and accompanying

documents, will detail the campaigns of the armies in the field since the date of the last annual message, and also the operations of the several administrative bureaus of the War Department during the last year. It will also specify the measures deemed essential for the national defense, and to keep up and supply the requisite military force.

The report of the Secretary of the Navy presents a comprehensive and satisfactory exhibit of the affairs of that Department of the naval service. It is a subject of congratulation and laudable pride to our countrymen that a navy of such vast proportions has been organized in so brief a period, and conducted with so much efficiency and success.

The general exhibit of the Navy, including vessels under construction on the 1st of December, 1864, shows a total of 671 vessels, carrying 4,610 guns, and of 510,396 tons, being an actual increase during the year, over and above all losses by shipwreck or in battle, of 83 vessels, 167 guns, and 42,427 tons.

The total number of men at this time in the naval service, including officers, is about 51,000.

There have been captured by the Navy during the year, 324 vessels, and the whole number of naval captures since hostilities commenced, is 1,379, of which 267 are steamers.

The gross proceeds arising from the sale of condemned prize property, thus far reported, amount to $14,396,250 51. A large amount of such proceeds is still under adjudication, and yet to be reported.

The total expenditures of the Navy Department of every description, including the cost of the immense squadrons that have been called into existence from the 4th of March, 1861, to the 1st of November, 1864, are $238,647,262 35.

Your favorable consideration is invited to the various recommendations of the Secretary of the Navy, especially in regard to a navy-yard and suitable establishment for the construction and repair of iron vessels, and the machinery and armature for our ships, to which reference was made in my last annnal message.

Your attention is also invited to the views expressed in the report in relation to the legislation of Congress at its last session in respect to prize on our inland waters.

I cordially concur in the recommendation of the Secretary as to the propriety of creating the new rank of vice admiral in our naval service.

Your attention is invited to the report of the Postmaster General for a detailed account of the operations and financial condition of the Post Office Department.

The postal revenues for the year ending June 30, 1864, amounted to $12,438,353 78, and the expenditures to $12,-644,786 20; the excess of expenditures over receipts being $206,652 42.

The views presented by the Postmaster General on the subject of special grants by the Government in aid of the establishment of new lines of ocean mail steamships and the policy he recommends for the development of increased commercial intercourse with adjacent and neighboring countries, should receive the careful consideration of Congress.

It is of noteworthy interest that the steady expansion of population, improvement, and governmental institutions over the new and unoccupied portions of our country has scarcely been checked, much less impeded or destroyed, by our great civil war, which at first glance would seem to have absorbed almost the entire energies of the nation.

The organization and admission of the State of Nevada has been completed in conformity with law, and thus our excellent system is firmly established in the mountains which once seemed a barren and uninhabitable waste between the Atlantic States and those which have grown up on the coast of the Pacific ocean.

The Territories of the Union are generally in a condition of prosperity and rapid growth. Idaho and Montana, by reason of their great distance and the interruption of communication with them by Indian hostilities, have been only partially organized; but it is understood that these difficulties are about to disappear, which will permit their governments, like those of the others, to go into speedy and full operation.

As intimately connected with and promotive of this material growth of the nation, I ask the attention of Congress to the valuable information and important recommendations relating to the public lands, Indian affairs, the Pacific railroad, and mineral discoveries contained in the report of the Secretary of the Interior, which is herewith transmitted, and which report also embraces the subjects of patents, pensions, and other topics of public interest pertaining to this Department.

The quantity of public land disposed of during the five quarters ending on the 30th of September last was 4,221,342 acres, of which 1,538,614 acres were entered under the homestead law. The remainder was located with military land warrants, agricultural scrip certified to States for railroads, and sold for cash. The cash received from sales and location fees was $1,019,446.

The income from sales during the fiscal year ending the 30th of June, 1864, was $678,007 21, against $136,077 95 received

43

during the preceding year. The aggregate number of acres surveyed during the year has been equal to the quantity disposed of; and there is open to settlement about 133,000,000 acres of surveyed land.

The great enterprise of connecting the Atlantic with the Pacific States by railways and telegraph lines has been entered upon with a vigor that gives assurance of success, notwithstanding the embarrassments arising from the prevailing high prices of materials and labor. The route of the main line of the road has been definitely located for one hundred miles westward from the initial point at Omaha City, Nebraska, and a preliminary location of the Pacific railroad of California has been made from Sacramento eastward to the great bend of the Truckee river in Nevada.

Numerious discoveries of gold, silver, and cinnabar mines have been added to the many heretofore known, and the country occupied by the Sierra Nevada and Rocky mountains, and the subordinate ranges, now teems with enterprising labor, which is richly remunerative. It is believed that the product of the mines of precious metals in that region has, during the year, reached, if not exceeded, one hundred millions in value.

It was recommended in my last annual message that our Indian system be remodeled. Congress, at its last session, acting upon the recommendation, did provide for re-organizing the system in California, and it is believed that under the present organization the management of the Indians there will be attended with reasonable success. Much yet remains to be done to provide for the proper government of the Indians in other parts of the country to render it secure for the advancing settler, and to provide for the welfare of the Indian. The Secretary reiterates his recommendations, and to them the attention of Congress is invited.

The liberal provisions made by Congress for paying pensions to invalid soldiers and sailors of the Republic, and to the widows, orphans, and dependent mothers of those who have fallen in battle, or died of disease contracted, or of wounds received in the service of their country, have been diligently administered. There have been added to the pension rolls. during the year ending the 30th day of June last, the names of 16,770 invalid soldiers, and of 271 disabled seamen, making the present number of Army invalid pensioners 22,767, and of Navy invalid pensioners 712.

Of widows, orphans, and mothers, 22,198 have been placed on the Army pension rolls, and 248 on the Navy rolls. The present number of Army pensioners of this class is 25,433, and of Navy pensioners 793. At the beginning of the year the number of revolutionary pensioners was 1,430 ; only twelve of them were soldiers, of whom seven have since died. The remainder are those who, under the law, receive pensions because of relationship to revolutionary soldiers. During the year ending the 30th of June, 1864, $4,504,616 92 have been paid to pensioners of all classes.

I cheerfully commend to your continued patronage the benevolent institutions of the District of Columbia which have hitherto been established or fostered by Congress, and respectfully refer, for information concerning them, and in relation to the Washington acqueduct, the Capitol, and other matters of local interest, to the report of the Secretary.

The Agricultural Department, under the supervision of its present energetic and faithful head, is rapidly commending itself to the great and vital interest it was created to advance. It is peculiarly the people's Department, in which they feel more directly concerned than in any other. I commend it to the continued attention and fostering care of Congress.

The war continues. Since the last annual message all the important lines and positions then occupied by our forces have been maintained, and our arms have steadily advanced; thus liberating the regions left in the rear, so that Missouri, Kentucky, Tennessee, and parts of other States have again produced reasonably fair crops.

The most remarkable feature in the military operations of the year is General Sherman's attempted march of three hundred miles directly through the insurgent region. It tends to show a great increase of our relative strength that our General-in-Chief should feel able to confront and hold in check every active force of the enemy, and yet to detach a well appointed large army to move on such an expedition. The result not yet being known, conjecture in regard to it is not here indulged.

Important movements have also occurred during the year to the effect of moulding society for durability in the Union. Athough short of complete success, it is much in the right direction, that twelve thousand citizens in each of the States of Arkansas and Louisiana have organized loyal State governments, with free constitutions, and are earnestly struggling to maintain and administer them. The movements in the same direction, more extensive, though less definite, in Missouri, Kentucky, and Tennessee, should not be overlooked. But Maryland presents the example of complete success. Maryland is secure to Liberty and Union for all the future. The genius of rebellion will no more claim Maryland. Like another foul spirit, being driven out, it may seek to tear her but it will woo her no more.

At the last session of Congress a proposed amendment of the Constitution, abolishing slavery throughout the United States, passed the Senate, but failed for lack of the requisite two-thirds vote in the House of Representatives. Although the present is the same Congress, and nearly the same members, and without questioning the wisdom or patriotism of those who stood in opposition, I venture to recommend the reconsideration and passage of the measure at the present session. Of course the abstract question is not changed; but an intervening election shows, almost certainly, that the next Congress will pass the measure if this does not. Hence there is only a question of time as to when the proposed amendment will go to the States for their action. And as it is so to go, at all events, may we not agree that the sooner the better? It is not claimed that the election has imposed a duty on members to change their views or their votes, any further than, as an additional element to be considered, their judgment may be affected by it. It is the voice of the people now, for the first time, heard upon the question. In a great national crisis like ours, unanimity of action among those seeking a common end is very desirable—almost indispensable. And yet no approach to such unanimity is attainable unless some deference shall be paid to the will of the majority simply because it is the will of the majority. In this case the common end is the maintenance of the Union: and, among the means to secure that end, such will, through the election, is most clearly declared in favor of such constitutional amendment.

The most reliable indication of public purpose in this country is derived through our popular elections. Judging by the recent canvass and its result, the purpose of the people, within the loyal States, to maintain the integrity of the Union, was never more firm, nor more nearly unanimous than now. The extraordinary calmness and good order with which the millions of voters met and mingled at the polls, give strong assurance of this. Not only all those who supported the Union ticket, so called, but a great majority of the opposing party also, may be fairly claimed to entertain and to be actuated by the same purpose. It is an unanswerable argument to this effect, that no candidate for any office whatever, high or low, has ventured to seek votes on the avowal that he was for giving up the Union. There have been much impugning of motives, and much heated controversy as to the proper means and best mode of advancing the Union cause; but on the distinct issue of Union or no Union the politicians have shown their instinctive knowledge that there is no diversity among the people. In affording the people the fair opportunity of showing, one to another, and to the world, this firmness and unanimity of purpose, the election has been of vast value to the national cause.

The election has exhibited another fact not less valuable to be known—the fact that we do not approach exhaustion in the most important branch of national resources—that of living men. While it is melancholy to reflect that the war has filled so many graves and carried mourning to so many hearts, it is some relief to know that, compared with the surviving, the fallen have been so few. While corps, and divisions, and brigades, and regiments have formed and fought and dwindled and gone out of existence, a great majority of the men who composed them are still living. The same is true of the naval service. The election returns prove this. So many voters could not else be found. The States regularly holding elections, both now and four years ago, to wit: California, Connecticut, Delaware, Illinois, Indiana, Iowa, Kentucky, Maine, Maryland, Massachusetts, Michigan, Minnesota, Missouri, New Hampshire, New Jersey, New York, Ohio, Oregon, Pennsylvania, Rhode Island, Vermont, West Virginia, and Wisconsin, cast 3,982,011 votes now against 3,870,222 cast then, showing an aggregate now of 3,982,011. To this is to be added 33,762 cast now in the new States of Kansas and Nevada, which States did not vote in 1860, thus swelling the aggregate to 4,015,773, and the net increase during the three years and a half of war to 145,551. A table is appended showing particulars. To this again should be added the number of all soldiers in the field from Massachusetts, Rhode Island, New Jersey, Delaware, Indiana, Illinois, and California, who by the laws of those States could not vote away from their homes, and which number can not be less than 90,000. Nor yet is this all. The number in organized Territories is triple now what it was four years ago, while thousands, white and black, join us as the national arms press back the insurgent lines. So much is shown affirmatively and negatively by the election. It is not material to inquire *how* the increase has been produced, or to show that it would have been *greater* but for the war, which is probably true. The important fact remains demonstrated that we have *more* men *now* than we had when the war *began;* that we are not exhausted nor in process of exhaustion; that we are *gaining* strength and may, if need be, maintain the contest indefinitely. This as to men. Material resources are now more complete and abundant than ever.

The national resources, then, are unexhausted, and, as we

believe, inexhaustible. The public purpose to reëstablish and maintain the national authority is unchanged, and, as we believe, unchangeable. The manner of continuing the effort remains to choose. On careful consideration of all the evidence acces·sible, it seems to me that no attempt at negotiation with the insurgent leader could result in any good. He would accept nothing short of severance of the Union—precisely what we will not and can not give. His declarations to this effect are explicit and oft-repeated. He does not attempt to deceive us. He affords us no excuse to deceive ourselves. He can not voluntarily re-accept the Union; we can not voluntarily yield it. Between him and us the issue is distinct, simple, and inflexible. It is an issue which can only be tried by war, and decided by victory. · If we yield, we are beaten; if the Southern people fail him he is beaten. Either way, it would be the victory and defeat following war. What is true, however, of him who heads the insurgent cause, is not necessarily true of those who follow. Although he can not re-accept the Union, they can. Some of them, we know, already desire peace and re-union. The number of such may increase. They can at any moment have peace simply by laying down their arms and submitting to the national authority under the Constitution. After so much, the Government could not, if it would, maintain war against them. The loyal people would not sustain or allow it. If questions should remain, we would adjust them by the peaceful means of legislation, conference, courts, and votes, operating only in constitutional and lawful channels. Some certain, and other possible, questions are, and would be, beyond the executive power to adjust; as, for instance, the admission of members into Congress, and whatever might require the appropriation of money. The executive power itself would be greatly diminished by the cessation of actual war. Pardons and remissions of forfeitures, however, would still be within executive control. In what spirit and temper this control would be exercised can be fairly judged of by the past.

A year ago, general pardon and amnesty, upon specified terms, were offered to all, except certain designated classes; and it was, at the same time, made known that the excepted classes were still within contemplation of special clemency. During the year many availed themselves of the general provision, and many more would, only that the signs of bad faith in some, led to such precautionary measures as rendered the practical process less easy and certain. During the same time, also, special pardons have been granted to individuals of the accepted classes, and no voluntary application has been denied. Thus, practically, the door has been, for a full year, open to all, except such as were not in condition to make free choice—that is, such as were in custody or under constraint. It is still so open to all. But the time may come—probably will come—when public duty shall demand that it be closed; and that, in lieu, more rigorous measures than heretofore shall be adopted.

In presenting the abandonment of armed resistance to the national authority on the part of the insurgents, as the only indispensable condition of ending the war on the part of the Government, I retract nothing heretofore said as to slavery. I repeat the declaration made a year ago, that "while I remain in my present position, I shall not attempt to retract or modify the emancipation proclamation, nor shall I return to slavery any person who is free by the terms of that proclamation, or by any of the acts of Congress." If the people should, by whatever mode or means, make it an executive duty to reënslave such persons, another, and not I, must be their instrument to perform it.

In stating a single condition of peace, I mean simply to say that the war will cease on the part of the Government whenever it shall have ceased on the part of those who began it.

ABRAHAM LINCOLN.

December 6, 1864.

Two Cabinet changes had occurred, since the retirement of Gov. Chase from the Secretaryship of the Treasury. At the time when an attempt was zealously made to divide the friends of the Administration on the basis of the Missouri classification of parties, it became the fashion, with those busiest in this work, to denounce Attorney-General Bates, and Postmaster-General Blair, as special representatives of "Conservatism" in the Cabinet. Mr. Seward had previously been regarded in the same light, but Messrs. Bates and Blair had a more direct relation to Missouri affairs, and they came to be more frequently assailed, during the summer of 1864, than the former, by the "Radicals." Mr. Lincoln had good reasons for reluctance to part with either of those gentlemen. Mr. Blair had almost alone, in the cabinet, stood firm against the policy—never favorably regarded for a moment by President Lincoln—of surrendering Fort Sumter to Rebel insolence, without a blow struck in its favor. That he was a prompt, watchful, and energetic officer, doing his executive work well, nobody ventured to question.   But he had made some speeches which were obnoxious to Republicans, almost universally This was particularly true of a speech made at Rockville, in Maryland, which was circulated in that State, with the intimation that it was an exposition of Mr. Lincoln's policy.   The views thus given out were construed as decidedly reactionary on the slavery question, and savored too strongly of old-fashioned denunciation of Abolitionism.   President Lincoln had certainly not only given no approval to the singular positions taken by Mr. Blair, in apparent backsliding from his former faith, but was even ignorant of the contents of this speech, at least for a long time after its publication.   Mr. Blair was scarcely less unfortunate in speeches made elsewhere, though less universally known.   Without attempting fully to account for the fact, it was certainly true that there had come to be a very general dissatisfaction with Mr. Blair as a Cabinet Minister.   The latter understood this feeling, and verbally proposed to relieve the President from any embarrassment, in the canvass, on his account.   Mr. Lincoln at first regarded this as mere clamor without just ground, and was disinclined to heed it.   Afterward, he became satisfied that the hostility was real and wide-spread—not to be appeased by a firm refusal, as previously in the case of Mr. Seward—and addressed Mr. Blair the following note :

EXECUTIVE MANSION,
WASHINGTON CITY, September 23, 1864.

MY DEAR SIR:
        You have generously said to me, more than once, that whenever your resignation could be a relief to me, it was at my disposal.   The time has come.   You very well know that this proceeds from no dissatisfaction of mine with you personally or officially.   Your uniform kindness has been unsurpassed by that of any friend, and while it is true that the war does not so greatly add to difficulties of your Department as it does to some others, it is yet, much to say, as I most truly can, that in three years and a half, during which you have administered the General Post Office, I remember no single complaint against you in connection therewith

Yours, as ever,   A. LINCOLN.

Hon. MONTGOMERY BLAIR.

To this letter, Mr. Blair replied as follows:

POST OFFICE DEPARTMENT,
WASHINGTON, September 23, 1864.

MY DEAR SIR:

I have received your note of this date, referring to my offers to resign, whenever you should deem it advisable for the public interests that I should do so, and stating that, in your judgment, the time has now come. I now, therefore, formally tender my resignation of the office of Postmaster-General. I can not take leave of you without renewing the expressions of my gratitude for the uniform kindness which has marked your course toward Yours, truly,

M. BLAIR.

The President.

Hon. William Dennison, Ex-Governor of Ohio, who had presided over the National Union Convention at Baltimore, was appointed Postmaster-General in Mr. Blair's stead, an appointment confirmed by the Senate at the beginning of the session.

Attorney-General Bates tendered his resignation soon after the Presidential election, to take effect on the 1st of December. Judge Bates had been the first member of Mr. Lincoln's Cabinet definitely decided upon, and whose appointment was mutually understood. He had many years before been offered a Secretaryship under a Whig Administration, but declined the honor. He was well-known throughout the country as an early and steadfast advocate of emancipation in Missouri, and had long ago shown the sincerity of his faith by freeing his own slaves. While in his official capacity, he was set down by some as a Conservative, he was on many questions of the time, fully up to the advance line of his associates, and lagged behind on none. His views were not, however, a mere echo of other men's opinions, or of those of the people indiscriminately. He was unwilling to go with the current when he believed it was wrong, but chose to use his influence toward directing it aright. Least of all could he brook factious dictation. Those who thoroughly understood him, felt little occasion to be proud of any difference with him. He was ever, while in office, a cordial friend and conscientious adviser of Mr Lincoln, having no under-current of hostile discontent when his counsels were not followed, or when his wishes were overruled. Judge Bates resigned, for personal reasons, an office he had never sought, and his resignation was accepted by Mr. Lincoln, as a favor to one whose presence he would gladly have retained. The Hon. James Speed, of Louisville, Ky., was appointed Attorney-General, and entered upon the duties of that office, soon after it was vacated by his predecessor, having been confirmed by the Senate on the 12th of December.

Chief Justice Taney died on the 12th of October, 1864. One of the most zealous upholders of slavery, he did not survive the day on which the people of Maryland, his native State, decreed the freedom of their slaves. His name will be forever associated with one of the last bulwarks of the doomed institution, known as the Dred Scott decision. Perhaps the most noted, if not the only specially memorable utterance of his life, was the strangely inaccurate assertion that, in the early days of the Republic, the colored race were regarded as having "no rights which the white man was bound to respect." He was a jurist of ability, though too strong a partisan to be always an impartial judge. He was a man of upright and irreproachable private character, and had remained true to the Government in whose service he spent so large a portion of his long life. The first President to whom he administered the oath of office was Martin Van Buren; the last, Abraham Lincoln. For all those intermediate, he had officiated in like manner. The news of the death of Judge Taney came unexpectedly at last; his health having permitted his attendence on the courts, with little interruption, to the end, although he attained the age of eighty-seven years.

During the vacation of the Supreme Court, there was no occasion for filling the important office thus made vacant. A decision was consequently deferred until the assembling of Congress, on the first Monday in December. During the intermediate time, the popular expression in favor of the Hon. Salmon P. Chase, of Ohio, became very general. This appointment, too, was in accordance with President Lincoln's original inclination. By the very fact of the strong contrast between Governor Chase and Judge Taney, on the great questions of the time, was this inclination strengthened, and the popular wish intensified. The nomination was promptly sent in on the meeting of the Senate, and at once confirmed without opposition. Mr. Chase had taken ground in favor of emancipation, at a time when no public honors were to be gained by espousing a cause so unpopular. From first to last, he has been known as the unswerving advocate of universal liberty and impartial equality of rights. To place a man of these principles in the position just now held by the author of the Dred Scott decision, was an almost incredible step in advance. This change moved the people to less enthusiastic demonstrations indeed, but not less profoundly, than the greatest victories of our armies. Chief Justice Chase took the oath of office, and entered on his high duties on the 15th day of December.

The action of the Canadian authorities in refusing to deliver up the St. Albans raiders for trial, on proper demand under the extradition treaty, produced intense feeling on the part of the people of the loyal States. Gen. Dix, in command of the Military Department including the frontier of New York and Vermont, promptly issued an order that marauding parties of like character, hereafter coming into the States from Canada, should be vigorously pursued, across the border if necessary, and captured or shot down wherever found. This order was undoubtedly warranted by recognized principles of international law. It met with a hearty response throughout the country, as did the arrest of Mason and Slidell on the Trent, by Commodore Wilkes, or more recently, the capture of the Rebel pirate-ship Florida, in Brazilian waters, by Commander Collins. But the policy of moderation, from high motives of expediency, still prevailed. There was an earnest desire on the part of the Rebels to embroil our nation with some strong foreign power, and the accomplishment of this object was probably one of the purposes entertained while organizing, in "neutral" British Territory, expeditions across the border. The President deemed it advisable that so much of Gen. Dix's order as authorized pursuit across the frontier should be rescinded. A rigid passport system was, however, adopted, which the hostile conduct of Canadians, and their encouragement to robbery and murder, openly avowed as acts of war, set on foot within their own territory by emissaries of Davis, rendered proper for protection. The regulation was extended to all travelers from a foreign country, except immigrant passengers directly entering an American port by sea.

On the 13th of December, a joint resolution was passed by the House of Representatives, authorizing the President to give the requisite notice to the Government of Great Britain for the termination of the treaty of the 5th of June, 1854, known as the Canadian Reciprocity treaty. This resolution, in a slightly modified form—subsequently agreed to by the House—passed the Senate on the 12th of January, 1865, by a vote of 33 to 8. The resolution as finally passed, and approved by President Lincoln, on the 18th of January, 1865, is in the following terms:

WHEREAS, It is provided in the reciprocity treaty concluded at Washington the 5th of June, 1854, between the United States of the one part, and the United Kingdom of Great Britain and Ireland of the other part, that this treaty "shall remain in force for ten years from the date at which it may come into operation, and further until the expiration of twelve months after either of the high contracting parties shall give notice to the other of its wish to terminate the same;" and whereas, it appears, by a proclamation of the President of the United States, bearing date 16th of March, 1855, that the treaty came into operation on that day; and whereas, further, it is no longer for the interests of the United States to continue the same in force, therefore,

Resolved by the Senate and House of Representatives of the United States of America, in Congress assembled, That notice be given of the termination of the reciprocity treaty, according to the provision therein contained for the termination of the same; and the President of the United States is hereby charged with the communication of such notice to the government of the United Kingdom of Great Britain and Ireland.

Another joint resolution, approved February 9th, 1865, ratifies the notice already given by the President on the 23d of

November, 1864, for the termination of the treaty with Great
Britain, for the reason, assigned in the preamble, that " the
peace of our frontier is now endangered by hostile expeditions
against the commerce of the lakes, and by other acts of lawless persons, which the naval force of the two countries, allowed
by the existing treaty, may be insufficient to prevent."

On the 19th day of December, 1864, President Lincoln, in
order to supply a deficiency of 260,000 men, on the previous
call of July 18, 1864, for 500,000, issued another call for
300,000 volunteers, to serve for one, two, or three years—any
portion of the quota for any locality not made up before the
15th day of February, to be filled by a draft commencing on
that day.

The proposed constitutional amendment prohibiting slavery
throughout the United States, and every where under its jurisdiction, had been defeated in the House of Representatives at
the previous session, as already seen.   Mr. Ashley's motion to
re-consider the vote by which the joint resolution was lost,
being called up, on the 6th of January, 1865, the question
was discussed at great length during the three weeks following.
The motion to re-consider prevailed on the 31st of January, by
a vote of 112 yeas to 57 nays—it being ruled by Speaker
Colfax that only a majority was needed for that purpose.   On
the final vote—two-thirds being required—the joint resolution
was concurred in, yeas 119, nays 56, as follows:

YEAS—Messrs. Alley, Allison, Ames, Anderson, Arnold,
Ashley, Baily, Augustus C. Baldwin, John D. Baldwin, Bax-
ter, Beaman, Blaine, Blair, Blow, Boutwell, Boyd, Brandegee,
Broomall, William G. Brown, Ambrose W. Clark, Freeman
Clarke, Cobb, Coffroth, Cole, Colfax, Creswell, Henry Winter
Davis, Thomas T. Davis, Dawes, Deming, Dixon, Donelly,
Driggs, Dumont, Eckley, Eliot, English, Farnsworth, Frank,
Ganson, Garfield, Gooch, Grinnell, Griswold, Hale, Herrick,
Higby, Hooper, Hotchkiss, Asahel W. Hubbard, John H.
Hubbard, Hulburd, Hutchins, Ingersoll, Jenckes, Julian,
Kasson, Kelley, Francis W. Kellogg, Orlando Kellogg, King,
Knox, Littlejohn, Loan, Longyear, Marvin, McAllister, Mc-
Bride, McClurg, McIndoe, Samuel F. Miller, Moorhead, Mor-
rill, Daniel Morris, Amos Myers, Leonard Myers, Nelson,

Norton, Odell, Charles O'Neill, Orth, Patterson, Perham, Pike, Pomeroy, Price, Radford, William H. Randall, Alexander H. Rice, Edward H. Rollins, James S. Rollins, Schenck, Scofield, Shannon, Sloan, Smith, Smithers, Spalding, Starr, John B. Steele, Stevens, Thayer, Thomas, Tracy, Upson, Van Valkenburgh, Elihu B. Washburne, William B. Washburne, Webster, Whaley, Wheeler, Williams, Wilder, Wilson, Windom, Woodbridge, Worthington and Yeaman—119.

NAYS—Messrs. James C. Allen, William J. Allen, Ancona, Bliss, Brooks, James S. Brown, Chanler, Clay, Cox, Cravens, Dawson, Denison, Eden, Edgerton, Eldridge, Finck, Grider, Hall, Harding, Harrington, Benjamin G. Harris, Charles M. Harris, Holman, Philip Johnson, William Johnson, Kalbfleisch, Kernan, Knapp, Law, Long, Mallory, William H. Miller, James R. Morris, Morrison, Noble, John O'Neill, Pendleton, Perry, Pruyn, Samuel J. Randall, Robinson, Ross, Scott, Wm. G. Steele, Stiles, Strous, Stuart, Sweat, Townsend, Wadsworth, Ward, Chilton A. White, Winfield, Benjamin Wood and Fernando Wood—56.

NOT VOTING—Messrs. Lazear, LeBlond, Marcy, McDowell, McKinney, Middleton, Rogers and Voorhees—8.

The result, up to the last moment, had been doubtful, and the affirmative decision of this momentous question was no sooner announced, than the members on the floor, and the spectators who thronged the galleries, spontaneously joined in enthusiastic and long-continued demonstrations of joy. Never was such a scene before witnessed in any legislative hall. The sensation produced, wherever the news was spread by telegraph, was one of universal satisfaction and gladness that the great work was accomplished. The Republic had at last proclaimed itself truly FREE—needing only the State ratification provided for by the Constitution, and sure to be obtained, to settle the question forever. President Lincoln promptly approved the measure, and State after State has echoed and re-echoed the popular ratification.

The inhuman conduct of the Rebel leaders toward our prisoners in their hands, will fill the darkest pages of the history of the great insurrection. Starvation, freezing, delirium, prolonged agony yielding to the slow-coming relief of death, were the lot of tens of thousands of true and valorous men, whom the fortunes of war had thrown into Rebel hands. The names of

Libby, and Belle Isle, of Salisbury, Millen and Andersonville, will be words of infamy forever—their black shadow resting as a pall over all the fancied military glories of Lee, and covering with shame all the imperial pride of the traitor Davis. Cruelty so brutal was inconsistent with no crime. Barbarism so astounding was not an unnatural fruit of the tyrannous system which the rebellion was designed to perpetuate. The facts stand fully proved, as in the clearest sunlight. The crime was deliberate and without palliation. The agony and torture endured by our imprisoned soldiers could hardly be paralleled by any outrage of the Inquisition, or by any torments inflicted by the savage. The first reports of these inhumanities seemed incredible, but the half was not told.

There were those who urged what they believed the only remedy, retaliation. This policy was discussed at great length in the Senate, and found earnest advocates, whose arguments, enforced by the citation in detail of some portion of these horrible atrocities, may have seemed to some minds almost irresistible. While the discussion continued, relief was happily found in a manner less revolting to humanity. No retaliation was ever practiced. Under no circumstances would public sentiment have tolerated it. No Rebel prisoner ever had occasion to complain. But on the heads of the real authors of these crimes, retribution could not but be fervently invoked.

It was after these facts were known, that certain aiders, abettors and sympathizers in England, enriched by blockade-running, or by the fitting out of Rebel cruisers, or allied in character to these wretched despots, raised a fund for the alleged purpose of relieving the wants—not of these Union prisoners, subjected to slow torture, and murdered by thousands, through the aid of hunger, thirst and cold—but *of the Rebel prisoners in our hands,* who had never lacked any thing consistent with their condition, and who were undisputedly and notoriously well fed, sheltered and cared for. The following correspondence shows the origin, purpose and result, of this insolent attempt to shield the Rebels from the infamy of their prison murders, and of their prison tortures, worse than murder :

MR. ADAMS TO MR. SEWARD.

LEGATION OF THE UNITED STATES, }
LONDON, November 18, 1864. }

Hon. Wm. H. Seward, Secretary of State, Washington, D. C.:

SIR: I have received from Lord Wharncliffe, the Chairman of the British Association, organized to give aid and comfort to the Rebel cause, a note, a copy of which is transmitted herewith.

I append a copy of my reply.

I have the honor to be, Sir, your obedient servant,

CHARLES FRANCIS ADAMS.

LORD WHARNCLIFFE TO MR. ADAMS.

WORTLEY HALL, SHEFFIELD, }
November 12, 1864. }

His Excellency, Hon. C. F. Adams:

YOUR EXCELLENCY: A bazaar has been held in St. George's Hall, to provide a fund for the relief of Southern prisoners of war. It has produced a clear sum of £17,000. In preference to any attempts to reach the intended object by circuitous means, a committee of English gentlemen has been formed to address you on this subject.

As chairman of this committee, I venture to ask your Excellency to request permission of your Goverment that an accredited agent may be sent out to visit the military prisons within the Northern States, and minister to the comfort of those for whom this fund is intended, under such supervision as your Government may direct.

Permit me to state that no political end is aimed at by this movement. It has received support from many who were opposed to the political action of the South. Nor is it intended to impute that the Confederate prisoners are denied such attentions as the ordinary rules enjoin. But these rules are narrow and stern. Winter is at hand, and the clothing which may satisfy the rules of war will not protect the natives of a warm climate from the severe cold of the North.

Sir, the issue of this great contest will not be determined by individual suffering, be it greater or less; and you, whose family name is interwoven with American history, can not view with indifference the sufferings of American citizens, whatever their State or opinions.

On more than one occasion, aid has been proffered by the people of one country to special classes, under great affliction, in another. May it not be permitted to us to follow these examples, especially when those we desire to solace are beyond the reach of their immediate kinsmen? I trust these precedents and the voice of humanity may plead with your Excellency, and induce you to prefer to the Government of the United States the request which I have the honor to submit.

I am Sir, your obedient, humble servant,

WHARNCLIFFE.

___

MR. ADAMS TO LORD WHARNCLIFFE.

LEGATION OF THE UNITED STATES, }
LONDON, November 18, 1864. }

LORD WHARNCLIFFE: *My Lord*—I have the honor to acknowledge the receipt of your letter of the 12th inst., asking me to submit to the consideration of my Government a request of certain English gentlemen, made through your lordship, to send out an accredited agent to visit the military prisoners held by the United States, and afford them such aid, additional to that extended by the ordinary rules of war, as may be provided by the fund which has been raised here for the purpose.

I am sure that it has never been the desire of my Government to treat with unnecessary or vindictive severity any of the misguided individuals, parties in this deplorable rebellion, who have fallen into their hands in the regular course of war. I should greatly rejoice were the effects of your sympathy extended to the ministering to the mental ailment, not less than the bodily sufferings of these unfortunate persons, thus contributing to put an end to a struggle which otherwise is likely to be only procrastinated by your labors.

Be that as it may, I shall be happy to promote any human endeavor to alleviate the horrors of this strife, and in that sense shall very cheerfully comply with your lordship's desire, so far as to transmit, by the earliest opportunity, to my Government, a copy of the application which has been addressed to me.

I beg your lordship to receive the assurance of my distinguished consideration.

CHARLES FRANCIS ADAMS.

___

MR. SEWARD TO MR. ADAMS.

DEPARTMENT OF STATE, }
WASHINGTON, December 5, 1864. }

SIR: I have received your dispatch of the 18th of November, No. 807, together with the papers therein mentioned, namely, a copy of a letter which was addressed to you on the

44 58

12th of November last, by Lord Wharncliffe, and a copy of your answer to that letter.

Your proceeding in that matter is approved. You will now inform Lord Wharncliffe that permission for an agent of the committee described by him to visit the insurgents detained in military prisons of the United States, and to distribute among them seventeen thousand pounds of British gold, is disallowed. Here it is expected that your correspondence with Lord Wharncliffe will end.

That correspondence will necessarily become public. On reading it, the American people will be well aware that while the United States have ample means for the support of prisoners, as well as for every other exigency of the war in which they are engaged, the insurgents, who have blindly rushed into that condition, are suffering no privations that appeal for relief to charity either at home or abroad.

The American people will be likely to reflect that the sum thus insidiously tendered in the name of humanity constitutes no large portion of the profits which its contributors may be justly supposed to have derived from the insurgents, by exchanging with them arms and munitions of war for the coveted productions of immoral and enervating slave labor. Nor will any portion of the American people be disposed to regard the sum thus ostentatiously offered for the relief of captured insurgents as a too generous equivalent for the devastation and dissolution which a civil war, promoted and protracted by British subjects, has spread throughout States which before were eminently prosperous and happy.

Finally, in view of this last officious intervention in our domestic affairs, the American people can hardly fail to recall the warning of the Father of our Country, directed against two great and intimately connected public dangers, namely : sectional faction and foreign intrigue. I do not think the insurgents have become debased, although they have sadly wandered from the ways of loyalty and patrtiotism. I think that, in common with all our countrymen, they will rejoice in being saved by their considerate and loyal Government from the grave insults which Lord Wharncliffe and his associates, in their zeal for the overthrow of the United States, have prepared for the victims of their unnatural and hopeless rebellion.

I am, sir, your obedient servant,

WILLIAM H. SEWARD.

An attempt of Lord Warncliffe, through the London *Times*, to give a color of propriety to the action thus summarily

brought to an end, by referring to statements of some menda-
cious correspondent in this country—as utterly destitute of
truth, as much of the correspondence of the London *Times*
and other English journals concerning American affairs—Professor Goldwin Smith, of Oxford University, who had candidly observed and judged our people in this conflict from the
first, and who had lately visited America, promptly met these
allegations with the following reply :

To THE EDITOR OF THE DAILY NEWS : *Sir:*—Lord Wharncliffe, in his letter published in the *Times* of yesterday, intimates on the faith of an American correspondent, whose letter
he does not produce in full, and whose name he does not give,
that the Confederate prisoners in the hands of the Federal
Government are suffering unusual privations, and that a pile
of them has been seen lying dead from want of nourishing food,
and he accuses Mr. Seward, in effect, of excluding the agent
of the Liverpool Southern Bazaar Fund from the prisons, lest
by his testimony these cruelties should be brought to light.

In the course of the tour in the United States, from which I
have just returned, I visited the prison at camp Douglas, near
Chicago, and the Prisoner's Hospital at Baltimore.   And I beg
leave again to express the conviction, stated in my former
letters, that the inmates of the prison were not suffering for
want of nourishing food, or from any unusual privation ; and
that the inmates of the hospital were treated with the utmost
liberality and kindness.   I have among my papers, and hope
to send you in the course of a day or two, the dietary of the
hospital, from which it will appear that there is no disposition,
in that case at least, to withhold a sufficiency of nourishing
food.

I beg leave, at the same time, to express my firm belief that
the sentiment of the people at the North is strongly as possible in favor of a humane and generous treatment of the prisoners, both as a matter of duty and as an instrument of ultimate
reconciliation, and this, notwithstanding that they are convinced, and in fact have the proof before their eyes, that their
own soldiers are treated with the greatest barbarity in Southern
prisons.   I am, etc.,
Manchester, Dec. 27.   GOLDWIN SMITH.

In a spirit not unlike that exhibited by Lord Wharncliffe,
certain officious intermeddlers in England, under the leadership
of a titled Briton. named De Houghton, had prepared an

address to the people of the United States, expressing an earnest desire for peace.   This paper, alleged to have received the signatures of three hundred and fifty thousand persons (" mostly fools," as Carlyle would say), in Great Britain, was first transmitted to Governor Seymour, of New York, who prudently declined the part assigned him of presenting it to President Lincoln.   Finally, an English messenger named Parker, undertook the task of delivering this precious parcel at the White House, and arrived in Washington for the purpose.   The Senate having, on the 6th of December, requested the President to furnish " any information in the Department of State, concerning any proposition or overture recently made by British subjects in aid of the rebellion," Mr. Seward next day transmitted to that body the following correspondence on the subject of the peace memorial in question.   It presents a rare example of diplomatic directness and brevity :

MR. PARKER TO MR. SEWARD.

WASHINGTON, November 26, 1864.

Hon. W. H. Seward, Secretary of State, etc.:

HON. SIR : I beg to inform you that I have been deputed to convey to this country an address from the people of Great Britain and Ireland to the people of the United States of America.   The address was presented to Governor Seymour, for him to present through the proper channel.

I was requested by him to convey it to the President of the United States, as the authorized channel of communication between the people of other nations and the people of the United States of America.

May I, therefore, ask the honor of an opportunity for so doing.

I am, Hon. Sir, yours most obediently,

JOSEPH PARKER.

MR. PARKER TO MR. SEWARD.

METROPOLITAN HOTEL, }
WASHINGTON, November 26, 1864. }

Hon. W. H. Seward, Secretary of State, etc.:

HON. SIR : In reply of your letter of to-day, permit me to state that the address which I have had the honor of being deputed by the parties signing it to bring to this country, and containing the signatures of some three hundred and fifty thousand of my countrymen, from the peer to the artisan, is *not* from the Government of Great Britain, nor from any political party. It is simply an expression of the earnest desire of the masses of the people of Great Britain to see peace again restored to this continent.

Waiting your favors, I am, Hon. Sir, yours, most obediently,

JOSEPH PARKER.

MR. SEWARD TO MR. PARKER.

DEPARTMENT OF STATE, ⎱
WASHINGTON, November 26, 1864. ⎰

To Joseph Parker, Washington, D. C.:

SIR : Your letter of this date, stating that you are the bearer of an address from the people of Great Britain and Ireland to the people of the United States, has been received.

Before answering the question which your letter contains, it is desirable to be further informed whether you have authority from the Government of Great Britain and Ireland for the purpose referred to, and whether your mission has been made known to the diplomatic agent of that Government accredited to the Government of the United States ?

I am, sir, your very obedient servant,

WILLIAM H. SEWARD.

MR. SEWARD TO MR. PARKER.

DEPARTMENT OF STATE, ⎱
WASHINGTON, November 26, 1864. ⎰

To Joseph Parker, Esq., Metropolitan Hotel:

SIR : The Government of the United States can not receive the address which was mentioned in your notes of this morning. Your request for an interview with the President, to present the address, is, therefore, declined.

I am, sir, your obedient servant,

WILLIAM H. SEWARD.

In marked contrast with these demonstrations of Wharncliffe and De Houghton—and perhaps called out by their acts—was the address of the English Workingmen to President Lincoln, congratulating him on his re-election. This paper first appeared in the *London News* of December 23d, 1864, and was transmitted to the President through Mr. Adams. It affords a fitting conclusion to the foregoing papers :

To Abraham Lincoln, President of the United States :

SIR : We congratulate the American people on your re-election by a large majority. If. resistance to the slave power were the reserved watchword upon your first election, the triumphant war-cry of your re-election is "death to slavery." From the commencement of the Titanic American strife the workingmen of Europe felt instinctively that the star-spangled banner carried the destiny of their class.

The contest for the territories which opened the dire epopee, was it not to decide whether the virgin soil of immense tracts should be wedded to the labor of the emigrant, or prostituted by the tramp of the slave-driver? When an oligarchy of three hundred thousand slaveholders dared to inscribe, for the first time in the annals of the world, slavery on the banner of armed revolt; when on the very spots where hardly a century ago the idea of one great democratic republic had first sprung up whence the first declaration of the rights of man was issued, and the first impulse given to the European revolution of the eighteenth century ; when on those very spots counter revolution, with systematic thoroughness, gloried in rescinding " the ideas entertained at the time of the formation of the Old Constitution," and maintained slavery to be a beneficent institution, indeed the only solution of the great problem of the relation of capital to labor, " and cynically proclaimed property in man " the corner stone of the new edifice ; then the working classes of Europe understood at once, even before the frantic partisanship of the upper classes for the Confederate gentry had given its dismal warning, that the slaveholders' rebellion was to sound the tocsin for a general holy crusade of property against labor, and that for the men of labor, with their hopes for the future, even their past conquests were at stake in that tremendous conflict on the other side of the Atlantic.

Everywhere they bore, therefore, patiently, the hardships imposed upon them by the cotton crisis, opposed enthusiastically the pro-slavery intervention importunities of their " betters," and from most parts of Europe contributed their quota of blood to the good cause. While the workingmen, the true political power of the North, allowed slavery to defile their own republic, while before the negro, mastered and sold without his concurrence, they boasted in the highest prerogative of the white-skinned laborer to sell himself and choose his own master, they were unable to attain the true freedom of labor, or to support their European brethren in their struggle for emancipation ; but this barrier to progress has been swept off by the red sea of civil war.

The workingmen of Europe feel sure that as the American

war of independence initiated a new era of ascendancy for the middle class, so the American anti-slavery war will do for the working classes. They consider it an earnest of the epoch to come, that it fell to the lot of Abraham Lincoln, the single-minded son of the working-class, to lead his country through the matchless struggle for the rescue of an enchained race and the re-construction of a social work.

Signed on behalf of the International Workingmen's Association, the members of the Central Council.

A cordial speech of Baron de Wetterstedt, the minister representing the kingdom of Sweden and Norway, on the occasion of the elevation of his mission to a higher grade by his Sovereign, and his official presentation on the 20th of January, to the President, drew from Mr. Lincoln the following deservedly friendly response:

BARON DE WETTERSTEDT: My memory does not recall an instance of disagreement between Sweden and the United States. Your predecessor was most agreeable in his intercourse with this Government, and I greet you with the same good feeling which was entertained for him while he resided with us. The consideration which your Government has manifested by raising the rank of its mission here, is acknowledged with sincere satisfaction. You may be assured that on my part every occasion will be improved to exhibit the sincere desire which this Government entertains for the prosperity and welfare of the Government and Kingdom of Sweden and Norway.

On the 25th of January, a delegation of ladies and gentlemen from Philadelphia, headed by the Rev. Dr. Suddards, waited on the President, to present him with a vase of leaves, gathered by the lady donors, on the battle-field of Gettysburg, and placed on exhibition at the great Sanitary Fair, held during the previous summer at the former place. Mr. Lincoln replied to the presentation speech as follows:

REVEREND SIR, AND LADIES AND GENTLEMEN: I accept, with emotions of profoundest gratitude, the beautiful gift you have been pleased to present to me. You will, of course, expect that I acknowledge it. So much has been said about Gettysburg, and so well said, that for me to attempt to say more may, perhaps, only serve to weaken the force of that which has already been said. A most graceful and eloquent tribute was paid to the patriotism and self-denying labors of the American ladies, on the occasion of the consecration of the National Cemetery at Gettysburg, by our illustrious friend, Edward Everett, now, alas! departed from earth. His life was a truly great one, and I think, the greatest part of it was that which crowned its closing years. I wish you to read, if you have not already done so, the glowing, and eloquent, and truthful words which he then spoke of the women of America. Truly, the services they have rendered to the defenders of our country in this perilous time, and are yet rendering, can never be estimated as they ought to be. For your kind wishes to me, personally, I beg leave to render you, likewise, my sincerest thanks. I assure you they are reciprocated. And now, gentlemen and ladies, may God bless you all.

The State of Tennessee, under the Military Governorship of Andrew Johnson, had been steadily advancing toward a better condition, though still disturbed by a large Secession element of its population, bitterly hostile to the Government. The loyal portion of the inhabitants had readily fallen in with the out-spoken anti-slavery policy of Gov. Johnson, as the only basis for re-organizing the State Government. The final defeat of the Rebel Hood, and his expulsion from the State— many of the worst enemies of the Union following him, as the same class had followed Price out of Missouri—left the party of malcontents and disunionists comparatively subdued and peaceful.

A State Convention, in calling which East Tennessee had taken the lead, inviting and receiving the co-operation of Middle and West Tennessee, assembled at Nashville on the 11th of January, 1865. Its object was the re-organization of a civil government for the State. No one who had borne arms in the Rebel service, or who had given aid and comfort to the rebellion, was permitted to take a seat in the convention. The number of votes to be cast for each county was at first determined on the basis of the vote against secession in 1861. This gave a decided preponderance to East Tennessee—ever the home of loyalty and freedom. As this created dissatisfaction among the delegates from other parts of the State, they were conciliated by a change, giving a more equal local representation. The Convention unanimously declared in favor of abolishing, and forever prohibiting slavery throughout the State. A further constitutional amendment was also agreed to, forbidding the Legislature from recognizing ' the right of property in slaves, or from giving compensation for those freed. The declaration of State independence, and the military league with the "Davis Confederacy," made in 1861, and all laws and ordinances made in pursuance of those measures, were declared abrogated. All official appointments made by Gov. Johnson, during the time of his service as Military Governor, were confirmed.

The action of the Convention was submitted to the people for ratification or rejection, the vote to be taken on the 22d of February—State officers and a Legislature to be chosen on the 4th of March, in case of a popular approval. Nearly three hundred delegates took part in the proceedings. The people approved the work of the Convention, ratifying these important changes in the organic law of the State. On the 4th of March, William G. Brownlow was elected Governor, and was duly installed in office. A Legislature was also chosen, and Tennessee has now a fully organized government as a Free State.

The policy pursued in Tennessee was entirely consonant in principle, though necessarily varied in some details, with that which the President had adopted in regard to Louisiana. In the former case, however, partly through the firm and energetic management of a Military Governor in the midst of people from whom he had received the highest honors in the gift of the State, the result was more complete. Gov. Johnson knew the men with whom he had to deal. They knew him as a statesman who had before been Chief Magistrate of the State by a popular election, and who had long represented them in the Senate. He had, too, a basis of immense strength in the indomitable spirit of freedom which pervaded East Tennessee, his own home, and which hailed the advent of universal liberty as the sole enduring foundation for the re-organization of civil order in the revolted States.

We have already seen something of the difficulties which

59

attended the like efforts in Louisiana. Only some of the more important localities, as New Orleans, and points on the Mississippi River chiefly, had been reclaimed by absolute military possession. The earlier Military Governors had not been citizens of Louisiana. Personal divisions and partisan factions had sprung up within the State, and had been fostered by ambitious men elsewhere. An energetic opposition to the President on this subject was organized in Congress. A firm and fair trial of his policy was thus interfered with, where cordial support was most of all needed. Unfortunately, too, the influence of Gen. Banks, to whom so important a part in this matter had been assigned, and who had so successfully conducted affairs in the earlier stages, had lost prestige somewhat, by the unexpected issue of the Red River expedition, which failed to sustain the reputation he had gained in the Port Hudson campaign.

The prominence given to this subject, and the factious opposition by which a small minority in the Senate succeeded, at the close of the session of 1864–5, in defeating, for a time, the final consummation by Congressional recognition of the long-continued efforts for the re-organization of a permanent local Government, gives importance to the following letter of the President, recently made public:

"EXECUTIVE MANSION,
WASHINGTON, August 5, 1863.

MY DEAR GEN. BANKS: While I very well know what I would be glad for Louisiana to do, it is quite a different thing for me to assume direction of the matter. I would be glad for her to make a new Constitution, recognizing the Emancipation Proclamation, and adopting emancipation in those parts of the State to which the proclamation does not apply. And while she is at it, I think it would not be objectionable for her to adopt some practical system by which the two races could gradually live themselves out of their old relations to each other, and both come out better prepared for the new. Education for young blacks should be included in the plan. After all, the power or element of "contract" may be sufficient for this probationary period, and by its simplicity and flexibility may be the better.

As an anti-slavery man, I have a motive to desire emancipation which pro-slavery men do not have; but even they have strong enough reason to thus place themselves again under the shield of the Union, and thus perpetually hedge against the recurrence of the scenes through which we are now passing.

Gov. Shepley has informed me that Mr. Durant is now taking a registry with a view to the election of a Constitutional Convention in Louisiana. This, to me, appears proper. If such convention were to ask my views, I could present little else than what I now say to you. I think the thing should be pushed forward, so that, if possible, its mature work may reach here by the meeting of Congress.

For my own part, I think I shall not, in any event, retract the Emancipation Proclamation; nor, as Executive, ever return to slavery any person who is free by the terms of that proclamation, or by any of the acts of Congress.

If Louisiana shall send members to Congress, their admission to seats will depend, as you know, upon the respective Houses, and not upon the President.   *   *   *

Yours, very truly,

(Signed.)   A. LINCOLN.

It is difficult to see how a State government, organized in a regular manner from this beginning, with a constitution prohibiting slavery, could be intrinsically obnoxious, except on the theory—having as yet few supporters—that all the disloyal States should be reduced to the " territorial " condition. And it was in fact the author of t.is theory in the Senate, who, backed by a small minority, and resorting to parliamentary tactics little at home in that body, succeeded, near the close of the session, in defeating the will of a decided majority of both Houses, as clearly manifested in favor of the recognition of the Louisiana State government. It was of no such act that his leading (but unsuccessful) coadjutor in the House, and one of his associates in this transaction in the Senate, had said, arraigning the President in the midst of the canvass of the previous summer, that " a more studied outrage on the legislative authority of the people has never been perpetrated."

Arkansas followed the fortunes of Louisiana, in this failure of recognition, despite the will of a majority of both Houses, in which the President also cordially concurred. That State, too, had been re-organized on the basis of a free State constitution, ratified by a large loyal vote. The rejection of its Congressional delegation, which, like that of Louisiana, was present, asking admission, turned upon the autocratic determination which refused recognition of Louisiana.

In determining what States should be allowed a representation in the electoral college, Tennessee, Louisiana and Arkansas had been excluded—a respectable minority of the Union members voting in their favor. When that vote was taken, however, it was expressly understood that this action was not to be regarded as prejudicing the question of recognizing the State governments and chosen Congressional representatives in the two last-named States, which alone had reached that stage of re-organization. It is not difficult to appreciate the distinction between counting the electoral votes of States, which had undertaken to participate in the Presidential election, before any determination as to their condition, and the recognition of loyal governments in such States, with representation in Congress. But it is very difficult, if not impossible, to see by what method these States, as such, should become entitled to recognition at all, except on such a basis as the organizations already perfected. The President had, in fact, the satisfaction of knowing that a decided majority of both Houses coincided with himself on this subject, though not of seeing their views prevail.

Soon after the Presidential election, there was a considerable clamor—at first raised by Democratic leaders, and afterward joined by the same persons who had taken an interest in the Niagara Falls correspondence with the Canada conspirators—for opening some kind of communication with the spurious government at Richmond, with a view to agreeing on terms for a general pacification. To the Rebels, in their still unbroken pride and presumption, such a proposition was more likely to appear as an indication of weakness than of magnanimity. To most loyal people, unquestionably, it was evident that Grant and Farragut, Sherman, Thomas and Sheridan, were intrusted with the only practicable powers for securing peace guarantees from "an authority that can control the armies now at war with the United States." This was the more especially believed, after the repeated exhibitions of indomitable insolence and inveterate malice on the part of those presuming to exercise civil functions as the chief rulers of a " Confederacy " based on the " corner-stone of slavery." President Lincoln himself, at least, was not deceived into any other supposition. While there were prominent individuals in Richmond who ventured to speak openly of making peace, on terms definitely involving a recognition of Secession, even these, as in the case of McMullen, were unable to secure a party of any strength to follow them. Foote, rather in bitter hatred of Davis, than from any real inclination to submit to rightful authority, had at the same time—just before Christmas—made a gloomy speech on the financial condition and military prospects of the rebellion, and sought to shield himself from the consequences of his rashness by flight. Re-captured, he was censured in such terms as to amount, in his estimation, to definite proscription. The Rebel Congress was discussing, in secret session, what Davis had vaguely hinted at as a necessity, and what his Secretary, Benjamin, as well as Lee and other generals, now openly urged as a last resort—the arming of slaves, with the promise of freedom.

A fiendish desperation had become more and more manifest, after the 8th of November. Schemes of an infernal character were devised, or sanctioned in Richmond, as already partly known to the Government, to be afterward more fully discovered, while their execution was mainly intrusted to the men " in the confidential employment " of Jefferson Davis, who were provided with ample funds, over the Canada border. Emissaries were set at work on Lake Erie, to seize vessels and to enact piracy—as in the case of Beall, afterward convicted and hung in New York. On the 25th of November, Howell Cobb Kennedy and others, tools of the same Thompson-Clay cabal, attempted to execute a plan of wholesale arson and murder in the city of New York, by setting fire to many hotels and to shipping in the harbor. A party of men, afterward zealously defended by the same Canada conspirators, and bearing commissions from the pretended government at Richmond, stole, in disguise, across the British border into the village of St. Albans, in Northern Vermont, on the 19th of October, and, by a surprise, robbed the banks in that place, committing assaults and murder, and rode back again into the same "neutral" territory. Their surrender to the proper authorities for trial, after some show of an inclination to act fairly under the extradition treaty, had been ultimately denied, after the assumption of the responsibility for these crimes, by the "belligerent power" having its seat at Richmond. All these facts were transpiring and were publicly understood, as these appeals to send peace commissioners to Richmond were continually reiterated.

Unwilling to be misconstrued on either hand, as determined unncessarily to prolong the war, and heartily desiring peace, if by any possibility it could honorably and justly be had, President Lincoln at length consented that F. P. Blair, Senior, who was personally well known to the leading men at Richmond, should, purely on his own responsibility, make a visit to the Rebel capital. This journey of Mr. Blair, for the time enveloped in mystery, resulted in a second visit, and in the appointment of "commissioners" to present to the Government the Rebel ultimatum, before repeatedly proclaimed. A conference was had with these parties on board a steamer in Hampton Roads, by Mr. Seward at the outset, who was afterward joined by President Lincoln. A concise version of this "negotiation" and its results was communicated by the Secretary of State in the following official dispatch to Mr. Adams, our Minister at the British Court:

DEPARTMENT OF STATE, }
WASHINGTON CITY, February 7, 1865. }

SIR: It is a truism that in times of peace there are always instigators of war. So soon as war begins, there are citizens who impatiently demand negotiations for peace. The advocates of war, after an agitation, longer or shorter, generally gain their fearful end, though the war declared is not unfrequently unnecessary and unwise. So peace agitators in time of war ultimately bring about an abandonment of the conflict, sometimes without securing the advantages which were originally expected from the conflict.

The agitators for war in time of peace, and for peace in time of war, are not necessarily, or perhaps ordinarily, unpatriotic in their purposes or motives. Results alone determine whether they are wise or unwise. The treaty of peace concluded at

Guadalupe Hidalgo, was secured by an irregular negotiator under the ban of the Government. Some of the efforts which have been made to bring about negotiations, with a view to end our civil war, are known to the whole world, because they have employed foreign as well as domestic agents. Others, with whom you have had to deal confidentially, are known to yourself, although they have not publicly transpired. Other efforts have occurred here which are known only to the persons actually moving in them and to this Government. I am now to give, for your information, an account of an affair of the same general character, which recently received much attention here, and which, doubtless, will excite inquiry abroad.

A few days ago, Francis P. Blair, Esq., of Maryland, obtained from the President a simple leave to pass through our military lines, without definite views known to the Government. Mr. Blair visited Richmond, and on his return he showed to the President a letter which Jefferson Davis had written to Mr. Blair, in which Davis wrote that Mr. Blair was at liberty to say to President Lincoln that Davis was now, as he always had been, willing to send commissioners if assured they would be received, or to receive any that should be sent; that he was not disposed to find obstacles in forms. He would send commissioners to confer with the President with a view to a restoration of peace between the two countries if he could be assured they would be received. The President thereupon, on the 18th of January, addressed a note to Mr. Blair, in which the President, after acknowledging that he had read the note of Mr. Davis, said that he was, is, and always should be, willing to receive any agents that Mr. Davis or any other influential person, now actually resisting the authority of the Government, might send to confer informally with the President, with a view to the restoration of peace to the people of our one common country. Mr. Blair visited Richmond with this letter, and then again came back to Washington.

On the 29th ultimo we were advised from the camp of Lieutenant-General Grant that Alexander H. Stephens, R. M. T. Hunter, and John A. Campbell were applying for leave to pass through the lines to Washington, as peace commissioners, to confer with the President. They were permitted by the Lieutenant-General to come to his headquarters to await there the decision of the President. Major Eckert was sent down to meet the party from Richmond at General Grant's headquarters. The Major was directed to deliver to them a copy of the President's letter to Mr. Blair, with a note to be addressed to them and signed by the Major, in which they were directly informed that if they should be allowed to pass our lines they would be understood as coming for an informal conference upon the, the basis of the aforenamed letter of the 18th of January to Mr. Blair. If they should express their assent to this condition in writing, then Major Eckert was directed to give them safe conduct to Fortress Monroe, where a person coming from the President would meet them. It being thought probable, from a report of their conversation with Lieutenant-General Grant, that the Richmond party would, in the manner prescribed, accept the condition mentioned, the Secretary of State was charged by the President with the duty of representing this Government in the expected informal conference. The Secretary arrived at Fortress Monroe in the night of the 1st day of February. Major Eckert met him in the morning of the 2d of February, with the information that the persons who had come from Richmond had not accepted in writing the condition upon which he was allowed to give them conduct to Fortress Monroe. The Major had given the same information by telegraph to the President at Washington. On receiving this information, the President prepared a telegram directing the Secretary to return to Washington. The Secretary was preparing at the same moment to so return, without waiting for instructions from the President. But at this juncture Lieutenant-General Grant telegraphed to the Secretary of War, as well as to the Secretary of State, that the party from Richmond had reconsidered and accepted the conditions tendered them through Major Eckert; and General Grant urgently advised the President to confer in person with the Richmoud party. Under these circumstances, the Secretary, by the President's direction, remained at Fortress Monroe, and the President joined him there on the night of the 2d of February. The Richmond party was brought down the James river in a United States steam transport during the day, and the transport was anchored in Hampton Roads.

On the morning of the 3d, the President, attended by the Secretary, received Messrs. Stephens, Hunter and Campbell on board the United States steam transport River Queen, in Hampton Roads. The conference was altogether informal. There was no attendance of secretaries, clerks, or other witnesses. Nothing was written or read. The conversation, although earnest and free, was calm and courteous and kind on both sides. The Richmond party approached the discussion rather indirectly, and at no time did they either make categorical demands, or tender formal stipulations or absolute refusals. Nevertheless, during the conference, which lasted four hours, the several points at issue between the Government and the insurgents were distinctly raised, and discussed fully, intelligently, and in an amicable spirit. What the insurgent party seemed chiefly to favor was a postponement of the question of separation, upon which the war is waged, and a mutual direction of efforts of the Government, as well as those of the insurgents, to some extrinsic policy or scheme for a season, during which passions might be expected to subside, and the armies be reduced, and trade and intercourse between the people of both sections resumed. It was suggested by them that through such postponement we might now have immediate peace, with some not very certain prospect of an ultimate satisfactory adjustment of political relations between this Government and the States, section, and people now engaged in conflict with it.

The suggestion, though deliberately considered, was nevertheless regarded by the President as one of armistice or truce, and he announced that we can agree to no cessation or suspension of hostilities except on the basis of the disbandment of the insurgent forces and the restoration of the national authority throughout all the States in the Union. Collaterally, and in subordination to the proposition which was thus announced, the anti-slavery policy of the United States was reviewed in all its bearings, and the President announced that he must not be expected to depart from the positions he had heretofore assumed in his proclamation of emancipation and other documents, as these positions were reiterated in his last annual message. It was further declared by the President that the complete restoration of the national authority everywhere was an indispensable condition of any assent on our part to whatever form of peace might be proposed. The President, assured the other party that while he must adhere to these positions, he would be prepared, so far as power is lodged with the Executive, to exercise liberality. Its power, however, is limited by the Constitution; and when peace shall be made, Congress must necessarily act in regard to appropriations of money and to the admission of representatives from the insurrectionary States. The Richmond party were then informed that Congress had, on the 31st ultimo, adopted, by a constitutional majority a joint resoluion submitting to the several States the proposition to abolish slavery throughout the Union; and that there is every reason to expect that it will be soon accepted by three-fourths of the States, so as to become a part of the national organic law.

The conference came to an end, by mutual acquiescence, without producing any agreement of views upon the several matters discussed, or any of them. Nevertheless, it is perhaps of some importance that we have been able to submit

45

our opinions and views directly to prominent insurgents, and to hear them in answer, in a courteous and not unfriendly manner.

I am, sir, your obedient servant,
WILLIAM H. SEWARD.

On the 8th of February, the House of Representatives adopted a resolution calling upon the President for information on the subject of this conference. On the 10th, he transmitted to that body the following response:

EXECUTIVE MANSION,
WASHINGTON, February 10, 1863. }

To the Honorable the House of Representatives:

In response to your resolution of the 8th inst., requesting information in relation to a conference recently held in Hampton Roads, I have the honor to state that on the day of that date, I gave Francis P. Blair, Sr., a card written on as follows, to-wit:

"Allow the bearer, F. P. Blair, Sr., to pass our lines, go south and return.
"December 28, 1864.　　　　A. LINCOLN."

That at the time I was informed that Mr. Blair sought the card as a means of getting to Richmond, Virginia, but he was given no authority to speak or act for the Government, nor was I informed of anything he would say or do on his own account or otherwise. Afterward Mr. Blair told me that he had been to Richmond and had seen Mr. Jefferson Davis, and he, Mr. B., at the same time left with me a manuscript letter as follows, to-wit:

MR. DAVIS TO MR. BLAIR.

"RICHMOND, VIRGINIA, January 12, 1865.

" *F. P. Blair, Esq.:*

SIR: I have deemed it proper, and probably desirable to you, to give you in this form the substance of remarks made by me, to be repeated by you to President Lincoln, etc.

I have no disposition to find obstacles in forms, and am willing now, as heretofore, to enter into negotiations for the restoration of peace; am ready to send a commission whenever I have reason to suppose it will be received, or to receive a commission, if the United States Government shall choose to send one.

That, notwithstanding the rejection of our former offers, I would, if you could promise that a commissioner, minister, or agent would be received, appoint one immediately, and renew the effort to enter into conference with a view to secure peace to the two countries.

"Yours, etc., JEFFERSON DAVIS."

Afterward, and with the view that it should be shown to Mr Davis, I wrote and delivered to Mr. Blair a letter, as follows:

"WASHINGTON, January 18, 1865.

"*F. P. Blair, Esq.:*

"SIR: You having shown me Mr. Davis' letter to you of the 12th inst., you may say to him that I have constantly been, am now, and shall continue ready to receive any agent whom he, or any other influential person now resisting the national authority, may informally send to me with a view of securing peace to the people of our one common country.

"Yours, &c., "A. LINCOLN."

Afterward Mr. Blair dictated for, and authorized, me to make an entry on the back of my retained copy of the letter last above received, which entry is as follows:

[INDORSEMENT.]

"JANUARY 28, 1865.

"To-day Mr. Blair tells me that on the 21st inst., he delivered to Mr. Davis the original of which the within is a copy, and left it with him; that at the time of delivering it Mr. Davis read it over twice, in Mr. Blair's presence, at the close of which he (Mr. Blair) remarked that the part about 'our one common country' related to the part of Mr. D.'s letter about 'the two countries,' to which Mr. D. replied that he so understood it.

"A. LINCOLN."

Afterward the Secretary of War placed in my hands the following telegram, indorsed by him, as appears:

[Cipher.]

"OFFICE U. S. MILITARY TELEGRAPH, }
"WAR DEPARTMENT. }

"The following telegram was received at Washington, January 29, 1865, M.:

"'FROM HEADQUARTERS ARMY OF THE JAMES, }
     "'January 29, 1865, 6.30 P. M. }

"'*Hon. E. M. Stanton, Secretary of War.*

"'The following dispatch, just received from Maj.-Gen. Parke, who refers it to me for my action. I refer it to you in Lieut.-Gen. Grant's absence.   "'E. O. C. ORD,
     "'Major-General Commanding.'"

"'HEADQUARTERS ARMY OF POTOMAC, }
     4 P. M., January 29, 1865. }

"'*Maj.-Gen. E. O. C. Ord, Headquarters Army of the James:*

"'The following dispatch is forwarded to you for your action. Since I have no knowledge of Gen. Grant's having had any understanding of this kind, I refer the matter to you as the ranking officer present in the two armies.
     (Signed,)   "'JOHN G. PARKE,
     "'Major-General Commanding.'"

"'FROM HEADQUARTERS NINTH ARMY CORPS, }
     "'January 29, 1865. }

"'*Major-General John G. Parke, Headquarters Army of Potomac:*

"'Alexander H. Stephens, R. M. T. Hunter and J. A. Campbell desire to cross my lines, in accordance with an under-standing claimed to exist with Lieut.-Gen. Grant, on their way to Washington as peace commissioners. Shall they be admitted? They desire an early answer to come through immediately. Would like to reach City Point to-night, if they can. If they can not do this, they would like to come through at 10 A. M. to-morrow morning.
     (Signed,)   "'O. B. WILCOX,
     "'Major-General Commanding Ninth Corps.'"

It appears that about the time of placing the foregoing telegram in my hands, the Secretary of War dispatched Gen. Ord as follows, to-wit:

[Copy.]
"WAR DEPARTMENT, WASHINGTON CITY, }
     "January 29, 1865, 10 P. M. }

"*Major-General Ord:*

"This Department has no knowledge of any understanding by Gen. Grant to allow any person to come within his lines as commissioners of any sort. You will, therefore, allow no one to come into your lines under such character or profession until you receive the President's instructions, to whom your telegram will be submitted for his directions.

(Signed,)   " EDWIN M. STANTON,
      " Secretary of War."
Sent in cipher at 2 A. M., 30th.

Afterward, by my direction, the Secretary of War telegraphed Gen. Ord as follows, to-wit:

" WAR DEPARTMENT, WASHINGTON, D. C.,
   10.30 A. M., January 30, 1865.
" *Maj.-Gen. E. O. C. Ord, Headquarters Army of the James:*
" By direction of the President, you are instructed to inform the three gentlemen, Messrs. Stephens, Hunter and Campbell, that a messenger will be dispatched to them at or near where they now are, without unnecessary delay.

(Signed,)   " EDWIN M. STANTON,
      " Secretary of War."

Afterward, I prepared and put into the hands of Major Thomas T. Eckert the following instructions and message:

" EXECUTIVE MANSION,
WASHINGTON, January 30, 1865.
" *Major T. T. Eckert:*
" SIR: You will proceed with the documents placed in your hands, and on reaching Gen. Ord will deliver him the letter addressed to him by the Secretary of War; then, by Gen. Ord's assistance, procure an interview with Messrs. Stephens, Hunter and Campbell, or any of them, deliver to him or them the paper on which your own letter is written, note on the copy which you retain the time of delivery and to whom delivered, receive their answer in writing, waiting a reasonable time for it, and which, if it contain their decision to come through, without further condition, will be your warrant to ask Gen. Ord to pass them through, as directed in the letter of the Secretary of War to him. If by their answer they decline to come, or propose other terms, do not have them passed through. And this being your whole duty, return and report to me.

" Yours, truly,   A. LINCOLN."

" *Messrs. Alex. H. Stephens, J. A. Campbell and R. M. T. Hunter:*
" GENTLEMEN: I am instructed by the President of the United States to place this paper in your hands, with the infor-

mation that if you pass through the United States military
lines it will be understood that you do so for the purpose of
an informal conference, on the basis of the letter, a copy of
which is on the reverse side of this sheet; and that if you pass
on such an understanding, and so notify me in writing, I will
procure the Commanding General to pass you through the
lines, and to Fortress Monroe, under such military precautions
as he may deem prudent; and at which place you will be met
in due time by some person, or persons, for the purpose of such
informal conference.   And further, that you shall have protection, safe conduct and safe return, in all events.
                                   " THOS. T. ECKERT,
                                        " Major and A. D. C.
     " CITY POINT, VIRGINIA, February 1, 1865."

                       [Copy.]
                  " WASHINGTON, January 18, 1865.
" *F. P. Blair, Esq.:*
     " SIR: You having shown me Mr. Davis' letter to you of
the 12th inst., you may say to him that I have constantly
been, am now, and shall continue ready to receive any agent
whom he, or any other influential person now resisting the
national authority, may informally send to me with the view
of securing peace to the people of our one common country.
          " Yours, &c.,   A. LINCOLN."

     Afterward, but before Major Eckert had departed, the follow-
ing dispatch was received from Gen. Grant:

                       [Cipher.]
          " OFFICE U. S. MILITARY TELEGRAPH, }
                    " WAR DEPARTMENT.   }
     " The following telegram received at Washington, M., Jan-
uary 31, 1865:

               " ' FROM CITY POINT, VIRGINIA, 10.30 A. M., }
                         " January 31, 1865.   }
" ' *His Excellency, Abraham Lincoln, President of the United
     States:*
     " ' The following communication was received here last
evening :

          " ' PETERSBURG, VIRGINIA, January 30, 1865.
     Lieut.-Gen. Grant, Commanding Armies U. S. A.:
     " ' SIR: We desire to pass your lines under safe-conduct, and

to proceed to Washington to hold a conference with President Lincoln upon the subject of the existing war, and with a view of ascertaining upon what terms it may be terminated, in pursuance of the course indicated by him in his letter to Mr. Blair, of January 18, 1865, of which we presume you have a copy, and if not we wish to see you in person, if convenient, and to confer with you upon the subject.

" ' Very respectfully, yours,

(Signed,)   " ' ALEXANDER H. STEPHENS,
          " ' J. A. CAMPBELL,
          " ' R. M. T. HUNTER.' ' "

"I have sent directions to receive these gentlemen, and expect to have them at my quarters this evening, awaiting your instructions.   " U. S. GRANT,
     " Lieutenant-General Commanding Armies U. S."

This, it will be perceived, transferred Gen. Ord's agency in the matter to Gen. Grant. I resolved, however, to send Maj. Eckert forward with his message, and accordingly telegraphed Gen. Grant as follows, to-wit:

[Telegram—Copy.]

" EXECUTIVE MANSION,
" WASHINGTON, January 31, 1865.

" *Lieut.-Gen. Grant, City Point, Virginia :*

" A messenger is coming to you on the business contained in your dispatch. Detain the gentlemen in comfortable quarters until he arrives, and then act upon the message he brings as far as applicable, it having been made up to pass through Gen. Ord's hands, and when the gentlemen were supposed to be beyond our lines.

(Signed,)   " A. LINCOLN."

Sent in cipher, at 1.30 P. M.

When Major Eckert departed, he bore with him a letter of the Secretary to Gen. Grant, as follows, to-wit:

[Letter—Copy.]

" WAR DEPARTMENT,
" WASHINGTON, January 30, 1865.

" *Lieut.-Gen. Grant, Commanding, etc. :*

" GENERAL: The President desires that you will please procure for the bearer, Major Thomas T. Eckert, an interview with

Messrs. Stephens, Hunter and Campbell ; and if, on his return to you, he requests it, pass them through the lines to Fortress Monroe by such route, and under such military precautions as you may deem prudent, giving them protection and comfortable quarters while there ; and that you let none of this have any effect upon your movements or plans.

"By order of the President.

    (Signed)   " EDWIN M. STANTON,
            " Secretary of War."

Supposing the proper point to be then reached, I dispatched the Secretary of State with the following instructions, Major Eckert, however, going ahead of him:

       " EXECUTIVE MANSION,
     " WASHINGTON, January 31, 1865.

" *Hon. Wm. H. Seward, Secretary of State :*

 " You will proceed to Fortress Monroe, Virginia, there to meet and informally confer with Messrs. Stephens, Hunter and Campbell, on the basis of my letter to F. P. Blair, Esq., of January 18, 1865, a copy of which you have.

 " You will make known to them that three things are indispensable, to wit :

 " 1. The restoration of the national authority throughout all the States.

 " 2. No receding by the Executive of the United States, on the slavery question, from the position assumed thereon in the late annual message to Congress, and in preceding documents.

 " 3. No cessation of hostilities short of an end of the war, and the disbanding of all forces hostile to the Government.

 " You will inform them that all propositions of theirs not inconsistent with the above, will be considered and passed upon in a spirit of sincere liberality. You will hear all they have to say, and report it to me.

 " You will not assume to definitely consummate anything."

  " Yours, etc.,   ABRAHAM LINCOLN."

On the day of its date the following telegram was sent to Gen. Grant:

       [Copy.]

       " WAR DEPARTMENT,
    " WASHINGTON, D. C., Feb. 1, 1865.

" *Lieut.-Gen. Grant, City Point, Va. :*

 " Let nothing which is transpiring change, hinder, or delay your military movements or plans.

    (Signed)   "A. LINCOLN."

Sent in cipher at 1.30 A. M.

Afterward the following dispatch was received from Gen. Grant:

[In cipher.]

The following telegram received at Washington, 2.30 P. M., Feb. 1, 1865:

" FROM CITY POINT, VA., }
" Feb. 1—2.30 P. M. }

" *His Excellency A. Lincoln, President of the United States:*

" Your dispatch received; there will be no armistice in conse quence of the presence of Mr. Stephens and others within our lines. The troops are kept in readiness to move at the shortest notice, if occasion should justify it.

" U. S. GRANT, Lieut.-Gen."

To notify Major Eckert that the Secretary of State would be at Fortress Monroe, and to put them in communication, the following dispatch was sent:

[Telegram—Copy.]

"WAR DEPARTMENT, }
" WASHINGTON, D. C., Feb. 1, 1865. }

" *Major T. T. Eckert, care Gen. Grant, City Point Va.:*

" Call at Fortress Monroe, and put yourself under direction of Mr. S., whom you will find there.

(Signed,) " A. LINCOLN."

Sent in cipher at 5.30 P. M.

On the morning of the 2d inst., the following telegrams were received by me respectively from the Secretary of State and Major Eckert:

" FORT MONROE, VA., }
" 11.30 P. M., February, 1, 1865. }

" *The President of the United States:*

" Arrived at ten (10) this evening. Richmond party not here. I remain here. " WM. H. SEWARD."

Received 4.30 A. M., Feb. 2, in cipher.

"CITY POINT, VA., 10 P. M., Feb. 1, 1865.

" *His Excellency A. Lincoln, President of the United States:*

" I have the honor to report the delivery of your communication, and my letter, at four fifteen (4.15) this afternoon, to which I received a reply at six (6) P. M., but not satisfactory.

" At eight (8) P. M. the following note addressed to Gen. Grant, was received:

60

" ' CITY POINT, VA., Feb. 1, 1865.

" ' *To Lieutenant General Grant:*

" ' SIR : We desire to go to Washington to confer in'ormally with the President personally in reference to the matters mentioned in his letter to Mr. Blair, of the eighteenth (18th) January ultimo, without any personal compromise on any question in the letter.

" ' We have the permission to do so from the authorities in Richmond.

" ' Very respectfully yours,

(Signed,) " ' ALEXANDER H. STEPHENS,
" ' R. M. T. HUNTER,
" ' J. A. CAMPBELL.'

" At nine-thirty (9.30) P. M. I notified them that they could not proceed further unless they complied with the terms expressed in my letter. The point of meeting designated in above note, would not, in my opinion, be insisted upon ; think Fortress Monroe would be acceptable. Having complied with my instructions, I will return to Washington to-morrow, unless otherwise ordered.

" THOS. T. ECKERT,
" Major and A. D. C."

Received in cipher, Feb. 2d.

On reading this dispatch of Major Eckert I was about to recall him and the Secretary of State, when the following telegram of Gen. Grant to the Secretary of War was shown me :

[In cipher.]

The following telegram received at Washington 4.35 A. M., Feb. 2, 1865 :

" FROM CITY POINT, VA., Feb. 1, 10.30 P. M.

" *Hon. E. M. Stanton, Secretary of War*

" Now that the interview between Major Eckert, under his written instructions, and Mr. Stephens and party has ended, I will state confidentially, but not officially, to become a matter of record, that I am convinced, upon conversation with Messrs. Stephens and Hunter, that their intentions are good and their desire sincere to restore peace and Union. I have not felt myself at liberty to express even views of my own or to account for my reticency. This has placed me in an awkward position, which I could have avoided by not seeing them in the first instance. I fear now their going back without any expression from any one in authority will have a bad influence. At the same time, I recognize the difficulties in the way of receiving these informal commissioners at this time and do not know what to recommend. I am sorry, however, that Mr. Lincoln can not have an interview with the two named in this dispatch, if not with all three, now within our lines. Their letter to me was all that the President's instructions contemplated to secure their safe-conduct, if they had used the same language to Major Eckert.

(Signed,)   "U. S. GRANT,
"Lieutenant-General."

This dispatch of Gen. Grant changed my purpose; and, accordingly, I telegraphed him and the Secretary of State respectively as follows:

"WAR DEPARTMENT,
"WASHINGTON, D. C., Feb 2, 1865.
"*Lieut.-Gen. Grant, City Point, Va.:*
"Say to the gentlemen I will meet them at Fortress Monroe as soon as I can get there.
(Signed,)   "A. LINCOLN."
Sent in cipher at 9 A. M.

Before starting the following dispatches were shown me. I proceeded, nevertheless:

"OFFICE U. S. MILITARY TELEGRAPH,
"WAR DEPARTMENT.

"The following cipher telegram received at Washington, Feb. 2, 1865:

"FROM CITY POINT, VA.,
"9 A. M., Feb. 2, 1865.

"*Hon. William H. Seward, Secretary of State, Fortress Monroe:*
[Copy to Hon. Edwin M. Stanton, Secretary of War, Washington.]

"The gentlemen have accepted the proposed terms, and will leave for Fort Monroe at 9.30 A. M.
"U. S. GRANT, Lieut.-Gen."

On the night of the 2d, I reached Hampton Roads, found the Secretary of State and Major Eckert on a steamer anchored off shore, and learned of them that the Richmond gentlemen were on another steamer, also anchored off shore in the Roads, and that the Secretary of State had not yet seen or communicated with them. Here I ascertained that Major Eckert had literally complied with his instructions, and I saw for the first time the answer of the Richmond gentlemen to him, which in his dispatch to me of the 1st he characterizes as "not satisfactory." That answer is as follows:

[COPY.]
"CITY POINT, VA., Feb. 1, 1865.

"*Thomas T. Eckert, Major and A. D. C.:*

"MAJOR: Your note delivered by yourself this day has been considered. In reply, we have to say that we were furnished with a copy of a letter of President Lincoln to Francis P. Blair, Esq., of the 18th of January, ult., another copy of which is appended to your note. Our instructions are contained in a letter of which the following is a copy:

"'RICHMOND, Jan. 28, 1865.

"'In conformity with the letter of Mr. Lincoln, of which the foregoing is a copy, you are to proceed to Washington City for informal conference with him upon the issues involved in the existing war, and for the purpose of securing peace to the two countries.

"'With great respect, your obedient servant,
(Signed,)   "'JEFFERSON DAVIS.'

"The substantial object to be obtained by the informal conference is to ascertain upon what terms the existing war can be terminated honorably.

"Our instructions contemplate a personal interview between President Lincoln and ourselves at Washington City, but, with explanation, we are ready to meet any person or persons that President Lincoln may appoint, at such place as he may designate. Our earnest desire is that a just and honorable peace may be agreed upon, and we are prepared to receive or submit propositions which may, possibly, lead to the attainment of that end.

"Very respectfully, yours,
(Signed,)   "ALEX. H. STEPHENS,
                      "R. M. T. HUNTER,
                      "JOHN A. CAMPBELL."

A note of these gentlemen, subsequently addressed to Gen. Grant, has already been given in Major Eckert's dispatch of the 1st inst.

I also here saw, for the first time, the following note, addressed by the Richmond gentlemen to Major Eckert:

[COPY.]

"CITY POINT, VA., Feb. 2, 1865.

"*Thomas T. Eckert, Major and A. D. C.:*

"MAJOR: In reply to your verbal statement that your instructions did not allow you to alter the conditions upon which a passport could be given to us, we say that we are willing to proceed to Fortress Monroe and there to have an informal conference with any person or persons that President Lincoln may appoint on the basis of his letter to Francis P. Blair, of the 18th of January ultimo, or upon any other terms or conditions that he may hereafter propose, not inconsistent with the principles of self-government and popular rights, on which our institutions are founded.

"It is our earnest wish to ascertain, after a free interchange of ideas and information, upon what principles and terms, if any, a just and honorable peace can be established without the further effusion of blood, and to contribute our utmost efforts to accomplish such a result.

"We think it better to add that in acccepting your passport we are not to be understood as committing ourselves to anything, but to carry to this informal conference the views and feelings above expressed.

Very respectfully yours, etc.,

(Signed,)   "ALEXANDER H. STEPHENS,
"J. A. CAMPBELL,
"R. M. T. HUNTER."

"NOTE.—The above communication was delivered to me at Fortress Monroe at 4:30 P. M., February 2d, by Lieut.-Col. Babcock, of General Grant's staff.

(Signed,)   "THOS. T. ECKERT,
"Major and A. D. C."

On the morning of the 3d, the gentlemen, Messrs. Stephens, Hunter and Campbell, came aboard of our steamer and had an interview with the Secretary of State and myself of several hours duration. No question of preliminaries to the meeting was then and there made or mentioned. No other person was present; no papers were exchanged or produced; and it was, in advance, agreed that the conversation was to be informal, and verbal merely.

On our part the whole substance of the instruction to the

Secretary of State, hereinbefore recited, was stated and insisted upon, and nothing was said inconsistent therewith; while by the other party it was not said that, in any event, or on any condition, they *ever* would consent to re-union, and yet they equally omitted to declare that they *never* would consent. They seemed to desire a postponement of that question, and the adoption of some other course first, which, as some of them seemed to argue, might or might not lead to re-union, but which course, we thought, would amount to an indefinite postponement. The conference ended without result. The foregoing, containing, as is believed, all the information sought, is respectfully submitted.

ABRAHAM LINCOLN.

This detailed report of the processes and result of a some time mysterious "negotiation," was quite satisfactory to the country. It demonstrated the futility of the "resources of statesmanship," in an attempt to settle issues that the Rebels had determined to leave to the arbitrament of arms. It gave a new impulse, throughout the loyal States, to united efforts for a decisive settlement at the tribunal to which the Secession party had been so prompt to appeal. The use made of this conference at the South, and the view publicly given to the affair by the Rebel leaders will appear from their version, which is subjoined, as published in the Richmond *Whig* of February 7.

To the Senate and House of Representatives of the Confederate States :

Having received a written notification, which satisfied me that the President of the United States was disposed to confer informally with unofficial agents that might be sent by me, with a view to the restoration of peace, I requested the Hon. Alex. H. Stephens, the Hon. R. M. T. Hunter, and the Hon. John A. Campbell to proceed through our lines, and to hold conference with Mr. Lincoln, or such persons as he might depute to represent him.

I herewith submit, for the information of Congress, the report of the eminent citizens above named, showing that the enemy refused to enter into negotiations with the Confederate States, or any of them separately, or to give to our people any other terms or guarantees than those which the conqueror may grant, or permit us to have peace upon any other basis than an unconditional submission to their rule, coupled with the acceptance of their recent legislation, including an amendment to the Constitution for the emancipation of all negro slaves, and with the right on the part of the Federal Congress to legislate on the subject of the relations between the white and black population of each State. Such is, as I understand, the effect of the amendment to the Constitution, which has been adopted by the Congress of the United States.

JEFFERSON DAVIS.

EXECUTIVE OFFICE, RICHMOND, Feb. 6.

RICHMOND, February 5, 1865.

To the President of the Confederate States:

SIR : Under your letter of appointment of the 28th ultimo, we proceeded to seek an " informal conference " with Abraham Lincoln, President of the United States, upon the subject mentioned in the letter.

The conference was granted, and took place on the 30th ult., on board of a steamer anchored in Hampton Roads, where we met President Lincoln and the Hon. Mr. Seward, Secretary of State of the United States. It continued for several hours, and was both full and explicit.

We learn from them that the message of President Lincoln to the Congress of the United States, in December last, explains clearly and distinctly his sentiments as to the terms, conditions, and method of proceeding by which peace can be secured to the people, and we were not informed that they would be modified or altered to obtain that end.

We understood from him that no terms or proposals of any treaty or agreement looking to an ultimate settlement would be entertained or made by him with the authorities of the Confederate States, because that would be a recognition of their existence as a separate power, which under no circumstances would be done ; and, for like reasons, that no such terms would be entertained by him from the States separately ; that no extended truce or armistice (as at present advised) could be granted or allowed, without a satisfactory assurance, in advance, of a complete restoration of the authority of the Constitution and laws of the United States over all places within the States of the Confederacy ; that whatever consequence may follow from the re-establishment of that authority must be accepted. But that individnals subject to pains and penalties under the laws of the United States might rely upon a very liberal use of the power confided to him to remit those pains and penalties, if peace be restored.

During the conference the proposed amendment to the Constitution of the United States, adopted on the 31st ult., was brought to our notice.

The amendment provides that neither slavery nor involuntary servitude, except for crime, should exist within the United States, or any place within their jurisdiction; and that Congress should have power to enforce this amendment by appropriate legislation.

Of all the correspondence that preceded the conference herein mentioned, and leading to the same, you have heretofore been informed.

Very respectfully, your obedient servants,

ALEX. H. STEPHENS.
R. M. T. HUNTER.
J. A. CAMPBELL.

The account to which the abortive negotiation was turned by the Rebel leaders, will also further appear from the following comment of the special organ of Jefferson Davis—the Richmond *Sentinel:*

Our advance, though invited, has been met with the most intolerable of insults. We have been fairly forced to the wall, and it is plain that there is no escape from utter ruin save such as we shall hew out with manful swords. There is literally no retreat but in chains and slavery. There are no peace men among us now. There is no room for one—not an inch of ground for one to stand upon. We are all war men.

As a consequence of sundry propositions and alleged secret movements at Richmond, earlier in the season, looking toward peace by an abandonment of Secession, the Rebel Congress unanimously adopted, in the latter part of January, a concurrent resolution for the appointment of a joint committee to prepare an address to the people of the " Confederate States," informing them of " the unalterable determination of Congress to continue, with all its energy, the struggle for independence, in which," they say, " we are engaged, and assuring them of the final triumph which, in our solemn judgment, must crown our efforts if we stand firm and united together, and wield our resources with strength and wisdom."

About the same time, Mr. Seddon, the Rebel Secretary of

War, resigned, in consequence of an expression of their want of confidence in him by the members of the Legislature of his own State, Virginia. He was succeeded by John C. Breckin-ridge, who, as an officer in the field, had hardly attained a standing commensurate with his former position in civil life. The Rebel Congress, about the 25th of January, finally passed a bill providing for a General-in-Chief to command all the "Confederate" armies. For this post Robert E. Lee was soon after selected. A resolution was also passed by the same body, recommending the restoration of Johnston to the command of the army from which he had been displaced by Davis, and which was now, so far as still in existence, under the command of Hood. In these, and various other ways—especially in the outspoken criticism of the press—dissatisfaction with the management of Davis was manifested. He was, in fact, rapidly losing his hold upon the people, if he had not already become actually odious. It was all the more necessary, therefore, to make an effort to improve the occasion of this conference as a means of uniting the South in his support. A large meeting of the people was held at Richmond, by which resolutions were adopted, indignantly spurning the terms of peace proffered by Mr. Lincoln; characterising the proffer as a premeditated insult; and renewing their pledges of devotion to the Rebel cause. Davis violently declaimed against " reconstruction;" predicted the triumph of his cause, and assured his hearers, very solemnly, that " with the Confederacy he would live or die." No condition but the independence of " the Confederacy," he affirmed, could ever receive his sanction. " Sooner than submit to re-union, he would willingly yield up everything he had on earth, and if it were possible, he would yield up his life a thousand times, rather than succumb." A Richmond journal proclaimed : " It is said that Mr. Stephens will return to Georgia and canvass the State for a vigorous prosecution of the war. He stated to a friend that the only hope now left for the people of the South was in strong arms and stout hearts."

In this manner, everywhere within the narrow " Confede-

61

46

rate " jurisdiction remaining, was the work of firing the slave-holding breast revived.

Davis himself, as his fortunes grew more desperate, became more tyrannical. He meditated reckless schemes, and delegated agents who, in various places, busied themselves with diabolical enterprises. A legion of demons, of whom Blackburn was but the type, was sent forth on " confidential employment "—whose doings were ere long to astonish the world by the depth of their depravity. The arch-traitor conscripted men and boys heretofore exempt, " robbing the cradle and the grave." He forced the negro into his service. He appropriated, in a way of his own, means and materials for carrying on his nefarious work. When Lee clearly foresaw and foretold the fatal result of further resistance, Davis only grew more sullenly unyielding. In vain did the more sagacious leaders about him strive to awaken a saner reflection that would avert the madness bent on ruining all. His commissioners at Hampton Roads had evidently other wishes than he permitted them to avow. He artfully perverted their mission to strengthen himself in his infatuated policy. Defiantly and persistently, he hastened on to the ignoble end of his self-willed career.

The movements of our armies were attended with a series of brilliant successes, prior to the 4th of March, that left the event no longer doubtful. The Congress which terminated with Mr. Lincoln's first Presidential term had well sustained him in his leading measures for suppressing the great insurrection, and had the gratification of knowing, ere its final adjournment, that the good work was substantially accomplished. The more prominent acts of this Congress have been chiefly indicated, while there remain some others which should not be passed unnoticed.

By an act approved on the 21st of December, 1864, the office of Vice-Admiral in the Navy was created, "whose relative rank with officers of the army shall be that of Lieutenant-General in the army." To this office, the President appointed Admiral D. G. Farragut. An act to prevent military interference in elections in the States, was approved February 25th, 1865. A voluminous act in amendment of the Internal Revenue laws, designed to give greater efficiency to the system, and to produce a larger income, was approved on the 3d of March, 1865. An act of the same date also modifies the tariff laws, with the like object.

Another important measure, resulting from the bill of Mr. Eliot, of Massachusetts, which passed the House of Representatives at the previous session, was the act to establish, in the War Department, a Bureau for the relief of freedmen and refugees, approved March 3d, 1865. This measure, as originally proposed, for the the benefit of freedmen alone, had received the earnest support of President Lincoln, who called the attention of Congress thereto, at the previous session, in the following special message :

To the Senate and House of Representatives of the United States:
Herewith I lay before you a letter addressed to myself by a committee of gentlemen representing the Freedmen's Aid Societies in Boston, New York, Philadelphia, and Cincinnati. The subject of the letter, as indicated above, is one of great importance, and one which these gentlemen, of known ability and high character, seem to have considered with great attention and care. Not having time to form a mature judgment of my own as to whether the plan they suggest is the best, I submit the whole subject to Congress, deeming that their attention thereto is almost imperatively demanded.
December 17, 1863. ABRAHAM LINCOLN.

One important appropriation bill was lost by the dictatorial action of Mr. Davis, of Maryland, who wished to compel Congress to enact into a law the views in regard to " military arrests," to which he had become an ardent convert. While he thus signalized the close of his career in Congress, by factiously insisting that irrelevant legislation (already rejected) should be linked with the appropriation, or the latter defeated— which he was able to accomplish under the rules—none of the more essential operations of the Government were thereby materially hindered.

Just preceding the time of counting the electoral votes, Congress adopted a joint resolution, the preamble of which sets forth that " the inhabitants and local authorities of the States of Virginia, North Carolina, South Carolina, Georgia, Florida,

Alabama, Mississippi, Louisiana, Texas, Arkansas, and Tennessee, rebelled against the Government of the United States, and were in such condition on the 8th day of November 1864—that no valid election for electors of President and Vice-President of the United States, according to the Constitution and laws thereof, was held therein on said day;" and which enacts, therefore, that the aforesaid States shall be excluded from representation at this time in the Electoral College for the choice of President and Vice-President. This resolution was sent to Mr. Lincoln, who gave it his signature on the 8th of February, and returned it with the following special message :

To the honorable the Senate and House of Representatives :

The joint resolution, entitled "Joint resolution, declaring certain States not entitled to representation in the Electoral College," has been signed by the Executive in deference to the view of Congress implied in its passage and presentation to him. In his own view, however, the two Houses of Congress, convened under the twelfth article of the Constitution, have complete power to exclude from counting all electoral votes deemed by them to be illegal ; and it is not competent for the Executive to defeat or obstruct that power by a veto, as would be the case if his action were at all essential in the matter. He disclaims all right of the Executive to interfere in any way in the matter of canvassing or counting electoral votes ; and he also disclaims that, by signing said resolution, he has expressed any opinion on the recitals of the preamble, or any judgment of his own upon the subject of the resolution.

ABRAHAM LINCOLN

EXECUTIVE MANSION, February 8, 1865.

The close of the session, at noon on the 4th of March, 1865, found the state of the country in marked contrast to that at the beginning of this Presidential term. Then, unknown storms were pending in the darkened clouds of the future. Now, the storm had mainly expended its fury, and the sunshine of peace—for four years hidden—began once more to appear. During the last three months, the triumphs of our arms—to be noticed in the ensuing chapter—had secured an effective pacification, and the second term of Mr. Lincoln was about to open with joyous omens.

CHAPTER IX.

Winter Campaigns of 1864–5.—Movement of Sherman from Atlanta to Savannah.—Fort McAllister Carried by Assault.—Communication Opened with Admiral Dahlgren's Fleet.—Savannah Occupied by Sherman.—Movements of Hood and Beauregard.—Campaign in Tennessee.—Battle of Franklin.—The Armies Before Nashville.— Raid of Stoneman and Burbridge.—Battle of Nashville.—Defeat and Rout of Hood's Army.—Movements Against Wilmington.— Failure of the First Attack on Fort Fisher.—Success of the Second Expedition.—Fort Fisher Captured by Terry and Porter.—Movements of the Army Before Petersburg.—Sherman's Campaign in the Carolinas.—Capture of Charleston and Wilmington.—Advance of Schofield and Terry on Goldsboro—Battles of Averysboro and Bentonville.—Occupation of Goldsboro and Union of the Three Armies in North Carolina.—Movements in Virginia.—Conference at City Point.

HAVING swept the army of Hood from the Atlanta and Chattanooga road into the wilds of North-eastern Alabama, Gen. Sherman made energetic preparations for a new campaign. The climate of Georgia permitted winter operations with little interruption, and no time was to be lost in following up the decided advantage everywhere gained. Gen. Thomas was left with an ample force in Tennessee to look after Hood, while the remainder of the army set forward on its "march to the sea." On the 12th of November, Gen. Sherman left Kingston, where his headquarters had been since his return from the pursuit of the enemy northward, and advanced to Atlanta. He had already caused the inhabitants of this place to remove—an act of some severity, which he justified as necessary to the execution of his military purposes. The depots and public property in the city were now destroyed, as well as the railroad between Atlanta and Kingston, and trains of supplies were in readiness for a long march—abandoning his base, to seek a new one on the Atlantic coast. This launching of a "movable column into the heart of the enemy's country, for a march of three hundred and fifty miles, might well seem a rash undertaking. Hood was manifestly incredulous, otherwise he would hardly have been now on a wild chase, far away from the State he had just been endeavoring to protect, and which his present movement was intended to relieve from the presence of the "invader." Even Gen. Sherman himself is believed to have doubted the practicability of this undertaking, when first indicated to him by Lieut.-Gen. Grant. The latter, nevertheless, had determined on thus testing his conviction that "the South was but a shell," and his order was given. As yet, the destination of the army was a secret to all but the leaders—friend and foe alike being left in mystery.

The forces taken on this expedition were the Fourteenth, Fifteenth, Seventeenth and Twentieth Corps, together with Gen. Kilpatrick's Division of cavalry—in all, about 70,000 men. The march from Atlanta commenced on the 14th of November.

The right, consisting of the Fifteenth and Seventeenth Corps, under command of Maj.-Gen. Howard, advanced in the direction of Macon, while the Fourteenth and Twentieth Corps, on the left, commanded by Maj.-Gen. Slocum, moved toward Augusta, both wings destroying the railroads in their march. On the 16th, Iverson was driven from Rough-and-Ready by Gen. Howard, who occupied Jonesboro and McDonough on the 17th, his advance skirmishing with Rebel cavalry and infantry. Gen. Slocum reached Covington and Social Circle on the day last named—destroying the depots and other property. On the 18th, the Macon railroad was cut at Forsyth, and the Georgia Legislature, then in session at Milledgeville, together with the State authorities, fled with precipitancy, in alarm at the close proximity of Gen. Sherman. On the 19th, Howard threw a bridge across the Ocmulgee River, advancing on the State Capital, while on the extreme left, the same day, a force entered Madison, on the Augusta railroad, destroying public property at that place. On the 20th, Griswoldville, east of Macon, on the Georgia Central railroad, was taken, and the railroad track and property destroyed. Instead of attacking

Macon, which was well fortified, and defended by State militia, our forces passed wide of the town, steadily advancing. Howard entered Milledgeville on the 20th, and Sherman's extreme left, on the same day, crossed the Oconee, and entered Greensboro, half-way from Atlanta to Augusta. On the 21st, after a slight cavalry engagement, Gordon, an important railroad junction, was reached by the right, and the chief remaining communication with Richmond by rail was severed. The following day was occupied in destroying the railroad, and some fighting occurred near Griswoldville, on the 23d; Wolcott's brigade, of the Fifteenth Corps, having made a reconnoissance toward Macon, and defeated a party of the enemy advancing for a similar purpose. The portion of the army proceeding along the Georgia Central railroad, crossed the Oconee River on the 26th, Kilpatrick encountering and defeating a Rebel force under Wayne, which contested the passage of the stream. This was the principal fighting done in the interior of the State during the campaign, and a victory over Kilpatrick was proclaimed by the Rebel press, after Sherman's entire force was beyond the Oconee, having destroyed the bridges in their rear. The Fourteenth and Twentieth Corps had crossed somewhat earlier at Milledgeville, forty miles above.

On the 28th, the Seventeenth Corps was at Sandersville, advancing toward the Ogeechee river, while to Slocum's command was left the work of destroying the Georgia Central railroad, between the Oconee and the Ogeechee. The Seventeenth Corps crossed the latter river on the 30th of November, following the railroad, while the Fifteenth Corps moved down the south bank of the same stream. During the next eight days, the army moved steadily on, in parallel columns, its flanks well guarded, and scarcely even annoyed by the enemy's cavalry. During all the march there had been liberal foraging; the men were well supplied, and the animals were in excellent condition, accessions being made also to their numbers. The incidents of this memorable procession, sweeping over a wide belt across the territory of the Southern Empire State, attracting the wondering eyes and elating the simple hearts of tens of thousands of the faithful race that hailed their deliverers from long-accumulating wrongs; flashing the light of divine ideas from columns of gleaming bayonets by day, and from cities of camp-fires by night, will live in the pages of history and romance while our country shall endure. For weeks enveloped in a cloud to the world around—even to the Rebels, mainly, who were often only ignorant when affecting to be reticent—tidings of the great expedition began to be anxiously awaited.   A fleet, under Admiral Dahlgren, was, meanwhile, arriving off the coast, near Savannah, prepared to rejoin the long-broken line of communication with Washington.

The enemy had thrown up some rude earth-works at the railroad bridge across the little Ogeechee, but retired before the First Division of the Seventeenth Corps, deployed for the purpose, had come within attacking distance.   The whole force of the enemy was found to be concentrated, on the 9th of December, behind intrenchments, in an apparently strong natural position, thirteen miles from Savannah.   A gallant charge of the single division just named, through a swamp in front of the enemy's position—the men sometimes marching waist deep—drove him from his works, in spite of a heavy artillery fire, and they were firmly held by our forces.   The Rebels retired within another line of works, three or four miles from the city, which were found, by reconnoissance on the 10th, to be covered by a more formidable swamp, artificially deepened by a canal cut from the Savannah to the Ogeechee river, and really impassable.   Destroying the Charleston railroad to the Savannah River, and the bridge across that stream, the Fourteenth and Twentieth Corps took position before the city.   The Fifteenth Corps having crossed the Ogeechee at King's Bridge, had previously struck the Gulf Railroad, at a point seven miles from Savannah, and the Seventeenth Corps moved to the right to relieve the Fifteenth, which was advanced toward the sea.

On the evening of the 13th of December, the Second Division of the Fifteenth Corps, commanded by Gen. Hazen, assaulted and carried Fort McAllister, at the point of the bayonet—a brilliant feat of arms, quickly executed, which opened communications with the fleet of Admiral Dahlgren, connecting the hitherto floating army with a secure base, and apprising the country of the success of "Sherman's march to the sea." Fort McAllister is four miles from the mouth of the Ogeechee river, where Dahlgren's fleet now lay.

During the next few days, there was some further destruction of railroads, and more or less shelling and skirmishing. The city of Savannah was taken possession of on the 21st of December, with some prisoners, and a large amount of cotton and other property. The enemy, under Hardee, mostly escaped across the Savannah river, toward Charleston. The grand culmination of this remarkable campaign gave joy to the nation, as the Christmas bells were sounding, giving new assurance of "peace," if not of "good-will," soon to be restored throughout the land.

Hood, who, aided by Beauregard, menacingly advanced into Tennessee, causing a temporary anxiety, had already ceased to be a subject of concern. The sanguine hopes of Davis in that direction had been terribly crushed. The movement of Hood westward, brought the scene of operations comparatively near the Mississippi and Ohio rivers, and their tributaries, so that re-enforcements and supplies were within easy reach of Gen. Thomas, while the cavalry of Grierson, and other forces, made destructive raids through the States of Mississippi and Alabama, in the enemy's rear. On the other hand, Thomas had a long line to defend, on portions of which annoying attacks were occasionally made by raiding parties. At Johnsonville, on the Tennessee, where he had a depot of supplies, Forrest made his appearance, planting batteries above and below the town, and capturing it on the 4th of November. Three "tin-clad" gunboats, a number of transports and barges, and a large amount of stores were destroyed. Near Bull's Gap, in East Tennessee, on the extreme left of Thomas' line, also, Gen. Gillem was attacked by a superior force and beaten, losing his trains and artillery, and falling back toward Knoxville.

The movement of Hood, after leaving Gaylesville, in Northeastern Alabama, to which place he was pursued by most of Sherman's force, had been southward to Jacksonville, from whence, he took a north-west course toward the Tennessee river, marching on the 22d of October. He remained for some time in the vicinity of Tuscumbia, while a corps of observation, sent out by Thomas, was watching the enemy's movements, at Florence, nearly opposite. The advance of the Rebels northward began about the 20th of November. Gen. Schofield withdrew to Pulaski, seventy-three miles from Nashville, on the 21st, concentrating there his command, consisting of the Fourth aud Twenty-third Corps, with some other forces. The First and Third Divisions of the Sixteenth Corps, under the command of Major-Gen. A. J. Smith, which had been watching for any signs of the the enemy's advance upon Memphis, or other points on the Mississippi river, hastened eastward to join Schofield, on learning the direction of Hood's movement.

On the 22d, Hood was reported to be approaching, within twenty miles of Pulaski, which place he had flanked on the west, by moving directly on Gaynesboro from Florence Thereupon Gen. Schofield fell back to Columbia, on the south side of the Duck river. Hood rapidly pursued, moving across to Mount Pleasant and Spring Hill, on the opposite flank, while Schofield continued his retreat, carefully covering his long trains, to Franklin. The enemy's advance was beginning to press closely on the rear of our forces, and more or less skirmishing took place between Columbia and Franklin. At Spring Hill, on the 29th, an attack was made upon the Union cavalry, which was driven in upon its infantry support, and the army was really in a critical condition, had Hood now been able to bring his main body of infantry into action. But this opportunity passed. Schofield's loss in the encounter was less than 300 men. He was not overtaken by the Rebel infantry south of Franklin, which place he reached about noon on the 30th. He had now fallen back for a distance of fifty-five miles, and was within eighteen miles of Nashville. He would have preferred to avoid a general engagement so far from the latter place, but it was now impossible. He accordingly formed his lines in a strong position, with Gen. Stanley on the right and Gen. Cox on the left, and prepared to give battle.

At four o'clock in the afternoon of the same day (the 30th of November) Schofield was vigorously attacked by two corps of the enemy (Cheatham's and Lee's.) The action continued until after dark, the Second Division of the Fourth Corps being the most hotly engaged. Hood was repulsed at all points, with very severe losses, those on the Union side being comparatively slight. The Rebel dead densely covered the ground for fifty yards in front of portions of our lines. About one thousand Rebel prisoners were taken, among whom was Gen. Gordon. The enemy's killed and wounded exceeded 5,000, including Maj.-Gen. Cleburne and five Brigadier-Generals killed, and five general officers wounded, while the Union loss was about 2,000. The great disparity of these losses will not seem remarkable when it is known that the Rebels, in dense masses—four lines deep—charged upon Schofield's line of batteries several times, being fearfully mowed down at each desperate and persistent advance, by well-directed artillery and musketry firing, often at close range. The re-enforcements under Gen. A. J. Smith arrived most opportunely, about seven o'clock in the evening.

During the night of the 30th, the Government forces were withdrawn toward Nashville, and took up a new position about three miles south of that city. The Rebels, further emboldened by this retrograde movement, confidently advanced on the next day (December 1st), and skirmishing again commenced in the evening. The Rebel cavalry had already made an attempt to cut the Chattanooga road, but without occasioning any serious interruption. Gen. Thomas had a force on his left at Murfreesboro, which was well fortified and garrisoned, Generals Milroy and Rousseau being in command, and considerable re-enforcements were moved up from Chattanooga. Gen. Cooper's brigade, and a brigade of colored troops, which garrisoned Johnsonville before its evacuation, and had been cut off from the main army, when it retired from Franklin, arrived safely at Clarksville. This retrograde movement was conducted with great skill, throughout, and was completed without any loss to Schofield's trains or artillery.

Hood established his headquarters about six miles south of

Nashville, on the Franklin pike, while his front occupied the residence of Mrs. A. V. Brown, near the lines of Thomas. They also planted a battery on a hill near the Hyde Ferry road, and extended their line of counter fortifications before Nashville, plainly visible from the State House, and from high points in the suburbs. Hood's forces were so disposed as also to threaten Murfreesboro and Chattanooga, and to prepare the way for securing the co-operation of the forces in East Tennessee, under Breckinridge. A timely movement of Gen. Burbridge, however, on the flank of Breckinridge, by Bean's Station, compelled the latter commander to retreat through Bull's Gap, early in December. Generals Stoneman and Burbridge pressed on by way of Bristol into Virginia, reaching Glade's Spring, on the railroad, thirteen miles east of Abingdon, on the 15th of December, destroying the track, and afterward ruining the principal salt works in that region of Southwestern Virginia. This raid was one of the most successful ones of the war, severing communication between Richmond and East Tennessee, and depriving the enemy of important public property.

For several days, there was some skirmishing going on around Nashville, with occasional Rebel attacks on points along the railroad toward Chattanooga. On the 4th, and several succeeding days, there was some fighting at Murfreesboro, and in the vicinity, in which the Rebels were beaten by Rousseau and Milroy. By means of careful reconnoissances, the movements of the enemy were closely watched, it being for some time uncertain whether his appearance before Nashville was not a mere demonstration to cover some other design. No purpose of crossing above Nashville could be discovered; but a force, estimated at 4,000 men, under the Rebel Lyon, passed the Cumberland, twenty miles above Fort Donelson, about the 8th of December, going into Kentucky. It became manifest, before many days, however, that Hood's forces were concentrating in earnest before Nashville. This plan of operations was the one which, of all others, Gen. Thomas was best prepared to meet. He had looked well to the defenses of the city, heretofore, and had now a strong force within his defensive lines. His left rested on the Cumberland river, eastward, while to the south-westward, on his right, he had constructed formidable works. Below, gunboats supported the lines on the right. The fortifications thus extended to the river on each side of the city, which was quite encircled with either natural or artificial defenses.

It was now determined to assume the aggressive—for Hood, who had overrun and still had at his mercy, the greater portion of Middle Tennessee, being able to support his army, for an indefinite period, off the country, evinced no haste to bring on an engagement. Gen. Thomas had disposed his forces in the following order: On the left, resting on the Cumberland, was the corps commanded by Gen. Steedman; next on the left center, the Fourth Corps, commanded by Gen. T. J. Wood (in the absence of Gen. Stanley, who was severely wounded in the battle of Franklin); on the right center, Gen. A. J. Smith's corps (two divisions), with Schofield's corps (the Twenty-Third) in reserve; and on the extreme right, was Gen. Wilson's cavalry, fighting dismounted, aided from the river by a division of the Mississippi Naval Squadron, under command of Rear-Admiral S. P. Lee.

At nine o'clock on the morning of the 15th of December, Gen. Wilson opened the battle on the right, his troops assaulting and carrying the enemy's breastworks in gallant style. The advantage was followed up, the other corps, except Steedman's, coming into action, until the enemy's left was driven from the river almost to the Franklin pike, a distance of more than five miles, and doubled upon his center and right—the center being also forced back from one to three miles. One of the most brilliant charges of the day was that made by six colored regiments on Rains' Hill, utterly routing the Rebel force which held that position. The enemy lost all his intrenchments—except for a mile or so on his extreme right, where no attack was made—sixteen pieces of artillery, the headquarters and trains of Chalmers, about 1,000 prisoners, and about 600 killed and wounded. The Union losses, this day, were not heavy, the killed and wounded numbering about 500.

Hood withdrew the right wing of his army from the river

on the night of the 15th, and took up a new position along the
" Granny White Hills," contracting his lines.   On the 16th
the attack was renewed by our forces—occupying, substantially,
the same relative position as on the previous day. As soon as
the clearing up of a dense fog disclosed the position of the
enemy, Schofield skillfully flanked the Rebel left, while Steedman advanced in front, Kimball's division impetuously sweeping the enemy from his advance works.   Thomas now ordered
a charge along the whole line, and the Rebel left and center
were completely broken.   Wood and Steedman now concentrated their forces on Hood's right, which, as yet, stood firm.
A sharp and severe contest followed, resulting in a decisive
rout of the enemy.   Hood was in full retreat soon after noon,
having suffered heavy losses in men and cannon, as well as in
the fallen left on the field in the hands of Thomas.   His killed
and wounded before Nashville were about 3,000.   The victory
gained by these two days' fighting was one of the most important of the war.   The retreating foe was vigorously pressed by
the victor, who followed Hood beyond Franklin, on the 17th,
on which day, Gen. Hatch, in a series of brilliant cavalry
charges, six miles beyond that place, dispersed the Rebel rear-
guard consisting of Stevenson's division of infantry and a
brigade of cavalry, and captured three guns and many prisoners.

Pursuit and attack were kept up for several days, by infantry
and cavalry, with disastrous effect upon the flying army, the
advance of which appears to have reached Florence and crossed
the Tennessee on the 21st, while another column moved further up stream, crossing at Bainbridge, or near the mouth of
the Elk river.   Gen. Wood, with the Fourth Corps, supported
Gen. Wilson's cavalry, in direct pursuit, while Gen. Steedman,
moving his troops by railroad to Limestone Creek, advanced
upon Decatur, on the 25th.   Hood, protecting his rear by Forrest's heavy cavalry force, escaped with little further loss to
the remnant of his army, moving back toward the interior of
Georgia.

Hood continued to make all haste in his flight, using such
strategy as he was able, to save a remnant of his command

By surrenders, desertions, and casualties in battle, he probably lost 20,000 men, or fully one-half the number with which he entered the State of Tennessee. Among his losses were eighteen general officers and sixty-eight pieces of artillery.

Beauregard had gone into Georgia, before Hood's advance into Tennessee—with the purpose of aiding in some way to interfere with Sherman's progress—his stirring appeal to the people to resist the invader having failed to produce any decisive effects. Lyon, who had gone on a raid into Kentucky, was compelled suddenly to retrace his steps, escaping southward as best he might. Tennessee and Kentucky had now seen their last invasion. Secessionists and sympathizers had suffered serious losses, as the like class had done during Price's invasion of Missouri; and in a similar manner the Rebel retreat had rid the country of many of its worst enemies, either by enlistment or conscription into the ranks of the enemy, on his haughty and exultant advance. None of these profitless expeditions were to be repeated. It was the last wave of the receding tide across a border, which was never again to be debatable ground between the armies of the Government and its Rebel enemies.

The port of Wilmington, in North Carolina, a few miles above the mouth of Cape Fear River, and the adjacent coast, were so situated as to afford great facilities to blockade-runners, whose trade had everywhere else been almost entirely broken up by the activity and vigilance of our large naval forces This continued defiance of the blockade was annoying to the Government, and a source of much advantage to the Rebels. It had long since been found that the navy could only partially interrupt this contraband traffic; but the army movements on foot had hitherto prevented the detachment of a sufficient force to warrant an attack on this strongly-guarded *entrepot* for foreign commerce with the pretended "Confederacy." The demonstrated impracticability of any effective naval operations against Richmond by the James River, rendered it expedient to employ elsewhere that portion of the North-Atlantic Squadron which had accompanied the movement of Gen. Butler to City Point. This fleet was accordingly enlarged and fitted out for an expedition against Wilmington, to be undertaken when ever the state of affairs before Petersburg and Richmond wouid warrant the detachment of an adequate supporting force from the army. Meanwhile, Admiral D. D. Porter had been transferred, in the summer of 1864, from the command of the Mississippi Squadron, to exchange places with Admiral S. P. Lee, and the naval preparations, commenced in the month of August, were under the charge of the former officer. A military force, under Gen. Weitzel, from the Army of the James, was organized and fitted out under the supervision of Gen. Butler, to co-operate in the attack on the defenses of Wilmington. The primary object of the expedition was the reduction of Fort Fisher, commanding the entrance to the Cape Fear river.

Gen. Weitzel's forces, accompanied by Gen. Butler, sailed from the Chesapeake Bay in the afternoon of the 14th of December, reaching the rendezvous the following night. Admiral Porter, waiting for the preparation of a vessel (the Louisiana), which was to be used in testing the effects of exploding a large amount of gunpowder near the Fort, did not leave Beaufort, North Carolina, until the 18th. A gale on the 20th delayed the operations of the navy. On the 23d, Commander Rhind proceeded with the Louisiana, which was disguised as a blockade-runner, to play his preliminary part in the assault on Fort Fisher. This he accomplished by making the vessel fast at four hündred yards distance from the walls of the Fort, and lighting a slow fuse. The whole accompanying party safely retired toward the fleet. The explosion took place near two o'clock on the morning of the 24th, the main fleet being about twenty-five miles distant. Admiral Porter records that "the shock was nothing like so severe as was expected." Gen. Butler believes that, of more than one hundred tons of powder on board the Louisiana—stowed in bags—"not more than one-tenth ever did burn—making an explosion, indeed, which is described as hardly more than would have been felt from a fifteen-inch gun."

This magnificent inane flash fitly pre-figured the result of the expedition. Waiting for the Louisiana to be got in readiness, wasted two or three fair days after Butler's forces were on the spot, ready for their work. Directly after Porter's arrival a severe gale compelled further delay, and the retirement of Butler's transports to Beaufort Harbor, sixty-five miles distant, where he was at the time of the great explosion, having understood that nothing was to be commenced by the Admiral without due notice to the Army. Re-enforcements from Wilmington reached Fort Fisher on the night following the Louisiana explosion.

On the 24th, about noon, Admiral Porter, without waiting for Gen. Butler to come up, attacked the Fort, his line consisting of the following vessels: The Ironsides, Canonicus, Mahopac, Monadnock, Minnesota, Colorado, Mohican, Tuscarora, Wabash, Susquehanna, Brooklyn, Powhattan, Juniata, Seneca, Shenandoah, Pawtuxet, Ticonderoga, Mackinaw, Maumee, Yantic, Kansas, Itasca, Quaker City, Monticello, Rhode Island, Sassacus, Chippewa, Osceola, Tacony, Pontoosuc, Santiago de Cuba, Fort Jackson and Vanderbilt. His reserve, of small vessels, consisted of the Aries, Howquah, Wilderness, Cherokee, A. D. Vance, Anemone, Eolus, Gettysburg, Alabama, Keystone State, Banshee, Emma, Lillian, Tristam Shandy, Britannia, Governor Buckingham and Nansemond.

After five hours' cannonading, some damage and loss of life having been suffered from the guns of the Fort, and from the explosion of a heavy gun on board the Ticonderoga, the attacking vessels withdrew. Two magazines are stated by Admiral Porter to have been exploded within the Fort, which was set on fire in several places, and its guns temporarily silenced.

Gen. Butler's forces arrived that night, and about noon on the 25th, the shore being covered by the navy, 2,200 men of his command were landed. The cannonading upon Fort Fisher had been renewed at an earlier hour the same day, and was continued while the troops were landing on the beach, five miles eastward. Gen. Weitzel advanced a skirmishing party, under cover of the bombardment, to within fifty yards of the Fort, after capturing two batteries near the beach, with a number of prisoners. After careful observation, he reported

47   62

against the expediency of attempting to carry the place by assault. The same evening, Gen. Butler ordered the troops to re-embark, and notified Admiral Porter that he should sail for Hampton Roads, as soon as the transport fleet could be put in order. He added: "The engineers and officers report Fort Fisher to me as substantially uninjured as a defensive work."

This termination of an expedition that had excited such universal interest and hope, was a great public disappointment. The want of hearty co-operation between the two branches of the service was manifest, and there is good reason to apprehend that disastrous failure would have resulted from an assault, under the circumstances then existing. On the report of Gen. Weitzel, a skillful engineer and a gallant officer, Gen. Butler could hardly do otherwise than as he did. His orders did not contemplate a siege, nor did he care, with a heavy storm approaching, to await an attack from Hoke's Division—larger than his entire force—then coming up in his rear.

Another trial was, however, determined upon, as apparently demanded by public opinion. The military forces, on this occasion larger in number, were placed under command of Maj.-Gen. Alfred H. Terry, who arrived off Fort Fisher on the night of the 12th of January, 1865. On the following day, his men were all landed, under cover of a heavy fire from the fleet. On the 14th, Gen. Terry made a careful reconnoissance, and determined to venture an attack on the Fort. The same day, he established a strong defensive line against any force of the enemy that might approach from the direction of Wilmington. This line, extending across the peninsula, was held by Gen. Paine's Division and Col. Abbott's Brigade, in all about 4,000 men, chiefly blacks. The assaulting party was to be the Division commanded by Gen. Ames, and a column of seamen and marines.

Soon after three o'clock on Sunday afternoon, the 15th of January, a heavy bombardment having been kept up for three hours previous, the assault commenced. The seamen and marines, fourteen hundred strong, led by Capt. Breese, advanced against the walls on the front, which had been considerably battered by the heavy fire of the fleet during the preceding three days, and succeeded in reaching the parapet. After a brief contest, they were checked, and thrown back in confusion. On the land side of the Fort, which was the most difficult, Curtis' Brigade, of Ames' Division, led the charge, simultaneously with that made by the men under Capt. Breese. Pennybacker's and Bell's brigades followed. The struggle was a severe one, the troops advancing little by little, under a destructive fire, but firmly maintaining their ranks, until, at five o'clock, half the land side was carried. The repulsed forces, under Capt. Breese, were then ordered to relieve Abbott's brigade, in the defensive line looking toward Wilmington, and the latter force was brought up to re-enforce the three brigades of Ames' division. The Rebel force in the Fort numbered about 2,200 men, who resisted desperately, defended successively by a series of seven traverses, each of which had to be carried by hard fighting. By signals understood between Gen. Terry and Admiral Porter, the guns of the navy rendered effective service, at intervals, by a well-directed fire—destructive to the enemy, without endangering the assailants. The conflict lasted until about ten o'clock at night, when the enemy had been driven out of the Fort and compelled to fall back to Federal Point—the extremity of the peninsula—pursued by part of the assailing force. It was near midnight when the Rebel Gen. Whiting unconditionally surrendered himself and his command, now reduced to about 1,800 in number, as prisoners of war.

The Union loss was estimated at about 800 in killed and wounded. Colonels Curtis and Pennybacker were severely, and Col. Bell mortally, wounded. Many other gallant officers fell. The Rebel loss was about 400 in killed and wounded. Both the army and navy heartily co-operated in this work, and shared its glory. The victory was hailed as one of the most important as well as brilliant of the war—hermetically sealing the great inlet heretofore so rejoiced in by the blockade-runner. It excited all the more public joy, for the disappointment which it so speedily followed.

Gen. Butler was relieved from the command of the Department of Virginia and North Carolina, on the 7th of January, and Maj.-Gen. E. O. C. Ord was appointed in his place. The organization of the Army of the James had been previously changed, by a general order of the War Department, under date of December 3d, 1864, which discontinued the Tenth and Eighteenth Corps, consolidating the white troops of those two corps into a new one called the Twenty-Fourth, and organizing the colored troops of the Department into a separate corps, called the Twenty-Fifth. Gen. Ord, by the same order, was put in command of the Twenty-Fourth, and Gen. Weitzel of the Twenty-Fifth Corps.

On the 1st of December, Gen. Gregg was sent southward, from before Petersburg, with his division of cavalry, to break up the enemy's communication by the Weldon railroad, and to destroy his supplies at Stony Creek Station, about twenty miles south from Petersburg. He captured the place on the same day, defeating the Rebel forces of infantry and cavalry, who were within defensive works and supported by artillery. Gregg captured two guns, nearly two hundred prisoners, and destroyed the depot, trains, and stores of various kinds, for the Rebel army. He also proceeded south to Duval Station, inflicting further damage, and returned safely to camp the same night.

For the purpose of still more effectually preventing the enemy from procuring supplies by the aid of the Weldon railroad, Gen. Warren's corps, with the Third Division (Gen. Mott's) of the Second Corps and Gen. Gregg's cavalry, was, a few days later (December 7th) sent down the road, destroying the track most effectually, and advancing to Hicksford, but declining to attack that place, which was strongly defended by the Rebels, occupying both sides of the Meherrin river. It appeared that one hundred cars, loaded with supplies, had passed over this part of the road every day. A general destruction of depots, mills, and other Rebel property, was made on the route passed over by Warren, who returned to his camp before Petersburg on the 12th of December. His losses were few, the principal fighting having occurred at Jarrett's Station on the return. Meanwhile, the two divisions of the Second Corps moved out toward Hatcher's Run, to the left of Meade's lines, on the 9th, to prevent the enemy from intercepting Warren's movements on the Weldon railroad, and returned the next day, without any serious engagement.

After resting nearly a month at Savannah, Gen. Sherman began a new campaign into the Carolinas, on the 15th of January. Before his arrival at Savannah, Gen. Foster had moved out from Beaufort, South Carolina, toward Grahamsville, on the Charleston and Savannah railroad, co-operating with Sherman's movement by attracting the enemy's attention to that quarter. It had been conjectured that Sherman's destination might be the harbor at Port Royal, and Foster's advance, strengthening this probability, led to the concentration of a superior Rebel force in Foster's front, under Hardee, and to his temporary repulse near Grahamsville. He gained a permanent foothold near the railroad, however, in the vicinity of Pocotaligo. At the outset of Gen. Sherman's new movement, his right wing, under Gen. Howard, was sent around by transports to Beaufort, and from thence the Seventeenth Corps, (Blair's) advanced without difficulty to the Charleston railroad, near Pocotaligo, effecting a secure lodgment there on the 15th of January. A depot of supplies was established at the mouth of Pocotaligo Creek, whence there was easy water communication with Port Royal Harbor.

The left wing of the army, commanded by Gen. Slocum, and the cavalry corps, under Gen. Kilpatrick, proceeded at the same time toward their first appointed rendezvous, near Robertsville and Coosawatchie, in South Carolina. Gen. Grant, meanwhile, had sent Grover's division of the Nineteenth Corps to garrison Savannah. He also withdrew Gen. Schofield, with the Twenty-Third Corps, from Tennessee, and sent him to the coast of North Carolina, to aid Generals Terry and Palmer, in their contemplated movement into the interior of the State, to co-operate with Sherman. Transferring the command of Savannah and its forts to Gen. Foster, who was to follow by the sea-coast to Charleston and elsewhere, as the advance of the main army might invite, Gen. Sherman embarked for Hilton Head, on the 22d of January, and there conferred with Admiral Dahlgren and Gen. Foster. On the 24th, he reached the encampment of Gen. Blair, at Pocotaligo. The Fifteenth Corps was not yet brought together—Wood's and Hazen's Divisions lying at Beaufort, Smith's marching by the coast road from Savannah, and Corse's still waiting at the latter place, his intended march having been intercepted by freshets and storms.

On the 25th, Gen. Sherman amused the enemy by demonstrating against his works on the Salkehatchie, where a line of defense had been established, on the supposition of an intended advance of the Government forces toward Charleston. Such a purpose was never entertained by Sherman. The demonstrations, having the effect to keep a considerable Rebel force in front, were continued until the freshets had so subsided on the route of Gen. Slocum as to enable him to move his forces up the Savannah river, on the west bank, to Sister's Ferry, where the crossing was for some time delayed by high water. The Fifteenth Corps entire having now arrived at Pocotaligo, and the wagon' trains being in readinesss, the march of the right wing northward toward Branchville commenced in earnest on the 1st of February.

Wheeler's cavalry had for some time previous occupied the roads to be traversed, obstructing them by felling trees and destroying bridges. Gen. Sherman's pioneer battalions, however, quickly rendered the ways passable. The Seventeenth Corps, moving directly along the right bank of the Salkehatchie, reached Rivers' Bridge on the 2d of February, while the Fifteenth Corps, at the same time moving by a route further west, arrived at Loper's Cross Roads. Gen. Hatch's division of Gen. Foster's command remained at Pocotaligo, keeping up the feint at the Salkehatchie railroad bridge and ferry, until the general movement, turning the enemy's line on that river, compelled him to fall back behind the Edisto.

From Loper's Cross Roads, communication was opened with Gen. Slocum, who was still delayed at Sister's Ferry by swamps and floods. The cavalry of Kilpatrick, and two divisions of the Twentieth Corps (Williams) had crossed to the east side of the Savannah. Hastening forward the remainder of the left wing as rapidly as possible, Gen. Williams was ordered to move on Buford's Bridge, and Gen. Kilpatrick by Barnwell Court House to Blackville, on the South Carolina railroad (from Charleston to Augusta.) Gen. Howard crossed the Salkehatchie, and moved directly toward Midway, on the same railroad. The enemy held the line of that river in force, having intrenched at Buford's and Rivers' bridges. The Seventeenth Corps crossed over by the latter, on the 3d of February, the divisions of Mower and G. A. Smith carrying the position, by wading through the swamp, nearly three miles wide, the division commander taking the lead on foot. The water was sometimes up to the breasts of the stalwart soldiers as they cheerily moved on, despite the bitter cold—many a man in the ranks, no doubt, recalling his readings of watery marches in the Netherlands, in the days of William of Orange. Effecting a lodgment below the bridge, they advanced upon the Rebel brigade which defended it, and drove the enemy in confusion toward Branchville. The Union loss was less than one hundred. The Rebels at once fell back behind the Edisto, guarding Branchville. The Seventeenth Corps pursued, menacing that place, so that the enemy burned the railroad bridge there, and also Walker's bridge below.

Sherman's whole force was now pushed along the South Carolina railroad, and proceeded to its thorough destruction, the Seventeenth Corps working from the Edisto up to Bamberg, and the Fifteenth Corps from Bamberg to Blackville. Kilpatrick moved beyond the latter point toward Aiken, demonstrating against Augusta, but avoiding any serious engagement. He had heavy skirmishing, however, both at Blackville and Aiken, with Wheeler's cavalry. These operations occupied until the 10th of February, at which date Slocum was fully up with the left wing, which continued the destruction from Blackville as far as Windsor. The whole army was now concentrated on the railroad, from Midway to Johnson's Station, being intercepted between the two portions of the enemy's forces, respectively at Augusta and Aiken westward, and at Branchville and Charleston on the east.

Blair's corps crossed the south fork of the Edisto at Binnaker's Bridge, on the 11th of February, and marched directly on Orangeburg, the Fifteenth Corps crossing at Holman's Bridge and moving to Poplar Springs, in support.   On the 12th, Blair carried the Orangeburg Bridge, in the face of stout resistance, and his whole corps entered the town at four o'clock in the afternoon.   He at once proceeded to destroy the railroad, continuing the work as far as Lewisville, and on the 14th drove the enemy across the Congaree, compelling him to burn the bridges. The left wing and the cavalry crossed the South Edisto at New and Guignard's Bridges, and proceeded to the Orangeburg and Edgefield road, awaiting the result of the movement on the former place.

After the occupation of Orangeburg, all the columns were put in motion toward Columbia.   The Seventeenth Corps moved by the State road, and the Fifteenth crossed the North Edisto.   On the 15th of February, the Fifteenth Corps encountered the enemy, in a strong position, at Little Congaree, with a *tete de pont* on the south side, and a fort on the north side, commanding the bridge.   In spite of the difficult nature of the ground, which was low and wet, the position, being skillfully turned by the division of Gen. Woods, was carried without any protracted fighting.   After nightfall, the column approached the bridge across the Congaree, in front of Columbia, and encamped in the vicinity.   During the night the enemy shelled the Union camps, from a battery above Granby, on the east side of the river.   In the morning (on the 16th), the bridge was found to have been burned.   The pontoons came up, and Gen. Howard crossed the Saluda near the factory, three miles above the city, and afterward the Broad river, approaching the city from the north, in the evening of the same day.   The left wing, under Gen. Slocum, crossed the Saluda at Zion Church, and moved directly toward Winnsboro, destroying, on his way, the railroads and bridges near Alston. The city was formally surrendered by the Mayor, on the morning of the 17th.   Wade Hampton, commanding the Rebel rear-guard of cavalry, had, in the mean time, ordered that all the cotton in the city, public and private, should be moved into the streets and burned.   The wind was blowing with fury, and the bales of cotton opened and fired, were piled in every direction, and the city in general conflagration, as Sherman's forces entered. Much of the town was burned in spite of the exertions of the Union soldiers.

During the day, the Fifteenth Corps passed through the place. The entire left wing and the cavalry passed some distance to the left, not coming within two miles of the city. The Seventeenth Corps, also, passed outside of the limits of the town, moving north-eastward toward Cheraw. In regard to the burning of Columbia, Gen. Sherman makes the following official statement:

Before one single public building had been fired by order, the smoldering fires, set by Hampton's order, were re-kindled by the wind, and communicated to the buildings around. About dark they began to spread, and got beyond the control of the brigade on duty within the city. The whole of Wood's division was brought in, but it was found impossible to check the flames, which, by midnight, had become unmanageable, and raged until about four A. M., when, the wind subsiding, they were got under control. I was up nearly all night, and saw Generals Howard, Logan, Wood, and others, laboring to save houses and protect families thus suddenly deprived of shelter, and of bedding and wearing apparel. I disclaim, on the part of my army, any agency in this fire; but, on the contrary, claim that we saved what of Columbia remains unconsumed. And, without hesitation, I charge Gen. Wade Hampton with having burned his own city of Columbia, not with a malicious intent, or as the manifestation of a silly "Roman stoicism," but from folly and want of sense, in filling it with lint, cotton, and tinder. Our officers and men on duty worked well to extinguish the flames; but others not on duty, including the officers who had long been imprisoned there, rescued by us, may have assisted in spreading the fire after it had once begun, and may have indulged in unconcealed joy to see the ruin of the capital of South Carolina. During the 18th and 19th the arsenal, railroad depots, machine shops, founderies, and other buildings were properly destroyed by detailed working parties, and the railroad track torn up and destroyed down to Kingsville and the Wateree Bridge, and up in the direction of Winnsboro.

Gen. Slocum reached Winnsboro on the 21st of February. The Twentieth Corps reached the Catawba, at Rocky Mount, on the 22d, and crossed over on a pontoon bridge the next day.

Kilpatrick's cavalry passed the same bridge during the night of the 23d, in the midst of a heavy storm of rain, and moved up to Lancaster, keeping up the appearance of a general advance toward Charlotte, N. C., on which place Beauregard and all the Rebel cavalry had retreated. Cheatham's corps, of Hood's army, returned from his disastrous campaign in Tennessee, was also known to be endeavoring to join Beauregard at the same place, having been cut off by Sherman's rapid march upon Columbia and Winnsboro.

Heavy rains and swollen streams rendered further movements nearly impracticable, until the 26th, on which day the Twentieth Corps reached Hanging Rock, there waiting for the Fourteenth to come up. On its arrival, the entire left wing was put in motion on the road to Cheraw, toward which point the right wing was already considerably advanced. The Seventeenth Corps had crossed by Young's Bridge, and the Fifteenth by Tiller's and Kelly's Bridges—detachments from the latter corps having entered Camden—ground already historic—and burned the railroad bridge over the Wateree, destroying stores and other public property. Detentions of the right wing at Lynch's Creek enabled the left to make up nearly all the time it had relatively lost in getting across the Catawba, and on the 2d of March, the advance division of the Twentieth Corps entered Chesterfield, encountering some slight resistance from Rebel cavalry. On the 3d, the Seventeenth Corps entered Cheraw, the Rebel force there retiring across the Pedee river and burning the bridge.

Meanwhile, these movements in the interior, in connection with the previous operations on the coast, and especially the capture of Fort Fisher, had rendered comparatively easy the work of successively occupying Charleston and Wilmington. Columbia was taken on the 17th of February, as already seen, and on the 18th Charleston was evacuated by the Rebel garrison, and taken possession of by Gen. Gillmore. This result was hastened by an advance of Union forces on the Edisto and from Bull's Bay. Among the captures of Rebel property were about two hundred pieces of artillery and a good supply of ammunition. The cotton warehouses, arsenals, army stores, and railroad bridges were burnt by the enemy, as well as two iron-clad boats, and a number of vessels in the ship-yard. Universal joy, throughout the loyal States, was manifested at the final subjugation of a city, in which was hatched the deadliest treason the world ever saw. The fearful retribution had come at last, and possession of the place revealed a picture of desolation beyond what the fancy, musing on "poetic justice," had as yet fully conceived.

On evacuating the city, a considerable quantity of ammunition and many cannon had been removed by the Rebels to Cheraw—not then apparently threatened—where they fell into the hands of Gen. Sherman.

On the coast of North Carolina, Gen. Schofield assumed command of the forces of the Department, on arriving with his corps from Tennessee, Gen. Terry taking command of a corps under him. Possession had already been gained of the remaining works near the mouth of Cape Fear river, but no serious advance was made upon Wilmington until the 11th of February. Meanwhile, in pursuance of a plan formed before the fall of Fort Fisher, to occupy and restore the railroad from Newbern toward Waynesboro and Raleigh, and to move a column by this route inland from the coast, co-operating with Sherman's army, a construction party, with a supporting force, was landed at the former place, under the direction of Gen. Schofield. On the morning of February 11th, the divisions of Gen. Ames and Gen. Paine, near Fort Fisher, attacked the Rebel lines across the peninsula, between Cape Fear river and the sea, and drove back the enemy. On the 17th, Gen. Schofield, with 8,000 men, advanced from Smithville, on the west side of the Cape Fear river, supported by a portion of Admiral Porter's fleet, and on the following day captured Fort Anderson and adjacent works, the last defenses of Wilmington. While the guns played upon the fort in front, Major-Gen. Cox led a force, by a circuit of sixteen miles, around the right flank of the enemy, completely turning his position, causing his immediate evacuation of the works assailed, and his retreat to Wilmington. On the 21st, our forces had a successful engagement, four miles from town, which resulted in its speedy occupation by Gen. Schofield.   The columns moving from the seaboard were to concentrate at Goldsboro, as pre-arranged with Gen. Sherman.

After a brief delay at Cheraw, Gen. Sherman resumed his march, passing into North Carolina and moving toward Fayetteville.   His right wing crossed the Pedee river at Cheraw, and his left and cavalry at Sneedsboro.   The Fourteenth and Seventeenth Corps entered Fayetteville on the 11th of March, driving back Wade Hampton's cavalry, which covered the rear of Hardee's forces, as they retreated across the Cape Fear river, burning the bridge behind them.   The next three days were passed at Fayetteville, during which the arsenal, including a large amount of machinery from the old armory at Harper's Ferry, were completely destroyed, as well as much other valuable property of use to the enemy.

The Rebel forces, hitherto successfully separated by Gen. Sherman in his march—those under Beauregard, including Cheatham's brigade, driven aside to Charlotte, as well as the troops which had garrisoned Augusta, and those under Hardee, which had escaped across the Cape Fear river—were now getting in a condition to form a junction with Johnston and Hoke, at or near Raleigh.   These several commands, united under Johnston—one of the most skillful of the Rebel generals—with a combined cavalry force superior to that under Kilpatrick, would constitute a formidable army, fighting on familiar ground against an invading force without a "base." By trusty scouts, Sherman opened communication with Gen. Terry, now in command at Wilmington, and with Gen. Schofield at Newburn, apprising them of his situation and plans. Communication was also opened by a gunboat, which now ran up to Fayetteville.   Both Schofield and Terry were ordered to advance at once on Goldsboro, toward which place Sherman himself moved on the 15th of March, first feigning an advance on Raleigh.   Kilpatrick moved out accordingly, on the road to Averysboro, followed by four divisions of Slocum's command, accompanied by Gen. Sherman, in person.   On the 16th—Kilpatrick having had some heavy skirmishing with the enemy's rear-guard, three miles beyond Kyle's Landing—the

Rebels were found in a fortified position, covering a point where the road branches off through Bentonville to Goldsboro. It was apparent to the commanding General that Hardee, whose force was estimated at 20,000 men, had made a stand here, on the narrow, swampy neck between Cape Fear and South rivers, in the hope of gaining time for a concentration of the various forces under Johnston, at some point beyond, toward Goldsboro. It became expedient, therefore, to dislodge the enemy as promptly as possible, and was necessary, as well for the purpose of continuing the feint on Raleigh, as of securing the use of the Goldsboro road. After a conflict, chiefly difficult from the nature of the ground, over which horses could not move, and which yielded to the steps of the men—two or three charges by brigades, and some artillery firing by a well-posted battery, comprising the sum of all—the enemy was forced back from his first and second lines, and made his escape in the darkness of the ensuing night. It was soon found that he had retired by the Smithfield road, and not toward Raleigh. The only Union forces engaged were portions of the Twentieth and Fourteenth Corps, the command of Gen. Slocum, who reported his losses as twelve officers and sixty-five men killed, and 476 wounded. The enemy left 108 dead on the field, his whole loss probably exceeding 700. Such was the battle of Averysboro, fought on the 16th day of March.

The left wing now took the Goldsboro road. Howard's column and the trains were already moving in the same direction on the right; Kilpatrick watching the right flank. Slocum encamped on the night of the 18th, at a point where the road from Clinton to Smithfield crosses the Goldsboro road, twenty-seven miles from Goldsboro, and five from Bentonville. Howard was at Lee's store, two miles south, and both wings had pickets thrown out for three miles, to where the two roads united in one. Not anticipating any further opposition, Howard was directed to advance, on the 19th, along the new Goldsboro road, by Falling Creek Church, while Sherman proceeded to join this column in person, desiring to open communications with the converging columns of Schofield and Terry, advancing from Newbern and Wilmington. Slocum had not gone far before Carlin's division, in the advance, encountered Dibbrell's division of Rebel cavalry, supported by infantry, which gained some advantage over him; and soon after it appeared that he was confronted, near Bentonville, by the whole of Johnston's army in position, under that officer in person. Sherman speedily made his dispositions for battle. Couriers from Schofield and Terry arrived at this juncture, reporting that the former was at Kingston, and could reach Goldsboro by the 21st, and that Terry was at or near Faison's Depot, some thirty miles south of Goldsboro, on the Wilmington railroad. Orders were issued to these commanders, with a view to secure their most effective co-operation, at the earliest moment, in the battle now pending.

Meanwhile, Slocum had protected himself by a line of barricades, and remained on the defensive, having with him but four divisions, to which the cavalry of Kilpatrick was added, after the latter had heard the sounds of battle. In this position, six successive charges were made on the left, by the combined forces of Hardee, Cheatham and Hoke, under the direction of Johnston himself. Each attack was repulsed, with heavy loss to the enemy. During the night of the 19th, the two divisions guarding the wagon train arrived, together with Hazen's division of the Fifteenth Corps, enabling Gen. Slocum to make his position secure. Gen. Howard, on advancing the Fifteenth Corps to form a connection with Slocum, found that Johnston's left occupied a strong position, fortified by a line of parapets across the Goldsboro road, thus interposing a barrier between Sherman's two wings. Howard, however, succeeded in forming a connection with Slocum's right, without engaging the enemy. Before nightfall, on the 20th, Sherman's united forces, in a strong line of battle, had Johnston on the defensive. On the 21st, Gen. Schofield entered Goldsboro without serious opposition, and Gen. Terry reached the Neuse river, ten miles above Goldsboro. The three armies were thus brought into communication, within supporting distance of each other—a triumphant success of the various movements.

During the day, on the 21st, it rained steadily, but Mower's division of the Seventeenth Corps, on the extreme right, gradually moved around on the enemy's flank, and had nearly reached the bridge over Mill Creek, Johnson's only line of retreat now left open. To prevent Mower from being overwhelmed by a superior force of the enemy, Sherman ordered his skirmishers to attack along the whole line, while Mower regained his connection with his own corps. During the night, the enemy retreated on Smithfield, leaving his pickets, with many unburied dead, and his wounded men in the field hospitals to fall into Sherman's hands. Pursuit was made for two miles beyond Mill Creek, on the morning of the 22d, and then suspended. Johnston had been completely foiled in his main attempt, and decisively beaten. Slocum reported his total losses at the battle of Bentonville, in killed, wounded and missing, as 1,247. Howard's entire losses numbered only 399—making an aggregate Union loss of 1,646. The Rebel dead, buried by our forces, numbered 267, and his entire loss in prisoners was 1,625—making an aggregate of 1,892. Johnston must have lost heavily, in addition to the foregoing, in his attacks on the left wing, on the 19th.

Sherman had now full possession of Goldsboro, accomplishing his purpose, and his forces thus combined constituted an army irresistible by any force that could be brought against him. He had now communications by the two railroads, rapidly put in running order, with the seaboard at Beaufort and Newbern.

Before Petersburg, Gen. Meade had continued to keep a strong hold upon Lee, breaking his communications, and extending the Union lines on the left. The effective fighting under Gen. Sheridan, in the Shenandoah Valley, had rendered the longer maintenance of any large force there unnecessary. The Sixth Corps had returned to Petersburg not long after the decisive engagements in the late autumn, and was assigned a position on the left, affording the opportunity for a further advance of Meade's lines toward the Southside railroad. The most important movement undertaken by the Army of the Potomac since the movement on the Weldon road under Warren and Gregg, in December, was that which resulted in the battle of Hatcher's Run, on the 6th and 7th of February, and by which the Rebel communications by the Boydton Plank road were broken. The Fifth, and a portion of the Sixth Corps, were engaged in this movement, the Third division of the Fifth Corps suffering heavily. Its aggregate loss in killed and wounded was 594. The losses in the Sixth Corps, acting mainly as a supporting column, were slight.

It was now manifest that the main Rebel armies under Lee and Johnson were becoming inextricably involved in the toils of Grant and his Generals. Only some unforeseen cause, or some serious blunder, could long delay the final termination of the struggle. A conference was now held at City Point, between President Lincoln, Lieut.-Gen. Grant, and Gens. Meade, Sherman, and other leading commanders, on the 27th of March. The closing movements were now fully considered and planned, with incidental discussions of the general policy to be pursued in the final exigencies ; and the several Generals returned to their commands, prepared to strike the last blows, and confident of their effect.

To President Lincoln, saddened and worn by four years of a strife so relentless and painful, the prospect of peace near at hand was inexpressibly gladdening. To each of the war-worn Generals, the culmination of all his cares and toils in a grand choral triumph, was a joyful hope that made music in his heart, as he moved away to his closing task.

CHAPTER X.

THE morning of the 4th of March, 1865, was dark with clouds and rain. The previous stormy night Mr. Lincoln, with the members of his Cabinet, remained at the President's room, in the north wing of the capitol, until a late hour, considering and signing bills which came thronging upon him, in the usual manner, during the closing hours of a Congress soon to be dissolved. The President had a somewhat care-worn look, but a cheerfulness of manner, manifesting itself in occasional pleasantry, or in the relation of some suggested incident or anecdote, as was his wont in his most seriously earnest moods. He had a genial word for occasional visitors, and a ready ear, as always, for whatever had any fair claim to his attention. Without a word as to the morrow, or as to the momentous hours of an eventful term of service now just

48

closing, his furrowed face spoke to the casual observer of sober thoughts, not unmingled with conscious satisfaction, in looking back upon the work of the four years of his unceasing watchfulness and assiduity in the service to which his country had called him. Some talked hopefully of brighter hours for the intended pageant of the coming day. To him, long used to more real and penetrating storms, the passing shadows and mists of a day seemed of no concern. More inspiring were the thoughts of an abiding calm and of the lasting sunshine of peace. But, again, he knew that with the close of the desolating strife of armed men in the field, a new struggle was to begin—one that must precede and accompany the evolution of order and repose from the chaos existing throughout the rebellious districts. For had he not clearly enunciated, four years ago, this undeniable truth: "Suppose you go to war, you can not fight always; and when, after much loss on both sides, and no gain on either, you cease fighting, the identical questions as to terms of intercourse are again upon you." In the angry commotion, excited by self-willed agitators, these persuasive words had passed unheeded. Battle had come, and had done its fearful work. The aggressors were about to yield to the national power they had defied. The "questions" at issue were already settled in part, yet much remained for the clear head, kind heart, and strong hand of the re-elected Chief Magistrate of the people.

While the President was thus waiting at the capitol, there came to the Secretary of War a telegraphic dispatch from Gen. Grant, announcing that the Rebel Gen. Lee had sought an interview with the Lieutenant-General, for the purpose of arranging terms of peace. It is now known that Lee had for several months despaired of any final success in the unholy work which he had deserted the United States Army to engage in, and that he prudently desired to end the war, accepting the best terms that could be made. This was a proposition to which Davis himself, then, as at the last moment, could only speak of with impatience. From his message to the Rebel Congress, however, it appears that the telegram to Gen. Grant, just mentioned, was sent with Davis' knowledge. He avers that one of his Commissioners at the Hampton Roads Conference, suggested to President Lincoln that his objections to treating with the "Confederate Government," or with any State by itself, might be avoided by adopting the method sometimes employed of a military convention, to be entered into by the commanding generals of the armies of the two belligerents—almost a precise foreshadowing of the mode sub sequently suggested to Gen. Sherman by Johnston and Breckinridge. This suggestion, Davis distinctly says, was not accepted by Mr. Lincoln. In the same message, Davis alleges that advances were afterward made by Gen. Ord to Longstreet, intimating the possibility of arriving at a satisfactory adjustment by means of a military convention, and that if Lee desired an interview on this subject, it would not be declined, if Lee were clothed with authority to act in the premises. He further states that Lee wrote to Gen. Grant, on the 2d of March, informing him that he was vested with the requisite authority for such negotiation.

It was Lee's letter, thus referred to, that formed the subject of Gen. Grant's dispatch to President Lincoln. This dispatch, Mr. Stanton informs us, "was submitted to Mr. Lincoln, who, after pondering a few minutes, took up his pen and wrote with his own hand the following reply, which he submitted to the Secretary of State and Secretary of War. It was then dated, addressed, and signed by the Secretary of War, and telegraphed to Gen. Grant: "

WASHINGTON, March 3, 1865, 12 P. M.

Lieutenant-General Grant:

The President directs me to say to you that he wishes you to have no conference with Gen. Lee, unless it be for the capitulation of Gen. Lee's army, or on some minor and purely military matter. He instructs me to say that you are not to decide, discuss, or confer upon any political question. Such questions the President holds in his own hands, and will submit them to no military conferences or conventions. Meantime you are to press to the utmost your military advantages.

EDWIN M. STANTON,

Secretary of War.

The morning of Saturday, the 4th of March, found the President again at his post at the capitol, while the world outside was still dismal with the continuing storm. Many thousands had come from far and near to witness the re-inauguration of a loved President. The condition of the skies and the streets was dismal. The procession, which would otherwise, perhaps, have surpassed any previous one in numbers and show, lost much of its attraction. Yet was there never a more numerous and sympathetic turn-out of the people at any like ceremony.

A committee to notify Mr. Lincoln, in a formal manner, of his re-election, had waited on him for that purpose, and Mr. Wilson, of Iowa, reported to the House, on the evening of the 1st of March, his response, which was in the following terms:

Having served four years in the depths of a great and yet unended national peril, I can view this call to a second term in no wise more flattering to myself than as an expression of the public judgment that I may better finish a difficult work, in which I have labored from the first, than could any one less severely schooled to the task. In this view, and with assured reliance on that Almighty Ruler who has so graciously sustained us thus far, and with increased gratitude to the generous people for their continued confidence, I accept the renewed trust, with its yet onerous and perplexing duties and responsibilities.

As the hour of twelve arrived, and the two Houses of Congress were declared finally adjourned, the rain had ceased, and a vast throng of citizens, with battalions of soldiers, white and black, stood in front of the stand erected at the east front of the capitol, awaiting the approach of the procession from the Senate Chamber. Meanwhile, Hon. Andrew Johnson had taken the oath of office as Vice-President, in presence of the compact audience assembled on the floor and in the galleries of the Senate. The new Senate, called by the President to meet in special session for Executive business, had organized. At twenty-five minutes past twelve o'clock, Mr. Lincoln, having now closed the Presidential labors of his first term, entered the Senate Chamber, accompanied by a committee of Senators and Representatives. The procession moved to the eastern portico in the following order: The Marshal of the District of Columbia; the Ex-Vice-President; the Supreme Court of the United States; the Sergeant-at-Arms of the Senate; the President of the United States, the President elect; the Vice-President and the Secretary of the Senate; the members of the Senate; the Diplomatic Corps; heads of Departments; Governors of States and Territories; the Mayors of Washington and Georgetown, and other persons admitted to the floor of the Senate Chamber.

As President Lincoln stepped upon the platform to address the many thousands present, the bright sunlight, hitherto obscured through all the morning, broke from the clouds, as if by miracle, and illuminated his face and form, as he bowed acknowledgment to the boisterous greeting of the people. With wonder and joy, the multitude accepted the omen as something more than unmeaning chance. The long hours of rain and cloud were over. The city roofs and spires, the trees and lawns, the hills and woods farther away, and all the landscape around were gladdened as with the freshness of the first created light.

Standing in this presence, with a clear voice, mellowed by the emotion of the hour and by the slightly plaintive tone usually pervading his utterances, Mr. Lincoln delivered the following

INAUGURAL ADDRESS.

Fellow-Countrymen:

At this second appearing to take the oath of the Presidential office, there is less occasion for an extended address than there was at the first. Then, a statement, somewhat in detail, of a course to be pursued, seemed fitting and proper. Now, at the expiration of four years, during which public declarations have been constantly called forth on every point and phase of the great contest which still absorbs the attention and engrosses the energies of the nation, little that is new could be presented. The progress of our arms, upon which all else chiefly depends, is as well known to the public as to myself; and it is, I trust, reasonably satisfactory and encouraging to all.

With high hope for the future, no prediction in regard to it is ventured.

On the occasion corresponding to this four years ago, all thoughts were anxiously directed to an impending civil war. All dreaded it; all sought to avert it. While the inaugural address was being delivered from this place, devoted altogether to *saving* the Union without war, insurgent agents were in the city seeking to *destroy* it without war—seeking to dissolve the Union, and divide effects, by negotiation. Both parties deprecated war; but one of them would *make* war rather than let the nation survive; and the other would *accept* war rather than let it perish. And the war came.

One-eighth of the whole population were colored slaves, not distributed generally over the Union, but localized in the southern part of it. These slaves constituted a peculiar and powerful interest. All knew that this interest was, somehow, the cause of the war. To strengthen, perpetuate, and extend this interest was the object for which the insurgents would rend the Union, even by war; while the Government claimed no right to do more than to restrict the territorial enlargement of it. Neither party expected for the war the magnitude or the duration which it has already attained. Neither anticipated that the *cause* of the conflict might cease with, or even before, the conflict itself should cease. Each looked for an easier triumph, and a result less fundamental and astounding. Both read the same Bible, and pray to the same God; and each invokes His aid against the other. It may seem strange that any men should dare to ask a just God's assistance in wringing their bread from the sweat of other men's faces; but let us judge not, that we be not judged. The prayers of both could not be answered; that of neither has been answered fully. The Almighty has His own purposes. "Woe unto the world because of offenses! for it must needs be that offense come; but woe to that man by whom the offenses cometh." If we shall suppose American slavery is one of those offenses which, in the providence of God, must needs come, but which, having continued through His appointed time, He now wills to remove, and that He gives to both North and South this terrible war, as the woe due to those by whom the offense came, shall we discern therein any departure from those divine attributes which the believers in a living God always ascribe to Him? Fondly do we hope, fervently do we pray, that this mighty scourge of war may speedily pass away. Yet, if God wills that it continue until all the wealth piled by the bondman's two hundred and fifty years of unrequited toil shall be sunk, and until every drop of blood drawn with the lash shall be paid by another drawn with the sword, as was said three thousand years ago, so still it must be said, " The judgments of the Lord are true and righteous altogether."

With malice toward none, with charity for all, with firmness in the right, as God gives us to see the right, let us strive on to finish the work we are in; to bind up the nation's wounds; to care for him who shall have borne the battle, and for his widow, and his orphan; to do all which may achieve and cherish a just and a lasting peace among ourselves and with all nations.

The oath of office was then administered to the President by Chief Justice Chase. Reverberating cannon, saluting the re-inaugurated Chief Magistrate, and giving voice to the people's joy, announced the close of the brief ceremony. The address, in the grand setting of events before and after, has an imperishable luster, and a priceless worth—to be recognized wherever the tongue in which it is written is known. Compared with that of four years previous, it shows the same kindly forbearance and good-will toward his enemies, the same yearning for restored harmony under the equal laws of a free republic. Yet wide was the contrast between the two addresses, and between the two occasions. He was no longer the comparatively inexperienced statesman, entering upon a position of unexampled trials, undertaking to lead the people, at their command, through a wilderness of untold dangers to the State. He had gained the last ridge, and paused to converse with them on the duties remaining, as they entered the longed-for land. Then, he had been willing, for the sake of peace—although he had ever felt that " if slavery was not wrong, nothing was wrong "—to leave the removal of this evil to the slow processes of time, through the convictions of those sustaining it, and the formalities of legislation; but now he rejoiced in his own decisive act, which had summarily ended this great wrong, striking down at once the cause and the support of the Rebellion. Then, he had taken his official oath before a Chief Justice whose most memorable act was an attempt, by a political decision, to render impregnable the bulwarks of slavery. Now, he was sworn by a Chief Justice who believed that no inherent right of manhood was dependent on the hue of the skin, or on the accident of birth. Before, treason was rampant, and armed Rebels gathering in Charleston, where the germ of secession had been for thirty years developing into sturdy growth. The same Charleston, almost a ruin, was now under the heel of the military power it had insulted, and proud South Carolina was overrun, from border to border, by unsparing Western soldiery. Four years—the most wonderful the nation had ever seen, or, perhaps, ever may see—years into which the ordinary history of generations had been condensed, had made the name of ABRAHAM LINCOLN more famous and enduring than any other American name in his century. As the procession returned from the Capitol to the White House, but little after midday, hundreds of persons were gazing upward at a bright star, visible in the heavens—not less marvelous than the favorable sunlight omen. A phenomenon so rare—to many spectators altogether unknown hitherto—was the subject of universal comment.

The public reception at the White House, on Saturday evening, was attended by perhaps greater numbers than ever before. The day had closed without serious accident. Vague rumors had been in the air of a plot of assassination, to culminate on that day; but no disorder of any kind occurred. Political opponents, heretofore the most hostile, now outwardly seemed quietly to assume the attitude of reverent acquiescence in the renewed leadership of the Chosen One of the people, the Elect of Providence.

Hon. William P. Fessenden, having been elected a Senator from the State of Maine, for the term of six years, commencing on the 4th of March, 1865, had resigned his office as Secretary of the Treasury, to take his seat in the Senate on that day. Mr. Fessenden had assumed the always responsible and trying position of Finance Minister, at a time of peculiar difficulty, when the country was comparatively depressed, in view of heavy losses in war without decisive victories, and when a heavy conscription impending, with its burdensome demands upon the Treasury, added to the heretofore severe strain upon the financial capabilities of the Government. Despite all the criticism and captiousness incident to such a time, Mr. Fessenden, by the even tenor of his course—avoiding hazardous experiments and visionary resorts—passed safely through the ordeal, and left to his successor no harder task than that he had himself assumed when taking the office. President Lincoln selected Hon. Hugh McCulloch, of Indiana, to fill the place made vacant by Senator Fessenden's resignation—an appointment not only promptly confirmed by the Senate, but cordially approved by the people. Judge McCulloch had organized the Currency bureau, and perfected the working of the National Bank system originated by Gov. Chase; and his later labors, as Secretary of the Treasury, have been attended with such marked success as to insure him a reputation in the office scarcely inferior to that of either of his predecessors under Mr. Lincoln's Administration.

This appointment of another Cabinet officer from Indiana, led to the resignation of Mr. Usher as Secretary of the Interior, to take effect on the 15th of May. Mr. Lincoln appointed Hon. James Harlan, a Senator from Iowa, to fill this vacancy, and his nomination, which was eminently satisfactory to the country, was at once confirmed by the Senate, on the 9th of March, in advance of the time at which he was to enter upon his duties at the head of the Department of the Interior. No other changes occurred in the constitution of Mr. Lincoln's Cabinet, at his entrance upon his second term of office.

The called session of the Senate terminated on the 11th of March. A large proportion of the nominations sent into that body, during this brief session, were promotions in the army and navy. Few changes were made in civil offices, the President having determined to adopt no general system of "rotation." The Executive Mansion was, however, thronged by unusual numbers, during the first two or three weeks, and his time continually occupied with visitors, on manifold business, the variety and amount of which was such as no President before him ever grappled with, or would have conceived as within the range of possible attention. Much of this tax upon his time and vital energy was levied for the mere personal interests of either the visitor himself, or some importunate friend or constituent. Mr. Lincoln was uniformly indulgent to such appeals, when made in no offensive manner; and a

64

positive element of the wasting weariness which these incessant calls occasioned him, was the sympathetic regret he felt
for the many whom he was daily compelled to disappoint,
whom yet he would gladly have gratified. Much of this
" pressure " related to other matters than official appointments.
Most of it was, perhaps, as unavoidable by the visitor, as it
was deemed to be by the President. But it was not, on this
account, any the less exhausting. These, and other cares of
graver sort, were manifestly telling upon his physical condition.
For some days prior to the 15th of March, he was obliged to
deny himself to visitors altogether. To those who had the
opportunity of occasionally meeting him, when in his office,
this change was doubtless generally apparent. It may be
readily seen by all who compare his photographic likenesses,
taken in the early part of the year 1864, with those of February and March, 1865. Not a little of this change was probably due to the anxieties he had continuously felt, and to the
labors he had undergone, in connection with the great military campaigns of the past twelve-month, which were now
near a final consummation.

On the 17th of March, Mr. Lincoln was present at the presentation to Gov. Morton, of Indiana, of a flag captured at
Fort Anderson, near Wilmington, by Indiana troops. The
ceremony occurred at the National Hotel, and the President,
responding to the request of those present, made the following
memorable speech from the balcony :

FELLOW CITIZENS : It will be but a very few words that I
shall undertake to say. I was born in Kentucky ; raised in
Indiana, and live in Illinois [laughter], and I now am here,
where it is my business to be, to care equally for the good people of all the States. I am glad to see an Indiana regiment on
this day able to present this captured flag to the Governor of
the State of Indiana. I am not disposed, in saying this, to
make a distinction between the States, for all have done equally
well.

There are but few views or aspects of this great war upon
which I have not said or written something, whereby my own
views might be made known. There *is* one : the recent
attempt of our erring brethren, as they are sometimes called
[laughter], to employ the negro to fight for them. I have

neither written nor made a speech upon that subject, because that was their business and not mine; and if I had a wish upon the subject, I had not the power to introduce it or make it effective.

The great question with them was, whether the negro, being put into the army, will fight for them. I do not know, and, therefore can not decide. [Laughter.] They ought to know better than we, and do know. I have in my life-time heard many arguments why the negro ought to be a slave; but if they fight for those who would keep them in slavery it will be a better argument than any I have yet heard. He who will fight for that ought to be a slave. [Applause]. They have concluded, at last, to take one out of four of the slaves and put him in the army; and that one out of the four, who will fight to keep the others in slavery, ought to be a slave himself, unless he is killed in a fight. While I have often said that all men ought to be free, yet I would allow those colored persons to be slaves who want to be; and, next to them, those white men who argue in favor of making other people slaves. I am in favor of giving an opportunity to such white men to try it for themselves. [Applause.]

I will say one thing with regard to the negro being employed to fight for them that I do know. I know he can not fight and stay at home and make bread too. [Laughter and applause.] And as one is about as important as the other to them, I don't care which they do. I am rather in favor of having them try them as soldiers. They lack one vote of doing that, and I wish I could send my vote over the river, so that I might cast it in favor of allowing the negro to fight. [Applause.] But they can not fight and work both. We must now see the bottom of the enemy's resources. They will stand out as long as they can, and if the negro will fight for them, they must allow him to fight. They have drawn upon their last branch of resources, and we can now see the bottom. [Applause]. I am glad to see the end so near at hand. [Applause.] I have said now more than I intended to, and will therefore bid you good-by.

Partly to break away from the throngs at the White House, and to recuperate his strength, but perhaps still more from the impulse which had several times before induced him to visit the army at important crises, Mr. Lincoln determined to pass some time at the headquarters of Gen. Grant, at Petersburg. It is scarcely necessary to say that his presence with the army in the field, was not, in this or any other instance, for the purpose of assuming any supervision of military affairs. He found a relief in an interchange of views with the commanding general, perhaps often not without profit to the latter, and a satisfaction in gaining such an exact knowledge of affairs as could only be obtained on the ground. More hopeful of an early consummation of decisive results than at any previous hour, his mind was now, in spite of all distracting influences, intently fixed on the chief work of disarming treason and ending the deplorable work of war.

It was a period of joyous hope to the whole country, now eagerly watching the culmination of a series of widely-extended, but harmonious movements. From New Orleans, and from points above, on the Mississippi river, expeditions were penetrating the Gulf States eastward—partly cavalry raids, and partly detachments for the occupation of State capitals or other prominent towns in the great cotton region. Sherman, having already overrun Georgia and the Carolinas, was uniting with the armies of Schofield and Terry, at Goldsboro, N. C., and preparing to occupy Raleigh, as well as to envelop and crush the army of Johnston. Sheridan's cavalry force was sweeping down from the Shenandoah Valley, by Charlottsville, thoroughly breaking the Virginia Central Railroad, destroying the James river canal, isolating Lynchburg, and cutting off all communications further west, as, while moving down upon Richmond, creating universal panic there, as he passed around to join Grant and Meade. Ord's army was holding its advance line, in the positions so gallantly carried at Fort Harrison and Chapin's Farm, months before.

The army under Gen. Meade, which had constantly occupied Lee, giving his forces no release through the winter, while all the remoter and more active operations were going forward, and while events were rapidly sweeping on to a central consummation, was now ready to strike the final blows for which it had awaited the fitting time. From the moment that Grant assumed the general control, the enemy had had no moment's respite. Neither summer's heat, nor winter's cold; neither drenching rains, nor "horrible" roads; neither insufficiency of supplies, nor the want of re-enforcements; neither heavy losses, nor temporary disappointments; no difficulty, no hazard, no subterfuge had prevented the irresistible onward tread and ceaseless pressure of our glorious legions upon the chief armies and the vital centers of the rebellion. For once, Mr. Lincoln's purpose had been fairly carried out. The Rebels had been given no coveted season for recuperation. The damage inflicted, they were allowed no leisure to repair. And thus the end was at hand.

President Lincoln was present at the memorable interview at Gen. Grant's Headquarters, at City Point, on the evening of the 27th of March, when the final movements in Virginia and North Carolina were arranged. Generals Meade, Sherman, Sheridan and Ord were among the leading commanders who participated in this conference. The terms to be made with the enemy, when decisively conquered, were, it may be presumed, incidentally considered, and Mr. Lincoln's policy, as definitely announced in the dispatch of Gen. Grant, of the 3d of March, already given, was left in full force. The military commanders were given no authority in making peace or establishing a basis of State re-organization, beyond the mere act of disarming and disbanding the Rebel forces. In regard to the conditions of surrender, a liberal course was deemed advisable, as may be inferred from the subsequent action of Gen. Grant.

It is not even alleged by Gen. Sherman, whose subsequent action was inconsistent with that of Gen. Grant, and with Mr. Lincoln's order of March 3d, that any authority was delegated to the military commanders, at this interview, or any other time, to enter into negotiations for peace. When examined before the Committee on the Conduct of the War, he explains his action in at first recognizing the Rebel State government of North Carolina, by stating that President Lincoln encouraged him to a similar course with the Governor of Georgia, when he (Sherman) was at Atlanta. He says he had " never received one word of instruction, advice or counsel, as to the plan or policy of the Government, looking to a restoration of peace on the part of the Rebel States of the South." In another part of his testimony, however, while still conceding that, at the time of his armistice with Johnston, he " did not know what the views of the Administration were" in regard to " reconstruction," he says : " Mr. Lincoln, up to that time, in letters and by telegrams to me, encouraged me, by all the words which could be used in general terms, to believe, not only in his willingness, but in his desire that I should make terms with civil authorities, Governors and Legislatures, even as far back as 1863." It is, therefore, plainly inferable that this subject was not formally discussed at the conference of the 27th of March. That no authority on these matters was delegated by the President to the military commanders, is thus apparent from Gen. Sherman's testimony. It is obvious that the views which might have been entertained by Mr. Lincoln in regard to the terms to be made with Gov. Brown, of Georgia, in order to detach him from the Rebellion, at the particular juncture named, might well be different from those he would contemplate after another long period of active warfare, and the Rebel armies were surrendered from necessity, and not by voluntary submission. But from what is otherwise known of Mr. Lincoln's policy on this subject, it may be fairly presumed that Gen. Sherman was under a misapprehension, in supposing that under any circumstances the Rebel State government of Georgia would have been recognized as legitimate.

This conference with the Generals was not a protracted one, for they had important work in hand. Sherman was back at Goldsboro on the 30th, and the combined forces under his command were soon in readiness to move against Johnston, whose army, much inferior in numbers, was concentrated about Smithfield, on the Neuse river, nearly half way to Raleigh. Sherman, however, awaited the result of the impending movement of Meade's forces against Lee.

Gen. Sheridan's cavalry, consisting of the First and Third Divisions, under the immediate command of Gen. Merritt, having marched from Winchester, cut all Lee's communications westward, effectually destroying his most important medium for transporting supplies—the James River Canal— crossed the James at Jones' Landing, on the 26th of March, and went into camp at Hancock's Station, near Petersburg, on the 27th. The Second Cavalry Division, under Gen. Crook, now reported to Sheridan, who was under the immediate command of Grant, increasing his force to an aggregate of 9,000. McKenzie's division of the Army of the James, 1,000 strong, reported to him on the 1st of April. On the 29th, Sheridan moved out by way of Reams' Station, and thence across Rowanty Creek, to Dinwiddie Court House, where his main force encamped for the night. On the morning of the 30th, the First Division, under Gen. Devin, was sent to gain possession of the Five Forks, on the White Oak road. The enemy was discovered, by reconnoissance, to be in strong force near this vicinity, and heavy skirmishing occurred before nightfall. On the 31st, the advance of the First Division reached the Five Forks, after serious opposition. In the mean time, the Second and Fifth Corps (respectively commanded by Generals Humphreys and Warren), by direction of Gen. Grant, crossed Hatcher's Run on the 29th. On the 30th, both corps further advanced, with some unimportant fighting, pressing the enemy's lines. On the 31st, Gen. Ayres' Division was sent by Warren to dislodge the enemy on the White Oak road. Ayres was repulsed and driven back upon Crawford, whose division in turn broke, and both retreated in some confusion to the position occupied by Griffin. The enemy then ceased pursuit, and rapidly turned upon Sheridan at Five Forks and Dinwiddie Court House, and threatened a movement in flank and rear upon the lines of Humphreys and Warren. A severe battle followed, in which the enemy's entire cavalry force and two divisions of infantry were kept in check by Sheridan's cavalry. During the night, Warren's corps was ordered by Gen. Grant to report to Sheridan, whose headquarters were now at Dinwiddie Court House.

On the 1st of April occurred the brilliant action at the Five Forks, in which the cavalry and the Fifth Corps, Sheridan commanding the combined forces, achieved an important victory. The enemy was driven back by the cavalry to the Five Forks, and forced within his works, while a feint was made of turning his right—the real purpose being to get between this force and Petersburg, and to cut off retreat. The design was well carried out, infantry and cavalry moving vigorously to

their work, and fighting with valor, under the inspiring presence of a popular commander. The enemy at length fled in
disorder, his artillery was captured, and over 5,000 prisoners
were taken. The fugitives were pursued for six miles by cavalry, being driven westward.

Meanwhile, the Sixth and Ninth Corps, under Generals
Wright and Parke, had remained in front of Petersburg.
After consultation with Gen. Grant, on the 1st of April, Gen.
Meade, believing that the enemy's forces before Petersburg
had been much reduced to meet the operations on the left,
ordered an attack by the Sixth and Ninth Corps on the lines
in their front, at four o'clock the following morning. Meanwhile the soldiers were jubilant over the news received the
same evening, of the victory at the Five Forks. The Sixth
Corps attacked at the hour appointed, driving the enemy at
all points, and capturing his strong works, with many guns
and prisoners. After reaching the Boydton plank road, Gen.
Wright turned to the left, sweeping down the Rebel line of
intrenchments nearly to Hatcher's Run, where he met the
Twenty-fourth Corps (two divisions), under Gen. Gibbon,
which had come in on the left. Wright then returned by the
plank road toward Petersburg, where he met the enemy in an
inner line of works immediately around the city. He deployed
his corps in front of these works, and was joined by the
Twenty-fourth and part of the Second Corps. Gen. Parke
also attacked the works in his front, at four o'clock on the
same Sunday morning, and carried the first line, capturing guns
and prisoners ; but was unable to carry the remaining works.
At three o'clock, the enemy had disappeared from the front of
Wright and Parke, and, on advancing, they found Petersburg
evacuated. Gen. Wilcox's division, of the Ninth Corps was
left to occupy Petersburg, and the Sixth Corps, with portions
of the Second and Ninth, at once moved up the Appomattox
river, reaching Sutherland's Station the same evening.

Sunday, the 2d of April, was a memorable day for Richmond
and the Rebellion. As the people of that city went to church
in the morning, they knew that during the last two or three
days there had been fighting on Lee's right, and among their

impressions of the result, that of a defeat of Meade's Fifth Corps was the most vivid. Not even Jefferson Davis or Gov. Smith, though better informed, had any thought, on that morning, that the last day of their power in Richmond had come. Davis was quietly seated in his pew. Prayers had been said. The reverend pastor had begun his discourse. Presently the sexton, moving softly up the aisle, put a telegraphic dispatch in the hand of the "Confederate President." That functionary rose, and, followed by many inquiring but not startled eyes, stalked out of the sanctuary. The discourse went on to the end, and the concluding exercises, even to the collection, were not omitted. The news was then broken to the minister, and speedily spread among his flock. The lines before Petersburg had been broken through by Grant's whole army, and Lee had apprised his superior that Richmond must be evacuated. Davis and his chief associates moved away that night toward Danville. On the following morning, Gen. Weitzel's colored troops, of the Army of the James, entered the city, which was now wrapped in flames kindled by Rebel hands. Despite the efforts of the soldiers to extinguish the conflagration, an important portion of the city was destroyed.

President Lincoln, who was awaiting at City Point the results of the movement commenced on the 29th of March, transmitted, successively, the following dispatches to Secretary Stanton :

CITY POINT, VA., April 2—8.30 A. M.

Hon. Edwin M. Stanton, Secretary of War :

Last night Gen. Grant telegraphed that Gen. Sheridan, with his cavalry, and the Fifth Corps, had captured three brigades of infantry, a train of wagons, and several batteries—prisoners amounting to several thousand. This morning, Gen. Grant, having ordered an attack along the whole line, telegraphs as follows :

"Both Wright and Parke got through the enemy's lines. The battle now rages furiously. Gen. Sheridan, with his cavalry, the Fifth Corps, and Miles' division of the Second Corps, which was sent to him since one o'clock this morning, is now sweeping down from the west."

All now looks highly favorable. Gen. Ord is engaged, but I have not yet heard the result in his front.

A. LINCOLN.

CITY POINT, VA., April 2, 1865—11 A. M.

Hon. Edwin M. Stanton, Secretary of War :

Dispatches frequently coming in. All going finely. Parke, Wright and Ord, extending from the Appomattox to Hatcher's Run, have all broken through the enemy's intrenched lines, taking some forts, guns and prisoners.

Sheridan, with his own cavalry, Fifth Corps and part of the Second, is coming in from the west on the enemy's flank, and Wright is already tearing up the Southside railroad.

A. LINCOLN.

CITY POINT, VA., April 2, 1865—2 P. M.

Hon. Edwin M. Stanton, Secretary of War :

At 10.45 A. M., Gen. Grant telegraphs as follows:

"Everything has been carried from the left of the Ninth Corps. The Sixth Corps alone captured more than 3,000 prisoners. The Second and Twenty-fourth Corps, both captured forts, guns and prisoners from the enemy, but I can not tell the numbers. We are now closing around the works of the line immediately enveloping Petersburg. All looks remarkably well. I have not yet heard from Sheridan."

His headquarters have been moved up to T. Banks' house near the Boydton road, about three miles south-west of Petersburg.   A. LINCOLN.

Later in the day, the President telegraphed—sending some further details from Gen. Grant:

All seems well with us, and everything quiet just now.

A. LINCOLN.

The news of the evacuation of Petersburg, and soon after, of the occupation of Richmond by Union troops, was received at Washington on the morning of the 3d of April. Expectation had been excited by the cheering dispatches of the previous day, and the decisive intelligence was not a surprise; yet never before was there witnessed at the National Capital any scene to be compared with the present spontaneous manifestations of joy. The streets were speedily filled; everybody was abroad, business was suspended, flags waved on every side, bands played national airs, batteries thundered in token of the universal delight. Processions visited the War Department. Vice

President Johnson, Secretary Seward, Secretary Stanton, and other public men, made speeches in answer to the calls of many thousands of jubilant listeners. A deep feeling of religious gratitude seemed to move the hearts of all speakers and all listeners, underlying all the superficial demonstrations of popular gladness. It was not the mere exultation of triumph over a fallen foe. In those ever-memorable hours, there was a gentle spirit of clemency diffused among the people, such as had but now become consciously present. To the colored race, the "jubilee" appeared indeed to have come—an hour earnestly longed for, and now welcomed with childlike exhilaration.

Similar was the reception of the news in all the great cities, and throughout the loyal portion of the land. Even those who least sympathized with the Government, found cause for gratification in the immediate prospect of peace. The joy was truly universal.

While the people were rejoicing over the capture of Richmond, Gen. Grant and the armies with him were eagerly endeavoring to make an end of the army of Lee, without which the work was incomplete. Anticipating the prompt retreat of the enemy from Richmond, Grant did not wait for " official information " that he was gone, but threw his men at once westward toward Burkesville, moving with great celerity, in order to intercept his retiring march. Sheridan, with the Fifth Corps, led the van. His cavalry pursued the forces retreating from Petersburg, routing the Rebel cavalry and taking many prisoners, on the 3d of April. During the two following days Grant's entire force, except those left in garrison at Petersburg, and the Ninth Corps, guarding the Southside railroad, was moving along the river and Namozine roads, the Second and Sixth Corps following after the Fifth, which was preceded by the cavalry.

On the 4th, learning from scouts that a body of the enemy was at Amelia Court House, a concentration at that point being probable, Sheridan ordered Crook's cavalry division to strike the Danville railroad between Jettersville and Burke's Station, advancing toward the former place. The Fifth Corps moved rapidly up to that point, and the fact was soon settled that Lee, with his whole army, was there, his retreat to Burkes-ville Junction having thus been intercepted.   He now endeav-ored to strike across the country by way of Deatonsville to Farmville, on the Lynchburg road.   The cavalry and the Sixth and Second Corps encountered Ewell's corps at Sailor's creek, on the 6th, surrounded it, and captured nearly all the force, including Ewell and other general officers.   On the 7th, the Fifth Corps was moved to the left, toward Prince Edward's Court House, south-west of Farmville.   The Second Corps continued the direct pursuit, coming up with the enemy at High Bridge, across the Appomattox, capturing eighteen of his guns.   Gen. Barlow's division advanced to the left, found the enemy evacuating Farmville, and hastened his movement by attacking the place.

Pursuit was continued on the 8th, by the Lynchburg stage road, and on the following day at noon, the advance of the Second Corps came up with the enemy, three miles from Appo-mattox Court House.   Meanwhile, Gen. Sheridan's cavalry had succeeded in getting beyond that point, on the 8th, and having reported the situation, with an urgent request for infan-try support, the Fifth and Twenty-Fourth Corps, with one division of the Twenty-Fifth, arrived in position on the Lynch-burg side of the enemy, who was now surrounded.

Gen. Grant, in the meantime, had sent the following note to the Rebel General-in-Chief, there being " no relaxation in the pursuit :"

April 7th, 1865.

Gen. R. E. Lee, Commanding C. S. A.:

GENERAL : The result of the last week must convince you of the hopelessness of further resistance on the part of the Army of Northern Virginia in this struggle.   I feel that it is so, and regard it as my duty to shift from myself the responsi-bility of any further effusion of blood, by asking of you the surrender of that portion of the Confederate army known as the Army of Northern Virginia.

Very respectfully, your obedient servant,
U. S. GRANT, Lieutenant-General,
Commanding Armies United States.

To this the subjoined reply was received:

April 7, 1865.

To Lieut.-Gen. U. S. Grant, Commanding Armies of the United States:

GENERAL: I have received your note of this date. Though not entirely of the opinion you express of the hopelessness of the further resistance on the part of the Army of Northern Virginia, I reciprocate your desire to avoid useless effusion of blood, and, therefore, considering your proposition, ask the terms you will offer on condition of its surrender.

R. E. LEE, General.

The remainder of this memorable correspondence is as follows:

GEN. GRANT TO GEN. LEE.

April 8, 1865.

Gen. R. E. Lee, Commanding C. S. A.:

GENERAL: Your note of last evening, in reply to mine of same date, asking conditions on which I will accept the surrender of the Army of Northern Virginia, is just received. In reply, I would say that peace being my first desire, there is but one condition I insist upon, viz.:

That the men surrendered shall be disqualified for taking up arms against tke Government of the United States until properly exchanged. I will meet you, or designate officers to meet any officers you may name for the same purpose, at any point agreeable to you, for the purpose of arranging definitely the terms upon which the surrender of the Army of Northern Virginia will be received.

Very respectfully, your obedient servant,

U. S. GRANT, Lieutenant-General.

GEN. LEE TO GEN. GRANT.

April 8, 1865.

GENERAL: I received at a late hour your note of to-day, in answer to mine of yesterday. I did not intend to propose the surrender of the Army of Northern Virginia, but to ask the terms of your proposition. To be frank, I do not think the emergency has arisen to call for the surrender of this army, but as the restoration of peace should be the sole object of all, I desire to know whether your proposals would tend to that end. I can not, therefore, meet you with a view to surrender the Army of Northern Virginia; but as far as your proposition may affect the Confederate States forces under my command, and tend to the restoration of peace, I should be pleased to meet you at 10 A. M. to-morrow, on the old stage road to Richmond, between the picket lines of the two armies.

Very respectfully, your obedient servant,

R. E. LEE, General,

Confederate States Army.

Lieut.-Gen. U. S. GRANT, Commanding United States Armies.

GEN. GRANT TO GEN. LEE.

April 9, 1865.

Gen. R. E. Lee, Commanding C. S. A.:

GENERAL: Your note of yesterday is received. As I have no authority to treat on the subject of peace, the meeting proposed for 10 A. M. to-day could lead to no good. I will state, however, General, that I am equally anxious for peace with yourself, and the whole North entertains the same feeling. The terms upon which peace can be had are well understood. By the South laying down their arms they will hasten that desirable event, save thousands of human lives; and hundreds of millions of property not yet destroyed.

Sincerely hoping that all our difficulties may be settled without the loss of another life, I subscribe myself, very respectfully,

Your obedient servant,

U. S. GRANT, Lieutenant-General.

GEN. LEE TO GEN. GRANT.

April 9, 1865.

GENERAL: I received your note of this morning on the picket line, whither I had come to meet you, and ascertain definitely what terms were embraced in your proposition of yesterday. With reference to the surrender of this army, I now request an interview, in accordance with the offer contained in your letter of yesterday for that purpose.

Very respectfully, your obedient servant,

R. E. LEE, General.

Lieut.-Gen. U. S. GRANT, Commanding United States Armies.

GEN. GRANT TO GEN. LEE.

April 9, 1865.

Gen. R. E. Lee, Commanding Confederate States Army:

Your note of this date is but this moment, 11.50 A. M., received, in consequence of my having passed from the Rich-

mond and Lynchburg road to the Farmville and Lynchburg
. road. I am at this writing about four miles west of Walter's
Church, and will push forward to the front for the purpose of
meeting you. Notice sent to me on the road where you wish
the interview to take place will meet me.

Very respectfully, your obedient servant,

U. S. GRANT, Lieutenant-General.

TERMS PROPOSED BY GEN. GRANT.

APPOMATTOX C. H., April 9, 1865.

Gen. R. E. Lee, Commanding C. S. A.:

In accordance with the substance of my letter to you of the
8th inst., I propose the surrender of the Army of Northern
Virginia on the following terms, to wit:

Rolls of all the officers and men to be made in duplicate;
one copy to be given to an officer to be designated by me, the
other to be retained by such officer or officers as you may
designate. The officers to give their individual paroles not to
take arms against the Government of the United States until
properly exchanged, and each company or regimental commander to sign a like parole for the men of their commands.
The arms, artillery, and public property to be packed and
stacked, and turned over to the officers appointed by me to
receive them. This will not embrace the side arms of the
officers, nor their private horses or baggage. This done, each
officer and man will be allowed to return to their homes, not
to be disturbed by United States authority so long as they
observe their parole and the laws in force where they may
reside.

Very respectfully,

U. S. GRANT, Lieutenant-General.

GEN. LEE'S ACCEPTANCE OF THE TERMS.

HEADQUARTERS ARMY NORTHERN VIRGINIA, }
April 9, 1865. }

Lieut -Gen. U. S. Grant, Commanding United States Armies:

GENERAL: I have received your letter of this date, containing the terms of surrender of the Army of Northern Virginia, as proposed by you. As they are substantially the same
as those expressed in your letter of the 8th inst., they are
accepted. I will proceed to designate the proper officers to
carry the stipulations into effect.

Very respectfully, your obedient servant,

R. E. LEE, General.

The intelligence of Lee's surrender put the seal of certainty on what was confidently hoped the week before. The main army of the rebellion, the only one that had successfully resisted the advance of our forces for any long period, was now disarmed and disbanded. All other insurgent forces must quickly succumb. PEACE was at last secured. Enthusiastic exhibitions of glad emotion were renewed, with even greater earnestness, and with a thankfulness more devout, than on the fall of the Rebel capital.

On the 4th of April, the day after Gen. Weitzel entered Richmond, President Lincoln visited that city. On arriving, he proceeded at once to the headquarters of the commanding general, which happened to be the late residence of Jefferson Davis. The appearance of Mr. Lincoln in Richmond might well excite universal attention and remark. He walked from the landing to headquarters—not a little distance—with but few attendants. Nor was his presence unknown, as he passed along the streets, for crowds came out to see him. By a portion of the residents, he was received with enthusiasm—by the negroes universally with their customary manifestations of uncontrollable emotion. He received calls of respect from many army officers and Richmond citizens, holding a sort of levee in the parlor of the late Rebel Executive. Subsequently, he rode through the city, looking at the burnt district, the Libby prison, and other objects of special interest. At night he slept on board one of the gunboats lying in the James. On the 4th, and again on the 5th, he had protracted interviews with Gen. Weitzel, and also with Judge Campbell, formerly a Judge of the Supreme Court of the United States, and recently Assistant Secretary of War to Jefferson Davis. The Ex-Judge had been one of the Rebel conferees at Hampton Roads, and was now more anxious than ever about terms of peace and re-organization. It was finally understood that Gen. Weitzel should permit the assembling of a number of the leading men of Virginia, to consult as to the re-establishment of a State government. It was manifestly not agreed to by Mr. Lincoln, however, that the Pierpoint government or the Alexandria free constitution should be set aside, and much less that William Smith and the Rebel State Legislature should be recognized.

On the 5th, the President returned to City Point. On the same day, Mrs. Lincoln, accompanied by Attorney-General Speed, Senator Harlan, and other friends, left Washington to join him. The two following days were occupied in visiting Petersburg, the scenes of military operations in the vicinity, and other interesting localities. Mr. Lincoln, meanwhile, was occasionally receiving dispatches from Gen. Grant, whose headquarters were now at Burkesville, announcing the progress of military events. These dispatches were in turn transmitted to the Secretary of War—the last one, announcing the brilliant victory at Sailor's Creek, having been sent from City Point on the morning of April 7th.

Mr. Lincoln passed most of the day, on the 8th of April, in visiting the sick and wounded soldiers in hospital at City Point. He said to the Medical Director that he had come to see the boys who had fought the battles of the country, and particularly the battles which resulted in the evacuation of Richmond. He expressed his desire to take these men by the hand, as it would probably be his last opportunity of meeting them. Though his will was good to see them in Washington, on their return from the war homeward, it would be impossible for him to meet so many of them again. The Medical Director had at first proposed some particular places for the President to visit, and was surprised to learn the extent and impartiality of his intentions. Mr. Lincoln devoted the entire day to shaking hands with over six thousand soldiers, many of them fresh from the fields of battle, and to giving them such words of cheer and sympathy, as the circumstances from time to time suggested. "It was," says one who visited the hospital the same day, "like the visit of a father to his children, and was appreciated in the same kindly spirit by the soldiers. They loved to talk of his kindness and unaffected manner, and to dwell upon the various incidents of this visit, as a green spot in the soldier's hard life. At one point in his visit he observed an ax, which he picked up and examined, and made some pleasant remark about his having once been considered a good chopper. He was invited to try his hand upon a log of wood lying near, from which he made the chips fly in primitive style. The 'boys' seemed to worship him; and the visit of the President to City Point Hospital will long be remembered by many a soldier who was only too happy in its enjoyment."

On the evening of the same day—Saturday, April 8th—the fate of Lee's army not being yet definitely known to him, but its capture a well assured result, Mr. Lincoln embarked on his way back to Washington, with Mrs. Lincoln and accompanying friends. During the voyage, he was at times occupied in reading the tragedy of Macbeth, a favorite drama in which he seemed now to take an unusual interest. Some passages he read aloud to the friends near him, adding remarks on the peculiar beauties that most impressed his mind. He dwelt particularly on the following lines, which he read with feeling, and again read, giving emphasis to his admiration:

> " Duncan is in his grave,
> After life's fitful fever he sleeps well;
> Treason has done his worst; nor steel, nor poison,
> Malice domestic, foreign levy, nothing
> Can touch him further."

President Lincoln, almost on the first occupation of Richmond, had visited the city—amid many anxious misgivings of his friends—but slightly guarded, for two days appearing more or less in the streets where his name had so lately been rarely mentioned except in scorn or hate. He was now returning homeward unharmed, gliding quietly along the Potomac, surrounded only by friends. Did a thought of coming danger visit him? To many hearts it was a relief to know that he had safely reached the White House, on Sunday evening, having witnessed the triumph of weary years of war. Late at night came the tidings which gladdened the land, and which on the morrow was to open again—more widely if possible, than on the preceding Monday—the floodgates of gladness. Lee had surrendered.

On the 10th of April, the country was jubilant with the glad tidings. The streets of the national capital again overflowed with enthusiastic crowds. Reverberations of cannon were heard in city, town, and hamlet throughout the land. Millions of flags were dancing to the movements of the winds. *Te Deum* was sung in New York, and thanksgiving notes of " peace on earth, good-will to men," in audible strain, or in the silent rhythm of the heart, swelled in one grand harmony through all the nation. A day which none now living can ever forget: a day which future generations will think of, bu never adequately imagine.

An unnumbered throng gathered before the White House, while cannon were resounding, and bands playing, and voices spontaneously joining in choral accompaniment. Mr. Lincoln, in response to the calls of the besieging multitude, appeared at the window above the main entrance, amid excited demonstrations of affectionate respect. Declining at this moment to make any extended speech, he only said:

I am very greatly rejoiced that an occasion has occurred so pleasurable that the people can't restrain themselves. I suppose that arrangements are being made for some sort of formal demonstration, perhaps this evening or to-morrow night. If there should be such a demonstration I, of course, shall have to respond to it, and I shall have nothing to say if I dribble it out before. [Laughter and cries of " We want to hear you now," etc.] I see you have a band. [Voices, " We have three of them."] I propose now closing up by requesting you to play a certain air, or tune. I have always thought " Dixie " one of the best tunes I ever heard. [Laughter.]

I have heard that our adversaries over the way have attempted to appropriate it as a national air. I insisted yesterday that we had fairly captured it. I presented the question to the Attorney General, and he gave his opinion that it is our lawful prize. [Laughter and cheers.] I ask the band to give us a good turn upon it.

" Dixie " was played with a vigor suited to the temper of the people, Mr. Lincoln still remaining at the window. As the music ceased, he proposed " three good, rousing, hearty cheers for Lieut.-Gen. Grant and all under his command," which were given. He then called for " three more cheers for our gallant navy," which were no less energetically given. The President then bowed and retired.

Considerable numbers were assembled in front of the Execu·
tive Mansion at several times during the day.   After five
o'clock in the evening, he again appeared at the window, in
answer to repeated calls of a large crowd, and made the following speech :

MY FRIENDS : I am informed that you have assembled
here this afternoon under the impression that I had made an
appointment to speak at this time.   This is a mistake.   I have
made no such appointment.   More or less persons have been
gathered here at different times during the day, and in the
exuberance of their feeling, and for all of which they are
greatly justified, calling upon me to say something, and I have,
from time to time, been sending out what I supposed was
proper to disperse them for the present. [Laughter and
applause.]

I said to a larger audience this morning which I desire now
to repeat.   It is this : That I supposed in consequence of
the glorious news we have been receiving lately, there is to be
some general demonstration, either on this or to-morrow evening, when I will be expected, I presume, to say something.
Just here, I will remark, that I would much prefer having
this demonstration take place to-morrow evening, as I would
then be much better prepared to say what I have to say than
I am now or can be this evening.

I therefore say to you that I shall be quite willing, and I
hope ready, to say something then ; whereas just now I am
not ready to say anything that one in my position ought to
say.   Everything I say, you know, goes into print. [Laugh-
ter and applause].   If I make a mistake it doesn't merely
affect me, or you, but the country.   I, therefore, ought at
least try not to make mistakes.

If, then, a general demonstration be made to-morrow evening, and it is agreeable, I will endeavor to say something, and
not make a mistake, without at least trying carefully to avoid
it. [Laughter and applause].   Thanking you for the compliment of this call, I bid you good evening.

On the evening of Tuesday, April 11th, Mr. Lincoln was
serenaded ; and the general expectation of a somewhat elaborate speech, giving a definite foreshadowing of his future
policy in regard to the Rebel States, attracted a very large
gathering of the people.   The remarks he designed to make
on this occasion were carefully written out, and will be ever

memorable as the final words of political counsel which he has left as a legacy to his country.

MR. LINCOLN'S LAST SPEECH.

We meet this evening not in sorrow, but in gladness of heart. The evacuation of Petersburg and Richmond, and the surrender of the principal insurgent army, give hope of a righteous and speedy peace, whose joyous expression can not be restrained. In the midst of this, however, He from whom all blessings flow must not be forgotten. A call for a national thanksgiving is being prepared, and will be duly promulgated. Nor must those whose harder part gives us the cause of rejoicing be overlooked. Their honors must not be parceled out with others. I myself was near the front, and had the high pleasure of transmitting much of the good news to you; but no part of the honor, for plan or execution, is mine. To Gen. Grant, his skillful officers and brave men, all belongs. The gallant navy stood ready, but was not in reach to take active part.

By these recent successes, the re-inauguration of the national authority, reconstruction, which has had a large share of thought from the first, is pressed much more closely upon our attention. It is fraught with great difficulty. Unlike the case of a war between independent nations, there is no authorized organ for us to treat with. No one man has authority to give up the rebellion for any other man. We simply must begin with and mold from disorganized and discordant elements. Nor is it a small additional embarrassment that we, the loyal people, differ among ourselves as to the mode, manner and means of reconstruction.

As a general rule, I abstain from reading the reports of attacks upon myself, wishing not to be provoked by that to which I can not properly offer an answer. In spite of this precaution, however, it comes to my knowledge that I am much censured from some supposed agency in setting up and seeking to sustain the new State Government of Louisiana. In this I have done just so much as, and no more than, the public knows. In the annual message of December, 1863, and accompanying proclamation, I presented a plan of reconstruction (as the phrase goes), which I promised, if adopted by any State, should be acceptable to, and sustained by, the Executive Government of the nation. I distinctly stated that this was not the only plan which might possibly be acceptable ; and I also distinctly protested that the Executive claimed no right to say when or whether members should be admitted to seats in Congress from such States. This plan was, in advance, submitted to the then

Cabinet, and distinctly approved by every member of it. One of them suggested that I should then, and in that connection, apply the Emancipation Proclamation to the theretofore excepted parts of Virginia and Louisiana ; that I should drop the suggestion about apprenticeship for freed people, and that I should omit the protest against my own power, in regard to the admission of members of Congress, but even he approved every part and parcel of the plan which has since been employed or touched by the action of Louisiana.

The new Constitution of Louisiana, declaring emancipation for the whole State, practically applies the proclamation to the part previously excepted. It does not adopt apprenticeship for freed people, and it is silent, as it could not well be otherwise, about the admission of members to Congress. So that, as it applies to Louisiana, every member of the Cabinet fully approved the plan. The message went to Congress, and I received many commendations of the plan, written and verbal ; and not a single objection to it, from any professed emancipationist, came to my knowledge, until after the news reached Washington that the people of Louisiana had begun to move in accordance with it. From about July, 1862, I had corresponded with different persons, supposed to be interested, seeking a reconstruction of a State government for Louisiana. When the message of 1863, with the plan before mentioned, reached New Orleans, Gen. Banks wrote me he was confident that the people, with his military co-operation, would reconstruct substantially on that plan. I wrote him, and some of them, to try it. They tried it, and the result is known. Such only has been my agency in getting up the Louisiana government. As to sustaining it, my promise is out, as before stated. But, as bad promises are better broken than kept, I shall treat this as a bad promise, and break it, whenever I shall be convinced that keeping it is adverse to the public interest. But I have not yet been so convinced.

I have been shown a letter on this subject, supposed to be an able one, in which the writer expresses regret that my mind has not seemed to be definitely fixed on the question whether the seceded States, so-called, are in the Union or out of it. It would, perhaps, add astonishment to his regret were he to learn that, since I have found professed Union men endeavoring to make that question, I have *purposely* forborne any public expression upon it. As appears to me, that question has not been, nor yet is, a practically material one, and that any discussion of it, while it thus remains practically immaterial, could have no effect other than the mischievous one of dividing our friends. As yet, whatever it may hereafter become, that question is bad, as the basis of a controversy, and good for nothing at all—a merely pernicious abstraction. We all agree that the seceded States, so-called, are out of their proper practical relation with the Union, and that the sole object of the Government, civil and military, in regard to those States, is to again get them into that proper practical relation. I believe it is not only possible, but in fact easier to do this without deciding, or even considering, whether these States have ever been out of the Union, than with it. Finding themselves safely at home, it would be utterly immaterial whether they had ever been abroad. Let us all join in doing the acts necessary to restoring the proper practical relations between these States and the Union, and each forever after innocently indulge his own opinion whether, in doing the acts, he brought the States from without into the Union, or only gave them proper assistance, they never having been out of it.

The amount of constituency, so to speak, on which the new Louisiana government rests, would be more satisfactory to all if it contained fifty, thirty, or even twenty thousand, instead of only about twelve thousand, as it really does. It is also unsatisfactory to some that the elective franchise is not given to the colored man. I would myself prefer that it were now conferred on the very intelligent, and those who serve our cause as soldiers. Still the question is not whether the Louisiana government, as it stands, is quite all that is desirable. The question is " Will it be wiser, to take it as it is, and help to improve it, or to reject and disperse it?" "Can Louisiana be brought into proper practical relation with the Union *sooner* by *sustaining* or by *discarding* her new State government?"

Some twelve thousand voters, in the heretofore slave State of Louisiana, have sworn allegiance to the Union, assumed to be the rightful political power of the State, held elections, organized a State government, adopted a free State constitution, giving the benefit of public schools equally to black and white, and empowering the Legislature to confer the elective franchise upon the colored man. Their legislature has already voted to ratify the constitutional amendment recently passed by Congress, abolishing slavery throughout the nation. These twelve thousand persons are thus fully committed to the Union, and to perpetual freedom in the States—committed to the very things and nearly all the things the nation wants—and they ask the nation's recognition and its assistance to make good that committal. Now, if we reject and spurn them, we do our utmost to disorganize and disperse them. We, in effect, say to the white men, "You are worthless, or worse, we will neither help you, nor be helped by you." To the blacks we say, " This cup of Liberty which these, your old masters, hold to your lips, we will dash from you, and leave you to the chances of gathering the spilled and scattered contents in some vague and undefined when, where and how." If this course, discouraging and paralyzing both white and black, has any tendency to bring Louisiana into proper practical relations with the Union, I have, so far, been unable to perceive it. If, on the contrary, we recognize and sustain the new government of Louisiana, the converse of all this is made true.

We encourage the hearts and nerve the arms of the twelve thousand to adhere to their work, and argue for it, and proselyte for it, and fight for it, and feed it, and grow it, and ripen it to a complete success. The colored man, too, seeing all united for him, is inspired with vigilance, and energy, and daring to the same end. Grant that he desires the elective franchise, will he not attain it sooner by saving the already advanced steps towards it, than by running backward over them? Concede that the new government of Louisiana is only to what it should be as the egg is to the fowl, we shall sooner have the fowl by hatching the egg than by smashing it. [Laughter]. Again, if we reject Louisiana, we also reject one vote in favor of the proposed amendment to the National Constitution. To meet this proposition, it has been argued that no more than three-fourths of those States, which have not attempted secession, are necessary to validly ratify the amendment. I do not commit myself against this, further than to say that such a ratification would be questionable, and sure to be persistently questioned, while a ratification by three-fourths of all the States would be unquestioned and unquestionable.

I repeat the question. "Can Louisiana be brought into proper practical relation with the Union *sooner* by *sustaining* or by *discarding* her new State government?" What has been said of Louisiana will apply generally to other States. And yet so great peculiarities pertain to each State, and such important and sudden changes occur in the same State, and, withal, so new and unprecedented is the whole case, that no exclusive and inflexible plan can safely be prescribed as to details and collaterals. Such exclusive and inflexible plan would surely become a new entanglement. Important principles may, and must, be inflexible.

In the present situation, as the phrase goes, it may be my duty to make some new announcement to the people of the South. I am considering, and shall not fail to act, when satisfied that action will be proper.

The change in the domestic situation, rendered it expedient to

FORD'S THEATER and THE HOUSE (opposite) WHERE MR. LINCOLN DIED.

67

take new ground in regard to the concession of belligerent rights to the Rebels, made by certain foreign powers. The following proclamation—issued at this time—speedily accomplished its purpose of utterly outrooting this international heresy:

BY THE PRESIDENT OF THE UNITED STATES OF AMERICA—A PROCLAMATION.

WHEREAS, for some time past, vessels of war of the United States have been refused, in certain foreign ports, privileges and immunities to which they were entitled by treaty, public law or the comity of nations, at the same time that vessels of war of the country wherein the said privileges and immunities have been withheld, have enjoyed them fully and uninterruptedly in ports of the United States; which condition of things has not always been forcibly resisted by the United States, although, on the other hand, they have not, at any time, failed to protest against and declare their dissatisfaction with the same. In the view of the United States, no condition any longer exists which can be claimed to justify the denial to them, by any one of such nations, of customary naval rights, as has heretofore been so unnecessarily persisted in.

Now, therefore, I, ABRAHAM LINCOLN, President of the United States, do hereby make known that, if, after a reasonable time shall have elapsed for intelligence of this proclamation to have reached any foreign country in whose ports the said privileges and immunities shall have been refused, as aforesaid, they shall continue to be so refused, then and henceforth the same privileges and immunities shall be refused to the vessels of war of that country in the ports of the United States, and this refusal shall continue until the war vessels of the United States shall have been placed upon an entire equality, in the foreign ports aforesaid, with similar vessels of other countries, the United States, whatever claim or pretence may have existed heretofore, are now, at least, entitled to claim and concede an entire and friendly equality of rights and hospitalities with all maritime nations.

In witness whereof, I have hereunto set my hand, and have caused the seal of the United States to be affixed.

Done at the city of Washington, this eleventh day of April, in the year of our Lord one thousand eight hundred and sixty-five, and of the Independence of the United States of America the eighty-ninth.   ABRAHAM LINCOLN.

By the President:

WILLIAM H. SEWARD, Secretary of State.

The following statement of Senator Sumner, in regard to President Lincoln's earlier views and actions on this question, with a citation of the striking terms used by him in relation thereto, has an abiding interest:

The President saw the painful consequences of this concession, and especially that it was a first step toward the acknowledgment of Rebel slavery as an independent power. Clearly, if it were proper for a foreign power to acknowledge belligerency, it might, at a later stage, be proper to acknowledge independence; and any objection vital to independence would, if applicable, be equally vital to belligerency. Solemn resolutions by Congress on this subject were communicated to foreign powers, but the unanswerable argument against any possible recognition of a new power founded on slavery—whether as independent or as belligerent—was stated by the President, in a paper which I now hold in my hand, and which has never before seen the light. It is a copy of a resolution drawn by himself, which he gave to me, in his own autograph, for transmission to one of our valued friends abroad, as an expression of his opinion on the great question involved, and a guide to public duty. It is in these words:

"WHEREAS, While heretofore states and nations have tolerated slavery, recently, for the first [time] in the world, an attempt has been made to construct a new nation upon the basis of human slavery, and with the primary and fundamental object to maintain, enlarge and perpetuate the same; therefore,

"Resolved, That no such embryo state should ever be recognized by, or admitted into, the family of Christian and civilized nations; and that all Christian and civilized men everywhere should, by all lawful means, resist, to the utmost, such recognition or admission."

On the 11th day of April, also, the President issued a proclamation closing certain ports of entry, in accordance with an act of Congress, approved July 13, 1861, "further to provide for the collection of duties on imports and for other purposes," and recognizing the fact that the blockade had been conditionally set aside or relaxed, "in consequence of actual military occupation by this Government," at Norfolk and Alexandria, Virginia; Beaufort, North Carolina; Port Royal, South Carolina; Pensacola and Fernandina, Florida, and New Orleans,

Louisiana.   The body of the proclamation, relating to the closing of Southern ports of entry, is in the following words :

" Now, therefore, be it known that I, ABRAHAM LINCOLN, President of the United States, do hereby proclaim that the ports of Richmond, Tappahannock, Cherrystone, Yorktown and Petersburg, in Virginia; of Camden (Elizabeth City), Edenton, Plymouth, Washington, Newberne, Ocracoke and Wilmington, in North Carolina; of Charleston, Georgetown and Beaufort, in South Carolina ; of Savannah, St. Marys and Brunswick (Darien), in Georgia; of Mobile, in Alabama ; of Pearl River (Shieldsborough), Natchez and Vicksburg, in Mississippi; of St. Augustine, Key West, St. Marks (Port Leon), St. Johns (Jacksonville) and Apalachicola, in Florida ; of Teche (Franklin), in Louisina ; of Galveston, La Salle, Brazos de Santiago (Point Isabel) and Brownsville, in Texas, are hereby closed, and all right of importation, warehousing and other privileges shall, in respect to the ports aforesaid, cease until they shall have again been opened by order of the President; and if, while said ports are so closed, any ship or vessel from beyond the United States, or having on board any article subject to duties, shall attempt to enter any such port, the same, together with its tackle, apparel, furniture and cargo, shall be forfeited to the United States.

President Lincoln had made repeated demands upon Great Britain for indemnity for losses to our citizens from the depredations of the Alabama, and other cruisers constructed and equipped in English ports since the commencement of the war.   Though refused by the British Government, Mr. Lincoln never relinquished the demand.   It was specially renewed at this time, with a manifest determination to press the matter to a favorable determination.

On the 11th of April, Lynchburg was surrendered to a scouting party from Griffin's division of the Fifth Army Corps, and McKenzie's brigade of cavalry was ordered to occupy the place. Gen. Sherman was now moving on Raleigh, with little opposition, Johnston falling back before him.   This advance was commenced by order of Gen. Grant, from Burkesville, with the apparent object of preventing a junction between Johnston and Lee, should the latter succeed in escaping Sheridan and getting off toward Danville.   Sherman occupied Raleigh on the 13th.   Gen. Canby captured Mobile on the following day.   Gen. Wilson, having taken Selma, was raiding through Alabama and Georgia at will.   Everywhere our arms were triumphant, and each Rebel army—it was now certain—must speedily follow the example of that in Virginia, under the Rebel General-in-Chief.   President Lincoln accordingly determined on an immediate reduction of the military force in the field, as announced in the following dispatch:

WAR DEPARTMENT, WASHINGTON, }
April 13, 1865—6 P. M.   }

Maj-Gen. Dix, New York:

The Department, after mature consideration and consultation with the Lieutenant-General upon the results of the recent campaign, has come to the following determination, which will be carried into effect by appropriate orders, to be issued immediately:

1. To stop all drafting and recruiting.
2. To curtail purchases for arms, ammunition, Quartermaster and Commissary supplies, and reduce the expense of the military establishment in its several branches.
3. To reduce the number of general and staff officers to the actual necessities of the service.
4. To remove all military restrictions upon trade and commerce, so far as it may be consistent with public safety.

As soon as these measures can be put in operation, it will be made known by public order.

EDWIN M. STANTON,
Secretary of War

In the evening of the 13th, the city of Washington was brilliantly illuminated, in honor of the great victories achieved, and in recognition of the near approach of peace.

On the 14th day of April, at the regular meeting of the Cabinet, the mode of dealing with the Rebel States and people was discussed at some length.   President Lincoln expressed himself decidedly in favor of lenient measures with the great mass of the offenders, and found, it is understood, no discordant opinion in his council.   The re-organization of the revolted States was determined upon substantially in accordance with the principles heretofore acted on in Virginia, Missouri and Louisiana—almost the identical policy since carried into effect.

The order of Gen. Weitzel, at Richmond, practically recognizing the disloyal Virginia Legislature, and William Smith as Governor of the State, was revoked by the President, who manifestly can not have intended to vest any authority of this sort in the military commander at Richmond, or to annul his former recognition of the Pierpoint Government.

On the same day—the cycle of war having now revolved quite around to its starting point—the flag hauled down from Fort Sumter, four years before, was again run up by the hand of Gen. Robert Anderson, who was then compelled to surrender the Fort to traitors; Henry Ward Beecher represented New England ideas in the city of Charleston; and William Lloyd Garrison spoke there, as he listed, of slavery.

The grand sweep of events since the 4th of March—six swift weeks—culminating in the complete downfall of the Rebellion, the unresisting submission of the traitors, the re-occupation and possession of all the Government forts, the destruction of slavery, and the restoration of peace, had, at length, under the guidance of a good Providence, crowned the Administration of Abraham Lincoln with immortal honor. His earnest grapple with the monster treason, that struck at the nation's life, had never relaxed until the work was done. It only remained that he should seal the great result with the sacrifice of his life.

CHAPTER XI.

Last Days of Mr. Lincoln.—His Assassination.—Attack on Mr. Seward.—Remains of Mr. Lincoln lying in State.—Obsequies at Washington.—Removal of the Remains to Springfield, Illinois.—Demonstration along the route.—Obsequies at Springfield.—The Great Crime, its authors and abettors.—The Assassin's End.—The Conspiracy.—Complicity of Jefferson Davis.—How assassins were trained to their work.—Tributes and Testimonials.—Mr. Lincoln as a Lawyer.—Incidents and Reminiscences.—Additional Speeches.— Letter to Gov. Hahn, on Negro Suffrage.—Letter to Mrs. Gurney.— Letter to a Widow who had lost five Sons in the War.—Letter to a Centenarian.—A letter written in early life.—A speech made in 1839.—Letter to Mr. Choate, on the Pilgrim Fathers.—Letter to Dr. Maclean, on receiving the Degree of LL. D.—Letter to Gov. Fletcher, of Missouri, on the restoration of order.—A message to the Miners.—Speech at Independence Hall in 1861.—Concluding remarks.

AFTER years of weary toil, Mr. Lincoln seemed now to be entering on a period of comparative repose. The first step had been taken for putting the army on a peace footing. A policy had been matured for the re-establishment of loyal local governments in the insurgent States. Forbearance, clemency, charity were to control the executive action in dealing with the difficult problems still awaiting practical solution. After the Cabinet meeting on the 14th of April,* the President was in unusually buoyant spirits. His remaining tasks evidently seemed lighter than ever before. His gladsome humor was noticed by his friends.

As he went on an afternoon drive with Mrs. Lincoln, she could not forbear an expression of slight foreboding, suggested

---

*At a Cabinet meeting at which General Grant was present to-day, the subject of the state of the country and the prospects of speedy peace was discussed. The President was very cheerful and hopeful, spoke very kindly of General Lee, and others of the Confederacy, and the establishment of Government in Virginia.—*Secretary Stanton's Dispatch, April 14th.*

by this change of manner: "It was thus with you," she said, "just before our dear Willie's death." The allusion to this event, the depressing effects of which, during more than three years, had never been effaced, cast a shadow on his heart. But in a moment he replied, speaking of the impossibility of accounting for such transitions of mood. The passing thought was quickly gone, to be recalled only by subsequent realities. Mr. Lincoln talked of the future, and of the hopes he indulged of happier hours during his second term than he had been permitted to enjoy during that which was passed—an expectation reasonably founded on the altered condition of national affairs, and on the assured confidence and love of the people, which would lighten the burdens undertaken on their behalf.

Gen. Grant had arrived in Washington in time to witness the grand illumination of the previous evening. There was a general desire to see the great commander, to whom, during the war, three Rebel armies had successively surrendered, and whose leadership had at length brought the military power of the rebellion to utter ruin. This desire had not been gratified. On the evening of the 14th, the places of public amusement were to be specially decorated in honor of the great victories achieved, and of the raising over Fort Sumter of the identical flag pulled down on that day four years before, at the opening of the war. Mr. Lincoln, who had been wont occasionally, though seldom, to seek a brief respite from his heavy cares by attending on a play, or an opera, thought proper to engage a private box at Ford's Theater, for this evening, intending that Gen. Grant should accompany him on the occasion. A messenger was accordingly sent on Friday morning to secure the upper double box, on the right hand side of the audience, before occupied by him, and the announcement was made in the evening papers, by the business manager of the theater, that the President and Gen. Grant would be present to witness the performance of "The American Cousin." Gen. Grant, however, had felt compelled to leave the city that evening, going north with his family, and he was accordingly excused.

There were visitors at the White House that night as usual, and it was somewhat late when Mr. Lincoln was ready to leave.

Mrs. Lincoln, as if some persentiment restrained her, seemed reluctant to go, but the President was unwilling that those who had seen the announcement should be totally disappointed by seeing neither himself nor the Lieutenant-General. Speaker Colfax, who was the last person received by Mr. Lincoln, walked with him and Mrs. Lincoln from the parlor to the carriage. Mr. Ashmun, who had nearly five years before presided over the National Convention, which first nominated Mr. Lincoln for the Presidency, came up at this moment, having hoped to obtain an interview. After salutations, a card was handed to Mr. Ashmun, written by the President as he sat in his carriage, directing the usher to admit that gentleman to the Executive room on the following morning. The carriage drove away, stopping to take up two young friends on the way—Maj. Rathbone and Miss Harris. It was not yet past nine when the party reached the theater, which was densely thronged. As President Lincoln entered and passed to his box he was greeted with enthusiastic cheering.

Mr. Lincoln occupied a chair on the side of the box nearest the audience, Mrs. Lincoln sitting next him. Their guests were seated beyond, in a portion of the box usually separated by a partition, which had been removed for this occasion. Each part was ordinarily entered by its own door, opening from a narrow passage, to which, near the outer wall, a door gives access from the dress circle. The last named door and the further one inside were closed, the other, through which the whole party passed, remaining open. Any intrusion upon this privacy, in the presence of so many spectators, was hardly to be thought of as possible. Every day of his life in Washington, the President had been in positions far more inviting to murderous malice or Rebel conspiracy.

During the hour that followed Mr. Lincoln's entrance into the theater, his attention seemed to be unusually absorbed in the scenes before him. His countenance indicated an appreciation of the lively caricature in which the good-humored audience manifested a high degree of delight. Yet it may safely be affirmed that there was, in his mind, a strong undercurrent of quite other thoughts and emotions than those which had to do with this mock presentation of human life and manners. One can not doubt, knowing his mental characteristics, that while partly enjoying this light diversion, his mind was active with more substantial realities, and actually most occupied with these, when apparently most intent in observing what passed on the stage.

In the midst of a scene of the third act, when but one actor was before the curtain, the sound of a pistol-shot was heard, and a man leaped from the President's box and disappeared behind the scenes. So sudden was all this, that only the screams of Mrs. Lincoln, a moment later, revealed its meaning. The President had been shot. His assassin had escaped. One of the audience promptly sprang upon the stage, following the fugitive, but was only in time to see him mount a horse at the rear of the theater, and ride away at a flying speed. Wild excitement swayed the audience now toward the stage, many leaping over the foot-lights, and now toward the door. Attention was earnestly directed, on the next instant, to the condition of Mr. Lincoln. He was found to be insensble, having fallen slightly forward, where he sat. Presently surgeons were admitted to the box, and soon after it was discovered that he had been shot in the back of the neck, just beneath the base of the brain, in which the ball was still lodged—a hopeless wound. In a few minutes more he was borne from the theater to a private house on the opposite side of the street.

The terrible news quickly spread through the city, and the streets near the theater were thronged with distressed and indignant thousands, anxious for a word as to the President's condition, that would give encouragement to hope—eager to know who was the author of this monstrous crime. Almost simultaneously came the intelligence that Secretary Seward, who had been lying seriously ill for many days past, had been brutally stabbed in his bed by a ruffian, who had wounded several others in making his escape from the house. It soon became known, also, that Frederick W. Seward, Assistant Secretary of State, had been so wounded, by the same hand, that his recovery was very doubtful.

In the room to which Mr. Lincoln had been removed, he remained, still breathing, but unconscious, surrounded by his distracted family—who sometimes retired together to an adjoining room—by his Cabinet, by surgeons, and by a few others, until twenty-three minutes past seven o'clock, on the morning of April 15th, when his great heart ceased to beat.

Never before was rejoicing turned into such sudden and overwhelming sorrow. A demon studying how most deeply to wound the greatest number of hearts, could have devised no act for his purpose like that which sent ABRAHAM LINCOLN to his grave. No man's loss could have been so universally felt as that of a father, brother, friend. Many a fireside was made doubly lonely by this bereavement. "Sadness to despondency has seized on all"—says a private letter from a resident of one of our largest cities, written on the fatal day. "Men have ceased business, and workmen are turning home with their dinner buckets unopened. The merchants are leaving their counting-rooms for the privacy of their dwellings. A gloom, intensified by the transition from the pomp and rejoicing of yesterday, settles impenetrably on every mind." And this was but a picture of the grief everywhere felt. Bells sadly tolled in all parts of the land. Mourning drapery was quickly seen from house to house on every square of the national capital; and all the chief places of the country witnessed, by spontaneous demonstrations, their participation in the general sorrow. In every loyal pulpit, and at every true altar throughout the nation, the great public grief was the theme of earnest prayer and discourse, on the day following. One needs not to dwell on what no pen can describe, and on what no adult living on that day can ever forget.

During the night of Friday, diligent efforts were made to discover the assassin, and to secure his arrest. It was early ascertained that J. W. Booth, an actor, was the perpetrator of the crime, and that he had probably escaped across the East Branch, into a portion of Maryland in warm sympathy with the rebellion. The circumstances attending the deed were eagerly inquired into, and testimony taken, from which it was learned that the assassination of Mr. Lincoln and the attempted murder of Mr. Seward, had their source in a conspiracy, of which Vice-President Johnson was also an intended victim

The statements of Major Rathbone, who was in the President's box, and of the actor (Mr. Hawk) who was alone on the stage, at the time of the murder, have a special value in relation to the circumstances attending its consummation. Maj. Rathbone, in an affidavit made on the 17th of April, said:

The distance between the President, as he sat, and the door was about four or five feet. The door, according to the recollection of this deponent, was not closed during the evening. When the second scene of the third act was being performed, and while this deponent was intently observing the proceedings upon the stage, with his back toward the door, he heard the discharge of a pistol behind him, and looking around, saw, through the smoke, a man between the door and the President. At the same moment deponent heard him shout some word which deponent thinks was "freedom!" This deponent instantly sprang toward him and seized him; he wrested himself from the grasp and made a violent thrust at the breast of deponent with a large knife. Deponent parried the blow by striking it up, and received a wound several inches deep in his left arm, between the elbow and the shoulder. The orifice of the wound is about an inch and a half in length, and extends upward toward the shoulder several inches. The man rushed to the front of the box, and deponent endeavored to seize him again, but only caught his clothes as he was leaping over the railing of the box. The clothes, as deponent believes, were torn in this attempt to seize him. As he went over upon the stage, deponent cried out with a loud voice, "Stop that man!" Deponent then turned to the President; his position was not changed; his head was slightly bent forward, and his eyes were closed. Deponent saw that he was unconscious, and supposing him mortally wounded, rushed to the door for the purpose of calling medical aid. On reaching the outer door of the passage way as above described, deponent found it barred by a heavy piece of plank, one end of which was secured in the wall, and the other resting against the door. It had been so securely fastened that it required considerable force to remove it. This wedge or bar was about four feet from the floor. Persons upon the outside were beating against the door for the purpose of entering. Deponent removed the bar, and the door was opened.

The actor who was at the moment on the stage, gave the following particulars in a letter to his father, written on the 16th of April:

I was playing *Asa Trenchard*, in the " American Cousin." The " old lady " of the theater had just gone off the stage, and I was answering her exit speech when I heard the shot fired. I turned, looked up at the President's box, heard the man exclaim, " *Sic semper tyrannis !*" saw him jump from the box, seize the flag on the staff and drop to the stage ; he slipped when he gained the stage, but he got upon his feet in a moment, brandished a large knife, saying, " The South shall be free !" turned his face in the direction I stood, and I recognized him as John Wilkes Booth. He ran toward me, and I, seeing the knife, thought I was the one he was after, ran off the stage and up a flight of stairs. He made his escape out of a door directly in the rear of the theater, mounted a horse and rode off.

The above all occurred in the space of a quarter of a minute, and at the time I did not know that the President was shot, although, if I had tried to stop him he would have stabbed me.

I am now under one thousand dollars bail to appear as a witness when Booth is tried, if caught.

All the above I have sworn to. You may imagine the excitement in the theater, which was crowded, with cries of " Hang him !" " Who was he ?" etc., from every one present.

On the morning of his death, Mr. Lincoln's remains were taken to the White House, embalmed, and on Tuesday laid in state in the East Room, where they were visited by many thousands during the day. On Wednesday, funeral services were held in the same room. An impressive discourse was preached by Rev. Dr. Gurley, pastor of the Presbyterian church which the late President attended ; the main portion of the Episcopal service for the burial of the dead was read by Rev. Dr. Hall (Episcopalian), and prayers were offered by Bishop Simpson (Methodist) and Rev. Dr. Gray (Baptist). The funeral procession and pageant, as the body was removed to the rotunda of the capitol, were of grand and solemn character, beyond description. The whole length of the Avenue, from the Executive Mansion to the capital, was crowded with the thousands of the army, navy, civil officers, and citizens, marching to the music of solemn dirges. From window and roof, and from side-walks densely crowded, tens of thousands along the whole route witnessed the spectacle. The remains again lay in state, in the Rotunda, and were visited by many thousands during the following day. On Friday morning the remains were borne to the rich funeral car, in which, accompanied by an escort of distinguished officers and citizens, they were to be borne on their journey of nearly two thousand miles to their last rest in the silence of the Western prairie. The funeral cortege left Washington on the 21st of April, going by way of Baltimore and Harrisburg to Philadelphia, where the body lay in state in Independence Hall, from Saturday evening, the 22d, until Monday morning. On the afternoon of the 24th, the train reached New York. All along the route, thus far, the demonstrations of the people were of the most earnest character, and at Philadelphia the ceremonies were imposing, profound grief and sympathy being universally manifested. At New York, on the 25th, a funeral procession, unprecedented in numbers, marched through the streets, while mottoes and emblems of woe were seen on every hand—touching devices, yet altogether vain to express the reality of the general sorrow. The train reached Albany the same night, remaining there part of the day on the 26th, while the same overflowing popular manifestations were witnessed as at previous places along the route. These were continued at all the principal points on the way from that city to Buffalo, where there were special demonstrations, on the 27th, as again at Cleveland on the 28th, at Columbus on the 29th, and at Indianapolis on the 30th. Wherever the funeral car and cortege passed through the State of Ohio, as through Indiana and Illinois, the people thronged to pay their sad greeting to the dead, and tokens of public mourning and private sadness were seen. At Chicago, where the train arrived on the 1st of May, the demonstrations were specially impressive, and the mournful gatherings of the people were such as could have happened on no other occasion. It was the honored patriot of Illinois, who had been stricken down in the midst of his glorious work, and whose lifeless remains were now brought back to the city which he had chosen to be his future home.

From Chicago to Springfield, the great ovation of sorrow was unparalleled, through all the distance. The remains of the martyred statesman were passing over ground familiar to his sight for long years, and filled with personal friends who had known him from early life. Yet even here, where all were deeply moved, there could scarcely be a more heartfelt tribute, a more universal impulse to render homage to the memory of the immortal martyr for liberty, than in every city and State through which the funeral car and its cortege had passed.

The final obsequies took place at Springfield, on Thursday, the 4th day of May, when the remains of Abraham Lincoln, in the presence of many thousands, were placed in a vault in Oak Ridge Cemetery. With the body of the late President, the disinterred remains of his son Willie, who died in February, 1862, had been borne to Illinois, and were now placed beside those of the father by whom he had been so tenderly loved. The ceremonies were grandly impressive. Mr. Lincoln's last inaugural address was read, the Dead March in Saul, and other dirges and hymns were sung, accompanied by an instrumental band, and an eloquent discourse was preached by Bishop Simpson. Rev. Dr. Gurley, of Washington, and other clergymen, participated in the religious exercises. In every part of the nation, the day was observed, and business suspended. Never, probably, was the memory of any man before so honored in his death, or any obsequies participated in by so many hundreds of thousands of sincere mourners.

The assassination of Abraham Lincoln was the culmination of a series of fiendish schemes undertaken in aid of an infamous rebellion. It was the deadly flower of the rank and poisonous weed of treason. The guiding and impelling spirit of Secessionism nerved and aimed the blow struck by the barbarous and cowardly assassin, who stole up from behind to surprise his victim, and brutally murdered him in the privacy of his box, and in the presence of his wife.

Large rewards were speedily offered for the capture of the chief assassin and of his principal known accomplices, Atzerodt and Herold. The villain who attempted the murder of Mr. Seward was first arrested—giving his name as Payne. Booth and his companion Herold were traced through the counties of Prince George, Charles, and St. Mary, in Maryland, and finally across the Potomac into King George and Caroline counties in

Virginia. They had crossed the Rappahannock at Port Conway, and had advanced some distance toward Bowling Green. By the aid of information obtained from negroes, and from a Rebel paroled prisoner, they were finally found in a barn, on a Mr. Garrett's place, early on the morning of the 26th of April, when Herold surrendered. Booth, defiant to the last, was shot by Sergeant Corbett, of the cavalry force in pursuit of the fugitives, and lived but a few hours, ending his life in miserable agony. In leaping from the box of the theater, he had broken a bone of his leg, impeding his flight and producing intense suffering during the eleven days of his wanderings. A swift and terrible retribution had overtaken the reckless criminal—perhaps the most fitting expiation of his deed.*

In addition to the arrests of Payne and Herold, were those of Atzerodt, O'Laughlin, Spangler, an employee at Ford's Theater; Dr. Mudd, who harbored Booth the day after the assassination, set the broken bone of his leg, and helped him on his way; Arnold, whose letter to Booth, found in the latter's trunk, signed "Sam," showed his connection with the conspiracy, and Mrs. Surratt, at whose house some of the conspirators were wont to meet, and who was charged with aiding the plans and the escape of Booth.

But the conspiracy was clearly traceable to a higher source than Booth and these wretched accomplices. Mr. Johnson, who had been inaugurated as President on the morning of Mr. Lincoln's death, issued, after the plot had become more fully unraveled, the following

---

* The wretched miscreant whose hand has spread mourning over a continent, and turned even hostility into sympathy for his victim, has perished in a manner that is perhaps the fittest penalty for his crime. Other assassins have invested their deed with a glow of heroism, by setting their own lives frankly against the life they smote, and daring vengeance in the name of justice. But Wilkes Booth was a cowardly villain, who crept secretly to strike his enemy in the back, and who thought to secure his own safety by a prepared flight. So it is best that he should not even have the dignity of dying by the hands of justice, but hunted like vermin to his lair, be put out of life by the pistol of a common soldier. It is best for the world that as speedily as possible it should be enabled to cease thinking of a nature so deformed, which had drawn to itself notoriety by a crime so inhuman.—*London Daily News.*

PROCLAMATION:

WHEREAS, It appears from evidence in the Bureau of Military Justice that the atrocious murder of the late President, Abraham Lincoln, and the attempted assassination of the Hon. W. H. Seward, Secretary of State, were incited, concerted and procured by and between Jefferson·Davis, late of Richmond, Virginia, and Jacob Thompson, Clement C. Clay, Beverley Tucker, George N. Sanders, W. C. Cleary, and other Rebels and traitors against the Government of the United States, harbored in Canada; now, therefore, to the end that justice may be done, I, Andrew Johnson, President of the United States, do offer and promise for the arrest of said persons, or either of them, within the limits of the United States, so that they can be brought to trial, the following rewards: One hundred thousand dollars for the arrest of Jefferson Davis; twenty-five thousand dollars for the arrest of Clement C. Clay; twenty-five thousand dollars for the arrest of Jacob Thompson, late of Mississippi; twenty-five thousand dollars for the arrest of George N. Sanders; twenty-five thousand dollars for the arrest of Beverley Tucker, and ten thousand dollars for the arrest of William C. Cleary, late clerk of Clement C. Clay.

The Provost-Marshal-General of the United States is directed to cause a description of said persons, with notice of the above rewards, to be published.

In testimony whereof, I have hereunto set my hand, and caused the seal of the United States to be affixed.

Done at the city of Washington, the second day of May, in the year of our Lord one thousand eight hundred and [L. S.] sixty-five, and of the independence of the United States of America the eighty-ninth.

ANDREW JOHNSON.

By the President: W. HUNTER, Acting Secretary of State.

A Military Commission was convened to meet on the 8th of May, for the trial of the parties arrested on the charge of "maliciously, unlawfully, and traitorously, and in aid of the present armed Rebellion against the United States of America, on or before the 6th day of March, A. D. 1865, combining, confederating and conspiring together, with one John H. Surratt, John Wilkes Booth, Jefferson Davis, George N. Sanders, Beverley Tucker, Jacob Thompson, William C. Cleary, Clement C. Clay, George Harper, George Young, and others unknown, to kill and murder, within the Military Department of Washington,

THE BURIAL SERVICES AT SPRINGFIELD.

and within the fortified and intrenched lines thereof, ABRA-
HAM LINCOLN, and at the time of said combining, confederating and conspiring, President of the United States and Commander-in-Chief the Army and Navy thereof; Andrew Johnson, then Vice President of the United States aforesaid, Wm.
H. Seward, Secretary of State of the United States aforesaid,
and Ulysses S. Grant, Lieutenant-General of the Army of
the United States aforesaid, then in command of the armies of
the United States, under the direction of the said Abraham
Lincoln; and in pursuance of and in prosecuting said malicious,
unlawful and traitorous conspiracy aforesaid, and in aid of said
Rebellion, afterward, to-wit, on the 14th day of April, 1865,
within the Military Department of Washington aforesaid, and
within the fortified and intrenched lines of said Military
Department, together with said John Wilkes Booth and John
H. Surratt, maliciously, unlawfully and traitorously murdering
the said Abraham Lincoln, then President of the United States
and Commander-in-Chief of the Army and Navy of the United
States as aforesaid, and maliciously, unlawfully and traitorously assaulting, with intent to kill and murder, the said Wm.
H. Seward, then Secretary of State of the United States as
aforesaid, and lying in wait with intent, maliciously, unlawfully
and traitorously, to kill and murder the said Andrew Johnson,
then being Vice President of the United States, and the said
Ulysses S. Grant, then being Lieutenant-General and in command of the Armies of the United States as aforesaid.''

In the course of the trial, positive evidence was furnished,
connecting Jacob Thompson, Jefferson Davis, and their associates named above, with President Lincoln's assassination.
This direct evidence is only the key-stone of an arch of circumstances, strong as adamant. We have already seen the
avowal, in the Greeley-Sanders peace correspondence, that several of these men were in Canada, in the " confidential employment " of Davis. This employment, after the failure of their
busy intrigues with Northern sympathizers, to defeat Mr. Lincoln's re-election, and the liberal waste of funds in sustaining
Northern Rebel journalism, had taken a form congenial to their
" chivalrous " instincts, in instigating and aiding piratical seiz-

51

ures on Lake Erie, robbery at St. Albans, hotel-burning and wholesale murder at New York, and in a broad-cast diffusion of, pestilence and death through the northern cities, by the efforts of the "philanthropic" Dr. Blackburn, who labored assiduously in his purpose of spreading malignant disease by means of infected clothing. What farther depth of iniquity needed these men to sound before organizing a conspiracy—at first for the avowed purpose of abducting, then of murdering outright, the President whom they so maliciously hated? That they did enter this scheme, is proved beyond doubt. That Jefferson Davis, in whose "confidential employment" all this while they were, was consulted as to the plan of assassination, and gave it his approval, is shown by positive testimony. And this suits the temper he had shown in his readiness to entertain McCullough's infamous plan for introducing into the "confidential" service a combustible which would obviate the "difficulties heretofore encountered" in burning hotels. It is strikingly confirmed by his language on hearing, at Charlotte, North Carolina, that Mr. Lincoln had been assassinated. Lewis F. Bates, of that town, in whose house Davis was then staying, gives the following testimony on this point, after stating that the latter received a dispatch from Breckinridge announcing the assassination:

Q.—Look at this (exhibiting to witness a telegram) and see whether it is the same dispatch?

A.—I should say that it was.

The dispatch was then read, as follows:

"GREENSBORO, April 19, 1865.—His Excellency, President Davis: President Lincoln was assassinated in the theater in Washington, on the night of the 14th inst. Seward's house was entered on the same night, and he was repeatedly stabbed, and is probably mortally wounded.

(Signed,)   "JOHN C. BRECKINRIDGE."

Q.—State what Jefferson Davis said after reading this dispatch to the crowd. Endeavor to recollect his precise language?

A.—At the conclusion of his speech to the people, he read this dispatch aloud, and made this remark: "If it were to be done, it were better that it were done well."

Q.—You are sure these are the words?

A.—These are the words.

Q.—State whether or not, in a day or two afterward, Jefferson Davis, John C. Breckinridge, and others, were present in your house in Charlotte?

A.—They were.

Q.—And the assassination of the President was the subject of conversation?

A.—A day or two afterward that was the subject of their conversation.

Q.—Can you remember what John C. Breckinridge said?

A.—In speaking of the assassination of President Lincoln, he remarked to Davis that he regretted it very much; that it was unfortunate for the people of the South at that time. Davis replied: "*Well, General, I don't know; if it were to be done at all, it were better it were well done; and if the same were done to Andrew Johnson, the beast, and to Secretary Stanton, the job would then be complete.*"

Q.—You feel confident that you recollect the words?

A.—These are the words used.

The expedient of assassinating Mr. Lincoln had long been a favorite one, beyond doubt, with many of the Southern traitors. It was no less unlawful, they might naturally reason, than levying war against the Government. That it was less manly, that it was infamous in the eyes of all nations, weighed little with many who had so long brazenly defied the sentiment of the civilized world. Mr. Lincoln, during the canvass of 1860, received letters threatening his life—in themselves of no consequence, but showing how easily Rebel notions even then took such a direction, and might sooner or later mature into act. It can not reasonably be doubted that there was a definite plan for assassinating Mr. Lincoln at Baltimore, in February, 1861. Northern Copperheads and Southern traitors kept the propensity alive by constant denunciations of the President as a tyrant, and by historic allusions, hightened in effect by poetic citations in praise of tyrannicide. These doctrines were fostered by the Copperhead secret orders—undoubtedly in affiliation with Thompson, Clay and Tucker, and receiving from them pecuniary aid. This spirit was rampant at the Chicago Democratic National Convention, as shown in previous pages, and during the subsequent canvass. All these ideas apparently originated in the South, and were propagated from thence. It was under such training that the assassin was prepared for the conception, and nerved to the execution of his monstrous crime.

When the youthful Col. Dahlgren fell a victim to Southern hate, in Kilpatrick's unsuccessful raid for the rescue of prisoners at Richmond, on the 4th of March, 1864, there was pretended to have been found on Dahlgren's person an order in his name, directing that the city be destroyed, "and Jeff. Davis and Cabinet killed." This "order," of which much was made in the Rebel States and abroad, has been satisfactorily shown to be a forgery, and it now but serves to reveal the dark undercurrent in the Southern mind, setting in the direction of a crime ultimately consummated.

There is positive proof, developed on the trial of the assassination conspirators, that, at the time of this raid of Kilpatrick, preparations were made for a wholesale massacre of several thousand Union prisoners, in case he had taken the city, by means of mines filled with gunpowder under the Libby prison. This fact has been officially conceded and justified in the report of a Rebel committee, which has recently come to light.

A lawyer of Alabama, named Gayle, perhaps quite as respectable as "philanthropist" Blackburn, published a notice (the authorship and genuineness of which are proved), on the 1st of December, 1864, in the *Selma Dispatch*, in these words:

ONE MILLION DOLLARS WANTED TO HAVE PEACE BY THE 1ST OF MARCH.—If the citizens of the Southern Confederacy will furnish me with the cash, or good securities, for the sum of one million dollars, I will cause the lives of Abraham Lincoln, William H. Seward and Andrew Johnson to be taken by the 1st of March next. This will give us peace, and satisfy the world that cruel tyrants can not live in a "land of liberty." If this is not accomplished, nothing will be claimed beyond the sum of fifty thousand dollars, in advance, which is supposed to be necessary to reach and slaughter the three villains.

I will give, myself, one thousand dollars toward this patriotic purpose. Every one wishing to contribute will address Box X, Cahaba, Alabama.

DECEMBER 1, 1864.

During the same winter there were intimations in Southern quarters, and in sympathetic circles abroad, as indicated through the public prints, that some great event was about to happen, which would startle the world. The spirit of assassination had been carefully nursed. The crime itself had been repeatedly meditated and plotted. This fact was known to Davis. Men in his "confidential employment," constantly at work, with his knowledge, on schemes the most infamous, were instigating and aiding the crime of Booth. Davis knew this crime to be intended, gave it his sanction, and rejoiced with no regret except that the plot was not more completely carried into effect. The assassination was not the mere freak of a madcap or fanatic. It was the natural outgrowth of the spirit which led the Rebellion, and which advanced on the same line to the vilest works of desperation. The barbarous oligarch and upstart autocrat who had deliberately starved thousands of Union prisoners, could have no compunction at seeing a chosen emissary stealthily murder the ruler to whose authority he must otherwise soon be forced to succumb.

Never, perhaps, has the death of any man called forth so many expressions of sorrow and respect, or inspired so many exalted tributes from orators, poets and authors, as well as from the people of every class. In British America, the shock seemed almost as universal as in the States. From all parts of Great Britain, from Germany, France, Italy, and the countries beyond, as from the diplomatic representatives of all nations at the National Capital, have come unaffected utterances of sympathy and high recognitions of the goodness and greatness of the departed. Letters of condolence were addressed to Mrs. Lincoln by Queen Victoria and the Empress Eugenie, with their own hands. Numerous public bodies and popular meetings—parliaments, associations, and gatherings of the people--throughout Europe as well as this country, have sent similar tokens. From the multitude of the higher tributes to the character of Mr. Lincoln, only a few brief extracts can be given here.

In the course of his oration, delivered in New York on the

occasion of Mr. Lincoln's death, our great historian, George Bancroft, said :

Those who come after us will decide how much of the wonderful results of his public career is due to his own good common sense, his shrewd sagacity, readiness of wit, quick interpretation of the public mind, his rare combination of fixedness and pliancy, his steady tendency of purpose ; how much to the American people, who, as he walked with them side by side, inspired him with their own wisdom and energy ; and how much to the overruling laws of the moral world, by which the selfishness of evil is made to defeat itself. But after every allowance, it will remain that members of the government which preceded his administration opened the gates of treason, and he closed them ; that when he went to Washington the ground on which he trod shook under his feet, and he left the republic on a solid foundation ; that traitors had seized public forts and arsenals, and he recovered them for the United States, to whom they belonged ; that the capital, which he found the abode of slaves, is now the home only of the free ; that the boundless public domain which was grasped at, and, in a great measure, held for the diffusion of slavery, is now irrevocably devoted to freedom ; that then men talked a jargon of a balance of power in a republic between slave States and free States, and now the foolish words are blown away forever by the breath of Maryland, Missouri and Tennessee ; that a terrible cloud of political heresy rose from the abyss threatening to hide the light of the sun, and under its darkness a rebellion was rising into indefinable proportions ; now the atmosphere is purer than ever before, and the insurrection is vanishing away ; the country is cast into another mold, and the gigantic system of wrong, which had been the work of more than two centuries, is dashed down, we hope forever. And as to himself personally, he was then scoffed at by the proud as unfit for his station, and now, against the usage of later years, and in spite of numerous competitors, he was the unbiassed and the undoubted choice of the American people for a second term of service. Through all the mad business of treason he retained the sweetness of a most placable disposition ; and the slaughter of myriads of the best on the battle-field, and the more terrible destruction of our men in captivity by the slow torture of exposure and starvation, had never been able to provoke him into harboring one vengeful feeling or one purpose of cruelty.

How shall the nation most completely show its sorrow at Mr. Lincoln's death ? How shall it best honor his memory ? There can be but one answer. He was struck down when he was highest in its service, and in strict conformity with duty was engaged in carrying out, principles affecting its life, its good name, and its relations to the cause of freedom and the progress of mankind. Grief must take the character of action, and breathe itself forth in the assertion of the policy to which he fell a sacrifice. The standard which he held in his hand must be uplifted again, higher and more firmly than before, and must be carried on to triumph. Above everything else, his proclamation of the first day of January, 1863, declaring throughout the parts of the country in rebellion the freedom of all persons who have been held as slaves, must be affirmed and maintained.

Referring to the deed of the assassin, and to the attempt to sever the Union, Mr. Bancroft said :

To that Union Abraham Lincoln has fallen a martyr. His death, which was meant to sever it beyond repair, binds it more closely and more firmly than ever. The death blow aimed at him was aimed not at the native of Kentucky, not at the citizen of Illinois, but at the man who, as President, in the executive branch of the government, stood as the representative of every man in the United States. The object of the crime was the life of the whole people ; and it wounds the affections of the whole people. From Maine to the South-west boundary on the Pacific, it makes us one. The country may have needed an imperishable grief to touch its inmost feeling. The grave that receives the remains of Lincoln, receives the martyr to the Union ; the monument which will rise over his body will bear witness to the Union ; his enduring memory will assist during countless ages to bind the States together, and to incite to the love of our one, undivided, indivisible country. Peace to the ashes of our departed friend, the friend of his country and his race. Happy was his life, for he was the restorer of the republic ; he was happy in his death, for the manner of his end will plead forever for the Union of the States and the freedom of man.

The venerable Lewis Cass, a life-long political opponent, after excusing himself from taking an active part in the great demonstration at Detroit, on account of infirm health, wrote as follows :

But in the numerous assemblages, which the impressive ceremonies will call together, there will not be one who will mourn more sincerely than I do the deplorable event which has spread sorrow and indignation through our whole country. He whom the nation loved and laments was called to his high station at a most portentous crisis, at the commencement of a war, almost without a parallel in human history in the sacrifices and exertions it required, and in the appalling circumstances that marked its progress.

The nature of the contest, an attempt to break up the happiest government ever enjoyed by man, gave rise to many new and difficult questions at home and abroad, and added strength to the passions which war usually calls into action. The departed patriot entered upon his new field of duty with an unwavering confidence in the justice of his cause and its final triumphant issue, and this confidence accompanied him during all the trials to which he was exposed, inaugurated the policy he felt called upon to adopt. And, as in the progress of events, he became better understood by the course of his administration, he became better appreciated by his countrymen. Though differences of opinion as to the measures to be adopted were inseparable from such a contest, involving many issues of weal and of woe, still his noble qualities inspired general confidence and commanded general respect, and his successful administration will be evidence, in all time to come, of his own worth and the wisdom of his measures.

The poet-scholar, Ralph Waldo Emerson, in his oration at Boston, used these words:

In this country, on Saturday, every one was struck dumb, and saw, at first, only deep below deep, as he meditated on the ghastly blow. And, perhaps, at this hour, when the coffin which contains the dust of the President sets forward on its long march through mourning States, on its way to his home in Illinois, we might well be silent, and suffer the awful voices of the time to thunder to us. Yes, but that first despair was brief; the man was not so to be mourned. He was the most active and hopeful of men; and his work had not perished; but acclamations of praise for the task he had accomplished burst out into a song of triumph, which even tears for his death can not keep down.

The President stood before us a man of the people. He was thoroughly American, had never crossed the sea, had never been spoiled by English insularity or French dissipation; a quiet, native, aboriginal man, as an acorn from the oak; no aping of foreigners, no frivolous accomplishments, Kentuckian born, working on a farm, a flatboatman, a captain in the Black-hawk war, a country lawyer, a representative in the rural

Legislature of Illinois—on such modest foundations the broad structure of his fame was laid. How slowly, and yet by happily prepared steps, he came to his place.

* * * * A plain man of the people, extraordinary fortune attended him. Lord Bacon says: "Manifest virtues procure reputation; occult ones, fortune." He offered no shining qualities at the first encounter; he did not offend by superiority. He had a face and manner which disarmed suspicion, which inspired confidence, which confirmed good will. He was a man without vices. He had a strong sense of duty which it was very easy for him to obey. Then he had what farmers call a long head; was excellent in working out the sum for himself; in arguing his case, and convincing you fairly and firmly.

Then it turned out that he was a great worker; had prodigious faculty of performance; worked easily. A good worker is so rare; everybody has some disabling quality. In a host of young men that start together, and promise so many brilliant leaders for the next age, each fails on trial; one by bad health, one by conceit or by love of pleasure, or by lethargy, or by a hasty temper—each has some disqualifying fault that throws him out of the career. But this man was sound to the core, cheerful, persistent, all right for labor, and liked nothing so well.

Then he had a vast good nature, which made him tolerant and accessible to all; fair-minded, leaning to the claim of the petitioner; affable, and not sensible to the affliction which the innumerable visits paid to him, when President, would have brought to any one else. And how this good nature became a noble humanity, in many a tragic case which the events of the war brought to him, every one will remember, and with what increasing tenderness he dealt, when a whole race was thrown on his compassion. The poor negro said of him, on an impressive occasion, "Massa Linkum am everywhere."

Then his broad good humor, running easily into jocular talk, in which he delighted, and in which he excelled, was a rich gift to this wise man. It enabled him to keep his secret, to meet every kind of man, and every rank in society; to take off the edge of the severest decisions, to mask his own purpose and sound his companion, and to catch with true instinct the temper of every company he addressed. And, more than all, it is to a man of severe labor, in anxious and exhausting crisises, the natural restorative, good as sleep, and is the protection of the overdriven brain against rancor and insanity.

He is the author of a multitude of good sayings, so disguised as pleasantries that it is certain they had no reputation at first

68

but as jests; and only later, by the very acceptance and adoption they find in the mouths of millions, turn out to be the wisdom of the hour. I am sure if this man had ruled in a period of less facility of printing, he would have become mythological in a very few years, like Æsop or Pilpay, or one of the Seven Wise Masters, by his fables and proverbs.

But the weight and penetration of many passages in his letters, messages and speeches, hidden now by the very closeness of their application to the moment, are destined hereafter to a wide fame. What pregnant definitions; what unerring common sense; what foresight, and on great occasions, what lofty, and more than national, what humane tone! His brief speech at Gettysburg will not easily be surpassed by words on any recorded occasion. * * * *

It can not be said there is any exaggeration of his worth. If ever a man was fairly tested, he was. There was no lack of resistance, nor of slander, nor of ridicule. The times have allowed no State secrets; the Nation has been in such a ferment, such multitudes had to be trusted, that no secret could be kept. Every door was ajar, and we knew all that befell.

Then what an occasion was the whirlwind of the war. Here was place for no holiday magistrate, no fair-weather sailor; the new pilot was hurried to the helm in a tornado. In four years— the four years of battle days—his endurance, his fertility of resources, his magnanimity, were sorely tried and never found wanting.

There, by his courage, his justice, his even temper, his fertile counsel, his humanity, he stood an heroic figure in the center of an heroic epoch. He is the true history of the American people in his time. Step by step he walked before them; slow with their slowness; quickening his march by theirs; the true representative of this continent; an entirely public man; father of his country; the pulse of twenty millions throbbing in his heart, the thought of their minds articulated by his tongue.

William C. Bryant, our venerable poet, composed the following immortal hymn for the obsequies in New York

ABRAHAM LINCOLN.

O, slow to smite and swift to spare,
    Gentle and merciful and just!
Who, in the fear of God, didst bear
    The sword of power—a nation's trust!

In sorrow by thy bier we stand,
　Amid the awe that hushes all,
And speak the anguish of a land
　That shook with horror at thy fall.

Thy task is done; the bond are free;
　We bear thee to an honored grave,
Whose proudest monument shall be
　The broken fetters of the slave.

Pure was thy life; its bloody close
　Has placed thee with the sons of light,
Among the noble host of those
　Who perished in the cause of Right.

Prof. Goldwin Smith, of Oxford University, in England, said:

America has gained one more ideal character, the most precious and inspiring of national possessions. * * * * * * * * * * * Lincoln has fallen a martyr to the abolition of slavery. He was not a fanatical abolitionist. He would have done nothing unconstitutional to effect immediate emancipation. In this respect, as in others, he was a true representative of the hard-headed and sober-minded farmer of the West. But he hated slavery with all his heart. He was himself one of a family of fugitives from its dominions. He said that "If slavery was not wrong, nothing was wrong;" and though these words were not violent, they were sincere. He said that the day must come when the Union would be all slave or all free; and here again he meant what he said. He did not, as President, suffer himself to hold fierce language against slavery; nor would he, though hard pressed by those for whose character and convictions he had a high respect, allow himself to be led into premature and illegal measures for its instant extirpation. But, biding his time with patient sagacity, he struck it deliberately and legally the blow of which it has died. It struck him in return the blow which will make him live in the love of the nation and of mankind forever.

The Count de Paris, in a letter to Senator Sumner, used these words:

I should not have presumed to add my voice to the unanimous expressions of sympathy offered by Europe to your fellow-citizens, if my personal relations with Mr. Lincoln, which henceforth will remain among the most precious recollections of my youth, had not added something in my eyes to the magnitude of that public calamity. My brother and myself will both always gratefully remember the way in which he admitted us, four years ago, into the Federal army, the opportunity he then gave us to serve a cause to which we already felt bound by our family traditions, our sympathies as Frenchmen, and our political creed.

Those who saw Mr. Lincoln during the great ordeal when everything seemed to conspire against the salvation of the Republic, will never forget the honest man who, without personal ambition, always supported by a strong perception of his duties, deserved to be called emphatically a great citizen. And when the dreadful crisis, during which he presided over the destinies of America, will belong to history—when its bloody track will disappear under the rapid growth of an invigorated nation and a regenerated community, people will only remember its beneficial results, the destruction of slavery, the preservation of free institutions, and will ever associate with them the name of Mr. Lincoln. In this struggle with slavery, his name will remain illustrious among those of the indefatigable apostles who fought before him, and who will achieve his work. But it will also be said of him that he secured the preservation of the Union through a tremendous civil war, without ceasing to respect the authority of the law and the liberty of his fellow-citizens; that in the hour of trial he was the Chief Magistrate of a people who knew how to seek in the fullest use of the broadest liberties the spring of national endurance and energy.

Victor Hugo characteristically wrote to a friend in Boston:

At the moment you were writing, the North was victorious and Lincoln alive. To-day Lincoln is dead. That death ennobles Lincoln, and confirms the victory. The South has gained nothing by this crime.

Slavery is abolished.

It is abolished by the glorious means with which it has been attacked, and through the execrable means by which it has been defended.

Long live liberty! Long live the Republic!

From M. Drouyn de Lhuys, and other eminent French publicists, citations of earnest eulogy and sympathy might be made, to an almost unlimited extent. Let us rather return to the utterances of an eminent American statesman and scholar, Charles Sumner, whose more strictly personal tribute—for he was one who knew Mr. Lincoln intimately in private intercourse—in his funeral oration at Boston, on the 1st of June, is specially memorable. In the course of his address, Mr. Sumner said:

In person, Mr. Lincoln was tall and rugged, with little semblance to any historic portrait, unless he might seem, in one respect, to justify the epithet which was given to an early English monarch. His countenance had even more of rugged strength than his person. Perhaps the quality which struck the most, at first sight, was his simplicity of manners and conversation—without form or ceremony of any kind, beyond that among neighbors. His handwriting had the same simplicity. It was as clear as that of Washington, but less florid. He was naturally humane, inclined to pardon, and never remembering the hard things said against him. He was always good to the poor, and in his dealings with them was full of those " kind little words which are of the same blood as great and holy deeds." Such a character awakened instinctively the sympathy of the people. They saw his fellow-feeling with them, and felt the kinship. With him as President, the idea of republican institutions, where no place is too high for the humblest, was perpetually manifest, so that his simple presence was like a proclamation of the equality of all men.

While social in nature, and enjoying the flow of conversation, he was often singularly reticent. Modesty was natural to such a character. As he was without affectation, so he was without pretence or jealousy. No person, civil or military, can complain that he appropriated to himself any honor that belonged to-another. To each and all, he anxiously gave the credit that was due.

His humor has also become a proverb. He insisted, sometimes, that he had no invention, but only a memory. He did not forget the good things that he heard, and was never without a familiar story to illustrate his meaning. When he spoke, the recent West seemed to vie with the ancient East in apologue and fable. His ideas moved, as the beasts entered Noah's ark, in pairs. At times, his illustrations had a homely felicity, and with him they seemed to be not less important than the argument, which he always enforced with a certain intensity of manner and voice.

He was original in mind as in character. His style was his own, formed on no model, and springing directly from himself.

While failing, often, in correctness, it is sometimes unique in beauty and in sentiment. There are passages which will live always. It is no exaggeration to say that, in weight and pith, suffused in a certain poetical color, they call to mind Bacon's Essays. Such passages make an epoch in State papers. No Presidential message or speech from a throne ever had anything of such touching reality. They are harbingers of the great era of humanity. While uttered from the heights of power, they reveal a simple, unaffected trust in Almighty God, and speak to the people as equal to equal.

* * * There was one theme in which latterly he was disposed to conduct the public mind. It was in the treatment of the Rebel leaders. His policy was never announced, and of course it would always have been subject to modification, in the light of experience. But it is well known that, at the very moment of his assassination, he was much occupied by thoughts of lenity and pardon. He was never harsh, even in speaking of Jefferson Davis; and only a few days before his end, when one who was privileged to speak to him in that way said, "Do not allow him to escape the law—he must be hanged," the President replied calmly in the words which he had adopted in his last Inaugural Address, "Judge not, that ye be not judged." And when pressed again and again by the remark that the sight of Libby Prison made it impossible to pardon him, the President repeated twice over these same words, revealing unmistakably the generous sentiments of his heart. The question of clemency here is the very theme so ably debated between Cæsar and Cato, while the Roman Senate was considering the punishment of the confederates of Catiline. Cæsar consented to confiscation and imprisonment, but pleaded for the lives of the criminals. Cato was sterner. It is probable that the President, who was a Cato in heart, would, on this occasion, have followed the counsels of Cæsar.

The leading minds of England had long since come to see the inadequacy and injustice of their first opinions of Mr. Lincoln. Of the many faithful estimates of his public conduct, after his death, that of the London *Spectator*, especially in the following passages, deserves to be cited:

We all remember the animated eulogium on Gen. Washington, which Lord Macaulay passed, parenthetically, in his essay on Hampden. "It was when to the sullen tyranny of Laud and Charles had succeeded the fierce conflict of sects and factions, ambitious of ascendancy, or burning for revenge; it was when the vices and ignorance which the old tyranny had engendered threatened the new freedom with destruction, that England missed the sobriety, the self-command, the perfect soundness of judgment, the perfect rectitude of intention to which the history of revolutions furnishes no parallel, or furnishes a parallel in Washington alone." If that high eulogium was fully earned, as it was, by the first great President of the United States, we doubt if it has not been as well earned by the Illinois peasant-proprietor and "village lawyer," whom, by some Divine inspiration of Providence, the Republican caucus of 1860 substituted for Mr. Seward as their nominee for the President's chair. No doubt he has, in many ways, had a lighter task than Washington, for he had not, at least, to produce a government out of chaos, but only to express and execute the purposes of a people far more highly organized for political life than that with which Washington had to deal. But without the advantages of Washington's education or training, Mr. Lincoln was called from an humble station, at the opening of a mighty civil war, to form a government out of a party in which the habits and traditions of official life did not exist. Finding himself the object of Southern abuse so fierce and so foul, that in any man less passionless it would long ago have stirred up an implacable animosity; mocked at for his official awkwardness, and denounced for his steadfast policy by all the Democratic section of the loyal States, tried by years of failure before that policy achieved a single great success; further tried by a series of successes so rapid and brilliant that they would have puffed up a smaller mind and overset its balance; embarrassed by the boastfulness of his people, and of his subordinates no less than by his own inexperience in his relations with foreign States; beset by fanatics of principle on one side, who would pay no attention to his obligations as a constitutional ruler, and by fanatics of caste on the other, who were not only deaf to the claims of justice, but would hear of no policy large enough for a revolutionary emergency : Mr. Lincoln has persevered through all without ever giving way to anger, or despondency, or exultation, or popular arrogance, or sectarian fanaticism, or caste prejudice, visibly growing in force of character, in self-possession, and in magnanimity, till in his last short message to Congress, on the 4th of March, we can detect no longer the rude and illiterate mold of a village lawyer's thought, but find it replaced by a grasp of principle, a dignity of manner, and a solemnity of purpose which would have been unworthy neither of Hampden nor of Cromwell, while his gentleness and generosity of feeling toward his foes are almost greater than we should expect from either of them.   *   *   *   *   *   *

Mr. Lincoln presents, more powerfully than any man, that quality in the American mind which, though in weak men it becomes boastfulness, is not really this in root, but a strange, an almost humiliated trust in the structural power of that political nature which, without any statesman's co-operation, is slowly building up a free nation, or free nations, on that great continent, with an advance as steady as that of the rivers or the tides. It is the phase of political thought most opposite to, though it is sometimes compared with the Cæsarism that is growing up on the European side of the Atlantic. The Emperor of the French thinks the Imperial organ of the nation almost greater than the nation—certainly an essential part of it. It is men like Mr. Lincoln, who really believe devoutly, indeed too passively, in the "logic of events," but then they think the logic of events the work of God. The Cæsar thinks also of the logic of events, but he regards himself not as its servant but its prophet. He makes events when the logic would not appear complete without his aid; points the slow logic of the Almighty with epigram; fits the unrolling history with showy, rhetorical *denouements;* cuts the knot of raveled providences, and stills the birth throes of revolution with the chloroform of despotism. Mr. Lincoln is a much slower sort of politician, but we doubt if any politician has ever shown less personal ambition and a larger power of trust.

Mr. Lincoln had entered the legal profession soon after he attained to manhood—struggling with many difficulties in educating himself for his chosen work, as already seen. It was to this profession that he devoted his efforts for the most of his life, aiming to acquit himself well in his honorable calling. Judged in this character alone, had he been raised to no high political position, he would have ranked among the first men of the nation. A just estimate of his professional character can, perhaps, best be found in the language of leading men, with whom he was intimately associated at the bar for a quarter of a century. His friend, Hon. David Davis, of the United States Supreme Court, bears this testimony :

I enjoyed for over twenty years the personal friendship of Mr. Lincoln. We were admitted to the bar about the same time, and traveled for many years, what is known in Illinois as the Eighth Judicial Circuit. In 1848, when I first went on the bench, the circuit embraced fourteen counties, and Mr. Lincoln went with the court to every county. Railroads were not then in use, and our mode of travel was either on horseback or in buggies.

This simple life he loved, preferring it to the practice of the law in a city, where, although the remuneration would be greater, the opportunity would be less for mixing with the great body of the people who loved him and whom he loved. Mr. Lincoln was transferred from the bar of that circuit to the office of President of the United States, having been without official position since he left Congress in 1849. In all the elements that constitute the great lawyer he had few equals. He was great both at *nisi prius* and before an appellate tribunal. He seized the strong points of a cause, and presented them with clearness and great compactness. His mind was logical and direct, and he did not indulge in extraneous discussion. Generalities and platitudes had no charms for him. An unfailing vein of humor never deserted him, and he was always able to chain the attention of court and jury, when the cause was the most uninteresting, by the appropriateness of his anecdotes.

His power of comparison was large, and he rarely failed in a legal discussion to use that mode of reasoning. The framework of his mental and moral being was honesty, and a wrong cause was poorly defended by him. The ability which some eminent lawyers possess of explaining away the bad points of a cause by ingenious sophistry, was denied him. In order to bring into full activity his great powers, it was necessary that he should be convinced of the right and justice of the matter which he advocated. When so convinced, whether the cause was great or small, he was usually successful. He read law books but little, except when the cause in hand made it necessary, yet he was usually self-reliant, depending on his own resources, and rarely consulting his brother lawyers either on the management of his case or on the legal questions involved.

Mr. Lincoln was the fairest and most accommodating of practitioners, granting all favors which he could do consistently with his duty to his client, and rarely availing himself of an unwary oversight of his adversary.

He hated wrong and oppression everywhere, and many a man, whose fradulent conduct was undergoing review in a court of justice has writhed under his terrific indignation and rebukes. He was the most simple and unostentatious of men in his habits, having few wants and those easily supplied. To his honor be it said, that he never took from a client, even when the cause was gained, more than he thought the service was worth and the client could reasonably afford to pay. The peo-

52   69

ple where he practiced law were not rich, and his charges were always small.

When he was elected President, I question whether there was a lawyer in the circuit who had been at the bar as long a time whose means were not larger. It did not seem to be one of the purposes of his life to accumulate a fortune. In fact, outside of his profession, he had no knowledge of the way to make money, and he never even attempted it.

Mr. Lincoln was loved by his brethren of the bar, and no body of men will grieve more at his death, or pay more sincere tributes to his memory. His presence on the circuit was watched for with interest, and never failed to produce joy and hilarity. When casually absent, the spirits of both bar and people were depressed. He was not fond of controversy, and would compromise a lawsuit whenever practicable.

Judge Drummond, from the bench of the United States Circuit Court at Chicago, paid the following tribute to the memory of Mr. Lincoln, as a member of the bar:

With a probity of character known to all, with an intiective insight into the human heart, with a clearness of statement which was itself an argument, with uncommon power and felicity of illustration—often, it is true, of a plain and homely kind—and with that sincerity and earnestness of manner which carried conviction, he was, perhaps, one of the most successful jury lawyers we have ever had in the State. He always tried a case fairly and honestly. He never intentionally misrepresented the evidence of a witness, nor the argument of an opponent. He met both squarely, and, if he could not explain the one or answer the other, substantially admitted it. He never misstated the law, according to his own intelligent view of it. Such was the transparent candor and integrity of his nature, that he could not well, or strongly, argue a side or a cause that he thought wrong. Of course, he felt it his duty to say what could be said, and to leave the decision to others; but there could be seen in such cases the inward struggles of his own mind. In trying a case, he might occasionally dwell too long upon, or give too much importance to, an inconsiderable point; but this was the exception, and generally he went straight to the citadel of the cause or the question, and struck home there, knowing, if that were won, the out-works would necessarily fall. He could hardly be called very learned in his profession, and yet he rarely tried a cause without fully understanding the law applicable to it; and I have no hesitation in saying he was one of the ablest lawyers I have ever known. If he was forcible before a jury, he was equally so with the court. He detected, with unerring sagacity, the weak points of an opponent's argument, and pressed his own views with overwhelming strength. His efforts were quite unequal, and it might happen that he would not, on some occasions, strike one as at all remarkable. But, let him be thoroughly roused—let him feel that he was right, and that some principle was involved in his cause—and he would come out with an earnestness of conviction, a power of argument, and a wealth of illustration that I have never seen surpassed.

It has been stated since he became President, even by some of his political friends, that he had no marked superiority of mind. Those who said so did not know him, or regarded him with some peculiarity of political bias. No intelligent man who ever watched Mr. Lincoln through a hard-contested case, at the bar, questioned his great ability. In 1838, he met one of the ablest debaters of the country, in a memorable political contest, and discussed questions of the highest importance, and no candid or impartial man ever claimed for his antagonist any superiority in the intellectual conflict. His mind was eminently of a practical, even of a mechanical turn, and he tried a difficult patent cause with a skill, clearness, and success which excited admiration. He was never a diffuse speaker. His language was not often elegant, or his style classical, but his meaning was unmistakable; and he was at times eloquent with the genuine eloquence of reason and of feeling. Independent of all this, there was pervading the whole man that delightful humor, that genial outflow of human sympathy, which those who knew him intimately can never forget. His frankness, his integrity, his kindness of manner, his sincerity and his goodness of heart (and his heart was as tender as a woman's), made him hosts of personal friends, and he grappled them to himself with hooks of steel. He would do, all his life, more for them than for himself. Simple in his habits, without pretension of any kind, and distrustful of himself, he was willing to yield precedence and place to others, when he ought to have claimed them for himself; and he rarely, if ever, sought office, except at the urgent solicitation of his friends. As he never won a cause by unfair means, so he never intentionally did a wrong to any one.

There have been few public men, with regard to whom more reminiscences of an interesting character could be collected than Abraham Lincoln. Unique, individual in his traits, of a melancholic temperament, underlaid by genial humor, warm-hearted and generous, simple, and at times almost childlike in his frankness of speech, he left abiding impressions upon every one who saw him—even during the most casual interview.

Mr. Lincoln had a remarkable memory—recalling countenances, dates, names and incidents, after long years might be thought to have effaced them from his mind. A gentleman who had been introduced to him at the White House, on one occasion, incidentally mentioned a mutual friend, Mr. C——, in Illinois, whom the former had known in boyhood in the State of their birth. "I have known him for now almost thirty years," said Mr. Lincoln. "My first board bill in Springfield began on the 15th of April, 1837; and C—— came along *about strawberry time.*" The coincidence of dates between this and the day of his decease, just twenty-eight years afterward, lends great interest to the fact stated. Referring to the late Senator Douglas, at one time, he spoke of the first occasion on which he met that distinguished man—then a mere youth, but recently come to Illinois. It was at Vandalia, during a session of the Legislature, of which Mr. Lincoln was a member. "He was then," said Mr. Lincoln, "extremely thin—being so short in stature, too—I think he was about *the least man I ever saw.*"

Mr. Lincoln had great quickness of perception, and fineness of sense beyond what many seem to have supposed. One evening, while the writer was conversing with him in his room, there was a rap at the door, and the President at once said, with a pleasant smile, "That is Charles Sumner"—and the Massachusetts Senator presently entered the room. On one of the last interviews it was ever my privilege to have with President Lincoln—rather late in the evening—he seemed unusually care-worn and weary, though cheerful in tone and kind in manner. Detaining him but a short time, I rose to go, when he requested me to wait for an instant, until he was gone. "I must have rest," said he, "and there are still persons waiting outside; I hear their voices now." He then hastily retired by the private way, which had recently been constructed in the rear of the ante-room. He either imagined the voices spoken of, or else his organs of hearing must have been preternaturally acute

Mr. Lincoln's powers of endurance were remarkable. Had

not this been the case, he could hardly have survived the first three months of his Presidency. Added to the distractions of the time, with a monster rebellion impending, and with the uncertain fidelity of many about him in positions that could hardly be immediately filled with new men, he gave unusual attention to the various applications and recommendations for place, treating all with courteous attention, and sympathetically considering their " claims." As time went on, his cares only increased. An immense army and a greatly increased navy were to be organized, and a multiplicity of business arose, such as his predecessors never knew, while none of the official duties common to them were diminished. It is an error to suppose, as some have done, that he had not superior administrative abilities. Without these, he could never have brought his work to the successful close which he lived to see. It was yet believed by many of his friends that he might have thrust aside more of the details of his office, without detriment to the public service, and with advantage to himself. He thought differently, and labored conscientiously, in view of his responsibility to the people, to satisfy the demands upon his personal attention. On one occasion the writer found him with a huge roll of manuscript before him, to which his consideration had been earnestly requested. It was the record in a court-martial case, of vital consequence to the party concerned, who hoped for some relief in the last resort. The amount of business to which he gave attention, of this character alone, was perhaps greater than any one of ordinary endurance should be charged with ; yet, to a ventured suggestion that he might feel warranted in turning this work over chiefly to the Bureau of Military Justice, he replied with emphasis : " I can not do it. The people would come in here in a mass, and turn me out of this place if I did it." He conscientiously felt that he was under obligation to exert to the utmost, the personal faculties the people had sought to employ in giving him executive power.

These and his manifold other labors told severely upon him, as could be especially seen in the last year or two of his life. He came to have a certain chronic weariness of the mind, which rest or recreation could only superficially relieve. As he sometimes expressed it, the remedy " seemed never to reach the tired spot."

Speaking once of a prominent man who had the year before been violent in his manifestations of hostility to the Administration, but was now ostensibly favoring the same policy previously denounced, Mr. Lincoln expressed his entire readiness to treat the past as if it had not been, and said : " I choose always to make my statute of limitations a short one."

His aversion to calls for a speech, that must be merely " offhand," was decided; yet, unwilling altogether to disappoint the crowds who perhaps too often made such demands of him, he seldom excused himself altogether from speaking. One evening, when the writer was conversing with him in his room, his quick ear caught the sound of approaching music, and his countenance suddenly changed, as he inquired, though readily divining, its meaning. This was presently announced by an usher, and Mr. Lincoln, as he arose to go forward to the front window, lingered a moment in his room, and said: " These serenade speeches bother me a good deal, they are so hard to make. I feel very much like the steam doctor, who said he could get along well enough in his way of practice with almost every case, but he was always a little puzzled when it came to mending a broken leg." The serenading party happened to be a delegation of colored men, whose upturned faces and hilarious manifestations, as he appeared before them would have made a study worthy of the greatest artist. They were rejoicing over emancipation in Maryland ; and Mr. Lincoln, in a really felicitous though entirely unstudied speech, never reported, gave most appropriate advice to his auditors as to the manner of turning to good account their privileges as freemen.

Mr. Lincoln was never willing to hear any disparagement of another, to impair his influence with the appointing power, or to further the interests of a rival candidate for place. A delegation of Californians waited on Mr. Lincoln soon after his first inauguration, presenting a written address intended to counteract what they considered an undue regard for the recommendations of a distinguished Pacific Senator, since deceased, and to remonstrate against some of the candidates of his choice. The paper was, perhaps, not too discreetly worded, and when it was put in Mr. Lincoln's hand, he warmly repelled the attack on his friend, and thrust the writing into the fire, as his answer to its representations.

Toward even those who had given him ample cause for hostility, he uniformly manifested feelings of kindness. He was never inclined to pursue a man who had fallen from favor. After the removal of McClellan, he once said that he would most gladly, were it in the nature of things possible, assign that general to another command, and relieve the unpleasantness of his position, in which he (Mr. Lincoln) found no gratification.

The sad failure of the Peninsular campaign, as the first anniversary of the Bull Run disaster approached, made a deep impression on Mr. Lincoln's mind. It was truly a critical time for the nation. In his great anxiety he determined to visit the army in person at Harrison's Landing, which he did on the 8th of July (1862). Whatever physical recreation he may have found in this visit, it did not change his feeling in regard to military prospects. It was no fitting time to divide the North, or to distract the army by displacing the unsuccessful commander, whose factitious fame still gave him a hold upon the army and the country. How far the loyal States would respond to new and heavy demands for more troops remained to be seen. A most important emergency had arisen, in which, were it possible, some new power must be brought to his aid. It was under these circumstances, and while on board the steamboat, returning from Harrison's Landing to Washington, that Mr. Lincoln wrote the first draft of his Emancipation Proclamation. This he retouched soon after reaching Washington, and read the document to his Cabinet. After due consideration, he approved the suggestion of Mr. Seward, that the proclamation would have more weight at some other time, when the military situation should be less dubious. The people nobly responded to the call for recruits, but meanwhile the division of our forces in Virginia, through McClellan's tardy movements, had resulted in further disasters. The battle of Antietam was fought on the 17th of September. " I remember," said Mr. Lincoln, in the conversation on which the foregoing statements are based, " when I heard, in the morning, that a battle was going on, it at once occurred to me that if we gained the victory, now would be the time to issue the proclamation." This he did, as is well known, on the 22d of September.

The subjoined incident is related by Hon. Schuyler Colfax, of Indiana:

One morning, over two years ago, calling upon him on business, I found him looking more than usually pale and careworn, and inquired the reason. He replied, with the bad news he had received at a late hour the previous night, which had not yet been communicated to the press, adding that he had not closed his eyes or breakfasted; and, with an expression I shall never forget, he exclaimed, " How willingly would I exchange places to-day with the soldier who sleeps on the ground in the Army of the Potomac."

Auguste Langel, a French writer, who visited this country not long since, gives, among other reminiscences, the following account of a visit to Ford's Theater—occupying the fatal box in company with Mr. Lincoln (some months before his death):

I was, as may be supposed, more occupied with the President than the performance. He, however, listened with attention, though he knew the play by heart. He followed all the incidents of it with the greatest interest, and talked with Mr. Sumner and myself only between the acts. His second son, a boy of 11, was near him, and Mr. Lincoln held him nearly the whole time, leaning on him, and often pressed the laughing or astonished face of the child on his broad chest. To his many questions he replied with the greatest patience. Certain allusions of *King Lear* to the sorrows of paternity caused a cloud to pass over the President's brow, for he had lost a young child at the White House, and never was consoled. I may be pardoned for dwelling on recollections so personal, which, under other circumstances, I should communicate only to a few friends; for it was on that very spot where I saw him with his child and his friends, that death struck down one so full of meekness, as gentle as a woman, as simple as a child. It was there he received the Parthian arrow of vanquished slavery, and fell the noble victim of the noblest of causes.

Rev. Dr. Thompson, of New York, mentions these incidents as within his own knowledge:

Mr. Lincoln was asked whether he thought the victory at Atlanta or the Chicago platform contributed most to secure his re-election. " I guess it was the victory," he observed ; " At any rate, of the two, *I would rather have the victory repeated.*" The death of the guerrilla Morgan being mentioned, Mr. Lincoln remarked: " Well, I wouldn't crow about anybody's death; but I guess I can take this death as resignedly as I can anybody's." Then he added, with indignation, that Morgan was a coward, a negro-driver, a kind of man that the North knows nothing about.

Mr. Carpenter, the artist, whose painting, " The Signing of the Emancipation Proclamation," is well known, makes the following statement :

It has been the business of my life, as you know, to study the human face, and I say now, as I have said repeatedly to friends, Mr. Lincoln had the saddest face I ever painted. During some of the dark days of last spring and summer I saw him at times when his careworn, troubled appearance was enough to bring tears of sympathy into the eyes of his most violent enemies. I recall particularly, one day, when, having occasion to pass through the main hall of the domestic apartments, I found him all alone, pacing up and down a narrow passage, his hands behind him, his head bent forward upon his breast, heavy black rings under his eyes, showing sleepless nights—altogether such a picture of the effects of weighty cares and responsibilities as I never had seen. And yet he always had a kind word, and almost always a genial smile, and it was his way frequently to relieve himself at such times by some harmless pleasantry. I recollect an instance told me by one of the most radical members of the last Congress. It was during the darkest days of 1862. He called upon the President early one morning, just after news of a disaster. It was a time of great anxiety, if not despondency. Mr. Lincoln commenced telling some trifling incident, which the Congressman was in no mood to hear. He rose to his feet and said, " Mr. President, I did not come here this morning to hear stories; it is too serious a time." Instantly the smile disappeared from Mr. Lincoln's face, who exclaimed, " A——, sit down ! I respect you as an earnest, sincere man. You can not be more anxious than I am constantly, and I say to you now, that were it not for this occasional vent I should die !"

The following reminiscences of the Hampton Roads conferrence, are taken from a Southern paper, and are understood to have been written by A. H. Stephens, or at his instance :

Mr. Lincoln declared that the only ground upon which he could rest the justice of the war—either with his own people or with foreign powers—was that it was not a war for conquest, but that the States never had been separated from the Union. Consequently, he could not recognise another government inside of the one of which he alone was President, nor admit the separate independence of States that were yet a part of the Union. " That," said he, " would be doing what you have so long asked Europe to do in vain, and be resigning the only thing the armies of the Union are fighting for."

Mr. Hunter made a long reply, insisting that the recognition of Davis' power to make a treaty was the first and indispensable step to peace, and referring to the correspondence between King Charles the First and his Parliament, as a reliable precedent of a constitutional ruler treating with rebels.

Mr. Lincoln's face then wore that indescribable expression which generally preceded his hardest hits, and he remarked : " Upon questions of history I must refer you to Mr. Seward, for he is posted in such things, and I don't profess to be bright. My only distinct recollection of the matter is, that Charles lost his head."   *   *   *

The special report made by Stephens, Hunter and Campbell, on this conference, as quoted in the article just cited from, says:

Mr. Seward then remarked : " Mr. President, it is as well to inform these gentlemen that yesterday Congress acted upon the amendment to the Constitution abolishing slavery."

Mr. Lincoln stated that was true, and suggested that there was a question as to the right of the insurgent States to return at once and claim a right to vote upon the amendment, to which the concurrence of two-thirds of the States was required.

He stated that it would be desirable to have the institution of slavery abolished by the consent of the people as soon as possible—he hoped within six years. He also stated that four hundred millions of dollars might be offered as compensation to the owners, and remarked : " You would be surprised were I to give you the names of those who favor that."

Mr. Hunter said something about the inhumanity of leaving so many poor old negroes and young children destitute by encouraging the able-bodied negroes to run away, and asked, what are they—the helpless—to do ?

Mr. Lincoln said that reminded him of an old friend in Illinois, who had a crop of potatoes, and did not want to dig them. So he. told a neighbor that he would turn in his hogs, and let them dig them for themselves. " But," said the neighbor " the frost will soon be in the ground, and when the soil is hard frozen, what will they do then ?" To which the worthy farmer replied, " Let 'em root !"

Mr. Stephens said he supposed that was the original of " Root Hog, or Die," and a fair indication of the future of the negroes.

Mr. Lincoln's private papers, in the possession of his family, include many letters, memoranda, and other embodiments of his thoughts, which will, no doubt, be hereafter given to the reading world. It must suffice to add here some portion of the writings of this character, not embraced in the preceding pages, on which the seal of privacy does not rest. A few brief speeches are also added.

MR. LINCOLN ON TEMPERANCE.

In response to an address from the Sons of Temperance, in Washington, on the 29th of September, 1863, Mr. Lincoln made the following remarks :

As a matter of course, it will not be possible for me to make a response co-extensive with the address which you have presented to me. If I were better known than I am, you would not need to be told that, in the advocacy of the cause of temperance, you have a friend and sympathiser in me.

When I was a young man—long ago—before the Sons of Temperance, as an organization had an existence, I, in an humble way, made temperance speeches, and I think I may say that to this day I have never, by my example, belied what I then said.

In regard to the suggestions which you make for the purpose of the advancement of the cause of temperance in the army, I can not make particular responses to them at this time. To prevent intemperance in the army is even a part of the articles of war. It is part of the law of the land, and was so, I presume, long ago, to dismiss officers for drunkenness. I am not sure that, consistent with the public service, more can be done than has been done. All, therefore, that I can promise you is (if you will be pleased to furnish me with a copy of your address), to have it submitted to the proper department, and have it considered whether it contains any suggestions which will improve the cause of temperance and repress the cause of drunkenness in the army any better than it is already done. I can promise no more than that.

I think that the reasonable men of the world have long since agreed that intemperance is one of the greatest, if not the very greatest, of all evils among mankind. That is not a matter of dispute, I believe. That the disease exists, and that it is a very great one, is agreed upon by all.

The mode of cure is one about which there may be differences of opinion. You have suggested that in an army—our army—drunkenness is a great evil, and one which, while it exists to a very great extent, we can not expect to overcome so entirely as to leave such successes in our arms as we might have without it. This, undoubtedly, is true, and while it is, perhaps, rather a bad source to derive comfort from, nevertheless, in a hard struggle, I do not know but what it is some consolation to be aware that there is some intemperance on the other side, too; and that they have no right to beat us in physical combat on that ground.

But I have already said more than I expected to be able to say when I began, and if you please to hand me a copy of your address, it shall be considered. I thank you very heartily, gentlemen, for this call, and for bringing with you these very many pretty ladies.

MR. LINCOLN'S " SHORTEST AND BEST SPEECH."

There appeared in the Washington *Chronicle*, of December 7, 1864, this little paragraph, including what Mr. Lincoln himself pronounced his shortest and best speech—the " report " being in his own words as he gave them:

On Thursday of last week two ladies from Tennessee came before the President, asking the release of their husbands, held as prisoners of war at Johnson's Island. They were put off until Friday, when they came again, and were again put off until Saturday. At each of the interviews one of the ladies urged that her husband was a religious man, and on Saturday, when the President ordered the release of the prisoners, he said to this lady: "You say your husband is a religious man; tell him when you meet him that I say I am not much of a judge of religion, but that, in my opinion, the religion that sets men to rebel and fight against their Government, because, as they think, that Government does not sufficiently help *some* men to eat their bread in the sweat of *other* men's faces, is not the sort of religion upon which people can get to heaven."

SPEECH TO OHIO SOLDIERS, AUGUST 18, 1864.

The following speech was made to a regiment of Ohio "hundred-days men," who paid him a visit of respect, as they were about to go home, at the close of their service:

SOLDIERS: You are about to return to your homes and your friends, after having, as I learn, performed in camp a comparatively short term of duty in this great contest. I am greatly obliged to you, and to all who have come forward at the call of their country. I wish it to be more generally understood what the country is now engaged in. We have, as all will agree, a free government, where every man has a right to be equal with every other man. In this great struggle this form of government and every form of human rights are endangered, if our enemies succeed. There is more involved in this contest than is realized by every one. There is involved in this struggle the question whether your children and my children shall enjoy the privileges we have enjoyed. I say this in order to impress upon you, if you are not already so impressed, that no small matter should divert us from our great purpose. There may be some inequalities in the practical application of our system. It is fair that each man shall pay taxes in exact proportion to the value of his property; but if we should wait, before collecting a tax, to adjust the taxes upon each man in exact proportion with every other man, we should never collect any tax at all. There may be mistakes made sometimes; things may be done wrong while all the officers of the Government do all they can to prevent mistakes. But I beg of you, as citizens of this great republic, not to let your minds be carried off from the great work we have before us. This struggle is too large for you to be diverted from it by any small matter. When you return to your homes, rise up to the hight of a generation of men worthy of a free government, and we will carry out the great work we have commenced. I return to you my sincere thanks for the honor you ·have done me this afternoon.

SPEECH TO OHIO SOLDIERS, AUGUST 31, 1864.

On a similar occasion, at a later day, Mr. Lincoln made the following speech to another regiment:

Soldiers of the 148*th Ohio:* I am most happy to meet you on this occasion. I understand that it has been your honorable privilege to stand, for a brief period, in the defense of your country, and that now you are on your way to your homes. I congratulate you, and those who are waiting to bid you welcome home from the war; and permit me, in the name of the people, to thank you for the part you have taken in this struggle for the life of the nation. You are soldiers of the Republic, everywhere honored and respected. Whenever I appear before a body of soldiers, I feel tempted to talk to them of the nature of the struggle in which we are engaged. I look upon it as an attempt on the one hand to overwhelm and destroy the national existence, while on our part we are striving to maintain the government and institutions of our fathers, to enjoy them ourselves, and transmit them to our children, and our children's children forever.

To do this, the constitutional administration of our Government must be sustained, and I beg of you not to allow your minds or your hearts to be diverted from the support of all necessary measures for that purpose, by any miserable picayune arguments addressed to your pockets, or inflammatory appeal made to your passions and your prejudices.

It is vain and foolish to arraign this man or that for the part he has taken, or has not taken, and to hold the Government responsible for his acts. In no administration can there be perfect equality of action and uniform satisfaction rendered by all. But the Government must be preserved in spite of the acts of any man or set of men. It is worthy of your every effort. Nowhere in the world is presented a Government of so much liberty and equality. To the humblest and poorest among us, are held out the highest privileges and positions. The present moment finds me at the White House, yet there is as good a chance for your children as there was for my father's.

Again, I admonish you not to be turned from your stern purpose of defending our beloved country and its free institutions, by any arguments urged by ambitious and designing men, but stand fast to the Union and the old flag.

Soldiers, I bid you God-speed to your homes.

LETTER TO GOV. HAHN, OF LOUISIANA.

EXECUTIVE MANSION,
WASHINGTON, March 13, 1864.

HON. MICHAEL HAHN—*My Dear Sir:* I congratulate you on having fixed your name in history as the first Free-State Governor of Louisiana. Now you are about to have a convention, which, among other things, will probably define the elective franchise. I barely suggest, for your private consideration, whether some of the colored people may not be let in, as, for instance, the very intelligent and especially those who have fought gallantly in our ranks. They would probably help, in some trying time to come, to keep the jewel of liberty in the family of freedom. But this is only a suggestion, not to the public, but to you alone.

Truly yours,   A. LINCOLN.

LETTER TO MRS. ELIZA B. GURNEY.

EXECUTIVE MANSION,
WASHINGTON, September 4, 1864.

ELIZA B. GURNEY—*My esteemed Friend:* I have not forgotten, probably never shall forget, the very impressive occasion when yourself and friends visited me on a Sabbath forenoon, two years ago, nor has your kind letter, written nearly a year later, ever been forgotten.

In all it has been your purpose to strengthen my reliance upon God. I am much indebted to the good Christian people of the country for their constant prayers and consolations, and to no one of them more than to yourself.

The purposes of the Almighty are perfect and must prevail, though we erring mortals may fail to accurately perceive them in advance.

We hoped for a happy termination of this terrible war long before this, but God knows best and has ruled otherwise. We shall yet acknowledge His wisdom and our own errors therein. Meanwhile we must work earnestly in the best light He gives us, trusting that so working still conduces to the great ends He ordains. Surely He intends some great good to follow this mighty convulsion, which no mortal could make and no mortal could stay. Your people, the Friends, have had and are having very great trials on principles and faith. Opposed to both war and oppression, they can only practically oppose oppression by war. In this hard dilemma some have chosen one horn and some the other. For those appealing to me on conscientious grounds, I have done, and shall do, the best I could and can, in my own conscience, under my oath to the law. That you believe this I doubt not, and, believing it, I shall still receive for our country and myself your earnest prayers to our Father in Heaven.

Your sincere friend,

A. LINCOLN.

LETTER TO A WIDOW WHO HAD LOST FIVE SONS IN THE WAR.

EXECUTIVE MANSION,
WASHINGTON, November 21, 1864.

DEAR MADAM—I have been shown, in the files of the War Department, a statement of the Adjutant-General of Massachusetts, that you are the mother of five sons who have died gloriously on the field of battle. I feel how weak and fruitless must be any words of mine, which should attempt to beguile you from the grief of a loss so overwhelming. But I can not refrain from tendering to you the consolation that may be found in the thanks of the Republic they died to save. I pray that our Heavenly Father may assuage the anguish of your bereavement, and leave you only the cherished memory of the loved and lost, and the solemn pride that must be yours, to have laid so costly a sacrifice upon the altar of freedom.

Yours, very sincerely and respectfully,

A. LINCOLN.

To MRS. BIXBY, Boston, Massachusetts.

LETTER TO DEACON JOHN PHILLIPS—104 YEARS OLD.

EXECUTIVE MANSION,
WASHINGTON, November 21, 1864.

MY DEAR SIR—I have heard of the incident at the polls, in your town, in which you acted so honorable a part, and I take the liberty of writing to you to express my personal gratitude for the compliment paid me by the suffrage of a citizen so venerable.

The example of such devotion to civic duties, in one whose days have already been extended an average life-time beyond the Psalmist's limits, can not but be valuable and fruitful. It is not for myself only, but for the country, which you have, in your sphere, served so long and so well, that I thank you.

Your friend and servant,   A. LINCOLN.

DEACON JOHN PHILLIPS.

AN OLD LETTER.

The following letter of Mr. Lincoln, but recently published, was written when he was at the age of twenty-seven. He was then a candidate for re-election to the Legislature of Illinois, having previously served one term of two years :

NEW SALEM, June 21, 1836.

DEAR COLONEL—I am told that during my absence last week, you passed through this place, and stated publicly that you were in possession of a fact, or facts, which, if known to the public, would entirely destroy the prospects of N. W. Edwards and myself at the ensuing election ; but that, through favor to us, you would forbear to divulge them. No one has needed favors more than I, and, generally, few have been less unwilling to accept them ; but in this case, favor to me would be injustice to the public, and, therefore, I must beg your pardon for declining it. That I once had the confidence of the people of Sangamon county, is sufficiently evident, and if I have since done any thing, either by design or misadventure, which, if known, would subject me to a forfeiture of that confidence, he that knows of that thing and conceals it, is a traitor to his country's interest.

I find myself wholly unable to form any conjecture of what fact, or facts, real or supposed, you spoke. But my opinion of your veracity will not permit me, for a moment, to doubt that you, at least, believed what you said. I am flattered with the personal regard you manifested for me ; but I hope that, on more mature reflection, you will view the public interest as a paramount consideration, and therefore determine to let the worst come.

I here assure you that the candid statement of facts on your part, however low it may sink me, shall never break the ties of personal friendship between us.

I wish an answer to this, and you are at liberty to publish both, if you choose. Very respectfully, A. LINCOLN.
Col. ROBERT ALLEN.

AN EARLY SPEECH.

In a debate in the Illinois House of Representatives, in December, 1839—near the opening of the Harrison canvass— Mr. Lincoln is reported * to have made a speech, from which the subjoined paragraphs are extracted:

---

* Without doubting its genuineness and general accuracy, I have not been able to verify this extract, which has appeared in the public prints.

 Many free countries have lost their liberty, and ours may lose hers; but if she shall, be it my proudest plume, not that I was the last to desert, but that I never deserted her. I know that the great volcano at Washington, aroused and directed by the evil spirit that reigns there, is belching forth the lava of political corruption in a current broad and deep, which is sweeping with frightful velocity over the whole length and breadth of the land, bidding fair to leave unscathed no green spot or living thing, while on its bosom are riding, like demons on the waves of hell, the imps of the Evil Spirit, and fiendishly torturing and taunting all those who dare resist its destroying course with the hopelessness of their effort; and knowing this, I can not deny that all may be swept away. Broken by it, I, too, may be; bow to it I never will. The probability that we may fall in the struggle, ought not to deter us from the support of a cause which we deem to be just. It shall not deter me.

If I ever feel the soul within me elevate and expand to those dimensions not wholly unworthy of its Almighty architect, it is when I contemplate the cause of my country deserted by all the world beside, and I standing up boldly and alone, hurling defiance at her victorious oppressors. And here, without contemplating consequences, before high Heaven, and in the face of the whole world, I swear eternal fidelity to the just cause, as I deem it, of the land of my life, my liberty and my love. And who, that thinks with me, will not fearlessly adopt the oath I take? Let none falter who thinks he is right, and we may succeed. But if, after all, we shall fall, be it so. We shall have the proud consolation of saying to our conscience, and to the departed shade of our country's freedom, that the cause approved by our judgments, and adored by our hearts in disaster, in chains, in torture, and in death, we never failed in defending.

LETTER TO MR. CHOATE, OF NEW YORK.

EXECUTIVE MANSION, ⎞
WASHINGTON, December 19, 1864. ⎠

MY DEAR SIR—I have the honor to acknowledge the reception of your kind invitation to be present at the annual festival of the New England Society, to commemorate the landing of the Pilgrims, on Thursday, the 22d of this month.

My duties will not allow me to avail myself of your kindness. I can not but congratulate you and the country, however, upon the spectacle of devoted unanimity presented by the people at home, the citizens that form our marching columns, and the citizens that fill our squadrons on the sea—all animated by the same determination to complete and perpetuate the work our fathers began and transmitted.

The work of the Plymouth emigrants was the glory of their age. While we reverence their memory, let us not forget how vastly greater is our opportunity. I am, very truly, your obedient servant, A. LINCOLN.

JOSEPH H. CHOATE, ESQ.

LETTER TO DR. JOHN MACLEAN, OF PRINCETON COLLEGE.

In December, 1864, the degree of Doctor of Laws was conferred upon President Lincoln, by a vote of the Board of Trustees of Princeton College, in New Jersey, of which fact he was duly notified by the President of that institution, Dr. Maclean. Mr. Lincoln sent the following letter, in acknowledgment of this honor:

EXECUTIVE MANSION,
WASHINGTON, December 27, 1864.

MY DEAR SIR—I have the honor to acknowledge the reception of your note of the of the 20th of December, conveying the announcement that the Trustees of the College of New Jersey had conferred upon me the degree of Doctor of Laws.

The assurance conveyed by this high compliment, that the course of the Government which I represent has received the approval of a body of gentlemen of such character and intelligence, in this time of public trial, is most grateful to me.

Thoughtful men must feel that the fate of civilization upon this continent is involved in the issue of our contest. Among the most gratifying proofs of this conviction, is the hearty devotion everywhere exhibited by our schools and colleges to the national cause.

I am most thankful if my labors have seemed to conduce to the preservvtion of those institutions under which, alone, we can expect good government, and in its train, sound learning and the progress of the liberal arts.

I am, Sir, very truly, your obedient servant,
A. LINCOLN.

DR. JOHN MACLEAN.

LETTER TO GOV. FLETCHER, OF MISSOURI.

EXECUTIVE MANSION,
WASHINGTON, February 20, 1865.

His Excellency, Gov. Fletcher:

It seems that there is now no organized military force of the enemy in Missouri, and yet that destruction of property and life is rampant everywhere. Is not the cure for this within easy reach of the people themselves? It can not but be that every man, not naturally a robber or cut-throat, would gladly put an end to this state of things. A large majority, in every locality, must feel alike upon this subject; and if so, they only need to reach an understanding, one with another. Each leaving all others alone solves the problem; and surely each would do this, but for his apprehension that others will not leave him alone. Can not this mischievous distrust be removed? Let neighborhood meetings be everywhere called and held, of all entertaining a sincere purpose for mutual security in the future, whatever they may heretofore have thought, said or done, about the war, or about any thing else. Let all such meet, and, waiving all else, pledge each to cease harassing others, and to make common cause against whoever persists in making, aiding or encouraging, further disturbance. The practical means they will best know how to adopt and apply. At such meetings, old friendships will cross the memory, and honor and Christian charity will come in to help.

Please consider whether it may not be well to suggest this to the now afflicted people of Missouri.

Yours, truly,   A. LINCOLN.

MR. LINCOLN TO THE MINERS OF THE FAR WEST.

On the fatal 14th of April, Hon. Schuyler Colfax, then about to start for the far-off mining regions, received from Mr. Lincoln a verbal message for the miners, which was thus given in a speech by Mr. C. in Colorado:

"Mr. Colfax, I want you to take a message from me to the miners whom you visit. I have," said he, "very large ideas of the mineral wealth of our nation. I believe it practically inexhaustible. It abounds all over the Western country—from the Rocky Mountains to the Pacific, and its development has scarcely commenced. During the war, when we were adding a couple of millions of dollars every day to our national debt, I did not care about encouraging the increase in the volume of our precious metals. We had the country to save first. But, now that the Rebellion is overthrown, and we know pretty nearly the amount of our national debt, the more gold and silver we mine, makes the payment of that debt so much the easier. Now," said he, speaking with much emphasis, "I am going to encourage that in every possible way. We shall have hundreds of thousands of disbanded soldiers, and many have feared that their return home in such great numbers might paralyze industry by furnishing suddenly a greater supply of labor than there will be a demand for. I am going to try and attract them to the hidden wealth of our mountain ranges, where there is room enough for all. Immigration, which even the war has not stopped, will land upon our shores hundreds of thousands more per year, from over-crowded Europe. I intend to point them to the gold and silver that waits for them in the West. Tell the miners, from me, that I shall promote their interests to the utmost of my ability, because their prosperity is the prosperity of the nation; and," said he, his eye kindling with enthusiasm, " we shall prove, in a very few years, that we are, indeed, the TREASURY OF THE WORLD."

HIS SPEECH AT INDEPENDENCE HALL.

These quotations from the written and spoken words of Mr. Lincoln, can not be more fitly closed than with the remarkable speech which he made at Independence Hall, in Philadelphia, on Washington's birthday, while on his way to the National Capital, to enter upon the duties of the Presidency. He had taken his life in his hand, as he well knew, in thus responding to the call of the people. He seems at the moment, to have almost foreseen the end which awaited him, and his unpremeditated words rise into prophetic grandeur, as he stands face to face with the possible—and now actual result:

I am filled with deep emotion at finding myself standing here in the place where were collected together the wisdom, the patriotism, the devotion to the principle from which sprung the institutions under which we live. You have kindly suggested to me that in my hands is the task of restoring peace to our distracted country. I can say, in return, sir, that all the political sentiments I entertain have been drawn, so far as I have been able to draw them, from the sentiments which originated and were given to the world from this hall in which we stand. I have never had a feeling, politically, that did not spring from the sentiments embodied in the Declaration of Independence. I have often pondered over the dangers which were incurred by the men who assembled here and adopted the Declaration of Independence. I have pondered over the toils that were endured by the officers and soldiers of the army who achieved that independence. I have often inquired of myself what great principle or idea it was that kept this Confederacy so long together. It was not the mere matter of the separa-tion of the colonies from the mother land, but something in that declaration giving liberty, not alone to the people of this country, but hope for the world for all future time. It was that which gave promise that in due time the weights should be lifted from the shoulders of all men, and that all should have an equal chance. This is the sentiment embodied in the Declaration of Independence.

How, my friends, can this country be saved upon that basis? If it can, I will consider myself one of the happiest men in the world if I can help to save it. If it can't be saved upon that principle, it will be truly awful. *But if this country can not be saved without giving up that principle, I was about to say, I would rather be assassinated on the spot than to surrender it.*

Now, in my view of the present aspect of affairs, there is no need of bloodshed and war. There is no necessity for it. I am not in favor of such a course, and I may say, in advance, there will be no bloodshed unless it be forced upon the Govern-ment. The Government will not use force unless force is used against it. [Prolonged applause, and cries of " That's the pro-per sentiment."] My friends, this is a wholly unprepared speech. I did not expect to be called upon to say a word when I came here. I supposed I was merely to do something toward raising this flag. I may, therefore, have said something indis-creet. *But I have said nothing but what I am willing to live by, and, in the pleasure of Almighty God, die by.*

From the cabin to the White House—from a lowly birth to an honored death, at the summit of human glory—these pages have imperfectly traced the earthly course of ABRAHAM LINCOLN. He is now where praise and blame alike fall unheeded " on the dull, cold ear " of the dead, yet one comes reluctantly to any final summing up of the labors and the character of one so lately gone, and still so spiritually present. He served the people. He saved the nation. He gave his life for his country. His name will be one of heroic grandeur for all time. His fame will be perennial as the sun. While Liberty lives, this her chief martyr will be the central figure among her most illustrious devotees. He finished his work, and its renown is not alone for a transient generation, but for the wide world and for the whole future.

What Robert Burns has, proverbially, been to the people of

his native land, and, to a certain extent, of all lands, as a poet, Abraham Lincoln early became to us as a statesman and a patriot, by his intimate relations alike with the humbler and the higher walks of life. By his own native energy and endowment, he rose from a place of humble obscurity to a commanding position and power among his fellow-men, and achieved an enduring fame. The experiences of the "toiling millions," whether of gladness or of sorrow, had been his experiences. He had an identity with them, such as common trials and common emotions produced. He had become in person, no less than in principle, a genuine representative man in the cause of free labor.

As a ruler, no man ever took the people into his confidence so unreservedly and fully—discarding the diplomatic devices of European statesmanship, which erect so many barriers between the governing and the governed. His policy was unfeignedly democratic. In accepting a great public trust, he endeavored always to be in harmony with those who gave it. He carried out the popular will, so far as in him lay, discarding the imperial idea which would force the masses into subjection to the will of one leading mind. He was " controlled by events," and " did not control them," after the vain imagination of a Napoleon. His strength lay in striving to embody and execute the mind of the nation, not to direct its thought and will. The greatness of Mr. Lincoln lay not in contesting, defying, or deluding the masses in their purposes, but in giving those purposes development and effect.

Mr. Lincoln knew how to be reticent, as occasion required, and how to be honest and open whenever matured decisions were passing into speech and act. He was never precipitate ; and when he " put his foot down," it was never to recall the step deliberately taken. He did not move forward rapidly enough for some ; he was in advance of many ; but always keeping near what may be termed his skirmishing line, he moved forward whenever it appeared that his main column could safely move with him. He was not of the material of which reformers, a whole generation in advance of their time, could be made; yet he recognized their uses, and was never indifferent to whatever in their aspirations had reality of promise.

He grew upon the affections and confidence of the people, which he had no art for suddenly captivating. He was never forced upon them by political management. His honors were duly ripened in the open air and sunlight—never forced to an artificial ruddiness or unnatural proportions under cover. The incident of his election as captain of volunteers in 1832—the confidence of his fellows outrunning his own aspiration—is a type of all his advancements, in his own State and in the nation. From the time of his first appearance in the Illinois Legislature, he was a man of mark as a politician in the best sense. From his earliest connection with the bar as an advocate and counsellor, more than ordinary success was expected of him. A sterling native ability was conceded to him. He wanted only development and cultivation. And to the necessary study for this end, it was at once remarked how closely he applied himself. As was said of him in those days, when not actively engaged, he was "always thinking." He was an "improving man." Such an one, with great inherent capacities, is capable of the highest attainment. Mr. Lincoln's life is a grand exemplar for the youth who worthily aspires. All the space, from the nethermost to the topmost round of the ladder—with the aid of no adventitious circumstances, and in spite of the most depressing hindrances—was thus surmounted by the once obscure worker.

This great success, it must not be overlooked, and can not be too earnestly impressed upon the young, was partly due to the remarkable purity of his private life and to the rugged honesty of purpose, in his earliest days as in his latest, which were at the basis of his character. He unhesitatingly and unswervingly believed in the right, the true, the good—not simply as on the whole preferable to their opposites, or even as infinitely worthier of his regard, but as the only possible objects of his faith. He had a reverent and abiding trust in a beneficent and all-controlling Providence. He saw the presence of God in all national and individual life, and devoutly sought His guidance and spiritual strength in all his trials. Though never demonstrative on this subject, and recoiling from any doubtful pretensions, he had profoundly earnest religious sentiments and convictions. His conscience was ever active, clear and strong. His faith in God, and his worshipful trust, came out more and more visibly during the later years of his life. Who, that knew him well, can point to any man in his whole circle of acquaintance, however wide, as a truer exemplar of the Christian character as set forth in the Sermon on the Mount? In certain outward restraints or formalities, and in merely negative virtues, others went beyond him, but few, very few in this world, have ever more truly *lived* the life of purity, of charity, of universal good-will, of gentle forgiveness, of self-denying devotion to the interests of humanity, of kindness to the poor, of sympathy for the oppressed, and of submission to the Divine will, as enjoined by the precept and example of Christ.

Mr. Lincoln's face was rather striking than attractive at the first view. Its plainness was proverbial. But the power of its expression, the winningness of its smile, were such, that you carried away the impression of a noble and pleasing countenance. It was written all over with the history of his struggles and triumphs. An olive complexion preserved the memory of his first seven years in a Southern clime. His deep-set, clear, steady eye, told of earnest study, of assured attainment, of confirmed self-mastery. He had no unsubdued passion—or, if a sense of indignation occasionally got the better of him, it was not from wrong to himself but to a friend, or to a class, or to the nation. A terrible civil war, which he greatly dreaded, and labored earnestly to avert, impressed numberless lines on his brow and cheeks. He had had, too, his private sorrows, which deepened the native sadness of his countenance—especially the loss of two tenderly-loved boys, the one before, the other after, his elevation to the Presidency. A wide range of emotions—the extremes of sunlight and shadow—passed successively over these masculine features, in all of which strength and power were manifest.

His humor was proverbial, yet nothing could be wider of the

mark than to represent him as a "jesting" trifler. A trifler he never was, or a jester in any proper sense. His "stories" had always a logical relation to his main subject of conversation. They were never his own inventions. He resorted to them for illustrations, or as a gentle method of putting off importunities, or of avoiding a committal for which he was unprepared. To a zealous advocate for more radical measures in regard to slavery, for instance, early in the war, he spoke of the vivid impression made on his mind by one of the fables of Æsop—an edition of which, illustrated by plain wood-cuts, he read in very early life—in which certain zealous philanthropists are represented as endeavoring to change the color of a negro's skin by assiduous washing; their labors effecting nothing except to give him a cold, of which he nearly died. This tale, with its rude illustration, had an abiding lesson for him, and when told in his peculiar manner, its moral could not be without effect, in at least parrying complaints, if not repressing untimely zeal. The genuine humor which he possessed, is of the kind nearly allied to genius, and its almost invariable accompaniment. It relieved many a hard exigency of his life, and saved him from an unbroken gloom, toward which, at times, he gravitated.

It is idle to conjecture what might have been, or how his life could have been spared from the stealthy malice bent on his destruction. His work was really finished. The "wrath of man" was permitted to accomplish its design, and so overruled as to serve the purposes of Providence. To that overruling power, the nation, and all who mourn the great bereavement, should reverently bow. The future of our nation, as the past has been, is in the keeping of a Being supremely wise and good, "who knoweth the end from the beginning," and ever "doeth all things well."

Any book in this list will be sent by mail for price annexed.
August, 1865.

THE LOGIC OF SIR WILLIAM HAMILTON, BART., Professor of Logic
and Metaphysics in the University of Edinburgh. Reduced and prepared
for use in Colleges and Schools, by HENRY N. DAY, D. D., LL. D., Author
of the "Art of Elocution," "Rhetorical Praxis," etc. 1 vol. 12mo, . $1 25

RHETORICAL PRAXIS. The Principles of Rhetoric Exemplified and Applied in Copious Exercises for Systematic Practice, Chiefly in the Development of the Thought. By H. N. DAY, D. D., LL. D., Author of
"Elements of the Art of Rhetoric," and formerly Professor of Rhetoric
in "Western Reserve College." 1 vol. 12mo, ... 1 12

THE ART OF ELOCUTION. Exemplified in a Systematic Course of Exercises.
By H. N. DAY, D. D., LL. D. Revised Edition. 1 vol. 12mo, . . . 1 50

THE ART OF BOOK-KEEPING. Methodically Unfolded in its Principles,
and Illustrated by Copious Exercises. By H. N. DAY, D. D., LL. D. 1
vol. 12mo, ... 75

MOFFAT'S ÆSTHETICS. An Introduction to the Study of Æsthetics. By
Rev. JAS. C. MOFFAT, D. D., late Professor of Greek in the College of New
Jersey, now Professor of Ecclesiastical History in the Theological Semi-
nary, Princeton. 1 vol. 12mo., muslin. 436 pages, ... 1 25

THE SCIENCE OF EDUCATION AND ART OF TEACHING. In two
parts. By JOHN OGDEN, A. M. 1 vol. 12mo., muslin. 478 pages. Sixth
Edition, ... 1 50

THE TEACHERS' INDICATOR and Parents' Manual. For School and
Home Education; consisting of elaborate essays on topics covering nearly
the whole field of Education, from the Pens of some of the most distinguished men in the country. 1 vol. 12mo., muslin. 450 pages . . . 1 25

THE WHEAT PLANT. Its Origin, Culture, Growth, Development, Composition, Varieties, Diseases, etc., together with a few remarks on Indian
Corn, its Culture, etc. By JOHN H. KLIPPART, Corresponding Secretary of
the Ohio State Board of Agriculture; Member of the Academy of Natural
Sciences, Cleveland; Honorary Mem. West. Acad. Natural Science, Cincinnati, etc. 1 vol. 12mo., muslin. Profusely Illustrated, . . . 1 75

BUCHANAN (Robert) on Grape Culture, and LONGWORTH (NICHOLAS) on the
Strawberry. Sixth Edition. 1 vol. 12mo., muslin, ... 75

HOOPER'S (E. J.) WESTERN FRUIT BOOK. A Compendious Collection
of Facts, from the Notes and Experience of Successful Fruit Culturists.
Arranged for Practical use in Orchard and Garden. Third Edition, completely revised. 1 vol. 12mo., with Illustrations. Muslin, . . . 1 50

KERN'S (G. M.) Practical Landscape Gardening. With reference to the Improvement of Rural Residences, giving the general principles of the Art,
with full directions for Planting Shade Trees, Shrubbery, and Flowers,
and Laying out Grounds. Third Edition, with Twenty-two illustrative
Engravings. 1 vol. 12mo., ... 1 50

THE THREE GREAT TEMPTATIONS of Young Men. With several Lectures addressed to Business and Professional Men. By SAMUEL W.
FISHER, D. D. Fifth Edition. 1 vol. 12mo., muslin, ... 1 25

MOFFAT'S (Rev. Jas. C., D. D.) Life of Chalmers, (Rev. THOMAS D. D., LL. D.) with Portrait on Steel. 1 vol. 12mo., muslin, ... $1 25

HUGH MILLER'S Scenes and Legends of the North of Scotland. Fourth Edition. 1 vol. 12mo., muslin. 446 pp., ... 1 50

MOFFAT'S (Rev. Robert) Missionary Labors and Scenes in Southern Africa. Twelfth Edition, with a Steel Portrait of the Author. 1 vol. 12mo., muslin, 409 pages, ... 1 25

RICE'S (Rev. N. L., D. D.) Romanism, the Enemy of Free Institutions and of Christianity. Third Edition. 12mo., muslin, 364 pages, . . . 1 25

THE CHRISTIAN PROFESSION. A Series of Letters to a Friend, on the Nature, Duties, Necessities, Trials and Supports of the Christian Profession. By JOSEPH CLAYBAUGH, D. D. Second Edition. 1 vol. 12mo., muslin, 216 pages, ... 75

CROTHERS' (Rev. Samuel, D. D.) Life and Writings. By Rev. ANDREW RITCHIE, Author of "Sacramental Catechism." 1 vol. 12mo., muslin, with Portrait, ... 75

HISTORY OF THE PURITANS, and Pilgrim Fathers. By STOWELL and WILSON. 1 vol. 12mo., 508 pages, ... 1 25

POETRY OF THE VEGETABLE WORLD. A Popular Exposition of the Science of Botany, and its relation to Man. By M. J. SCHLEIDEN, M. D. Edited by ALPHONSO WOOD, M. A. Illustrated with Engravings. Second Edition. 1 vol. 12mo., muslin. 356 pages, ... 1 50

THE COURSE OF CREATION. With a Glossary of Scientific Terms added to the American Edition. By JOHN ANDERSON, D. D. With numerous Illustrations. Third Edition. 1 vol. 12mo., muslin, 384 pages, . . 1 50

FARR'S (Edward) ANCIENT HISTORY. Containing the History of the Egyptians, Assyrians, Chaldeans, Medes, Lydians, Carthagenians, Persians, Macedonians, the Seleucidæ in Syria, and the Parthians. From Authentic Sources, Ancient and Modern. 4 vols. 12mo., 1334 pages. Library Sheep, marble edges, ... 4 50

THE BLENNERHASSETT PAPERS. Embodying the Private Journal of Harman Blennerhassett, and the hitherto unpublished Correspondence of Burr, Alston, Comfort Tyler, Devereaux, Dayton, Adair, Miro, Emmett, Theodosia Burr Alston, Mrs. Blennerhassett, and others, their cotemporaries; developing the purposes and aims of those engaged in the attempted Wilkinson and Burr Revolution; embracing, also, the first account of the "Spanish Association of Kentucky," and a memoir of Blennerhassett. By WILLIAM H. SAFFORD. 1 vol. 8vo., muslin, 665 pages, . . 3 50

ROSECRANS' CAMPAIGN WITH THE FOURTEENTH ARMY CORPS; or the Army of the Cumberland. A Narrative of Personal observations, with an Appendix, consisting of an Official Report of the *Battle of Stone River.* By W. D. BICKHAM. With a Topographical Sketch of the Battle-field. 1 vol. 12mo., 476 pages, ... 2 00

BAYARD TAYLOR'S CYCLOPEDIA OF MODERN TRAVEL. A Record of Adventure, Exploration, and Discovery for the past Sixty Years. Comprising Narratives of the most distinguished Travelers since the beginning of this century. Prepared and arranged by BAYARD TAYLOR. 2 vols., royal 8vo. Neatly bound in dark leather, Embellished with five fine Portraits on steel, by BUTTRE, and Illustrated by over fifty Wood Engravings, by ORR, and thirteen authentic Maps, by SCHONBERG. *Sold to Subscribers only.*

THE TRIALS FOR TREASON AT INDIANAPOLIS, Disclosing the Plans for Establishing a North-Western Confederacy, Being an Official Record of the Trials before the Military Commission convened by Special Orders No. 129, Headquarters District of Indiana; Brevet Major-General A. P. Hovey, Commander of the District. Brevet Brigadier General Silas Colgrove, President; H. L. Burnett, of the Department of the Ohio and Northern Department, Judge Advocate of the Commission. Containing the Testimony, Arguments, Finding and Sentence, in the case of Harrison H. Dodd; also of William A. Bowles, Andrew Humphreys, Horace Heffren, Lambdin P. Milligan, and Stephen Horsey. Developing the Origin, History, Extent, Names of Officers, etc., of the Secret Orders of Knights of the Golden Circle, the Circle of Honor, the Order of American Knights, and Order of the Sons of Liberty—their Organization, Rituals, Passwords, Grips, Oaths, Obligations and Penalties; their ostensible and real purposes. With accurate Illustrations of the Greek Fire Shells, Hand Grenades, Rockets and Infernal Machines of the Conspirators, introduced in Evidence on the Trials. To which is added the full Report of Judge Advocate General Holt on the Order of American Knights, *alias* the Sons of Liberty; a Western Conspiracy in aid of the Southern Rebellion. Edited by Benn Pitman, Recorder to the Military Commission. 1 vol. 8vo., with five Portraits. *Sold to Subscribers only.*

MEDICAL BOOKS.

BEACH'S (Wooster, M. D.) THE AMERICAN PRACTICE, Condensed, or the Family Physician, being the Scientific System of Medicine on Vegetable Principles, designed for all Classes. In Nine Parts. This work embraces the character, causes, symptoms, and treatment of the Diseases of men, women and children of all climates. By W. Beach, M. D, member of the Medical Society of the City and County of New York; of the Medical and Physiological Society of Wetterau, Germany; of Leipsic, Saxony; of the Medical Society of Bamberg, Bavaria; member of the Royal College of Physicians and Surgeons of Berlin, Prussia, etc., etc. Illustrated with nearly Two Hundred Engravings. Fifty-fifth Edition, Revised. Complete in one volume, octavo, 873 pages. Sheep, ... $5 00

BEACH'S (Wooster, M. D.) AMERICAN PRACTICE OF MEDICINE. Revised, Enlarged, and Improved; being a Practical Exposition of Pathology, Therapeutics, Surgery, Materia Medica and Pharmacy, on Reformed Principles; embracing the most useful portions of the former work, with corrections, additions, new remedies, and improvements; and exhibiting the results of the author's investigations in Medicine in this country, and in a year's tour in Europe. By W. Beach, M. D. Illustrated with Three Hundred Engravings, colored to life. In three vols., royal 8vo. Sheep, 36 00

BEACH'S (Wooster, M. D.) IMPROVED SYSTEM OF MIDWIFERY, Adapted to the Reformed Practice of Medicine. Illustrated by numerous Colored Plates. To which is annexed a Compendium of the Treatment of Female and Infantile Diseases, with remarks on Physiological and Moral Elevation. By W. Beach, M. D. New and Revised Edition. I vol. large quarto. Sheep, ... 8 00

KING'S American Eclectic Obstetrics. By John King, M. D., Professor of Obstetrics and the Diseases of Women and Children, in the "Eclectic Medical Institute of Cincinnati." With Seventy Illustrations. 1 vol. royal 8vo. Sheep, 800 pages, ... , . . . 5 00

THE AMERICAN DISPENSATORY. By JOHN KING, M. D., Professor of Obstetrics, and Diseases of Women and Children, in the "Eclectic Medical Institute, Cincinnati." The Sixth Edition, Revised and Enlarged. PART I contains an account of a large number of medicinal plants indigenous to this country, many of which were for the first time presented to the profession in this work, giving their botanical descriptions, general chemical histories, therapeutical properties and uses, together with a large amount of information relative thereto, of practical value to the chemist, pharmaceutist and physician. PART II contains practical pharmacy, and a description of the various pharmaceutical compounds in use among Medical Reformers, especially of that class to which the author belongs, known as Eclectics. The various chemical and pharmaceutical processes described are mainly those of recent date, and such as have been found by ample experience to be the best; these are fully and clearly explained, so that every apothecary may be enabled to prepare, without difficulty, all or any of the more modern preparations of Reformers, whenever ordered. PART III is devoted to the various mineral medicines, their chemical histories, therapeutical virtues and uses, together with a vocabulary explaining the Latin words and abbreviations frequently met with in medical prescriptions; tables of doses; weights and measures; chemical composition of mineral waters; specific gravities; hydrometrical equivalents; solubility of salts, acids, bases, etc., etc., all of which are of much utility and indispensable to the chemist and pharmaceutist. The work contains a full and complete index. so arranged that any medicine, compound, or table, etc., may be promptly found without any delay or difficulty. 1 vol., royal 8vo., 1509 pages, ... $10 00

KING'S Chart of Urinary Deposits. Paper, ... 50

GUNN'S NEW FAMILY PHYSICIAN; or, Home Book of Health, Forming a Complete Household Guide; giving many Valuable Suggestions for avoiding Disease and Prolonging Life, with plain directions in cases of emergency, and pointing out in familiar language the Causes, Symptoms, Treatment and Cure of Diseases incident to Men, Women and Children, with the simplest and best Remedies; presenting a Manual for nursing the Sick, and describing minutely the properties and uses of hundreds of well-known Medicinal Plants. By JOHN C. GUNN, M. D., author of "Gunn's Domestic Medicine." With supplementary treatises on Anatomy, Physiology and Hygiene, on Domestic and Sanitary Economy, and on Physical Culture and Development. Hundredth Edition, Revised and Enlarged. Newly Illustrated and Re-stereotyped. 1 vol. royal octavo, 1218 pages. *Sold to Subscribers only.*

JONES. The American Eclectic Practice of Medicine. By I. G. JONES, M. D., late Professor of the Theory and Practice of Medicine, in the "Eclectic Medical Institute of Cincinnati," etc., etc. Extended and Revised at the request of the author, by WM. SHERWOOD, M. D., formerly Professor of General, Special and Pathological Anatomy, in the "Eclectic Medical Institute of Cincinnati," etc. 2 vols. 8vo. Sheep, 1600 pages, . . . 10 00

KOST'S Elements of Materia Medica and Therapeutics. Adapted to the American Eclectic or Reformed Practice, with numerous Illustrations. By J. KOST, M. D., Professor of Materia Medica, Therapeutics and Botany, in the American Medical College, Cincinnati, etc., etc. 1 vol. 8vo., 700 pages. Sheep, ... 5 00